MEDIEVAL
COLONIALISM

BOOKS BY THE SAME AUTHOR

Medieval Colonialism is number three in a continuing series of related but independent works on crusader Valencia. The following have appeared or are ready for press:

The Crusader Kingdom of Valencia: Reconstruction on a Thirteenth-Century Frontier. Cambridge, Mass.: Harvard University Press, 1967.

Islam under the Crusaders: Colonial Survival in the Thirteenth-Century Kingdom of Valencia. Princeton: Princeton University Press, 1973.

Medieval Colonialism: Postcrusade Exploitation of Islamic Valencia. Princeton: Princeton University Press, 1975.

The Crusader-Muslim Predicament: Colonial Confrontation in the Conquered Kingdom of Valencia, forthcoming.

MEDIEVAL COLONIALISM

Postcrusade Exploitation of

Islamic Valencia

Robert Ignatius Burns, S.J.

PRINCETON UNIVERSITY PRESS

PRINCETON, NEW JERSEY

Library of Congress Cataloging in Publication Data will
be found on the last printed page of this book

Publication of this book has been aided by
the Whitney Darrow Publication Reserve Fund of
Princeton University Press

This book has been composed in Linotype Granjon

Printed in the United States of America by
Princeton University Press
Princeton, New Jersey

They took gold and silver, more than they
                          could handle.
All the Christians became rich on those spoils . . .
Footmen made themselves knights. The gold and
                  silver; who could count it?

All were rich . . .
They gaze over the huerta, lush and wide.
They raise their arms to thank God for gains
                so great and wonderful.

Song of the Cid
(cantos 40, 74, 87)

Valencia is far greater in revenues and profit than the County of
Barcelona [Catalonia].

Pope Innocent IV (1251)

CONTENTS

CONTENTS

ILLUSTRATIONS

MAPS

PREFACE

MAN'S RECORDS echo his mortality. They drift astray, rot, crumble into dust, or go up in flames. As kingdoms pass away, so does much of the documentation that mirrored their glory. This spreading dissolution meets resistance from two institutions: the church, which bridges kingdoms; and taxes, whose relevance and precedent abide. Though time wreaks havoc even there, the historian's industry can salvage such a run of records as to open a great window on some corner of man's past. Having told the story of Reconquest reconstruction as seen from the vantage of the church-as-frontier-institution in *The Crusader Kingdom of Valencia*, therefore, I propose now to approach the colonialized Muslim via his tax burden.[1] As the church volumes revealed the European society in its exploitation of religious dynamism for expansionist practicalities, the present study will explore the dying or at least traumatically transculturating Islamic society as reflected in the tax system and its ambience.

Each book wears a double face. The church volumes, in their surface or narrative capacity, recaptured in detail the planting of myriad ecclesiastical institutions; at the same level, the tax approach must trace each fee or levy in the total complex, assess its relative impact, explain its manner of collection or exemption, and weigh its meaning both to the realm and to Islamic-Christian relations. But there is a deeper level. Though more obliquely conveyed, the same story exposes the subject Islamic community from a hundred sides, surprising a vision of life from prosaic money-affairs. Follies emerge, from treasure-fever to the crimes that occasioned fines. Varied social strata from aristocrat and merchant to artisan, farmer, and slave put in their appearance. Images gather—the Muslim in his public bath, tavern, and fields, or while shopping, fighting, trading, dining, or irrigating his crops. One catches glimpses of his house, law, daily customs, language, and finances. Temptation to romanticize is contained, however, by the hard realities of the economic frame, so that the abundant human life assumes a corresponding reality.

[1] *The Crusader Kingdom of Valencia: Reconstruction on a Thirteenth-Century Frontier*, 2 vols. (Cambridge, Mass., 1967).

Taxes thus reflect Islamic society as viewed from one vantage, and simultaneously they reflect the colonialist crusades as seen from that vantage—limited in depth of focus but affording a wide-screen comprehension. This view is so special, so stubbornly involved with matters that properly pertain to revenue, that I refrained from incorporating it into my more ambitious *Islam under the Crusaders: Colonial Survival in the Thirteenth-Century Kingdom of Valencia*; it stands by itself, supplementing but in no way repeating that larger enterprise. Readers desiring closer, more formal acquaintance with Valencian Mudejars, or subject Muslims, their society on the eve of crusade, their adaptations and continuance, and all the elements of religion, law, culture, commerce, social classes, governmental apparatus, or inner dynamics, may turn to *Islam*.[2] The elaborate interplay of encounter and recoil between the two populations—what current jargon wrongly terms "race relations"—will be extensively studied in a sequel, *The Crusader-Muslim Predicament*.

The reader may therefore take up the present book for any of several reasons: as a freestanding socioeconomic monograph or as one contribution to a continuing larger project, as the first study in depth of Mudejar taxation, as an unusual approach to crusade history, as an essay in medieval revenues over the spectrum of feudal, royal, and seignorial, as a rare glimpse into the obscure subject of late Almohad society, or finally as a crossroads for examining the converging societies of Christendom and Islam. A glance through the table of contents with its multiple subtopics will reveal the general plot, if not the full scope, of the work. The first chapter, borrowing from my previous books, will supply the background required for entering this world and meeting its people. They are

[2] Princeton, 1973. For the wider relations between the two societies see Robert Ignatius Burns, "Christian-Islamic Confrontation in the West: The Thirteenth-Century Dream of Conversion," *American Historical Review*, LXXVI (1971), 1386-1434, with bibliographical orientation especially in n. 3; and the study on adventurers, businessmen, and renegades from both peoples, below, Chapter V, n. 51. *Mudéjar* (Catalan *mudèixar*) deriving from Arabic *mudajjan*, "allowed to remain," gained currency among Christians only from the late fifteenth century; its plural often lacks an accent in older, and occasionally in current, books. In the crusade period formal Latin usually employed "Saracen" for every kind of Muslim or Mudejar; Catalan favored "Saracen" but also used "Moor." On the Valencian phase of the Reconquest as a formal crusade, duly proclaimed by the pope and aided by the universal crusade tithe, see Burns, *Islam under the Crusaders*, preface and its n. 1.

the Muslims of the postcrusade generation especially, those who lived under James the Conqueror for some forty years, until his death in mid-1276 during their great revolt, and then for a decade under his son Peter the Great.

Valencian Muslims under the Christians left no body of public records, no memoirs or histories, no codes of religious or social life. Literary fragments, passing references, and an isolated document or two have survived, but not enough to suggest even an outline of life under the Christian conquerors. To some extent this gap is intelligible in the light of the contemporary turmoil and the ravages of subsequent eras; Christian records also suffered wholesale destruction, survivals being largely either from the crown and regional archives or from the collections of religious corporations. Many Muslim men of letters moved to more genial surroundings, especially during the exodus from Valencia city. The lack of documentation owes most however to the structure of Islamic public life, which was more informally designed than the Christian. The Muslim lacked the European's obsession for legally incorporating every group function from cathedral chapter to hospital, an orientation that proliferated undying corporate personalities, each treasuring its archives. Since the Valencian Muslim surfaces in Christian records, therefore, and since these are of the most disparate and fragmentary character, he must appear on the page of history only gradually, as each piece of data aligns itself with others until a pattern stands clear.

Though a number of archives have contributed to the process in this book, the manuscripts at the royal archives in Barcelona helped most. Its unique registers alone, which owe their existence to the crusaders' capture of the celebrated paper mills at Játiva, contain many thousands of documents on every aspect of Valencian life during the postcrusade decades. In the narrow terms of taxation itself, this concentration of documents makes for imbalance; regalian taxes obscure the seignorial and the lesser local or municipal. But the king was by far the most extensive landholder in the new kingdom, with a special jurisdiction over all Mudejars; and, as a subchapter will show, the profile of taxes under the royal landlord during this very early period did not differ appreciably from the seignorial. Sufficient extrinsic evidence survives to assure us that, on the damaged and wasted pages of these paper registers and in the whole population of fugitive manuscripts at other archives, Islamic Valencia still lives.

The scant bibliography available about Mudejars touches only tangentially upon taxes—a section of some article, a chapter here and there, or advertence to Mudejars during more general discussion of revenues. Bibliography and footnote citations pay my respects to these partial investigations by men like Chabás, Fernández y González, García y García, Gual Camarena, Macho y Ortega, Piles Ros, and Roca Traver. No scholar has devoted separate study to this subject, however, much less explored it in depth.[3]

What of the antecedent tax system, which the conquered Muslims carried into their surrender negotiations and which they preserved substantially? Islamic taxation in the ideological or ideal order, by which scholastic jurists labored to bend contemporary tax customs into some acceptable Koranic shape, is not difficult to reconstruct.[4] As Løkkegaard emphasizes, however, the tax reality was not the generalities and disputes of the *fiqh* but rather "the complex and motley" mingling of the traditional with the local.[5] Lévi-Provençal notes that Islamic taxation is a very obscure subject, much in need of light, "and it is evident that this light is not going to come from

[3] Winfried Küchler does devote an article to the mixed subject of Jewish and Moorish taxes, for a much later era; see "Besteuerung der Juden und Mauren in den Ländern der Krone Aragons während des 15. Jahrhunderts," *Gesammelte Aufsätze zur Kulturgeschichte Spaniens*, xxiv (1968), 227-256, and the attack on it by Miguel Gual Camarena, "¿Depiste o plagio?" *Caudernos de estudios medievales* (Granada), 1 (1973), 132-133.

[4] See, e.g., the general treatises by Nicolas P. Aghnides, *Mohammedan Theories of Finance, with an Introduction to Mohammedan Law and a Bibliography* (New York, 1916), or S. A. Siddiqi, *Public Finance in Islam* (Lahore, 1952). See also such classic theoretical treatises of medieval Islam, accessible in translation, as Abū Yūsuf (d. A.D. 798), Qudāma b. Ja'far (d. 932?), and Yahyā b. Ādam (d. 818), in *Taxation in Islam*, ed. Aharon Ben-Shemesh, 2d edn. rev., 3 vols. to date (Leiden, 1965ff.); and the pertinent entries in both the old and new editions of the *Encyclopaedia of Islam*, ed. H. M. Houtsma *et alii*; 2d edn. rev., ed. H.A.R. Gibb *et alii*, 4 vols. each (Leiden, 1913-1936; and 1960ff. with last volume in progress). Studies of individual taxes like D. C. Dennett's *Conversion and the Poll Tax in Early Islam* (Cambridge, Mass., 1950) have been cited only when directly pertinent (see the use of Zayas on the *zakāt*, e.g., below in Chapter IV, n. 98).

[5] Frede Løkkegaard has produced the best general study of early Islam in the east, *Islamic Taxation in the Classic Period with Special Reference to Circumstances in Iraq* (Copenhagen, 1950). Cahen and others feel that this rejection of the *fiqh* literature has now gone too far, and that ingenuity can extract from the jurists some measure of practical information.

Hispano-Arabic documentation." His own diffidently offered outline for the caliphal period in Spain has passed from author to
author, fleshed out with gleanings from a handful of medieval
Muslim writers: a standard scheme of the canonical tenth, the
territorial tax as its anomalous substitute, and that vague range of
extralegal impositions about whose multiplication Ibn Ḥazm complained.[6] The details of Mudejar taxes in Valencia, however, reveal
much more than that about the immediately antecedent Islamic
taxation there, as well as about Islamic society immediately before
and after the crusade.

In framing this Mudejar data, certain constants as well as analogies are afforded from the systems of other countries, though taxation varied widely throughout the Islamic world. Cahen's many
articles and the complex volumes both of Goitein and of Lapidus
supply valuable information.[7] Among general considerations of
taxation in North Africa, Islamic Sicily,[8] or Egypt, the recent study
by Rabie (Rabī') is particularly welcome because it deals in detail
with the thirteenth century, despite the fact that Egypt was the most
atypical economic regime of medieval Islam.[9] Nasrid Granada, as
analyzed in the tax articles by Álvarez de Cienfuegos and Ladero
Quesada, can supply some points of reference, though this line of
research has favored a later era.[10] More useful because closer in time

[6] Évariste Lévi-Provençal, *Histoire de l'Espagne musulmane*, on the caliphal
period only, 2d edn. rev., 3 vols. (Paris, 1950-1953), more generally available in an
improved edition, rev. and trans. by Emilio García Gómez, *España musulmana hasta
la caída del califato de Córdoba*, 2 vols., as vols. IV-V of *Historia de España*, ed.
Ramón Menéndez Pidal, 12 vols. to date (Madrid, 1957ff.), V, ch. 1, part 3. S. M.
Imamuddin [Imām ad-Dīn], *Some Aspects of the Socio-Economic and Cultural
History of Muslim Spain, 711-1492 A.D.* (Leiden, 1965), pp. 53-58, is even more
summary in its tax aspects.

[7] See Bibliography for all three, and citations passim. Rabie (see below, n. 9) includes fifteen of the more pertinent Cahen items in his bibliography.

[8] Ad-Dāwūdī, *Kitāb al-amwāl*, ed. and trans. H. H. Abdul Wahab and F.
Dachraoui, in "Le régime foncier en Sicile au moyen âge (ix et x siècles)," with
fragments on Islamic Spain, in *Études d'orientalisme dediées à la mémoire de Lévi-
Provençal*, ed. Emilio García Gómez et alii, 2 vols. (Paris, 1962). For taxes in nearby
North Africa see Hady Roger Idris, *Berbérie orientale sous les zīrides, xe-xiie siècles*,
2 vols. (Paris, 1962), II, 608-621, and J.F.P. Hopkins, *Medieval Muslim Government
in Barbary until the Sixth Century of the Hijra* (London, 1958), ch. 3.

[9] Hassanein Rabie, *The Financial System of Egypt, A.H. 564-741 / A.D. 1169-1341*
(London, 1972), esp. ch. 3 on taxation and ch. 4 on collection.

[10] Isabel Á[lvarez] de Cienfuegos, "Régimen tributario del reino mudéjar de
Granada (la hacienda de los nasríes granadinos)," *Miscelánea de estudios árabes y*

are the fragments conveyed by Ibn 'Abdūn within his general *ḥisba* treatise for twelfth-century Seville.[11] Works treating early modern Islamic revenues have very little direct application.[12] Surprisingly, the excellent recent histories of Islamic Valencia by Sanchis Guarner and Huici do not touch on taxation.[13]

For the Christian side the substantial researches carried through on medieval taxes and public finance all but exclude Spain, as a glance through the text and book lists of the compendious *Cambridge Economic History of Europe* demonstrates.[14] Investigations into more northerly systems, besides, do not illuminate very much the idiosyncratic Spanish tax experience. Mitchell's survey of English taxes in the twelfth and thirteenth centuries, for example, in its preoccupation with tallage, reflects a quite different fiscal-political reality, as does Kaeuper's analysis of how Edward I incorporated the Riccardi bankers of Lucca into England's tax system, or Lyon's and Verhulst's monograph on Flemish as compared to English governmental finance in the twelfth and thirteenth centuries.[15] Medieval

---

hebraicos, VIII (1959), 99-124. For Ladero Quesada's briefer contributions see below, Chapter IV, n. 82.

[11] Ibn 'Abdūn (Muḥammad b. Aḥmad b. 'Abdūn at-Tujībī), *Séville musulmane au début du xiie siècle, le traité d'Ibn 'Abdūn*, trans. Évariste Lévi-Provençal (Paris, 1947), pp. 10-14, 66-70.

[12] See, e.g., the remarkably detailed work by Stanford J. Shaw, *The Financial and Administrative Organization and Development of Ottoman Egypt, 1517-1798* (Princeton, 1962), and the subsequent operations as discussed under "Taxation and Finance" in H.A.R. Gibb and Harold Bowen, *Islamic Society and the West: A Study of the Impact of Western Civilization on Moslem Culture in the Near East*, I vol. to date (London, 1969), I, ch. 7.

[13] Manuel Sanchis Guarner, "Època musulmana," in Miguel Tarradell Mateu *et alii*, *Història del país valencià*, I vol. to date (Barcelona, 1965), I, 207-362; and Ambrosio Huici Miranda, *Historia musulmana de Valencia y su región, novedades y rectificaciones*, 3 vols. (Valencia, 1970), a political history with little attention to revenues (see I, 50-51, 262). On the *waqf*, or secular revenue alienated to Islamic religious purposes in Valencia, see below, p. 207.

[14] Eds. M. M. Postan, H. J. Habakkuk, *et alii*, 6 vols. (Cambridge, 1941-1965), esp. III, *Economic Organization and Policies in the Middle Ages*, ch. 6, part 5, and pp. 644-647.

[15] Sydney K. Mitchell, *Taxation in Medieval England*, ed. Sidney Painter (New Haven, 1951). R. W. Kaeuper, *Bankers to the Crown: The Riccardi of Lucca and Edward I* (Princeton, 1973). Bryce Lyon and A. E. Verhulst, *Medieval Finance: A Comparison of Financial Institutions in Northwestern Europe* (Providence, 1967). More specialized is Michael Prestwich, *War, Politics and Finance under Edward I* (London, 1972), and the revenue study by H. G. Richardson, *The English Jewry under Angevin Kings* (London, 1960).

France displays its own strong variation from the Spanish models.[16]
The German experience, with its reliance on Italian revenues in this
century, is particularly unhelpful. The thoroughly researched papal
finances, both local and international, have relatively few points of
practical application here.[17] The Italian communes, in fiscal analyses
like those of Herlihy, do provide more useful analogues, though the
points of difference balance and sometimes cancel the similarities.[18]
Taken as a whole, the body of research on thirteenth-century
European taxation can provide background and trends, and is
especially useful for credit operations and public finance. A range
of current studies on the period immediately following, which is
richly documented and reflects an evolved, well-structured state
finance, is ably represented outside the Spanish peninsula by the
recent works of Bowsky and Henneman.[19] Less relevant here are

[16] The major studies are cited in Martin Wolfe's recent "Medieval and Renaissance
Fiscal Systems—A Perspective," in his *The Fiscal System of Renaissance France*
(New Haven, 1972), ch. 1. Though it stresses the later medieval period, see also
Joseph R. Strayer and Charles H. Taylor, *Studies in Early French Taxation* (Cam-
bridge, Mass., 1939). See also É. Barabier, *Enquêtes sur les droits et revenus de
Charles Ier d'Anjou en Provence, 1252 et 1278, avec une étude sur le domaine comtal
et les seigneuries de Provence au xiiie siècle* (Paris, 1969). W. Percy is preparing for
publication his doctoral dissertation on Charles of Anjou, "Taxes and the Sicilian
Vespers" (Princeton University, 1968).

[17] Both the incidental information and the solid outlines of comparative levels of
prosperity are of use in the *Rationes decimarum Hispaniae (1279-1280)*, ed. José
Rius Serra, 2 vols. (Barcelona, 1946-1947). Volume one covers Catalonia, Majorca,
and Valencia; volume two, Aragon and Navarre, together with documents about
the collection mechanisms for this universal crusade tithe. I have used the data to
help reconstruct the parish networks and to comment on the economic condition of
the Valencian kingdom in my *Crusader Valencia*. The classic survey is W. E. Lunt,
Papal Revenues in the Middle Ages, 2 vols. (New York, 1934), supplemented by his
extensive *Financial Relations of the Papacy with England to 1327* (Cambridge, Mass.,
1939). Daniel Waley surveyed local taxation (about ten percent of the papacy's total
revenues) and its bibliography in *The Papal State in the Thirteenth Century*
(London, 1961), ch. 8. Léon Poliakov is concerned almost exclusively with later
periods in his *Les banchieri juifs et le saint-siège du xiie au xviie siècle* (Paris, 1965).
Other ecclesiastical taxation, a field in itself, has only occasional relevance to the
present subject. On German taxation see Matthew M. Fryde, "Studies in the History
of Public Credit of German Principalities and Towns in the Middle Ages," *Studies
in Medieval and Renaissance History*, 1 (1964), 221-292, with works cited.

[18] See especially the chapters on direct and indirect taxes in David Herlihy, *Pisa
in the Early Renaissance: A Study of Urban Growth, ca. 1250-1310* (New Haven,
1958), chs. 5, 6; and his contribution to the symposium *Finances et comptabilité
urbaines du xiie au xvie siècle; colloque international* (Brussels, 1964). See also
Bowsky in the next note.

[19] W. M. Bowsky, *The Finance of the Commune of Siena, 1287-1355* (Oxford,

the continuing contributions to the remote background, including the evolution from Roman to early medieval taxation and the coordinate, indirectly influential Byzantine system.[20]

For Arago-Catalonia, Usher's ambitious investigation of Catalan and Mediterranean banking touches on many themes of public finance, though less for the thirteenth than later centuries.[21] Standard surveys of taxation, such as those of Asso or Macanaz for the realms of Aragon, or the classic by López de Ayala for Castile, tend to become either recitations of tax genres or antiquarian essays on regalian claims, with no pretense to depth.[22] Among overviews of Spanish institutions that incorporate a summary view of the main taxes and fiscal systems, García de Valdeavellano is easily the most compendious and serviceable. López Dapena is currently investigating the revenues of Sancho IV of León-Castile (d. 1295).[23] For the

1970). J. B. Henneman, *Royal Taxation in Fourteenth Century France: The Development of War Financing, 1322-1356* (Princeton, 1972).

[20] Recent examples are Walter Goffart, "From Roman Taxation to Mediaeval Seigneurie, Three Notes," *Speculum*, XLVII (1972), 165-187, 373-394, on sixth-century tax operations, transitional to the estate-management approach, and Charles M. Brand, "Two Byzantine Treatises on Taxation," *Traditio*, xxv (1969), 35-60.

[21] Abbott Payson Usher, *The Early History of Deposit Banking in Mediterranean Europe*, 1 vol. to date (Cambridge, Mass., 1943), useful for our Chapter VII. Scholars in medieval banking history, such as Raymond de Roover, seem to prefer to investigate the better documented and more developed later periods, or to deal with themes that have little relevance to Valencian governmental finance.

[22] Ignacio de Asso (Ignacio Jordán de Asso y del Río), *Historia de la economía política de Aragón* (Zaragoza, [1798] 1947), esp. ch. 6. Melchor de Macanaz, *Regalías de los señores reyes de Aragón, discurso jurídico, histórico, político*, a report of 1713 to the Spanish king, ed. Joaquín Maldonado Macanaz (Madrid, 1879), esp. chs. 2, 3. Jerónimo López de Ayala Álvarez de Toledo y del Hierro [conde de Cedillo], *Contribuciones é impuestos en León y Castilla durante la edad media* (Madrid, 1896), ch. 3 on the thirteenth century. Less well known is the survey of the same title, publisher, place, date, and even prize, by Ramón Sánchez de Ocaña. It prefers a topical rather than chronological format and is much less useful. Ample general works include Francisco Gallardo Fernández, *Origen, progresos y estado de las rentas de la corona de España, su gobierno y administración*, 7 vols. (Madrid, 1805-1808). Such older titles, intriguing until examined and found wanting for our purpose, might be multiplied here to little effect.

[23] Luis G[arcía] de Valdeavellano y Arcimís, *Curso de historia de las instituciones españolas de los orígenes al final de la edad media*, 2d edn. rev. (Madrid, 1968), esp. book 4. Far less useful is an older, standard work, Ernesto Mayer, *Historia de las instituciones sociales y políticas de España y Portugal durante los siglos v a xiv*, 2 vols. (Madrid, 1925-1926), e.g., 1, 313ff. on Mudejars. For a textbook résumé of taxes and finance in their historical evolution as part of Spain's general economic history,

kingdom of Valencia the finance official Branchát elaborated a survey of historical and eighteenth-century taxes, which can be supplemented by incidental information from the constitutional study of his fellow Valencian of the previous century, Matheu y Sanz.[24] A brief booklet on Valencian medieval taxes by García de Cáceres in 1909 was based largely on Branchát. A subsequent doctoral thesis on the same subject by Ferraz Penelas is jejune and disappointing.[25]

For particular taxes the articles of current scholars like Aragó Cabañas, Bisson, Gual Camarena, Mateu y Llopis, Moxó, Russell, and Soldevila will be cited at pertinent places. A continuing interest in commercial taxes, such as *peajes*, is reflected in the ample bibliography for the realms of Aragon by Gual Camarena in his recent *Vocabulario* (see my Bibliography). For Spain as elsewhere the post-thirteenth-century periods are currently attracting attention: Ladero Quesada and Ulloa are among those who have addressed themselves to the postmedieval Castilian tax system, and Zabalo Zabalegui has gone deeply into fourteenth-century Navarrese taxes.[26] Later Valencia, though boasting a strong current of economic studies, lacks such larger syntheses. The abundant tax materials for medieval Spain in general, despite the inroads indicated, still await the historian's hand. The Arago-Catalan situation particularly invites attention, as an amalgam of Mediterranean communes and fed-

---

see Jaime Vicens Vives (with Jorge Nadal Oller), *Manual de la historia económica de España*, 7th edn. rev. (Barcelona, 1970); and as *An Economic History of Spain,* trans. F. M. López-Morillas (Princeton, 1969); ch. 19 for the realms of Aragon, ch. 22 for Castile, with bibliographical orientation.

[24] Vicente Branchát, *Tratado de los derechos y regalías que corresponden al real patrimonio en el reyno de Valencia* . . . , 3 vols. (Valencia, 1784-1786). Lorenzo Matheu y Sanz, *Tractatus de regimine regni Valentiae . . .* (Lyons, [1654] 1704).

[25] Francisco García de Cáceres, *Impuestos de la ciudad de Valencia durante la época foral* (Valencia, 1909). Félix M. Ferraz Penelas, *El maestre racional y la hacienda foral valenciana* (Valencia, 1913). I am excluding specialized topics about the tax history of later medieval Valencia, though these will be cited where pertinent as with Aliaga Girbés and Ferrer i Mallol. García y García, in studying the more northerly portion of medieval Valencia, includes reference to taxation but draws mostly on *cartas pueblas* (see Chapter III, n. 1).

[26] Miguel Ángel Ladero Quesada, *La hacienda real castellana entre 1480 y 1492* (Valladolid, 1967). Modesto Ulloa, *La hacienda real de Castilla en el reinado de Felipe II* (Rome, 1963). For Navarre see Javier Zabalo Zabalegui, *La administración del reino de Navarra en el siglo xiv* (Pamplona, 1973), part 2 on taxes (pp. 225-227 on Mudejar taxes).

erated royal states; within it, as my first chapters indicate, the Valencian tax situation was unique.

Grouping or categorizing taxes poses a problem, and not only because many taxes remain obscure or unstudied. The nature of the taxes themselves was changing, as a new-model government and a world grown suddenly more complicated confronted medieval men. The purist historian might still insist on classifying as domanial income such items as fees, rents, agrarian shares, quitrents, aids, procurations, and a range of jurisdictional prerogatives from escheats to scutage, fastidiously reserving "tax" for exactions of an origin and nature closer to our modern acceptance of that term. Bluff common sense suggests arranging the whole chaos of charges into direct and indirect taxes, characterizing apart such recalcitrant species as customs duty or justice profits.[27] If Islamic sensibilities were consulted, the project would assume further complications; the monthly shop rent paid to the government, for example, seemed to many a license, while tolls, market fees, and purchase taxes were not always clearly distinguished.

To avoid an archaic division that stresses historical continuity with origins, or an overly abstract division based on hindsight and knowledge of the developments of latter centuries, it may be more effective to view the thirteenth-century charges as Catalan contemporaries did. Though aware of origins, they hungrily stressed taxes as distinct but correlative categories of a whole. The proto-modern state, beset by novel budget demands, arrogated to itself as many sources of public income as it dared or could devise, careless of their title claims, expanding its obligations to the limits of its power. A more professional cadre employing new techniques assumed stewardship, a generation distinct both from its feudalized predecessors and from the specialized treasury bureaucracy that was to succeed it. Though framework and nomenclature remained, in imperfect disengagement from nonrevenue functions, the authorities in charge were no longer really feudal lords involved in manorial management but heads of fledgling states, experimenting with bureaucratic treasury systems, however embryonic and undifferentiated.

[27] As Herlihy does (see n. 18). Bowsky's more complex grouping as gabelles does not correspond to the Valencian actualities; I have found the word itself used mostly to mean a salt monopoly (see below, Chapter V, part 3; for later Castile see *alcabala*, from *qabāla*, in Chapter IV, n. 25).

If thirteenth-century men viewed old taxes in new perspective, they did so not only by reason of the new needs and opportunities that were allied to the general commercial revolution in business techniques and organization; the machinery itself for tax imposition underwent radical change during those very years of Valencia's postconquest surge of settlement. At that time Europe's major countries experienced a "profound transformation" into more centralized and heavily administered states; parallel to this metamorphosis came "the difficult period of fiscal reform during which western society was adjusting itself to the painful necessity of taxation." From mid-century, borrowing became extensive and public credit highly developed. "By the second half of the thirteenth century the systematic and continuous borrowing practiced in some western states began to resemble the use of credit by modern governments." Neither random nor feckless, this "wise and efficient use of credit lies behind some of the most successful achievements of medieval history."[28] The results are most visible for the last decade or two of the century and the opening decades of the next. The Mudejar taxation studied in this book, despite its unconventional or eccentric aspects, affords a fascinating panorama of the earlier, transitional decades, regarding both substantive taxes and fiscal procedure.

In the novel, changing context, such traditional feudal banalities as ovens and mills, to take a random illustration, assumed the color of indirect taxation. Just as folk songs can be subsumed into a symphony, the older tax elements, remaining recognizable, became in fact transformed. For that reason it is not improper to apply to each banality, rent, or even fee the generic name "tax." In this same

[28] E. B. and M. M. Fryde, in the section on medieval public credit, *Cambridge Economic History of Europe*, III, 431-433. Though personal and governmental revenues and budgets were intermixed, rulers did distinguish their personal debts from the needs of the realm and did respect their predecessors' debts so as to provide continuity. As an introduction to the altered social psychology and viewpoint in Spain around mid-century, see the two essays by José Antonio Maravall, "Del régimen feudal al régimen corporativo en el pensamiento de Alfonso X" for thirteenth-century Castile, and "La formación del régimen político territorial en Cataluña (la obra del jurista Pere Albert)," reprinted in his *Estudios de historia del pensamiento español*, first series, Edad Media (Madrid, 1967), pp. 87-140, 141-156. In the last decades of the thirteenth century and the first decades of the fourteenth, the further shift is characterized by Herlihy for the Pisa commune as a transfer from participatory or democratic finance systems to a more rigidly state or bureaucratic situation, simultaneously with a major expansion of revenues and important changes in indirect taxation.

fashion King James could speak of his revenues in general as *rendes*, a term he applied also to the complex of Islamic taxes to which he fell heir by conquest.[29]

A lesser problem of nomenclature is the application of tax terms familiar to medievalists but burdened with historical contexts that render them inexact for other times and places, such as corvée, scutage, or gabelle. To spare the reader as much as possible, I have tried to find equivalents that convey the nature of the tax without modernizing too brashly. Some terms useful for communication with the modern reader, conversely, do not bear the same technical meaning they had in medieval times; but context should clarify the sense intended. When the king "mortgaged" a tax, for example, this does not necessarily imply the medieval meaning, a usurious arrangement by which all products produced from the basic pledge went to the creditor without their reducing the debt (unlike a "live" gage or pledge). Formulas were probably sonorous legal phrases to be taken as a unit, rather than strictly translated by an exegesis of component elements; but I have tried to stay with one meaning for each element when translating such phrases as "redditus, exitus, proventus, fructus, et iura nostra."

In presenting so unsettled a time, one may perhaps take liberties with structure as well. I have chosen to arrange the taxes according to several broad categories, followed by a looser mixtum-gatherum in Chapters V and VI to fill in the interstices. Thus the salt fee does not come under the monopoly-utilities, nor labor service under work. This procedure was suggested not only by logical interrelations of taxes, or by such adventitious factors as surviving quantity of source materials or merciful regard for the needs of the reader, but more particularly by the role of a given tax in illuminating Mudejar life. In a social history technical rigor must yield to larger purpose, and logic to art. In a purely tax discussion, too, budgets and disbursements would have had a central place, as well as assessment of the relative weight of the several revenues, and of Christian as against Mudejar totals.

However radicated in taxes, this book remains at bottom a study of society, and implicitly of two confronting and mutually acculturative societies. Its focus is people, in their solidarities and institutions.

[29] See, e.g., Chapter II, nn. 3, 8 ("les rendes que solia p[r]endre l·arais").

Tax records yield meager results in this direction until placed within the context of converging scholarship in other fields of Hispanic and Islamic studies, not to mention the context of so many areas of medieval researches recently transformed. These have amassed an indirect bibliography that allows more sophisticated use of Valencia's tax records. Hardly anything remains for the Arabist in this task, either by way of literary exercises or proper documents; if the Muslims of this diaspora can come alive, it will be owing to the pens of European bookkeepers—a reimbursement long overdue those acquiescent taxpayers.

As described at greater length in previous prefaces, I follow a number of procedural simplifications. Words like huerta, solidus, and Sunna are adopted into English. Geographical names appear in their modern Spanish form, with a rare exception like Guadalaviar for Turia River or Murviedro for Sagunto. Given-names I Anglicize as far as possible, sometimes leaving surnames in the modern Castilian spelling and accent. Aragon's Jews similarly translate with Anglicized first names and Romance-shaped surnames (Alconstantini), with Ben replacing Ibn to clarify this non-Muslim status. Such names, and especially the conjecturally reconstructed Arabic names so corrupted by scribal ear and copyist's eye, usually have their original in the notes, accessible via the index. My Arabic transliteration follows the international program but prefers dh to ḍ, gh to ġ, j to ǧ, kh to ẖ, and sh to š; this coincides with the *Encyclopaedia of Islam* scheme, except for minor simplifications like th for ṯẖ, j for dj, and q for ḳ. The elision of *al* to the first letter of a personal name (aṭ-Ṭanjī), a speech pattern, I preserve for its pragmatic uses.[30] Arabic words, once explained, can be checked by forgetful readers through their index entries. A special section will discuss money. Land measures depended upon extrinsic variables; in the theoretical order, six tafullas made a fanecate (831 square meters), six fanecates a cafizate, and six cafizates a jovate or yoke (one day's plowing). Dates coincided in the nativity and incarnational calendars from January 1 to March 24, but only occasionally do I provide both years in such cases.

This volume grew out of several years' research in European

[30] This affects names beginning in d, dh, n, r, s, ṣ, sh, t, ṭ, z, and ẓ, and helps correlate Latin or Romance distortions with the Arabic.

archives, cast into rough draft in the late 1950's. Further materials were added during a *voyage paléographique* as Guggenheim Fellow in Spain in 1963 and 1964. Finishing touches became possible during travels for my next project in 1971 and 1973 under the auspices of the National Endowment for the Humanities, and in 1972 as a Fellow of the American Council of Learned Societies and a member of the Institute for Advanced Study at Princeton. Auxiliary funds also came from the faculty grant program of my own university.

ROBERT IGNATIUS BURNS, S.J.
UNIVERSITY OF SAN FRANCISCO

Valencia
1974

ABBREVIATIONS

ACCV	*Anales del centro de cultura valenciana*
AEM	*Anuario de estudios medievales*
AHDE	*Anuario de historia del derecho español*
Aldea Charter	Carta puebla de Aldea, February 12, 1258
Alfandech Charter	Carta puebla de Alfandech, April 15, 1277
Arch. Cat.	Archivo de la Catedral de Valencia
Arch. Cat. Tortosa	Archivo de la Catedral de Tortosa
Arch. Crown	Archivo de la Corona de Aragón
Arch. Mun. Alcira	Archivo Municipal de Alcira
Arch. Mun. Val.	Archivo Municipal de Valencia
Arch. Nac. Madrid	Archivo Histórico Nacional
Arch. Reino Val.	Archivo General del Reino de Valencia
Arch. Vat.	Archivio Segreto Vaticano
Aureum opus	*Aureum opus regalium priuilegiorum ciuitatis et regni Valentie*
Bibl. Nac. Madrid	Biblioteca Nacional (MSS)
Bibl. Univ. Val.	Biblioteca, Universidad de Valencia (MSS)
BRABLB	*Boletín de la real academia de buenas letras de Barcelona*
BRAH	*Boletín de la real academia de la historia*
BSCC	*Boletín de la sociedad castellonense de cultura*
CHE	*Cuadernos de historia de España*
Chelva Charter	Carta puebla de Chelva, August 17, 1370
Chivert Charter	Carta puebla de Chivert, April 28, 1234
Colección diplomática	A. Huici, ed., *Colección diplomática de Jaime I*
Congrés (I, III, IV, or VII)	*Congrés d'història de la corona d'Aragó*
EEMCA	*Estudios de edad media de la corona de Aragón*
EI¹, EI²	*Encyclopaedia of Islam*, old and new editions
Eslida Charter	Carta puebla de Eslida, May 29, 1242
Fori	*Fori antiqui Valentiae* (1967, Latin text)
Furs	*Fori regni Valentiae* (1548, Catalan text)
Itinerari	J. Miret y Sans, *Itinerari de Jaume I*
Játiva Charter	Carta puebla de Játiva, January 23, 1251 or 1252
Llibre dels feyts	James I, *Crònica* (autobiography)
Masones Privilege	Tax exemption by James I to the Mudejars of Masones in Aragon, 1263
RIEEIM	*Revista del instituto egipcio de estudios islámicos en Madrid*
Second Eslida Charter	Rephrased Carta puebla de Eslida, June 27, 1276
Tales Charter	Carta puebla de Tales, May 27, 1260
Tortosa Charter	Carta puebla de Tortosa, December 1148
Tortosa Convention	Agreement on Taxes, June 18, 1174
Tudela Charter	Carta puebla de Tudela, February 22, 1119
Uxó Charter	Carta puebla de Uxó, August 1250
Valencia Capitulation	Surrender Treaty for Valencia City, September 28, 1238

MEDIEVAL
COLONIALISM

CHAPTER I

The Crusader Kingdom of Valencia

KING JAMES the Conqueror had just turned twenty-five when he rode out of Teruel, late in the spring of 1233, to lead his invading army down a hinterlands road into the heart of the Moorish kingdom of Valencia. Young in years, he was haloed by the charisma of greatness. Already he had humbled the island principality of Majorca, littering its battlefields with slain Muslims and taking its walled capital bloodily by storm. Now, as he rode under the crimson-and-gold barred standard of his confederated Arago-Catalan realms, his royal person caught even the casual eye. "This king was the most imposing man in the world," observed the contemporary Desclot, "taller than any other by a palm, well proportioned and perfect in every member, and he had a large face fair and ruddy, a nose long and very straight, a generous, well-made mouth, large white teeth resembling pearls, eyes of unequal color, good reddish hair like gold thread, large shoulders, a body long and elegant, arms sturdy and well made, good hands, long fingers, sturdy thighs, legs long and straight and thick for their size, and feet long and well made and elegantly shod." To match this impressive form, the young monarch bore a lion's heart: "he was very bold, knightly in battle-skills and strong, brave, generous in giving, cordial to everyone, and very merciful; and he bent all his heart and all his will to battle against Saracens."[1]

Disinterred in modern times, the king's skeleton helps confirm this description and displays as well the great cut along his skull,

[1] Bernat Desclot, *Llibre del rei En Pere,* also called *Crònica,* ed. Miguel Coll y Alentorn, 5 vols. (Barcelona, 1949-1951); also in *Les quatre grans cròniques,* ed. Ferran Soldevila (Barcelona, 1971); ch. 12. I omit identification of other quotes, as well as citations generally, from this introductory chapter, whose positions and details are elaborately documented in my *Crusader Kingdom of Valencia* and its sequel *Islam under the Crusaders.* My theses on Mozarabic absence and on the pattern of Mudejar expulsion are drawn from work currently in preparation. The chronology for revolts and the stages in Játiva's fall are argued in *Islam.* The specialized Bibliography for the present book contains some general works and biographies for readers impatient of searching out my more elaborate previous bibliographies.

3

soon to be sustained in combat under the walls of Valencia city. Troubadour romantic by temperament, cold realist under the iron demands of circumstance, King James could hardly have hoped to wrest more than a border section from his Islamic adversaries. A deeper ambition burned in him, nevertheless, a dream from childhood on, that by conquering Valencia he would prove himself "the best king in the world and the one who has done the most." The Cid was more than a century dead; it was time for a new Cid to ride.

THE CRUSADE

What force had converted the interminable border wars of this northeastern peninsular kingdom into a surging crusade that would double its territory, fill its coffers, and help make it the master seapower of the western Mediterranean? Nothing in the young giant's boyhood had promised such a future. His dissolute father, Peter the Catholic, had continued the southern expansion of Arago-Catalonia by snatching three outlying towns at the western margin of the Valencian region, but Peter's concern to reinforce his dynasty's wide feudal power in Languedoc led to catastrophic defeat and death in 1213 on the Muret battlefield at the hands of Simon de Montfort's Albigensian crusade.

The child James had inherited an oddly yoked set of territories, basically a heavily feudal upland region that lent its name, Aragon, and its royal title to the confederation, and the more mercantile city-state culture along the coast with an agricultural hinterland under the generic name Catalonia. Barcelona was the center of gravity for the Catalan counties as Zaragoza was for the Aragonese, though in practical affairs Lérida at their border served James I as a kind of capital or center of operations. Both regions backed onto the Pyrenees, the Catalans spilling over especially to include the Roussillon county and a far-flung network of feudal lords in Languedoc. King James himself was born in 1208 at Montpellier, a city on whose affairs and celebrated university he kept a close eye, making visitations during eighteen, or nearly half, of the latter forty years of his reign. Aragonese and Catalans differed in language, social structure, money system, laws, parliaments, landscape, economy, traditions, and temperament. Neither yielded to the other in its devotion to the king of Aragon, of the county-house of Barcelona, under whose "Crown" or realms they cooperated.

At the age of seventeen James, having survived the multiple perils and baronial turmoil of his minority—partly owing to the protective authority of Innocent III—launched his first invasion or raid in 1225 against Islamic Valencia. Unwisely he targeted the mighty offshore castle Peñíscola; his abortive adventure gained only a face-saving annual tribute from the Valencian *walī*. James did not return for nearly a decade, but by that time much had changed. The boy had metamorphosed into the Conqueror, leader of an amphibious crusade preached by the papal legate and bitterly fought through 1229 and 1230, by which he had become master of strategic Majorca. His Languedocian prospects had meanwhile grown less tenable. The upland Aragonese, jealous of Catalan preponderance in this Balearics enterprise, desired a countervailing expansion into Valencia. Most important of all, the monolithic Almohad empire of North Africa and Spain had come unstitched like some long-rotten garment, and King James found himself advantageously allied with one faction of the ensuing civil war dividing Valencia.

James had been an infant when western Islam's time of troubles began. Las Navas de Tolosa, that stunning victory of the Spanish Christian states in 1212, portended the end of the Almohad caliphate and the downfall of its capital, Marrakesh, at the edge of the Sahara. Less causative than catalytic, the battle triggered a series of misfortunes, intrigues, revolts, and failed opportunities. A victim of this terminal convulsion fragmenting both North Africa and Spain, the *walī* or governor of Valencia Abū Zayd found himself retreating north under the attacks of the usurper Zayyān. Murcia, the neighboring region to the south, which Abū Zayd ineffectively claimed, had earlier fallen to the popular hero Ibn Hūd. Local dynasts entrenched themselves at internal enclaves like Játiva. Desperate for allies, the cultivated *walī* entered alliance with Aragon in 1229, transforming the nominal tribute into partnership and surrendering to James whatever the Christians might conquer during their joint war plus a fourth of general revenues.

By the time the Conqueror could disengage from the Balearics to take advantage of his bargain, Abū Zayd found his own position so deteriorated that he had to sign away to James all revenues from

Valencia city and its huerta. While the white standard of the Almo-hads took its place beside the crimson bars of Aragon in chivalrous show, the canny lawyers computed crown profits, arranged for prop-erty redistribution, and in general prepared the colonial regime. Four years later Abū Zayd reduced himself to vassalage, saw James borrow the title "king of Valencia," which the *walī* had employed in deal-ings with the Christians, and as a convert began like the Cheshire cat to diminish and then disappear from the public scene.

The crusade itself falls into three general stages—for the north, the center, and the south. In 1232 a baronial incursion took over Morella and its mountainous northwest region. The next year James led his first invasion down the Teruel road. His strategy during these first years was to fasten upon key points, starting with the crucial city of Burriana, so as to isolate subsidiary castles and induce their sur-render on terms. It was a game of guile as much as of force, mini-mizing a feudal king's intermittent and imperfect control of his military resources but leaving him at the mercy of evolving contin-gencies as the years wore on. By 1235 James had overrun the north; in early 1236 he installed a symbolic little garrison on the hillock of Puig, within distant sight of Valencia city. He had accomplished this with very little damage to property or interruption of the economy, except for a siege at Burriana with expulsion of its populace.

Assiduously he rounded out his military efforts by a multiplicity of local capitulations, involving charters or constitutions which guaranteed privileges and spelled out the main revenue conditions. Though overextended, he had succeeded beyond expectation. With the road open into central Valencia, James found himself in position to inaugurate a more massive national effort. Rallying his realms by a joint parliament at Monzón in 1236, he assumed the royal title over Valencia and returned to the attack in impressive force. This time the crusade, again formally preached in the name of Rome, attracted warriors widely, from Languedoc, Provence, and Italy.

The Islamic hosts gathered in 1237 for their major offensive effort, a pitched battle intended to overrun Puig and roll back the Christian front. It failed dismally. Zayyān fell back within Valencia city, re-signed to a siege. From April until late September the vise tightened, until famine stalked the town's arabesque of streets. It was a half-year of epic incident—sallies by the defenders, close combat under the walls, heavy artillery sullenly thudding, even a staged tournament of Islamic and Christian champions. Meanwhile Christian armies ranged the area in slashing raids, while James kept up his reliable trick of separate surrenders. The celebrated poet and chancellor Ibn al-Abbār contrived to slip out from the stricken city and make his way to Tunis, now an independent power; his eloquence unleashed a fleet and army to lift the siege, but the crusaders repulsed it at Valencia's shores and the garrison of Peñíscola beat back its landing in the north. In faraway England Matthew Paris recorded how "the splendid and indefatigable warrior the lord king of Aragon so ravaged the great city of Valencia by bloody war, and so closely invested it, as to force its surrender." On September 28, 1238, Zayyān handed over all his holdings down to the Júcar River. Valencia city's population followed Burriana's into exile.

There the crusade might have rested, with the lower third of the former "kingdom" and Murcia beyond that as surviving Islamic states. At the Júcar, however, James realized that Játiva castle under the Banū 'Īsā dynasty "was the key to the kingdom, and I could not be king of the kingdom of Valencia if Játiva were not mine." Appetite had fed on conquest. Just as at Puig the king had realized that Valencia was ripe for the taking, if only he could rally his kingdom to the cause, so now on a visit to Játiva he eyed its castle and panorama with "great joy and great happiness in my heart," for God surely destined it for Christendom. A pseudo-siege in 1239 failed to bluff the ruling qā'id. In 1240 James sent a second host, this time securing the small prize of minimal vassalage. Soon the king's sly eye discerned a technical breach of feudal contract. He suffered the embarrassment of having the Banū 'Īsā countermove by shifting their vassalage to Castile, bullied the Castilian king into a partition agreement at the treaty of Almizra, and in 1244 negotiated the isolated qā'id into releasing the lesser castle (with surrender of the main castle due by 1246) in return for a powerful but less central fief of Montesa. Meanwhile Alcira, on an island in the Júcar, followed a pattern resembling Játiva's, while other towns of the south fell like ripe fruit into the Aragonese basket. Biar's surrender in 1245 marked the end of the crusade and its southern limits.

Fighting did not wholly stop. Castile's share from the Almizra treaty was Murcia; a restive garrison state of Castile from 1243, it boiled into revolt in 1264. Alfonso the Learned, embroiled in the wider revolt throughout Andalusia, invoked the military aid of

Aragon. James sent his son Peter twice at the head of armies in 1265, conducted the final decisive campaign himself in 1266, then honorably restored the region to Alfonso. Castile had not slumbered idly while the Conqueror labored in Majorca and Valencia. The whole Spanish front had surged forward, Cordova falling in 1236, Jaén in 1246, Seville in 1248, and Cadiz in 1265. Behind mountain ramparts at the peninsula's tip, the last remnants of Spanish Islam had organized itself as Granada, relict and heir of glories departed. Across the straits, Morocco's new Marinid dynasty had settled in at Fez, while the Hafsids at Tunis presumed to affect the caliphal title and a strong principate emerged between the two at Tlemcen.

In conquered Valencia, King James's lot was not a happy one. Revolts recurred so continuously that their chronology still confuses modern historians, every decade counting one major uprising and the longest period of peace lasting less than a decade. Patriot heroes like al-Azraq used their Mudejar fiefs as bases to rally rebellion and harry the ill-secured country. My own reconstruction of this moot and muddled story puts a first phase of revolt beginning shortly after the close of the crusade and probably before the traditional date of 1247, running through late 1249; a second phase began in early 1257, continuing through June 1258; an interim period of unrest disturbed the kingdom between 1252 and 1256, with some disquiet as postscript in the early 1260's.

All these troubles proved minor compared to the rebellion that rocked Valencia, and indeed all Spain, from 1275. James struggled desperately to retain his new kingdom, until death overtook him in July 1276 on the Valencian frontier, with no time for the niceties of a proper entombment at the royal pantheon of Poblet. His thirty-six-year-old son and successor, Peter the Great (1276-1285), soon to become liberator of Sicily by the War of the Sicilian Vespers and to go down in history as Dante's troubadour hero, had to put off his coronation. As his contemporary Muntaner remarked, Peter was forced to "conquer part of the kingdom of Valencia a second time." The new king describes succinctly how the Valencian Muslims "rebelled with many castles and strongholds," bringing in armies from Islamic Granada and from "the regions of Barbary," so that his own "large armies" had to subdue Valencia "with great slaughter, toil, and expense."

8

Trouble had begun by December 1275; in March 1276 James was convoking an army from all his realms; by June the rebels controlled forty castles and the king had established his base at Játiva. After a heavy defeat at Luchente, followed by the old king's untimely death, Peter contrived a three-month truce, which began in September. Slow progress throughout 1277, culminating in the Montesa campaign that fall, with mopping-up operations and diminuendo echoes thereafter, finally secured the Valencia kingdom. Castile had not been so lucky; from mid-1275 it had to contend with invasions led by Morocco's ruler Abū Yūsuf as well as with general revolt of its Moorish subjects into 1279, followed by civil war among the Castilians.

These alarums and excursions bore relevance to the revenue scene in Valencia. They did not result in general repression or loss of privilege, but they ended Mudejar nobiliary control over large segments of the country, dealt the *coup de grâce* to lingering hopes for Islamic restoration, disorganized collections temporarily, occasioned their tighter organization afterwards, introduced successive drafts of Christian immigrants, diminished some town populations of Muslims into Moorish quarters, and in general hastened the demographic rearrangement, the displacement of Muslims from high commerce and from establishment or control situations, and the intensification of colonial grip that made Valencia by 1285 a far different human situation than it had been at crusade's end in 1245.

Colonial Mudejarism

King James had inherited the pattern by which Arago-Catalonia absorbed and administered subject Moors; it reflected general Mediterranean experience and had analogies in Islamic and Byzantine lands. Treatment of Jews, and to a lesser extent of foreigners like the Genoese within Spain, betrayed this same mentality. Neither tolerance nor discriminatory ghetto, it pragmatically accepted parallel, antipathetic societies. Where such an enclave existed as a unitary religio-social entity, it became in effect a second established religion in the realm, protected in its liturgies, subject to its separate law and courts, enjoying its local officers of rule, conducting its schools, living by its proper calendar, and in general standing apart carapaced in limited autonomy and alien cultural forms. The system permitted any anomaly proper to each society, from polygamy to the Mecca pilgrimage, but sternly forbade crossing over—Christian to Jew for example, or Jew to Muslim. Theoretically the host society welcomed and even sought converts; in practice Valencia's Christians demonstrated lively prejudice against them as cultural aliens, and her barons resisted the economic loss to tithes and the untidy repercussions in life, law, and real estate exchange.

Administrative practice so readily fell in with the concept of parallel societies that Alfonso VI, conqueror of Toledo, had styled himself "ruler of two religions," while King James's crusading colleague St. Ferdinand III of Castile was to flaunt on his tombstone inscriptions in Latin, Arabic, Hebrew, and Castilian. If city conditions encouraged, and feebly enforced, an apartheid residence, this rather resembled the clustering of artisan or immigrant groups according to their specialties or places of origin; only in the fourteenth century would this situation become the base for extended restrictive legislation in Valencia. In most towns and over the countryside however, Christians and Muslims lived cheek by jowl. Life tended to mix the two populations. They met and mingled at a hundred levels—in business, entertainment, agriculture, markets, travel, domestic service, social life, vice, and crime. At some levels a distance was kept; Muslims had their own days at city baths, and their dietary laws and distinct tax structure encouraged separate public utilities such as meat-stalls or mills. The Islamic society also found itself interpenetrated by Christian officialdom and customs at the overlapping edges—intersocietal lawsuits, major crimes, public order, appeals to the king or local lord, or contributions of army contingents.

If King James inherited the Mudejar pattern, he had to apply it in terms so unique as to mutate the experience qualitatively. The scale of the Valencian enterprise—immersing Christian immigrants in a sea of Muslims, clustered in city atolls or more often scattered adrift—altered the balance of traditional Mudejarism. The sheer size of the new acquisition, strung out along the open sea and connected to the homeland mostly along its northern hinterlands, provided in its own way a novel frame. Sea lanes and geographical determinants tied it to the progressive commune world of Catalonia, intruding the Christian community into the Islamic not only at multiple points but in the most advanced modern form—that is to say, in the form farthest evolved from what had once been common to Christian and Islamic societies.

Mudejarism was an acculturative phenomenon. The impact of a conquering society inevitably introduced disorientation and change in the defeated, as well as osmotic but superficial borrowings of life-style in both directions. A deliberately transformative society, how-ever, no matter how protective of its dissident majority, worked larger mischief, eroding boundaries by which a society maintains its identity, and sapping confidence in its self-image. As the Arago-Catalan forms took over, Gothic churches altered the skyline, access streets shattered the expressive city maze, Christian calendars and money dominated the daily round, and Christian officials or busi-nessmen dictated the pace and style. The Muslims became mere guests in their own home as these new owners moved in. The mobile rich among the conquered, along with the artistic and intellectual leaven they supported, plus the most zealously pious and most dy-namically adventuresome, chafed at the new order and progressively drifted toward Granada or Tunis. Though the myth of mass expul-sion cannot stand close examination, except for exceptions like Burriana and the capital, the loss of leadership was real.

Those staying behind, a remnant in psychological rather than demographic terms, tended to divide into the intransigents, frozen in their basic cultural forms and sterilely recapitulating the past, and the compromisers, who moved with the times and lost their sense of self. This cruel dilemma did not pose itself at once, but emerged only as the decades wore on, its outlines clarified more rudely with every rebellion suppressed. The Valencian Mudejar long retained his proper dress, beard, and diet, responded to the keening call of the muezzin from the ubiquitous minarets, comfortably observed how his Islamic names and customs still defined even the Christian ambience, normally went before his own judges, swore all his oaths on the holy Koran, bought and sold land freely, engaged in high finance or any enterprise, moved freely overseas—and suffered pro-found dislocation of spirit. Every strain of his environment betrayed the infidels' pollution; every scene was distracted by the infidel presence at the corner of his eye. Tolerance was not enough; this Disneyland replica of his father's world stood as an affront. Most Mudejars stayed, immobilized by their past, surviving with dry-eyed courage, turned in upon themselves and the old ways. The more brutally transformative Mudejarism of past centuries, soon assimilating all but the hard core, might have proved more merciful. Valencia remained a curiously schizoid land, its colonialist society scarcely adverting to the native host-body, its minority-status majority persevering listlessly as an irrelevant curiosity, its cultural ecology somehow askew.

For forty years, nevertheless, the better part of a lifetime, Valencian Islam persisted with relatively little change, in a kind of twilight before the dark closed down. To discern its configuration during that period, even as seen through brisk business documents, means to discover as well the previous Almohad century so obscure in the region's Islamic history. There is no room to recapitulate here what my previous book uncovered concerning social classes, from slave and prostitute, through artisan and *exaricus* sharecropper, to aristocrat and high merchant. Nor is there time to discuss again the complex ethnic strains, whether Yemenite as opposed to Syriac Arabs or whether al-Butr as opposed to al-Barānis Berbers; each ethnic group intermixed with the Visigothic-nuanced Iberian peoples of the coast and with the continually evolving cosmopolitan mélange, which ranged from the misnamed "Slave" stratum to the seaport hodgepodge of immigrants. Rustic differed from city dweller, though not decisively since urban folk often held country farms, while farmers lived in towns or villages more often than in isolated cottages (*barracas*).

Islamic society tended to the undifferentiated or rather interpenetrating, so that a single individual might simultaneously enjoy mercantile, religious, administrative, and intellectual roles, with the several elites or solidarities in each of these categories converging in family communities and cutting across the diversity of subcommunities. Actual power, and this supporting establishment-power, resided in the main families of town or village, who provided the local notables and town council, often with a princeling or military despot holding the balance for a given neighborhood. No clear distinction appears between the nobiliary-military and the mercantile-notable strata at this exalted level in Valencia, a situation that recalls the overweening upper classes of Renaissance Florence.

Executive power, especially at the lesser levels, worked through an administrative team. Historians have described this as comprising an *alamí* with one to four assistant *adelantats*, advised by a council of sheiks. This reflects later evolution. The *amín* by terminology was vaguely any faithful agent; in the Valencian executive or intra-aljama context he stands forth as a specific officer. Ubiquitous and prominent, he appears rather in the guise of a fiscal agent with some juridical and governmental influence. As a consequence he made a convenient bridge between the Islamic and Christian communities, taking on functions that only embryonically foreshadowed the central administrator into which he later evolved. At this early period the *qāḍī* and at times the *qā'id* was easily a more exalted figure of civil government. In Valencia, a land dotted by more than fifty major fortifications with numerous supporting defenses, the indeterminate title *qā'id* frequently stood for a castellan, whether princely or serving some outlying tower. The civil ruler, even at humble levels, often enough went under this title, his military attribution probably becoming secondary or absent in most places during the postcrusade period.

The religio-judicial *qāḍī*, whose name the Christian scribes sometimes confounded in its Latin or even Romance form with that of *qā'id*, had long fallen heir to civil government in many places of Islamic Spain, and even to a military dynastic role. A Valencian community at this period normally spoke through its representative *qāḍī*. The general term *faqīh*, meaning jurist or savant, at times apparently concealed a *qāḍī* ruler. Other community officers, like the *ṣāḥib aṣ-ṣalat* or the fascinating *muḥtasib*, stand out in the records but need not detain us here. A certain hierarchy or clientage wove the disparate units into regional and eventually provincial integrity; the informal solidarities, at levels like the religio-legal rite or the family, filled this function more solidly.

The Mudejar population is difficult to total. Valencia city and Játiva, at a time in the thirteenth century when both cities had drastically reduced their Moorish quarters, each held about 300 households or some 1,300 Muslims. Valencia city's total population stood at about 15,000. (Large cities in Aragon—Barcelona and Zaragoza aside—counted less than 10,000, while most were under 1,000 or even 500.) Historians variously conjecture the Valencia kingdom's total, García de Valdeavellano recently suggesting 150,000 Mudejars for Valencia and Majorca together. King James complained, toward the end of his life, that only 30,000 Christians had settled the new kingdom, where safety demanded at least 100,000. Whether the royal figures represent individuals or households, they convey some appreciation of relative strength. Sixteenth-century Moriscos or neo-Christians, remnant of Valencia's Mudejars, numbered 30,000 households or 135,000 individuals out of 300,000—in a Spain whose full population may have reached eight or nine million. At that time the Dutch geographer Blaeu reckoned Valencia's whole populace as 100,000 families in four cities, sixty walled towns, and a thousand villages.

THE KINGDOM AND ITS RECONSTRUCTION

Valencia extended down a long ribbon of coastland, from just below Tortosa on the Ebro River to just above Alicante near Murcia; James's grandson James II was to add an Alicante-Orihuela tail. It comprised a series of irrigated huertas and lively commercial cities, set like a necklace of emeralds and pearls against the baser pastoral zones, badlands, and marginal dry lands. The opposition was not clear-cut; heterogeneity prevailed, with each bloc or zone displaying a different balance of lush and dry, town and rural, valley, plain or pastoral. Just as rural merged with urban, with townsmen frequently holding farms, so the farmer commonly owned a mixture of dry land (olives, vineyards, grain) and irrigated land (fruits and vegetables). Backed against the Castilian escarpment and the uninviting highlands of Aragon proper, the Valencian faced out to sea, his chain of cities buzzing with seagoing commerce, every class from knight to ambitious farmer involving itself in trade.

Jurisdictionally the realm fell naturally into some hundred town-cum-countryside divisions, each englobing smaller village-countryside entities, with about twenty-five principal divisions. Each city-state or councilled-town set the pace for its region and satellite towns, the Christian jurates replacing the local conventicle of sheiks. A dozen major towns stood preeminent—Morella in the mountainous northwest; Peñíscola and Burriana on the north coast; Murviedro, Valencia, and Cullera on the central coast, with Liria and Segorbe inland and Alcira as a riverport on the south; and Játiva castellating a strategic ridge in the southern tumble of mountains closing the kingdom, with Denia and Gandía at the coast. The Guadalaviar River ran past Valencia in the center, while the Mijares

14

River cut off the north, as did the Júcar River the south. In Islamic times the main entities had combined variously, Játiva and Valencia tending to play the role of province capitals, the bleaker north rather assimilating to Tortosa.

James organized these areas as a separate kingdom, its rulers' names to be numbered distinctively, with special money and with a unique code of public law. His son served as procurator general, having a lieutenant as vicegerent and two sublieutenants dividing the country at the Júcar. For property and fiscal affairs, two general bailiffs at Játiva and Valencia city presided over the chaos of local bailiffs, tax farmers, castellan-debtors, and special collectors. Here too the heterogeneity seen in geography and society recurs, rather than a rationalized pattern. In the cities, elected jurates and the court's justiciar stand out. These several jurisdictions, each encased in its bureaucracy, overlapped; they existed alongside alodial, baronial, or ecclesiastical holdings, each providing its own lord-and-bailiff organization. King James himself devoted more attention to Valencia than to any of his other principalities, making assiduous visitation there. In his struggle to rise from feudal suzerain to Roman-law king, he cherished Valencia as a lever.

The crown immediately became dominant landholder, keeping most cities of importance and at least a third of the land. It distributed the rest to barons, knights, ecclesiastical lords like the Templars, or alodial tenants. Significantly, large baronial estates were few, mostly encumbering the north. Holdings tended to be modest and often lay under almost token rents. The distance between landlord-farmer and proud knight could appear minimal. Here again heterogeneity marked the land; rather than a feudal pyramid, the scene reveals rather a landlord and share-farmer (*exaricus*) pattern, with the farmer free to add to his holdings or to sell and leave. Crown and seigniors both brought in immigrants, sometimes Muslims from overseas; to open a bloc of land they often set up a group of settlement-leaders armed with a charter of privileges and obligations. The pace and pattern of Christian immigration remains obscure, though the collection of distribution-notes called the *Repartimiento* allows some reconstruction. Morella and Burriana in the north took sudden influxes, as did patchy areas wherever revolt failed; the main inpouring came at the center, between the Mijares and Júcar but especially at Valencia city with its huerta. Alcira, Játiva, Gandía, and the southern mountains showed increasing Christian settlement from mid-century.

By the crusade era, no body of Mozarabs remained to ease the transition, though individuals may have survived in negligible number. The Jews, more favored than the unitary ideology of contemporary Europe allowed, filled this intermediary role, serving as secretaries or diplomats in Islamic affairs and looming prominently in revenue collection and finance. In ecclesiastical matters, the diocese of Tortosa took over much of the north, and Valencia diocese the center and south, with an upstart diocese of Segorbe-Abarracín pushing in at the center-rear over loud protests. Military orders, mendicants, prayerful Benedictines, hospital and ransom groups—a bewildering array of independent energy points—devised their own maps of the new kingdom and busily set about their proper tasks.

In the burgeoning thirteenth century, this new frontier held out special and varied promise. The farmer sought free land, the knight estates, the Dominican many converts by his Arabic language schools, the merchant sudden profits from the Tunis trade, the surprising flocks of lawyers fame and fortune, the lowly cleric one of the many benefices, the schoolmaster a role in the university then forming, the artisan a part in such industries as paper, ceramics, or shipbuilding, the stockman a foothold along the celebrated sheep-walks, the banker a stall at some busy port, and the architect his chance at a Gothic church. The defeated Muslim could only observe this bustle with stoic sullenness or growing dismay, and cry with the poet ar-Rundī:

> Ask Valencia what became of Murcia,
> And where is Játiva, and where is Jaén?

CHAPTER II

The Economics of Crusade Victory

AT THE IDEOLOGICAL level, the subordination of Islam was the main preoccupation of the crusaders. At the more immediate human or social level the theme of chivalric function was repeatedly sounded. In terms of abiding advantage, however, the permanent acquisition of tax sources moved crusade leaders deeply. Understanding of the crusade begins here, according to one historian of Valencia, so that explanations in terms of opposed religions disorient the researcher by posing a false problem; to get taxes the crusaders would concede almost anything.[1] He makes his point too strongly, but it remains true that official and administrative leadership saw taxation as the practical foundation of rule and society. The North African, Ibn Khaldūn, generalized this principle of government in the next century in his famed study of social mechanisms. Taxes had further importance in Valencia as the point of closest frequent contact between the two peoples, as the greatest contribution by the Mudejar community to the total combined society, as the basis for a mutual relationship of respect, and as a motive for official protection of the dissident majority.

All this was reasonable. The nature of the conquered kingdom—an unusually fat and prosperous land—elevated the reasonable to a matter of passionate concern. In the Conqueror's lifetime and before any considerable Christian immigration, the lawyer-pope Innocent IV brought to the settlement of a royal inheritance dispute the sober finding of his experts, that Valencia's public revenues "much exceed" those of mercantile Catalonia. James himself estimated the total revenues of Islamic Valencia's governor at 500,000 besants or 1,875,000 solidi. The struggle to acquire these revenues, and their consequent deployment in the king's wars, were to comprise an important factor in transforming the realms of Aragon from a feudal to a constitutional monarchy. Valencian prosperity, moreover, contrasted with

---

[1] Francisco A. Roca Traver, "Un siglo de vida mudéjar en la Valencia medieval (1238-1338)," *EEMCA*, v (1952), 138-139. See also Vicens Vives, *Economic History of Spain*, p. 71.

the economic depression then afflicting both Aragon proper and Catalonia, making the expansive new realm even more desirable as a revenue source. This wealth represented the continuing economy of the precrusade Muslims. As their tax records demonstrate, the post-conquest Mudejars kept a goodly share of it; the Játiva aljama alone, to forestall expulsion after revolt, was able to offer King James a hundred thousand besants annually. In the new kingdom of Valencia, therefore, both peoples held a considerable stake in the economic *status quo*—the crusaders as heirs to a commercial and agrarian cornucopia, and the Muslims as profiting from a stable social order after decades of turmoil.[2]

COLONIAL TAXATION

To a king chronically short of money, his reach always exceeding his financial grasp, the economic dimension formed the most im-portant single aspect of the new kingdom. In his memoirs King James described how "all the rents in Aragon and Catalonia were held in pawn," and how 570 of 700 crown fiefs had been sold or alienated. He blamed his father for a foolish generosity and squan-dering, "through which his revenues and estates" were diminished

[2] Arch. Vat., Reg. Vat. 22, Innocent IV, fol. 88v, curiales, ep. 46 (March 5, 1251): "quod in redditibus et proventibus comitatum barchinonensem multum excedit." On the Játiva offer, see King James I, *Llibre dels feyts*, or *Crònica*, ed. Josep M. de Casacuberta, 9 vols. in 2 (Barcelona, 1926-1962); see also Soldevila, *Les quatre grans cròniques*, ch. 368; 100,000 besants in 1257 were worth some 375,000 solidi (see below, p. 80). Usher devotes a chapter of his classic *Early History of Deposit Banking in Mediterranean Europe* to the relations between the Arago-Catalan kings and the banking system (ch. 15); unfortunately it is concerned almost exclusively with the modern system appearing from about 1360, but he gives close attention to our region throughout his work and closes with an 80-page glossary of Catalan financial terms. He argues that "the wars of the thirteenth century led to the systematic development of new sources of revenue, which rapidly lost their purely feudal character," drawing the parliament into an ever more active role until "a strictly feudal state" became during that century "in fact a constitutional monarchy." If the decisive role here was that of constitutional mechanisms in controlling and exploiting both old and new revenues, first to take and hold Valencia and then to finance the Sicilian adventure, Valencian revenues constituted a main lodestone and resource. For the depressions and Valencia, see Antonio Ubieto Arteta, *Ciclos económicos en la edad media española* (Valencia, 1969), pp. 109-110; Islamic Valencia shared the Almohad economic crisis, but improved after the crusade, falling into recession again at the end of the century.

to a crippling degree. James remembered especially the day as boy-king at Monzón "when I had nothing to eat, so ruined and mort-gaged was the land!" Pope Innocent III, as protector of the young ruler, and his cardinal legate had intervened, briskly forbidding "castles or other properties or revenues to be given or alienated to anyone or bound by mortgage" without "express consent"; Innocent ordered the Jews and Mudejars to pay their taxes to the master of the Knights Templar, who was under strict obligation to turn these and all income "to liberating the realm from mortgages." The pope had to call on "all citizens of Catalonia and Aragon to contribute timely funds" for redeeming the pledged revenues. Eventually King James placed a Templar apiece over Aragon and Catalonia as bailiffs general, with their master as treasurer, "both for discharging the mortgages and for supervising and receiving all our revenues and income."[3]

James grappled with finances during the next fifteen years with limited success and few enduring results. Even after he stood before Christendom as the Conqueror, master of the Balearics and of northern Valencia with Burriana, his counselors urged military retreat, grimly warning that he was falling into "great expense": "for you know and we know just as well with you, that you do not possess a treasury, neither do you hold large rents, nor do you have bread anywhere at all but are hard put for subsistence as you wander about your realms." Neither James nor his successor Peter, as the latter confessed, "ever established or had a treasure" but existed by budgeting current revenues. In Valencia itself, after the conquest, barons and religious orders held their estates tax-free, while the crown had to reduce the amount of obligations to lure the all-too-

---

[3] *Llibre dels feyts*, ch. 11: "toda la renda que nostre pare havia en Arago e en Catalunya era empenyorada"; "e no haviem a un dia . . . que menjar, si era la terra destroida e empenyorada!"; ch. 6: "tant donava que ses rendes e ses terres ne valien menys." On problems involved in the first text, see below, p. 245. *La documenta-ción pontificia hasta Inocencio III (965-1216)*, ed. Demetrio Mansilla Reoyo (Rome, 1955), doc. 537 (Jan. 23, 1216): "castra vero vel alie possessiones aut redditus nulli donentur vel alienentur seu pignorari obligentur nec etiam aliqua loca de novo incastillentur absque . . . expresso consensu"; "ad regni pignora liberanda . . . [et] in redemptionem pignorum convertantur nec in alios usus idem magister expendere valeat." Doc. 538 (same date): "universis civibus Cathalonie et Aragoniae mandatur, ut pro redemptione . . . subsidium opportunum impendant." Doc. 539 (same date) to all Montpellier residents, for their taxes to be used to pay the king's living expenses.

rare immigrants; and Valencian grants tended to evolve into economically alodial status.[4]

The tax structure for Mudejars on crown lands therefore had special importance. The most plentiful, exact crown records about Muslims consequently were bound to be financial. This prosaic money documentation affords rare glimpses into aspects of life under the Christians. It also tells much, in revealing exploitation or restraint, about official policy and Christian attitudes. A Mudejar expected to pay annual tribute plus a number of rents. The consecrated pattern of Mudejarism reconciled the defeated to this need, and a relatively prosperous Moor would not have been disposed to quibble over fair taxes. His situation was not essentially different anyway from that of his Christian neighbor paying tithes and rents. In much the same way, the Mozarab minority living under Islamic rule had turned over a fifth of produce (double the amount paid by his Muslim neighbors) plus a head tax on adult males; an ordinary Christian laborer with no status might have surrendered a third if resident on Islamic state lands, four-fifths if on quasi-seignorial lands.[5]

[4] *Llibre dels feyts*, ch. 180: "una gran messio . . . car vos sabets, e nos sabem ho aitambe con vos, que vos no·n havets tresaur, ni vos no havets gran renda, ni no havet pa en loch del mon, ans sots enbargat de viure anan per vostra terra." At Burriana, King James had just borrowed the food and equipment for a Burriana garrison for two months from merchants, promising the knights 16,000 morabatins as well. Before storming the capital of Majorca previously, he had arranged to buy supplies for 60,000 pounds (1,200,000 solidi) and later to hire 100 extra knights at 1,000 solidi per knight (chs. 82, 92, and see chs. 99, 165, 205, 216); if the "pounds" were really "besants," as only the Latin MS by Pedro Marsili says, the first figure would be closer to a quarter million solidi. Ferran Soldevila, *Pere el Gran*, 2 parts in 4 vols. (Barcelona, 1950-1962), part I, 1, 93: "nec nos vel alii predecessores nostri nunquam fecerimus nec habuerimus thesaurum." On Valencian land as tending to the alodial, see José Martínez Aloy, *La diputación de la generalidad del reino de Valencia* (Valencia, 1930), pp. 4-10, 17-18. On the crown's financial crises see also Ferran Soldevila, *Els primers temps de Jaume I* (Barcelona, 1968), pp. 85-87, 183-186, 195-196, and Charles de Tourtoulon, *Don Jaime I el Conquistador, rey de Aragón, conde de Barcelona, señor de Montpeller, según las crónicas y documentos inéditos*, 2d edn., rev. and trans., Teodoro Llorente y Olivares, 2 vols. (Valencia, 1874), I, 131-133.

[5] An exemplar document in one of the incunabula at the Arch. Reino Val., for practical use in drawing contracts, affords a view of the main Mudejar taxes collected from the thirteenth through the fifteenth centuries. This "Venditio cuiusdam loci populati sarracenorum," after covering fields and waters, ovens, mills, shops, taverns, and the like, lists "monetatico sive morabatino terciodecimo agrariis censibus laudimiis faticis çofris almagramis biscuicis alfardis herentiis peytis questis demandis

Mudejarism furnished a bare outline, which in detail assumed varying patterns. At each surrender, though deeper factors like religion raised little debate, money matters inspired protracted haggling. It was precisely with rents and dues that King James showed himself most canny. In his autobiography he boasts of petty victories in such transactions, obviously pleased with his cleverness. After the essentials were yielded to an aljama, revenue questions left room for making the most of a given strategic situation or for bettering it by recourse to bluff. The overall result was an acceptable tax structure not too dissimilar from that of the preconquest Muslim or of the Christian immigrant. The assumption that Valencian Moors bought their administrative and religious liberties dearly, paying "gravosísimas extorsiones," in the words of a respected authority,[6] is not true. There is reason to suspect that taxation under the Christian ruler proved less onerous than under the unstable local kinglets of post-Almohad Islamic Spain. Ibn Khaldūn posits the principle that fragmentation of political authority leads to the creation of novel and crushing taxation, as "happened in Spain at the time of the petty kings"—the *reyes de taifas*—until the Almoravids "put an end to it."[7] Perhaps affairs had not degenerated so badly in eastern Spain by the time of the crusade, but deterioration of the tax structure must already have begun.

King James can say: "So I had Alcira and got the revenues that the governor [*ra'īs*]—that is, the lord—used to get." At Uxó he summed the obligations: "they should give me the taxes just as they did to their king," and "all those rents that they used to pay before

---

et actionibus penis caloniis atque multis civilibus et criminalibus oste et cavalcata redemptionibusque eorundem et aliis servitutibus et ademprimis [*for* adempriviis] atque cum . . . ," followed by jurisdictional detail (*Formularium diversorum contractuum et instrumentorum secundum pratiquam et consuetudinem civitatis et regni Valentie* [Valencia, 1499 (?)], fols. xxviiii-xxx). On the Mozarabic Christian's taxes under Islam, see Isidro de las Cagigas, *Los mozárabes*, 2 vols. (Madrid, 1947-1948), II, 320-321; and Florencio Janer, *Condición social de los moriscos de España, causas de su expulsión y consecuencias que esta produjo en el orden económico y político* (Madrid, 1857), p. 13.

[6] Francisco Fernández y González, *Estado social y político de los mudejares de Castilla, considerados en sí mismos y respecto de la civilización española* (Madrid, 1866), p. 271.

[7] Ibn Khaldūn ('Abd ar-Raḥmān b. Muḥammad Walī ad-Dīn b. Khaldūn), *The Muqaddimah: An Introduction to History*, trans. Franz Rosenthal, 2d edn., 3 vols. (Princeton, 1967), II, 92, (ch. 3, sec. 37).

the Moors left the land." The Uxó charter spelled out these dues, which on examination prove not to differ strikingly from those prevailing elsewhere in Valencia; the basic crown taxes owed by all subject Muslims therefore were much the same as they had delivered to their own rulers. Some fees, like Eslida's fines and Uxó's castle services, were specified as following preconquest pattern. In detail as in generality, the tax arrangements furnished a link with the past and facilitated the transition from independence to Mudejarism.[8]

Total Revenues

Taxes from Valencia's aljamas mounted up to a considerable sum. A preliminary impression of their richness, in several local contexts, will prepare the way for consideration of each separate tax; only after the evidence of subsequent chapters has been weighed, including those on collecting, can one form a fuller and more satisfactory idea of totals. A decade after the closing battles of the crusade, King James imposed a levy of nearly 30,000 solidi on thirty Mudejar communities.[9] The total for any such given tax, however, does not reveal as much as the total for all taxes taken at any one spot. The rustic

[8] *Llibre dels feyts*, ch. 250: "e qu·ens donassen dretura aixi con fayen al lur rey"; ch. 332: "e prenguem les rendes que solia p[r]endre l·arais d·Algezira, ço es, lo se[n]yor." The same policy was followed by the Spanish monarchs as late as the surrender of Granada, whose surrender treaty of 1491 included: "los dichos moros non hayan de dar, nin den nin paguen, a sus altezas mas derechos que aquellos que acostumbraban dar e pagar a los reyes moros," and that Muslim merchants "non paguen mas derechos . . . de las que pagan los cristianos." The formula turns up elsewhere, as at the surrender of Almería (1490): "non . . . mas derechos de aquellos que debian e acostumbraban pagar a los reyes [moros] . . . antiguamente." Salaries, community taxes or fees, and religious income from foundations were guaranteed as a matter of course. See Fernández y González, *Mudejares de Castilla*, appendix, docs. 85, 86 (esp. nos. 25 and 29), 87. The Uxó Charter (Aug. 1250) is in *Colección de documentos inéditos para la historia de España*, ed. Martín Fernández Navarrete et alii, 112 vols. (Madrid, 1842-1896), xviii, 42-50; *Colección diplomática de Jaime I, el Conquistador*, ed. Ambrosio Huici Miranda, 3 vols. (Valencia, 1916-1922), doc. 383; Fernández y González, *Mudejares de Castilla*, appendix, doc. 23. Eslida Charter (May 29, 1242), is in *Documentos inéditos de España*, xviii, 55-58. "Carta puebla de Eslida, Senqueir, Pelmes, Ayn, Veo, Suela," is in "Colección de cartas pueblas," no. 63, *BSCC*, xviii (1943), 159-160; *Colección diplomática*, doc. 241; Fernández y González, *Mudejares de Castilla*, appendix, doc. 17; Janer, *Moriscos de España*, doc. 15.

[9] Arch. Crown, James I, Reg. Canc. 8, fol. 36 (Nov. 24, 1257): "anno domini mcclvii, viii kalendas Decembris, iactavit dominus rex has peitas sarracenis civitatis et regni Valencie."

Alfandech Valley, which contributed only 4,000 solidi to that tax, in 1275 yielded a total of 12,000 solidi. At the same time a rental of its revenues for the coming three years was assessed at almost double this sum per annum; the king farmed or sold "for three years all the revenues, returns, and income, and all our receipts" at an agreed price of "20,000 solidi of Valencia in each of those three years."[10] Five years earlier a lesser though considerable sum had been reckoned for Alcira. This "sale" for a three-year period included "all revenues, receipts, returns, income, and other rights of our bailiwick of Alcira and of the Saracens of the Moorish quarter and of its countryside, as well as their *alfarda*, for 13,500 solidi of Valencia in each of the aforesaid years."[11] With such a quantity of money involved, officials entered the contract into two separate registers.[12]

An arrangement recorded in 1275 ran "for the Saracens of Pego and its valley for three years in the same way [annually], for 8,000 solidi."[13] Such a rental price did not represent the full payment by Muslim taxpayers, since expenses and the collector's ten percent profit were not expressed. Three years previously the king had sold "to our bailiff those 12,500 solidi of Valencia, which the Saracens of Pego Valley are obliged to pay us as tribute."[14] The revenues of Gallinera and Alcalá in 1267 came to 2,500 besants—at least three times that figure when expressed in solidi.[15] At Montesa in 1281 "the lord king sold all the revenues, returns, and income of the town and

[10] *Ibid.*, Reg. Canc. 17, fols. 13, 21 (1275); Reg. Canc. 20, fol. 245 (April 22, 1275): "omnes redditus, exitus, et proventus, ac iura nostra omnia de quibus teneamini respondere . . . , pro viginti millibus solidorum regalium Valencie . . . in unoquoque ipsorum trium annorum."

[11] *Ibid.*, Reg. Canc. 37, fol. 14v (March 19, 1270): "omnes redditus, fructus, et exitus, proventus, et alia iura baiulie nostre Algazire et sarracenorum morarie et termini eiusdem, ac etiam alfardam ipsorum pro tredecim millibus quingentis solidorum regalium Valencie in unoquoque predictorum annorum." On the *alfarda* see Chapter V, part 1.

[12] *Ibid.*, Reg. Canc. 35, fol. 56v (same date), same wording but with a hole obscuring *quingentis*.

[13] *Ibid.*, Reg. Canc. 30, fol. 245 (April 27, 1275): "item aliam, sub eadem forma et anno quo superius, sarracenis de Pego et vallis eiusdem ad tres annos similiter pro octo millibus solidorum."

[14] *Ibid.*, Reg. Canc. 37, fol. 51v (Oct. 11, 1272): "vendimus . . . baiulo nostro illos duodecim millia et quingentos solidos regalium, quos sarraceni vallis de Pego nobis tenentur dare et solvere pro tributo."

[15] *Ibid.*, Reg. Canc. 15, fol. 88 (March 1, 1267): "precio videlicet duorum millium et quingentorum bisantiorum quolibet ipsorum duorum annorum." On the equivalence between besant and solidus see p. 80.

of the holdings" of the community of the Saracens of Montesa for one year at 12,000 solidi.[16] It is fair to add that taxes may have been high in 1281 because of the threatening international situation.

In 1275 Alcira's Mudejars yielded 12,000 solidi; Gandía's 10,000; Burriana's 4,000; Pego's 8,000; Cullera's with Corbera's 7,000; Onteniente's, 2,000; Cárcer's 1,000; and Liria's 1,000.[17] In 1281 King Peter farmed a series of Mudejar revenues for the coming year: "from Sagra, Vall de Laguart [Alaguar], Pop, Jalón, Callosa with Algar, Confrides, Guadalest, and Castell, all our revenues, returns, income, and receipts, and all fines, and our other proceeds."[18] In solidi the assessments for these places became respectively 1,100, 4,500, 3,000, 2,200, 2,500, 3,000, 3,500, and 3,000; yet this income excludes criminal justice and the profitable *alfarda*.[19] Though the listed towns were relatively small, their sums were impressive. The last place, Castell, had been rented, with certain reservations, for three years at a thousand besants, amounting to over 3,000 solidi a year.[20] Tax lists obscure the Mudejar totals frequently, not only by offering mixed Christian-Mudejar entries alongside the purely Moorish but also omitting those tax classifications contracted to other tax farmers or creditors. In 1263 the bailiff at Alcira took 199 solidi as "revenues of the Moorish quarter," another 329 as head tax, 24 in "rents," 23½ as fines, and an indeterminate amount from the presumably mixed categories like mills, ovens, and shops. The same reckoning puts 5,400 solidi as "revenues from the Saracens" at Gandía, alongside presumably mixed entries such as meat market,

---

[16] *Ibid.*, Peter III, Reg. Canc. 51, fol. 24 (Jan. 11, 1281): "dominus rex vendidit ... omnes redditus, exitus, et proventus ville et posessionum de Muntesa."

[17] *Ibid.*, James I, Reg. Canc. 17, fols. 13, 21 (1275); since both the Pego and Alfandech sums in this document only equal the Mudejar revenues of those places for the same year (given in Reg. Canc. 20, fol. 25 [April 27, 1275]), the accompanying figures are probably also for Muslims. The argument, not very strong, is strengthened by remarking the relatively small contribution from Burriana (4,000 solidi), an important Christian center but one that, like Valencia city, had lost many Muslims by expulsion.

[18] *Ibid.*, Peter III, Reg. Canc. 51, fol. 27 (March 3, 1281): "vendimus ... ad unum annum proximum venturum vobis aliamis sarracenorum de Çagra, de Alaguar, de Pop, de Xalon, de Callosa et Algar, de Confrides, de Godalesth, et de Castell omnes redditus nostros, exitus, proventus, et fructus, et omnes calonias et alia iura nostra."

[19] *Ibid.*: "exceptis iusticiis criminalibus, alphardis, et thesauro invento, que nobis specialiter retinemus ad nostram voluntatem faciendam infra dictum tempus."

[20] *Ibid.*, James I, Reg. Canc. 15, fol. 135v (Feb. 9, 1268): "vendicionem vobis facimus precio millium bisanciorum quolibet ipsorum trium annorum."

fish market, dye concession, shops, and tariffs. For Onteniente it has 50 solidi in head tax and 20 in fines, and for Liria 500 unspecified solidi, thrown into a grab bag of varied items.[21]

King James could casually incur a debt of 18,000 solidi in 1258, arranging to satisfy it from the revenues of the Mudejar community at Valencia city.[22] In 1268 he similarly settled a debt of 20,000 solidi from Mudejar taxes at Tárbena.[23] García Pérez, owed 5,412 solidi for his service as castellan at Castalla and for loans to the crown, was paid in 1266 by assigning that amount on the next tax from Alcira; though this money came from both Christians and Muslims, few Christians then lived at Alcira.[24] Even a small place like Beniopa rented for 15,000 solidi a year, involving "all the revenues . . . we receive or should receive from Beniopa and from the Saracens who live there and in its districts."[25] Játiva's Muslims, in an incidental tax transaction of 1280, "had paid to the lord king 846 gold *doblas*."[26]

The meager financial evidence for Christian tithes supports the

[21] *Ibid.*, Reg. Canc. 17, fols. 27-32 (Dec. 30, 1263): "item redditus morerie"; "censualia"; "redditus sarracenorum [Gandie], v millia cccc solidorum." See the equally detailed and ambiguous lists in Reg. Canc. 35, fols. 3-4, 7-8 (1257).

[22] *Ibid.*, Reg. Canc. 10, fol. 58v (April 28, 1258): "confitemur nos debere tredecim millia quingentos et octuaginta solidorum . . . et sic debemus vobis inter hoc totum decem et octo millia solidorum regalium"; "exitus morarie Valencie."

[23] *Ibid.*, Reg. Canc. 14, fol. 94 (April 5, 1268): "et sic debemus vobis, inter omnia, xx millia solidorum regalium."

[24] *Ibid.*, fol. 82 (June 26, 1266): "recognoscimus nos debere vobis Garcie Petri de Castalla quinque millia et quadringentos duodecim solidorum regalium Valencie, quos vos debemus racione custodie quam fecistis de castro de Castalla et pro omnibus debitis . . . [et sunt percipiendos] super primis peitis . . . tam in christianos quam in sarracenos."

[25] *Ibid.*, Reg. Canc. 37, fol. 60v (Jan. 23, 1272): "omnes redditus . . . quos percipimus et percipere debemus in Beniopa et in sarracenis qui morantur ibidem et [in] terminis eiusdem." At non-Valencian Masones, when exempting the Moors from certain taxes in 1263, King James asked 1,500 solidi of Jaca yearly; since this was not rental but compensatory payment for the privilege, it fell considerably below the sum normally taken. The Masones privilege did not cover important taxes like justice, moneyage, herbage, and court fines—retained to the crown and still to be paid (*ibid.*, James I, perg. 1,738 [April 12, 1263], published in Fernández y González, *Mudejares de Castilla*, appendix, doc. 45).

[26] *Ibid.*, Peter III, Reg. Canc. 48, fol. 6v (April 29, 1280): "in Algeciram sigillimus quondam literam . . . recognitionis sarracenorum Xative, videlicet quod solverant domino regi octingentas quadraginta sex duplas." *Dupla* was used for the Almohad gold *dinar* or for similar gold coins such as the *dupla* of Castile or of Granada; these *doblas* were of course different from the *moneta de duplo sive de dupleto sive doblenca*, a vellon money of James I in 1221.

picture of prosperity in the Mudejar hinterland. Roderick Díaz, lord of Benaguacil and Almonacid castles, rented or more accurately kept during his lifetime the tithe of both places except for transient flocks, for a compromise yearly sum of 1,200 solidi; this means that Roderick was enjoying a minimum of ten times that amount, or 12,000 solidi in profit from these relatively unimportant spots. The real sum would have been at least 18,000 because, with the predeductions of patron or lord, he owed only a two-thirds tithe. It should be remembered that this was Roderick's own tithe from his Mudejar rents rather than a tithe paid by Muslims on their much higher personal totals. Since lump-sum compromises always fell below the real totals involved, sometimes absurdly below like a token refund, this figure must be expanded again. If Roderick's rents came mostly from rustic Muslims, they were very well off.[27] For Paterna and Manises, Artal of Luna eventually agreed to hand over a hundred besants a year as the price for keeping the tithe and first fruits; he allowed a further 35 besants annually to the local rector, if and when one arrived. This implies a revenue from his Muslims of 4,000 besants or over 12,000 solidi; it actually came to a great deal more since Artal, who had previously refused to part with a penny, yielded this token precisely for the privilege of keeping the full third of his personal tithe.[28]

Marcel Pacaut has pointed the way toward a methodology for assessing total taxation for a kingdom from partial figures; applying it rigorously to yield the Mudejar total in the Valencian kingdom would require tediously elaborate detail work.[29] Pacaut categorizes the several properties or tax sources characteristic of the France of Louis VII, then establishes a norm for each from available fragmentary documentation such as a total from a typical city of medium size; multiplying the revenues of that norm by all the representatives of its category results in a minimal tax total within each category. Thus, knowing that Valencia's aljama brought 18,000 one year, and Alcira's 12,000, one might reasonably suggest that the equivalent

[27] Arch. Cat., perg. 2,430 (Sept. 12, 1268); the document has "tam a christianis quam a sarracenis," because it is looking to eventual settlement, but there were few if any Christians here yet.

[28] *Ibid.*, perg. 2,432 (June 14, 1277).

[29] Marcel Pacaut, *Louis VII et son royaume* (Paris, 1964), pp. 119-160; John F. Benton analyzes the method, criticizing and amending it carefully, in "The Revenue of Louis VII," *Speculum*, XLII (1967), 84-91.

towns in that class or size paid a similar amount—some 13,000 a year from Mudejar Játiva or Murviedro—and multiply the number by four. If both Gandía and Montesa were worth 10,000 one year, their total revenues might place these lesser towns in a revenue category not too inferior to the large cities suffering from grosser immigration by Christians. Linked castles with a considerable countryside still in Muslim hands could easily match a single big city's aljama; in this category Alfandech Valley brought 12,000 one year but 20,000 on three other years and 13,000 another time, while the Pego Valley brought 8,000 twice and 12,500 once. A medium class of town was worth some 7 or 8,000 solidi—Tárbena castle and town for example, at 6,600, or Cullera with Corbera 7,000. At the bottom were lesser towns, though heads of their little regions, worth a thousand, like Liria and Cárcer.

This profile serves rather as an illustration of the method, applied to the figures in the section just covered. A reasonable total approximation in each category of rent requires its own research, and a satisfactory set of land categories has to be devised. If the two sets of categories are not confounded, and if each aljama can be assigned to its proper category, the door lies open to a deeper understanding of early Mudejar prosperity and to a comparison of it with the more easily documented prosperity of the Christian colonists.

Figures for specific taxes, displayed in detail in the following chapters, support the impression of well-being conveyed by this preliminary selection of totals; the profits evident in later chapters on collection will confirm the impression. Even the earliest general list of Valencian taxes, dating from a decade after the close of the crusade, in 1255, reveals an already robust sum drawn from the Muslim communities.[30] So imposing is the volume of revenue that some authors perversely take the document as proof of King James's

[30] Arch. Crown, James I, Reg. Canc. 8, fol. 21v (Nov. 26, 1255): "anno domini mccl quinto, vi kalendas Decembris, iactavit dominus rex has peitas in regno Valencie." See the similar formula above in note 9. The expulsion of the Moriscos from Valencia over three centuries later, stripping away twenty to thirty percent of that kingdom's total mixed population, was a stunning blow to prosperity and taxes; by that period the mass of Mudejars, a minority, was badly exploited and under seignorial control. See especially the conclusions of Pascual Boronat y Barrachina, *Los moriscos españoles y su expulsión*, 2 vols. (Valencia, 1901), II, ch. 10; and most recently the elaborate statistical study, moving beyond the data of Henri Lapeyre and Tulio Halperín Donghi, by Juan R. Torres Morera, *Repoblación del reino de Valencia, después de la expulsión de los moriscos* (Valencia, 1969), pp. 133ff.

exploitation of the helpless Moors. Wherever detail is available to elucidate Mudejar taxes, however, they are not severe. Nor is there any reason for agreeing with those who believe that taxes occasioned the later rebellions. King James boasted to the Murcians about his general treatment of Mudejars; in his memoirs he professed himself shocked by the seemingly motiveless rising of aljamas he had treated so well. Details of revenue merely underline what the king, Muslim writers, contemporaries like Desclot, and other evidence so often repeat. Valencia was a land of wealth in industries, commerce, and agriculture.

MONEYS

A sound currency promotes economic prosperity. It was particularly advantageous in a set of realms with diverse and fluctuating coinage systems. At the close of the crusade, King James made it one of his first tasks to devise and in 1247 promulgate a new money for his conquered kingdom, advertising it in colonial-ideological terms as destined "to reform [Valencia] for the better into a proper condition according with the life-style [*mores*] of Christians." It was to bear "the saving sign of the cross" above a tree and "the name of the kingdom of Valencia," with the reverse side displaying "the image and name" of King James. Regulated as to "weight, shape, name, lettering, value, imprint, and size" this "crown [*reyal*] of Valencia" commonly went under the name solidus, comprising like the solidus of neighboring regions twelve pence. Any resident or transient, expressly including Muslims, who used another money for reckoning major business transactions in the Valencia kingdom became "a violator of the royal ordinance and guilty of lese majesty," subject to property confiscation and corporal punishment.[31]

The law expressed an ideal, operative rather in urban centers; in the hinterlands, custom may have yielded slowly to fiat. The solidus

---

[31] *Aureum opus regalium priuilegiorum ciuitatis et regni Valentie cum historia cristianissimi regis Iacobi ipsius primi conquistatoris*, ed. Luis de Alanya (Valencia, 1515), doc. 23, fols. 9-11 (May 8, 1247): "in statum debitum iuxta christianorum morem in melius reformare . . . monetam cudi fecimus"; "sub signo salutifere crucis supra florem [arbor ad modum floris] et nomen regni Valentie posite, nostre etiam ymaginis et nominis insignis figuratam"; "pondere, figura, nomine, literatura, valore, signo, et magnitudine"; "tanquam transgressor regie ordinationis et lese maiestatis reus."

was employed directly in its penny (*denarius*) and half-penny (*obolus* or *mealla*) form; though King James insisted on its use as the official money of account, the solidus itself was in fact a ghost money. Applicable to tribute, taxes, and debts, it could be replaced, in the case of rents (*censualia*), by other gold or silver money. The rate of exchange imposed by the crown valued the twelve-pence solidus at eighteen Barcelona pennies, fifteen Jaca, sixteen Melgorian or fifteen Tours (both popular at Montpellier), and four silver pennies. Forty-eight Valencian solidi converted into a silver mark (not 38 as the exchange erroneously states), 4 into a gold Josephine mazmodin (of Moroccan origin), 3½ into the Christian copy or pseudo-Josephine, 6 into a gold Alfonsine morabatin (of Castilian origin), 8½ into a gold morabatin (of Almoravid origin), and 3¾ into a silver besant. Alas for the Conqueror's dream! The rate of exchange proved inconstant, fluctuating with the vagaries of time, place, and market. Of the basic four moneys minted in the realms of Aragon, the Valencian was the least stable, declining steadily between 1247 and 1310 from an equivalent of 18 Barcelona pence to below 15, and from 16 Jaca pence to 8. Tax amounts reckoned in Valencian solidi for 1250 differ therefore from the same figure entered for 1280.[32]

[32] *Ibid.*, doc. 22, fol. 9 (same date), for exchange rates: "exceptis censualibus rebus." Felipe Mateu y Llopis, *Glosario hispánico de numismática* (Barcelona, 1964), discusses the kinds of solidi at length, with bibliography (pp. 189-195), and also morabatins (pp. 115-120) and mazmodins (pp. 124-127). On the history of the Valencian solidus, whose vellon *denarii* and *oboli* were copiously minted by James I as a policy stratagem, see his *La ceca de Valencia y las acuñaciones valencianas de los siglos xiii al xviii: Ensayo sobre una casa real de moneda de uno de los estados de la corona de Aragón* (Valencia, 1929), especially ch. 1. He seems to define rents in terms of feudal agrarian contracts in *Materiales para un glosario de diplomática hispánica, corona de Aragón, reino de Valencia* (Castellón de la Plana, 1957), *sub* "censal," "censaler," "censalista," "censals"; it can also mean salary or pension (Arch. Crown, James I, Reg. Canc. 9, fol. 29v [May 4, 1258]) and income from buildings or land (*Rationes decimarum Hispaniae*, 1, 259, 264). Charles Emmanuel Dufourcq traces the inflationary process with a chart relating Valencian to neighboring moneys in *L'Espagne catalane et le Maghrib aux xiiie et xive siècles, de la bataille de Las Navas de Tolosa (1212) à l'avènement du sultan mérinide Abou-l-Hasan (1313)* (Paris, 1966), pp. 526-530; on money and prices, especially toward the end of the century, see the full part 3, ch. 5, and pp. 169-170; on cargoes and prices see pp. 171-176. In 1283 the crown adjusted the exchange "pro morabat[ino] censuali vii solvantur tantum novi solidi regalium, et pro mazmodina censuali vii solidi eiusdem monete"; this is not a different kind of Arabic coin, as some have thought, but the exchange imposed upon crown bailiffs and nonregalian landlords for rents (*Aureum opus*, doc. 18, of Peter III, fol. 32). On the relation of solidus to pound, see Chapter IV, n. 60.

Sometimes a tax document incorporated and imposed its own current exchange. In 1263 the bailiff of Alcira collected "the besants of the Saracens: 94 besants, which equal 329 solidi"; in 1262 the crown assigned 90 besants from the Moors at Pop and Denia, "computed at the rate of 3 solidi and 4 pennies for each besant."[33]

The exchange value, whether official or market, affords no idea of the real worth of the solidus. A typical knight's revenue, out of the hundreds given by the king of Aragon, transposed into 373 solidi. King James once rebuked the stinginess of the barons in Aragon proper, as against the generosity of Catalonia, by reminding them they held lucrative fiefs from him—"some of 30,000, some of 20,000, others of 40,000 solidi"; in Valencian money these exalted and relatively rare incomes ran from over 25,000 to over 50,000 solidi.[34] A plush ecclesiastical living for a Valencian rector around 1280 brought 300 solidi.[35] During the crusade King James scolded a mounted crossbowman for deserting his lord on the battlefield: "If you were captured, you could get free for 150 or 200 solidi"; if the king means Barcelona money, the Valencian equivalent according to his exchange rate of 1247 would be respectively 100 and 130 solidi; if he means Jaca money, the Valencian equivalent would be 120 and 160 solidi.[36] This was not too much above the traditional ransom price for the average Christian, Jew, or Muslim throughout the Mediterranean economy.[37] A more considerable prisoner could command a much higher ransom; in 1245 one knight brought his captor 100 morabatins and another knight 500.[38]

[33] Arch. Crown, James I, Reg. Canc. 17, fol. 27 (Dec. 30, 1263); Reg. Canc. 14, fol. 10 (Feb. 20, 1262): "qui bisancii computentur ad rationem de tribus solidis et quattuor denariis pro quolibet bisancio."

[34] Burns, *Crusader Valencia*, I, xii, with further prices and salaries. *Llibre dels feyts*, ch. 392.

[35] Burns, *Crusader Valencia*, II, appendix 3, ecclesiastical tax lists for Valencian dioceses in detail.

[36] *Llibre dels feyts*, ch. 229.

[37] Solomon D. Goitein, *A Mediterranean Society: The Jewish Communities of the Arab World as Portrayed in the Documents of the Cairo Geniza*, 2 vols. to date (Berkeley, Calif., 1967ff.), I, 329; I interpret his figures, given by the *dīnār*, in terms of Valencia. Eliyahu Ashtor reckons the price of a slave at the end of the thirteenth century at 140 to 320 solidi of Barcelona, commenting that these prices had recently increased steeply both in the east and the west (*Histoire des prix et des salaires dans l'orient médiéval* [Paris, 1969], p. 504).

[38] Joaquín Miret y Sans, *Itinerari de Jaume I "el Conqueridor"* (Barcelona, 1918), p. 172 (May 9, 1245).

The *qā'id* of Valencia city's aljama in 1267 was receiving an annual salary of 100 solidi, as was his counterpart at Játiva in 1260; by 1315 the standard salary for this official in communities below the Júcar River was 180 solidi.[39] In 1268 Prince Peter employed "92 Moorish bowmen for five days at the rate of four pence per Moor per day, which equals 153 solidi, 4 pence [of Valencia?]"; on a trip from Valencia to Toledo he paid "to the Moor trumpeters and Moor entertainers 50 morabatins, which equal 375 solidi."[40] Many castellans enjoyed incomes varying from 1,000 solidi to over 3,500; the justiciar of Valencia city had 2,000. The crown advanced a salary of 150 solidi annually apiece for fifteen men garrisoning Alfandech castle under a knight in the war crisis of 1276; at Guadalest castle the rate was 30 solidi a month for sixty men, an annual salary of 360 solidi apiece. In 1302 Muslim mercenaries for the Catalan governor of Djerba island off North Africa got a besant per day (3 solidi, four pence then) plus keep; but Christian knights loaned as mercenaries to North Africa at the same time received half that sum or 50 solidi a month.[41] A Mudejar widow's pension ran to 60 solidi yearly (much of this may have gone to the crown); a Majorcan artisan expected about 1 solidus per day, and a sailor a few pence. A personage or wealthy man enjoyed 2 Valencian solidi or more per day; the ordinary man, not so well documented for us, contented himself with sums far less handsome.[42]

---

[39] Arch. Crown, James I, Reg. Canc. 15, fol. 85 (March 14, 1267): "in tota vita tua centum solidos regalium habendos . . . racione predicti officii tue [*sic*] alcaldie." *Ibid.*, Reg. Canc. 11, fol. 191v (Jan. 20, 1260): "c solidos regalium quolibet anno dum alcadiam . . . tenueris." The 1315 figure is in *Rentas de la antigua corona de Aragón*, ed. Manuel de Bofarull y de Sartorio, in *Colección de documentos inéditos del archivo general de la corona de Aragón*, ed. Próspero de Bofarull y Mascaró *et alii*, 41 vols. (Barcelona, 1847-1910), xxxix, 115.

[40] Peter's Moors are in the documents of Joaquín Miret y Sans, *Viatges del infant En Pere, fill de Jaume I en els anys 1268 y 1269* (Barcelona, 1908); could his "trombadors et . . . juglars" be meant for troubadours and their jongleurs?

[41] Arch. Crown, James I, Reg. Canc. 20, fol. 341v (April 24, 1276); see also *Itinerari*, p. 532 (May 5, 1276), payment of 400 solidi for a supplement of 14 knights serving in the war or 29 solidi each but with length of service not specified here. The Guadalest figure, with an added 120 solidi to feed two guard dogs for one year, is in Ferran Soldevila, *Pere el Gran*, part 2, i, appendix, doc. 13 (Sept. 1, 1276). The salaries of 1302 are in Ashtor, *Histoire des prix*, p. 538.

[42] Dufourcq, *Espagne catalane et le Maghrib*, pp. 173-175. Besides the prices in Burns, *Crusader Valencia*, i, xii, the price of grain in the wartime year 1276 suggests basic values; Alcira sent 1,000 cafizes of barley at 12,000 solidi, or 12 solidi each; Ben Vives purchased at Alcira 200 cafizes of barley for the army at 2,100 solidi, or

Valencian Mudejars, though undoubtedly acquainted with a range of coinage, apparently thought in terms of Arabic money like the *mithqàl* for domestic purposes. The gold *mithqāl* of Valencia, though no longer minted, was the money used in a Mudejar marriage contract at Murviedro. Various coins of that name had continued to circulate, while the generic *mithqāl* served as Islamic money of account in gold transactions, just as the *dirham* served for silver.[48] The Valencian tax collector probably accepted a variety of

10½ each; Albalat charged 1,560 solidi for 130 cafizes of wheat and barley—perhaps 12 solidi per cafiz of each; another purchase came to 254 cafizes of wheat at 4,580 solidi of Jaca or 18 each; Corbera sold 50 cafizes of wheat and 250 of barley for a total 4,750 solidi or under 16 solidi per cafiz if equally distributed; Arnold of Montroig lent 1,284 solidi for purchasing 107 cafizes of barley, a price of nearly 13 solidi each. The money in these transactions, with the exception noted, was Valencian.

[48] Murviedro contract in *Spanisch-islamische Urkunden aus der Zeit der Naṣriden und Moriscos*, ed. Wilhelm Hoenerbach (Berkeley, 1965), doc. 4 (1297). The Almoravids coined the gold *dīnār* at Valencia, Játiva, and Denia in imitation of the Byzantine solidus or besant. The Almohads coined silver money at Valencia, as did Zayyān just before the crusade, but the Christian mint of Toledo at the end of the twelfth century produced an imitation Valencian and Murcian *dīnār* with the name *mithqāl*. The *mithqāl balansiya* is found also in twelfth-century Zaragoza; a dowry document long after our period equates its version to two solidi of Jaca. In thirteenth-century Spain *mithqāl* also designated the Castilian gold double *dīnār* and was loosely used for any kind of *dīnār*; thus the *aureus* or morabatin (*maravedí*) from 1172 by Alfonso VIII, in imitation of the Almoravid *dīnār*, was also a *mitcal de oro alfonsi*. The gold *dīnār* varied in value according to whether it was produced by the Almohad, Hafsid, or Marinid mint. There were further nuances in these Aragonese and Islamic moneys; each realm of Aragon developed its own mark; "Saracen besants" were distinguished from those of Ceuta (*ceptini*); mazmodins could be double, small, or quarter. See Ibn Khaldūn, *Muqaddimah*, ii, 57 on the Almohad *dīnār* and pp. 56-58 on the *mithqāl*; Lévi-Provençal, *España musulmana*, V, 137-138, 146-147, where the *mithqāl* is a ghost money; Eulalia Rodón Binué, *El lenguaje técnico del feudalismo en el siglo xi en Cataluña* (*contribución al estudio del latín medieval*) (Barcelona, 1957), pp. 75-77 on "uncias auri Valencie"; Sanchis Guarner, "Època musulmana," pp. 348-350; Jacinto Bosch Vilá, "Referencias a moneda en los documentos árabes y hebreos de Aragón y Navarra," *EEMCA*, vi (1956), doc. 2; R. García de Linares, "Escrituras árabes pertenecientes al archivo de Nra. Sra. del Pilar de Zaragoza," in *Homenaje á D[on] Francisco Codera en su jubilación del profesorado. Estudios de erudición oriental*, ed. Eduardo Saavedra et alii (Zaragoza, 1904), doc. 2; Joaquín Botet y Sisó, "Nota sobre la encunyació de monedes aràbigues pêl rey Don Jaume," *Congrés d'història de la corona d'Aragó, dedicat al rey En Jaume I y a la seua época*, 2 vols. paginated as one (Valencia, 1923), hereafter cited as *Congrés I*, pp. 944-963, and on the besant pp. 945-946; and his *Les monedes catalanes*, 3 vols. (Barcelona, 1908-1911), ii, 52-66; Enrique Bayerri y Bertoméu, *Historia de Tortosa y su comarca*, 8 vols. to date (Tortosa, 1933ff.), vii, 360; and

currencies from his Mudejars, adjusted these to the current rate, and entered his accounts under the headings of Valencian solidi or of besants. When the Muslims of Gallinera and Alcalá farmed their own revenues in 1267, they reckoned the results in besants.[44] The long list of *peites* from the Moors in 1257 also went down as besants. On the other hand the reduced besant, a head tax of that name, was accounted for at the city of Valencia in solidi.[45] Arabic money crops up in the Mudejar tax lists for Valencia. King James minted Arabic counterfeit in his several realms, letting one contract to Arnold Lawrence of Valencia city in 1262 for the regular manufacture of the silver *millarès*, or *dirham*, a coin of widely unequal value. What the sober lands of northern Europe regarded as a scandal went unnoticed in the realms of Aragon.[46] Embellished with Koranic texts

the monetary studies by Mateu y Llopis grouped in my Bibliography. Goitein has an appendix on the *dīnār* and *qīrāṭ* (24 to the *dīnār*), explaining the *mithqāl* as originally denoting a full-weight *dīnār* or a specific issue, being the preferred term for *dīnār* in Spain and North Africa; he has a further, extensive appendix on exchange rates of gold and silver coins (*Mediterranean Society*, I, 359-360, 368-392); against a common persuasion, he argues that gold was not always merely a money of account among ordinary people (p. 391).

[44] Arch. Crown, James I, Reg. Canc. 15, fol. 88 (March 1, 1267): "omnes redditus ... precio videlicet duorum millium et quingentorum bisantiorum."

[45] *Ibid.*, Reg. Canc. 8, fol. 36 (Nov. 24, 1257): for example "Eslida, ccc bisantios"; on the *peita* see Chapter IV, part 3. The Valencia city besant is on p. 80.

[46] Botet y Sisó, "Encunyació de monedes aràbigues pêl rey Don Jaume," p. 947 and doc. of June 20, 1262 on pp. 956-957. The *dirham*, as Goitein notes, varied from local, base coins, to a common coin relating at 36 or 40 to the *dīnār*, up to the pure silver coin relating at 13½ to the *dīnār* (*Mediterranean Society*, I, 360). Relating the *millarès* to this fluctuating coin is difficult, but the *millarès* equaled roughly four Barcelona pence or a third-solidus. On the besant, a common money of account for Valencian Muslims dealing with the crown, and on its relation to the constituent *millareses*, see below, Chapter IV, part 1. See also Mateu y Llopis, *Glosario hispánico de numismática*, pp. 131-133 on *millarès*, pp. 133-135 on *mitcal*, and pp. 17-20 on *besant*. It was only after Capetian administration was long in control of Toulouse that St. Louis IX of France forbade coinage of Arabic money there, noting that it bore the name "perfidi Mahometi, et dicatur ibi esse propheta Dei, quod est ad laudem et exaltationem ipsius"; see too the prohibition of the practice by Clement IV to the count-bishop of Maguelonne: "quis enim catholicus monetam debet cudere cum titulo Mahometi?" (Botet y Sisó, "Encunyació de monedes aràbigues pêl rey Don Jaume," p. 946). The crusader states of the Holy Land coined "besants sarracenats," a gold *dīnār* imitating a Fatimid coin though worth a third less; and from the mid-thirteenth century they struck an original *dīnār* displaying a Christian legend in Arabic; see Claude Cahen, "Notes sur l'histoire des croisades et de l'orient latin: orient latin et commerce du Levant," *Bulletin de la faculté des lettres de Strasbourg*, XXIX (1951), 337.

and indistinguishable from the originals, these coins facilitated international trade at great ports like Valencia.

Mudejar tax lists represent for the most part cash and not kind. Agrarian rents in the realms of Aragon had been evolving for a generation into a fixed money-tax. The rents of Christian settlers combined a mixture of money, produce, and a symbolic gift.[47] Crown officials collected their share of agricultural tithe in produce, apparently storing and marketing it as did the diocesan authorities. A mixed rent, such as money with some wine, was not unknown. The king's household in travelling levied foodstuffs such as chickens. Agriculture was big business, however, with a class of wholesalers to purchase, transport, and store its products, while the small farmer hawked his kitchen-garden surplus in the town square.[48] Thus it is no surprise to find coins stipulated for inconsiderable taxes from Moors, like the penny on each beehive at Tales or the similar trifling fees in the charters of Aldea, Chivert, Játiva, and Uxó.[49]

[47] Rafael Gibert y Sánchez de la Vega, "Los contratos agrarios en el derecho medieval," *Boletín de la universidad de Granada*, xxii (1950), 322-323.

[48] On tithe collecting by king and bishop see Burns, *Crusader Valencia*, i, 147, 168ff., and on domestic sales p. 152. A rent on buildings of "75 gold pieces and 75 quarters of wine" appears in the *Repartimiento de Valencia*, ed. Prospero de Bofarull y Mascaró, in *Documentos inéditos de Aragón*, xi, 269. A *quarter* was a variable wholesale measure for liquids; rental for shops, or perhaps a purchase price, is a hundred quarters of wine in an item on p. 265.

[49] Chivert Charter (April 28, 1234), ed. Manuel Ferrandis e Irles, in *Homenaje á Codera*, pp. 28-33; with slight differences in "Colección de cartas pueblas," no. 76, *BSCC*, xxiv (1948), 226-230. The background and evolution of tenant obligations on the lands of the Knights Templar in the realms of Aragon, useful for appreciating the demands of their Chivert charter, is surveyed by A. J. Forey, *The Templars in the Corona de Aragón* (London, 1973), chs. 4, 6. Aldea Charter (Feb. 12, 1258), in "Colección de cartas pueblas," no. 60, *BSCC*, xvi (1935), 289-291. La Aldea, as it is called today, is not properly Valencian, being situated just above Valencia's northern border as a Knights Hospitaller holding in the Tortosa region. It did become englobed in the seignorial territory of the Valencian monastery of Benifasá in the fourteenth century, and even in the thirteenth must have belonged as much to the Mudejar world of Valencia as to the politically more immediate environs of the Ebro Valley; it was dominantly Mudejar, despite its nominally Christian status since 1148, and its 1258 charter probably derived from the pacification following the Valencia Mudejar revolt. José M. Font y Rius gives the charter and some comment in his *Cartas de población y franquicia de Cataluña*, i vol. to date (Madrid, 1969), i, doc. 303 and pp. 785-787. The Játiva Charter (Jan. 23, 1251 or 1252) is in *Documentos inéditos de España*, xviii, 62; *Colección diplomática*, doc. 412; Fernández y González, *Mudejares de Castilla*, appendix, doc. 24. Tales Charter (May 27, 1260) in "Colección de cartas pueblas," no. 84, *BSCC*, xxviii (1952), 437-438. Uxó Charter.

Shops and Stalls

The Islamic province of Valencia had enjoyed an urbanized economy for centuries; towns focused the countryside, with the specialization and marketing this implied. The teeming bazaars of Valencian towns proved a lucrative source of revenue for the Christian crown, with outlying villages contributing their share. As in the older towns of North Africa today, the main *sūq* or market comprised a labyrinth of little stalls and workshops; normally each lane or area devoted itself to a single product so as to form a subordinate *sūq*. The shops threaded their way around larger establishments and public services—khans, ovens, baths, mosques, and notaries' stands—while public entertainers functioned in appropriate fringe areas. The class of tradespeople busy there can be distinguished as craftsmen (*ministrales*) and shopkeepers (*tenderii*); this official division was not so mutually exclusive as the tidy mind might desire, nor yet completely adequate to the proliferating variety of shop merchants. King James made efforts to promote and increase this class of Muslim in Valencia. These people enter our present story not as a social or industrial phenomenon but solely as a tax source.[50]

Shops paid tax-rental to king or lord, or else to men subholding the concession. Corresponding to the well-established craftsman was the *operatorium*, properly a workshop fronting on the street as a salescounter. The shoptender served his *tenda*, which was a stall or awning-protected stand. The *tenda* may always have been a less substantial booth, rigged up especially near baths, mosques, and city gates; or perhaps the grander kind of shop could outshine the cramped workshop of some less successful craftsman; or finally, the conjoined words may cover indifferently every type of shop establishment. Though no organized statistics are available for Valencia city, at the comparable community of Palma de Mallorca the king's half of the conquered town contained 320 *operatoria*; each of the city's eight divisions held about 80 such shops. Around a plaza in the Valencian mountain-town of Morella in 1260, fifty crown *operatoria* faced each other, now in Christian hands.[51] Alcira held some

---

[50] See Burns, *Islam under the Crusaders*, ch. 4, part 2.

[51] *Itinerari*, p. 308 (Nov. 2, 1260): "que est ante illa quinquaginta operatoria nostra." *Repartimiento de Mallorca*, ed. Próspero de Bofarull y Mascaró, in *Docu-*

77 shops, in a tax list of 1263, only one in seven actually owned by Muslims. Either absentee Christians held title to the shops of Alcira's Moorish quarter, or else the seven Moors here may have operated in the Christian sector; it seems improbable that only eight Muslims, their names tightly grouped at the end of this long list, form a complete roster of shops serving Alcira's Moorish quarter.[52]

Not all shops clustered in the main market; there were also auxiliary, specialty, and neighborhood markets. At Játiva, small plazas gave space respectively for the cattle *sūq* and for pottery manufacture; the potters' firing ovens, paying an annual besant apiece at Játiva, might have fallen under the heading of shops. The Játiva charter granted the Muslims a market every Friday in St. Michael's plaza, presumably a monopoly drawing customers, traders, and peddlers from the surrounding countryside.

In dividing Valencia city, the conquerors reveal something of the placing of shops. Some stood near the main mosque, where one Christian received in nonrental alod a workshop with upstairs studio (*algorfa*). Others fronted on the mosque that became St. Martin's.[53] Real estate transactions show shops in the vicinity of the mosque that became Holy Savior's, at the southern gate alongside a mosque that owned them, at Játiva next to the mosque acquired by the Franciscans, and at Alcira in the plaza before the mosque that became St.

---

mentos inéditos de Aragón, xiii, 116ff. For a *tenda* as a *domus* or building, with the *tabula* or counter within, as against the multiple *tendae* that formed one concession, see Chapter III, n. 24. On license fees for shops in Islam, see Rabie, *Financial System of Egypt*, pp. 105-106; for the incidence of rents transferred from shops, bakeries, mills, and baths for pious foundations, see Ira M. Lapidus, *Muslim Cities in the Later Middle Ages* (Cambridge, Mass., 1967), appendix A, lists.

[52] Arch. Crown, James I, Reg. Canc. 17, fol. 26v (Dec. 30, 1263): "Jucef Fetdar, i operatorium, i bisancium; Mahomet alcadi, i operatorium, i bisancium; Abdela Abolaix, i operatorium, duos solidos; Ali Alferrero, i operatorium, unum [sic] bisancium; Mafumet Allongo, i operatorium, unum bisancium; Jucef Fetdar, i operatorium, unum bisancium; Maçror, unum operatorium, unum bisancium; Brachim Almaymo, una barracha, duos solidos." On fol. 37r (July 2, 1265) a list for Gandía includes "item Aladrach fuster, i obrador, iii solidos, iv denarios"; this carpenter or woodworker, al-Azraq, appears later in the list (fol. 38r) as having received 30 solidi from the crown the previous year, perhaps for services rendered.

[53] Arch. Cat., perg. 1,229 (June 6, 1270): "operatorium meum cum sua algurfa" in St. Mary's parish, fronting on the bishop's *cellarium* and here being sold; see Leopoldo Torres Balbás, "Algunos aspectos de la casa hispanomusulmana: almacerías, algorfas, y salezidos," *Al-Andalus*, xv (1950), esp. pp. 181-182. *Repartimiento de Valencia*, p. 281: "ante ecclesiam Sancti Martini."

Catherine's church.[54] Shopping centers seem to have flanked neighborhood mosques throughout a city like Valencia; the shops themselves were of unequal value, renting in a range from one to ten morabatins a year.

King James insisted that his Valencia city bailiff "make all Saracen shopkeepers and craftsmen of Valencia, present or future, have their shops and work their crafts in our stores and workshops in the Moorish quarter of Valencia city, and hold them for us at rent and not in other workshops [or] stores, nor elsewhere in Valencia." The fine was severely punitive, a hundred solidi for each offence. A Muslim could build or subrent a shop from anyone "for an appropriate rental," as long as the king's own rental rights were respected.[55] By the pact of Játiva each *tenda* paid the king a besant a year.[56] One transaction of 1273 reveals eight shops under construction there for Muslims, the rents to go to King James.[57] At Játiva too the head of the Valencia city aljama maintained a shop for "two morabatins' lease, which you are obliged to pay me [the king] annually."[58]

Christians owned properties from the beginning in the "Saracen quarter" of Valencia city, some of which were shops. The stall granted to Muḥammad b. Ṣāliḥ, or perhaps of Salā (de Sale), in that quarter was bounded by three other shops belonging to Christians; possibly they were converts as was the previous holder of this shop, all huddled in one place.[59] Peter Ferrer owned a large building

---

[54] Arch. Cat., perg. 4,713 (April 13, 1252), a *tenda* at Játiva. Arch. Crown, James I, Reg. Canc. 10, fol. 62 (April 28, 1268): "operatorium in A[l]gezira in placia Sancte Katarine" on the main street; fol. 69 (July 3, 1258): "illis quattuor operatoriis . . . in partida Sancti Salvatoris." *Repartimiento de Valencia*, pp. 254-256, 259, 299, 311, 485-486.

[55] Arch. Crown, James I, Reg. Canc. 19, fol. 107v (Feb. 26, 1274): "quod faciatis sarracenos omnes tenderios et ministrales Valencie presentes et futuros habere suas tendas et operari sua ministeria in tendis et operatoriis nostris ravalli Valencie et que a nobis tenentur ad censum, et non in aliis operatoriis seu tendis nec in alio loco Valencie"; "sub competenti censu."

[56] Játiva Charter.

[57] Arch. Crown, James I, Reg. Canc. 21, fol. 151v (June 7, 1273): "que modo construistis."

[58] *Ibid.*, Reg. Canc. 19, fol. 30v (July 8, 1273): "duos morabatinos censuales quos annuatim nobis facere tenetis." The Çahat Abenache here can be identified with Çahat Abinafia or Abinhaia (see Chapter VII, n. 55).

[59] *Ibid.*, Peter III, Reg. Canc. 44, fol. 163 (Nov. 22, 1279); on Muḥammad see Burns, *Islam under the Crusaders*, ch. 16, n. 75. Christians owning property in these

complex "with seventeen porticos," or openings, inside the city's quarter; because he was able to sell the place in 1283 for the unusual sum of 650 solidi, it has been argued that these were archways used as shops.[60]

Possibly the crown conveyed most shops in the Valencia city quarter, and most farms in the city's countryside, into the hands of Christian owners due to the unconditional surrender of that area; on the other hand, just as the Muslim tenants for the new owners continued to operate their farms in the countryside by the terms of the city's capitulation, so within the quarter Muslims may have manned all the shops. The phenomenon appears more visibly in the dual ownership of certain public utilities. Muslims did not object to remote supervisory or financial control over these by Christian owners; they did insist, as in the Játiva pact, that Christians and Jews not "conduct" (conducere) shops that were social amenities, like public ovens and baths.[61]

A number of ambiguous fees might be assimilated to shop rents, except that pronounced differences shunt them into categories apart. Wineshops, butcher shops, and similar utilities call for their own chapter. Market and commercial taxes, though allied, can be identified as a distinct group. Industrial licensing for highly specialized arts, esteemed and promoted by the authorities, comprises a subclassification; their charges, when not waived to encourage the vocation, tended to be higher than those for prosaic craftsmen. Such skilled professions are revealed in the crown exemptions to attract Muslim dye masters and silk processers to Valencia; in the waiving of fees for ceramics, pottery, and glass at Játiva and Valencia city; and in King James's ability to assign a hundred solidi as salary for Játiva's qāḍī, to be taken "every year from the millage [almaxera] on paper that the said Saracens pay."[62] The term logerium (Catalan lloguer),

---

sectors eventually had to share in certain Mudejar taxes for them (Leopoldo Piles Ros, "La situación social de los moros de realengo en la Valencia del siglo xv," Estudios de historia social de España, 1 [1949], 232).

[60] Roca Traver, "Vida mudéjar," p. 169: "ab xvii portals . . . en la moreria de Valencia."

[61] Játiva Charter. On the huerta farms retaining their exarici, see the Valencia Capitulation, in Fernández y González, Mudejares de Castilla, appendix, doc. 15.

[62] Arch. Crown, James I, Reg. Canc. 11, fol. 191v (Jan. 20, 1260), transcribed more fully below in Chapter VII, n. 54; almaxera derives from the Arabic for a grinding-mill, the Catalan almàssera or (usually animal-driven) olive press being

a derivative of *locarium*, often stands for shop rent; its broader meaning as rental of any kind, however, allows it to cover pasturage fees
or even the complex of revenues owed under the rubric of rents or
tribute to the crown.[63]
The dyeworks in any of King James's cities were so indispensable
to a clothes-conscious generation, as well as to the ubiquitous cloth
trade, that they almost amounted to a public utility. The cauldron
fee (*caldera*), collected by the crown on each vat used by any class
of citizen including nobles and clerics, rose at Lérida from 200 solidi
early in James's reign to a thousand by mid-reign and to many
thousands by the time the king died. At Valencia city in 1252 James
took ten pennies for each pound of indigo used at the vat. "Dyeworks" appears among the Mudejar rents listed at Biar in 1267; at
Gandía in 1263 the mixed Christian and Mudejar revenues from the
dyeworks came to 80 solidi net.[64] Muslim masters of dyes were
prized. A number of them appear in Valencian records as objects of
the king's solicitude, and he legislated to promote their craft. 'Alī al-
Lūrī (Allauri), master at Játiva, won particular favor. At Valencia
city the three masters Muḥammad al-Ghazāl (Algacel), Ibrāhīm
al-Hammānī (Alhameni), and another Muḥammad got from King

---

the same word. For exemptions see Chapter IX, part 3. Utilities are in Chapter III,
commercial taxes in Chapter IV.

[63] The Aldea Charter waives all pasturage "sine aliquo logerio." An arrangement
for Alcira Mudejars farming their own revenues speaks of: "tributo seu logerio
quod sarraceni debent nobis dare et facere pro emptione reddituum Algezire"
("Sección de documentos," ed. Roque Chabás y Lloréns, *El archivo*, II [1887-1888],
doc. 56, pp. 403-406 [July 18, 1245]). A 1315 summary for Valencia city's shops,
apparently Christian and Muslim alike, records that "munte lo loguer dels obradors
de la soch" to 1,725 solidi; at three solidi apiece, the city would have held 575 shops,
but the rents were not so uniform (*Rentas de Aragón*, p. 88). A guard over the
shops drew a yearly salary of 60 solidi (p. 99). At Tarazona in 1294 the Mudejars
paid "logueros de las tiendas" to the king, and sixteen proprietors not in the normal
shop area paid "el loguero de los moros otros menestrales" (p. 225).

[64] Arch. Crown, James I, Reg. Canc. 15, fol. 84 (1267): "tintureriam"; Reg. Canc.
17, fol. 28 (Dec. 30, 1263): "tinturaria, lxxx solidos." *Colección diplomática*, doc.
416 (March 10, 1252) and doc. 400 (June 26, 1251); "qui tinxerit vel tingi fecerit in
caldaria tintorerie nostre civitatis Valencie colorem indi de bagadell"; though
bagadell was a near Eastern cloth, *indi de bagadell* meant the finest of the three
classes of indigo dye. On all such words, consult the appropriate entry in Miguel
Gual Camarena, *Vocabulario del comercio medieval, colección de aranceles aduaneros
de la corona de Aragón (siglos xiii y xiv)* (Tarragona, 1968), *bagadell* being on p.
225, and *purpura* of the next note on pp. 400-401. The Lérida tax is in *Llibre dels
feyts*, ch. 34.

James, "for their lifetime, buildings next to St. Mary's [cathedral] so as to manufacture dyes in them."[65] The Játiva charter took care to include dyeshops among crown monopolies, as they had been under Islamic rule, but it listed them in the midst of the utilities and as a separate item from the equally monopolized *operatoria*.

The Valencian Muslims were a nation of shopkeepers as much as agriculturists. The two spheres interacted, the agrarian serving and supplying the commercial, and the shopkeeper class involving itself with farming.[66] This fascinating urban scene, obscured behind the rural communities that survived longer, until Moor and peasant come to seem interchangeable terms, emerges again in the rental documentation. With its resurrection the social scene of crusader Valencia and the structure of the Mudejar community take on rich vitality. In protecting its revenues, the crown preserved at least for a while a Mudejar commercial society.

[65] On 'Alī "Allauri" see p. 91. The *Repartimiento de Valencia* has "Mahomet Algacel Abrahim Alhamemi Mahomat filius de Cobich teneant in vita sua domos iuxta Sanctam Mariam ut in eis faciant purpuras" (pp. 285-286); I translate *purpurae* in the several contexts here loosely as dyes; on p. 275 are houses "in quibus solebant fieri purpure," and on p. 443 "in domibus magistri purpurarum." Cobich perhaps garbles some name like al-Qubbashī or al-Khabbaz. Ibn 'Abdūn wanted all dye shops outside the town, and issued a warning against a fraudulent blue and green that could fade (*Séville musulmane, le traité*, pp. 111, 112). On the dye business see also César E. Dubler, *Über das Wirtschaftsleben auf der iberischen Halbinsel vom xi. zum xiii. Jahrhundert, Beitrag zu den islamisch-christlichen Beziehungen* (Erlenbach-Zurich, 1943), pp. 62-63.

[66] Burns, *Islam Under the Crusaders*, ch. 5, part 3.

CHAPTER III

Public Monopolies and Utilities

COMMUNITY SERVICES, centering on some establishment vital to daily living, were often reserved as a monopoly for tax purposes. Such a rental harvest inevitably provided a basic source of crown income. The concomitant records open a window on the life of the common man. Service concessions recur constantly in Christian property grants, sometimes released to a vassal, community, or individual, sometimes retained for farming at a share of profits or for a flat rent, and sometimes managed by a salaried executive responsible to the local bailiff. Mudejar communities, when not sharing the Christians' utilities, operated their own in much the same fashion. The Eslida charter specified mills, ovens, baths, and fonduks; the tax on each continued to be the portion of revenue previously given under Islamic rule. At Valencia city a number of these utilities clustered along the north and northeast of the Mudejar quarter, where shops and caravanserai were convenient also to non-Muslims. Neighborhood utilities of more modest scope flourished outside the area of this main *sūq*. These were primary utilities; revenues from salt or the upkeep of roads and waterways might be understood as part of their wider pattern. Some authors would include as well hunting, fishing, smithy, treasure trove, public weights and measures, and even less likely services.[1] King or lord looked carefully before alienating utilities, and saw to the proper collection of their valuable revenues.

TAVERNS AND BUTCHERIES

Despite fulminations of the orthodox, wineshops flourished in Spanish Islam. During an earlier era the Cordova caliphate had briefly conducted a state wine market. Not long after the Valencian crusade Peter III of Aragon demanded the surrender of half the Tunis excise on wine as part payment for helping a pretender to

[1] Honorio García y García, *Estado económico-social de los vasallos en la gobernación foral de Castellón* (Vich, 1943), p. 52.

41

plot seizure of the caliphate.[2] In the next century a Castilian charter, when reserving the Mudejar tavern to a local lord, forbade "any Moor ever to buy wine or to drink it in another tavern, and anyone who buys or drinks it in another tavern is to pay me a fine of 60 maravedis for each offence"; in the Valencian towns along the Chelva River, at the same time, the *taberna* was similarly a customary reservation of the local lord.[3] In the crusade period, before rents became itemized in greedy detail, Valencian charters do not explicitly mention the wineshop. Muslim-owned vineyards were ubiquitous in the kingdom before and after the crusade however; wineshops appear in a number of records, and Valencian Muslims relished their wine. Presumably the aljama officials, like their counterparts in Islamic lands, acquiesced in Christian operation of these embarrassing facilities.

The Játiva charter, regulating commercial activities, did allow that "no Saracen be made to pay for wine that he keeps or sells in his home."[4] When the Biar aljama in 1258 undertook to collect Mudejar revenues by a farming contract for three years, the excep-

---

[2] Ramón Muntaner, *Crònica*, ed. Enrique Bagué, 9 vols. in 2 (Barcelona, 1927-1952); see also the edition by Soldevila in *Les quatre grans cròniques*; ch. 31. In ch. 85 casks of red and white wine were gifts selected as acceptable presents for Barbary Muslims. In 1357 a temperance faction raided the wine and hashish parlors of Damascus, but the bibbers subdued them and counterattacked their mosques (Lapidus, *Muslim Cities*, p. 106; see also pp. 82, 173, 268). Alcoholic liquors were also made by Spanish Muslims from figs, roses, and violets (April), apples and pears (June), pomegranates (August), and other fruits; wine became a taxable commodity in the eleventh century (Imamuddin, *Socio-Economic and Cultural History of Muslim Spain*, pp. 105-106). Goitein provides new materials on the popularity of wine in eastern Islam (*Mediterranean Society*, I, 122-123). Ibn Khaldūn has an illuminating story about the wine impost at Fez in the early decades of the fourteenth century (*Muqaddimah*, II, 339-340). Ibn ar-Raqīq wrote a monograph on the several caliphs' attitudes toward wine and on their wine-drinking (Franz Rosenthal, *A History of Muslim Historiography*, 2d edn. rev. [Leiden, 1968], p. 419n.).

[3] Chelva Charter (Aug. 17, 1370), *Documentos inéditos de España*, XVIII, 69-74; Fernández y González, *Mudejares de Castilla*, appendix, doc. 71: "retengo . . . furnos, molinos, taberna"; following the custom of established aljamas here, the charter provided three kinds of land for each Muslim settler—"en secano como en regadio, e de las viñas." The Palma del Río Charter is in Fernández y González, *ibid.*, doc. 72 (1371): "que ayades taberna por quenta que me dedes, e que ningun moro que non compre vino ni ne beua en otra tauerna [*sic*], e qualquier que lo comprare e beuiere en otra tauerna, que peche a mi en pena por cada vez que lo fiziere sesenta maravedis."

[4] Játiva Charter: "nullus sarracenus teneatur dare caloniam pro vino quod habuerit vel emerit in domo sua." Strictly, *calonia* is a penalty (see below, Chapter V, n. 162).

tions reserved were "manslaughter fines and the tavern." Since these revenues included the few Christian contributions at Biar, one might argue that homicide and drink were preoccupations solely of the Christian community, but this seems unlikely.[5] A second tavern operated within Biar's concession for foreign Muslim merchants.[6] During the thirteenth century no parish was erected at Eslida because, according to a witness testifying in court, "no one lives there except Saracens, nor are any Christians there except the castellan and some taverners [*tabernarii*] selling wine."[7] No further hints survive from crusader Valencia; this is hardly surprising, since Muslims considered taverners among the disreputable classes along with usurers, prostitutes, professional mourners, and street entertainers, about all of whom the less said the better.

A valuable regalian monopoly among Christian and Muslim subjects was the butchery or meat market. As with the Jews, Mudejar operation of a separate butchery amounted to an extension of religious privileges. Muslims took ritual precautions when slaughtering, and shunned pork. The word "butchery" (*carnicería*) comprehended all phases of the meat industry from slaughtering, skinning, and dressing to retail sales. Thus the Christian butchery at Játiva consisted of both a meat market (*macellum*)—twenty stalls renting at three mazmodins yearly apiece—and an adjacent slaughterhouse enclosure "for preparing meat."[8] Hygiene as well as access to livestock counseled the siting of butcheries near a town gate; at Valencia city the Christians took over the butchers' *sūq* just inside the wall to

---

[5] *Itinerari*, pp. 275-276 (June 16, 1258): "exceptis homicidiis et taberna." As used by authors like Lull, *homicidium* (Catalan *homicidi* and *homei*), in its general sense can be murder; in a legal sense it rather implies manslaughter. On the fine called *homicidium* see Rodón Binué, *Lenguaje técnico del feudalismo*, p. 136.

[6] *Itinerari*, p. 261 (Sept. 4, 1257): "et tenere tabernam."

[7] Honorio García y García, "La parroquial del Santo Ángel de la Vall de Uxó," *BSCC*, XXII (1946), 320: "non habitent ibi nisi sarraceni, nec sint ibi christiani nisi alcaydus et aliqui tabernarii vina vendentes." At Uxó in 1469 the only Christians were the winesellers too (Honorio García y García, *Notas para la historia de Vall de Uxó* [Vall de Uxó, 1962], p. 81). See also Burns, *Crusader Valencia*, I, 77.

[8] *Repartimiento de Valencia*, p. 439 (1248): "placiam sibe [*sic*] carrariam . . . ubi modo est macellum" with an adjoining yard or corral "ad excoriandas carnes"; each keeper of a stall or *tabula* also received a farm of two fanecates in size. The stages *occidere, excoriare* (*vestire*), *scindere* (*taylare*), *tenere*, and *vendere* appear in the notes below. The *escorxador* who dressed the animal, and the *maell* or butcher, may often be the same man under names emphasizing his dual functions.

the west of the southern gate.[9] At neighboring Tortosa, on the Valencian kingdom's northern border, the law code allowed Christians to buy fresh meat not only at the gate but also at stalls behind the cathedral; cured meat, birds, and wild meat brought in by hunters went on sale anywhere as long as it was already dressed.[10]

Meat markets also handled fish, an everyday commodity in Valencian coastal towns; at Tárrega in Catalonia the Christians had a single "butchery or meat market for meat and fish," while at Valencia city a settler from Lérida rented "ten stalls for the fish business in the place adjoining the butchery." This Valencian city fish market of the Christians appears once or twice in the records, as does the collector of the king's fifth on private and commercial fishing in the Valencian kingdom; fishing by Muslims also comes up, but not references detailing their public sale of fish there.[11] The stalls of the meat market and fish market of Murviedro, with the fanecates of land assigned to them along the inner town-wall, served both Murviedro and its *ravallum*—presumably the Moorish quarter. At Alcira, in renting "the whole meat market for selling all meat and the whole fish market for selling all fish" to revenue farmers in 1274, the bailiff of Valencia excepted "the stalls for meat and fish of the Jews and Saracens." He further ordered "all Christian butchers of the town or quarters of Alcira not to butcher or cause to be butchered, or to sell, meat or fish in the stalls of the Saracens or Jews"; Mudejars and Jews, on the other hand, were not "to allow butchering or sales in the stalls of their own meat market for any

---

[9] *Ibid.*, p. 256: "ante ecclesiam Sancte Cathaline circa carniceriam"; pp. 536-539, the "vicus de carnificibus" with 58 owners, many of whom were not butchers; see also p. 508, buildings at Murviedro "que fuerunt cuiusdam sarraceni carnicerii," and the butchers' inn below, n. 85.

[10] Bayerri, *Tortosa*, vi, 343-345, from the *Costums*. Ibn 'Abdūn has a number of regulations on the slaughter, display, and sale of meat and fish in twelfth-century Seville; his segregation of poultry and rabbits away from the main mosque and in a special area suggests that the Tortosan Christian stalls continued a precrusade custom (*Séville musulmane, le traité*, pp. 95, 98-99, 106, 128-129; see p. 69 on fixed taxes for butchered meat).

[11] *Itinerari*, p. 77 (April 4, 1229): "carniceria sive macellum ad carnes et pisces." *Repartimiento de Valencia*, p. 309: "x tabulas ad opus piscaterie in loco illo iuxta carniceriam." The mixed Christian-Mudejar rents at Cullera in 1263 yielded nearly twice as much from the fish as from the meat stalls (Arch. Crown, James I, Reg. Canc. 17, fol. 28 [Dec. 30, 1268]: "ius piscium, xxx solidos," "carniceria, xvii solidos, iii denarios").

Christian at any time." The three meat markets were to continue as a regalian monopoly.[12]

Two taxes were at issue. The regalian *carnicería* fee properly fell on the shops, not the meat. A separate range of exactions affected the animals, domestic or wild, brought in for slaughter; these went under names like *carnatge* or *carnalatge* (slaughter fee) and *cabeçatge* (head-of-stock charge). Chivert's aljama was exempt from fees on "animals that they kill in their butchery" and on "all fishing in fresh or salt water"; but had to surrender "on greater quarry only a fourth portion of the meat." Rabbits, always important to Spanish Islamic towns, came under a special yearly fee for the crusader masters as probably they had before: "two brace of rabbits, dressed."[13] At Játiva the animals commonly slaughtered fell into two tax groupings: three obols or subpennies at the killing of "a ram, sheep, male goat, and female goat, and for a beef six pence."[14] The Aldea charter describes the *cabeçagium*, or penny per head of stock killed for table meat; it

[12] Arch. Crown, James I, Reg. Canc. 13, fol. 289r,v (Oct. 27, 1275): "tabulas carnicerie et piscaterie Muriveteris cum fanecatis terre ipsis tabulis assignatis." Arch. Mun. Alcira, Canc. Real, perg. 010.6 (Dec. 30, 1274) gives: "totam carniceriam omnium carnium et totam pischateriam omnium piscium vendendi . . . in villa de Algesira et ravallibus suis universis, exceptis tabulis carnicerie et pischaterie iudeorum et sarracenorum . . . , immo mandamus de presenti omnibus carnificiis christianis presentibus vel futuris ville vel ravallium Algesire quod non scindant vel scindi faciant sive vendant carnes vel pisces in tabulis sarracenorum . . . mandantes etiam iudeis et sarracenis quod non dimittant scindere sive vendere in tabulis carnicerie eorum alicui cristiano ullo tempore."

[13] Chivert Charter: "de bestiis autem quas occident in carniceria sua nichil dare teneantur"; "in omnibus piscacionibus aque salse et dulcis"; "venatores dent de venacione grossa quartam partem de carne tantum et non de alio" (*grossa* may rather mean serious or commercial in this context); "venator venacionis cuniculorum dent . . . quo [duo?] paria de cunicullis vestitis." The revenues at Benaymir (Benámer?) in Valencia include rabbit hunting; see Arch. Crown, James I, Reg. Canc. 35, fol. 4v (1268): "cassa de los conils, xi solidos, viii denarios"; fol. 7 (1269): "item la casça dels conils, xi solidos, vii denarios." See also below, pp. 155ff. On the variety of wild animals in Islamic Valencia see Dubler, *Wirtschaftsleben*, pp. 78-79, and the animal index on pp. 174-175. Animals to be hunted were regarded somewhat as movable properties by Valencian lords (García y García, *Estado económico-social de Castellón*, pp. 61-62), but they normally granted universal license, sometimes asking token or license fees. On hunting privileges, see too the *Fori antiqui Valentiae*, ed. Manuel Dualde Serrano (Valencia, 1967), rub. cxxiv, no. 12.

[14] Játiva Charter: "statuimus etiam quod de unoquoque capite arietis, ovis, hirci, et caprae, qui in ravallo nostro interfecti fuerint, persolvantur tres oboli regalium; et pro unoquoque capite bovis, vel baccae, sex denarii nobis vel nostris."

appears again after the turn of the century in an application of these pennies to the repair of Denia's fortifications.[15] The ordinary tax on sea fish was a tenth of the catch, and on fish from the Albufera lagoon a fifth, with no fee on actual selling of fish at home or abroad.[16] Snaring of sea or land birds remained free on crown lands and where the laws of Valencia city prevailed.[17] These details, besides telling something of the market and tax aspects of Mudejar life, broaden our insights into the protein content of the Valencian Moors' diet.

Upon the fall of Valencia city King James limited its Christian meat stall to a single locality accommodating forty men to "cut and butcher, sell or keep meat for sale." The only exceptions were Jews and Muslims, "who can each have a butchering place for their own purposes."[18] Segregation did not necessarily mean isolation of butchering facilities; Jews for example sold ritually slaughtered meat to Christians and won the privilege at Valencia of buying ritual meat also from the Christian butchery.[19] Ten years after the capitula-

[15] "Sección de documentos," doc. 36, p. 360 (1308, revealed in a transfer to their lord Gonzalbo García by James II in 1314). *Cabeça* or *cabessa* can be the head of a person or a head of stock (esp. *cabeçes de bestiar*); after the turn of the century the large sums listed for Elche (4,500 solidi), for Elda (2,000 solidi), for Aspe (1,500), and for Novelda (1,500) raise a suspicion that personal head tax may have been meant there (*Rentas de Aragón*, pp. 123ff.); since *cabeçes* and *alfarda* appear together at a place like Aspe (1,500 versus 2,000), the problem of the *alfarda* may be related (see below, Chapter V, part 1).

[16] *Fori antiqui Valentiae*, rub. cxxiv, no. 12. *Aureum opus*, doc. 36, fols. 12v-13 (Jan. 21, 1250). Valencia city, above, in the early fourteenth century contributed 24,000 solidi as "la quinta del peix" from Christians and Moors alike—double the revenue from the rich "gabella de la sal" (*Rentas de Aragón*, p. 87). Background details on fishing in Islamic Spain are in Dubler, *Wirtschaftsleben*, p. 80.

[17] See Burns, *Islam under the Crusaders*, ch. 5, part 3; see also the cattle-tax information below, p. 156. Hunting played a larger role in Islamic patrician life than it did among Christians, but it appears indirectly in Valencian sources on the Mudejars; see Maurice Lombard, "La chasse et les produits de la chasse dans le monde musulman (viiie-xie siècle)," *Annales, économies, sociétés, civilisations*, xxiv (1969), pp. 572, 576-577.

[18] *Colección diplomática*, doc. 193 (Dec. 21, 1238): "nec audeat aliquis scindere vel taylare, vendere vel tenere carnes ad vendendum in aliquo civitatis . . . nisi fuerit sarracenus vel iudeus, qui possint inter se habere locum carnicerie ad suum opus." Goitein distinguishes four classifications of butchers in Islamic society— slaughterer, butcher, meat carver, and meat seller, with a separate division for goat slaughterers (*Mediterranean Society*, i, 115).

[19] Francisco de A. de Bofarull y Sans, *Los judíos en el territorio de Barcelona (siglos x a xiii), reinado de Jaime I, 1213-1276* (Barcelona, 1910), pp. 93-94 (July

tion and expulsion a separate Mudejar meat stall can be discovered in operation—"one stall for butchering and selling meat, near the gate of the quarter of the Saracens at Roteros of Valencia." This was a monopoly. "No other Christian, Jew, or Saracen can set up stalls for selling meat elsewhere in the said quarter except at the said stall, ever at any time."[20]

The owner, a Christian named Dominic Cavall, returned two Alfonsine morabatins a year to the crown; as concessionaire Dominic probably sublet the operation itself to Muslim butchers. Occasional documents continue to locate "the butchery of the Saracens of Valencia," which soon became profitable and elaborate. Either the concessionaire paid the king a share of the profits as well as the rental, or the stalls of the quarter multiplied, or the king renegotiated the butchery contract. At any rate the crown was able to draw the salary of an official of the aljama in 1267 by assigning a claim of a hundred solidi "to be had and collected from our revenues and receipts in the meat stalls of the Saracens of Valencia." Smaller Moorish centers, of course, returned far less revenue. In 1268 Pego paid some 30 solidi into royal coffers from its meat market, a third of the sum returned by Pego's shops.[21] The repugnance expressed by

---

20, 1271); for the same privilege confirmed for Majorca, see doc. 221 (Aug. 25, 1273). Jewish as well as Christian scruples had to be overcome; see Yitzhak Baer, *A History of the Jews in Christian Spain*, trans. Louis Schoffman *et alii*, 2 vols. (Philadelphia, 1966), I, 159-161, including the 1268 privilege for Catalan Jews. Jews did not always have separate butcheries; see Abraham A. Neuman, *The Jews in Spain: Their Social, Political and Cultural Life During the Middle Ages*, 2 vols. (Philadelphia, 1942), I, 273, citing Ben Adret; a Christian woman had the Jewish oven at Barcelona under James I. The animals normally slaughtered at Valencia city's meat market for Christians may offer further clues to Mudejar local diet as well, pork aside: "videlicet bove, vacca, porco, ariete, yrco, capra, et ove, edulis, atque agnis" (Arch. Crown, James I, Reg. Canc. 13, fol. 160 [April 6, 1264]).

[20] *Colección diplomática*, doc. 362 (Sept. 13, 1249): "prope portam morerie sarracenorum de Roteros de Valencia unam tabulam ad taliandum et vendendum carnes," the king decreeing "in perpetuum quod nullus alius christianus, iudeus vel sarracenus possit alibi in dicta moreria . . . tabulas ad vendendum carnes facere . . . nisi tantum in dicta tabula tua, nunquam in aliquo tempore." In 1322 James II awarded 2 morabatins to the Puridad convent, taken yearly from the rentals of the meat stalls in Valencia city's Moorish quarter (Branchát, *Derechos y regalías de Valencia*, I, 432).

[21] Arch. Crown, James I, Reg. Canc. 15, fol. 85 (March 14, 1267): "habendos et percipiendos annuatim in redditibus et iuribus nostris carnicerie sarracenorum Valentie." A reference of 1273 to the quarter's butchery is in Reg. Canc. 19, fol. 30v

the Muslims in Játiva's charter, against Christians operating Mudejar utilities, indicates that Christians sometimes did so in person. Even at Játiva a Christian concessionaire may have presided over the butchery complex. Each stall there owed the crown an annual silver besant; a separate entry in the charter took care to reserve the butchery in perpetuity.[22]

It is difficult to distinguish Muslim control of utilities at the operational level from the profitable supervisory role of the concessionaire. A privilege from the fourteenth century, though too late to employ probatively for the present study, does illumine this dual control. In 1376 the Valencia city aljama, burdened with debts, received the butchery concession, its profits committed to reducing the community's obligations. Generously phrased to allow removal and more formal construction, the grant "allows you to build, make and maintain a butchery within the boundaries of the said quarter, wherever you prefer, and to cut and sell in it any kind of meat you want to anyone at all; and likewise to impose and regulate the price you want not only for buyers among themselves but any others [buying] the said meat, [and] to farm and administer [the tax] as you decide best, for as long as it pleases us."[23]

Muslims, whether united as an aljama or dispersed in negligible groups, commonly enjoyed this privilege of a separate butchery. The custom is underlined by another document of the fourteenth century, when the Calatayud Muslims complained that they remained the exception. "Considering that in all cities and towns of the kingdom of Aragon, where Saracens live or where a Saracen aljama exists, the aljama or the Saracens have their own legal, separate meat shop

---

(July 8, 1273): "affrontat cum carneceria sarracenorum Valencie," referring to a Muslim-owned *operatorium*. Pego is in Reg. Canc. 35, fol. 3v (1268): "item la carniceria—viii besants, v millareses"; this segment, collected in besants and with the specific Mudejar tax of the besant nearby, probably refers only to the Mudejar community.

[22] Játiva Charter: "retinemus . . . in perpetuum carniceriam"; "et pro unaquaque tenda carnicerie, unum besancium similiter." See also the Chivert Charter: "in carniceria sua."

[23] Roca Traver, "Vida mudéjar," doc. 30 (July 18, 1376): "vobis liceat construere, facere et tenere infra limites morarie prefate, ubi magis elegeritis, carniceriam, et in ea scindere et vendere carnes quascumque et quibuscumque volueritis, et in et super carnibus nedum inter vos sed etiam quoscumque alios ementes de dictis carnibus, imposicionem quam volueritis, dum nobis placuerit, ponere et ordinare eamque exhigere et levare, vendere et administrare prout magis duxeritis eligendum."

(*macellum*) and butcher who kills and cuts according to their rite or Sunna the meats they need," the king remedied the defect by permitting "a building or shop" on a specified street in the Christian section of Calatayud or in a similar place of the Moorish quarter. Here the "butcher," perhaps the concessionaire, had to be a Christian, though elected by the Muslims to "kill and cut meat according to your rite and Sunna." The butcher's fee was one obol higher, for each pound of meat "of any kind whatsoever," than was paid at the Christian butchery; Christians purchasing at the Mudejar butchery also had to give the extra obol. The crown impressively ornamented this extended parchment with its seal in red wax. Though derived from a generation restricting Mudejar rights, it tells something about the rooted customs fifty to seventy-five years before. Strangely enough, its editor read the privilege in an opposite sense, assuming it to represent an "extreme" of tolerance peculiar to Calatayud.[24]

Bakeries and Mills

Though a variety of industrial kilns fell under taxes, the common *furnum* was the monopoly oven for baking a neighborhood's bread. Daily bread was the staff of life, making the *furnaticum* (Catalan *fornatge*) collected at its cooking site correspondingly lucrative. As with other utilities, three tax agencies might be involved—the baker on salary, the concessionaire or tax farmer, and the crown. The taxpayer surrendered his loaf in twenty or so; occasionally the community might arrange to give a fixed sum to lord or concessionaire, presumably also providing the baker's salary. Domestic ovens, where allowed to bake bread, paid their private *furnaticum*. King or local lord sometimes surrendered this revenue, in effect exempting public and private bakeries. The traditional Valencian oven, freestanding or fitted into the wall of a building, resembled a large, dome-shaped

---

[24] Fernández y González, *Mudejares de Castilla*, appendix, doc. 69 (1354): "attendentes quod in omnibus civitatibus et villis regni Aragonum, ubi sarraceni habitant seu aliama est sarracenorum, quod ipsa aliama seu sarraceni habent macellum proprium, et signatum, et separatam, et carnificem qui occidat et scindat carnes eis necessarias, secundum eorum ritum sive çunam . . . in una domo seu tenda . . . et ibidem parare seu habere unam tabulam carniceriae, intus dictam domum seu tendam; . . . attamen quod carnifex sit christianus . . . et quod possitis vos eligere illum carnificem, quem vobis placuerit, qui occidat et scindat carnes vobis necessarias secundum ritum et çunam vestram; insuper vobis concedimus quod ille carnifex christianus quem vobis duxeritis eligendum possit habere [*one obol more*]."

hive, with aperture for fueling with wood and for inserting the loaves, and with a hole at the top as chimney and observation control.

In licensing one of the Christian bakehouses, King James located it at Valencia city's seashore, "in the place where the cottages [*barrache*] now stand"; anyone could "bake biscuits and other bread as in the ovens of Valencia city," the king's rental being half the profits.[25] Another Christian bakehouse, located in the city market, paid yearly to the king "four Alfonsine morabatins in gold of good gold and legal weight," plus one morabatin as rental of the shop space. A third Christian oven, a continuation and later a rebuilding of the original Islamic oven for the northeast corner of the city near the gate called Bāb Ibn Ṣajar, illustrates the careful jurisdiction assigned to such ovens, tracing its monopolistic area from the gate eastwards to the Dominicans' priory and from the town-wall to the canal of the Guadalaviar River.[26] Mudejar communities normally supported their own bakeries, since each oven was able to serve only a limited, neighborhood clientele.

[25] *Itinerari*, p. 458 (Jan. 20, 1272): "in loco ubi modo sunt barrache . . . in quo quidem furno possit quicumque voluerit bescuytum et alium panem decochere sicut in furnis civitatis Valencie." The *bescuit*, as its name indicates, was baked twice; *pa* would be a loaf from one of several kinds of flour. On this tax see Agustín Coy Cotonat, "El derecho llamado 'furnatico' en el siglo xiii," *Congrés I*, 190-193. On Valencian ovens see also my *Crusader Valencia*, I, 192, where the Templars in the city charged one loaf in twenty; p. 235, where an Alcira convent gets annual rents from Játiva ovens of 30, 22, 20, and 40 solidi; and II, 483. García y García found that the crusader lords of northern Valencia were even more tenacious in retaining Christian ovens than mills; only six small settlements got them free; sometimes the seigniors even forbade use of ovens belonging to other villages. The tax varied from 1 loaf in 30, 1 in 25 or 27, and 5 in 20, to a fraction suitable to lesser portions. At Culla the Christians could bake in their houses, though they had to pay a *fornagium*. See García y García, *Estado económico-social de Castellón*, pp. 54-56. Ovens are treated in the *Fori antiqui Valentiae*, rub. ccv, no. 26 (on careless bakers causing fires), rub. cxxxiv, no. 6 (Muslim bakers to close on Sundays and feasts), and rub. cxxxv, no. 2. At Aranda in Aragon in 1294 "el tributo de los fornos de los moros" was paid in grain—two cafizes of barley (*Rentas de Aragón*, p. 250). The payment of a proportion of the bread baked, by the individual customer to the baker, prevailed also in Islamic Seville (Ibn 'Abdūn, *Séville musulmane, le traité*, pp. 107, 118-119). Rabie includes Islamic sales taxes and license fees on bakeries, mills, and the like, in his *Financial System of Egypt*, p. 105.

[26] Arch. Crown, Reg. Canc. 16, fol. 202v (July 31, 1270): "pro censu dicti furni donetis . . . quattuor morabatinos alfonsinos in auro boni auri et iusti ponderis cum illo videlicet morabatino quem inde facere debebas pro censu loci." Reg. Canc. 11, fol. 167v (June 21, 1259): "furnum sive furnos a porta que dicitur [Babaza]char . . . usque ad se[quiam de] Godalaviar."

At Aldea just north of Valencia the Muslims paid their lords the Hospitallers a fixed sum of fifteen solidi yearly for ovens. "No other Christian or Saracen may build any oven there nor may they bake bread anywhere except in this oven." The Eslida Moors "may bake your bread in your ovens which were built in the time of the Saracens"—a privilege renewed by the crown in 1276. At Játiva the crown "retained for ourselves the ovens."[27] At towns of mixed populations too small to support separate ovens, Moors and Christians shared the town utility; in 1258 "all the inhabitants of Navarrés, both Christians and Saracens, present and future, are bound to come for baking their bread" to the newly constructed municipal bake-house, paying to its concessionaire the standard fee "according to the custom of the kingdom of Valencia."[28]

Aside from general notices in charters, specific ovens crop up in the documentation from time to time as the crown assigned them to concessionaires. The wealthy lady Andrea of Arnet, whose investment portfolio rather ran to ovens, acquired in 1278 the right to build a bakery in the Moorish quarter of Alcira.[29] At Valencia city in 1245 King James licensed a Christian to have "an oven beyond the walls in the Moorish quarter," at two mazmodins every Christmas.[30] Arnold of St. Vincent (does the name conceal a baptized Moor?) rented a bakery at Valencia city; in 1256 King James reconfirmed "that oven that you hold at rent from us in the Moorish quarter of Valencia and also all the buildings you bought in the said quarter," adding a promise to permit no others in the immediate vicinity. In

[27] Aldea Charter: "et aliquis alius christianus vel sarracenus non possint [sic] construere nec possint coquere panem aliumde [sic] nisi tantum in ipso furno." Second Eslida Charter (Arch. Crown, James I, Reg. Canc. 38, fol. 3v [June 27, 1276]): "et possitis decoquere panem vestrum in furnis vestris quod constructum erat [sic] tempore sarracenorum." The (first) Eslida Charter requires a tenth "de furnis" as in "tempore paganorum." Játiva Charter: "retinemus tamen ibi nobis . . . furnos."

[28] Arch. Crown, James I, Reg. Canc. 9, fol. 58 (July 30, 1258): "ad quod furnum teneantur venire ad decoquendum panem suum omnes populatores tam christiani quam sarraceni de Navarres . . . secundum consuetudinem regni Valencie."

[29] Ibid., Peter III, Reg. Canc. 43, fol. 126v (Dec. 1, 1278); she got another in Valencia city, an interest in a third, and yet another in Benifayó, and also exported grain to Genoa. She was probably related to the former bailiff of Alcira, of the same name, and did own properties in Alcira.

[30] Repartimiento de Valencia, p. 319 (1245): "Dominicus Sancii Fortun: furnum extramuros in moreria"; one Dominic Sanxez, an official (porter) of King James, may be the same man.

1258 John of Borgia, a lesser crown official, acquired at a rental of four Josephine mazmodins the right to "build and construct one oven for baking bread in the Moorish quarter of Valencia in a certain small building of Yūsuf."[31]

General tax lists provide some idea of profit for the crown from ovens, and thus of their larger prosperity for the holders. Ovens plus chickens at Pego in 1269 brought over 100 besants, including costs of collection; the same heading, with labor service added, brought over eight solidi from every Mudejar house at Sumacárcel and Sueca in 1269 and somewhat less than that in 1268; the mixed revenues from Gandía in 1263 assigned a total tax of 225 solidi to ovens.[32]

In the *sūq* near each large mosque there seems to have stood a public oven. As with Mudejar shops, these are most easily discerned in the confiscated city of Valencia—an oven near the mosque that became St. Thomas' church, another in front of the St. Andrew's mosque, others near the Holy Cross and St. Martin's mosques, one at the southern or market gate "between the two gates," another in the Tarragona sector and another in the Jews' quarter, with others listed less precisely. At least two grants date from 1238, five from 1239, and one from 1240; one grant demands 60 solidi "as entry fee" plus 50 solidi rental every Christmas.[33] Poring over the book of land

---

[31] *Colección diplomática*, doc. 543 (Aug. 10, 1256): "illud furnum . . . quod pro nobis ad censum tenes in moreria Valencie et domos eciam omnes quas emisti in dicta moreria." Though context makes one suspect a convert, he may have come from a town of that name or have belonged to one of the Catalan families named Santvicenç; in any case he is an obscure person. (On St. Vincent as patron of Valencia and identified with Valencian Mozarabs, see Burns, *Crusader Valencia*, i, ch. 15.) Arch. Crown, James I, Reg. Canc. 10, fol. 59v (April 8, 1258): "quod possitis hedificare et construere unum furnum ad coquendum panem in moraria Valencie in quadam casali Iusefi alamini [*hole in manuscript*] eiusdem morarie."

[32] Arch. Crown, James I, Reg. Canc. 35, fol. 7 (1268): "çofra e besant e galinas e forn, xxiiii cases, cclxviii sous," and fol. 8 (1269): "de xxiii cases, xii sous, i diner per quada casa, ccxc sous"; I've subtracted the besant to give the reckoning in my text. Reg. Canc. 17, fol. 28 (1263): "furni, ccxxv solidos."

[33] *Repartimiento de Valencia*, pp. 290, 318, 324, 325, 382-383 (sixty solidi "pro intrata"), 536-539. The Jewish quarter was laid out with one of its boundary references the "furnum de Abinnulliz" (p. 290). Other names include: of Abenbalbo or Abinfaldon (pp. 324, 382); Amalgazen on Tarahifi street (pp. 324, 382); Chaher (p. 187); Fauha, on that street (p. 251); of the Fig Tree, in that plaza (p. 383); of the Forge, on that street (p. 325); and Laxacof or Laxacef, on that street (pp. 324, 382). Recalling the equivalence of street and quarter, Islamic names for some of the city's quarters emerge here (see Burns, *Islam under the Crusaders*, ch. 5, part 3).

divisions, the Valencian historian Chabás contrived to isolate about a dozen city ovens carried over from the Islamic period, though a few may be ambiguous repetitions.[34] The fuller listings at Majorca show that the king's half of the captured capital supported 24 ovens; the allotment was 6 to each eighth of the divided city.[35] The forge or smithy (*fabrica*) proves very difficult to find; though some may lie concealed under the plural *furni*, this sounds improbable.[36] The ceramics kilns, which gained a special fame for both Islamic and Christian Valencia, belong to another context, since they were not among the utilities.

Water-driven mills served as an ordinary source of power. They proliferated within the towns and over the countryside, lining the banks of the humblest watercourse. No mention appears of Valencian windmills, nor of the animal mills and presses that must have functioned on upland farms. Depending on the kind of stream, a watermill might be a multi-wheeled monster, a small mobile mechanism, an unambitious wheel designed to turn only at moments of water flow in a ditch, ' _ a solid edifice around which settlement tended to accumulate. Certain mills catered to the grinding of industrial products like henna, or served the manufacture of paper or the processing of cloth; an occasional mill-type wheel, fitted with buckets, lifted water to higher levels. Most mills, however, met the daily needs of farmers and townsmen by pulverizing wheat and barley, or by carrying water to houses and gardens.

The Valencian poet Ibn al-Abbār (d. 1260) rang the changes on a conventional theme in his "The Wheel," seeing the waterwheel as a prisoner on a chain, or as alternately drinking and pouring, or as a heavenly sphere "where star never burns." His predecessor, the twelfth-century Sa'd al-Jayr, indited a similar effusion to the waterwheel spraying over a garden, responding by its creaking to the coo of doves, and weeping from its wooden eyeducts.[37] King James

---

[34] Roque Chabás y Lloréns, "El libro del repartimiento de la ciudad y reino de Valencia," *El archivo*, III (1888-1889), 222.

[35] *Repartimiento de Mallorca*, pp. 116ff.

[36] See García y García, *Estado económico-social de Castellón*, pp. 56-59, on the forge in Christian settlements of northern Valencia.

[37] Ibn Saīd ('Alī b. Mūsā b. Sa'īd, al-Andalusī al-Maghribī), *The Pennants*, anthology of 1243 trans. by A. J. Arberry as *Moorish Poetry* (Cambridge, 1953) has the first poem on p. 135, the second on p. 137; see also Emilio García Gómez, *Poemas arábigoandaluces*, 4th edn. (Madrid, 1959), p. 139. Only the Tarragona windmill is

contemplated mills under a more prosaic light. When settling Valencian lands, the utilities he most frequently reserved, besides ovens, were mills. He distributed them to concessionaires with frugal care, and allowed new constructions only by explicit privilege. No distinction or description appears in most cases, so that it is hard to say whether he lumped industrial machines and domestic water-lifters into the same category, adjusting his fees by known custom. Probably the documents follow the usage of the early Valencian *Furs*, the word "mill" normally referring to the grinding of cereals, though paper or fulling or other mills fell under the same regalian control.[38]

King James appointed a special collector for mills, and from the revenues of the Valencia city mills in 1271 he alienated to the mistress of his declining years, Berengaria Alfonso, a gift of 3,730 solidi. When he donated the great Moncada irrigation system to Valencia city in 1268, he retained the charge on mills for the use of the canals' water force.[39] King James founded a convent of Alcira nuns in good part with rents from local mills, and he was not ashamed to award the Knights Hospitaller a fifth share in a Burriana mill. The millers' brotherhood early formed a guild in Valencia city, and one of the

mentioned by Muslim authors of any period discussing Islamic Spain, but Lévi-Provençal believes windmills were used then as now on the uplands (*España musulmana*, v, 154). On mills see also the *Fori antiqui Valentiae*, rub. cxxxiv, "de molendinis." See also García y García, *Estado económico-social de Castellón*, pp. 52-54, with discussion of the charge in each Christian charter of northern Valencia, and two examples of alienation in return for grinding the lord's grain; Ferraz Penelas, *Maestre racional y la hacienda foral valenciana*, pp. 27-28; Branchát, *Derechos y regalías de Valencia*, I, ch. 5. The detailed study by N. P. Gómez Serrano, "Contribució al estudi de la molinería valenciana mijeval," *III Congrés d'història de la corona d'Aragó*, 2 vols. (Valencia, 1923), II, 695-766, treats only the fourteenth and fifteenth centuries, though enlightening in some ways for the previous period. See also the works of Glick and Cuvillier below, Chapter V, nn. 1, 2, and the allied discussion of water.

[38] *Fori antiqui Valentiae*, rub. cxxxiv. On noncereal mills, see Branchát, *Derechos y regalías de Valencia*, I, 288-290.

[39] *Aureum opus*, doc. 78, fol. 23v (May 9, 1268). For Berengaria, see Arch. Crown, James I, Reg. Canc. 21, fol. 10v (Aug. 18, 1271): "de redditibus et iuribus nostris molendinorum Valencie." Some comparisons with the mills of Christian neighbors can be drawn from Agustí Altisent's "Un poble de la Catalunya nova, els segles xi i xii, L'Espluga de Francolí de 1079 a 1200," *AEM*, III (1966), esp. pp. 209-210 discussing the parts of the mill, the rental third, and the concept of public tax rather than seignorial mill monopoly.

first disputes waged by the city's Dominican friars was with a miller over an adjoining watercourse.[40]

The list of vacated lands distributed to Christians describes Islamic mills with three, four, five, and six waterwheels, plus one giant boasting fourteen wheels.[41] The crown controlled the placing of new mills, the number of waterwheels, and the rental-tax, sometimes alienating a single wheel of a complex. Thus King James in 1239 permitted the Dominicans "one wheel only, on that irrigation course going toward the [five-wheel] mill of Bernard of Teruel, and they can raise it only so high as is required to draw one full measure of water day and night continually."[42] James tells of destroying canals of the Muslims around Játiva as part of a siege, "to cut off the water used for irrigating and for grinding at the mills."[43]

The Mudejars' Eslida charter reserved mills to the crown, designating the same payment as given "in the time of the pagans." Mills undoubtedly came under Játiva charter's "all the other [utility] revenue claims."[44] The mills of Uxó, not specifically mentioned in the Mudejar charter, remained in crown hands. King James turned over four of these to the aljama in 1260, apparently as consolation for the irrigation system stripped from them by judgment rendered in the king's court that same day. "You are to have and hold by my gift a half share of the four mills that I have in the Uxó country, so that from now on you are not bound to give me or mine anything from the revenue and income of those four mills except only a third portion"; he carefully excluded "any expenses" being deducted

[40] Burns, *Crusader Valencia*, I, 185, 213, 235, 471: the dispute was "super . . . decursu acquarum" in 1271; the Burriana fifth was given in 1235.

[41] *Repartimiento de Valencia*, esp. pp. 320-326, 379-381; on a bridge, p. 480; fourteen-wheeled, rented for half the profits, p. 432; rental of a third of profits, p. 322; "i rotam in molendino," p. 242; license to build unlimited number of wheels in Peñíscola mill, p. 263. *Repartimiento de Mallorca*, pp. 40-42, has 32 on one waterway. The *rota* or wheel in the records was the turbine wheel against which the water struck from above or below, and should not be confused with the *mola* or millwheel grinding.

[42] *Repartimiento de Valencia*, p. 326 (Dec. 17, 1239): "i rota tantum in illa cequia que vadit ad molendina Bernardi de Turolio et possint eam tantum elevare ita ut possit abstrahere unum bonum riguarium de aqua de die et nocte et continue et semper"; the five-wheeled mill of Bernard is on pp. 321-322.

[43] *Llibre dels feyts*, ch. 321: "de tolre l•aygua on devien reguar e molre los molins."

[44] Eslida Charter: "de molendinis . . . tempore paganorum." Játiva Charter: "balnea, furnos, operatoria, et omnia alia iura censualia."

from this annual rent.[45] Since King James in a similar contract demanded from a Christian lessee half the wheat and barley collected as fees, this Uxó grant stands out as generous.

The olive press or mill for making olive oil was a commonplace everywhere in the realm; in 1283 King Peter was to allow any Valencian not only to mill his "cereals, olives, henna, flax, rice, and everything else" at any legal mill he chose, but also "to construct on his own property, without tax, mills for oil." Since mills varied widely in their capacities, the rent fluctuated from a third to two-thirds of profits or was set at a fixed measure of wheat or some money rate like 3 morabatins, 1 mazmodin, or 9 solidi. Mudejar oil mills in a list of 1268 brought the crown a tax in kind valued at 45 besants. At Pego that year the receipts totaled 31 besants or some 115 solidi; next year they came to 193 besants or over 700 solidi.

A mill producing oil and another grinding grain appear in a lease-renewal for an Alfandech Muslim, at a rent of over 60 solidi. "We assign to you, 'Abd Allāh ad-Dāyah [Adayo], our Saracen of Alfandech de Marignén, our mills that had already been yours, namely one for oil and another for flour, all the days of your life; and for these you are bound to give us every year as rent on the feast of St. Michael in September twenty besants, all clear, without any expenses on our part."[46] The joint treatment here indicates that

---

[45] Arch. Crown, James I, Reg. Canc. 11, fol. 184 (Nov. 12, 1260): "per nos et nostros damus et concedimus vobis sarracenis de Uxo quod teneatis et habeatis ex donacione nostra ad medietatem quattuor molendina que nos habemus in termino de Uxo quod decetero vos nec vestri non donetis nec dare tenebamini nobis vel nostris de redditibus et exitibus istorum iiii molendinorum nisi tantum tertiam partem, sed ipsam tertiam partem nobis tenebamini dare annuatim in perpetuum sine aliqua nostri et nostrorum missione, et cetera; datum Valencie, ii idus Novembris anno domini mcclx." For *missio* see Rodón Binué, *Lenguaje técnico del feudalismo*, p. 180.

[46] Arch. Crown, James I, Reg. Canc. 37, fol. 52v (Nov. 10, 1272): "stabilimus vobis Abdala Adayo sarraceno nostro de Alfandech de Marayen [*sic*] molendina nostra que iam fuerant tua unum videlicet de almazara et aliud de farina . . . diebus vite sue; et teneatis inde nobis dare quolibet anno pro censu . . . in festo Sancti Michaelis Septembri viginti bisancios quitios sine aliqua missione nostra." The Latinized form of the Arabic name here might also relate to the tribe like the Banū ad-Dayyān, or with *al* join some descriptive title like *da'i*, or less probably conceal a name like Ayyūb. The 1268 taxes are in Reg. Canc. 35, fol. 3: "item l'almaçara 1 roves d'olio contat a iii sous el arrova, que fa xlv besants"; for Pego, "item almaxira, vi besants," and "de las almaçaras, xxiiii besants"; in 1269, "item almaxira, vi besants," and "item dreyto de las almaçaras cxxv kaficis . . . [que fa] clxxxvii besants e mig." Branchát, *Derechos y regalías de Valencia*, iii, 138, doc. 9 (1283):

the oil press was water-powered. Another oil mill turns up in northern Valencia, singled out by the bishop of Tortosa as retained to himself when he brought in Christian settlement.[47] Most Valencian mills continued under Muslim operation, especially in the countryside where Muslim *exarici* or tenant farmers outnumbered the intruders so grossly. Only the recipient of the customary taxes changed.

BATHS AND FONDUKS

Public baths supplied an essential element of social life for Muslim and Christian alike. Like the Roman baths from which these establishments derived, they filled the functions of club, business rendezvous, recreation center, retreat from life's hurly-burly, meeting room, and news exchange. For the harem women they provided a place of leisured reunion, and for Muslims in general they held an echo of Koranic precepts on washing. A Spanish poet of the Almohad pre-crusade era sang the pleasures of the public baths in one poem, then satirized them in another as places filled with smoke, noisy with clamor, and so dirty that the customer went in white and came out black.[48] Muslim authors in the earlier period claimed that Cordova

"quilibet possit molere bladum, olivas, alquenas, linos, arrocium et omnia alia ubicumque voluerit"; "quilibet in toto regno possit facere in hereditate et loco suo libere almaçeras olei et habere molendina olei olivarum. . . ." Probably Mudejars owning land participated in this privilege. Branchát gathers a series of mill grants and rents by King James, pp. 245-247. The grant in 1286 of Montaberner with its mixed Mudejar and Christian population to the high official, Conrad of Lanza, included: "et [cum] molendinis et almaceris facientibus oleum" (Arch. Crown, Alfonso III, Reg. Canc. 63, fol. 18 [January 13, 1286]).

[47] García y García, *Estado económico-social de Castellón*, p. 54. The Valencian town Almácera takes its name from the oil press; see also Dubler, *Wirtschaftsleben*, p. 96. The *almaxera* on millage for paper is above, Chapter II, n. 62. *Almassera* (Castilian *almazara*) derived from the Arabic for oil mill, and was used both for mill and millage.

[48] Abū Ja'far b. Sa'īd (d. 1164), in A. R. Nykl, *Hispano-Arabic Poetry and its Relations with the Old Provençal Troubadours* (Baltimore, 1946), p. 323. On baths in Spain's Islamic communities, see Leopoldo Torres Balbás, "Los baños públicos en los fueros municipales españoles," *Al-Andalus*, xi (1946), 443-445; his "Los edificios hispanomusulmanes," *RIEEIM*, i (1953), 103-104; and his archeological articles below in n. 57. In his reception address before the Real Academia de la Historia, Torres Balbás devoted a chapter to "Baños mudéjares," largely of a survey nature (*Algunos aspectos del mudejarismo urbano medieval* [Madrid, 1954], pp. 47ff.); but nothing on baths was included in the posthumous collection *Ciudades hispanomusulmanas*, ed. Henri Terrasse, 2 vols. (Madrid, 1971). Ibn 'Abdūn refers both to the owner or

had 300 baths within its walls and later 600, half of them reserved for women. More realistically the crusaders' partitioning of Majorca's capital reveals five baths grand enough to attract the greed of magnates; two of these went to the king.[49] In describing the sights of Tortosa, al-Himyarī tells of a five-nave main mosque, four public baths, and a bustling bazaar; undoubtedly he ignored whatever squalid minor baths lay tucked away in neighborhood corners.[50]

The fourteenth-century traveler Ibn Baṭṭūṭa marveled at the sumptuous baths of Bagdad, where each of the many cubicles held two

---

entrepreneurial administrator and the lowly bath caretaker, as well as to the masseurs and barbers sometimes allied (Séville musulmane, le traité, pp. 68, 108, 110). Dubler describes constructing a bath and refers to the medicinal baths near Játiva (Wirtschaftsleben, pp. 36-37). The arrangement of rooms, and the stages in bathing, are in "Hammām," EI¹, II, 253. For the wider Islamic world too, Aly Akbar Mazahéri discusses baths and bathing in his La vie quotidienne des musulmans au moyen âge, xe au xiiie siècle (Paris, 1951), pp. 18, 21, 68-69, 175-176. On Christian Spanish baths, see Aníbal Ruiz-Moreno, "Los baños públicos en los fueros municipales españoles," CHE, III (1945), 152-157, and Francisco Carreras y Candi, "Les aygues y banys de Barcelona," in his Miscelánea histórica catalana, 2 vols. (Barcelona, 1905-1906), I, 182-208, esp. pp. 200-204. On Valencian baths see the survey by José Martínez Aloy in the Geografía general del reino de Valencia, ed. Francisco Carreras y Candi, 5 vols. (Barcelona, 1920-1927), I, 587-590; José Sanchis y Sivera, "Los baños públicos (vida íntima de los valencianos en la época foral)," ACCV, VIII (1935), 1-13; and Burns, "Baths and Caravanserais in Crusader Valencia," Speculum, XLVI (1947), 443-458. The Fori antiqui Valentiae treats of baths in rub. XLVII, no. 6 (against the establishment's damp ruining a neighbor's wall), and rub. CXXXIV, no. 6 (close on Sunday and feasts, even for Moors, and have men and women bathe separately); it cites them also as an example of properties that could be co-owned by multiple sharers who cannot conveniently divide the establishment itself (rub. L, no. 2).

[49] Repartimiento de Mallorca, p. 119: "alia tria fuerunt de magnatibus."

[50] Al-Himyarī (Muḥammad b. Muḥammad b. 'Abd al-Mun'im al-Himyarī), Kitāb ar-rawḍ al-mi'ṭār, trans. M. P. Maestro González (Valencia, 1963), p. 254; see also the edition and translation by Évariste Lévi-Provençal as La péninsule ibérique au moyen-âge d'après le Kitāb ar-rawḍ al-mi'ṭār fī ḫabar al-aḳṭār d'Ibn 'Abd al-Mun'im al-Himyarī . . . (Leiden, 1938). Juan Torres Fontes, editor of the Repartimiento de Murcia, has gathered all the information available on Murcian baths of the crusader era in the introduction to his Colección de documentos para la historia del reino de Murcia, no. 1, Documentos de Alfonso X el Sabio (Murcia, 1963), pp. lx-lxiii. Julio González, in the critical study prefacing his edition of the Repartimiento de Sevilla, offers notes on Islamic baths at Jaén and Cordova, then lists nineteen baths of postcrusade Seville including some later constructions and probable repetitions in his sources (2 vols. [Madrid, 1951], I, 520-525). Ibn Shaddād (1216-1285), compiling lists of public buildings in Syria, found 156 baths (plus 31 in private homes) at Aleppo, two especially large (N. A. Ziadeh, Urban Life in Syria under the Early Mamluks [Beirut, 1953], p. 90).

basins, each with hot and cold water piped in, and where every customer luxuriated in a wasteful three towels; fresh from North Africa, he was scandalized to find that the men wore no waist-covering in the baths at Minya in Egypt, and he did not rest until he got the governor to rectify the situation by orders to the lessees of the various bathhouses.[51] A more famous North African contemporary, Ibn Khaldūn, observed that "public baths do not exist in medium-sized towns" but "only in densely settled cities of a highly developed civilization resulting from luxury and wealth."[52] Islamic Valencian towns of all sizes did support baths, however, indicating perhaps a widely spread commercial and luxury class. At conquered Tortosa to the north, each woman during the women's days at the baths could bring along a servant and child without increase of entry fee, though a boy had to be under seven. The municipality there owned all commercial baths, charged a fixed fee per customer, kept the places open night and day, and regulated hygiene and the supply of hot and cold water—procedures probably reflecting Islamic antecedents.[53]

The Játiva charter reserved its plural baths to crown ownership; a separate entry decreed that only Muslims could operate them.[54] The Eslida surrender agreement stipulated that the bath tax remain

[51] Ibn Baṭṭūṭa (Muḥammad b. 'Abd Allāh b. Muḥammad b. Ibrāhīm b. Baṭṭūṭa aṭ-Ṭanjī), *Travels*, trans. H.A.R. Gibb, 3 vols. (Cambridge, 1958-1971), I, 63 and II, 329-330.

[52] *Muqaddimah*, II, 302. The wide distribution of baths in Valencia tends to support Ira Lapidus' controversial thesis on the nature of Muslim urban-rural arrangement, where the city was less differentiated from the hamlet than has been claimed; see, besides his ampler *Muslim Cities*, his symposium on *Middle Eastern Cities* (Berkeley, 1969), part 2, ch. 2, esp. pp. 60ff.

[53] *Costums de Tortosa*, as *Código de las costumbres de Tortosa*, ed. Bienvenido Oliver, appended to his *Historia del derecho en Cataluña, Mallorca y Valencia*, 4 vols. (Madrid, 1876-1881), IV, part 9, rub. 13. Twice during crises in his Valencian crusade, the anguished King James sweated through a sleepless night—"suavem tam·be con si fossem en i bany" (*Llibre dels feyts*, chs. 237, 363); as Torres Balbás perceived, the identical wording suggests a popular saying; Christian enthusiasm for public baths later diminished and disappeared, he notes, under the impact of plague and Renaissance viewpoints.

[54] Játiva Charter: "retinemus . . . balnea"; "aliquis christianus vel iudeus non possit conducere balnea vel furnos qui sunt vel pro tempore [unquam] erunt infra ravallum praedictum." Among the baths surviving into the postcrusade era at Játiva was the establishment along the edge of the meat market, given in grant to a Christian on condition that no shops be established in it (Arch. Crown, Reg. Canc. 10, fol. 60v [April 25, 1258]: "illa balnea seu cellarium").

what it had been in Islamic days. The second Eslida charter recalled the detail that Islamic custom was to regulate baths, and "no one may compel you to use the baths except in the manner that pleases you."[55] Squat, with heavy walls and domed ceilings, bathing establishments required a complex of small service buildings or rooms, patios, heating equipment, conduits, and various apparatus. The assignment of Alcira's Christian baths to the Jewish tax farmer Joseph b. Shaprut in 1273, at a profit of two hundred solidi a year, specified free water, "central sweat room, and other appurtenances."[56] A Mudejar community's bath at the village of Torres Torres, northwest of Murviedro, typified the modest rural bath. It stood just outside town in a lovely huerta, positioned to take advantage of a main canal. Mudejars in the kingdom of Valencia attended baths on Sundays as on other days, a scandal soon corrected by a decree in the *Furs*.[57] In 1277 King Peter established one Ḥusayn (Foçain) as *faqīh* of Chelva, confirming him and his family in possession of "the bath of Chelva with its rights and appurtenances, just as you had and held them hitherto"; apparently a reward or conciliation connected with rebellious Chelva's recent surrender, the action shows a Mudejar patron controlling the community's baths.[58]

---

[55] Second Eslida Charter: "aliquis non potest compellere vos ad balneandum nisi secundum quod vobis placuerit."

[56] *Itinerari*, p. 483 (June 16, 1273): "cum caldaria et aliis apparamentis ipsorum balneorum." On the financier Ben Shaprut (Avinxaprut) see below, p. 287. The *caldaria* or *sudatio* (*harāra*) was the main sweat room (*EI¹*, II, 253). King James gave another Jewish financier, the Tortosan Astruc Jacob Shishon serving as a local bailiff in Valencia, "licentiam et plenum posse" to construct "balneum seu balnea" on his personal holdings at Campanar near Valencia city, to be open to all wishing to bathe (Arch. Crown, James I, Reg. Canc. 16, fol. 268v; in Francisco de A. de Bofarull y Sans, "Jaime I y los judíos," *Congrés I*, pp. 907-908, doc. 99 [Dec. 1, 1270]).

[57] Leopoldo Torres Balbás, "El baño de Torres Torres (Valencia) y otras levantinas," *Al-Andalus*, XVIII (1952), 176-186. He also discusses, and offers drawings of, the ruins of a Mudejar bath at Játiva, an establishment averaging about ten feet of width for each of its three rooms, of which only some arches remain; it is difficult to assign a preconquest date to any such bath ("Crónica arqueológica de la España musulmana," no. 42, *Al-Andalus*, XXIII [1958], 144, 154-155). *Fori antiqui Valentiae*, rub. cxxxiv, no. 6.

[58] Soldevila, *Pere el Gran*, part 2, I, appendix, doc. 53: "confirmamus vos Foçain alfaquino de Celva et placet nobis quod tu et tuis teneatis [et] habeatis balneum de Celva cum iuribus et pertinenciis suis sicut ipsum hucusque tenuistis et habuistis." Peter's announcement to Castile of Chelva's surrender is in doc. 54 (Jan. 24, 1277). In settling Muslims at Peñíscola in 1286, King Alfonso gave instructions "quod

At Valencia city, at least ten such Islamic bathhouses turn up in the land distribution records, bearing names like Baths of the Vizier, of the Market, of the Fig Tree, of Ibn Mālik, and of the Bāb al-Warrāq or north-central gate. An important bath went to the crusader Nuño, powerful count of Roussillon; located at the northeast corner of the city, adjacent to the Santiago Knights' church, it became the property of the Knights Hospitaller in 1241. Another, named after Abū Bakr the vizier (Ubecar alguasqui), stood near St. Catherine's mosque-church in the south-central part of town. Repeated in the records because it marked a terminus for the Jewish portion of the city, the baths of Ibn Mālik (Dabenmelich) lay a short distance inside the main eastern gate. St. Bartholomew's must have served the west-central neighborhood.[59] The law code for the conquered kingdom reveals that one establishment, converted to other uses, stood to the west of the city walls, perhaps somewhat to the northwest; a statute located the Christians' extramural market as running "from the place in which Saracen baths had formerly stood, [thence] toward the city gate called Bāb al-Ḥanash [Bebalhonig], [and thence] toward the irrigation canal that goes straight to Ruzafa, up to the church of St. John" and the Boatella gate.[60]

Of all the city's Islamic or Mudejar establishments, archaeology

---

detis et dividatis ipsis vineam et domum balneorum diruptorum et alias terras et possessiones," an emphasis that suggests that these ruined baths were an important property (Arch. Crown, Alfonso III, Reg. Canc. 64, fol. 129 [Oct. 15, 1286]); cf. also his "collectoribus sive emptoribus . . . balneorum morarie Valencie" (Reg. Canc. 82, fol. 89 [Dec. 18, 1290]).

[59] *Repartimiento de Valencia*, pp. 256 (of Abenadup), 602 (of Abinegama), 226, 294 (of Aliasar, Rabat Alicar), 646 (of Barbo), 261 (near the gate Bebuarach), 217, 256, 257, 274, 290, 307 (of Abdolmelich, Almeli, Avenmelich, Dabenmelich, Nalmelig), 308, 539, 650 (of Algacir, of Ubecar alguasqui in Rabatalcadi), 230 (of St. Bartholomew's), 188 (Damrem), 229, 244 (of the Fig Tree), 284 (of the Hospital), 483 (of the Market), 286, 631 (of Nuño), 510 (of Polo of Tarazona); the Fig baths may be those of Ibn Mālik, the houses of a Jew being "circa balneum apud figeram"; see also pp. 283, 286, 309, 608. See also *Itinerari*, pp. 202 (1250) and 550n. (May 15, 1240); and Chabás, "Libro del repartimiento de Valencia," 219-220. On Nuño's baths see Burns, *Crusader Valencia*, I, 188; Mudejars had to refrain from the baths on Sunday (p. 55).

[60] *Fori antiqui Valentiae*, rub. LXXIV, no. 2: "a loco in quo heddificata sunt balnea quondam sarracenica, versus portam que vocatur Bebalhonig, versus cequiam que vadit ad Rozafam recta via, usque ad ecclesiam sancti Iohannis." If "quondam" is really "quedam," the baths may still have been in use and for Mudejars of the Moorish quarter nearby.

has rescued only one, the Baths of 'Abd al-Malik, also called by the crusaders "of Ibn Mālik," or often the Baths of the Admiral, situated toward the city's east. Constructed in the eleventh or twelfth century, it comprised a squared building of three main chambers, each flanked by smaller compartments, with a complex of entry rooms and with domed vaults admitting light. An underground system piped water from nearby wells. Several confiscated baths can be discerned in records for the capital during the postcrusade decades, including one held sometime before 1267 by William of Plana at twenty mazmodins' lease in the shoemakers' section, another named for Sir (En) Polo, and another rented by the king's mistress in 1279.[61]

A special establishment for the Mudejars of Valencia city lay outside the walls of their quarter in the open countryside, presumably connected with the canal there. Since historical reconstructions of the quarter locate the baths inside, as the largest building in the northeastern part of the quarter, the extramural baths may have been auxiliary or perhaps the original. King James describes them in 1272 as "some baths located alongside the Moorish quarter of Valencia, with their buildings and courtyards." They represented an investment the king was anxious to recover, since he bought them in exchange for "the entry plaza of the Valencia city gate toward Roteros, and the towers and moat at the barbican, which is near the monastery of St. Eulalia," the Mercedarian religious house outside the southern wall. These baths had been consigned to Geoffrey of Loaysa (Luesia) "with a charter publicly drawn." Their recovery by the crown seems part of the pattern examined below with the fonduk. The arrangement of "buildings and courtyards" indicates a sizable establishment.[62]

---

[61] Arch. Crown, James I, Reg. Canc. 15, fol. 82 (Feb. 22, 1267): "illas viginti macemutinas censuales quas habemus in balneis que fuerunt Guillelmi de Plana et sunt in capateria Valencie"; on the Polo baths encountered previously (see note 59), see the published but misdated document discussed in Burns, *Crusader Valencia*, II, 472, n. 73. In Reg. Canc. 44, fol. 151 (July 12, 1279), Agnes Zapata rented a city bathing establishment. The Valencia city remains are described by Elías Tormo y Monzó, "Los baños árabes del Almirante, en Valencia," *BRAH*, CXIII (1943), 241-248; see the reservation above in n. 57. Some idea of the baths prevalent in Western Islam and Spain may be gathered from the plates and elaborate plans in Henri Terrasse, "Trois bains mérinides du Maroc," *Mélanges offerts à William Marçais par l'institut d'études islamiques de l'université de Paris* (Paris, 1950), pp. 311-320.

[62] Arch. Crown, James I, Reg. Canc. 21, fol. 40v (June 2, 1272): "plateam intratus porte Valencie civitatis de Roteros et turres et vallum ad barbacanum que

It was replaced or supplemented by another large bath house inside the quarter. Perhaps this existed from the beginning, but it comes into view fairly late, during a transfer of custodianship in 1338. King Peter IV assigned to a functionary of his household, Justus of Miravet, "the baths, buildings, sweat rooms, and apparatus" inside "the suburb of the Moorish quarter of Valencia city." Justus received all its crown rents, except 400 solidi, which continued to go as pension to Teresa, the widow of the lord of Rebollet in southern Valencia. A few years later, confirming the concession and noting that it could be canceled at any time by paying Justus 6,000 solidi of Barcelona, the crown as a further favor extended this ownership to his heirs indefinitely.[63] Here was the same situation as with the fonduk and butchery—a Christian concessionaire enjoying the revenues and apparently subletting actual operation to Muslims.

Illuminating statistics from 1310 and 1315, nearly seventy years after the close of the crusade, indicate how lucrative were baths, despite the pittance required from customers. In the Moorish quarter of Valencia city they yielded 1,200 and 1,150 solidi in the respective years, almost as much as the quarter's other revenues together. Peter Bou, probably the custodian, received 500 solidi from them each year. Assuming a thousand inhabitants over the age of seven, these must have consumed many an afternoon in steamy chambers to raise 14,400 pence in profits, not to mention expenses and salaries.[64]

sunt circa [?] monasterium Sancte Eulalie . . . in excambium et permutationem quorundam balneorum sitorum iuxta moreriam Valencie cum domibus et corrallis, que quidem erant dicti Iaufridi cum instrumento . . . publico confecto." The critical word *iuxta* here is clearly not *intra*, and is important in a contract locating and exchanging pieces of real estate. On the Moorish quarter's baths, see also Arch. Reino Val., Real Cancillería, codex 612, fols. 104-105v, series of documents.

[63] Roca Traver, "Vida mudéjar," doc. 28 (Feb. 27, 1338): "balnea nostra que habemus in ravallo morarie Valencie, cum domibus, calderia et omnibus aliis apparatibus inibi existentibus quoquomodo"; the bailiff is ordered forthwith to put Justus "in corporalem possessionem" of these elements, repeated again. Teresa had been the wife of Francis Carroz. The confirmation is doc. 29 (June 11, 1346).

[64] Arch. Reino Val., Real Cancillería, codex 612, fol. 267v (1310), where the *morería* baths bring in "mcc solidos." *Rentas de Aragón*, pp. 88, 96, 123: "item bany de la moreria de la dita ciutat, mcl solidos"; "item pren en la renda del bany de la moreria En P. Bou per violari, d solidos"; at Novelda, "los bayns del dit loch cascun any" brought 400 solidi. See also *Censo de Catalunya ordenado en tiempo del rey Don Pedro el Ceremonioso*, ed. Próspero de Bofarull y Mascaró, *Documentos inéditos de Aragón*, xii, 262. An oblique reference to the various par-

A fascinating institution among both Muslims and Christians was the fonduk or khan, at once a public inn, goods depository, mail drop, center for any notarial or customs services, and exhibit hall. Often a walled compound or square, with baggage and beasts on the ground floor and merchant-lodgers on the second, it could elaborate into a home-away-from-home in the form of a small quarter. By the thirteenth century, Islamic fonduks were often large establishments, put up by rulers or men with capital. The traveler Ibn Baṭṭūṭa in the early fourteenth century preferred the *māristān*, a religious hospital-hospice run by brotherhoods who proffered "many conveniences and medicament" to pilgrims and transients; but he also described the post station fonduks running serially from Cairo to Syria. Each was "a *funduq*, which they call a *khān*, where travelers alight with their beasts," taking free water from a well in front and purchasing anything needed for self or beast from a shop.[65] Main Valencian towns apparently held several, the capital boasting as many as Da-

---

ticipants of the revenues from Valencia city's Mudejar baths appears in a crown directive of December 1290 (Arch. Crown, Alfonso III, Reg. Canc. 82, fol. 89).

[65] Ibn Baṭṭūṭa, *Travels*, I, 43, 71. Goitein has some information on fonduks in his *Mediterranean Society*, I, 349-350. *Funduq* derives from Greek through Aramaic (p. 349), the Catalans taking their form from the Arabic. See also Dubler, *Wirtschaftsleben*, p. 141n.; Ibn 'Abdūn on the state tax on fonduks, *Séville musulmane, le traité*, p. 110; Reinhart P. A. Dozy and Willem H. Engelmann, *Glossaire des mots espagnols et portugais dérivés de l'arabe*, 2d edn. rev. (Leiden, [1869] 1965), pp. 79 (*alcaicería*), 139 (*alhóndiga*), 270 (*fonduk*); Arnald Steiger, *Contribución a la fonética del hispano-árabe y de los arabismos en el iber-románico y en el siciliano* (Madrid, 1932), pp. 114 (*fúndaq*) and 216 (*fúnduq*). Mazahéri describes the daily order of the Near Eastern khans, their specialized types (grains, dates, salt fish, luxury articles, etc.), their function as bourse, and their clustering by the dozen, or at Bagdad by the hundred, along the quais or near the port (*Vie quotidienne des musulmans au moyen âge*, pp. 193-195). Roger Le Tourneau complains that "no work exists dealing specifically with *funduks*" ("Funduk," *EI²*, II, 945). Jean Sauvaget supplies Syrian information in "Les caravansérails syriens du Ḥadjāj du Constantinople," in *Ars Islamica*, IV (1937), 98-121, and "Les caravansérails syriens du moyen âge," VI (1939), 48-56, and VII (1940), 1-20. *Funduq* is the Syrian and Moroccan term corresponding to the Persians' *khān* (*EI¹*, "Funduk," II, 117). Some authors give it the meaning of a warehouse, though this may be a matter of emphasis (cf. *EI²*, II, 284). Vicens Vives distinguishes the fonduk as a warehouse, for storing merchandise of nonlocal businessmen, from the khan or inn where they were housed (*Economic History of Spain*, pp. 116-117, but cf. pp. 134, 194). The *Fori antiqui Valentiae* regulated inns and stables for merchants, requiring honest dealing with guests; probably the provisions covered fonduks as well as Christian inns (rub. XXXI, and rub. XLVIII, no. 10).

mascus[66] though doubtless on a smaller scale; later the postcrusade fonduk catered to merchants from Islamic lands.

What the essential nature of the fonduk meant for aliens can be seen in its more developed overseas form of a trading concession; there it became a diplomatic enclave protecting and serving the European merchant community within an Islamic city, providing church and religious life, military guard, tavern, oven, baths, shops, and similar amenities.[67] It served both as extension of the local ruler's hospitality and as encouragement for commerce. It seemed appropriate, consequently, that the crusader king should reserve to the crown a fair number of these establishments, letting them out to concessionaires.

The *alfundicum* in the crusaders' records conceals a semantic trap, however; evolutions of meaning allowed the word to stand for "a public market for common articles" and also for a grain exchange.[68]

---

[66] Lapidus, *Muslim Cities*, pp. 59-60, where the Mamluk emirs owned 3 of the 5 khans, the others being held by merchants; the emirs also had 6 out of 9 of the establishments called a *qaiṣāriya* (see below, p. 75), 7 of 12 markets, and 12 of the 15 baths. Al-Ḥimyarī praises "the khans and bazaars" of Alcira, then open by river to the commerce of the sea (*Kitāb ar-rawḍ al-mi'ṭār*, pp. 213-215). Postcrusade sources speak of various inns and hospices, but it is not clear which of these were newly contrived, as some were, and which may have been converted fonduks. For example on March 2, 1276 King James granted Aaron Allatefi, a Valencian Jew, permission to join his two hospices by a bridge over the street: "super viam que transit inter duo hospicia que habes in Valencia, per quem possit homo transire de uno hospicio ad aliud" (*Itinerari*, p. 529); Jesús E. Martínez Ferrando's catalogue reads the name as Allacefi (*Catálogo de la documentación relativa al antiguo reino de Valencia contenida en los registros de la cancillería real*, 2 vols. [Madrid, 1934], I, no. 1938). On Christian hospices or hospitals see Robert Ignatius Burns, "Los hospitales del reino de Valencia en el siglo xiii," *AEM*, II (1965), 135-154.

[67] Dufourcq gave some attention to this kind of fonduk in his *L'Espagne catalane et le Maghrib* and in his earlier articles cited there; he studies them closely in his "Les consulats catalans de Tunis et de Bougie au temps de Jacques le Conquérant," *AEM*, III (1966), 469-479; those of Tunis and Bougie were "of the king" and therefore better documented, whereas the Alexandria fonduk from 1272 was run by the Barcelona townsmen. See also Robert Brunschvig, *La Berbérie orientale sous les ḥafsides*, 2 vols. (Paris, 1940-1947), I, ch. 7, part 2. An aliens' fonduk could be established for a Christian group in a Christian country. As lord of conquered Majorca and by the request of "my blood relative" King James, Peter of Portugal arranged "for building a fonduk" there for all Genoese, out of various large and small buildings, including a bakery and a mosque to serve as chapel (*Itinerari*, pp. 103-104 [May 17, 1233]).

[68] See Bayerri, *Tortosa*, VI, 346, and Imamuddin, *Socio-Economic and Cultural History of Muslim Spain*, p. 121 ("public market," but see p. 197). On these forms

When contemporaries could even speak of an *alfondega* for salt, caution is obviously needed in interpreting the documents.[69] Bayerri, familiar with the daily life of medieval Tortosa, contends that *alfondech* in old Catalan almost always bore the sense of market or exchange, or even of a warehouse or deposit near a port, rather than a hostelry.[70] King James described a true caravanserai, at Biar in southern Valencia, about a decade after the close of the crusade. He ordered the establishment refurbished, with its wineshops, "stables, beds, and everything necessary for merchants to lodge comfortably with their merchandise, animals, and possessions." Since Biar housed a border customs control, its local fonduk took on added importance. James awarded the concession to a Christian businessman, Sancho Pérez of Cabeçó; rental was set at half the profits. A decade later the king rented the establishment for four years directly "to the community of the Saracens of Biar and the totality of Saracens of the same community, present and future."[71] Located inland, such a fonduk emphasized garage facilities for pack trains, which explains

---

see especially Torres Balbás, "Edificios hispanomusulmanes," pp. 112-116, and his "Las alhondigas hispanomusulmanas," *Al-Andalus*, xi (1946), 447-480. Catalan *fonda* and *alfòndic*, and Castilian *fonda* and *alhóndiga* reflect these meanings of inn, market, and grain exchange. Eero K. Neuvonen studies the forms in their contemporary evolution (*Los arabismos del español en el siglo xiii* [Helsinki, 1941], pp. 37-38). Du Cange defines the European fonduk as a market, shops, bourse, public granary, and the like, offering documentation from Italy and other areas as well as Spain (*Glossarium mediae et infimae latinitatis*, 10 vols. [Paris, 1937-1938], I, 176, III, 542, under *alfundicus, fondaceus*, and esp. *funda*).

[69] *Repartimiento de Murcia*, ed. Juan Torres Fontes (Madrid, 1960), p. 244: "alffondega de sal." See also the *Repartimiento de Sevilla*, on both *alhóndiga* and *alcaicería* (I, 311, 342, 483, 501, 512, 513, 530, 544 for map, 548; and II, 320, 352, 353, 364, 378).

[70] Enrique Bayerri y Bertoméu, *Llibre de privilegis de la vila de Ulldecona, cartulario de la militar y soberana orden de San Juan de Jerusalén (ahora de Malta) en su comendadoría de Ulldecona desde mediados del siglo xii hasta finales del xvi* (Tortosa, 1951), p. 192.

[71] Arch. Crown, James I, Reg. Canc. 9, fol. 33v (Sept. 4, 1257): "totum illud alfondicum ab integro . . . paratum de stabilis, lectis, et aliis omnibus necessariis ut mercatores et alii advenientes possint ibi bene hospitari cum mercibus, bestiis, et rebus suis"; "et tenere tabernam" for wine. Further improvements came in 1262: "et facere ante portam alfondici iii operatoria, et etiam cohoperire quandam domum in illo alfondico" (Reg. Canc. 12, fol. 40 [May 5, 1262]). See also *Itinerari*, p. 261. Arch. Crown, James I, Reg. Canc. 15, fol. 84 (ca. March 16, 1267): "vobis aliame sarracenorum de Biar et universis sarracenis eiusdem aliame presentibus et futuris . . . alfa[n]dicum."

why the Arabic word list attributed to Raymond Martí in this century equated *funduq* with Latin *stabulum*.[72]

A seaside fonduk, resembling the kind serving the port city of Valencia and therefore a useful analogue, was described by King James in a 1243 charter giving protection to "all men coming to lodge and live in the fonduks . . . at Barcelona at the harbor" and to the "goods and merchandise" stored with them. Peter Lissac held these three fonduks for the king; instead of half the profits, as at Biar, Peter paid a flat 160 Alfonsine morabatins in annual lease. The plural fonduks there, with their complex of shops, buildings, and "oven of the fonduk," proved so valuable a property that King James was able to exchange his rights in them for Altea castle in Valencia. Illustrating the complexity of shareholding in such enterprises, a suit brought by Lissac against the subholder of the fonduk's oven, William Burgués, forced an increase in the seven solidi Lissac had retained from the oven, because inflation had caused this sum to decline in value by a third. The administrative pyramid conducting this fonduk shows Moncada as alodial lord in place of the king, Lissac as life executive, and businessmen like Burgués managing the component elements, probably through hired operatives.[73]

[72] *Vocabulista in arabico, pubblicato per la prima volta sopra un codice della biblioteca riccardiana di Firenze*, ed. Celestino Schiaparelli (Florence, 1871), p. 590. Though its attribution to Ramón Martí is not certain, the work does belong to eastern Spain's Reconquest zone and to the thirteenth century. See also Bayerri, *Tortosa*, VI, 673.

[73] *Colección diplomática*, doc. 258 (Aug. 8, 1243): "omnes homines venientes hospitari et habitari in alfundicis que tu Petrus de Lissach a nobis tenes in Barchinona iuxta mare"; no one is to dare "eorum aliqua bona et merces invadere, capere, detinere, impedire, offendere"; the king's officials were to protect these "in predictis alfundicis hospitantes et habitantes." *Itinerari*, p. 278 (July 30, 1258): "omnia illa alfundica et domos et operatoria que nos habemus in civitate Barchinone iuxta litus maris cum furno qui est in uno ipsorum"; p. 293 (Sept. 23, 1259); p. 302 (June 26, 1260); p. 369 (April 13, 1265), a license to the fonduk's oven-holder William Burgués to arrest some culprits; p. 398 (May 3, 1267), Lissac renting Barcelona mills. The king solved Lissac's suit by setting a new exchange: for seven of the old solidi *de duplo*, Lissac's pension, four solidi and eight pence of the new would be given. Miguel Gual Camarena has studied one profitable concession of foreign merchants' inns, with special reference to Valencia and probably applying as well to its Mudejar fonduks—the official "host," a skilled intermediary who collected sales taxes, facilitated business, and oversaw contractual arrangements and sales ("El hospedaje hispano-medieval, aportaciones para su estudio," *AHDE*, XXXII [1962], 527-541; see more generally Frances Garrison, "Les hôtes et l'hébergement des étrangers au moyen âge, quelques solutions de droit comparé," *Études*

Surrender charters provided for continuance of local fonduks. At Tudela in 1119, for example, the treaty had assured this monopoly to the Mudejars, probably through a Christian acting as crown lessee: "that Saracens and Christians of the merchant class have access to Tudela and that they lodge in those fonduks." A patent miscopy of the manuscript converts this item into a restriction on the number of Christian merchants taking quarter in the fonduks.[74] King James's grandfather, Alfonso I, had made pregrant of a fonduk to the bishop of Tortosa to gain his help for a projected Valencian crusade.[75] During James's own crusade, the Eslida region's surrender charter specified that Moors could conduct their own fonduks, paying to the crown the rent previously handed to Islamic authorities.[76] These merchant hostels seem to have been common in the Valencian kingdom, and even the smaller khans were looked on as suitable gifts for prominent crusaders. King James gave three Islamic Valencian fonduks as prizes to the highest churchman of his realms, the archbishop of Tarragona.[77]

Among the welter of gifts distributed at Burriana in 1233 to the crusading Knights of Calatrava, the king singled out for special mention "one fonduk that belonged to al-Manṣūr [Almaçor]" with the associated "properties and buildings and garden of the fonduk with their frontages."[78] A second fonduk at Burriana went that same

---

d'histoire du droit privé offertes à Pierre Petot [Paris, 1959], pp. 199-222, and *Fori antiqui Valentiae,* rub. CXLIV, on *hostalagium*).

[74] Tudela Charter, in Fernández y González, *Mudejares de Castilla,* appendix, doc. 2 (March 1119), and in *Colección de fueros municipales y cartas pueblas de los reinos de Castilla, León, corona de Aragón y Navarra,* ed. Tomás Muñoz y Romero (Madrid, [1847] 1970), p. 415: "quod intrent in Tutela sarraceni vel christiani [*sinon v christianos*] de mercaders, et quod pausent in illas alfondecas." The accepted reading in italics, perhaps a scribal slip, makes little sense. The traditional date still commonly cited, March 1114 or 1115, .was corrected to February 22, 1119 by José M. Lacarra in "La fecha de la conquista de Tudela," *Príncipe de Viana,* v (1946), 657-694.

[75] Bibl. Nac. Madrid, MSS, no. 13,079, Dd. 98, p. 1.

[76] Eslida Charter: "[de] alfondicis ... [ut in] tempore paganorum."

[77] *Repartimiento de Valencia,* p. 636.

[78] Arch. Nac. Madrid, Ords. milits., Calatrava, privs. reales, no. 265 (Oct. 27, 1233): "et damus vobis unum alfundicum quod fuit de Almaçor ... et hereditates et domos et ortum alfondici cum suis affrontationibus." The name might also be a distorted script for Abū Ma'shar. Arch. Crown, James I, Reg. Canc. 16, fol. 237 registers the document with slight differences: "illud alfondicum ... de Almazor."

year to the knight William Assalit, buildings "that were a fonduk in the time of the Saracens."[79] The gift of a fonduk at Murviedro and its subsequent withdrawal so disturbed the king's conscience—a notoriously lax faculty in his makeup—that he devised a codicil about it for his will as he lay dying: "likewise we order to be fulfilled and observed the charter of grant to Raymond Falconer of Alcira, which we made to him about a certain fonduk located in Murviedro, as is contained in that [charter], if we unjustly confiscated the same from him."[80] Falconer was the king's long-term bailiff of Alcira.

At Denia King James turned over an Islamic fonduk for a hospice or hospital of the ransomer Mercedarians; as the former "alfundicum christianorum" under the Muslims, in its own quarter or suburb, this was disposable, unlike the hostelries still required to lodge Muslim merchants. The Denia area contained a number of such confiscated fonduks, since King James expressly arranged for their alienation in 1246.[81] At Pego in 1269 the Mudejar fonduk paid the crown a rental of some 70 solidi, reckoned in besants. At Onteniente in 1263 "the king's fonduk" brought 42 solidi, as much as the meat market that year and more than the Mudejar head tax.[82] At Játiva the king gave a fonduk to Ferrer of Monzón, then transferred it in 1266 to Peter Escrivá for conversion into a hospital. Sancho Martin of Oblites acquired two fonduks in the same city; in 1270, after his death, Simon of Tovía got them.[83] King James himself retained

[79] *Itinerari*, p. 109 (Nov. 16, 1233): "que fuerunt alfandicum tempore sarracenorum."

[80] Tourtoulon, *Jaime I*, II, doc. 22 (July 23, 1276): "item mandamus exsequi et observari R. Falconerii de Algizira cartam donacionis quam sibi facimus de quodam fundico sito in Muroveteri prout in ea continetur si iniuste emparavimus ipsum ei." The "alfondega Marie de Mengit" stood at Segorbe's "portam de mercatali," with public roads running along three sides (Arch. Crown, James I, Reg. Canc. 11, fol. 186v [Dec. 19, 1260]).

[81] Arch. Nac. Madrid, Clero sec. y reg., Merced, legajo 2,034, arm. 44, fab. 2 (Aug. 6, 1245). See the document of different provenance in *Itinerari*, p. 174. The Denia document is also in *Itinerari*, p. 176 (Feb. 4, 1246), to Carroz, lord of Rebollet; besides houses and farms, James specified shops, mills, baths, and fonduks.

[82] Arch. Crown, James I, Reg. Canc. 35, fol. 4 (1269): "item el alfondech, xviii besants." Reg. Canc. 17, fol. 29 (Dec. 30, 1263): "a[l]fondicum domini regis, xlii solidos," in a context suggesting a dominantly Muslim population.

[83] *Ibid.*, Reg. Canc. 13, fol. 287v (Jan. 5, 1266): "Petro Scribe illud alfondicum . . . ad opus hospitalis"; the Martínez Ferrando catalogue erroneously reads the owner as Peter Soler. Reg. Canc. 16, fol. 196 (June 15, 1270): "duos fundicos."

"the fonduk of the king," which faced the Franciscan priory in Játiva.[84]

Charters sometimes described a single fonduk in the plural, suggesting a complex of related inns that had multiplied around or expanded from the original nucleus. This may indicate specialization of facilities in larger towns, to serve merchants of different regional origins, unequal economic status, or specific commodities. The number of khans visible in land-distribution lists of the crusaders, when taken in the context of their siting, indicates that a neighborhood *sūq* usually boasted its own fonduk hard by a secondary mosque. At Valencia city, confiscated Islamic fonduks stood on Lérida square, and next to or near the mosques that became the churches of St. Catherine, St. Thecla, and the cathedral, as well as at the northwest gate of Bāb al-Qanṭara and the southern Bāb Baiṭāla. The "fonduk for butchers" seems to be a misnomer. Others were undoubtedly included within the mass grants of whole segments of the city.[85] A real-estate record located its property as near two fonduks. The crusaders commandeered another, obviously of imposing dimensions, as temporary residence for the king.[86]

When a city was divided, crusaders taking over their part, the fonduk for transient Muslim merchants might be expected to relocate in the Mudejar quarter, convenient to the religious, legal, dietary, and social facilities. The dismantling or conversion of a number of the city's fonduks further encourages this conjecture. Though Valencia's trade with Islamic lands continued as a firm foundation of its commercial prosperity, the crusade had shifted the kingdom into Christendom's economic sphere and made its ports vastly more inviting to European merchants. A shift of merchant life-style began, foreign merchants fitting into the general life of the city and probably seeking quarters at private inns catering to commercial travelers. The changeover came only gradually, however,

---

[84] Arch. Cat., perg. 4,713 (April 13, 1252): "cum alfundico regis."

[85] *Repartimiento de Valencia*, pp. 244: "alfundicum [quod] est ante ecclesiam [cathedralem] Sancte Marie"; 262: "alfundicum ante ecclesiam Sancte Tecle"; 282: "alfondica in vico Rahabat Alcadi," near St. Catherine's; 261; 287; 636; the "alfundicum carniceriarum" on p. 284 may merely locate the street, referring to the "Rahabat Alcadi" fonduk, since St. Catherine's was next to the butchers' quarter (see p. 256).

[86] *Ibid.*, pp. 29, 244: "in quo hospitabamini."

and the first location of the main Mudejar fonduk reflects this transitional phase. It was "in Valencia [city]," as distinguished from the next site "in the Moorish quarter" by the only extant document that treats of both. Whatever its location—and the western gate near the quarter seems the logical choice—this fonduk won the monopoly on foreign Muslim merchants.

A plum, it naturally fell into the hands of an influential citizen, one of several Williams in the prominent Valencian family of the Escrivá. Guillemo or Guillmon (forms of William), conducted it, collecting profits wholly or partly for himself at a lease of five Josephine mazmodins. A personage so eminent as an Escrivá would have been a financier rather than an entrepreneur; retaining control, he sublet the fonduk to the businessman and "resident of Valencia," Bernard Botí, for life at eight mazmodins, clearing a handsome profit. As befitted a trust of this magnitude, the contract involved a charter from King James to Bernard. The arrangement proved satisfactory over three decades; then King James announced plans for a new fonduk within the quarter. Reasons are not far to seek. Provisional leases after the conquest had been designed to attract talent and capital for the reconstruction of the kingdom; as the decade of the 1270's opened, James could justly feel that this phase had passed. The crown required more income for its enterprises also, and a judicious reassessment of utilities could uncover it. Trade with North Africa, assiduously encouraged and now flourishing, called for capital improvements to maintain its dynamism. Finally, a spirit of segregation was abroad, demanding mitigation of the easy inter-course between the two peoples in Valencia. These reasons may have stayed in abeyance until death terminated Escrivá's life tenure.

Ironically the new financial arrangement was to be the reverse of the old, the king retaining the fonduk's profits and the lessee taking a straight salary, with Botí forcibly ejected by a kind of eminent domain but compensated through a claim "in perpetuity on those five Josephine rental mazmodins that we receive and ought to re-ceive." Botí now had the king's rent, and James had the fonduk. In a letter to Botí the king described his project: "I shall cause a fonduk to be established for the advantage of the Saracens in the Moorish quarter, in which [fonduk] all Saracens coming to Valencia must lodge by my command"; as a consequence "Saracens will not lodge in your fonduk."[87] The new building stood at the northeast corner, tucked back against the eastern wall some distance from the noisy main gate of the suburb. It was accessible to merchants landing at the port village (Grao) and bringing their goods by muleback along the north bank of the Guadalaviar to the western or main bridge. It was also convenient to overland merchants, since it stood hard by the city's western gate, terminus of local inland routes, and below a bridge vital to north-south traffic.

In 1273 King James awarded its life-custody to Berengar of Torrent, charging him to collect crown revenues under the watchful eye of the bailiff resident in the city. Berengar bore maintenance expenses and staff salaries; his gross recompense amounted to ten pennies daily, which meant over 300 solidi a year or almost a knight's fee, far more than the king had previously received from the enterprise. It is tempting to think that the new custodian was someone like the politically powerful jurist Berengar of Torres; the form of the name, and perhaps the office, points rather to an obscure investor of Botí's status.[88] Berengar duly got from the crown "a charter

[87] Arch. Crown, James I, Reg. Canc. 19, fol. 83 (Dec. 17, 1273). "Quia nos Iacobus dei gratia rex Aragonum, Maioricarum, et Valencie, comes Barchinone et Urgel, et dominus Montispessulani concessimus tibi Bernardo Botini habitatori Valencie, cum carta nostra quam a te recuperavimus, quod sarraceni advenientes apud Valenciam hospitantur in fundico tuo quod habeas in Valencia, de quo Guillmonus Scriba facit et facere tenetur nobis quinque maçmutinas censuales quod tu ab ipso tenes ad censum octo maçmutinarum, nos modo fecerimus [?] fieri fundicum ad opus sarracenorum in moreria in quo omnes sarraceni advenientes Valencie habent hospitari in nostro mandato, idcirco [ad] emendam et satisfactionem dampni quod tu sustines vel sustinebis in futuro quia sarraceni in dicto fundico tuo non hospitaverint, per nos et nostros damus et concedimus tibi dicto Bernardo Botini et tuis imperpetuum illas quinque maçmutinas iucefias censuales quas nos percipimus et percipere debemus in dicto fundico ut est dictum . . . Damus etiam tibi dicto Bernardo Botini in tota vita tua tantum quadringentos solidos regalium Valencie annuales pro vita tua . . . [ex] iuribus nostris tabule Valencie singulis annis dum vita fuerit." The phrase "ad opus sarracenorum" may mean to the advantage and strengthening of the aljama or of foreign merchants, or merely for the needs of merchants while there. The several Escrivá Williams are untangled in Burns, *Crusader Valencia*, I, 239-240, II, 487; the elder William died before 1272 and may be the *Guillmonus* here.

[88] Torrent[e] castle and town was a Knights Hospitaller possession a few kilometers southwest of Valencia city, early settled and made a parish (see Burns, *Crusader Valencia*, I, 81-82, 86, 136, 143, 185-187, 189). Berengar, who later received from King Alfonso the advocacy of St. James's altar at the cathedral, was probably a not inconsequential citizen from this small settlement, or from one of

sealed with the greater seal," together with assurance of such salary "as holders of the said fonduk have usually received." The new king incorporated this information in a renewal and confirmation of October 1276, referring to the more detailed charter in the possession of Berengar.[89] A companion message of the same month settled the matter of salary, always a touchy point as devaluation introduced the dilemma of letter versus spirit behind any customary sum.[90] King Peter again confirmed to Berengar this fonduk "of the Moorish quarter of Valencia," with its salary, early in 1279.[91]

Within five months Berengar had either died or retired. Casting about for a suitable successor, King Peter chose Matthew Jordán, aide to his ex-mistress Agnes Zapata, a lady to whom the infatuated monarch had presented extensive Valencian properties and four bastard children.[92] Jordán, a native of Jaca in Aragon, appears in one

---

several similar towns of the name in Catalonia, and I cannot identify him with any contemporary bearing Torrent merely as a family name.

[89] Arch. Crown, Peter III, Reg. Canc. 38, fol. 48 (Oct. 2, 1276). "Infans Petrus etc. laudamus concedimus et confirmamus tibi Berengario de Torrente donacionem et concessionem tibi factam a domino rege bone memorie patre nostro cum instrumento sigillo maiori suo sigillato quod sis custos alfondici nostri morarie Valencie diebus omnibus vite tue dum bene et legaliter in ipso officio te habebis, et quod habeas et recipias inde pro tuo officio et labore tantum quantum alii dictum alfundicum tenentes consueverunt inde recipere et habere pro suo officio et labore . . . Laudationem concessionem et confirmationem facimus de predicta donatione tibi facta a dicto domino rege in vita tua et quod teneas dictum alfundicum sicut melius dici potest et intelligi ad tuum bonum et sanum intellectum prout in instrumento dicti domini regis plenius continetur. Datum Valencie, vi nonas Octobris anno domini mcclxx sexto."

[90] *Ibid.*, fol. 66v (Oct. 24, 1276): "infans Petrus fideli suo baiulo Valencie salutem et gratiam; nos intelleximus quod custos alfundici morarie consuevit recipere pro labore suo qualibet die decem denarios regalium Valencie, quare mandamus vobis Berengario de Torrentibus tenenti dictum alfondicum pro nobis qualibet die pro suo salario et labore x denarios regalium Valencie."

[91] *Ibid.*, Reg. 44, fol. 170 (Feb. 23, 1279): "laudamus . . . et concedimus vobis Berengario de Torrente donacionem et concessionem [Iacobi] . . . cum carta sua de custodia morarie Valencie, volentes quod dum vixeris et bene et legaliter in dicta custodia te habueris sis custos dicti alfundici et habeas ibi servitia [?] tua ac recipias et colligas ius nostrum et redditus dicti alfundici, de quibus respondeas baiulo Valencie pro nobis, concedentes et . . . quod pro tuo salario et labore inde recipias decem denarios regalium qualibet die dum . . . legaliter te habueris super eo. Mandantes universis officialibus. . . ."

[92] *Ibid.*, fol. 148 (July 22, 1279): "nos Petrus dei gratia etc. damus et concedimus de gratia speciali tibi Matheo Iordani de Iacca scutifero Agnetis Çappate [dis-

document as her esquire (*scutifer*) and later as her secretary, roles in which he contrived "many welcome services" for the king. Though the new custodian received "the care of merchandise or anything else in our fonduk of the Moorish quarter of Valencia" from 1279 provisionally, it was only in 1284 that he entered into possession with full and permanent formality. He could serve the office himself or "through another or others whom you may wish to substitute in the said office in your stead." The charge went under the capitalized title "Office of Guarding or of Custody of the fonduk of our Moorish quarter of the city of Valencia."[93]

Less than two years passed, when yet another owner assumed responsibility for the fonduk. This was Bernard of Bolea, in possession by September of 1286 and still operating the concession as late as 1315. Thus the history of the fonduk, after earlier shifts of administration, displays a steady period of some thirty years under one man—broken only by the usual renewals of ownership, the occasional assignation of some portion of revenues to a crown creditor, and several intrusions by civic officialdom that were firmly rebuked by the crown. In 1315 the continuing prosperity of the fonduk comes into view in a summation of crown rentals at the city: "the lord

---

trictum] . . . de mercimoniis vel aliis rebus in fundico nostro morarie Valencie." Agnes gave the king three sons and a daughter before the Sicilian wars; of these Peter became lord of Tous in Valencia, and Ferdinand lord of Albarracín on its border; King Peter granted Agnes (Iñes) the cities of Alcira and Liria, a share in the Játiva saltworks, properties at Burriana and elsewhere in Valencia, and baths and other buildings at Valencia city.

[93] *Ibid.*, Reg. Canc. 43, fol. 94 (Dec. 30, 1284). "Noverint universi quod nos Petrus dei gratia Aragonum et Valencie rex propter multa et grata servicia que vos Matheus Iordani scriba nobilis domine Agnesie Çapata nobis fecistis et cotidie facere non cessatis de gratia speciali damus et concedimus vobis dum nobis placuit, Officium Guardarie sive Custodie alffondici nostri morarie civitatis Valencie ut Berengarius de Torrent qui ipsum tenebat et dimisit ipsum melius habebat ex concessione domini Iacobi dei gratia regis Aragonum felicis recordationis patris nostri, ita quod vos de cetero per vos vel per alium vel alios quos in dicto officio substituere volueritis loco vestro utamini predicto officio bene et legaliter prout officium est, et habeatis et capiatis de redditibus ipsius alffundici pro vestri [*sic*] salario et labore id quod predictus Berengarius consuevit percipere et habere ut in instrumentis sive gratia [?] plenius continetur. Mandantes baiulo nostro Valencie presenti scilicet et futuro et aliis officialibus et subditis nostris quod vos deceterom habeant pro guardiano et custodia dicti alffundici, et vobis vel cui volueritis persolvant et persolvi faciant salarium predictum ac predicta firmiter habeant et observent ut superius continetur. Datum Turolii, tertio kalendas Ianuarii anno domini mcclxxx quarto."

king owns a fonduk in Valencia that Sir Bernard of Bolea holds at a rental of 400 solidi by grant from the lord king, of which the lord king has granted that he keep for life 300 solidi each year and the surplus that the said fonduk is worth each year."[94] The city's fonduk eventually served also as residence for crown officials and as collecting station for regalian revenues from local Mudejars.[95]

Another commercial institution under the ruler's protection but not to be confused with the fonduk was the *qaiṣārīya*. Originally a

[94] *Rentas de Aragón*, p. 88 (1315): "item ha lo senyor rey en Valencia un fondech lo qual te En Bernat de Bolea a cens de cccc solidos per atorgament del senyor rey dels quals lo senyor rey li ha ortogat ques retenga de vida sua ccc solidos cascun any et la sobre que val cascun any lo dit fondech." Bernard of Bolea had served as crown procurator in Valencian business of 1284, and Peter of Bolea was named justiciar of Bolea town in 1323. A run of eight documents in the reign of Peter's successor Alfonso III touches on Bolea's reception of the fonduk (Sept. 20, 1286), his efforts to get it from Valencian officials (Oct. 18, 1287), his displacement by William of Massanet from some of its revenues (Feb. 27, 1288), his reappointment (Sept. 15, 1288 and March 7 and 29, 1289), and his struggle to control (March 18, 1291). His salary in 1289 remained ten pence daily. See, e.g., Arch. Crown, Alfonso III, Reg. Canc. 64, fol. 119 (Sept. 20, 1286): "propter multa grata et idonea servitia que vos fidelis portarius noster Bernardus de Bolea illustrissimo domino regi Petro etc. exhibuistis et nobis etiam, et adhuc facere non cessatis, idcirco concedimus vobis alfondicum in nostra morarie Valencie," at the king's will and the usual recompense; Reg. Canc. 74, fol. 6 (Oct. 18, 1287), rebukes officials who blocked Bernard's possession of "alfondicum nostrum morarie civitatis Valencia"; Reg. Canc. 78, fol. ii v (Sept. 15, 1288) extends to a life-concession "alfondegum morerie nostre Valencie . . . [et] recipiatis salarium et alia iura que alii tenentes ipsum alfondegum consueverunt habere." The Tunis fonduk had been administered in much the same fashion; a document of Aug. 18, 1277 explains that King James had retained proprietorship, selling the usufruct to Raymond Ricard and Philip of Denia, who in turn sublet or resold it to Bernard of Rubió. King Peter revoked the usufruct and declared the sublease invalid as having occurred after King James's death; Peter then farmed the entire operation to Bernard for two-thirds of the profits, waiving his share until it had repaid a loan by Bernard—"alfundicum cum consulatu, furno, scribaniis notarie videlicet et duane, butigiis, maczeniis, et taberna" (Soldevila, *Pere el Gran*, part 2, 1, appendix, doc. 91). The history of the fonduk in Valencia city's Moorish quarter may be followed into the next century; see, e.g., Arch. Reino Val; Cancillería Real, codex 612, fols. 1-8.

[95] Roca Traver, "Vida mudéjar," pp. 137-138. An entry for Novelda in 1315 puts the king's rent from its "l'alfondech" at 40 solidi (*Rentas de Aragón*, p. 123). Further references appear in Alfonso's documents; see, e.g., the visitations by the "officium custodie tabule pensi Valencie, ita quod eans per ianuas murorum Valencie et per alfundica. . . ." (Reg. Canc. 64, fol. 118v [Sept. 20, 1286]); the possession by the Mudejar Ibrāhīm Bellido "illorum operatoriorum que se teneat cum alfondico dicti regni Valentie" (Reg. Canc. 82, fol. 170v [Dec. 18, 1290]); and especially the arrest of a Muslim "pro eo quia invasit alfundicum nostrum Valencie et abstraxit furtim papirum ut dicitur" (Reg. Canc. 67, fol. 78v [Sept. 20, 1286]), a rare reference to paper as a commodity.

silk exchange, it had evolved into a carefully guarded luxury bazaar and warehouse, a kind of covered market sometimes amounting to a distinct commercial ward embracing many submarkets. In classical form it was a semiprivate building with the markets arranged around its inner courtyard and galleries, constituting a component element of the larger public market; but it could take other shapes, such as a blocked-off street or a section of the town. A *qaiṣārīya* or two may possibly lie concealed under the generic name *alfundicum*. The *qaiṣārīya* within the Mudejar quarter of Valencia city does appear in a transfer of its revenues in 1258 from one creditor to another. The only meaning assigned by Catalan lexicographers to *alcaçeria* is "merchandise," but this transfer explicitly regulates the number and revenues of shops "in the aforesaid *alcaçeria*." The writ forbids "any Jew, Saracen, or convert to have or own any shop in which merchandise is sold in the city or surroundings of Valencia" without the creditor's permission, "except in the aforesaid *qaiṣārīya*," and then only if "some shop is empty there."[96] The phrasing suggests that *qaiṣārīya* at Valencia comprised the whole Mudejar main market-place, unless the context of the time and place imposed an unstated restriction on the kind of "merchandise" meant.

Other establishments might be classed as utilities, such as the salt-works with their monopoly, discussed below, or the office for col-

---

[96] M. Streck, "Ḳaiṣārīya," *EI*[1], II, part 2, 659-670, with the traditional derivation from the Byzantine Greek for "imperial market." Arch. Crown, James I, Reg. Canc. 10, fol. 61 (April 28, 1258): "illorum operatoriorum alcaçerie que fuerunt Guillelmi de Porciano"; and the same shops again (April 29): "operatoriorum omnium Alqueçerie"; "nullus iudeus, sarracenus, vel babtizatus audeat habere vel tenere operatorium aliquod in quo aliqua mercatoria vendantur in civitate vel in suburbio Valencie . . . nisi tantum in predicta Alqueçeria [dum] tamen aliquod operatorium ibi vaccet." See also fol. 14 (Nov. 30, 1257): 2,135 solidi of Barcelona assigned to be repaid to a creditor of the crown from the taxes and rents "omnium illorum operatoriorum alchacerie que fuerunt Guillelmi de Porzario, salva tamen vendicione inde facta ad tempus Arnaldo de Romanino." See too the restricted meaning allowed *alcaceria* (the Catalan bears no accent) by Antonio Alcover *et alii* in the encyclopedic *Diccionari català-valencià-balear*, 10 vols. (Palma de Mallorca, 1930-1962), I, 445. Torres Balbás, "Alcaicerías," *Al-Andalus*, XIV (1949), 431-455; and for Valencia city's around 1200, pp. 433-434. See also his *Ciudades hispano-musulmanas*, I, 345-368; Dubler, *Wirtschaftsleben*, p. 147; Goitein, *Mediterranean Society*, I, 194; and Neuvonen, *Arabismos del español*, p. 89. Ibn Baṭṭūṭa describes an eastern *qaiṣārīya* with iron gates, its interior "encircled by shops and chambers, one upon the other, of skilful construction" (*Travels*, II, 349; cf. I, 97, where one encircles a mosque).

lecting the king's fifth on commercial fishing in Valencia, or the weights and measures service retained by the crown. These fell completely under Christian management, the Mudejars having recourse to them like other citizens. The most obvious among them was the public granary or *bladerium* (Catalan *almodí*), which appears in the documentation of Valencia city as a large establishment under the control of a permanent administrator, with a guardhouse annexed for protection.[97] Spanish Muslims were skilled at storing grain so as to preserve it over many years; this continuing tradition and need accounts for the privilege sought by Valencian Muslims, guaranteeing continued access to public granaries. The Játiva charter provided for buying "grain of all kinds just as the Christian inhabitants of Játiva";[98] at Uxó the Moors could "buy every grain at Burriana and other places of our lordship."[99]

The utilities, from butcheries to fonduks, provided a steady stream of commonplace taxes. Christian and Muslim alike accepted them; the Mudejar merely transferred these customary fees to his infidel conqueror.[100] The socioeconomic life of both cultures, before and

[97] Arch. Crown, James I, Reg. Canc. 14, fol. 114 (June 1, 1271), where Arnold of Fores receives "officium Rasorie . . . in tota vita tua" as overseer of "bladium" here; in Reg. Canc. 21, fol. 74 (Nov. 15, 1272) the watchman's building is commissioned. These directives comprise part of a half dozen unpublished documents during the reigns of King James and King Peter which, with two further documents from the next king, Alfonso, attest to the importance of Valencia city's *almodí*. Sale of its revenues to a speculator in 1290 brought 18,000 solidi. On weights and measures in northern Valencia's Christian settlements, see García y García, *Estado económico-social de Castellón*, p. 70; for twelfth-century Seville, see Ibn 'Abdūn, *Séville musulmane, le traité*, pp. 85ff. On the salt and road taxes, see below, Chapter V, parts 3 and 4.

[98] Játiva Charter: "possitis emere triticum, ordeum, panicium, et quodlibet aliud genus bladi, sicut christiani vicini Xativae."

[99] Uxó Charter: "puxen comprar tot blat per a llavor á ops de la llur terra en Borriana e en altres lochs de la nostra senyoria." Torres Balbás, "Alhóndigas hispanomusulmanas," 447-480. On storehouses see Imamuddin, *Socio-Economic and Cultural History*, pp. 80-81; wheat could be stored ten years at Toledo without spoiling, according to ar-Rāzī, while other authors multiplied the figure by 5 to 8 times. *Bladum* (Catalan *blat*) meant any cereal, only later narrowing to mean wheat, so these storehouses served an ample need; see *Glossarium mediae latinitatis Cataloniae, voces latinas y romances documentados en fuentes catalanes del año 800 al 1100*, ed. M. Bassols de Climent *et alii*, 1 vol. to date (Barcelona, 1960), 1, 274.

[100] Ibn 'Abdūn has a regulation for anyone renting a public bath, mill, shop, or boat from the state's domain, as well as references to the taxes on ovens, baths, butcheries, and the like (*Séville musulmane, le traité*, pp. 68, 110).

after the crusade, followed a pattern so assimilated at the level of basic diet and employment that such taxes became universally meaningful. Subjects hardly welcomed any taxes, but they knew that these fell equitably on all communities and reflected an understandable governmental control over services in constant, wide demand.

CHAPTER IV

Life and Work: Household, Community, Commercial, and Agrarian Charges

BESIDES THE daily utilities to which a steady flow of customers had recourse, the most obvious sources of Mudejar tax revenue were static social units and productive activity. The units were family and aljama; the economic activity was commercial or agrarian. A central tax fell in each area, with auxiliary taxes as circumstances warranted. Of auxiliary taxes, the irrigation and military were important enough to require separate consideration in the next chapter, where lesser auxiliary charges can join them in a miscellany of the pastoral, esoteric, occasional, or relatively trivial. Antecedent to all else were the fundamental taxes on life and work—the household, community, and primary commercial-agrarian demands.[1]

HOUSEHOLD BESANT OR HEAD TAX

The tax encountered most frequently is the besant. On the surface this term might seem a synonym for general Mudejar revenue as indicated by the Arabic coin in which it was reported; in fact it stood for a specific tribute. Christians and Jews under Islam paid a capitation or poll tax as a sign of their alien, inferior position. Every adult male contributed yearly a sum adjusted to the levels of affluent, moderate, and poverty income. Theoretically this *jizya* was not onerous, especially when balanced against the tithe-alms *zakāt* paid by Muslims; in fact it became a feared and at times nearly intolerable burden. In crusader Valencia Mudejars owed a similar though much lighter head tax under the name besant. Unlike the *jizya* it fell upon households rather than upon all adolescent and adult males in the family, and it amounted to a considerably smaller sum. The crown

---

[1] Several of this chapter's themes, revised here, comprised my preliminary report (in Spanish) on "Mudejar Life and Work" before the Primer congreso internacional del país valenciano in April 1971, published in its *Acta* (see Bibliography).

did impose it universally, however, and was reluctant to alienate it or to grant exemptions. The equivalent capitation in Aragon proper and in the Balearics underwent a different and sometimes puzzling evolution; the clearest documentation on this tax comes from Valencia.[2]

Besant was the Western word for a *dīnār* originally minted by Islamic countries in imitation of the Byzantine gold solidus. So useful was the silver besant, worth a fourth or a fifth of the gold coin, that King James deliberately counterfeited its components as *millareses*, with all Islamic trappings, in official mints of Aragon, Catalonia, Montpellier, and Valencia. At first its value in terms of the favored new Valencian money fluctuated from $3\frac{1}{4}$ solidi (3 solidi, 3 pence) to $3\frac{3}{4}$ or 4 solidi. The equivalence varied as inflation hurt the Valencian solidi, until by 1288 a besant brought nearly five solidi. Vagaries of local exchange also affected the besant's worth; around 1285 five silver besants could buy a gold *dīnār* in Hafsid Tunis, whereas the same transaction required twelve besants at nearby Tlemcen. Sometimes the taxpayer found relief from these fluctuations of the money market when the crown arbitrarily adjusted the equivalence of silver besant to solidi. At Alcira in 1263, where the total was expressed in both moneys, the rate adopted was $3\frac{1}{2}$ solidi to the besant; at Onteniente it was $3\frac{1}{3}$. Considering the falling value of the solidus over these years, the rates reflect a substantial lowering of the real value paid in tax.[3]

[2] Claude Cahen, "Ḏjizya," *El²*, II, 559-562. Løkkegaard, *Islamic Taxation*, ch. 6. Siddiqi, *Public Finance in Islam*, ch. 9. Lévi-Provençal, *España musulmana*, v, 20-22. Goitein, *Mediterranean Society*, II, ch. 7, section C2, a revisionist presentation on the onerous nature of the tax, including thirteenth-century evidence; individuals, not the community, were responsible, and paid directly to Muslim officials, not through the community (p. 389). Reckoned by the *dīnār*, the sum varied from $4\frac{1}{8}$ to $1\frac{5}{8}$ with further adjustments according to local circumstances (p. 387). For Aragon proper, see Francisco Macho y Ortega, "Condición social de los mudéjares aragoneses (siglo xv)," *Memorias de la facultad de filosofía y letras de la universidad de Zaragoza*, I (1922-1923), 181. On the Balearics see Elena Lourie, "Free Moslems in the Balearics under Christian Rule in the Thirteenth Century," *Speculum*, XLV (1970), 647-648, where the equivalent *morabatí* was owed "ratione standi in terra ista."

[3] Arch. Crown, James I, Reg. Canc. 17, fol. 27 (Dec. 30, 1263): "bisancia sarracenorum que receperunt, xciiii bisancia que faciunt cccxxix solidos." Fol. 29 (Dec. 31, 1263): "bisancia sarracenorum, xv bisancia que faciunt l solidos." For Valencia in 1258, and Valencia-Játiva in 1290, see notes 14, 15; for table of equivalence, see above, p. 29. See also Botet y Sisó, "Encunyació de monedes aràbigues pêl re Don Jaume," pp. 946-951, with documents; Lévi-Provençal, *España musulmana*, v, 146,

In the conquered kingdom of Valencia every Mudejar householder paid an annual besant as special tribute over and above his rents. Whether or not this involved an actual besant coin, or its component ten *millareses*, is difficult to say; the crown followed its own preferred coinage, drafting relief measures in terms of solidi and pence waived. Though assessed by house, the besant differed from the house or property rental. Játiva's charter specified the annual besant "for their houses." The Tales charter required it "by way of tribute from each household," defined "in such wise that each house," both in the town and in "its countryside and holdings," was to give "us and ours every year one silver besant as tribute."[4] At Onda as at Tales authorities collected the besant on St. Michael's Day—the warrior archangel's principal feast in September, which celebrated Christendom's movement of reconquest against Islam. An exemption awarded to three towns near Onda in 1258 "retains however the single besant paid to us and ours every year" on St. Michael's Feast, drawn from "every household."[5]

The crown registers noted the tax of "our besants" over the Játiva district in 1273, 1279, and 1281,[6] at Biar in 1268, in 1268 and 1269 at

---

on the kind of *dirham* of which twelve made up the *dīnār* besant; Felipe Mateu y Llopis, "La repoblación musulmana del reino de Valencia en el siglo xiii y las monedas de tipo almohade," *BSCC*, xxviii (1952), 35-36. In 1268, 150 silver besants equaled 325 Barcelona solidi; in 1291 five besants equaled a gold *dīnār*, and in 1288 a gold *dīnār* was worth 14 to 15 Valencian solidi (16 in 1302), making the besant worth roughly 5 of these later solidi (Dufourcq, *L'Espagne catalane et le Maghrib*, pp. 169-170, 526-530, 556). On Saracen and Ceuta besants, and the coining of gold and silver besants at Valencia, see above, Chapter II, n. 43.

[4] Játiva Charter: "pro domibus suis." Tales Charter: "ita quod unusquisque cassatus . . . in predicta alquaria et eius terminis et pertinenciis . . . donet nobis et nostris annis singulis . . . unum dargenti bessancium pro tributo"; "pro tributo pro unoquoque cassato."

[5] Arch. Crown, James I, Reg. Canc. 11, fol. 168v (Sept. 1, 1259): "in festo Sancti Michaelis Septembris . . . illos singulos bisancios." St. Michael's principal feast and the dedication of Monte Gargano was Sept. 29, which some places including parts of Spain celebrated on Sept. 6. Reg. Canc. 10, fol. 79 (May 31, 1258): "salvo tamen uno bisancio solvendo nobis et nostris annis singulis in festo Sancti Michaelis quod in unoquoque cassato ipsorum perpetuo retinemus."

[6] *Ibid.*, Reg. Canc. 21, fol. 141 (June 7, 1273): "a prestacione bisanciorum nostrorum." Peter III, Reg. Canc. 42, fol. 226v (Feb. 20, 1279): "quod exigat a sarracenis Xative et termini eiusdem tam militum quam aliorum bisancium et universa alia iura." Reg. Canc. 50, fol. 118 (July 7, 1281): "universis sarracenis locorum termini Xative . . . quatenus solvatis baiulo Xative presenti bisancios istius anni sicut consuetum est solvi in aliis locis nostris," or force will be used.

Pego, and in 1275 at Pego and at "Alfandech and its valley."[7] The besant tax can be seen at Nuches near Jijona[8] and Alcocer near Cocentaina in 1258,[9] at the villages of Montesa in 1259,[10] and—later but reflecting settled custom—at Algar and Albalat in the neighborhood of Murviedro in 1280.[11] The small settlement of Ayelo left record in 1259 of its obligation to pay a besant of good silver yearly. At the village of Benejama in 1258 "every household of Saracens that may be there will give us and ours every year one besant of silver." An exemption for Muslim tenants of Jews throughout the kingdom of Valencia in 1262 referred in a universal way to "that besant that we are accustomed to have from each of the said Saracens every year."[12]

To attract Muslim settlement the crown sometimes renounced this tax temporarily for a particular locality—as at Burriana in 1268 and the Alcira region in 1274.[13] In 1258, apparently as part of his program to bring Muslims to Valencia city, King James lowered the

[7] *Ibid.*, James I, Reg. Canc. 15, fol. 84 (1268): "bisancios." Reg. Canc. 20, fol. 25 (April 27, 1275): "Alfandech et vallis eiusdem." For Pego see the following document on the same folio, and Reg. Canc. 35, fol. 3v (1268): "item el besant, xliii besants, vi millareses"; fol. 4 (1269): "item el besant, liii besants." Did these rather low totals indicate partial collection, an agreed lump sum, or a reduced total for some *ad hoc* reason?

[8] *Ibid.*, Reg. Canc. 9, fol. 55v (Feb. 13, 1258): "quattuordecim domos in alcheria que vocatur Nahuges que est de termino de Sexona . . . de quocumque sarracenorum illorum . . . habeamus quolibet anno unum bisancium argenti, prout hoc est consuetum facere in regno Valencie."

[9] *Ibid.*, Reg. Canc. 10, fol. 83r,v (July 1, 1258): "alqueriam de Alcoçer que est in termino Coçentanie . . . de prestatione bisancii."

[10] *Ibid.*, Reg. Canc. 11, fol. 152 (Sept. 29, 1259), really a temporary exemption for a new settlement by the *qā'id* of Montesa, "que dicitur Yocor que est in terminis Xative," but by implication paid at his other places.

[11] *Ibid.*, Peter III, Reg. Canc. 48, fol. 159 (Sept. 24, 1280): "a sarracenis loci de Albalat . . . bisancium." For Algar see Reg. Canc. 42, fol. 220 (Feb. 15, 1279): "non compellatis homines sarracenos d[e] Algar . . . racione bisanciorum quos nobis dare tenentur," until a legal difficulty is resolved.

[12] *Ibid.*, James I, Reg. Canc. 11, fol. 151v (Sept. 29, 1259): "in alqueria de Yello . . . unusquisque casatus eorum det . . . unum bisantium boni argenti." Reg. Canc. 10, fol. 82 (June 28, 1258): "unusquisque casatus sarracenorum qui ibi sint [*sic*] donet nobis et nostris annis singulis unum bisancium argenti et preter hoc nichil aliud nobis vel nostris donent." Benixamen near Almizra must be Benejama. Reg. Canc. 12, fol. 44v (May 10, 1262): "illum bisancium quod ab unoquoque dictorum sarracenorum quolibet anno habere consuevimus."

[13] *Ibid.*, Reg. Canc. 19, fol. 124 (April 16, 1274): "subtus cequiam Algezire . . . [a] bisantiis et tributo." See also Miguel Gual Camarena, "Mudéjares valencianos, aportaciones para su estudio," *Saitabi*, VII (1949), 188 on Burriana (March 26, 1268).

tribute from each household of its quarter. "We allow and decree forever to you, each and every Saracen of the Moorish quarter of Valencia city, that you do not give that silver besant annually as tribute, [but] only four solidi and six pence in the money of Valencia."[14] The crown reduced the obligation further in 1290, asking only three solidi and four pence. The diminution prevailed also at Játiva.[15] In each case it was an expedient to solve the financial problems of the local aljama. In 1259 at Onda the obligation was doubled but all other taxes waived. At the same time, the aljama stood surety as a community against default by any single household. At Crevillente in 1273 King James permanently absolved the whole aljama from the besant and voided the lost Arabic document imposing it.[16]

A very late document, if used with caution, throws some light on the Valencia and Játiva Moorish quarters of our earlier period. Dating from the mid-fourteenth century, after both aljamas had suffered in numbers and prosperity, it shows that Játiva supplied the crown with an annual net of 1,492 solidi by way of the besant tribute, while Valencia city mustered 1,150.[17] At 3¼ solidi according to equivalence in payment of the besant, therefore, and allowing four souls to a household, Játiva had a Mudejar population of at least

[14] Arch. Crown, James I, Reg. Canc. 10, fol. 81v (July 2, 1258): "indulgemus ac statuimus vobis universis et singulis sarracenis morerie Valencie . . . imperpetuum quod non donetis . . . de illo bisancio argenti . . . annis singulis pro tributo [nisi] tantum iii solidos et vi denarios regalium Valencie." At Perpunchent in 1316 the Muslims paid three solidi six pence (Gual Camarena, "Mudéjares valencianos, aportaciones," p. 188), and the 1258 reduction may involve a scribal error of "iiii" for "iii," unless inflation explains the equivalence.

[15] Roca Traver, "Vida mudéjar," doc. 25 (Sept. 9, 1290): "pro bisanciis non detis . . . nisi tres solidos et quattuor denarios regales . . . tantum quantum sarraceni morerie nostre Xative nobis donant."

[16] Arch. Crown, James I, Reg. Canc. 11, fol. 168v (Sept. 1, 1259): "non donetis illos singulos bisancios quos unusquisque casatus vestrum dare debebatis in dicto festo . . . et si aliquis casatus vestrum non poterit solvere dictos duos bisancios, vos omnes ipsos duos bisancios pro eo donetis et solvatis." Reg. Canc. 19, fol. 98v (Feb. 5, 1273): "a solucione illorum bisanciorum argenti in quibus vos nobis tenebamini cum carta sarracenica."

[17] In a 1315 list, immediately following the "tribute" of the Jews at Játiva, comes the entry: "item munten cascun any los besans del dit loch de Xativa tro a ccccxlviii que valen a rao de iii solidos iiii diners per besant . . . mccccxcii solidos iii diners" (Rentas de Aragón, p. 93). The figures remain thus at mid-century, suggesting that a conventional figure based on some 400 to 500 households had been determined early. See the Censo de Catalunya, pp. 208, 262; the latter assessment ("item la moreria de la dita ciutat") must be the besants, from comparison with the Játiva entry.

450 households or almost 1800 people. Valencia city and its immediate environs would have counted about a hundred houses fewer.

A Muslim owning no property still paid the tributary besant. For the Alcira region in 1270, after thirty years of taxes, King James remitted all burdens on such folk but retained the besant. "We grant to you, each and every Saracen laborer resident in Campanar and in the district of Alcira who does not have properties or any possessions there, that henceforth you are not bound to give or pay us, any of you, anything except one besant every year."[18] A similar humanity was shown at Mogente in 1279, where each household paid six solidi but "those who do not have houses are to pay according as they are able."[19] The Mogente incident may represent a distinct house tax however, such as appears in the Tales charter; there the king demanded, besides the rent on each piece of land and the besant, a supplementary tribute of three solidi yearly.[20] The house besant at Játiva did not multiply for several houses owned by a single man, as long as he merged them "to make quarters [*staticum*]" amounting to a unit.[21]

Some charters, even when as detailed as those at Chivert and Eslida, do not mention the besant. Since this tax was universal, the omission provides another reason for seeing such documents as partial and as requiring interpretation by local custom. Privileges of exemption rarely included the besant, though the crown might temporarily suspend its payment as an expedient. Charters dismissing a range of taxes usually reserved this tribute. The Valencian *Furs* incorporated it. Legal reforms of 1283 retained it, though restoring to their proper lords those besants collected on noncrown lands:

[18] Arch. Crown, James I, Reg. Canc. 16, fol. 217 (Oct. 2, 1270): "concedimus vobis universis et singulis sarracenis laboratoribus habitantibus in Campanar et terminis Aliazire qui non habetis hereditates seu possessiones aliquas ibidem quod non teneamini dare vel solvere nobis decetero nisi unum bisancium quilibet vestrum anno quolibet."

[19] *Ibid.*, Peter III, Reg. Canc. 42, fol. 133 (Nov. 3, 1279): "e los qui casas no han que pagen segond lur poder."

[20] Tales Charter. See also Arch. Crown, Peter III, Reg. Canc. 42, fol. 175v (Nov. 19, 1279): "al alcayt de Muxen . . . que cascu dels moros casats de Muxen donassen vi sous." Reg. Canc. 60, fol. 19 (Jan. 29, 1282) more ambiguously has: "compellatis omnes illos sarracenos . . . , quibus stabilivit seu locavit almuniam suam, ad solvendum eidem illud quod ei solvere teneantur ratione ipsius almunie iuxta tenorem carte sarracenice." These seem to be distinct from the community tax or *peita* below.

[21] Játiva Charter (1251): "ad opus statice." *Staticum* or *estatge* was a staying place (*statio*), apartment, or the like.

"the lords of an estate are to have the besants of the Saracens."[22] Muslim slaves did not pay besants, but tenants of lords and landlords did. Dismissal in such cases might amount only to transfer of payment from regalian to seignorial status. In either case the besant bore the character of a tribute, at once a sign of alienation and of incorporation.

It was not the only tax, however, that could be understood as tribute.[23] Sometimes the Mudejar head tax or tribute went under the name *alfarda*; confusingly, so did the irrigation tax. Was the *alfarda*, on which a fair amount of detail survives for Valencia, distinct from the besant and from the tenth or fifth of agricultural rents? Resolution of the problem will come more readily after consideration of the rents below and of the water tax in the next chapter.[24]

TARIFF AND TRANSPORT

Commercial taxes burdened Muslims as well as Christians. Tolls, sales taxes, and duties could proliferate irritatingly, adding their weight to the shop rental and the overhead expenses of conducting business. In the lively commercial world of the southwestern Mediterranean, it is probable that the iron laws of profit had effected an osmosis of usage, so that Islamic and European commercial taxes did not differ markedly in the final reckoning. Theoretically the Muslim merchant paid a tenth of the value of his wares to the Islamic treasury, under title of religious *zakāt* on trade, or as import or export duties; in fact these ad valorem duties, transit tolls, or market fees were more like $2\frac{1}{2}$ percent. European merchants could pay duties of up to twenty percent on imports. As in Europe, a complex of many

[22] *Furs de València*, lib. VIII, rub. viii, c. 28: "et quod bisantios sarracenorum habeant, et recipiant ab ipsis dominis hereditatis prout continetur in foro." Besides the nuclear code of James I, cited already in its Latin version as *Fori antiqui Valentiae*, there are several editions of the Catalan, evolved version, of which the *Fori regni Valentiae*, ed. Francesc J. Pastor and P. J. de Capdevila, 2 vols. (Monzón, 1547-1548) is the more available and useful. The *Furs de València*, ed. Germán Colón and Arcadio García, 2 vols. to date (Barcelona, 1970ff.), contains as yet only the first segment, but its elaborate introduction furnishes full bibliographical orientation. According to Tourtoulon (*Jaime I*, II, 296) and Bofarull ("Jaime I y los judíos," p. 831), James imposed the extra tax of the besant but the *Furs* removed it wherever a lord admitted that code as public law.

[23] See pp. 107ff. It is distinct from the tribute in the document quoted in n. 13 but identified with it in that of n. 14.

[24] See Chapter V, part 1.

small charges affected merchandise, but the totals were predictable and not unreasonable.[25]

In crusader Valencia, the main commercial taxes, paired as often by way of exemption as of imposition, were the *lleuda* and *peatge*, respectively a charge on merchandise arriving for sale and on its transit. Depending on circumstances they assumed the color of local market taxes or of international export-import tariffs. The officials charged with their collection were addressed sometimes as a group apart; a directive could distinguish "all castellans, bailiffs, justiciars, tariff agents (*lezdarii*), and transit officers (*pedagiarii*), and all other officials and subjects."[26] The *lleuda*, deriving from Latin *licita*, translates as customs duties or as tariffs on imports, though it could also affect exports. A number of major cities of a region like Valencia each imposed its own set of tariffs on goods entering that region; frontier land- or dry-ports, and towns strategically sited on major highways, thus had their tariff lists. These tariffs were distinct from municipal taxes on commerce, though the municipality retained a considerable share before sending the bulk to the crown. In general the *lleuda* fell on foreign importers or purchasers of exports, though "foreign" in this context meant any nonresident of the given tariff-city and its district. Fixed by published lists, the tariff at a city fell upon specifically stated items or categories of commerce and upon such classes of debarking persons as slaves and visiting Muslims.

Sea tariffs provided a particularly rich income for the crown and made the harbor customs officer (*lezdarius*) an important man locally.[27] In the Valencian kingdom, Biar and Játiva were the major

[25] Lévi-Provençal, *España musulmana*, v, 25, 178. Qudāma b. Ja'far b. Qudāma al-Kātib al-Baghdādī, *Kitāb al-kharāj*, in *Taxation in Islam*, ii, ch. 13. Rabie, *Financial System of Egypt*, pp. 89-104. On the imitation by Castile of a market value-tax under the borrowed name *alcabala*, see García de Valdeavellano, *Instituciones españolas*, pp. 607-608; its later expansion and evolution is traced by Salvador de Moxó, *La alcabala, sobre sus orígenes, concepto y naturaleza* (Madrid, 1963). See Siddiqi, *Public Finance in Islam*, ch. 8 on Islamic tolls and customs; and Aghnides, *Mohammedan Theories of Finance*, pp. 261-282. On the Mudejar merchant class in Valencia, see Burns, *Islam under the Crusaders*, ch. 5, part 2, and on artisans part 1.

[26] Arch. Crown, James I, perg. 1,466 (Jan. 18, 1257): "mandantes alcaydis, baiulis, iusticiis, lezdariis, et pedegiariis et universis aliis officialibus et subditis."

[27] Dufourcq has studied this *lleuda*-as-sea-customs; sometimes a *lleuda* vessel stationed within view of a port demanded payment from coastal ships passing (but see *ribatge* or riverage below in n. 46). He cites varied schedules of tariffs on wheat, wine, slaves, and the like, but is unsure whether it was paid by nonforeigners; at Majorca it all went to the king, at Barcelona local authorities took half. It could

land ports, Valencia city and Denia the preeminent seaports, Alcira the vital river port, and the coastal towns Murviedro and Burriana main revenue stations for goods traveling to or from the north. Tariffs provided the largest volume of commercial taxes recorded for the realms of Aragon in the thirteenth century. Valencian documents preferred a circumlocution to the word *lleuda.*[28]

Peatge, literally footage, translates as a transit or carrying duty on commercial use of the roads. The Valencian *Furs* set transit duty on a foreign Muslim at four pence, a horse two solidi, and a mule twelve pence. At Valencia city the collecting station stood by the city gates.[29]

---

fall on exports also, or on individuals as well as merchandise; in general it was not excessive. See his *L'Espagne catalane et le Maghrib*, pp. 62-65. On collection at the port of Valencia, see *Aureum opus*, doc. 15 of Peter III, fol. 31v (undated).

[28] Gual Camarena, *Vocabulario del comercio medieval*, p. 31; on Valencia see p. 28 and notes, pp. 33-34, and docs. 3, 6, 7, and 12. The Latin *leuda*, Catalan *(l)leuda*, and Castilian (and Latin variant) *lezda* also turn up in forms like *ledda* and *ledde*. The Latin *lezdarius* was the Catalan *lleuder* or *leuder* operating at a *lleudari* (Latin *leudarium*) or *taula de la lleuda*; the last phrase indicates why *tabula* stood for *leuda*, as in the phrase "tabula aut pedaticum" in *Aureum opus*, doc. 35, fol. 11Cr,v (1250). See also the treatment by Rodón Binué with illustrative examples in her *Lenguaje técnico del feudalismo*, p. 162. A sixteenth-century moral theologian, rigorously assessing each tax required in Valencia, found that the crown had three main revenues left: *peatge, quema* (a later export-import tax), and the combined sea-tenth and fish-fifth. The *peatge* brought 12,000 *aureos*, more than the others together (9,000); it stood at four pence per twenty solidi of value, was justified as owed for security and order on the road, and was challenged by some authors as an unjust tax. The municipality had taken over the six pence (nine pence for some merchandise from 1286) per solidus worth on vendibles, and also collected *cisa* on staples like bread, meat, and wine. See José Aliaga Girbés, "Moralidad de las exacciones tributarias del reino de Valencia en el siglo xvi según Miguel Bartolomé Salón O.S.A. (1539?-1621)," *Anthologica annua*, xvi (1968), 115-122, 124, 132. For our own purposes, his subsequent book adds only detail and leisured narrative: *Los tributos e impuestos valencianos en el siglo xvi: Su justicia y moralidad según Fr. Miguel Bartolome Salón, O.S.A. (1539?-1621)* (Rome, 1972). An allied treatment is Elizabeth A. R. Brown, "Taxation and Morality in the Thirteenth and Fourteenth Centuries: Conscience and Political Power and the Kings of France," *French Historical Studies*, viii (1973), 1-28, useful both because it has wider extension than its title indicates and because the Catalan Raymond of Penyafort provided the main formative influence.

[29] *Furs*, lib. ix, rub. xxxiv, c. 81. *Pedaticum*, relating originally to a foot journey as its name indicates, became the Catalan *peatge* or *pedatge* (collected by a *peatger*), Castilian *peaje*, and French *péage*; a variant Latin form was *peagium*. Rodón Binué equates *passaticum* or passage fee, which confused Dufourcq (*Espagne catalane et le Maghrib*, p. 64), with *pedaticum* and offers her own explanation of both in *Lenguaje técnico del feudalismo*, pp. 190-191. Christians paid nothing *pro persona*, and Mudejars could have this unequal burden lifted as at Játiva. A notary was

Occasionally "tariff or transit duty" appears as a single customs tax. These were not the only commerce or market charges paid by Muslim and Christian. Tax lists mention portage, riverage, market dues, bridge tolls, road tolls and the like.

Portaticum (Catalan *portatge*) could apply to any toll on passing goods and is easily confused with the *peatge*. In 1267 the Mudejars of Gallinera and Alcalá, buying or taking at farm all the taxes on their communities for the next two years, included *portatge*.[30] *Pontaticum* (Catalan *pontatge*) was a bridge toll. *Ribaticum* or *riberaticum* (Catalan *ribatge*) was a shore toll on wares passing a toll point by water or disembarking there. *Passaticum* or *passatge*, due on the "passage" of wares, was sometimes a separate toll and sometimes an alternate name for *lleuda*. *Mensuraticum* (Catalan *mesuratge*) was a fee on mandatory public measurement of commercial products, including grains; *pes* or *pesatge* was the same for official weighing, not to be confused with the differently derived *pesatge*, which is *pedatge* with *d* converted. *Mercatum*, a marketplace, and *teloneum*, a tax-collecting station, could involve small fees of the same name; the *teloneu* or *toloneu*, however, tended to identify with *portatge*. Fees to support road repair included *rotaticum* on wheeled carts, *passaticum* or *pulveraticum* on animals, and generically *cespitaticum*. *Cisa* (Castilian *sisa*, Latin *scissa*) fell on designated foodstuffs, directly on the consumer at the market. Few of these taxes appear by name in the Valencian Mudejar revenue documentation. Usually tariffs and transit duty stood alone or figured most prominently in partial lists. Lesser tolls must have been included under the more general rubric.

---

appointed as "collector pedagii porte Valencie vocate dels catalans" (*Itinerari*, p. 451 [July 30, 1271]); presumably other collectors controlled the other gates. *Lleuda* and *portatge* were collected only at Valencia city for the great sweep of territory bounded by Murviedro on the north, Requena on the west, and Alcira on the south, according to a law of 1250, which explicitly excludes the twenty-two towns within this circle that were likely to attempt collection (*Aureum opus*, doc. 35, fol. 11Cr,v).

[30] Arch. Crown, James I, Reg. Canc. 15, fol. 88 (March 1, 1267): "portagia"; appearing only in the second of two illustrative and incomplete listings, in this sale of all the aljama's revenues, its plural form may stand for more than one species of commercial tax. On such taxes as *almodinatge, barcatge*, and *tiratge* on foreign commerce arriving at Valencia, and *almorantazgo* on exports, which do not appear in our early documents, see Ferraz Penelas, *Maestre racional y la hacienda foral valenciana*, pp. 22-23, 31, 37.

Transit duty and tariffs did not encumber only the remotely professional or the long-distance trade but entered the life of the ordinary Muslim. Unless exempted, the farmer or townsman found himself paying them on relatively small transactions incidental to making his daily living. Some documents consequently aligned them with other ordinary local taxes, and the farming of the Biar revenues en bloc in 1258 singled them out.[31] Either main tax, though small in itself, could return a considerable sum in the aggregate. At Alcira in 1255 the crown share of tariffs reached a total of 3,000 solidi.[32] At Gandía in 1263 "the tariff, market fee, and transit duty" for the crown came to 1,930 solidi.[33] Such totals allow no distinction between Christian and Muslim contributors. A further ambiguity in revenue documents is their listing of income from specific produce without indicating whether the items represent vendibles or agricultural rents. A passage in the king's memoirs, unfortunately resting on an ambiguous reading, claims that the crown took from the relatively unprosperous Mudejars of Minorca island, just "for transport of cattle," an annual 200 besants or some 750 solidi.[34]

The Moors of Benizarjó, a crown village in the district of Gandía, can be seen paying both tariffs and transit duty, in a letter clarifying their tax status.[35] These fees figured also at the Gandía market in King James's time, paid by that region's Christian, Jew, and Muslim inhabitants. Subsequently the municipal authorities of Gandía annoyed King Peter by interfering with the collection of the two

[31] Arch. Crown, James I, Reg. Canc. 10, fol. 103v (June 16, 1258): "pedagia," though not *lleuda* despite Biar's prominence as entrepôt for land commerce.

[32] *Ibid.*, Reg. Canc. 8, fol. 21v (Nov. 26, 1255): my own addition, the manuscript offering no total.

[33] *Ibid.*, Reg. Canc. 17, fol. 28 (Dec. 30, 1263): "lezda, mercatum, et pedaticum, mille dcccc xxx solidos."

[34] *Llibre dels feyts*, ch. 121. The standard older reading, from the Mariano Aguiló edition of the *Crònica* (Biblioteca clássica catalana; Barcelona, 1873 [1905]) has "y doscents besants per bestiar a passar." The 1926-1962 Casacuberta critical edition has "e cc barques per bestiar a passar" (my own reading of the standard, "Poblet" MS) with no indication of variant readings. Ferran Soldevila, in the latest editing of James, finds both readings acceptable but "barques" more intelligible (*Quatre grans cròniques*, p. 253, n. 12). By either reading, the Mudejars were being required to provide transport for this tax-in-kind.

[35] Arch. Crown, James I, Reg. Canc. 19, fol. 109v (Feb. 26, 1273): "sarraceni habitantes in alqueria nostra vocata Benizarjo sita in termino Gandie non teneantur dare nec donent nec faciant . . . salvis tamen et exceptis nostris pedagiis et lesdis que et quas non intelligimus in predictis." Martínez Ferrando read the name as Benizario for his catalogue and identified it as Benisá; it is more likely Beniarjo.

taxes, "which the Saracens ought to give and were accustomed to pay."[36] In 1261 the crown assigned to a consortium of five financiers all the revenues of the Denia region, including "tariffs both on sea and land, and the transit duty"; a special proviso noted "the tariff, from all the Saracens resident in the aforesaid places and environs, on figs and raisins and other commodities that the said Saracens sell to knights or any other persons, according as they are accustomed to pay the said tariff on these."[37] Muslims on seignorial holdings at Alcira and Gandía who were freed from regalian taxes in 1274 nevertheless had to give these two.[38]

Those Muslims on lands belonging to the bishop and chapter of Valencia won exemption from tariffs and transit duty upon their nonprofessional commerce in 1257, an action implying that Muslim tenants of even the highest ecclesiastics normally fell under both. The terms of the exemption help explain the two taxes. King James made his "grant to Brother Andrew bishop of Valencia, our chancellor, and to the Valencia chapter and your successors forever, that any Christian or Saracen residents of your castles, towns, and any other places that you hold or will hold in the kingdom of Valencia, are not to give or pay or be bound to pay in any place of our dominion transit duty, tolls, or tariffs on any objects or merchandise that they buy or sell, or carry for buying or selling, unless they shall be common and manifest merchants; but throughout our whole jurisdiction, on land as on sea, they are to be frank, free, and immune from these taxes."[39] This privilege remained in force; after

[36] Ibid., Reg. Canc. 17, fol. 114v (March 12, 1267): "de . . . lezda [et] pedatico . . . ville de Gandie et omnium terminorum." Peter III, Reg. Canc. 46, fol. 177v (April 10, 1284): "quam sarraceni debent dare, et solvere consueverunt."

[37] Ibid., James I, Reg. Canc. 11, fol. 197v (March 27, 1261): "recipiatis lezdam ab omnibus sarracenis habitantibus in locis et terminis predictis de ficubus et de adçebib et de aliis mercibus quas dicti sarraceni vendent militibus vel quibus[cumque] p[ersonis] prout dictam lezdam inde dare [c]onsueverunt."

[38] Ibid., Reg. Canc. 19, fol. 107 (Feb. 23, 1274): "dictos sarracenos nec aliquem ipsorum a pedagio seu lezda in aliquo loco nostro dicti regni."

[39] Ibid., James I, perg. 1,466 (Jan. 18, 1257): "noverint universi quod nos Iacobus dei gratia rex Aragonum . . . per nos et nostros concedimus . . . fratri Andree episcopo Valencie cancellario nostro et capitulo valentino et successoribus vestris imperpetuum quod aliqui christiani vel sarraceni habitatores castrorum, villarum et quorumlibet aliorum locorum que habetis et habebitis in regno Valencie non donent nec solvant nec solvere teneantur in aliquo loco dominationis nostre pedagium, portaticum, neque lezdam pro aliquibus rebus vel mercibus quas emant vel vendant, vel portabunt ad emendum vel vendendum, nisi mercatores fuerint communi et

inspection in 1277, Peter renewed it.[40] A special section below will study tax exemptions, but these documents convey such valuable information on the two revenues that some anticipation may be excused.

A similar exemption went to the Muslim and Christian subjects of the baron Blasco Simon (Eximèn) of Arenós in 1268,[41] and another in 1276 to Arnold of Romaní. Arnold's text ran: "During his lifetime his people, Christians and Saracens alike, are not required to give or pay the tariffs or transit duty or any charge by reason of the things that they will buy or sell or carry, throughout the realm of Valencia, for their own use, unless these shall be [professional] merchandise transported to be marketed."[42] Though not a usual privilege when serious commerce was in question, exemption might attach to the grant of a small market, as in 1280 for all Muslims or Christians coming to do business at the market of Pego. An individual Moor could secure exemption, especially to encourage the craft he represented. This happened in the case of the cloth processor 'Alī in 1273: "Know that we have dispensed 'Alī a Saracen, master of dyes, resident in Játiva, and Muḥammad and Bakr [Bocaron] his sons, along with the silk and gold and other things looking to and necessary for the making of silks, for their whole lives from any tariffs and transit duty and from any of our taxes while they keep residence in Játiva and remain there and pursue their business of dyes." Another dye master, though privileged, explicitly had to pay these taxes;

---

manifesti, set sint inde per totam iurisdictionem nostram tam in mari quam in terra franchi et liberi et immunes."

[40] *Ibid.*, Peter III, Reg. Canc. 39, fol. 330 (July 21, 1277); there is a copy of the same date appended to the original privilege as perg. 1,466 *bis*; "noveritis nos vidisse quoddam instrumentum illustris domini Iacobi inclite recordationis regis Aragonum . . . in quo continebatur quod conceditur episcopo et capitulo valentino quod aliqui homines ipsorum tam christiani quam sarraceni residentes in aliquibus castris seu locis eorum regni Valencie non tenerentur solvere in aliquo loco denarios seu aliquod pedagium, portaticum sive lezdam pro aliquibus mercibus seu rebus quas emerent, venderent seu portarent."

[41] *Ibid.*, James I, Reg. Canc. 15, fol. 87v (March 29, 1268): "non donent pedagium neque lezdam."

[42] *Ibid.*, Reg. Canc. 20, fol. 317 (Feb. 5, 1276): "homines sui tam christiani quam sarraceni in vita sua non teneantur dare vel solvere leçdam vel pedagium nec aliud ius racione rerum suarum quas ement vel vendent aut portabunt per regnum Valencie ad usus suos proprios nisi fuerint res mercatorie quas causa mercandi portent."

'Abd al-'Azīz and his company or household of "twenty Saracen persons, men and women" enjoyed crown protection in his export-import business with Granada and North Africa, "giving tariffs and transit duty and all other taxes due and customary."[43]

Trivial local sales were commonly exempt; by their charter Chivert's residents "are free in all their merchandise and sales and purchases" on or off the roads, on rivers or at sea. The Uxó charter similarly exempted certain vegetables and fruits except for public sale. By the Játiva charter Muslim sellers gave no permit dues or transit duty in all the realm—"pro persona sua"—though professional merchants coming to the area did pay. A special exemption from both tariffs and road duty covered the case of Játiva Muslims purchasing or redeeming slaves from lords, as long as the slaves settled at their town.[44]

Other charters, as at Aldea and the two at Eslida, make no reference to these taxes, but should probably be understood to regulate them in a like sense by custom.[45] Favoring this conjecture is the consideration that Christian settlement charters included the exemption, and in 1239 King James dispensed all Christian settlers coming

[43] *Ibid.*, Peter III, Reg. Canc. 48, fol. 194v (Dec. 8, 1280): "enfranquimus et francos et immunes facimus ab omni lezda seu pedagio que dari debeat in mercato de Pego omnes tam christianos quam sarracenos qui venerint ad dictum mercatum hinc usque ad unum annum." James I, Reg. Canc. 19, fol. 84 (Dec. 21, 1273): "noveritis [nos] infranquisse Aly sarracenum magistrum purpurarum habitantem in Xativa et Machometum et Bocaron filios eius cum serico et aliis rebus omnibus spectantibus et necessariis ad pannos sericos faciendos, in tota vita eorum ab omni lezda et pedagio [et] de alio iure nostro dum in Xativa residentiam fecerint et manebunt et operabunt ibi officio purpurarum." Bocaron may be Bakr on the analogy of "En Bugron" or Bogron, the lord of Constantine in North Africa during King Peter's reign, Abū Bakr b. al-Wazīr (see Muntaner, *Crònica*, chs. 44, 50); Bakr with additive became King Bugron. Peter III, Reg. 40, fol. 63 (Feb. 14, 1277): "te Abdolaçis tinturarium sarracenum et filium tuum Mahometh cum familia vestra ... ac mercibus vestris ipsius familie ... cum illis viginti duabus personis sarracenorum inter homines et mulieres ... in dictis partibus Almerie seu Barberie aut ubicumque volueritis et redire ac stare per totam terram et iurisdictionem nostram ... negociandi et mercandi ... solventibus leçdas et pedagia et iura alia omnia debita et etiam consueta." Reg. Canc. 42, fol. 149v (July 16, 1279), a review and confirmation of the original surrender charter of the Cuart Muslims, on the occasion of a subsequent surrender after rebellion, protected their commercial activities "ipsis solventibus pedagia et alia iura prout consueverunt et continetur in carta."

[44] Aldea, Chivert, Eslida, Játiva, and Uxó charters; "sint franchi in omnibus suis mercedibus [*for* mercibus] et vendicionibus et empcionibus."

[45] *Ibid.*, and the second Eslida Charter.

to crown lands from any "measuring fee, tariffs, road duty, toll, or riverage on any kind of merchandise" carried, bought, sold, or exported. The privilege did not include outsiders and therefore many professionals, so that the two taxes continued to figure prominently in Valencian law.[46]

In 1249 King James reduced tariffs at Alcira, listing the rates on horses, cattle, and other merchandise.[47] Coming soon after Alcira's conquest, the items reflect settled trade patterns of the Muslims, and comprise wheat and wine (exempt unless sold locally), other cereals, rice, raisins, oil, butter, lard, sugar, honey, pepper, figs, almonds, ginger, cinnamon, liquorice, salted fish, beans, sheep, ewes, goats, pigs, cows, bulls, rabbits, work horses, mules, horses arriving to be sold, horses in transit for sale elsewhere (double tariff), tallow, soap, hides of wild animals, rabbit fur, lambskin, sheepskin, goat and cattle hides, plain leather, bright red leather (*cordouanum vermellum*), wool, linen, cotton, cotton thread, gauze, silk, hemp, gold thread, purple dyes (two kinds), indigo (two), vermilion, verdigris (green dye), saffron, plain alum, fuller's earth, gum, mastic, madder, soda ash (for glassmaking), lead, brass, iron, pitch, quicksilver, cumin, caraway seeds, wax, incense, coats, blankets, Moorish cloaks (*alquice de barragans*), dyed cloth, island (Majorcan?) cloth, serge, cotton-linen fustian, fabrics of Rheims, Trier, Narbonne, and probably Alexandria (*bagadell*), other cloth, Muslim slaves, and free Muslim travelers. The only table vegetable is beans (*ffaves*); were these therefore either a kind of fodder or an industrial raw material? The tax applied "whether the aforesaid merchandise and goods

[46] *Aureum opus*, doc. 7, fol. 2 (Nov. 20, 1239): "mensuraticum, lezdam, pedaticum, portaticum, vel ribaticum de quibusvis mercibus . . . quos portaverit vel duci vel vendi fecerit . . . vel inde extraxerit vel extrahi fecerit." See also doc. 4 of Peter III, fol. 29v (Dec. 1, 1283). The *Fori antiqui Valentiae* freed all "residents and settlers" of the capital city's countryside, and other territories of the realm falling under its laws, from local tariff, transit duty, riverage, transit charges, and weight and measure fees, on goods belonging to themselves, whether conducted personally or sent via agent, being sold or exported; imports, exports, or materials handled by a resident as agent for a nonresident fell under the taxes (rub. CXLIV, nos. 1-3). On Christian charters see José M. Font y Rius, "Orígenes del régimen municipal de Cataluña," *AHDE*, XVI (1945), 489-490, and his recent *Cartas de población de Cataluña*, I, introduction.

[47] "Sección de documentos" (Chabás), doc. 55 (March 10, 1249); Miret y Sans prefers the alternative date, 1250 (*Itinerari*, p. 203). *Leuda*, applied to goods in transit, seems to become *portaticum* or rather to include the latter as subform of the more general term.

pass through Alcira or are sold there," but Alcira natives were exempt from all tariffs and transit charges.

Two years later James regulated them for Burriana and Murviedro in the north, and for Játiva and Biar in the south, setting exact fees for the several items.[48] Jews from all of his realms won exemption in the kingdom of Valencia from both tariffs and road duty in 1247 "in any castle or town, and in Burriana or Peñíscola or any other place of the kingdom of Valencia, applicable to their persons or to any animals they personally ride."[49] Since Mudejar charters were not more onerous than those of Christians, the crown probably showed itself equally lenient to Mudejars in this matter. Such privileges encouraged local commerce and transport, as well, the increased prosperity justifying the relatively small tax loss. The circumstance of exemption being sought by individual lords indicates that exemption was considered in some way a privilege rather than a routine concession, however, and that it may have been refused to seignorial lands as often as it was allowed to crown places. Perhaps the classic pattern of the frontier was emerging; as the crown made concessions in order to promote settlement, resultant economic health in town and country left the barons in the unenviable position of having to follow suit tardily.

The general designation (al)moixerifat may have covered all export-import tariffs collected by the crown. A tax list of 1315 defines "the almoixerifat of the custom office of the Christians" of Elche as "the tax that Christian merchants pay on the merchandise they buy and sell"; it totaled, or by permanent arrangement was set at, 1,500 solidi a year. Under the title quirat or (al)quilat, after the money in which authorities originally reckoned it, the Elche Muslims paid some 10,000 solidi a year. At the lesser towns of Aspe, Elda, and Novelda the quirat totals were 2,300, 3,200 and 3,500—considerable sums for their respective places.[50] All these cities belonged to the

---

[48] *Aureum opus*, doc. 40, fols. 12v-13r (Sept. 1, 1251), with lists; reedited in Gual Camarena, *Vocabulario*, doc. 7. Free Muslims quitting the realm at these points each paid half a besant, as against the half-solidus in the Alcira list of 1249.

[49] *Aureum opus*, doc. 24, fol. 11r (June 15, 1247): "quod in aliquo castro [et] villa nec in Burriana vel Panniscola seu quolibet alio loco regni Valentie non donent lezdam portaticum sive pedatgium: nec aliquid aliud, ratione personarum . . . nec etiam ratione bestiarum in quibus personaliter equitaverint."

[50] *Rentas de Aragón*, pp. 109, 112, 121, 123, 124: "lalmoxerifatt de la duana dels christians del dit loch ço es lo dret quels mercaders christians paguen de les merca-

Alicante region acquired long after the death of King James; their orientation toward the Castilian forms that characterized Murcia would explain the borrowing of the Arabic word for customs duties.

Almoixerifat recurs, however, as a general tax on Mudejars throughout the kingdom of Valencia. Had the ad valorem tariffs, or at least those associated with transit, evolved for the Valencian Muslims into a fixed sum, accumulated from individual assessments? Perhaps the aljama had arranged the commutation of this variable tax into a steady annual amount, well below the likely minimum, prorating the total. This would explain why Valencia city's Muslims paid "two pennies for the *almoixerifat*" during the reign of King James, a circumstance disclosed by a confirmation issued toward the end of the century—"just as you were accustomed to pay before the riots" of 1275.[51] The same arrangement prevailed at Játiva, and seems to have been normative. Uxó's community arranged full exemption in 1273: "I grant to you, the Saracens of Uxó, that you cannot be required, ever at any time, to pay anything toward the *almoixerifat* but that you be frank and free"; actually these Mudejars paid King James 400 solidi for the privilege.[52] An alternative explanation of the nature of this fee, to which the mind must remain open, is that the *almoixerifat* was a distinct rental or sales tax, applicable not only to customs (export-import) items but to all or at least

deries que compren et venen cascun any tro a md solídos"; "lo quirat que es dret quels dits moros paguen per les coses que compren et venen." The Aspe total includes as well the *alcahieda*, probably an allied commercial tax. Fernández y González translated the *quirat* as *alquiler* (*Mudejares de Castilla*, p. 271n.), for which the Catalan equivalent would be *lloguer*, the Latin *logerium*, for rental or hire (but see its usage below in Chapter V, n. 98). At Elche in 1315 "el quirat de la duana de la vila Delch ab tendes forns molins banys et calonies" totaled 14,500 solidi after salaries and expenses were deducted; since most of this was the *quirat*, and derived from buying and selling, it had to be either the tariffs, a sales tax, or the bill for lodging merchants with their stock (*Rentas de Aragón*, p. 109).

[51] Roca Traver, "Vida mudéjar," doc. 25 (Sept. 9, 1290), a confirmation of the "sunnam vestram et consuetudines" granted by James I: "duos denarios pro almoxerifatu prout ante barrigium dare consuevistis, tantum videlicet quantum sarraceni morarie nostre Xative nobis donant."

[52] Arch. Crown, James I, Reg. Canc. 21, fol. 148v (May 20, 1273): "concedimus vobis sarracenis de Uxo quod non teneamini unquam . . . dare aliquid racione almoxerifatus set sitis franchi et liberi." The document sets no time limit, since it reflects a previous agreement ("bonum et sincerum intellectum"); for a permanent dispensation it seems a bargain, but for a short respite it suggests a considerable tax.

to larger transactions. The name will find an echo in Chapter VIII, when the *moixerif* himself comes under consideration.[53]

A review of the evidence cited suggests that the average Muslim engaged in amateur, small-scale selling. This impression receives backing from the tithe history of Valencia, which shows the Christian immigrants extensively involved in this very activity.[54] Another insight afforded by comparison of the two communities, with respect to commercial taxes, is that Muslim and Christian appear on a nearly equal footing in the market place. When considered in the light of the Muslims' overwhelming numerical superiority, the circumstance furnishes a valuable index to social relations as well as background for understanding the concern of Christian authorities to maintain a social wall against Islamic influence.

COMMUNITY INCOME TAX AND OTHER *Peites*

Few taxes are so amorphous and irritating to the investigator as the *peita*.[55] Its meaning can vary treacherously, from taxes in general,

---

[53] Catalan [*al*]*moixerifat* derives from the Islamic offices of tax collector, finance minister, and customs man (see Chapter VIII, part 2). The Valencian *almoixerifat* can hardly be a salary or supplementary fee, because the totals are too large; it cannot be all or most taxes, because the totals are too small. In Arch. Crown, James I, Reg. Canc. 37, fol. 64v (May 10, 1273), the *almoixerifat* from Alfandech over the past five years amounted to 4,696 solidi and 9 pence, after expenses; but crown income from Alfandech ranged from 12,000 to 20,000 solidi a year (see Chapter II, n. 10 and text).

[54] Burns, *Crusader Valencia*, I, 151-152.

[55] Latin and Catalan *peita*, Castilian *pecha*, derives from earlier Latin *pacta*. The lowest serfs had been called *peitarii* (Eduardo de Hinojosa, "Mezquinos y exáricos, datos para la historia de la servidumbre en Navarra y Aragón," *Homenaje á Codera*, p. 527). In the early Middle Ages the usual land rents were called *pectum* as well as *censum* or other names; the nonexempt taxpayer in the realms of Aragon was a *pechero* because he paid this *pectum, pecta, pechos,* or *pechas*. The general tax on Jewish communities according to population and wealth was called the *peita*; so was the hundred thousand solidi the Jews of Aragon-Catalonia paid in 1271, though this seems only to mean their total tax revenues (Neuman, *Jews in Spain*, I, 66-67). A series of "hereditates villanorum" formerly belonging to Muslims paid their *peita* at Tudela in Aragon at this time; see "Documentos para el estudio de la reconquista y repoblación del valle del Ebro" [part 2], ed. José M. Lacarra, *EEMCA*, III (1947-1948), doc. 400. Gual Camarena sees the Mudejar *peita* as a house rent in money or kind ("Mudéjares valencianos, aportaciones," p. 191). By the fifteenth century, the Mudejars' *peita ordinaria* in Aragon proper was the lump-sum compromise for all but a handful of specific taxes (Macho y Ortega, "Mudéjares aragoneses," pp. 32, 35). See also Tourtoulon, *Jaime I*, II, 332; and Vicente Traver Tomás, *Antigüedades*

through lump-sum substitutes for a number of taxes, to small charges over and above a basic rent. Etymologically it denotes anything asked (*petita*) and thus relates to *demanda* or *quèstia*. Its most common special sense linked it with *quèstia*, to be considered next, as an arbitrary and resented occasional tax or subsidy. In Valencia it acquired a precise technical sense, besides the meaning conveyed by general formulas, because James I regulated a special *peita* for the colonists in 1252.

A quarter-century previously, when the *wālī* Abū Zayd agreed to pay as truce-tribute a fifth of his revenues or rents, he deducted and retained what King James called *peites*. In the surrender charter at Uxó, *peita* seems to have meant additional or extraordinary levies, its normal or general sense; after settling agricultural rents King James added that "if any *peita* or exaction [*demanda*] is made by me or my agent on the Moors in the territory of Valencia," the local Moors "are then bound to pay" whatever share the crown assigns them toward these general or common "*peites*." At Eslida too exemption from other or perhaps additional "*peita* on your farms" appeared in a context of setting the basic agricultural rent.[56] In a time of crisis extraordinary levies fell alike on Christian and Muslim. Thus

---

de Castellón de la Plana, estudios histórico-monográficos de la villa y su vecindario riqueza y monumentos (Castellón de la Plana, 1958), pp. 17-22 and passim; Macanaz, *Regalías de Aragón*, p. 67 (specific tax on real estate) and p. 79 (taxes in general); García de Valdeavellano, *Instituciones españolas*, pp. 251, 589, 602-603, on the thirteenth-century *peita* or *pecha* of Aragon and Navarre by each householder on his real and movable properties, but by a prorated community sum; Jean-Guy Liauzu, "La condition des musulmans dans l'Aragon chrétien aux xie et xiie siècles," *Hespéris-Tamuda*, ix (1968), 190-191, on movables and real estate; García de Cáceres, *Impuestos de la ciudad de Valencia*, p. 35. Though etymologically allied, *peita* should not be confused with the exceptional loan *petitum*, which by the twelfth century had evolved into a usual tax in Castile (Claudio Sánchez-Albornoz, "Notas para el estudio del 'petitum,'" *Homenaje a Don Ramón Carande* [Madrid, 1963], pp. 383-418). The form does appear at least once, however, in Valencian Mudejar taxes, in Arch. Crown, James I, Reg. Canc. 10, fol. 77r,v (June 16, 1258): "ab omni peyta et questia, pedido, cena. . . ."

[56] *Llibre dels feyts*, ch. 25; *rendes* and *les peytes*; on Gayangos' confusion of these *peytes* with the *zakāt* or charity tax see his notes to the translation by John Forster, *The Chronicle of James I, King of Aragon, Surnamed the Conqueror* (2 vols. [London, 1883], p. 49n.). Uxó Charter: "si per nos o procurado nostre es feyta alguna peyta o demanda als moros, los quals son en la tinença de Valencia, ladonchs sien tenguts pagar ço que per nos seran taxats en les peytes." Eslida Charter: "et non faciant aliquam frangam vel hostem, nec peitam super hereditatibus excepta decima tritici, ordei, panicii. . . ."

Mudejars paid a considerable amount to help finance King James's abortive crusade to the Holy Land. Descriptive lists of taxes for payment or exemption often included *peita*. Sometimes, in singular or plural, it was among the valued revenues specifically retained by the crown when making a grant.[57] *Peita* was included in the taxes conveyed in 1300 to "Constance, formerly empress of the Greeks," when she was granted the Uxó and Pego regions.[58]

Used technically, *peita* could mean an annual levy or direct tribute on all property holders, Christian or Muslim, by a specified schedule —in short, a community income tax, assessed according to the size and wealth of the group. As a regular exaction from Jewish communities alone, paid in installments on St. John's Day and at Christmas, it brought 50,000 solidi both in Catalonia and Aragon, and 25,000 in Valencia (6,500 in 1271 by an exemption).[59] The first document regulating and perhaps initiating the general *peita* for Valencia dates from early 1252. It provided for the election of two or more substantial citizens from each parish; they assessed each Christian householder's movable and immovable properties, not excluding the knights and Mendicant friars, but by law concealed their conclusions even from the king. They took a base of five

---

[57] Arch. Crown, James I, Reg. Canc. 10, fol. 40 (Feb. 22, 1257): "a christianis et sarracenis . . . excepta cena et peita," for four years. Fol. 140 (May 29, 1259): "çofram et peitas ac cenas quando nos iactabimus eas in dicto loco . . . et omnia a[lia] iura nostra que a christianis et sarracenis . . . recipere debemus." Reg. Canc. 9, fol. 39r,v (Sept. 19, 1257): "cum questiis, peytis, cenis, donis, servitiis, ademprivis," a long list involving also Moors. The Holy Land tax is below, p. 308. Joseph F. O'Callaghan has studied the levying of extraordinary taxes or subsidies in contemporary Castile (1252-1284), instructive also for the realms of Aragon, "The Cortes and Royal Taxation during the Reign of Alfonso X of Castile," *Traditio*, XXVII (1971), 379-398. For the corresponding contribution in Islamic lands, see Siddiqi, *Public Finance in Islam*, p. 13.

[58] Francisco Martínez y Martínez, "Pego, su población y primeros señores," *Congrés I*, doc. on pp. 68-69 (Nov. 17, 1300).

[59] Neuman, *Jews in Spain*, II, 66-68. García de Valdeavellano describes the tax in Aragon and Navarre as dating at least from the end of the twelfth century, paid in cash by family heads for both movables and immovables, and sometimes lumped by compromise into a fixed sum on a given community; called *peyta* or *pecha*, it fell on Moors as well as Christians in Aragon proper but not on nobles, clergy, or big towns like Zaragoza and Huesca (*Instituciones españolas*, p. 602). García y García analyzed the tax as it fell on Christian settlements in northern Valencia; he found it the most general and often named, going to the king or by alienation to a lord, with clerics, nobles, and Jews exempt; each municipality or rural equivalent kept its *Llibre de peyta*, taking inventory and assessing the movables and immovables of each resident (*Estado económico-social de Castellón*, pp. 39-40).

percent of the assessment—one solidus per pound or per twenty solidi assessed—and this they taxed at ten percent. The terms raised discontent, and soon both nobles and clergy won exemption.[60] The *peita*, though easily confused with the besant, apparently differed for Mudejars; the two can stand side by side on the same list.[61] Even then doubt persists, since one might argue that the first taxes in the list represented inclusive generalities.

A 1257 list of places responsible for something ambiguously called *peita* constitutes the earliest surviving systematic tax record for Valencia's Mudejars. It included no less than thirty communities, though it omitted many others, such as Biar, Játiva, Murviedro, and Pego. The crown required from the aljamas over 7,000 besants or more than 26,000 solidi. It remitted 4,000 besants, well over half, either to the lord as at Guadalest, or to the Mudejar community itself as at Alfandech. Alfandech had to give 800 besants; Uxó and Carbonera 600 each; Guadalest 500; and Cortes, Mogente, Rugat, and Tous with Tárbena 400 each. Lesser collections ranged from 100 to 300; Eslida gave 300 but Valencia city only 200 (with 50 of these remitted). Important towns like Alcira and Segorbe paid a mere 100 apiece, while smaller places like Jijona and Dues Aigües (Dos Aguas) each managed 300.[62] Perhaps the imbalance reflects some expulsion from cities during the recent revolt, with a corresponding importance attaching to the countryside.

It is difficult to analyze these uneven shares with any confidence. A similar imposition of *peites* two years earlier cannot be correlated

[60] *Aureum opus*, doc. 43, fols. 14v-15, also in *Colección diplomática*, doc. 413, and see *Itinerari*, p. 219 (Feb. 12, 1252). The pound (*lliura*, Latin *libra*) was a ghost money containing 20 solidi or 240 pennies. At Ricla in Aragon in 1294, Christians and Moors paid together; besides the public utilities and fines, a listing gives "la peyta et el tributo de los christianos et de los moros los quales peytan ensenble" at 2,000 solidi (*Rentas de Aragón*, p. 246), a somewhat ambiguous description. Asso treats of the tax and notes that the Mudejars were never exempt except by some special privilege (*Economía política de Aragón*, p. 293).

[61] Both appear, for example, in a list of 1274 in Arch. Crown, James I, Reg. Canc. 19, fol. 124 (April 16, 1274): "ab omni scilicet peyta sive questia, bisanciis, et tributo. . . ."

[62] *Ibid.*, Reg. Canc. 8, fol. 36v (Nov. 24, 1257). See also "Primera contribución conocida impuesta a los moros del reino de Valencia," ed. Roque Chabás y Lloréns, *El archivo*, 1 (1886), 255-256; Chabás gives the date as September. The document begins: "iactavit dominus rex has peytas sarracenis civitatis et regni [Valencie] quos [co]lligit Petrus Guillelmi portarius suus"—the name of the realm is trimmed away, and "colligit" is crippled by a hole.

with these in its pattern or details; this earlier document, though not marked expressly as Mudejar, could hardly have included many Christians yet for places like Uxó or Buñol.[63] Either list may represent a mixture of assorted taxes, or both could be extraordinary levies, perhaps in connection with Valencia's Mudejar rebellions. The loose usage of *peita* for taxes in general does appear in an immunity granted by King Peter in 1278; it attracted Muslim settlers to Valencia city's aljama by promising a year's freedom "from all *peita* that they are required to give."[64] This was surely a general tax exemption; dismissal of the community levy alone, especially for a single year, would hardly have constituted an attraction, nor would it have accorded with the practice, found in similar documents, of granting sweeping exemptions.

On the other hand, a tax lease of 1263 to the Masones aljama in Aragon proper employed the term in its specific sense, exempting five other taxes by name, reserving five more by name, and speaking of the rest only generally; the lease defined the *peita* also as among tributes "that you have been accustomed to give us up to this date."[65] The ambiguity carries over into the term's verbal form. At Cocentaina in 1264 King James allowed various villages "to *peita*" with the main town; did this involve them in the community levy of Cocentaina or in its total tax collectory? Muntaner employs the verb to mean taxes in general, telling how a North African ruler sent an army to enforce tax collection—"to make [those] lands *paytar*."[66]

At Gandía in 1258 King James assigned a pension to a Muslim functionary, to be drawn from the *peita* at Beniopa, noting its annual collection there. "We grant you Muḥammad of Baymen [Bairén, or b. Yumn?] Saracen messenger of Gandía, as a pension all the years of your life, thirty solidi of Valencia, which we assign to be had and collected from the *peita* that the Saracens of Beniopa give us; and you are to receive this every year."[67] The *peita* of 200 solidi claimed

---

[63] Arch. Crown, James I, Reg. Canc. 8, fol. 21v (Nov. 26, 1255): "has peytas," sums much larger than in the 1257 document, from 30,000 solidi down to 400.

[64] *Ibid.*, Peter III, Reg. Canc. 40, fol. 102 (May 5, 1278): "ab omni peyta quam nobis teneantur dare."

[65] Masones Privilege: "que nobis dare consuevistis usque in hunc diem."

[66] Arch. Crown, James I, Reg. Canc. 13, fol. 236 (Nov. 6, 1264): "simul vobiscum peytare in omnibus." Muntaner, *Crònica,* ch. 30: "per fer paytar les terres."

[67] Arch. Crown, James I, Reg. Canc. 9, fol. 29v (May 4, 1258): "concedimus tibi Mahometo de Bayman anagario sarraceno de Gandia diebus omnibus vite tue tri-

from the Muslims of Navarrés formed the subject of a crown order in 1259.[68] A salary payment of 1266 referred to the next *peites* on Alcira and all Valencia below the Júcar River, from both Christians and Muslims.[69] Muslims of Biar gave the tax on a list of 1258, those of Chulilla on a list of 1270, and those along the Alcira irrigation canal on a list of 1274. To meet expenses contracted during the recent Murcian war, King Peter in 1267 drew upon the *peita* given by Muslims throughout the kingdom of Valencia.[70] The entrepreneur 'Alī al-Lūrī (Ali Allauri) had to contribute until his exemption in 1273.[71]

It would be easy to multiply examples of this ambiguously named tax, but in few cases can one be sure it is not a synonym for a tax or taxes quite other than community income tax. Moreover, *peita* lists usually do not distinguish between Christian and Mudejar contributors, or reveal whether Mudejars were involved in a given *peita*. The most practical use for such a list is for setting categories of cities, and there are too many hidden variables, as well as vanished contexts, to inspire confidence in the results. Thus one can rank Játiva, at 20,000 solidi, as the most tax-productive city after the capital in a *peita* list of 1272, with Alcira, Morella, and Murviedro bringing in

---

ginta solidos regalium Valencie censuales quos assignamus habendos et percipiendos super peyta quam sarraceni de Beniopa nobis donant, et ipsos recipias quolibet anno." *Itinerari* (p. 274) incorrectly includes Anagari as part of his name. De Baymen is more likely to indicate a place (e.g. Bairén) than a family name; an apparently related document from Peter's reign, however, suggests that Muḥammad b. Yumn or a similar form is here grossly distorted (see below, p. 238). Catalan *enagar* or *anagar* meant "to initiate" or "incite," *enaiguar* "to put in water" or "to water," so the Latin *anagarius* might perhaps stand for a crown or irrigation office.

[68] Arch. Crown, James I, Reg. Canc. 10, fol. 108v (April 8, 1259): "quas iactaveramus pro peyta."

[69] *Ibid.*, Reg. Canc. 14, fol. 82 (June 26, 1266): "super primis peytis quas iactabimus."

[70] *Ibid.*, Reg. Canc. 10, fol. 103v (June 16, 1258): "peitas," first in a list of eight taxes; Reg. Canc. 16, fol. 229v (Jan. 28, 1270): "questia sive peita," *sive* acting as disjunctive; Reg. Canc. 10, fol. 124 (April 16, 1274): "ab omni scilicet peyta sive questia"; Reg. Canc. 14, fol. 83v (Jan. 16, 1267): "in peytis sarracenorum."

[71] *Ibid.*, Reg. Canc. 19, fol. 53 (Sept. 7, 1273): "ab omni scilicet peita sive questia, cena. . . ." The text supports an interpretation either of general reference to tax, followed by specifics, or a list of specific taxes, including *peita*. Since "Alaor[us]" had been the Spanish Christians' version of al-Ḥurr (b. ar-Raḥmān), third governor (715-718) after the invasion, Allaurus here may reasonably be conjectured as a related form; on balance, al-Lūrī may seem preferable.

8 to 9,000 or less than half of Játiva's return. Burriana, Cocentaina, Gandía, Onda, Onteniente, and Segorbe come next with 2 to 3,000. Alcoy, Alpuente, Cullera, Liria and Peñíscola follow, in a 1 to 1,500 solidi bracket. Ademuz and Castielfabib have 800 each; Albaida, Jijona, and Luchente 500; and Bocairente and Castalla 200. The Jews gave separately: 10,000 from Valencia, 2,000 from Murviedro, 1,000 from combined Burriana-Onda-Segorbe, 1,000 from Játiva, 700 from Gandía, and 300 from Alcira. The Mudejars may be included in each city district's total, or they may have had their own collectors, with the results englobed in more general listings of Mudejar taxes.[72]

At first glance *quèstia* (Latin *questia* or *questa*) seems to assimilate to *peita*. It derives from the equally general Latin verb *quaero*, appears in some contexts to stand for regalian taxes as such or for an undefined range of such taxes, turns up frequently in the paired phrase "peita et questia," and on occasion designates any tax demand.[73] It might even be interpreted as the genus—direct taxes irregularly or arbitrarily imposed on group or individual—to which *peita* was a species or for which *peita* was a more acceptable substi-

[72] *Ibid.*, Reg. Canc. 18, fols. 47v-48 (March 1, 1272): "has peytas."

[73] Latin forms include *questa, questia, quistia, quities, chesta,* and *kesta.* See Rodón Binué, *Lenguaje técnico del feudalismo*, pp. ix, 212, with allied *forcia* on pp. 121-122, *tolta* on pp. 244-245, and *usaticus* on p. 251. García de Valdeavellano, like most authors, omits consideration of *quèstia* under that name, nor does he discuss it in connection with Catalonia's classic six *mals usos* (*Instituciones españolas*, pp. 253-254, 360-361). Ferraz Penelas in his *Maestre racional y la hacienda foral valenciana*, p. 33, confines it to royal towns. Muntaner uses *quèstia* in a relatively general sense for taxes (*Crònica*, ch. 212: "e pot fer questes"); Ferran Soldevila similarly speaks of "las quisties o tributaciones anuales de los municipios" (*Historia de España*, 8 vols. [Barcelona, 1952-1954], II, 81). The parliament of Lérida in 1214, dispensing from "omnibus questiis" for a time, allowed "semel omni anno moderate questie" on certain crown lands (*Cortes de los antiguos reinos de Aragón y de Valencia y principado de Cataluña*, 26 vols. in 27 [Madrid, 1896-1922], I, part 1, p. 95). At Burriana in 1233 King James encouraged Christian settlement by abolishing *peita, questia, tolta, forcia,* moneyage, measurage, bovage, and other resented taxes (*Itinerari*, p. 108; other examples on pp. 73, 91). Perhaps an example of *quèstia* as occasional tallage is the contribution required toward the 30,000 solidi salary of the Valencian procurator or lieutenant in 1291, the bastard son of King James; a series of six letters to each "*amín* and aljama" in one Valencian region required 750 solidi from Játiva, 550 from Gallinera with Ebo, 550 from Vall de Laguart, 750 from Jalón, 800 from Tárbena, and 950 from Guadalest, "alias mandamus eundem [Bernardum Çabaterii] quod vos et bona vestra inde pignorari faciat et compelli" (Arch. Crown, Alfonso III, Reg. Canc. 85, fol. 131v [April 1, 1291]).

tute. *Quèstia* has a darker side. Its more normal meaning of arbitrary forced exaction placed it in the list of "bad customs" resented by the king's subjects and somewhat embarrassing to the king himself.[74] Charters or privileges that record it are often waiving it or establishing controls. It can take on the color of a voluntary donation, appear as a community levy prorated on individuals, or refer to provision gifts like chickens or prepared ham.

The Knights Hospitaller required *quèstia* from all their Mudejar subjects, as a tithe adjustment in 1243 reveals, levying it "in matters just or unjust."[75] The *quèstia* paid at Gandía, Alcira, and other crown places held by Prince Peter became a subject of dispute in 1274 when the knights who had acquired estates in those areas petitioned King James for tax relief; the king's decision removed this and other regalian taxes not paid by Muslim tenants of knights on crown lands elsewhere in the Valencia kingdom.[76] Thus it appears that crown lands, when alienated by alod or subinfeudation to knights,

---

[74] *Quèstia* comes under consideration in many contemporary Catalan charters far more frequently and less ambiguously than *peita*; see *Cartas de población de Cataluña*, 1, doc. 255 (1231): "questia que eis fieri consueverant in civadis, in pernis, gallinis"; doc. 260 (1233): "quities, forces, acaptes, . . . e altres mals usos"; doc. 261 (1233); doc. 262 (1234): "de questiis, toltis, forciis, de intestis et exorquis"; doc. 266 (1236); doc. 269 (1237); doc. 270 (1237): "neque opus neque ulla mala usatica neque questiam nisi quod dicitur superius"; doc. 290 (1248): "[de] consuetudinibus eisdem indebite positis . . . [nec] teneamini de aliquo facere questiam"; doc. 292 (1250); doc. 299 (1255): "de cugucia et exorquia et intestia et quistia, tolta, forcia"; doc. 314 (1265): "omnes questas, toltas, et rapinas, et omnes iniurias"; doc. 315 (1267) no *quèstia* "nisi in casibus a iure concessis"; doc. 317 (1269); docs. 325 and 326 (1274); doc. 332 (1278): "a questia, tolta, força, et opera"; doc. 325 (1279): "de omni questia et tolta et de omni servitio compulso domino exhibendo"; doc. 366 (1302): "teneamini contribuere in questiis cum hominibus de Seros, item concedimus quod cum questia iactabitur seu imponetur, . . . duo vestrum . . . interesse possint iactationi et computacioni." This sampling compensates for the lack of information on the elusive *quèstia*, though Valencian documents more frequently follow the formula of doc. 321 (1272): "questia, cena, et qualibet alia exactione regali," frequently pairing with *peita*; see the examples above in nn. 70, 71.

[75] Arch. Cat., perg. 4,104 (Oct. 29, 1243): "quod redditus omnes sive proventus quos dicti fratres a sarracenis percipiunt decimentur, excepta questia sive exaccione in iusta vel iniustis." See also Hipólito de Samper, *Montesa ilustrada. Origen, fundación, principios, institutos . . . de la real, ínclita y nobilissima religión militar de N. S. Santa María de Montesa y San George de Alfama*, 2 vols. (Valencia, 1669), part 4, pp. 828-832 (1243).

[76] Arch. Crown, James I, Reg. Canc. 19, fol. 107 (Feb. 23, 1274): "questias, cenas, et alias exacciones regales . . . aliquid ratione questie, cene, seu alterius exactionis regalis."

commonly ceased to pay many regalian taxes. Outside of crown lands, and after revocation within crown lands, this tax, like the besant, may finally have gone to the landlord.

At Almonacid in 1277 King Peter remitted the Mudejars' *quèstia* for a year. *Quèstia* stood among the "regalian exactions" paid by Muslims at Chulilla in 1270[77] and at Biar until 1267.[78] It continued to hold a place in the usual list of Mudejar taxes in Valencia two centuries later.[79] Since by its very nature it assumed variant forms or specific names in its occasional visitations, it is rarely encountered under its proper title outside of formulas or tax lists. The Islamic world was no stranger to such "bad usages" or arbitrary demands and confiscations;[80] probably the transition from the troubled decades of Almohad decline to the stable and improving tax milieu of the Catalan crusaders spelled progress for the Muslims in this particular respect.

A final tax remains to be considered here. It resembles the *peita* so closely as to raise suspicions that it is a synonym, until one finds both words separately in the same revenue lists. This is the *almagran* or *almagram*. From the Arabic for "tribute," its true nature is not easy to establish. In 1780 the historian Villarroya consulted "the most learned men of Spain" as to its specific meaning, with no success. The monumental Catalan lexicon by Alcover in our own day has penetrated no farther into the mystery, repeating earlier descriptions of it as "a tax Moors paid" annually.[81] The revenue history of later Islamic Granada, and of Mudejar rents in that area when it was conquered, compounds the difficulties of investigation. There the

[77] *Ibid.*, Reg. Canc. 16, fol. 229v (Jan. 28, 1270): "ab omni scilicet questia sive peita, çofra . . . ," a life exemption. For Almonacid see Peter III, Reg. Canc. 39, fol. 151 (Jan. 20, 1277): "remittimus vobis universis et singulis sarracenis de Al-moneçir et alqueriis et terminis suis omnes questias et alia iura"; Almonacid's surrender notice follows on this folio.

[78] *Ibid.*, James I, Reg. Canc. 15, fol. 84 (March 1267): "bisancios, peitas sive questias, atque cenas"; the list includes other taxes both before and after these, making one series, so that besants and *peites* appear as obviously distinct taxes.

[79] *Formularium diversorum contractuum*, fol. xxviiii-xxx: "questis."

[80] Rabie, *Financial System of Egypt*, ch. 3, part H; Siddiqi, *Public Finance in Islam*, p. 13; Lévi-Provençal, *España musulmana*, v, 21-22.

[81] Joseph Villarroya, *Real maestrazgo de Montesa, tratado de todos los derechos, bienes y pertenencias del patrimonio y maestrazgo de la real y militar orden de Montesa y S. Jorge de Alfama*, 2 vols. (Valencia, 1787), 1, 56-57n. See also Alcover, *Diccionari català-valencià-balear*, 1, 130. The Dozy and Engelmann *Glossaire* gives it only as a tax (p. 152).

magran or *magraner* was a ten percent import or sales tax paid by the consumer. It also became confused with the *almaguana* and sometimes stood for that tax, a two and a half percent ad valorem charge on real property; Granadans regarded this as illegal, an arbitrary imposition devised outside the framework of classical or even necr̃ssary taxes in Islam.[82] Neither of these meanings applied in Valencia.

The Valencian *almagran* was akin to the *peita*, insofar as it involved every householder, but it differed in that it fell on the land alone and within water communities only. It was more closely allied to the shares-of-produce, the "tribute" examined immediately below, since it substituted for these on some huerta properties. *Almagran* might seem to assimilate to agrarian rents with difficulty; at Biar the civil tenth appears alongside it, as do "the tributes or rents" at Mudejar Tárbena and Jalón, and in a general notarial formulary for Valencia "the agrarian rents."[83] From our meager information on its nature in Valencia, however, the equivalence of this species of *peita* with the tribute shares seems clear.

It fell upon sections or units of land. At Pego in 1269 it was entered as *"almagran* of the land sections of Pego . . . [on] 930 sections, assessed at one besant for each section, which equal 930 besants" or over 3,000 solidi. Since the besant or household capitation appears in this list as bringing only 53 besants, *almagran* was not only the largest single revenue at Pego but almost twenty times larger than the important besant. This same set of accounts, when compared to those of the previous year on a preceding folio, reveals that the complicated entry under *almagran* in 1269 is almost the same entry one finds under the rubric *rendas de Pego* in 1270; *almagran* therefore is a synonym for agricultural rents or for some portion of them.[84]

---

[82] M. A. Ladero Quesada, "Dos temas de la Granada nazarí," in *Estudios sobre la sociedad castellana en la baja edad media,* ed. Salvador de Moxó (Madrid, 1969), 324-325; and Ladero Quesada, *Granada, historia de un país islámico (1232-1571)* (Madrid, 1969), pp. 52-53. See also Álvarez de Cienfuegos, "Régimen tributario del reino mudéjar de Granada," pp. 104, 108. Goitein finds that the word was used for any very special tax or surcharge, whatever its nature.

[83] The formulary is in n. 79, Biar in n. 85 (1263), and Tárbena and Jalón in n. 86 (1268).

[84] Arch. Crown, James I, Reg. Canc. 35, fol. 4 (1269): "almagram de las alfabas de Pego . . . et axi romane[n] dccccxxx alfabas comtadas a i besant cada alfaba, que fan dccccxxx besants." An *alfaba* varied from two to five or more *tafullas* of land (Castilian *tahulla*), according to its productivity; a *tafulla,* still used in parts of

King James included *almagran* when farming the Mudejar revenues of Biar to its aljama in 1258, in a four-year renewal in 1263, in a two-year renewal in 1267, and in an exemption in 1270.[85] Cárcer, Sumacárcel, and Tous included it in their revenue lists of 1257 and 1258, Tárbena and Jalón in a 1268 list, Alcalá and Gallinera in a revenue farming of 1270, and Chulilla in an exemption that same year.[86] Pego listed it in 1258 and again in 1259. Both the Alfandech and the Pego valleys recorded it among regular regalian taxes in 1275. It appears at Serra, Torres Torres, and Polop in 1271, near Jalón in 1272, at Vallada in 1274, and at Luchente in 1277.[87]

In the transference of Sagra to Raymond of Villanueva in 1296 it figured prominently among the revenues. A very late charter, at Chelva in 1370, called it "the *almagra* of the land [*tierras*]," setting it at 800 solidi for the community. In a list of 1315 for four towns below the Júcar—Elche, Elda, Aspe, and Novelda—the "almagera" or assessment stood in first place for three of the four places and ranked as by far the largest revenue. At Aspe it provided a third of the Mudejar taxes, at Novelda two-thirds of the total, and at Elda three-fourths; at Elche no tax approached its volume, though the *alfarda*, water, and butchery charges together equaled two-thirds of the huge *almagran*.[88]

Valencia, was one-sixth of a fanecate (*faneca*). Fol. 3v: "rendas de Pego son las alfabas por todos dccclxi alfaba et media . . . que munta i besant per quodam alfaba que son dccci besants."

[85] *Ibid.*, Reg. Canc. 10, fol. 103v (June 16, 1258): "almagran." Reg. Canc. 12, fol. 119 (Oct. 1, 1263): "almagrams" (*sic*). Reg. Canc. 15, fol. 84 (March 1267): "almagram." Reg. Canc. 16, fol. 229v (Jan. 28, 1270): "almagrama." *Itinerari*, pp. 275-276, publishes part of the first document.

[86] Arch. Crown, James I, Reg. Canc. 10, fol. 40 (Feb. 22, 1257): "et cum almagram et omnibus aliis redditibus." Fol. 64 (April 30, 1258): "cum almagram et cum aliis redditibus." Reg. Canc. 15, fol. 105v (May 4, 1268): "almagramis." Reg. Canc. 16, fol. 193 (May 1, 1270): "almagramam et calonias et alia iura nostra." Fol. 229v (Jan. 28, 1270): "ab . . . almagrama."

[87] *Ibid.*, Reg. Canc. 10, fol. 66 (May 14, 1258): "et cum almagram." Reg. Canc. 20, fol. 245 (April 27, 1275), a form document circulated to both valleys. Reg. Canc. 16, fol. 254v (June 6, 1271): "almagranis, questiis, et cenis." Reg. Canc. 21, fol. 47 (July 4, 1272): "çofris, alfardis, bisanciis, et almagranis." Peter III, Reg. Canc. 40, fol. 66v (Feb. 19, 1277): "et almagranis." The "law of *magram*" is also in the Alfandech Charter, Arch. Crown, James II, Reg. Canc. 196, fol. 164 (1277), Spanish translation in José Toledo Girau, *El castell i la vall d'Alfandech de Marinyèn des de sa reconquesta per Jaume I, fins la fundació del monestir de Valldigna per Jaume II* (Castellón de la Plana, 1936), pp. 75-76.

[88] Arch. Nac. Madrid, Ords. milits., Arch. Uclés, caj. 307, no. 1 (Sept. 26, 1296):

The *almagran* played a prominent role in the revenues of Valldigna, the region of Valencia just north of Gandía. The Moors here paid a proportional part of the tax, in money rather than kind, and were thus exempt from giving shares of produce as rent. King James did exempt a property of a financial aide, the Jew Samuel b. Vives, or rather his tenant, with "a privilege that he not pay *magram* for all his life" on a half jovate of irrigated farmland here. The valley's Register of Magran Tax (*Cappatró del dret de magram*) recorded the amount owed by each unit of land. Christians paid no *almagran* here at first, since they had no access to the traditionally apportioned water except indirectly as landlords. After a mid-fourteenth-century revolt, the status of these Mudejars came under review and shares were imposed as rent upon the irrigated land, running between a third and a fourth of the produce. The *almagran* itself continued but may have diminished in volume and importance, becoming "a small cash sum," long fixed, for holding the best land.[89]

In Valencian records generally, the *almagran* is distinguished by the infrequency of its appearance, the considerable volume it represents whenever a sum is expressed, the subordinate role indicated by its position within lists, and a lack of information. Though only Muslims paid under this Arabicized name of "tribute," their situation was not thereby marked off from that of Christian taxpayers. Huerta land with access to irrigation water naturally paid higher taxes. Its form here represented for the Muslim continuity with his Valencian past.

Tribute as Agrarian Rents

Muslims lived in Christian Valencia "sub tributo," to the modern ear a circumstanced sign of subjection. The term, though it also bore

---

with "almagraniis." Chelva Charter: "por almagran de las tierras." *Rentas de Aragón*, p. 111: "lalmagera quels dits moros paguen" (14,500 solidi at Elche); p. 120 (12,895 Barcelona solidi at Elda); p. 122 (12,173 at Novelda); pp. 123-124 (4,600 for Aspe). The *alfarda* is erroneously copied at 57,000 for Elche instead of 7,000; on this and the relation with the water entry, see below, Chapter V, part 1. The later lists include 5,000 solidi for "delmes" (at Elche, where the *almagran* totaled 20,000), and elsewhere "delmes de la alfarra"; the *almaçera* service charge on oil-presses appears independently in the lists.

[89] José Toledo Girau, *Las aguas de riego en la historia de Valldigna* (Castellón, 1958), pp. 10-15, 20, 22, 36; definitions on pp. 10, 12.

that connotation, had long stood for ordinary agrarian rents. *Tributum* in early medieval charters was synonymous with *censum*, and a *tributarius* was a taxpayer. This meaning had evolved from the conjunction of the ancient territorial tax or tribute with the private agrarian rents.[90] Since Muslim provinces did pay tribute to powerful Christian neighbors, however, and, since Mudejars did live in a peripheral subsociety, the agrarian rents of Valencia's Moors probably shared the character of tribute as subjection. When the Moors of non-Valencian Masones won exemption from "all tenth and tribute," they may have shed a specific tribute like the besant, though the pairing of agricultural rents makes this interpretation dubious.[91] When Mudejar settlers along the Alcira irrigation system held exemption from specified taxes, on the other hand, "tribute" stood in their list without qualification.[92]

A Christian ruler, after overawing an Islamic province, usually demanded a fraction of state revenues as protection money or tribute, called *paria(s)*.[93] At Valencia this had long been a fifth, delivered to

[90] García de Valdeavellano, *Instituciones españolas*, pp. 251, 348, 352, 353, 590. The final quote is from James Casey, "Moriscos and the Depopulation of Valencia," *Past and Present*, L (1971), 33.

[91] Masones Privilege: "et ab omni decima et tributo." For Valencia later in the century Alfonso III seems to use tribute for taxes in general, for example complaining that "quidam sarraceni Algeçire contradicunt et denegant solvere tributa et quedam alia iura que nobis solvere consueverunt et tenentur" (Arch. Crown, Alfonso III, Reg. Canc. 81, fol. 171v [Aug. 26, 1290]). These are probably the same converts from Islam at Alcira who kept their "Saracen" lands, "non solvendo inde censum seu aliquod tributum pro eisdem," to Alfonso's distress (fol. 144 [Aug. 4, 1290]). Inviting fugitives back to Játiva after a revolt, Alfonso offered "domos, ortos, et alia sensualia nostra, sub eo scilicet sensu et tributo quod [*sic*] dabantur et solvantur pro ipsis domibus et sensualibus . . . et solvant tributa que consueverunt solvere tempore dicti domini regis Iacobi et postmodum usque nunc" (Reg. Canc. 75, fol. 5 [May 3, 1287]).

[92] Arch. Crown, James I, Reg. Canc. 19, fol. 124 (April 16, 1274). At Zaragoza in 1294 Mudejar shop rents were called "tributo de tiendas"; at Aranda it applied to mill and oven fees ("tributo de los fornos de los moros . . . tributo de tres molinos que tienen los moros"), as well as to the fourth of agricultural income paid the crown ("el tributo de las heredades de los ditos moros"); see *Rentas de Aragón*, pp. 236, 249, 250.

[93] On the etymology, meaning, and forms of the *paria* or *palia* (Castilian *parias*), usually employed in the plural, see Rodón Binué, *Lenguaje técnico del feudalismo*, p. 188 and Ramón Menéndez Pidal, *La España del Cid*, 4th edn. rev., 2 vols. (Madrid, 1947), I, 76-78, 199, 355, 508-510; the Cid paid the fifth to the king of Castile and received fifths from his troops. See too the fifth paid in the first decade

Aragon by the disconcerted Almohad *wālī* from the time of the calamitous battle at Las Navas; here the *paria* assimilated to the *quinta*, the fifth of booty given to one's overlord after raid or battle, a custom adopted from the Muslims. King James boasted that as a child-king he had received "the fifths of Valencia and Murcia." Later Abū Zayd offered James a fifth of Valencia's revenues if he would desist from his raids, a sum the Christian king estimated at a hundred thousand besants, excluding income from the Murcian region; Zayyān in 1238 proposed a compromise of half that amount, or 50,000 besants, to forestall the crusade threatening Valencia.[94] The treaty of 1229 between Abū Zayd and James promised the king one-fourth the revenues of places he could conquer; the treaty of 1236 assigned him a fifth of what Abū Zayd might acquire by truce. In 1245 James released his ally from these fourths on revenues from his castles and towns.[95]

The tribute of the individual Mudejar, where the term does not designate the besant or loosely the tax obligations as such, was his agricultural rents. Both for Muslim and Christian these comprised the primary acknowledgment of direct overlordship. From a quantitative viewpoint, they were the most significant of Mudejar revenues. Giménez Soler believes that their variations also marked "the only real distinction" between Christian and Muslim.[96] Since freedom from tithes and firstfruits more than compensated for the burden of the besant, any difference in economic status between the two populations must be sought in agricultural rents and charges.

---

of the fourteenth century by the Catalan mercenary armies to their leaders, in Muntaner, *Crònica*, ch. 225. Menéndez Pidal makes analogies with Cortés and Pizarro, and indicates the Koranic origins. Siddiqi, *Public Finance in Islam*, takes up the fifth on booty (pp. 10ff.); see also Frede Løkkegaard, "Fay'," *EI²*, ii, 869-870, and n. 112 below.

[94] *Llibre dels feyts*, chs. 25, 275. On Mudejar practice generally see Janer, *Moriscos de España*, p. 13; and Pilar Loscertales, "Exáricos," *Diccionario de historia de España*, ed. Germán Bleiberg, 2d edn. rev., 3 vols. (Madrid, 1968-1969), i, 1,059-1,060. Hinojosa, "Mezquinos y exáricos," pp. 523-531.

[95] Roque Chabás y Llorens has the treaties of 1229 and 1236 with translations in his "Çeit Abu Çeit," *El archivo*, v (1891), 147-151, 153-156. See also *Colección diplomática*, docs. 68 (1229), 151 (1236), and 279 (1245).

[96] Andrés Giménez Soler, *La edad media en la corona de Aragón*, 2d edn. rev. (Barcelona, 1944), p. 294: "la única distinción" was the slightly higher fifth, eighth, or ninth; "fuera de esto su condición era idéntica" with that of Christians.

Spanish Muslims had tended to be hostile to the idea of a fixed agricultural rent, so that it rarely prevailed under Islamic rulers. The common practice had been to give the landlord a set percentage of the yield, most often a fifth. In Islamic Spain the sharecropper might pay anything from a tenth to a fifth and sometimes as much as three-fourths, depending on the kind of crops, local custom, and the farmer's status. In theory a proprietor-farmer surrendered a tenth, which might diminish to a twentieth on artificially watered or difficult land. The true sharecropper in Islamic Spain would have been a member of the rural proletariat who contracted to work a piece of land for anything from three-fourths to a fourth of the profits. Such a man was probably not the norm, however, in a region of multiple individual farms like the Valencian huerta. His title, "sharer," and a contract analogous to his, had spread among the fairly independent proprietor-tenants both of Islamic and Christian Spain. Hinojosa's conclusion that the "sharer" was equivalently a serf on his landlord's property does not accord with the facts. The question of agricultural rents has been complicated by such interpretations of Islamic Spain's *ash-sharīk* and his Mudejar counterpart and namesake the *exaricus*.

In crusader Valencia the most typical *exaricus* was a proprietor-tenant, a permanent resident essentially independent and enjoying limited ownership rights, including the right to sell his property—in effect a small farmer under hereditary lease but not formally bound to the land, who owed his landlord a share of profits according to traditional tenant obligations. Beyond this base meaning or common usage, *exaricus* constituted a relative or analogous concept, embodying a proportional rather than a univocal meaning; when not confined to its prime analogue, it meant any Mudejar with rural properties, from grand lord to humble sharecropper.[97]

Islamic exegetes constructed an elaborate theoretical structure for agrarian taxes, based upon objective classification of lands, diversity

[97] The question of the Mudejar farmer and the *exaricus* is treated in Burns, *Islam under the Crusaders*, ch. 5, part 3, with opinions cited also by Liauzu, Loscertales, Hinojosa, and others. The "Abrahim exarchi iudeus Valentie et uxor eius Moyna" owning property near Valencia city in 1282 (Arch. Nac. Madrid, Clero sec. y reg., Valencia, Puig, Merced, legajo 2,043, arm. 44, fab. 2), who appears in the crown registers as "exarq[u]i," more probably had a descriptive name like ash-Sharqī. See also Lévi-Provençal, *España musulmana*, v, 150-152, correcting Hinojosa on p. 151n.

of crops, ability to pay, and similar factors;[98] but the real tax structures evolved less from this artificial juridicism than from historical
evolution in a given region. In Islamic North Africa agricultural
contracts ran to a fourth of cereals, or higher; if the landlord furnished seed and tools the share became a fifth; the shares adjusted
however according to irrigation advantages and variety of crops.[99]
In both Islamic and Christian Spain, Hinojosa has the Muslim *exaricus* surrendering a fifth to the authorities or local concessionaire. In
conquered Valencia in the late eleventh century the Cid had asked
only a tenth from his Moors, to be easy on them. García y García

[98] Ben-Shemesh has a brief analysis of each tax affecting land in the older, general system, with commonsense criticism of the overly theoretical description often
given them (*Taxation in Islam*, III, introduction, esp. pp. 19-20, 25-32); he particularly takes issue with the interpretations of Farishta G. de Zayas, *The Law and
Philosophy of Zakat: The Islamic Social Welfare System* (Damascus, 1960). Ben-
Shemesh sees *zakāt* as very shortly becoming a purely individual matter and, despite
the theorists, never really entering the public or state domain, much less becoming a
supervised tax. In this he takes issue, as well, with Siddiqi. On land and crop taxes
see also Løkkegaard, *Islamic Taxation*, pp. 109ff.; on rates for kinds of land, and
flexibility (p. 109); on theorists urging a third of farm revenues for family support, a
third for capital improvement and expenses, and a third for tax, with other opinions
ranging from a tax of a tenth to a tax of a half (p. 110); on olives taxed most dearly,
then vines, palms, sugar cane, cotton, wheat, barley, vegetables, and soft fruits (p.
117), with trees and bushes moot (pp. 122-123), new plantings exempt for three
years (p. 124), and as many as four rates for differing kinds of irrigation available
(pp. 120-121). Aghnides, *Mohammedan Theories of Finance*, part 2, ch. 2, *zakāt* of
agriculture; pp. 282-295 (some theorists denied the tenth is *zakāt*); and pp. 364ff.,
377-397. Imamuddin, *Socio-Economic and Cultural History of Muslim Spain*, ch. 5 on
agriculture, with shares varying from a half to a sixth (p. 55). Siddiqi, *Public
Finance in Islam*, chs. 2-5 on *zakāt* and ch. 6 on *kharāj*, both proportional (a half,
third, fourth) and fixed. Perishable vegetables should be free of *zakāt* (p. 10); the
tenth should fall to a twentieth on unirrigated land (p. 9); the same property should
not be subject both to *zakāt* and *kharāj*, nor an animal fall under both the *zakāt* of
trade and of animals—though some theorists do allow such double taxation (p. 61).
On "seignorial" taxes see A. N. Poliak, "La feodalité islamique," *Revue des études
islamiques*, x (1936), 254ff. See also his "Classification of Lands in the Islamic Law
and its Technical Terms," *American Journal of Semitic Languages and Literature*,
LVII (1940), 50-62; Joseph Schacht, "Zakāt," *EI¹*, IV, part 2, 1,202-1,205; Claude
Cahen, "Ikṭaʿ," *EI²*, III, 1,088-1,091. For the crusader Holy Land, see Cahen, "Notes
sur l'histoire des croisades et de l'orient latin: le régime rural syrien au temps de la
domination franque," *Bulletin de la faculté des lettres de Strasbourg*, XXIX (1951),
286-310; before the crusades, the shares here ran from a fourth to a half of the
harvest (p. 287); Ibn Jubayr found them a half, during the crusader regime, in the
Syrian backlands (pp. 300ff.).

[99] Idris, *Berbérie orientale*, II, 622ff.

found that in the northern sector of crusader Valencia Christian agrarian rents, when they were not the direct feudal gift to acknowledge granted dominion, varied from stipulated shares to fixed measure and to money; at Villahermosa the share was a tenth, for example, and at Arñuel a fourth.[100] In general, Islamic and Christian practice converged in the matter of shares; viewed in another context, the Mudejar resembled the Christian who surrendered on terms to an Islamic power in expectation of paying a head tax plus a fifth-share of produce.

Such shares in crusader Valencia comprised the main direct rent, prescinding from minor services and charges. There is reason to see the agricultural rent of the proprietor-*exaricus* as a state tax, given to the crown on directly regalian lands and to the lord on seignorial land. When the intervening proprietor held his land in essential independence almost as an alod, as a number of Christians did in Valencia, this income effectively disappeared, except for rents contracted from his tenant or tenants. The dispersed nature of land tenure in Valencia, in a multiplicity of relatively small holdings, meant a corresponding dispersal of alienated share-payments.[101]

Muslim lords surrendering a bloc of land without losing economic

[100] Menéndez Pidal, *España del Cid*, I, 489. García y García, *Estado económico-social de Castellón*, pp. 34-35.

[101] The remarkable variety of Valencian soil and crops is explored in detail by J. M. Houston, "Land Use and Society in the Plain of Valencia," in *Geographical Essays in Memory of Alan G. Ogilvie*, ed. R. Miller and J. W. Watson (London, 1959), 166-194; the huerta comprises only ten percent of the modern province but supports three-fourths of its agriculture and eighty percent of its population (p. 166); a remarkable gradation of contrasting subsoils, from gravel to silt, runs from hills to coast (p. 172); the Romans prized the area for its cereals, oil, and wine, and the Arabs brought fodder and dye crops, fruit trees, rice, mulberries, and other produce, which the crusaders rather increased or intensified than altered (pp. 175-177); remarkable changes in crops, manner of tenure, and intensity of cultivation make applications from modern centuries to the past dangerous (pp. 187-189). See also Alice Foster, *The Geographic Structure of the Vega of Valencia* (Chicago, 1936) on the several huertas, dry-farming highlands, types of crop, and four geoponic land types; and V. L. Simó Santonja, *La agricultura en los fueros valencianos* (Sagunto, 1970), for background data on contracts, rental, and the like. Very technical but with some attention to historical antecedents and evolution are Vicente Fontavella González, *La huerta de Gandía* (Zaragoza, 1952), esp. the chapters on physical setting, crops, and agrarian structure; and Eugenio L. Burriel de Orueta, *La huerta de Valencia, zona sur, estudio de geografía agraria* (Valencia, 1971), e.g., pp. 147ff., 515ff.

control of it agreed to a shared-tax system, as Muntaner noted.[102] Where Christian landlords took over, the Mudejars' precise rents had to be worked out with the new owners; in much of the surviving documentation this was the king. At the surrender of Valencia city he told the huerta Muslims to "make contracts with the lords who will hold the farms."[103] What was the incidence of shares as against fixed rents? Christian settlers in Valencia often paid money rents; a run of twenty grants of three jovates each, for example, asked ten solidi per jovate. When the Mercedarians settled the Mudejar Ādam (Edam) on a farm or garden (*ortum*) near Valencia city in 1263, they stipulated property improvement plus six solidi a year; perhaps the fixed rent was designed to lure settlers or to sell a property rather than to exploit land already settled.[104]

In the kingdom of Valencia a fifth of crops was often the norm. When the crown took over the rents of Simon of Urrea at Sollana and Trullars or Trullás in 1270, directing the Mudejars to "give and pay us and ours that tribute you gave and paid" to Simon, under the same "contracts and conditions," it also decreed that any new land brought under cultivation must "pay to us and ours the fifth part in full from all produce of the said land." If any of them purchased land from a Christian, he had to recontract (*componere*) with the crown concerning the rents to be paid.[105] At Chulilla in 1260 the Muslims gave a fifth on irrigated farms, and a tenth on dry-farmed lands, with some taxes waived to balance these shares; the document may have had in view new lands being broken to cultivation. "We vouchsafe to you, each and every Saracen of Chulilla present and to

---

[102] *Crònica*, ch. 9: "e tots aquells empero ab qui ell feu traves li responien de cosa sabuda lany."

[103] Valencia Capitulation: "et quod componant cum dominis qui hereditates tenuerint."

[104] Arch. Nac. Madrid, Clero sec. y reg., Valencia, Puig, Merced, legajo 2,043, arm. 44, fab. 2 (Aug. 9, 1263): "vobis Edam sarraceno et vestris imperpetuum ad laborandum, plantandum, et meliorandum unum ortum."

[105] Arch. Crown, James I, Reg. Canc. 16, fol. 213 (Sept. 21, 1270): "volumus et concedimus vobis universis et singulis sarracenis de Suyllana et de Trulars quod illa tributa detis et solvatis nobis . . . et eos pactos et condiciones nobiscum habeatis quos et quas cum dicto Eximino de Urrea habebatis; verumtamen si vos vel aliquis vestrum recipiatis seu scaliaveritis terram heremam . . . solvatis nobis et nostris quintam partem integriter de omnibus fructibus dicte terre quam recipiatis seu scaliaveritis." Trullars and Trullás are forms of the same name.

come forever, that for any labor you shall expend in lands irrigated or arid ... you are not obliged to pay us anything ... except only the fifth part."[106] At Fula and Atalla a hundred Moors taking farms in 1249 promised a fifth of their produce to the crown.[107]

The bailiff of Gandía included in his accounts to the crown in 1276 for the preceding six months "the fifth that you received from the Saracens and their possessions at Beniopa."[108] Such wording can be deceptive, however, applying rather to the lord's fifth of booty during times of rebellion or unrest. Another report on fifths, three months earlier, clearly concerns that military fifth: the king orders the castellan of Penáguila, the knight Berengar of Latera, "to give William of Entenza the full fifth of men and women Saracens and of anything else that the same Berengar had, by title of fifths, from infantry and their officers, out of the booty of the Saracens of Penáguila and its region." Entenza was then to render account to the officials specified.[109]

The share was also frequently the classic tenth, as at Biar in 1263.[110] In 1273 on a grant "in the valley of Jalón in the district of Tárbena," the owner "Ṭalḥa b. Zidri [Talba Abincedrey] the Saracen" under-

---

[106] *Ibid.*, Reg. Canc. 11, fol. 186 (Dec. 17, 1260): "indulgemus vobis universis et singulis sarracenis de Xulella presentibus et futuris in perpetuum quod de tota laboratione quam feceritis in bega sive regadivo ... nec teneamini dare nobis et nostris nisi tantum quintam partem; et quod de laboratione quam feceritis in secano ... non donetis ... nisi tantum decimam partem." *Bega* or *vega* here stands for irrigated land.

[107] *Colección diplomática de los documentos a que se refiere la disertación del feudalismo particular e irredimible de los pueblos del feudalismo del reino de Valencia, de donde salieron expulsos los moriscos en el año 1609,* ed. Miguel Salvá and Pedro Sáinz de Baranda, in *Documentos inéditos de España,* XVIII, 55.

[108] Arch. Crown, James I, Reg. Canc. 22, fol. 63v (July 14, 1276), confirmation of the report made to the bishop of Huesca as agent of the king: "de quinta quam recepistis de sarracenis et rebus suis de Beniopa."

[109] *Ibid.*, Reg. Canc. 33, fol. 124 (April 10, 1276): "mandavit dominus rex Berengario de Latera alcaydo Penaguile quod det Guillelmo de Entenza totam quintam sarracenorum et sarracenarum et quorumlibet aliorum que idem Berengarius racione quinte habuit a pedonibus et almotacenis de preda sarracenorum Penaguile et termini sui." An *almotacenus*, Catalan *almugatén* and Castilian *almocadén*, was a captain of footmen.

[110] *Ibid.*, Reg. Canc. 12, fol. 119 (Oct. 1, 1263): "decimam ... in Biar ... a sarracenis ibi habitantibus." Sometimes the customary share is left unstated as at Les Alcuces ("Las Alcuças") that same year (fol. 24 [Feb. 15, 1263]): "solvere teneatis partem tuam pro iovatis predictis prout alii faciunt qui hereditates habent ibidem"; along one boundary was the farm of 'Alī b. Ghālib (Aben Galip).

took to turn over a tenth of his crops.[111] This recalls the conquests of Tudela in 1119 and Tortosa in 1148 where a tenth had been stipulated. The Tales charter required of the Mudejars "that you give us a tenth part of all the fruits." Eslida, along with the towns sharing the conditions of its charter, specified a tenth of grain, vegetables, wine, and other items; to prevent fraud, agents collected these shares in kind on the field during harvesting (*in era*). The later Eslida charter repeated the condition.[112]

Carlet, Alcudia, and Alharp comprised a fief held for King James by Peter of Montagut and subsequently by that knight's son Peregrine. In 1241, when only Muslims inhabited these regions, Montagut agreed to pay the bishop of Valencia "a tithe from [his own] tenth," until "it ever happens that the said castle [and country] be populated by Christians," at which time the church could take its direct tithe from tenants.[113] At Uxó, though the tenth fell on chickens, figs, and other items, the general rule established payment of "the eighth part of all fruits." The charter summed up the Uxó rents however as "their obligations and tenth [*lur dret e delme*]." At Chivert Muslims gave "well and faithfully the sixth part to the

---

[111] *Ibid.*, Reg. Canc. 19, fol. 64 (Oct. 21, 1273): "in valle de Xalo termino de Tarbena," to "Talba Abencedrey sarraceno," the dues being "decima omnium fructuum eiusdem raffalli." Reconstruction of this name is unsatisfactory; the manuscript clearly has Talba, not Galba, suggesting the Companion of the Prophet named Ṭalḥa. Cedrey could reflect a distortion of anything from ṣadr, an official, to Zidri, a form of Isidro.

[112] Tales Charter: "quod detis nobis . . . decimam partem omnium fructuum." Eslida Charter. Second Eslida Charter. Tudela Charter: "teneant illos in lure decima: et que donent de x unum." But the Tudela Charter also states ambiguously: "si aliquis moro donaverit suam terram ad moros ad [l]aborare, et non poterit illam laborare suum xarico prendat suum quinto de horto et de vinea"; does this mean that wealthier farmers normally subfarmed to their own *exarici* at a rental of a fifth of produce, in turn paying their own fifth (in effect a fifth of the poor farmer's rental fifth) to the crown (see the case of the Cid in n. 93)? Tortosa Charter, *Documentos inéditos de Aragón*, IV, 130-134, also in Fernández y González, *Mudejares de Castilla*, appendix, doc. 5 (Dec. 1148, misdated as 1143): "sic est fuero in lure lege, id est, quod donent decima . . . de totos lures fructos et totos lures alçatas."

[113] Arch. Cat., perg. 2,341 (Feb. 7, 1241): "et sciendum est quod decima predicta debet deduci non tantum de decima set de omnibus que vos haberetis a sarracenis illius castri aliquo iusto vel consueto modo sive que habueritis ex consuetudine sarracenorum seu christianorum qualibet fraude et dolo exclusis"; "si unquam contigerit quod predictum castrum popularetur de christianis deducatur fideliter decima de castro supradicto." On Montagut see Burns, *Crusader Valencia*, I, 66-67, 84, 161-163.

Brothers [Templars]," and "of the vintage they are likewise to give the sixth part"; there is no doubt they gave these in kind, since each farmer had to bear the cost of transport to the collection depot. At Aldea, rental tax soared to a fourth of the crops, though the Hospitallers offered other advantages to woo Valencian Muslims to this settlement. At Aldaya, south of Cuart in a heavily irrigated huerta, St. Vincent's monastery collected a third from its Mudejars; by their surrender charter Muslims at Cuart itself paid the crown "a third of all fruits and production of their holdings."[114] The variety of crops and soil even in a single locality like Almonacid could result in a broad range of rents, described as "fifths, fourths, ninths, and tributes" in 1259; the early date suggests that Almonacid's taxpayers, "men and women Christians and Saracens," were largely Muslims.[115]

[114] Uxó Charter: "la huytena part de tots los fruyts a nos." Chivert Charter: "bene et fideliter sextam partem fratribus"; "de vindemia similiter dent sextam partem." Aldea Charter. For Aldaya, see Burns, Crusader Valencia, 1, 289, with circumstances of land tenure. The restatement of Cuart's charter is in Arch. Crown, Peter III, Reg. Canc. 42, fol. 149v (July 16, 1279): "solvant terciam partem omnium fructuum et expletorum possessionum suarum."

[115] Arch. Crown, James I, Reg. Canc. 10, fol. 147r,v (Feb. 13, 1259): "castrum et villam de Almonezir cum omnibus terminis . . . quintis, quartis, novenis, et tributis, et omnibus aliis redditibus . . . ab omnibus hominibus et feminis christianis et sarracenis ibi habitantibus et habitaturis." Though there was the military "fifth" already seen and a judicial "fourth" (treated below, p. 176), the placing of taxes in this list makes it improbable that these are meant. So general a time sweep, toward an indeterminate future, may suggest that a range of taxes are merely anticipated here; but the specific choices, plus the generic burden already carried by "tributis," argues that these were the common taxes actually collected then at Almonacid. In Aragon the treudo (from tributo), as the farm-produce shares were called from at least the thirteenth century, was a ninth part, so that novena became its synonym; in all the regions of Spain's reconquest, it was paid in kind, rarely in money (García de Valdeavellano, Instituciones españolas, p. 599). Macanaz makes the later share or treudo of the crown of Aragon a fanega of grain per house, another for every cafizate of land sown, and the eighth part "of wine, oil, and other produce [frutos]," in his Regalías de Aragón, p. 69 (cf. Catalan cafís and faneca below, Chapter V, n. 72). Macho y Ortega found the Mudejar shares in fifteenth-century Aragon proper varying from ninth through fourth, with grains commonly paying either a fifth or sixth, "thread" products like flax and hemp a sixth, vegetables and wine often a sixth, saffron a sixteenth, hill farms an eighth or ninth, irrigated farms a fourth, with variations, exemptions, and even amelioration by renegotiation ("Mudéjares aragoneses," pp. 201-202). At roughly our own period in Aragon proper (1294), the Mudejar crown rent at Nabal was "el noveno de los fruytos de sus campos"; at Alagón, "el diezmo de todos lures fruytos" plus one morabatin per house (noted as originating in the reign of James I); and at Huesa a third of produce from irrigated lands, a third of grapes and nuts, sixteen cafizes of wheat and

The charters display divergences also in detail. At Eslida the tenth fell on grapes as on grain; at Uxó grapes went unspecified though vineyards were named. Garden vegetables, perhaps only those consumed at home, won exemption in the Játiva, Uxó, and Eslida charters. Figs at Chivert and fruit trees at Eslida paid nothing. The Játiva tenth specifically included carob pods, popular as fodder. Rents apparently fell heavily on main crops but diminished or disappeared in the case of produce for domestic use or for sale in negligible quantity. Crown arrangements proved more generous than did seignorial.[116] The revenue picture altered in the next century, when agrarian rents of a fourth or a third became common.[117] Whatever the division of tax shares, the base wealth must have been considerable. From the small island of Minorca—which "was very poor and on that island there wasn't space to raise grain for the tenth part of the people"—James had arranged in the surrender charter to receive "every year three thousand quarters of wheat, and a hundred cows, and five hundre . mixed goats and sheep," as well as "eighty-four kilograms of fresh butter" every year.[118] The agrarian tax potential of Valencia was immeasurably greater.

"The tribute that the Saracens of Liria" gave the crown was so impressive that James assigned a debt of 5,500 solidi to be satisfied from it in 1257; when the tribute did not meet this sum, the king had to substitute an equivalent crown income "from all mills held for us in the region of Valencia city."[119] Lists of taxes in 1268 and

---

eight of barley (*Rentas de Aragón*, pp. 214, 255, 301). In fifteenth-century Islamic Granada the share on cereals ran to a tenth (Álvarez de Cienfuegos, "Régimen tributario del reino mudéjar de Granada," p. 103).

[116] Chivert, Eslida, Játiva, Uxó Charters. The Eslida tenth included "tritici, ordei, panicii, milli, lini, et leguminis." *Hortalissa* are vegetables, the Eslida charter defining them as "hortalicia, videlicet de cepis, cucurbitis, nec de aliis fructibus terrae nisi de suprascriptis."

[117] Gual Camarena, "Mudéjares valencianos, aportaciones," pp. 190-191.

[118] *Llibre dels feyts*, ch. 121. The butter was measured as two *quintars*, each about 42 kilograms (a kilogram being over two pounds); this was not the metric *quintar* of 100 kilograms. The *quartera*, not to be confused with the *quarter*, was a variable dry weight of nearly 70 liters of cereal, the total here amounting to 210,000 liters of wheat; a liter today is .906 of a dry quart.

[119] Arch. Crown, James I, Reg. Canc. 10, fol. 40 (March 7, 1257): "in tributo quod nobis faciebant [sarraceni Lirie] . . . [et] in omnibus molendinis que pro nobis tenentur in termino Valencie." This witness is unsatisfactory, because the words in brackets are largely reconstruction from fragments around a hole. In Reg.

1269 show the Muslims of Pego giving "the tenth of wheat: 30 cafizes minus 6 *almuds*, at a reckoning of 10 solidi and 6 pence the cafiz, which make 313 solidi [and] 8 pence, which equal 94 besants and 1 *millarès*." Similar entries follow for five other cereals, for flax, for 66½ baskets of figs (of which 55 brought a sales total of over 70 besants, while 11½ brought 11½ besants), for cucumbers (321 *arroves*—some 80 *quintars* or just over 3,300 kilos—at a total sales of 16 besants and 7 pence), grapes, and nuts. An allied tax list from Pego entered over 28 besants for figs, 107 besants for olives, 375 more for the tenth on olives as a separate entry, a presumable but illegible 161 besants for 100½ baskets of figs also entered as a tenth, and so on. Several of the items have a double entry, perhaps representing rent plus church tithe. Out of the total tax for Sumacárcel in 1268— 1,076 solidi—over 600 derived from such farm entries, of which 437 solidi was the sale price of 58 cafizes of a cereal (*panis*) at 8 solidi per cafiz.[120]

A listing of Alcira rents in 1263 has eleven entries under the rubric "cereals of the tenth" for a total of 5,941 solidi, but these rents mix Christian and Mudejar contributions together. A similar mixed list that year for Gandía yields an addition of just under 300 solidi for its "cereals of the tenth"; a companion list for Cullera has cereals that total some 1,380 solidi, as well as 43 solidi as "tenth on wine," and 20 solidi as tenth on oil.[121] Such lists are instructive for current prices and local wealth; expanded by a multiple of ten or less, they suggest the extent and value of the crops named. As tax information, how-

---

Canc. 16, fol. 178 (Aug. 27, 1269), the "entire bailiwick" of Valencia city included prominently among its farmed taxes: "ac tributa iudeorum et sarracenorum." Later in this document the crown assigned to Prince Peter "cccc solidos qui sibi deficiunt de sarracenis de Liria."

[120] *Ibid.*, Reg. Canc. 35, fols. 3-4, 7-8 (lists for 1268 and for 1269): "item diesmo de trigo, xxx kafices minus vi almuts a rao de x sous e vi diners lo kafiz que fan cccxiii sous, viii diners, que son xciiii besants, i millares"; "item figues, lxvi sportas e media e fueron vendidas las lv sportas a xiii millareses que fan lxxi besants, v millareses, e las xi sportas e media a i besant que fan xi besants e medio e assi son por todos lxxxiii besants."

[121] *Ibid.*, Reg. Canc. 17, fols. 27-32 (Dec. 30, 1263): "bladum de decima: spelta . . . avena . . . ordeum . . . frumentum . . . panicium . . . tramela . . . adassa . . . milium . . . lentiles . . . ciurons . . . guixe. . . . Summa v millia dcccc xli solidorum, vii denarios"; "decimum vini . . . decimum canabi et lini . . . decimum olei. . . ." The last three items under *bladum* translate as lentils, chickpeas or garbanzos, and blue vetch.

ever, they suffer both from mixing Christian and Mudejar data and in leaving doubt over their possible connection with the ecclesiastical tithe.

Amplification of one's Valencian holdings usually extended the existing services. When the Moors of Cuart in 1257 got a tract of land with houses: "from these let there be given to us the service that is had from your other lands."[122] The Pego Valley aljama in 1272 bought another section from the king, "in such wise that you may hold, possess, and use [it] . . . with all its appurtenances and rights, according to your way of holding other properties in the aforesaid valley."[123] A grant to an individual at Pego that year fell under the same conditions by which "the other Saracens of the same valley" held theirs.[124] Mudejars farming properties "in the village of Benibairon" in 1268 did so according to the services rendered by those of Alfandech—"and besides you are bound to reside there and improve the place."[125]

Like Christians, Valencian Mudejars had to contend with an entry fee when acquiring new land, and a sales tax when selling their land; but these expenses belong more properly to the schedule of fees discussed below. Similarly the taxes a farmer expected to pay on his domestic animals or on flocks may logically be deferred to the consideration of pastoral and grazing taxes. The countergift or symbolic offering to a landlord, less an agrarian tax than a feudal echo, can fit under the category of miscellany below, though some consider it along with produce shares as belonging to *treudo* or tribute. Labor services likewise belong to a wider category than farm taxes.[126]

In summation, a considerable diversity manifests itself in Mudejar agrarian taxes, even on crown lands, though convention favored a fifth or more often a tenth. The seignorial charters for Tales and

---

[122] *Ibid.*, Reg. Canc. 10, fol. 8 (Aug. 11, 1257): "et quod inde fiat nobis servicium quod fiet de aliis hereditatibus vestris."

[123] *Ibid.*, Reg. Canc. 37, fol. 57v (Dec. 22, 1272): "ita videlicet quod teneatis possideatis et expletetis . . . cum omnibus pertinenciis et iuribus ipsius prout tenetis alias hereditates . . . in predicta valle."

[124] *Ibid.*, fol. 48 (June 25, 1272): "sicut alii sarraceni eiusdem vallis possint facere de hereditatibus suis."

[125] *Ibid.*, Reg. Canc. 17, fol. 101v (March 2, 1268): "in alcheria de Benibayron"; "immo teneatis facere in ea residenciam et meliorare eandem."

[126] See below, Chapter VI, part 3 on land-sale taxes, with n. 67 on the countergift, and Chapter V, part 3 on pastoral taxes and part 4 on labor services.

Chivert proved more generous than some crown charters, though Aldea's was more restrictive. Differences may reflect bargaining power at time of surrender, or continuance of a diversity already evolved under preconquest regimes. The king's autobiography leaves the impression that Mudejar taxes remained basically the same as those previously paid to Islamic overlords, but it also shows some hard bargaining. Documents touching specific areas or cases support this impression and indicate a pattern not very different from the Christian tax structure, with expected minor divergences.

One key to differences may have been the agricultural prosperity of a given place. Beniopa and Sollana for instance stood in rich huertas; the towns of the Eslida charter dotted an unproductive mountain area. Such a solution remains tentative and admits of exceptions, since many variables enter such as irrigation, roads, soil, and the advance of cultivation; a bad wheat field might make a good vineyard. Mudejars could not have considered any part of the tax structure onerous simply because of its form. Chivert gave a tenth in its charter, yet had surrendered under circumstances assuring consideration and favor; Aldea gave a full fourth but as part of a charter designed to attract volunteer Muslim settlers. Obviously the crusaders had made a commonsense attempt to integrate these Islamic provinces into the Christian economy upon terms not too dissimilar from those of their Christian neighbors or from those to which Muslims had long been accustomed. Accommodation to the facts of the conquered society, and determination to maintain and encourage production, stand out as pillars of King James's economic policy.

CHAPTER V

Spectrum: Water, War, Salt, Moneyage, Livestock, Labor Services, Hospitality, and Fines

THE TRIBUTARY, monopoly-utility, industrial, commercial, and agrarian charges framed in turn a complex of lesser burdens. The Valencian Muslim paid compulsory religious alms and a salt gabelle; his aljama yielded its share of punitive fines. A baker's dozen of general impositions completed the structure: especially the water tax, host and cavalcade, hospitality, labor services, moneyage, pasturage, stock fees, protection money, treasure trove, and contract fees. Some of these varied their names, bred allied subforms, or found multiple application; into the interstices of their structure the purely local or specialized taxes fitted. Though often collected separately, hardly any were uniquely Mudejar.

WATER TAX: THE PROBLEM OF THE *Alfarda*

The intricate canal networks distributing rivers and springs over the lush huertas of the medieval Valencian kingdom have fascinated historians and hydraulic engineers for centuries. Like a coequal system lacing through the historical literature on medieval Spain, spirited disputes have developed concerning the origins, evolution, and intercultural significance of this irrigation marvel. The thirteenth century is particularly critical for such studies, because with the Reconquest began that amassing of documentation that allows detailed examination. The century itself, naturally but unfortunately, is the least rewarding for irrigation records in the neo-Christian era; the Reconquest with its immediate aftermath of revolts reached past the mid-century mark, while subsequent resettlement, reconstruction, and accumulation of local archives were painfully slow developments. Since irrigation affairs proceeded by custom, and irrigation disputes resolved themselves normally in summary oral courts, this earlier documentation tends to be of a scattered, indirect nature. All the more valuable therefore are the records of water-related charges, with their glimpses of the Mudejar water communities.[1] During the previous century, the renaissance of Roman law had encouraged the claim of the crown as universal proprietor of all waters, including lakes, rivers, and irrigation networks.[2] This claim was more sweeping for the kingdom of Valencia, owing to the right of conquest over public and private waters. Even when alienating waters or irrigation systems, the crown in theory retained residual dominion. The crusaders particularly prized Valencia's irrigation networks and improved or extended them somewhat, though hindered by the larger tasks of reconstruction and embarrassed by a paucity of settlers to use existing facilities. The crown ordered rebuilding at Cuart, and improved the Alcira system extensively.[3] It built a Burriana canal, opened two new ones at Bairén, and intervened in the appointment of the "master" overseeing each.[4]

[1] Thomas F. Glick has a full-scale study, *Irrigation and Society in Medieval Valencia* (Cambridge, Mass., 1970), starting from the thirteenth-century antecedents and elaborating in detail the workings of the irrigation communities through the next two centuries; its able bibliographical and narrative materials fill out the wider irrigation scene in Valencia. See also Burns, "Irrigation Taxes in Early Mudejar Valencia: The Problem of the *Alfarda*," *Speculum*, XLIV (1969), 560-567; and the bibliography by Vicente Vicent Cortina, *Bibliografía geográfica del reino de Valencia* (Zaragoza, 1964). Jean-Guy Liauzu examines the irrigation system just above the Valencian border, "Un aspect de la reconquête de la vallée de l'Ebre aux xie et xiie siècles, l'agriculture irriguée et l'héritage de l'Islam," *Hespéris-Tamuda*, v (1964), 5-13.

[2] Jean Pierre Cuvillier, "La propriété de l'eau et l'utilisation des ouvrages hydrauliques dans la Catalogne médiévale (xiiie et xive siècles): essai d'histoire économique et sociale," *Miscellània històrica catalana*, III (1970) [*Homenatge al Pare Jaume Finestres*], 243-257. Branchát, *Derechos y regalías de Valencia*, chs. 6-8, an extensive treatment. Leopoldo Piles Ros, *Estudio documental sobre el bayle general de Valencia, su autoridad y jurisdicción* (Valencia, 1970), p. 88.

[3] Arch. Crown, James I, Reg. Canc. 21, fol. 79v (Jan. 1, 1272) for the ruined Cuart system, with all helping: "omnes illos, tam christianos quam sarracenos." Reg. Canc. 14, fol. 14 (March 1, 1262), applying Teruel revenues, including "omnes redditus et exitus iudeorum Turolii, ad faciendum expensas in cequia Aliasire necessarias." In Reg. Canc. 19, fol. 105v (Feb. 24, 1273), the king gave a farm to "Arnaldo Vitalis, magistro operis cequie Algesire" (and see his connection with constructing the kingdom's cathedral, in Burns, *Crusader Valencia*, II, 378). In all, a handful of documents refers to the new Alcira system.

[4] The Burriana network, from Arch. Crown, James I, Reg. Canc. 21, fol. 84v (Nov. 11, 1272), is in *El "Repartiment" de Burriana y Villarreal*, ed. Ramón de María (Valencia, 1935), p. 88. The Bairén two appear in Reg. Canc. 19, fol. 100v (Feb. 14, 1273). The masters, as tax gatherers, are of direct interest; see Reg. Canc. 10, fol.

Though Alcira appears most often in crown documents, and the "master of its works," Arnold Vidal, is the only engineer whose name has survived, King James probably made his most creative contribution in constructing a system at Villarreal where he brought in Mudejar settlement. In preparation for this colonization he caused an important Knight Hospitaller to submit the financial accounts for building or extending the system. "We acknowledge that you, Fray Peter Peyronet, commander at Burriana and our almoner, returned sound, correct, and legal accounts for each and every penny that you, or any other for you, received . . . for the construction [improvement?] of the canal for our settlement of Villarreal, and for each and every expenditure or outlay through yourself or another . . . on construction of the aforesaid canal, and for the construction and administration of the same canal and of the aforesaid settlement."[5]

In grappling with the irrigation tax, two problems must be faced from the outset. To begin with, was *sequiatge* (Latin *cequiagium*) or "canal-age" really what some historians assume it to be—only a maintenance tax? The bulk of maintenance, except for the central canal of a given system, was the business of each farmer along his own small section; further policing, improving, or litigating required relatively small expense, if the average wage of functionaries and laborers is considered. The ultimate destination of *sequiatge* income might be argued either way merely from its amount. St. Vincent's monastery, to which King James alienated the Cuart canal system in the western part of the Valencian huerta, got "twenty-seven cafizes of barley that it receives as *sequiatge* from [each of] those who irrigate by means of the said canal." A fairly large system like the Moncada, one of those in Valencia city's huerta, brought enough *sequiatge* to make it a suitable gift to the crown agent and

---

131v (March 14, 1259) to "Bonfil, cequiario et magistro cequie Algezire . . . pro vestro magistratu et labore cequie Algezire"; see below, n. 7, on his successor Bortach.

[5] Arch. Nac. Madrid, Ords. milits., Montesa, privs. reales, no. 132 (Jan. 15, 1275): "confitemur vobis fratri P. Peyronet commendatori Burriane et elemosinario nostro vos reddidisse nobis bonum et rectum ac legale computum de omnibus et singulis denariis quos vos vel alius pro vobis recepistis . . . ad opus cequie populacionis nostre Ville Regali[s] et de omnibus etiam et singulis expensis et missionibus per vos vel alium . . . in opere antedicto, et de opere et administratione eiusdem cequie et populacionis predicte." On Peyronet or Peironet, see Burns, *Crusader Valencia*, I, 194, II, 465.

financial officer, Nicholas of Vallvert, in 1266. King James awarded it for life, stipulating that Nicholas was to administer the temporalities of the system "at his own expense"; presumably Nicholas supported a staff, met all expenses of maintenance and management, and still enjoyed a personal income worthy of the royal giving.

The value of such a post becomes clearer in the charter appointing Bortach of Montornés "custodian or head *sequier*" for life over the "new canal system of Alcira, which we are now having built"; Bortach was "to collect the entire *sequiatge* from the farms along the said canal," rigorously enforce its payment by property confiscation if necessary, present the tax accounts to the crown, and retain for himself the very comfortable annual income of 500 solidi. If this salary represented ten or even twenty percent of the total *sequiatge* collected on this one system at Alcira, then the tax was hardly a maintenance or inconsiderable fee. The impression of a true tax of sizable dimensions is strengthened by consideration of the money fief with which James encumbered the *sequiatge* revenues of Alcira's system in 1271, awarding an "honor" or estate of 2,000 solidi every year to the Provençal magnate Hugh of Baux.[6]

A dispute between some huerta farmers and St. Vincent's monastery, at Cuart in 1272, throws light on the obligations assumed by the holder of this income. A section of channel between Manises and Cuart had collapsed "from age and the force of the current." St.

[6] Arch. Crown, James I, Reg. Canc. 15, fol. 12v (April 7, 1266): "carta donationis Nicholai de Valle Virida in tota vita sua, de cequia or[te Va]lencie vocata de Moncada, et de cequiatico eiusdem et iuribus que dominus rex habebat seu habere poterat in possessionibus que ex ipsa rigantur, et quod dictus Nicholaus propriis missionibus conducat dictam cequiam." The other *iura* here may, however, include a separate *almagran* or *alfarda*. Reg. Canc. 16, fol. 185 (June 27, 1269): "concedimus tibi Bortaco de Montornes in tota vita tua custodiam cequie nove Algezire quam modo fieri facimus, ita quod tu sis custos seu cequiarius maior tocius ipsius cequie . . . et recipias pro nobis et nostris cequiaticum totum . . . de hereditatibus que subtus dictam cequiam sunt, de quibus respondeas bene et fideliter nobis . . . [et] habeas singulis annis de cequiatico dicte cequie toto tempore vite tue quingentos solidos regalium Valencie pro tuo officio et labore, quos tibi annuatim de cequiatico retineas." The money fief is in Soldevila, *Pere el Gran*, part I, III, appendix, doc. 31 (March 15, 1271): "nobili Hugoni de Balcio duo mille solidos [*sic*] regalium pro honore . . . in cequiatico et iuribus nostris cequie quam fieri fecimus in Algezira." For St. Vincent's see next note. The Arabic *as-sāqiya* or canal gave rise to the Catalan equivalent *sèquia* or *sìquia*, more commonly in thirteenth-century Catalan *cèquia* (and cf. Castilian *acequia*), whence the tax *sequiatge*, *cequiatge* (Castilian *acequiaje*), and Latin *cequiagium*.

Vincent's obligation "to clean and maintain that canal," because of the *sequiatge* it received from each farmer, did not cover this less routine accident. King James therefore ordered "all those Christians and Saracens who irrigate with water from the said canal," to pay shares "toward repairing and rejoining the canal." The king also noted that if the cost had fallen on the monastery, "all the revenues of the prior himself for one year would hardly suffice."[7]

One student of Valencian rural life surmised that the charge fell only on nonirrigational use of water, as for mills or operations of the cloth industry, an interpretation unsatisfactory for this region.[8] It is more commonly defined as "a tax on the use of water from an irrigation canal."[9] That description may be misleading; by the generous provisions of the Valencian *Furs* all rivers, waterways, waterworks, waterfronts, and water became accessible to the public and essentially free. This did not of course preclude reasonable service fees, collected by holders of the *dominium utile*. Whether the crown retained or alienated an irrigation network, the *Furs* make it clear that the *sequiatge* fell on land having access to water, not upon water as such or upon the landowner directly. In the river huertas, right to water inhered in the irrigation-area properties and was conveyed

[7] Arch. Crown, James I, Reg. Canc. 21, fol. 79v (Jan. 1, 1272). "Intelleximus quod aliqua pars voltarum cequie de Quarto que sunt inter Quartum et Maniçes impetu aque seu propter nimiam vetustatem est destructa; et licet prior seu ecclesia Sancti Vincencii Valencie teneatur ipsam cequiam mundare et condirectam tenere racione xx^{tl} et vii^{em} cafizarum ordei que pro cequiatico percipit ab illis qui rigant de cequia antedicta, non tamen sane intentionis est quod si dicta cequia vel pars eius impetu fluminis vel racione inundacionis aquarum seu nimia vetustate destruitur quod dictus prior Sancti Vincencii ipsam debeat reparare, cum ad eius reparationem omnes redditus ipsius prioris unius anni vix possent sufficere. . . . Visis presentibus, compellatis et distringatis omnes illos tam christianos quam sarracenos, undecumque et cuiuscumque sint, . . . ad ponendum partem suam simul cum dicto priore Sancti Vincencii ad reparandam et reintegrandam cequiam et voltas predictas." *Volta*, a turn, curve, or arc, may designate a return canal or perhaps a supporting arch. St. Vincent's had received Cuart itself in 1244; see Burns, *Crusader Valencia*, I, 289 and II, 508. Glick has a map showing the Moncada, Cuart, and other systems (*Irrigation in Medieval Valencia*, pp. 24-25) and a discussion of canal maintenance at a later period (pp. 48-51).

[8] José M. Casas Torres, *La vivienda y los núcleos de población rurales de la huerta de Valencia* (Madrid, 1944), p. 170.

[9] Alcover, *Diccionari català-valencià-balear*, IX, 852: "impost sobre l'ús de l'aigua de la sèquia." For a Valencian situation see Toledo Girau, *Castell i la vall d'Alfandech*, p. 39: "una contribució que pagaven els moros per l'aprofitament de les aigües d'una sèquia." See also his "Aguas de riego de Valldigna," p. 12.

by the sale of any lot; in spring-source huertas its usufruct, though capable of a more complex relationship to the land, was essentially private.[10] There may be truth in both the maintenance and the water-charge interpretations. On the one hand, local collectors probably prededucted maintenance charges before entering the profits as a tax result; on the other, remote origins of the tax probably involved regalian prerogatives over public waters.

It is possible that the *sequiatge* transformed itself into a maintenance tax, to some extent at least, after the crown alienated it to a given water community. Right after the fall of Valencia city, in December 1238, King James handed over the canal systems of its huerta, "with [their] water," to the city in perpetuity, excepting the "royal" or Moncada network later given to Nicholas of Vallvert.[11] The privilege, embedded in a larger context of tax enfranchisement, presumably concerns some release from *sequiatge* as much as acquisition of jurisdiction. This becomes explicit from a grant thirty years later, presumably after the death of Nicholas, when King James surrendered the Moncada system to its users, including water and its agricultural or industrial uses, upon payment of a stiff privilege fee of 5,000 solidi; he remitted regalian taxes, retaining indeed nothing beyond the rent from crown-owned mills.[12] From 1238, therefore, and for this last canal from 1268, the *sequiatge* of Valencia city's huerta may have diminished into a milder local charge under the same name.

In the fourteenth- and fifteenth-century documentation he perused,

---

[10] *Fori antiqui Valentiae*, rub. cxxiv, no. 14, conveying "aque et aquarumductus, . . . fontes, basse aquarum et flumina, portus et litus maris" to free public use; rub. cxli, on not disturbing any part of the irrigation system or custom, on paying *sequiatge*, and on related matters; rub. xlvii, nos. 2, 10, 16-20, 27, 28, 32, 37. See also García y García, *Estado económico-social de Castellón*, pp. 50-51; this freedom applied also to marshes, lakes, and ponds. Some Christian charters specify the irrigation systems: at Benifasá "torrentibus ac ripis . . . et cum acquis et acqueductibus"; at Area "cum suis aquis et cequiis et capud cequiis"; at Fredes "cum fontibus et aquis at aquarum ductibus"; at Benicarló the people warn the lord he cannot sell water.

[11] *Aureum opus*, doc. 8, fol. 2r,v (Dec. 29, 1238), giving "omnes et singulas cequias . . . maiores, mediocres, et minores cum aquis et aquarum ductibus."

[12] *Ibid.*, doc. 78, fol. 24v (May 8, 1268), the rent from mills being "censum vel certum tributum." The privilege allowed all owners and lords along the network to irrigate, run mills, or otherwise use the water without retention of tax or interference by anyone, enjoying it "liberam et francham ab omni servitute et exactione regali et personali."

Glick found that the *sequiatge* in the Valencian kingdom was always a maintenance charge assessed by the irrigation community on its members, or by a town on irrigators, for upkeep and cleansing of the canal.[13] Does this subsequent state reflect an evolution beyond a transitional thirteenth-century tax, or an unchanged practice? Was the *sequiatge* ever a regalian fee, or did its collection as a maintenance tax ever involve a margin of profit to the crown, reductively joining the regalian income?

The second problem lies in terminology. *Alfarda*, used also for a different tax, can bear the same sense as *sequiatge*—a duty paid for irrigating, or a charge upon the right to water. Some lexicons give this as its unique meaning; others reduce it to a secondary meaning, proper to Aragon, and make its primary meaning a tax for remaining as Muslim or Jew under Christian rule.[14] An eighteenth-century erudite, consulting the antiquarian commentators of his time on Valencian taxes, and noting the section on *alfarda* in the *Fueros* of Aragon proper, ended by adopting both meanings in interpreting an important Valencian document of 1319; he translated it "tributos," annotated it as a tax Muslims and Jews paid to the kings of Aragon, and added the opinion of Portolés that it was instead a tax used "to

---

[13] *Irrigation in Medieval Valencia*, pp. 38, 97, 294-295.

[14] Thus the standard *Pallàs diccionari català illustrat* (rev. edn. [Barcelona, n.d.]), defines it as "tribut per dret d'aigües que es pagava antigament," while the popular schoolbook *Cassell's Spanish Dictionary* (New York, 1960) has "duty paid for the irrigation of lands." Imamuddin's recent survey, *Socio-Economic and Cultural History of Muslim Spain*, interprets it the same way (p. 196). García de Valde-avellano, however, makes it the head tax or agrarian rental shares (*Instituciones españolas*, p. 604). Alcover's monumental *Diccionari català-valencià-balear* gives the first meaning as "tribut que pagaven al rei d'Aragó els moros que eren sos vassalls," followed by "dret que té l'arrendador de l'aigua de les sèquies, de cobrar un tant per faneca de regadiu" (i, 489). Dozy and Engelman have its first meaning as the tax Mudejars paid to live in a Christian land, but say that the fee paid for irrigation waters in Aragon has the same name and origin (*Glossaire*, pp. 108-109). Liauzu, working with Lacarra's Ebro Valley documents of the Reconquest, makes it one of the four main Mudejar taxes; "exigés comme droit de prise d'eau" ("Musulmans dans l'Aragon chrétien," p. 187); "c'est plus particulièrement un droit d'irrigation" (p. 191). The 1970 edition of the *Diccionario* issued by the Real Academia Española makes its main meaning "cierta contribución" paid by Jews and Muslims under Christian rule, with the special meaning for Aragon "contribución por el aprovecha-miento de las aguas." See also Álvarez de Cienfuegos, "Régimen tributario de Granada," p. 109; Martí, *Vocabulista in arabico*, p. 154; Neuvonen, *Arabismos del español*, p. 302, where the word becomes popular in Castilian only from the thirteenth century.

clean the irrigation canals"—in effect, the *sequiatge* seen at its most restrictive in terms of maintenance or labor service.[15] A number of documents for Aragon proper do relate *alfarda* to irrigation, regrettably without details. In 1250 a twenty-year concession of canal revenues to the Hospitallers at Jaca described it as the "*alfarda* of the said irrigation canal."[16] Over a century before, in 1138 at Zaragoza, "the count and marquis of Barcelona and prince of Aragon," Raymond Berengar IV, threw open a tract of wasteland "that does not pay *alfarda* to the irrigation canals of Zaragoza."[17]

In Valencian documents, one cannot identify *alfarda* with the poll-tax tribute or besant, since that charge appears in tax lists alongside the primary imposition.[18] *Alfarda* cannot be *almagran*, in the latter's sense of a tax on produce of irrigated land as a substitute for produce shares, because that tax also turns up beside *alfarda*.[19] Is it an alternate name for *sequiatge*, perhaps the Mudejar equivalent? Both words derive from Arabic so that one cannot be explained on linguistic grounds as the Christian equivalent of the other; since Christians and Mudejars already paid a number of taxes under Arabic-derived nomenclature identical for both peoples, moreover, it is hard to see why the names would differ in this particular case. *Alfarda* does occur mostly within a rectangle or trapezoid whose upper parallel runs from Alcira to the coast and whose lower boundary runs from Biar to the coast, where Islamic rule and population dominance remained strongest during the postcrusade decades, though it can turn up as far north as Uxó. The trapezoidal area, which received Christian colonists only slowly and tardily, may offer our best clue to the mystery. Thus *sequiatge* may have predominated for Christians or for mixed but largely Christian areas of irrigation, the name diminishing or disappearing from crown records as the munic-

---

[15] Villarroya, *Real maestrazgo de Montesa*, 1, 56n., 11, doc. 13 (July 22, 1319).

[16] *Itinerari*, pp. 206-207 (July 15, 1250): "alfardam dicte cequie," arranging to farm its collection for a period of twenty years.

[17] "Documentos para la reconquista del valle del Ebro" (part 1, *EEMCA*, 11 [1946]), doc. 91 (October, 1138): "barchinonensis comes et marchio ac princeps aragonensis . . . scilicet illam terram que non donat alf[ar]dam ad illas cequias de Zaragoza."

[18] Both "alfardam" and "bisancios" appear, e.g., in the Biar tax list for March 1267 (Arch. Crown, James I, Reg. Canc. 15, fol. 84); in the similar Alfandech list for April 27, 1275 (Reg. Canc. 20, fol. 245) are "bisancios, almagram, alfardam."

[19] *Ibid.*, Reg. Canc. 35, fol. 4r,v (1269), where besant, *alfarda*, and *almagran* all appear at Pego, with sums collected for each.

ipalities took over the irrigation systems. Meanwhile Moors on crown huertas whose canals had not been alienated may have continued to give their own *sequiatge* or *alfarda* to the crown. Why the term *alfarda*, belonging to the code and traditions of Aragon proper (and to Castile when used in a non-water, tributary context), should have invaded this dominantly Catalan area of conquest is not clear.

It is also possible that a certain carelessness affected the use of both *almagran* and *alfarda* as collected on irrigated lands of Valencian Mudejars; since each tax brought considerable totals from relatively small communities, the clear separation found in routine formulas or tax-conveyance lists may on occasion have disappeared when it came to collecting the canal-oriented charges on a given community. Such a hypothesis of *alfarda-sequiatge* conjoining in practice with *almagran* and collected under either name, or even perhaps concealed under agrarian shares in some revenue accounts, helps explain the relative infrequency of either word in Valencian tax records as well as the large sums entered under both words, and in any event arranges the data in a neat pattern. At some places, however, the two not only appeared in rote lists but actually brought separate totals into the local accounts; thus at Pego in 1269, where the besant tax indicated 53 Mudejar households (at least of the relatively prosperous type, holding land), the *almagran* came to 930 besants or nearly 3,500 solidi while the *alfarda* was 660 besants or something under 2,500 solidi.[20] Arabic theorists on irrigation taxes shed little light, and the tax may well have assumed various meanings, after the fashion of *peita*. Documentation later in the century seems to make it an occasional levy prorated among aljamas, like the *fardas* of post-conquest Granada.[21]

Collectors at least sometimes took the *sequiatge* of Christian settlers in kind, subsequently converting it by sale.[22] It was clearly distinguished from the universal labor service owed by huerta farmers. In 1251, about seven years after the formal close of the

[20] *Ibid.*

[21] See, e.g., Qudāma, "On Irrigation," a chapter on taxes earlier in the east; he does describe how share-rental varied with the mode of irrigation prevailing (*Kitāb al-kharāj*, ch. 16, pp. 40-41, 60-62). For Granada see Ladero Quesada's two works as cited in Chapter IV, n. 82. On the Arabic original as something apportioned or made obligatory, and bearing as well a technical, dogmatic sense, see T. W. Juynboll, "Fard," *EI²*, II, 790. The Valencian *alfarda* as levy is below, n. 48.

[22] As in the arrangement in n. 6.

Valencian crusade, King James published regulations for irrigation canals of the kingdom, addressed primarily to Christian immigrants but undoubtedly reflecting the generally received custom of the Muslims. He insisted that every class of citizen from noble to cleric, "whatsoever be his dignity," share in paying *sequiatge* and also in caring for the canals. People of status could not class the service obligation among the "sordid duties" beneath them. Only lands attached to an irrigation system bore the burden; these had to pay "even though lords of such vineyards and farms refuse to admit the irrigation waters." When a newcomer wished to attach his farm to the system, he merely paid the usual sum and no one could hinder him. A double obligation was described: "cleaning the canals and branches, and paying *sequiatge*."[23]

Custom law regulated the manner of keeping one's own canal section in good repair, while maintenance of the system at large required inspectors and functionaries. These were obliged to clean out the main canals thoroughly once a year, as well as to weed them, according to a 1250 decree for Valencia city; only after the municipal jurates showed themselves satisfied with a job well done could water flow again. Each system's *sequier* (Latin *cequiarius*) had to repair breaks within one week or in winter two weeks, to oversee proper distribution by proportioning the available volume of water to the current extent of cultivated land, and to "impose the fines set by custom" upon farmers failing to send water back out of their fields in time. Under the watchful eye of the communally elected *sequier* of a given system, farmers had to clean out secondary branches in or by their lands and to repair the little bridges used mainly by locals.[24] The various obligations amounted to a utilities service in huerta areas, but much of the kingdom was not involved in such water economy.

[23] *Aureum opus*, doc. 38, fol. 13v (June 19, 1251), for realm: "quantecunque dignitatis sit"; "[ad] mundacionem cequiarum et braçallorum et ad prestandum cequiagium de suo conferre teneantur"; "sordida munera"; "que possint rigari donent cequiagium, licet domini ipsarum vinearum et hereditatum accipere ad rigandum noluerint."

[24] *Ibid.*, doc. 34, fols. 11v-12 (Jan. 19, 1250), attached to a mixed heading, "De stillicidiis . . ."; "conductores sive cequiarii" see that the canals are cleaned, especially "de erbis," including their "braçalli," and repair "rupturas cequiarum." Abuse of "cequias vel cequiarum filiarias" or delay in returning water "ad matrem" was punished: "exigant . . . penas constitutas in consuetudine." The *sequier* or *siquier* is the *acequiero* of Castilian.

None of the Mudejar surrender or settlement charters extant for Valencia bothered to speak directly of the water tax. The lengthy Chivert treaty exempted mosque waters and their waterways, but rocky Chivert was hardly a huerta.[25] The Eslida Moors, together with the communities associated in their charter, were allowed to "draw their water supply as was done in the time of the Saracens, and divide it among them according to their custom"; this custom may have demanded a water tax.[26] Their charter's *azofra* on water, however, referred to a different tax, discussed below. A stipulation in the pact for the Játiva region mentions the higher irrigation officer on his rounds, a Christian who was required to bring along a Muslim companion from the central aljama whenever he "asks or receives water" both on entering Mudejar towns or sections of town and again at the individual Muslim's residence.[27]

The silence of the charters is countered by a documentation betraying strong interest on the part of the kings in Mudejar irrigation activities. One such record, either a legal decision following appeal or a grant by title of overlord for the place, shows how minute this attention could become. It was only to be expected that longstanding interregional quarrels should have commanded royal attention.[28] With equal solemnity, however, King James concerned himself here over the watering of four village fields near Valencia city: "we concede to all you present and future Saracens of Aldaya, a hamlet of Cuart, that you may provide a canal check in the canal that flows through Alacuas, for irrigating those four fields that you hold, according as was done of old in the time of the Saracens."[29]

[25] Chivert Charter: "aljupum quod est in mezquita maiori cum omnibus plateis per quas aqua venit et currit ad aljupum." Catalan *aljub* means a reservoir or covered cistern.

[26] Eslida Charter: "explectent aquas suas, sicut fuit tempore sarracenorum, et dividant eas sicut inter eos consuetum est." "Divide" bore a technical meaning here, the effecting of proportional quotas by divisors (see the method in Thomas F. Glick, "Levels and Levelers: Surveying Irrigation Canals in Medieval Valencia," *Technology and Culture*, IX [1968], 175 and plate).

[27] Játiva Charter: "aliquis cequiarius Xative non intret domos vel ravallos vestros pro aqua petenda vel accipienda, nisi cum uno sarraceno ravalli predicti." On *azofra*, see part 4 of this chapter.

[28] See the protracted dispute between the Mudejars of Eslida and Uxó over an irrigation system, in Burns, *Islam under the Crusaders*, ch. 11, part 1.

[29] Arch. Crown, James I, Reg. Canc. 15, fol. 90 (April 10, 1268). "Per nos et nostros concedimus vobis universis sarracenis de Aldaya alqueria de Quarto, presentibus et futuris, quod possitis facere parada in cequia que fluit apud Alacuas,

More promising than judicial notices is the information deriving from *alfarda*, if indeed that tax does relate to irrigation. One of the earlier Mudejar tax lists devotes itself to the *alfarda* from Prince Peter's holdings, located in that portion of southern Valencia where it flourished, and reports substantial sums. Four successive annual reports appear at this part of the royal register. One shows Alfandech de Marignén in 1269 giving 1,400 besants; Pego 1,500; Alcira 500; Beniopa near Gandía 1,500; and Sumacárcel 500.[30] A list for the same holdings the following year does not greatly differ; in the identical order, the sums amounted to 1,500, 1,000, 1,000, 1,200, and 300 besants.[31] By the official equivalence of besant to solidus, the figures increase nearly fourfold to fit the normal money pattern of the kingdom. It is clear that income from these holdings was considerable. The places involved represent both city huerta watered from a major river and backwoods mountain-valley huerta using very small rivers and springs.

As with household and commercial taxes, the crown sometimes singled out the *alfarda* for special mention from the mass of revenues, indicating its honored position. A sale in 1270 conveyed "all revenues, fruits, receipts, income, and other fees of our bailiwick of Alcira and of the Saracens of the Moorish section of its district, and

---

ad rigandum illos quattuor campos, quos vos tenetis, prout antiquius tempore sarracenorum fuit consuetum. Mandantes firmiter vicariis, baiulis, curiis, iusticiis, et universis aliis officialibus et subditis nostris presentibus et futuris, quod super hoc nullum vobis impedimentum vel contrarium faciant nec fieri ab aliquo vel aliquibus permittant ullo modo. Datum Valencie, iiii idus Aprilis, anno domini mcclx octavo." A *parada* or canal check was an obstructing slat, positioned to divert water, either permanently or during the time for irrigating a field. It is hard to say whether the "olden" custom here refers to the Aldayans' right to divert this water or to the procedures now to be followed in effecting the diversion.

[30] *Ibid.*, Reg. Canc. 35, fol. 32 (Nov. 18, 1269): "dominus infans iactavit sarracenis suis regni Valencie alfardas inferius nominatas." Of these the prince remitted ("dimisit") respectively 300, 900, 200, 500, and 370 besants; did they represent capital improvement or other extraordinary expense?

[31] *Ibid.*, fol. 32v (Nov. 13, 1270), one of the four on fols. 32r-v and 33, and representative: "saccavit dominus infans . . . alfardas a sarracenis suis regni Valencie / Alfandech de Marynnen, md bisantii recipia[n]tur / Algazira, mille . . . / Pego, mille . . . / Beniopa, mcc / Suma carcel, ccc." Fol. 32v (1269): "petiit dominus infans has alphardas a sarracenis suis regni Valencie"; Alfandech gave 1,600 besants, Alcira 500, Pego 900, Beniopa 1,200; and Sumacárcel 300. Fol. 33 (Oct. 13, 1272): "iactavit has alfardas"—Alcira 1,000 solidi [*sic*], Alfandech 1,500 besants, Beniopa 1,200 besants, and Sumacárcel 300 besants.

also their *alfarda*."[32] At Beniopa in 1272 the *alfarda* not only got separate mention but had its sum specified—"all the revenues [of the Moors] . . . and also the *alfarda* of 1,200 besants"; accounts for 1268 show these came also from the region or countryside, and that 100 of the besants went into costs of collecting.[33] At Alcira in 1270 the formula ran: "all the revenues . . . and also the *alfarda* of these Saracens."[34] When King Peter sold the income of Callosa, Castell, Confrides, Guadalest, Jalón, Pop, Sagra, and Vall de Laguart in 1282, he retained three important taxes, including the *alfarda*, "which we especially reserve to do with as we wish during the same period."[35] He had made the same reservation previously when selling the revenues of Vall de Laguart and Pop.[36]

The *alfarda* also occurs at Biar in 1267, joined with other taxes paid in a single sum;[37] at Tárbena and Jalón in 1268;[38] at Pego in

[32] *Ibid.*, Reg. Canc. 37, fol. 14 (March 19, 1270): "omnes redditus, fructus et exitus, proventus et alia iura baiulie nostre Algazire et sarracenorum morarie et termini eiusdem ac etiam alfardam ipsorum sarracenorum." See also the identical but canceled document of the same date in Reg. Canc. 35, fol. 56v.

[33] *Ibid.*, Reg. Canc. 37, fol. 60v (Jan. 23, 1272): "omnes redditus [sarracenorum] . . . et cum alfarda millium ducentorum bisanciorum." Reg. Canc. 35, fol. 3 (1268): "lalfarda de Beniopa e del termino, m besants c; item collidura, c besants."

[34] *Ibid.*, Reg. Canc. 35, fol. 56v (March 19, 1270): "omnes redditus . . . ac etiam alfardam ipsorum sarracenorum."

[35] *Ibid.*, Peter III, Reg. Canc. 51, fol. 27 (March 3, 1282): "nos Petrus dei gratia rex Aragonum vendimus a kalendis proximi preteriti Ianuarii, ad unum annum primum venturum, vobis aliamis sarracenorum de Çagra, de Alaguar, de Pop, de Xalon, de Callosa, et [*sic*] Algar, de Confrides, de Godalesth, et de Castell omnes redditus nostros, exitus, proventus, et fructus, et omnes calonias et alia iura nostra locorum predictorum, scilicet vobis de Çagra redditus, fructus, et omnia iura de Çagra pro mille et c solidis regalium, et vobis aliame de Alaguar. . . ." At the end of the total reckoning the crown applied the sale to all these places: "exceptis . . . alphardis . . . , quas nobis specialiter retinemus ad nostram voluntatem faciendam infra dictum tempus."

[36] *Ibid.*, Reg. Canc. 42, fol. 215v (Feb. 8, 1279): "nos Petrus etc. vendimus vobis aliame de Pop a kalendis mensis Ianuarii proventus ad unum annum videlicet çofras, calonias, et alia iura nostra dicti castri, retentis nobis alfarda . . . et iusticiis in criminalibus, precio ii millium [solidorum]. . . ." *Ibid.*, separate document: "similis fuit facta aliame de Alaguar precio iii millium et cccc solidorum, solvendorum in festo Sancti Michaelis medietatem et aliam medietatem per totam mensem Decembris; datum ut supra."

[37] *Ibid.*, James I, Reg. Canc. 15, fol. 84 (March 1267): "alfardam."

[38] *Ibid.*, fol. 105v-106 (May 4, 1268): "et alfardis, çofris, almagramis, bisanciis." Eighteen towns of these regions are named as included, "cum terminis et alqueriis suis."

1269, where it brought 660 besants minus 60 for collection costs;[39] at Alfandech in 1275;[40] at Vall de Gallinera in 1278;[41] at Beniopa again in 1282;[42] at Játiva in 1283;[43] and as one of the important regalian revenues from the Pego and Uxó valleys at the end of the century.[44] The Gallinera letter has special interest; the king ordered his Valencian lieutenant to surrender two-thirds of Gallinera's *alfarda* to Simon (Eximèn) López of Embún, either to pay a debt or as a boon, and to leave the rest with the aljama "on account of the damage and loss they suffered by reason of the war"—a valuable reference to the great revolt of the 1270's. A contribution to more general knowledge about the *alfarda* under King James comes from King Peter's 1280 order to his bailiffs, castellans, and tax farmers for the Valencian kingdom's aljamas. The officials were to put aside for the church, among other items, a tenth of the *alfarda* due to the crown in those quarters, "just as in the time of Friar Andrew, the deceased bishop of Valencia, ... it had been the custom for [this] to be given to the bishop and chapter."[45] The document, heavily interlineated and corrected, exempts some *alfarda*, perhaps as not going directly to the

[39] *Ibid.*, Reg. Canc. 35, fol. 41r,v (1269): "item alfarda de Pego, dc besants; collidura, lx besants."

[40] *Ibid.*, Reg. Canc. 20, fol. 245 (April 27, 1275): "alfardam."

[41] *Ibid.*, Peter III, Reg. Canc. 40, fol. 103v (May 12, 1278). "Petrus dei gratia rex Aragonum viro nobili et dilecto Roderico Eximini de Luna procuratori regni Valencie, salutem et dilectionem. Sciatis quod Eximinus Lupi de Embu petivit a nobis dare [*canceled?*] quod mandaremus ei dari a sarracenis de Gallinera alfardam consuetam anni preteriti, quia ipse emit redditus dicti loci. Quare mandamus vobis quatenus si dicti sarraceni consueti [?] sunt dare alfardam quolibet anno, de ipsa alfarda faciatis eidem Eximino Lupi dari duas partes, et residua etiam proinde remanere volumus dictis sarracenis propter dampnum et detrimentum quod passi sunt racione guerre. Datum Dertuse, vi idus Madii, anno domini mcclxx octavo."

[42] See the long document in note 46, directed to its *amin.*

[43] Arch. Crown, Peter III, Reg. Canc. 60, fol. 91 (April 18, 1283): "baiulo Xative: intelleximus quod illi sarraceni Xative, qui collegerunt alfardas quas sarraceni ipsius loci dederunt domino regi, collegerunt et receperunt ab ipsis sarracenis ratione ipsarum alfardarum plus quam deberent et quam dederunt domino regi, quare vobis mandamus quatenus si sit ita dictos sarracenos et bona sua [?] compellatis ad ... restituendum incontinenter. ..."

[44] Document in Chapter IV, n. 58.

[45] Arch. Crown, Peter III, Reg. Canc. 48, fol. 176 (Nov. 8, 1280): "sicut tempore fratris Andree [Albalat] quondam episcopi valentini ... dari fuerat [*sic*] consuetum episcopo et capitulo." *Frater* because he was a Dominican friar, Albalat served as third bishop of Valencia from 1248 to 1276; in a resounding quarrel during his tenure, the problems of tithes and firstfruits were threshed out to a settlement in 1268 (see Burns, *Crusader Valencia*, I, 25-27 on Albalat, and ch. 9 on the tithe fight).

king. Particularly significant is the fact that the reference to the bishop's time makes the *alfarda* payment a general thing in the kingdom from at least 1268 to past 1280.

A strange document of 1282, routine in nature, seems to say that something under twenty solidi was not too much to expect from each household. Directed "to the *amīn* of the aljama of Saracens of Beniopa," it deals with the complaint of James Castellá "that you force his Saracens of Beniarjó to contribute in the same way as you do to that sum of money that we currently wish to have as *alfarda*." The crown must have found the charge justified; it concluded: "since the said Saracens pay us twenty solidi for every house every year, a fact we believe you know, we order you not to compel them to contribute to the aforesaid *alfarda*, unless they are bound to do so under the treaty made between them and me, or unless another just reason warrants it, which warranting reason you are to convey to me."[46] There is a complication here. The twenty solidi was not a substitute for *alfarda*. Peter had recently imposed a novel charge of twenty solidi, which the parliament of the next year at Valencia would force him to annul.[47] If he meant this temporary tax, then the letter represents a suspension of *alfarda* where the new charge proved burdensome. If the incident implied any equivalence between the taxes—improbable in view of the normal *pro rata* manner of assessing unequal landowners unequally—it might easily be under-

---

[46] Arch. Crown, Peter III, Reg. Canc. 46, fol. 78v (April 11, 1282). "Alamino aliame sarracenorum Benioppe. Intelleximus per Iacobum Castellani quod vos compellitis sarracenos suos de Beniiarion ad contribuendum simile vobiscum in ista quantitate pecunie, quam a vobis modo habere volumus pro alfarda. Unde cum dicti sarraceni dent nobis viginti solidos pro quolibet casato quolibet anno secundum quod vos scire credimus, mandamus vobis quatenus non compellatis eos ad contribuendum in predicta alpharda [*sic*], nisi ex pacto facto inter nos et ipsos facere teneantur vel nisi alia iusta causa subsit, quam si subsit ad nos transmittatis. Datum Valencie, iii idus Aprilis, anno domini [mcclxxii]." The pact may be the original surrender during the crusade, but probably is a renegotiated treaty or confirmation after the 1275-1278 revolt.

[47] *Furs*, lib. VIII, rub. viii, c. 28: "illos viginti vel duodecim solidos nec alia quae erant de novo imposita." Unless the besant is meant, this may be the tax to whose collection King Peter appointed Judah b. Manasseh: "pro colligendis dictis denariis," explaining that "quolibet anno dare tenentur pro quolibet casato sarracenorum"; see David Romano Ventura, "Los hermanos Abenmenassé al servicio de Pedro el Grande de Aragón," *Homenaje a Millás-Vallicrosa*, 2 vols. (Barcelona, 1954-1956), appendix, doc. 8 (Jan. 29, 1283).

stood how the tax simultaneously maintained the canals and enriched the overlord.

Tracking *alfarda* through the reign of Peter's successor, Alfonso III, raises two impressions: the geographic focus continues to be the mountainous south rather than the central huertas, and the meaning shifts to suggest a special levy. It appears again in grants alongside every other tax, so as to preclude identification with any major imposition, and again it involves considerable sums. Alcira, Uxó, and Valencia city recur, but the main contributors are located from Játiva and Alfandech south or southeast. In 1290 Alfonso required Gallinera, Játiva and Vall de Laguart to give 3,000 solidi each; Guadalest, Jalón, and Uxó 2,000 each; and Tárbena 1,000. "Because of the present war we have with the Zaragozans and some nobles of Aragon, we need a great deal of money," Alfonso wrote in 1287 to nearly two dozen Mudejar communities of Valencia, demanding from each a specified sum as *alfarda*, totaling 47,000 solidi. After remitting 18,000 of this, Alfonso took the following sums in solidi from each (the previous year's rather similar and adjusted *alfarda*-as-subsidy appears in parentheses for comparison): Alcira 200 (200), Alfandech 8,000 (3,000), Beniopa 3,000 (2,000), Callosa with Algar 1,000 (400), Carbonera with Rugat 1,000 (300), Castell 1,000 (750), Cocentaina 500 (200), Finestrat 500 (missing), Gallinera with Alcalá 3,000 (3,000), Guadalest 1,200 (1,200), Jalón 1,000 (200), Játiva 4,000 (8,000), Mogente 1,000 (2,000), Montesa 1,000 (4,500), Pego 500 (750), Pop 1,500 (750), Sagra missing (300), Sumacárcel with Cárcer 500 (300), Tárbena missing (400), Uxó 2,000 (1,500), Valencia 500 (400), and Vall de Laguart 3,500 (1,500). Just after the turn of the century "the *alfarda* that the said Moors pay to the lord king" below the Júcar at Elche amounted to over 7,000 solidi every year (erroneously copied by a modern editor as 57,000); separate accounts for Aspe show it contributing 2,000 solidi annually.[48]

---

[48] Arch. Crown, Alfonso III, Reg. Canc. 82, fol. 72 (1290 ?): "fuit scriptum aliame sarracenorum de Alaguar quod dent pro alfarda iii millia solidorum regalium; Exalone ii millia solidorum; Galinera iii millia solidorum; Tarbena m solidos; Godalest ii millia solidorum; istas colligit Bernardus Sabater pro Arnaldo de Bastida; [d]e Xativa iii millia solidorum; Uxon[e] ii millia solidorum; istas colligit Iacobus de [V]allo." Reg. Canc. 68, fol. 62 (Nov. 21, 1287), a form letter, with list of other addressees appended: "fidelibus suis aliame sarracenorum de Algezira [*Alcira*] salutem et gratiam; cum ratione presentis guerre quam habemus cum Cesaraugustaniis et aliquibus nobilibus Aragonie peccuniam quamplurimam neces-

An air of mystery persists. The ambiguity of the term *alfarda*, both in its remote Arabic etymology and in its Catalan medieval form, cautions against proposing generalizations. Taking it as head tax, levy, residential fee, tribute, agrarian rents, or in some other nonirrigation sense, the *alfarda* represents an outstanding Mudejar contribution to the crown coffers. Taking it as identified with the water tax or as in some coordinate way allied to irrigation or irrigated land, it provides one of the many indications of agrarian continuity in the conquered kingdom. The placing of important aljamas, from *alfarda* documents surviving in random pattern, may reflect the persistence of exclusively Mudejar water communities at places like the Alcira huerta as well as in the more inhospitable south. Payment on the scale described shows that the Moorish communities continued to be prosperous and, in point of land ownership and operation, functioned fairly independently. By falling on central aljamas like Alcira and Pego the *alfarda* stresses again the close connection between the Islamic town and its surrounding hinterland, a pattern repeated in Valencian Christian society.

---

sariam habeamus, mandamus vobis quatenus detis nobis pro alfarda. . . ." Reg. Canc. 68, fols. 48v-49 (Sept. 19, 1286), a form letter with similar list: "alamino et toti aliame sarracenorum de Muntesa, cum ratione negotiorum in [necessitatibus] sumus . . . donetis nobis pro alfarda. . . ." See also Reg. Canc. 81, fol. 80 (March 24, 1290): "exigendis pro nobis alfardas seu quascumque alias exacciones a sarracenis montanearum Valencie [ultra] Xucharum." Reg. Canc. 82, fol. 170v (Dec. 18, 1290), assigning "super alfardis sarracenorum Valentie, Xative, et Uxonis" a debt of 2,400 solidi, "ratione illorum aparatiorum que se tenet cum alfondico dicti regni Valencie." Reg. Canc. 78, fol. 15v (Nov. 16, 1288): "de d[enariis] alfardarum sarracenorum regni Valencie." Reg. Canc. 82, fol. 89v (Dec. 13, 1290): "collectoribus alfardarum sarracenorum Valentie, Xative, et Uxonis ut observent . . . assignacionem." Reg. Canc. 78, fol. 29v (Jan. 22, 1289): "racione alfardarum seu cenarum vestrarum," to be kept by Empress Constance at Alcalá, Alfandech, and Beniopa. Reg. Canc. 78, fol. 24 (Jan. 13, 1289): a debt assigned "super alfardis sarracenorum de Xativa et de Uxone et super alfarda de Gallinera." Reg. Canc. 63, fol. 18 (Jan. 13, 1286), grant of Montaverner "cum questiis, cenis, caloniis, censualibus, tercia parte decimarum, bisanciis, soffris, almagranis, et alfardis." *Rentas de Aragón*, doc. 30, p. 111; "pot valer cascun any lalfarda quels dits moros paguen al senyor rey tro a lvii millia solidos"; careful addition of surrounding sums makes this enormous figure a transcription error for 7,000; ambiguous headings make it probable that these come only from Elche. Aspe is on p. 125: "val la alffarda . . . ii millia solidos." Elda, Novelda, and Aspe also submitted "los delmes ab la quels moros . . . donen," but as the Aspe confrontation of both taxes shows, this is a different tax. Elche had a separate entry besides for "laygua quel senyor rey ha en Elch, la qual se ven es partex per cascun dia als moros de las alqueries del dit loch Delch."

137

MILITARY OBLIGATIONS

Christian Spain had a long tradition of municipal militia, each town fielding its contingent of commoner soldiers. The obligation, especially for those not drafted in person, also assumed the form of a tax. The common military exactions, apart from the fifth of booty already discussed, were host and cavalcade. Host (*hostis*, Catalan [*h*]*ost*) or army duty (*exercitus*, Catalan *exèrcit*) meant a considerable gathering for offensive war on a time-consuming expedition; it implied an organized army led by the king or some other distinguished figure. By the thirteenth century it was often a money commutation. Both King James and Muntaner describe the Valencian crusaders as a royal "host." Cavalcade involved a raid or a coordinated series of forays. Whereas cavalcade represented rather the action of a posse, host suggested a campaign. Catalonia's *Usatges* had understood cavalcade as a limited action for one day and district, as against wider military efforts called host.

By the Valencian crusade era, on the other hand, the paired phrasing "host and cavalcade" may have come to assume together the meaning of any formal military foray, or its corresponding indemnity, without too explicit an awareness of the opposed elements it combined; thus the Villafranca Christian charter stipulated host and cavalcade at the individual settler's expense for a month throughout the kingdom of Valencia, while other Valencians gave the name cavalcade to their wider adventures over many days elsewhere in Spain. Distinct from these offensive actions, at least in theory, stood the more universal obligation of local defense. Defensive drafts of a minor nature like castle guard, assistance or contribution for the baggage train, and construction or repair of defenses, were also allied in spirit.[49]

[49] Antonio Palomeque Torres discusses military obligation at length in his "Contribución al estudio del ejército en los estados de la reconquista," *AHDE*, xv (1944), 205-351; on host, see p. 219 and esp. pp. 231ff. García y García devotes a section to the Valencian Christian's military obligation (*Estado económico-social de Castellón*, pp. 42-43), with the Villafranca case. See also Mateu y Llopis, *Glosario hispánico de numismática*, pp. 274, 290; Rodón Binué, *Lenguaje técnico del feudalismo*, pp. 51-52, 142-143; García de Valdeavellano, *Instituciones españolas*, pp. 612-628; James in *Llibre dels feyts*, ch. 39; Muntaner, *Crònica*, ch. 43. *Usatges de Barcelona i commemoracions de Pere Albert*, ed. Josep Rovira i Ermengol (Barcelona, 1933), *text antic*, nos. 28-29, with note on p. 284. James F. Powers, who has a detailed study in preparation on medieval Castilian militia, wrestles with the several terms and their

The sums corresponding to host and cavalcade amounted, whether for commoner or noble, to commutation of service into money. In the Valencian kingdom this had particular relevance for Muslims. King James might have demanded military service. He did employ Muslims in his armies and contingents of Muslim allies on his Valencian crusade; in similar fashion Spanish Christians served in Islamic ranks both at home and in North Africa. In a colonial situation like Valencia, however, especially where the alien masses retained such strength, prudence counseled the gathering of funds rather than an armed host. Mudejar communities could substitute money for militia or for the maintenance of their share of soldiery. Precedent existed in James's realms for such a policy; the Tudela charter of 1119 had guaranteed Muslims against being forced to do military service, presumably substituting a money contribution. Valencian Christians occasionally substituted large sums in place of service; facing threats from abroad in 1285, the city of Valencia alone amassed a host and cavalcade of no less than 80,000 solidi.[50] Substitution of military taxes does not mean that Valencian Muslims went free of offensive, as against defensive, military service. The story of the Mudejar as warrior under the banner of Aragon, however, belongs less to a discussion of taxes than of political organization.[51] The more prevalent tradition of Christian Spain stressed reliance on Christian armies,

---

implications in "The Origins and Development of Municipal Military Service in the Leonese and Castilian Reconquest, 800-1250," *Traditio*, xxvi (1970), 91-111. These taxes were akin to the *tallia militum* on some Italian cities and to the feudal scutage. For Islamic war taxes and services, and on digging trenches, see Goitein, *Mediterranean Society*, ii, 393; Rabie, *Financial System of Egypt*, pp. 117-118, on war taxes such as the 1260 *dinār* per male or female taxpayer and the "cavalry tax" of an-Nāṣir in 1300, with Jews and Christians also paying; Siddiqi, *Public Finance in Islam*, pp. 127-128, on contributions to equip soldiers; and Lévi-Provençal, *España musulmana*, v, ch. 2, on the armies of caliphal Spain, including volunteers.

[50] Arch. Crown, Peter III, Reg. Canc. 58, fol. 94v (May 15, 1285): compare this with the Holy Land sums from Mudejars, below, p. 308. The Tudela Charter of 1119 provided: "et non faciat exire moro in apellito per forza in guerra de moros, nec de christianos . . . et non devetent nullus homo ad illos moros lures armas." *Apellido* (summons, or police alarm) technically involved local defense, though here it takes on a more aggressive form; see its use in *Llibre dels feyts*, ch. 151, and in Muntaner, *Crònica*, ch. 121.

[51] On Muslims and Valencian Mudejars in the service of Aragon, see Burns, *Islam under the Crusaders*, ch. 12; on troops from Christian Spain serving Islamic countries, see Burns, "Renegades, Adventurers, and Sharp Businessmen: The Thirteenth-Century Spaniard in the Cause of Islam," *Catholic Historical Review*, lviii (1972), 341-366.

drawing upon the minorities for financial support of the military and to some extent for auxiliaries and local defense.[52]

"Army duty [*exercitus*] and cavalcade and their money equivalents" show up as Mudejar regalian fees in 1273 at Játiva, and in 1270 at Chulilla. Both places appear by indirection, when King James exempted from the general obligation 'Alī al-Lūrī (Ali Allauri) of Játiva and " 'Īsā al-Waṣī [Ayca Alauxi] a Saracen of Chulilla."[53] The requisition of pack animals for military transport, a form of army tax called *atzembles* (Latin *azemile*) or "beasts of burden," also fell on Valencian Muslims. An incomplete list, drawn during James's preparations in 1273 to help Alfonso of Castile against a threatened invasion from North Africa, demanded 25 animals from the Mudejars of Biar, 12 from Cuart, 30 from Mogente, 6 from Onda, 9 from Segorbe, 16 from Sollana, and 24 from Uxó.

---

[52] Argument against a war tax on Christians, during a Monzón parliament a century later (1376), stressed that in the past Christians gave service, while Mudejars and Jews contributed money; see Salo W. Baron, *A Social and Religious History of the Jews*, 2d edn. rev., 15 vols. to date (New York, 1952ff.), XI, 112.

[53] Arch. Crown, James I, Reg. Canc. 19, fol. 53 (Sept. 7, 1273): "exercitu et cavalcata et eorum redempcionibus"; Reg. Canc. 16, fol. 229v (Jan. 20, 1270): "ab exercitu et cavalcata et eorum redemptionibus"; "Ayça Alauxi sarracenum de Xulela . . . [ab] exercitu et cavalcata et eorum redempcionibus." Alauxi may be genitive, or the suffix may form part of the name; al-Waqqashī (al-Uacaxi), leader of a Valencian faction in the Cid's day, also suggests itself, deriving from Huecas near Toledo, as do names like that of the jurist al-Awzāʿī or the Banū Aws; *aw, au, ue,* and *ua* can sustain alarming transpositions and stand for a variety of originals. Allowing for vagaries of Christian retranscription, the two names Allauri and Alauxi may be closer than their present forms indicate. Ayça resembles a number of names in Spanish Islam; Ibn Ayixa (Ibn 'Āisha) for example in 1091 conquered Murcia, and his son took Almeria. Axa is a very common first name on the thirteenth-century eastern coast, however, a variant being Eça, pointing to 'Īsā. *Exercitus* could appear along with host and cavalcade, as in a privilege King James gave at Valencia (Arch. Crown, James I, Reg. Canc. 16, fol. 215v [Oct. 21, 1270]): "tu Mahomat ballistarius Tutele de officio et magisterio ballisterie multipliciter commendaris, et residere in nostro dominio et mansionem in villa nostra Calatayubie facere elegistis; volentes tibi facere gratiam specialem racione predicti tui officii et quia sub spe nostri ad terram nostram venisti ad morandum, idcirco per nos et nostros enfranquimus et franchum et liberum facimus et imunem te Mahomat predictum et omnia bona tua ab omni ostia, peita, cena, exercitu, cavalgata ac qualibet alia exaccione regali vel redempcionibus eorundem . . . in quocumque loco dominationis nostre volueris comorari." Later in the letter the series omits *ostia*. At Zaragoza in 1286 a payment "de denariis alfonsaderie sarracenorum" designated redemptions of military service, but the term does not occur among Valencian Mudejars; see Arch. Crown, Alfonso III, Reg. Canc. 67, fol. 105 (Oct. 24, 1286), and on fol. 110 see Salimah (En Calena) "alcalde sarracenorum, magister ingeniorum" or armaments specialist for the crown.

The same list required contributions from fourteen towns of southern Valencia not formally designated as "Saracen" but of dominantly Muslim population, probably as a levy on their Christian overlords; items include 12 animals from Confrides, 20 from Gallinera with Alcalá, 40 from Guadalest, 25 from Penáguila, and 50 from "Tárbena with its countryside."[54] The more general terms "host" and "cavalcade" probably included this lesser obligation, since Mudejar charters do not advert to it explicitly; non-Valencian Masones, whose Muslims won freedom from many taxes in 1263, aligned it as a separate charge: "host, cavalcade and *atzembles*, and their money equivalents." Guard dogs for castle defense, a Moorish custom long adopted by Christians and used in Valencia at this time, do not appear explicitly in Mudejar documentation.[55]

In 1274 the crown freed Mudejar settlers along the Alcira irrigation system from "army duty [*exercitus*] and cavalcade, and the money equivalents of these."[56] The charter of Eslida, Veo, Ahín, and allied towns dismissed the obligation: "and they are not to make any redemption or host." The charter's term was not *redempciones* as in the previous privilege but *franga*, apparently a derivative of *francum* or free, meaning payment in lieu of military offensive operations.[57] Chivert's concession released the aljama from host and

---

[54] Arch. Crown, James I, Reg. Canc. 18, fol. 51r,v (May 16, 1273): "dominus rex misit pro acemilis inferius scriptis, pro viatico Yspanie . . . : sarraceni de Segorbe iii, vi [azemilas]; sarraceni de Onda ii, iv; sarraceni de Uxo ix, xv; sarraceni de Cuart v, vii; sarraceni de Suylana vi, x; sarraceni de Moxen x, xx; sarraceni de Biar x, xv. . . . Tarbana cum terminis xx, xxx." Miret y Sans puzzled over the "curiosa anotació" about "Yspania" and conjectured a raid on Granada; he does not give the document, but like myself interprets the double numbers as cumulative rather than corrective (*Itinerari*, p. 482). On the Moorish custom of guard dogs see Menéndez Pidal, *España del Cid*, I, 480. Castle guard may have been part of the vigilance or guard tax called *guaita* or *gueta* (Rodón Binué, *Lenguaje técnico del feudalismo*, pp. 126-127).

[55] Masones Privilege: "hoste, cabalgata et asemyles et eorum redemptionibus." *Atzembla*, Castilian *acémila*, derives from Arabic *az-zāmila*, beast of burden. See García de Valdeavellano, *Instituciones españolas*, p. 603; Dozy and Engelmann, *Glossaire*, p. 33; Steiger, *Contribución*, p. 146. When the Mudejars of Majorca joined with Christians and Jews to equip galleys for war, it is not easy to say whether their ship tax, or perhaps voluntary contribution, assimilates to redemption of armed service (see Lourie, "Free Moslems in the Balearics," p. 641).

[56] Arch. Crown, James I, Reg. Canc. 19, fol. 124 (April 16, 1274): "et exercitu ac cavalcata et redempcionibus eorum."

[57] Eslida Charter: "et non faciant aliquam frangam vel hostem." The word cannot come from Catalan *franga* or *franja* (fringe), or *fragua* (a form of *fabrica*),

cavalcade against Muslim or Christian, while retaining the obligation of defensive war in the event of Muslim or Christian attack against the local castle, "and then the Moors of Chivert should defend themselves and their property together with the Brothers [Hospitaller] as best they can." This involved actual service at the side of the knights who garrisoned the castle.[58] The Mudejar communities of Alfamén and Almonacid, who paid the military charges until King James exempted them, have been erroneously cited as Valencian examples; when Moses of Portella attempted to collect there during the 1277 revolt, King Peter wrote from his siege camp at Montesa to "desist for now from the demand you are making or should make . . . by reason of the army obligation or its redemption," since each of these aljamas had "a charter of exemption."[59]

Uxó's charter mentioned only services to the castle, given according to past Islamic custom; from subsequent directives it becomes apparent that the Uxó Moors also fell under army taxes. In 1284 King Peter ordered Conrad Lanza "to reduce the contributions that the said Saracens made for the work of [Uxó] castle, namely in construction work."[60] By this concession the king meant to ease Uxó's burden in meeting army obligation—a link between castle service

---

or *tragina* (haulage); on the other hand the common Latin derivatives of *francum* in Catalonia were *franquitia, franchidia, franchitas, francheda,* etc. The word does not appear in any of the *Cartas de población de Cataluña* of Font y Rius.

[58] Chivert Charter: "insuper serraceni non teneantur facere hostem vel cavalcatam contra sarracenos alios aut christianos nisi forte aliqui sarraceni aut christiani facerent aliquod malefficium vel forciam vel gravamen castro suo et rebus, et tunc mauri Exiverti una cum fratribus deffenderent se suaque secundum posse suo."

[59] Arch. Crown, James I, Reg. Canc. 39, fol. 234v (July 28, 1277): "Petrus dei gratia rex Aragonum fideli suo Muçe de Portella baiulo et merino nostro, salutem et gratiam; mandamus vobis quatenus a peticione quam faciatis seu facere debetis alyami sarracenorum d'alfamem racione exercitus vel redempcionis eiusdem cum carta nostra desistatis ad presens . . . propter cartam franquitatis quam habent a domino Iacobo inclite recordacionis regis Aragonum." The place, also here as "de lalfamem" entered the Martínez Ferrando *Catálogo* (I, no. 259) as Valencian but is Alfamén, between Daroca and Zaragoza. Its companion place ("simile fuit missa eidem Muçe super facto sarracenorum d'Almonazir") is not Valencian Almonacid but Almonacid de la Sierra, near Alfamén. See also Chapter IV, n. 115.

[60] Arch. Crown, Peter III, Reg. Canc. 46, fol. 221v (July 9, 1284): "faciat temperamentum de missionibus quas dicti sarraceni fecerunt in operibus de castro videlicet de manobres." Uxó Charter. García de Valdeavellano distinguishes *castellaria*, personal work on castles, from *castellaje*, a commercial tax on traveling salesmen (*Instituciones españolas*, p. 252).

and army payment that throws light on both. A transfer of taxes to a new lord at the end of the century makes it clear that both the Uxó and Pego regions regularly paid "army dues and cavalcades and their redemption." Eslida's charter, already free of army charges, also dismissed "any service for castles," a plural reservation because it involved half a dozen districts.[61] One list of expenditures from 1255, shortly after the crusade, may reflect direct Mudejar taxes or else income derived by a local man from his Muslims and few Christians; items include 1,500 solidi "for the work of the castle" at Segorbe, and 3,000 "for work on the walls" at Gandía.[62] Precedents existed for widespread commutation of a military labor; eighty years before, for example, the crown had permanently dismissed service on castle works by Tortosa's Muslims in return for 400 "mazmodins of pure gold"; the decision applied to defensive works anywhere in Tortosa or its surrounding jurisdiction.[63]

By nature sporadic, and often enough realized by actual manpower rather than money substitute, the host and cavalcade are naturally difficult to find in revenue accounts. One such list, drawn in 1275 to meet a threat of invasion from North Africa together with a local Mudejar rebellion, distinguished contributors as Mudejars in only one entry. The list contains thirteen towns above the Júcar to which a form letter had gone out, requiring from each a specific sum as commutation of "army service," and another list of nine towns below the Júcar, with special entries for Jewish communities. From Valencia city the king expected 40,000 solidi and waived another 20,000; from Alcira, Játiva, and Morella he asked 10,000 each; from Murviedro 7,000; from Cullera, Gandía, Onda, and Segorbe 4,000 each; from Alcoy, Burriana, Corbera, and Onteniente 3,000 each; from Alpuente, Cocentaina, and Liria 2,000 each; from Ademuz, Albaida, Castielfabib, Luchente, and Peñíscola, 1,000 each; and from Bocairente only 500. Though ten Jewish communities gave a total of 9,000 solidi, the only Muslims specified were those of Játiva, at 1,000

---

[61] Martínez y Martínez, "Pego," doc. on pp. 68-69 (1300): "exorcitibus [sic] et cavalcatis et redemptionibus eorum." Second Eslida Charter: "servitutem castrorum."

[62] Arch. Crown, James I, Reg. Canc. 8, fol. 21v (Nov. [?] 26, 1255): "pro opere castri"; "in opere murorum."

[63] Tortosa Convention, negotiated a quarter-century after the surrender charter, in Fernández y González, *Mudejares de Castilla*, appendix, doc. 9 (June 18, 1174), and in *Documentos inéditos de Aragón* VIII, 50-52: "faciat operam . . . neque in castris."

besants or some 3,750 solidi.[64] By this date Játiva was the most important Mudejar community in the realm, the focus for rebellion and Islamic culture alike. Perhaps the other Mudejar populations contributed along with their Christian neighbors to the total of over 100,000 solidi given by the twenty-two towns as described.

Records for this same tax, drawn severally from sixteen Mudejar communities of Aragon proper at this very time, show that Zaragoza, Calatayud, Daroca, Tarazona, and Teruel together mustered only 3,900 solidi, almost the same as the single contribution of Játiva.[65] In the Aragonese list, six towns ranked at the level of 750 solidi; only four paid as high as 1,250 to 1,500 each; three paid 225 each; one gave 650, one 150, and one 80. Thus Játiva was giving an extraordinarily high commutation fee when compared to the Aragonese cities' contribution for the same troubles.

Eventually the Aragonese aljamas were summoned for actual military service in 1277 in Valencia; the crisis passed, however, so the crown commuted this to a large quantity of money: 3,000 solidi of Jaca from each of three towns, 2,000 each from two more, and 1,000 from a last; the crown also ordered the Catalan and Aragonese aljamas to forward forthwith a massive supply of crossbow bolts.[66] When France invaded Aragon a decade later, King Peter ordered every Valencian aljama to send its contingent of Muslim troops north, "well-equipped and well-trained"; a 600 man unit did special service at the siege of Gerona. Despite the obligatory nature of this draft, the crown paid the Muslims "a good salary." When the king's procurator in Valencia attempted to collect army charges from aljamas that had sent men, the king sharply ordered him to desist.

[64] Arch. Crown, James I, Reg. Canc. 23, fol. 8v (July 23, 1275): "item iactavit dominus rex sarracenis Xative mille bisancios et debet eos recipere Guillelmus de Turribus."

[65] Ibid., Reg. Canc. 17, fol. 8v (April 11, 1275), four lists, in column, with two more (Exea and Jaca merinates) on fol. 9; only the list on the Zaragoza merinate and list four name "Saracens."

[66] Soldevila, Pere el Gran, part 2, 1, appendix, doc. 83 (July 25, 1277): "placeat nobis quod remaneatis ab exercitu in quo ad partes Valencie vos venire mandavimus et quod donetis pro redempcione eiusdem duo mille solidorum iaccensium"; six copies were sent, to as many aljamas of Moors. In doc. 86 (Aug. 5, 1277), the king demands that the Mudejars send "v mille vel vi mille treites et v balestes de tornio et sagetes ad earum pertinentium" (no addressee), with another 10,000 from the "aliama sarracenorum Cesarauguste"; 10,000 from Huesca's Moors; 5,000 from Tarazona's; 5,000 from Calatayud's; 10,000 from Daroca; 5,000 from Teruel; and 2,000 from Catalonia's Lérida.

Muslim army groups would continue to attend the Spanish Christian wars; and as late as the end of the fifteenth century at Valencia, the standard list of Mudejar obligations, as recorded in a notarial form, included "host and cavalcade, as well as their money commutations."[67]

The evidence suggests widespread military obligation or at least money commutations, with exemption for some areas and occasions. No clear pattern emerges. Why should Chulilla, Játiva, and Uxó fall under the burden, for example, when Eslida did not and Chivert only partially? Did this sort of exaction fall within the area of bargaining during surrender negotiations? More probably a clue to the answer lies in contemporary Christian charters; Font y Rius, in the absence of military services in many charters, argued a trend toward excluding such service. Gual Camarena, along the same line of thought, believed Mudejars commonly won exemption. García y García, on the other hand, though observing that most Christian charters of northern Valencia omitted express mention of host and cavalcade, concluded that the obligation held universally, except when expressly exempted. Valencian Mudejars, as their service in the French war suggests, may have come into the same pattern.[68] Insofar as tax structures mirrored the economic societies of Christian and Muslim, the two peoples again show similarity; presumably they were capable of mutual sympathy at this level, and of assimilation to common patterns of life.

SALT, MONEYAGE, AND LIVESTOCK CHARGES

Other general taxes can be grouped into several miscellanies. Some were obviously important; others formed part of that multiplicity of small fees that research seems never to exhaust. Valencian sources unfortunately saw fit to chronicle specific taxes only spo-

---

[67] *Formularium diversorum contractuum*, fols. xxviiii-xxx. At the turn of the century, as a relief measure for Murcia's Mudejars, who had suffered much "por razon de las guerras e de los otros males," Ferdinand IV of Castile decreed: "tengo por bien que los dichos moros no vayan en hueste si no con el dicho concejo de Murcia en uno e syn departimiento de ellos"; redemption from host would not be allowed here to individuals but only to the whole body. See Juan Torres Fontes, "Los mudéjares murcianos en el siglo xiii," *Murgetana*, xvii (1961), repaged offprint, doc. 2 (April 20, 1305). On the French war see the citations above, n. 51.

[68] Font y Rius, "Régimen municipal," part 1, p. 490. Gual Camarena, "Mudéjares valencianos, aportaciones," p. 194. García y García, *Estado económico-social de Castellón*, p. 43.

radically, as part of a normally undifferentiated complex presumably familiar to Muslims by custom. Salt monopolies comprised a significant and at times vexatious imposition on both Christian and Mudejar. The crown had never quite succeeded in establishing a de facto monopoly over salt mines and salt pans, though its control in a new kingdom like Valencia was stronger than in lands where entrenched privilege already flourished. The crown would manage successfully to impose a tax on sale of salt by private holders in 1300.[69]

In the Valencian kingdom important salt monopolies existed at the Albufera lagoon near Valencia city, at Alcira, Burriana, Calpe, Játiva, and especially Peñíscola; later in the century the Templars assumed control of the Peñíscola salt. Arcos, on the western border but outside Valencia proper, also served the new kingdom. In 1263, when renting the revenues of Játiva and its district to a Christian knight, King James made a point of including its saltworks, defined here as located at Castellón de Játiva (Villanueva de Castellón) and at Calpe; the king added a promise that he would "make each and every person of the kingdom of Valencia, who lives from the Júcar River south, Christians as well as Jews, and Saracens as well as the subjects of knights, religious orders, clerics, the crown, or of anyone else, use the salt of the aforesaid saltworks and not any other salt." The condition of Valencia's Mudejars in connection with this monopoly was exactly that of their Christian neighbors. This rental of revenues was transferred in 1267 to the castellan of Biar and Alcoy.[70]

---

[69] See as background Miguel Gual Camarena, "Para un mapa de la sal hispánica en la edad media," in *Homenaje a Jaime Vicens Vives*, 2 vols. (Barcelona, 1965), 483-497; Reyna Pastor de Togneri, "La sal en Castilla y León, un problema de la alimentación y del trabajo y una política fiscal (siglos x-xiii)," *CHE*, xxxvii-xxxviii (1963), 42-87; and Rafael Arroyo Ilera, "La sal en Aragón y Valencia durante el reinado de Jaime I," *Saitabi*, xi (1961), 253-261. The Gual Camarena study is the more useful, and includes a bibliography. See also García de Valdeavellano, *Instituciones españolas*, pp. 601-602 on salt in medieval Aragon; Asso, *Economía política de Aragón*, pp. 297-298, Piles Ros, *Bayle general de Valencia*, p. 91; for tariff on salt import see Gual Camarena, *Vocabulario*, p. 413, with documents 12 and 13 on Valencia city.

[70] Arch. Crown, James I, Reg. Canc. 12, fol. 147v (1263): "et salinas de Castilione et de Calp . . . promittentes per nos et nostros vobis et vestris quod faciemus universos et singulos homines regni Valentie qui sunt a rivo Xucari ultra, tam christianos quam iudeos et tam sarracenos et tam homines militum, ordinum, clericorum, nostrorum quam quorumlibet aliorum, uti de sale salinarum predictarum et non de aliquo alio sale." The date must be conjectured from the document's placing in the register. Reg. Canc. 15, fols. 53v-54 (April 9, 1267) has the later rental of

In 1263 also, the king rented to a consortium of five businessmen the salt revenues of the upper part of the Valencian kingdom, from the Cenia River marking its northern border down to Oropesa near Castellón; they were to make sure that every inhabitant purchased "the salt necessary in their homes" from the royal saltworks at Peñíscola. In drawing from this monopoly (*gabella*), customers were to pay for each cafiz of salt "the price contained in the *Furs* of Valencia." The king realized 1,500 solidi per year from this farming of the Peñíscola salt.[71] The crown emphasized its monopoly for the southern part of the Valencian kingdom in 1270 when farming "our saltworks of Játiva and the monopoly of salt of the same place for the kingdom of Valencia from the Júcar River down." The king "desired and decreed that each and every male or female Saracen, of towns or places either our own or of knights and religious orders and of anyone else from the Júcar River down, who is older than seven years, is bound to receive, just as is customary, and is to receive from the said salt, individual *barcelles* per person in each of those years"; Christians were similarly obliged. The revenue farmers had the further privilege "of making salt in the said saltworks of Játiva and in all our other saltworks that exist from the Júcar River down." This form letter was reissued in 1273 to the same entrepreneur, its wording altered to apply instead to Játiva and the kingdom of Valencia above the Júcar. Where the crown had asked 8,000 solidi

---

"redditus etiam salinarum nostrarum Xative." A lease of the Arcos monopoly contains technical information, in Reg. Canc. 14, fol. 18 *bis*, r-v (May 8, 1263): "quod teneatis caldiras in quibus decoquitur sal ipsarum salinarum"; "xv denarios iaccenses pro qualibet fanecha, sive cruda fuerit sive decocta." On the faneca, see n. 72.

[71] *Ibid.*, Reg. Canc. 12, fol. 153 (March 10, 1263): "vendimus vobis . . . gabellam nostram salis Peniscole . . . et omnes homines . . . comorantes infra terminos infrascriptos utantur de dicto salo [*sic*] et non de aliquo alio videlicet de rivo de Uldecona usque ad gradum Oropesie . . . [et] nullus sit ausus uti de aliquo alio sale nisi de sale gabelle predicte, et quod veniant cum omni sua missione ad accipiendum sal quod habuerit necesse in domibus suis ad dictam meam gabellam et debeant dare vobis et vestris pro unoquoque kafitio salis ad mensuram Valencie pretium in foro Valencie contentum." On the cafiz see n. 72. Mudejars are not specifically mentioned, but the universal application of the monopoly here, as well as analogy with the more explicit salt-document for the south of Valencia that year, indicates their inclusion. The crown, in speaking of "sal quod modo est in gabella Peniscole," uses the word throughout in the sense of "monopoly"; its more common sense means a tax upon staples; it derives probably from Arabic *qabāla* (cf. *alcabala* in Chapter IV, n. 25).

annually for three years, it now expected 9,000. Though not excluding Christians, the mandate again emphasized Mudejars, crown and seignorial.[72]

Possibly as a routine confirmation but more probably owing to the activity of private salt dealers, King Peter in 1278 reminded the Mudejars of their obligation to purchase royal salt. "To the Saracens beyond the Júcar who have been accustomed to receive salt from the monopoly of our saltworks, greetings and good wishes: we order that you receive of the aforesaid salt just as has been the custom." He warned of customary punishments for violators. The "custom" probably goes back into Islamic times; the Mudejar charter at Alfandech, for example, in retaining Islamic customs, included buying salt as of old.[73] So far these documents have concerned the northern or southern portions of the realm. In 1279 the crown caused the bailiff of Valencia city to issue a like reminder for the central part, that Christians, Saracens, and Jews all "take and use salt from our Valencian monopoly according to the laws of Valencia." The bailiff was to "take care and have care taken lest any of the aforesaid use other salt."[74]

---

[72] *Ibid.*, Reg. Canc. 14, fol. 101 (May 9, 1270): "salinas nostras nostras [*sic*] Xative et gabellam salis eiusdem loci regni Valencie a rivo Xucari ultra . . . , volentes ac statuentes quod omnes et singuli sarraceni et sarracene villarum et locorum [tam] nostrorum quam militum et ordinum ac quorumlibet aliorum a rivo Xucari ultra qui quidem sunt maiores vii[tem] annis teneantur prout fieri est consuetum accipere et accipiant de dicto sale singulas barcellas pro persona in unoquoque ipsorum annorum . . . ; volumus etiam et concedimus vobis quod possitis facere sal in dictis salinis Xative et in omnibus aliis salinis nostris que sunt a rivo Xucari ultra et ipsum vendere." Reg. Canc. 19, fols. 104v-105 (Dec. 19, 1273): "a rivo Xucari citra, cum iuribus nostris omnibus salinarum et gabelle predictarum et salis predicti." The *citra* is quite clear, and repeated. The Catalan *barcella* (Castilian *barchilla*), from Latin *particella*, was a grain measure varying according to place and time; medieval Tortosan law set 25 *barcelles* to the cafiz (not the land-measure cafizate above in the preface) as against 5 at Majorca. Eighteenth-century Valencia city had a *barcella* of 16¾ dry liters, and 12 *barcelles* or 6 *faneces* or 201 liters made a *cafís*. The *Aureum opus* set 8 *almuds* to the *faneca* and 6 *faneces* to the *cafís* (doc. 30, fol. 11 [Nov. 16, 1249]). Salt was paid at set times and "by houses and families" in Valencia into the sixteenth century, and its income was early set aside for common needs (Aliaga Girbés, "Moralidad de las exacciones tributarias de Valencia," pp. 130-131).

[73] Arch. Crown, Peter III, Reg. Canc. 40, fol. 84v (April 5, 1278): "Petrus sarracenis ultra Chucarum qui consueverunt recipere sal de gabella salinarum nostrarum Xative salutem et gratiam: mandamus vobis quatenus recipiatis de predicto sale prout consuetum est." Alfandech Charter.

[74] Arch. Crown, Peter III, Reg. Canc. 41, fol. 60 (April 5, 1279): "quod omnes

During these years a number of less general documents concerned the Mudejars' use of salt. King James adverted to the profitable salt income of southern Valencia in 1267 when he released the revenues of Gallinera and Alcalá to their respective aljamas but retained several taxes, including "sale of our salt."[75] In a charter of 1269 arranging administration for the district of Polop along with adjoining villages, he directed its Muslims to use the saltworks of Játiva. The context here involved a privilege by which the Mudejar nobiliary figure Abū Jaʿfar, "and the Saracens resident in the said places, be frank and free from that third-measure of salt that you were required to take every year at our saltworks of Játiva, in such wise that you or the Saracens of Polop and the aforesaid villages cannot be forced to accept the third-measure of salt; but you and these Saracens are to use our salt of the saltworks of Játiva or of Calpe, and no other salt, for your use and that of these Saracens and of your flocks and theirs." No charge was stated since a broker held all revenues here for 600 solidi a year to the king.[76]

The farmers of salt revenues, in their zeal to close the stubborn gap between law and practice, so increased their importunities that they precipitated a reaction. In defense of their own Mudejar revenues, Valencian barons induced King Peter in 1283 to legislate protection: "so that the Saracens not be compelled to take salt, except for what they wish to purchase in small quantity." The *Furs*

---

tam christiani quam sarraceni quam iudei qui accipere debent et uti iuxta forum Valencie sale nostro gabelle Valencie accipiant et utantur . . . [et] custodias et custodiri faciatis ne predicti utantur alio sale." On the saltworks of the Albufera lagoon, see Francisco de P. Momblanch y Gonzálbez, *Historia de la Albufera de Valencia* (Valencia, 1960), p. 45, and Carmen Caruana Tomás, *Estudio histórico y jurídico de la Albufera de Valencia, su régimen y aprovechamientos desde la reconquista hasta nuestros días* (Valencia, 1954), pp. 148-149, 189-190.

[75] Arch. Crown, James I, Reg. Canc. 15, fol. 88 (March 1, 1267): "et venditionem salis nostri."

[76] *Ibid.*, Reg. Canc. 16, fol. 156 (April 22, 1269): "concedentes tibi quod tu et sarraceni habitantes in dictis locis sitis franchi et liberi ab illa tertia quantitatis salis quam singulis annis percipere tenebamini in salinis nostris Xative, ita quod ad tertiam quantitatem salis accipiendam tu vel sarraceni de Polop et alqueriarum predictarum compelli non possitis; tu vero et ipsi sarraceni utamini sale nostro salinarum Xative vel de Calp et non alio sale ad usus tuos et ipsorum sarracenorum et ganatorum tuorum et suorum." On the addressee, a nephew of al-Azraq here miscopied by the Christian scribe as "Aliafer," see Burns, *Islam under the Crusaders*, ch. 14, part I.

incorporated this law, increasing its impact.[77] The crown did not back away however from its firm position. In mid-1284 Arabic letters went out "to all Saracens of the lord king in the kingdom of Valencia," instructing them anew to patronize only the royal works—"that they take his salt."[78]

Moneyage (*monetaticum*, Catalan *monedatge*) was a newly reformulated tax in the realms of Aragon. As a substitute for governmental tampering with coinage, it guaranteed merchant and household a firm currency. From an occasion of lively discontent among all classes when devised or renamed in 1205, it soon became the "least disliked of medieval taxes."[79] Eventually even the Castilian

[77] *Furs*, lib. VIII, rub. viii, c. 28: "et quod sarraceni non forcientur accipere sal nisi illud quod emere voluerint per minutum."

[78] Arch. Crown, Peter III, Reg. Canc. 46, fol. 221v (July 9, 1284): "fuit scriptum in arabico universis sarracenis domini regis regni Valencie quod reciperent de sale suo." The wording may restrict this order to Muslims on crown lands; in any case, exemptions doubtless existed.

[79] J. C. Russell, "The Medieval Monedatge of Aragon and Valencia," *Proceedings of the American Philosophical Society*, CVI (1962), 483. Ferran Soldevila, *Història de Catalunya*, 2d edn. rev., 3 vols. (Barcelona, 1962), I, 228 (discontent). Thomas Bisson has carefully untangled the antecedents and origins of the *monedatge* and placed it in its European context; the mintage tax, the Peace of God security on money, the regulative *confirmatio monete*, and the purchase or commutative *redemptio monete* all converged to produce *monedatge*. He has kindly allowed me to read the manuscript of his forthcoming book on money legislation. For a preview, arguing that *monedatge* continues a traditional tax under a new name and formula, see his "Sur les origines du *monedatge*: quelques textes inédites," *Annales du midi*, LXXXV (1973), 91-104. See also Felipe Mateu y Llopis, " 'Super monetatico' o 'morabetino' (breve noticia documental sobre el impuesto de monedaje en Aragón, Cataluña, Valencia, Mallorca, y Murcia, 1205-1327)," *Mélanges offerts à René Crozet*, ed. Pierre Gallais and Yves-Jean Riou, 2 vols. (Poitiers, 1966), I, 1115-1120; his "La regalía monetaria en la corona de Aragón y en especial en el reino de Valencia hasta Fernando el Católico," *Cuadernos de historia Jerónimo Zurita*, IV-V (1956), 55-79; and his "Para el estudio de monedaje en Aragón, Tortosa, y Lérida en el siglo XIV," in *Martínez Ferrando archivero: miscelánea de estudios dedicados a su memoria*, ed. anon. (Barcelona, 1968), 315-322, with references to notes on the topic in his other articles. His "Nómina de los musulmanes de las montañas de Coll de Rates del reino de Valencia en 1409," *Al-Andalus*, VI (1942), 299-335, on collection of the later *monedatge* from certain Mudejar areas of Valencia, is drawn from fifteenth-century codices in Arch. Reino Val. See also Asso, *Economía política de Aragón*, pp. 293-294. In 1284 Huesca alone brought nearly 7,000 solidi of Jaca from this tax, while in 1321 Aragon proper yielded over 707,000 solidi. Macho y Ortega, "Mudéjares aragoneses," p. 186, and Miguel Gual Camarena, "Los mudéjares valencianos en la época del Magnánimo," *IV Congrés d'història de la corona d'Aragó*, 2 vols. (Palma de Mallorca and Barcelona, 1959-1970), I, 471, discuss the tax for fifteenth-century Mudejars.

realm of Murcia petitioned for the right to Valencian coinage, offering to pay the allied moneyage. Crown land bore the weight of the tax; since lay and ecclesiastical lords were disinclined to admit unwonted taxes, a small crisis erupted whenever such a lord contrived to buy crown property.[80] Among the few who did win exemption were powerful nobles and poor people.

Consisting of one morabatin on St. Michael's Day in September every seventh year, on a house or property assessed at a minimum value of fifteen morabatins, moneyage came to be called simply "the morabatin." The gold *morabati* or *morabeti*, in origin an Almoravid money as its name indicates, was pegged for purposes of the tax at seven Valencian solidi. Thus the tax in Valencia translated at 6.66 percent over seven years on a unit of minimal value or over, but more practically at under 1 percent in the form of one solidus for any given year, affecting heads of households with properties worth at least 105 solidi. It fell on Christian and Mudejar alike.[81] Reorganized by the Monzón parliament of 1236, probably because of expenses connected with the Valencian crusade, the tax formally entered Valencian public law in a 1266 edict requested by the townsmen. Though Russell, a student of this tax, suspects that Valencians "did not grant it to the king" until that year, it may well be that the edict was meant rather as confirmation of previous documents issuing from the crown chancellery.[82] After all, Valencia had enjoyed its own special coins, mints, and coinage legislation for almost twenty years before towns and king arranged the culminating edict of 1266. In the decades after the fall of Valencia city, moneyage fell due throughout all of James's realms: in 1243 and 1250 (probably too early for the prostrate Valencian kingdom), 1257, 1264 (followed by a popular appeal and the king's edict of 1266), 1271, 1278, and 1285. The dates of actual collection in the kingdom of Valencia obeyed an understandably less tidy rhythm.

[80] Martínez Aloy, *Diputación de Valencia*, pp. 82-83.

[81] Russell, "Monedatge," pp. 489-490 on percentages and on collection from Mudejars in centuries after our own. In Aragon itself the minimum worth of property tax rose to 210 solidi, making for the far lighter tax rate of 3.33 percent as reckoned on the minimum alone.

[82] The 1266 decree is in *Aureum opus*, doc. 68, fols. 19v-20v (April 14). Felipe Mateu y Llopis also has the law of 1266 establish the tax; see his "Sobre el curso legal de la moneda en Aragón, Cataluña, Valencia, y Mallorca, siglos xiii y xiv," *VII Congrés d'història de la corona d'Aragó*, 3 vols. (Barcelona, 1963-1964), ii, 519; see also p. 523.

Probably the belated collection of moneyage below the Júcar River in 1268 at places such as Albaida depended upon Muslim sources, at least in good part, considering the slow pace of Christian settlement there.[83] During the 1271 collection, when taking moneyage from Valencian subjects of the Calatrava Knights, the crown specified Muslims as well as Christians.[84] Templar lands, on the other hand, may have paid no moneyage; in 1236 when James reorganized the tax, the Templar provincial master allowed its temporary collection, to help the crusade against Valencia, but reiterated his order's contrary privilege.[85] Such an occasional tax can turn up only in brief glimpses. A long accounting of revenues garnered to pay the expenses of King James's crusade into Murcia, to put down the Mudejar rebellion there in 1266, acknowledged the collection "of the moneyage of the kingdom of Valencia below the Júcar," in a context of collections "from the Christians of Aragon, Catalonia, and Valencia and from the Jews as also from the Saracens."[86] In transferring the largely Mudejar districts of Tárbena and Jalón to his mistress in 1268, King James included their "moneyage."[87]

One universal record for these early years remains, to demonstrate how widely and in what pattern King James took this tax from his Mudejars of Valencia. Since this was a directive rather than a receipt, no sums appear. The king ordered the castellan of Uxó to take "moneyage from the Saracens of the kingdom of Valencia" down to the Júcar River from 15 crown holdings, grouped into 12

[83] Arch. Crown, James I, Reg. Canc. 15, fol. 101 (May 5, 1268): "de monetatico . . . in villa de Albayda et omnibus aliis" below the Júcar.

[84] *Ibid.*, Reg. Canc. 16, fol. 248 (July 18, 1271): "tam christianis quam sarracenis qui sunt ordinis Calatrave." See *ibid.*, document of the same date appointing the tax collector.

[85] *Itinerari*, p. 125 (Nov. 15, 1236).

[86] Arch. Crown, James I, Reg. Canc. 50, fol. 40v (Jan. 9, [1266, for] 1267): "tam super christianis Aragonie, Catalonie, [et] Valencie, et iudeis, quam etiam sarracenis . . . et de monedatico regni Valencie citra Xucarum quod vos pro nobis colligi fecistis et recepistis." The obligation remained in the normal formula for Mudejar lands in the late fifteenth century: "monetatico sive morabatino" (*Formularium diversorum contractuum*, fols. xxviiii-xxx). On an apparently different use of *morabati*, as a Mudejar tax in Majorca, see Lourie, "Free Moslems in the Balearics," pp. 641-644.

[87] Arch. Crown, James I, Reg. Canc. 15, fol. 105v-106 (May 4, 1268): "et monedatico aliisque iuribus." At non-Valencian Masones, when most taxes paid "habitually" by the Moors were commuted to a lump sum, moneyage stayed among the essentials singled out for collection as usual (*ibid.*, perg. 1,738 [April 12, 1263]: "excepto monetatico").

units, as well as "from all the Moors of the church and of knights and of orders and other persons, and those [Moors] who work farms if they do not belong to castles of high barons or of knights or of townsmen with surrounding jurisdictions." An identical order went to another collector, covering Valencia from the Júcar southwards, naming 43 towns grouped into 29 units. The northern and central aljamas included Alcira, Almenara, Burriana, Cullera, Chulilla, Dos Aguas, Madrona, Millares, Murviedro, Onda, Peñíscola, Segorbe, Sollana, Valencia city, and Uxó. Below the ·Júcar the lists gave Albaida, Alcalá, Alcoy, Alfandech, Almizra, Benejama, Beniopa, Biar, Bocairente, Callosa, Calpe, Carbonera, Cárcer, Castalla, Castell, Cocentaina, Confrides, Denia, Gallinera, Gandía, Garig, Guadalest, Ibi, Jalón, Játiva, Jijona, Mogente, Onteniente, Palma, Pego, Penáguila, Polop or Pop, Relleu, Rugat, Sagra, Sierra de Finestrat, Sollana, Sumacárcel, Tárbena, Teulada, and Vall de Laguart. With Teulada was Morera, and with Benejama Negrete; Carbonera and Relleu were listed twice. This comprises one of the most complete listings of Mudejar aljamas during the period after the early revolts and before the great revolt of 1275. The south displays many more units, but the northern aljamas in general represent far stronger and wealthier cities.[88]

For comparing the weight of Islamic taxation against European equivalents for Mudejars, extraordinary and widely-spaced charges like moneyage offer little scope. Moneyage would probably have seemed to the Valencian Mudejar a not particularly onerous fee, of the kind his Islamic governors had multiplied according to whatever handy pretext suggested itself. The root of moneyage at this period in the realms of Aragon, like the root of such extraordinary taxes in Islam, lay not so much in the material, visible cause as in the ruler's need for money in a world of growing complexity and crisis.

Livestock provided a special source of taxes. Arabs and Berbers had a long tradition as skilled herdsmen, and the wool they produced in eastern Spain was highly valued for industrial products like cloth and carpets. Spanish Christians had long been stockmen too, with a solid tradition of transhumance either native or borrowed

[88] *Ibid.*, Reg. Canc. 18, fols. 94v-95 (Dec. 1, 1272): "dominus rex fecit monetaticum a sarracenis regni Valencie . . . item de tots los moros de la eglesia e de cavallers e dordens e altres persones e que lauraren jovades, si no son de castels ab termens de richs homens o de cavallers o de ciutadans"; in the second list the phrase "ab termens" comes at the end.

from their Berber neighbors in whole or part. Transhumance, whose controversial origins for Christian Spain are not relevant here, involved the pasturing of flocks in the highlands during the summer, then removing them to protected lowland pastures in winter, a skilled profession with considerable logistical problems. Wool constituted the raw material for medieval Europe's great cloth industry, and every advance of the Reconquest increased Spain's role in providing that wool. Both Muslims and Christians in Spain used sheep and goats as the basic source of fresh meat; Christians added pigs. Farmers in both communities, of course, kept domestic stock such as oxen and mules. Valencia's conquest made that area immediately a favorite seasonal grazing grounds for most of the Aragonese and many Castilian transhumants. The northern part of the new kingdom, and the uplands away from the huertas particularly favored stock raising.[89]

Given the importance of grazing in the new kingdom, it is not surprising that settlers coveted free pasture rights. Nearly all the Christian settlement charters of northern Valencia explicitly claimed them, though at Chivert for example the Knights Templar reserved pasturage to their own flocks. One of the first rubrics in Valencia's law code, drawn from a privilege of January 1240, guaranteed free grazing throughout "the territories of towns, knights, clerics, and religious, from pasturage to pasturage [and] from irrigation canal [network] to irrigation canal," though traffic laws excluded flocks from vineyards and huertas. Valencian Christians paid no pasturage, herbage, or watering tax in the capital's district.[90] The Mudejars showed themselves equally zealous over grazing privileges, and shared as well in the privileges of their Christian landlords.[91]

[89] On Valencia's sheep, goats, and cows see Burns, *Islam under the Crusaders*, ch. 5, part 3, and *Crusader Valencia*, I, 221-222. See also Dubler, *Wirtschaftsleben*, pp. 51-60; Lévi-Provençal, *España musulmana*, V, 21-22, 168-169. Imamuddin, *Socio-Economic and Cultural History of Muslim Spain*, pp. 91-95; García de Valdeavellano, *Instituciones españolas*, pp. 263-271, 606, 649; Matheu y Sanz, *De regimine regni Valentiae*, ch. 5, parts 1 and 2; Branchát, *Derechos y regalías de Valencia*, I, ch. 4; Asso, *Economía política de Aragón*, p. 295.

[90] *Fori antiqui Valentiae*, rub. II, nos. 1-4. García y García, *Estado económico-social de Castellón*, pp. 47-48, on the north.

[91] See the Mudejar charters cited in nn. 98 and 99. The Cullera settlers could freely pasture on certain Templar meadows, a privilege that probably included their Mudejar *exarici* (*Colección diplomática*, doc. 418 [April 4, 1252]). Such areas (*boalars*) were not part of the general exemption the king had given Valencians.

Charges could fall on livestock in a variety of ways in either Islamic or Christian Spain, depending upon local historical evolution, kind of stock, choice of variable or fixed fees, or decisions as to taxing domestic stock or taking shares of flock increase. Some cattle exactions pertained rather to import and transport duty, sales tax, or butchery charges, and have already appeared under those guises. In Islam the classic Koranic contribution of the *zakāt* on "growth" objects affected herds as well as produce and trade. Muslim moral theologians tended to exclude from it riding and pack animals as well as those that fell under trade. They allowed the herd tax on horses (not a common stock in Valencia) but rejected it for mules and asses, since these did not pasture in the technical sense. Various schools estimated the tax differently; for a string of 5 to 9 camels, for instance, one might pay the authorities a goat. Sheep and goats paid nothing until their number reached 40, when one was taken; at 120 two went, at 200 three, and so on.[92]

One theorist in the canon of tax commentators devoted a complicated chapter to the complexities of "*Ṣadaqāt* from Camels, Cattle, and Sheep." He provided a range of opinions on the age, kind, and number taken, distinguishing five classifications of sheep, such as "a ewe feeling its lamb moving in its womb" or "a buck needed for breeding," that were exempt. On flocks numbering between 40 and 120, one ewe was taken. The author spent a further chapter on causes to which this levy had to be devoted. As one moves from theological speculation to the given historical reality, however, it is clear that the pastoral tax schedule of Islamic Spain cannot be reconstructed. In fact, valuable light derives more from the continued taxes retained by Mudejars and entered into Christian documentation. In the eleventh century Ibn Ḥazm did make reference to novel, extraordinary taxes being directly placed upon flocks, causing popular resentment. Some analogy might be seen too in contemporary Egypt,

---

When King James gave an exemption from pasture tax to his Jewish counselor Judah de la Cavallería, "ipse et exeriqui sui possint pascere seu pasturare mille cabecias ganati ipsius Iahudani et suorum exeriquorum" in the places named (*ibid.*, doc. 1,415 [Nov. 22, 1273]). In Arch. Crown, Reg. Canc. 10, fol. 140 (May 29, 1259), in renting the "iura nostra, que a christianis et sarracenis" were due at Confrides, King James included "pasturas."

[92] Aghnides, *Mohammedan Theories of Finance*, pp. 200-201, 244-261. Siddiqi, *Public Finance in Islam*, pp. 14, 53-54.

which had a choice between a fixed charge on pasture land and a head-of-stock or variable per capita tax, with an additional fixed fee to cover collection.[93] In Christian Spain flocks fell under several charges, not easily fitted into a corresponding Islamic pattern; *pasquer* (*pascuarium* or *pascuaticus*) had been an early title for the basic demand. Such charges were probably much the same for both peoples; for the Mudejars they remained what they had been in precrusade Valencia, only the ultimate recipient changing with the conquest.[94] Several standard taxes on stock turn up in crusader Valencia: pasturage (*pasturatge*), watering tax or beverage (*beuratge*), sheepwalk toll or mountain transit (*muntatge* or *montatge*), a special grazing fee (*herbatge*), and a direct head-of-stock charge (*bestiar*). Some confusion can arise from the word *carneratge* or *carneraje*, the substitute in Aragon proper for Catalan *muntatge* and Castilian *montazgo*. The butchery tax called *carnatge* or *carnalatge* (Latin *carnagium*), also served to designate a technique used against tax fraud; it appears in Valencia's *Furs* in a context suggesting that on occasion it replaced the word *muntatge*.[95] Similarly the word *herbatge* seems to have been used too loosely at times in the general sense of pasturage. These charges were regalian; landlords with rights of private jurisdiction might claim their own fees for pasturage of alien flocks into their Valencian regions.

The most important of the taxes was the novel *herbatge* (Latin

[93] Qudāma, *Kitāb al-kharāj*, chs. 9, 18. *Ṣadaqa* involved almsgiving, both voluntary and (as *zakāt*) obligatory; see above, Chapter IV, n. 98. Rabie, *Financial System of Egypt*, pp. 79-80. See also Álvarez de Cienfuegos, *Régimen tributario de Granada*, p. 104. For the complexity and local variations these pastoral taxes could assume, see, e.g., the document of 1497 outlining the stock taxes for the Mudejars of the Málaga region, appended to Ladero Quesada, "Granada nazarí," pp. 327-328.

[94] See nn. 98, 101. On earlier pasturage taxes like *pascuarium*, see Rodón Binué, *Lenguaje técnico del feudalismo*, p. 189.

[95] King James in the *Furs* exempted Valencians from "carnatge, herbatge, e beuratge" (cited in n. 90), and Branchát treated of "herbage y carnage." James uses *montaticum* in the 1246 exemption, cited below in n. 96. Asso distinguished only two stock taxes for Aragon proper: *herbage* on pasturing and *carnerage* on transhumant passage (*Economía política de Aragón*, p. 295); García de Valdeavellano seems to extend this to all the realms of Aragon (*Instituciones españolas*, p. 606). Macanaz preferred *merinaje* as counterpart to Castile's *montazgo* in the realms of Aragon (*Regalías de Aragón*, p. 68). Alcover's *Diccionari català-valencià-balear* makes no room for *carneratge* or its variants, and explains *carnatge* in the butchery sense (II, 1,042 and 1,043); see above, also, Chapter III, part I. For *carnatge* as counterfraud, see *Congrés VII*, II, 435 and its n. 26.

herbagium, herbaticum) introduced by James I. As described for Valencia in a privilege given for transhumants from Teruel a few months after the crusade, it took six out of every thousand lambs and kids born during a given year. In return for this light tax, the crown waived all pasturage and passage fees. A clear description, with universal application, occurs in a Mudejar document. In 1257 James granted to Yaḥyā b. Muḥammad b. 'Īsā (Yafia Abenmafomat Abenaiça), lord of Montesa and Vallada on a transhumant route, "that you may take the *herbatge* on all stock of Aragon and Castile in the jurisdiction of Montesa and Vallada, namely six lambs on a thousand sheep bearing young, and six kids on a thousand goats bearing young, just as we take the said *herbatge* in the jurisdictions of our other places of the kingdom of Valencia." In cases of attempted fraud this standard fee doubled. The Mudejars of Chelva and Tuéjar collected the tax from alien flocks but encountered trouble when they demanded it in 1277 "illegally and unjustly" for the grazing on Campo de Banacacira, claimed by Alpuente. King Peter suspended "collection of the tenth and *herbatge*" there while he investigated the merits of Alpuente's claim.[96] Revenue accounts at Pego in 1269, possibly mixed but probably Mudejar, reported an income of "79 besants" or roughly 300 solidi under *herbatge*; at Sumacárcel in 1268 similar accounts reported 150 solidi.[97]

Surrender and settlement charters for Valencia's Mudejars lumped pasturage demands into a general category, relying upon immemorial custom to supply details. The charter of Eslida said simply that Mudejars could pasture flocks throughout the district as in the

---

[96] Arch. Crown, James I, Reg. Canc. 9, fol. 24 (Feb. 27, 1257): "quod possitis accipere [er]bagium de omnibus ganatis Aragonie et Castelle in termino de Montessa [et] de Vallata, videlicet de mille ovibus parturientib[us sex] oves, et de mille cabris parturientibus sex capras, si[cut] nos dictum erbagium recipimus in terminis aliorum [locorum] nostrorum regni Valencie." Bracketed parts are missing; a modern hand has supplied "castrorum" in the last bracket. Peter III, Reg. Canc. 40, fol. 42v (Nov. 12, 1277): "alfaquimo et aliame sarracenorum de Xelva et de Tuhexa . . . quod vos indebite et iniuste tam de bestiario eorum quam de aliorum hominum . . . accepistis decimum et herbagium." The Teruel privilege is in *Colección diplomática*, doc. 294 (Feb. 5, 1246), from *Aureum opus*, doc. 19, fol. 8: "racione herbatici, pasquerii, montatici ganatorum suorum non donent . . . nisi semel in quolibet anno de mille ovibus parideriis tantummodo sex carnerios . . ."; Catalan *paridora*, Castilian *paridera*, has the same meaning as Latin *parturiens* in the previous quotation.

[97] Arch. Crown, James I, Reg. Canc. 35, fol. 4 (1269): "item erbatge, lxxix besants"; fol. 8 (1268): "item lerbatge, cl sous."

time of Islamic rule. Similarly their colleagues at Tortosan Aldea could "pasture beasts—namely, cows, mares, asses, sheep, and goats— without any charge [*logerium*]." Uxó Muslims retained "all their pasturages and their stock, at Uxó and Nules and Almenara, and the grazing of Urmell in the Plana" just as "in the time of the Moors," and their stock "can go over all the pasturage of Chova." Chivert's people pastured freely "on the wastelands far and near to the four quarters." The markedly commercial-industrial charter of Játiva did not bother to specify stock or grazing taxes, except for a butchery fee.[98]

An apparently universal livestock obligation was the direct head-of-stock (*bestiar*). Though Chivert Mudejars gave neither pasturage nor butchery fee, they did owe one penny of Jaca every year "for each head of lesser livestock: sheep or goats, large or very small." The distinction was standard between such "lesser livestock," or *bestiar menut*, and *bestiar gran*, the latter including such larger animals as mules or oxen. The tax may have used these terms quite differently, as Piles Ros suggests, opposing newborn stock of any kind to stock over a year old. Since the *bestiar gran* was waived in these documents, such an understanding of the *bestiar menut* would make the fee a growth tax not unlike the *herbatge* though more severe. It would lie somewhere between a head-of-stock charge and a classical *zakāt*. When the tax appears in the general run of Valencia's Mudejar charters, however, it seems clearly a direct head-of-stock charge. As at Chivert, the Mudejars at Tales gave a penny in April for every goat, ram, or sheep. At Aldea, just beyond Valencia's northern border, the penny fell likewise "on each head of sheep and goats."[99]

---

[98] Eslida Charter. Chivert Charter. Aldea Charter: "ad pascendum bestias, scilicet vaccas, equas [*sic*], asinas, oves et capras sine aliquo logerio." Uxó Charter: "e que hajen tots lurs termens e lurs bestiars de Uxo, e Nulles, e Almenara, o lo terme de Urmell en la Plana . . . segons que ja seren deputats a ells en temps de moros; e que pusca anar lo lur bestiar en tot lo terme de Xova, segons que a ells ja legut." *Terme*, the "countryside" or jurisdiction in this book, here bears a technical meaning of agreed pasture area or waste; *bestiar*, though not including the same animals everywhere, in its widest sense applied to all domesticated four-legged work or meat stock, whether pigs, cows, sheep, horses, goats, or mules. Chivert Charter: "in heremo longe et prope ad quattuor partes." The Chelva Charter of 1370 provided free grazing.

[99] Tales Charter. Aldea Charter. Chivert Charter: "unum denarium monete iaccense pro unoquoque capite bestiarii minuti ovini aut caprini tam magni [*BSCC*

At Castellón de Burriana the Mudejars paid the yearly penny "on your smaller animals [*minuta*]."[100] This recurrent *bestiar menut* goes into the actual revenue rolls under the title *zaque del bestiar*. Eslida's charter explained it as the "*açaque* on stock according as they were accustomed" to pay under their *wālī*. Uxó's charter explained the "claim of *bestiar*" not as a head charge but as the classic growth tax: "out of forty, one." The differing explanation here need not exclude the head-charge penny, since each charter's stock obligations were presented as continuing in the context of precrusade custom. Uxó's tax may relate to a different pattern, however, more along the lines of the requirement written into the Tortosa surrender charter a century before: "to give direct *ṣadaqa* on their sheep as is their custom and their Law."[101]

This "livestock *zaq*" at Jaraco and Jeresa in 1268 fetched 11 solidi and 2 pence. At Pego in 1268 it brought 13 besants or about 48 solidi, a third more than the meat market but only half the profit from bees; a special entry listed "a tenth on lambs" at over 13 besants. The next year's accounts repeated the *bestiar* sum, which compared very unfavorably with the *herbatge* there, amounting to less than a sixth of that larger total. At Benamer that same year, the *atzaque* was a little over 14 solidi; this rose in 1269 to 18 solidi and 4 pence. Sumacárcel in 1269 had a grand total of over 48 solidi. Cárcel with Sueca in 1268 listed no *atzaque* but rather "the third on the kids, 7

---

edn.: magnili] quam sutili." The Latin *grossum et minutum* corresponds to medieval Catalan *bestiar gros e menut*, and *su[b]tile* to *sotil*, the latter term meaning inconsiderable or scrawny. Piles Ros, working from later materials, explains the *bestiar menut* as a tax of six out of each thousand newborn animals, or a money equivalent, though he distinguishes it from *herbatge*, and the *bestiar gran* as a tax of three Jaca pennies on animals more than a year old, but two pennies per pig (*Bayle general de Valencia*, p. 88). See also Alcover, *Diccionari català-valencià-balear*, II, 460.

[100] *Itinerari*, p. 308 (Nov. 5, 1260): "de animalibus vestris minutis nisi tantum pro unoquoque unum denarium in anno."

[101] Eslida Charter: "et dent açaque ganatorum secundum quod consueverunt." Uxó Charter: "e que sien tenguts de pagar lo dret de bestiar . . . ço es de cuaranta una." Tortosa Charter: "donent sua açadaga directa de suas oves, sic est lure fuero et lure lege." The Tudela Charter had: "vadat ganado . . . securament, et prendant illum azudum de illas oves, sicut est foro de azuna de illos moros." Dozy and Engelmann, *Glossaire*, p. 222 (*azadeca*); Steiger, *Contribución*, p. 146 (*az-zakā*). Later Catalan also favored a form assimilating the Arabic article: *atzaque*. On the nontax nature of *zakāt* and more generally *ṣadaqa*, and the challenge of Ben-Shemesh to Siddiqi and Zayas in this matter, see above, Chapter IV, n. 98.

solidi" and "19 lambs of the tenth, 22 solidi and 2 pence." Both places omitted these items in 1269, substituting an *atzaque* of 69 solidi and 3 pence.[102] Corbera in 1263 reported a tithe on kids amounting to only 3 solidi, Gandía a "tenth on animals" of 7 solidi, Cullera a *bestiar* tenth of 17 solidi, and Onteniente a similar tenth at over 10 solidi; but these are more probably mixed than Mudejar revenue.[103] Perhaps in line with the third and the tenth of stock just cited, or perhaps in connection with pasturage, King Peter in 1279 ordered his functionaries at Olocau "not to demand from these Saracens of Barbagena any of our fifth on livestock."[104]

Specific returns in money accounts are hard to come by, and the series quoted appears at times to be mixed Christian and Mudejar payment. Nor is there any assurance that the scribes were not grouping the minor livestock returns under one heading. The major towns of Valencia and the centers for pastoral activity undoubtedly brought larger sums than these to the treasury. After the turn of the century a fiscal report noted that the *atzaque* returns from Aspe in the Alicantine region amounted to 350 solidi every year, from Elda 300, from Novelda 350, and from Elche 500. These sums contrasted with 1,000 solidi at Elche from "the *herbatge* of the flocks that enter to graze in the district," though this entry included Christian shepherds and applied rather to alien flocks. At Gallinera *herbatge* from Muslims alone reached the surprising annual figure of 10,000 solidi, from which the crown assigned pensions of 1,000 and of 240 solidi to Christians.[105]

---

[102] Arch. Crown, James I, Reg. Canc. 35, fol. 3 (1268): "zaq del ganado, xi sous, ii diners." Fol. 3v (1268): "zaque del bestiar"; "item diesmo de corderos, xiii besants, v millareses." Fol. 3v (1269), the same. Fol. 4v (1268): "zaque del bestiar, xiiii sous . . . iii diners"; fol. 7 (1269): "zaque del bestiar"; fol. 7 (1268, Sumacárcel); fol. 7v (1268): "item corderos de diesmo, xxii sous, ii diners," and "item el tierço de los cabritos, vii sous." Fol. 8 (1269): "zaque [del b]estiar, lxix sous, iii diners."

[103] *Ibid.*, Reg. Canc. 17, fol. 28 (Dec. 30, 1263): "decima de corderiis, iii solidos"; "decima animalium, vii solidos"; fol. 29: "decimum bestiarii, xvii solidos minus i denarium"; fol. 29v: "decimum bestiarii, x solidos, v denarios, obolum."

[104] *Ibid.*, Peter III, Reg. Canc. 42, fol. 133 (Aug. 26, 1279), though this year he was not to take it: "non exigatis ab ipsis sarracenis de Barbagena aliquam nostram quintam ganati."

[105] *Rentas de Aragón*, pp. 92, 102, 110 ("latzaque quels dits moros paguen por lo bestiar menut que tenen . . . tro a d sous"), p. 112 ("lerbatge de les cabanes que entra pexer en lo terme"), p. 120 ("munta latzaque del bestiar del dit loch cascun any tro a ccc sous"), pp. 122, 124; the adjoined tax is "les gallines," and all figures

Bees are not commonly considered as livestock today, but in Valencia bees shared the *atzaque* tax and were listed along with cattle. Their tax went under the name of *colmenes* (hives) or under the rubric "*zaque* of bees." At Uxó the hives followed the classic one-out-of-forty assessment. At Aldea, Chivert, and Tales each beehive yielded a penny. At Pego in 1268 this tax on bees or beehives came to 7 besants, 4 *millareses*, and 2 pence; for some reason Mūsā had his hive entered separately at 3 *millareses*. In 1269 the same item totaled 17 besants and 6 *millareses* after deduction of expenses for collecting, or about 64 solidi. At Benamer it was only 5 solidi and 8 pence in 1268, dropping to 3 solidi and 6 pence in 1269. At Suma-cárcel in 1269 the bee income entered into the accounts has lost its sum to manuscript deterioration.[106] At Chulilla in 1260, when arranging rents with the local Mudejars, King James gave careful attention to crops but expressly imposed a tax on only two animals: a penny for every goat and "one Valencian penny for every hive of bees."[107] The various entries for bees, and the governmental attention they attracted, point up Islamic Valencia's apiculture.

The charge on chickens might logically sit beside that on bees, but revenue lists preferred to associate it, along with physical labor required from tenants owning work animals, among the service

are net after collection expenses. Many places return lumped, unitemized tax totals. The *carnatge* for Gallinera every year was merely 100 solidi.

[106] Arch. Crown, James I, Reg. Canc. 35, fol. 3v (1268): "item zaque de las colmenas, vii besants, iiii millareses, ii diners"; "i colmena que fue de Musça, iii millareses." Fol. 4 (1269): "item zaque de las abellas, xvii besants, vi millareses; colidura, xvii millareses, ii diners." Fol. 4v (1268): "item çaque de las abellas, v sous, viii diners [de Benaamira]." Fol. 7 (1269): "item zaque de las abellas, iii sous, vi diners." Fol. 7v (1269): "zaque de las abel[as . . .]." Beehives led the list in a confiscation of agricultural goods at Montesa from emigrating Mudejars in 1287: "concedimus vobis Bernardo de Pulcrovisu [*Bellvís*] omnes colmenas, panicium, adassam, et stopam, et lanam et estoras, que fuerunt sarracenorum de Muntesa qui nunc recesserunt ab ipso loco de Muntesa" (Alfonso III, Reg. Canc. 75, fol. 2 [May 1, 1287]). Uxó Charter: "pagar lo dret . . . de colmenes." Chivert Charter: "et pro unaquaque arna de apibus similiter unum denarium eiusdem monete [iaccensis]."

[107] Arch. Crown, James I, Reg. Canc. 11, fol. 186 (Dec. 17, 1260): "de qualibet arna apium donetis et dare teneamini nobis et nostris unum denar[ium] regale tantum, et de unaquaque capra i denarium tantum." Honey served as the poor man's sugar, and a tax on hives was common in Islam. Qudāma has a passage on this moot honey tax and various opinions concerning its amount (*Kitāb al-kharāj*, pp. 39-40). See also Imamuddin, *Socio-Economic and Cultural History of Muslim Spain*, p. 89.

impositions treated below. The equally popular rabbit and its fee belong to the section on revenue from hunting and meat markets. *Bovatge* or oxen tax, though etymologically a cattle tax and in its remote origins a levy on yokes of oxen, had become by King James's day a recognition of sovereignty, voted by the *corts* or parliament around coronation time. Originally assessed on spans of oxen, it became a direct tax drawn from specified movables and semimovables, in theory demanded only once during each king's reign. King James, imitating his father, managed to impose it again as an extraordinary contribution for the Balearics crusade. Though Mudejars would have been involved as much as Christians, their early tax records do not refer to their participation.[108]

LABOR SERVICE

Some scholars believe that service by Valencian Mudejars began only after the thirteenth century, though becoming by the fifteenth a painful burden.[109] This is too sweeping a conclusion. Physical labor for one's lord did not loom large in the thirteenth century; it certainly existed, however, and it was not always replaced by money commutation. The word "service," susceptible of several meanings as an exaction, was not the preferred term for such works. The formal designation was *sofra*, a word derived from its Arabic equivalent *as-sukhra*; the prevailing Latin form in Valencian documents was *çofra*, both Catalan and Latin usually diverging from the *azofra* form that entered Castilian.[110]

---

[108] *Llibre dels feyts*, ch. 50. On bovage see the description by Jerónimo Zurita, *Anales de la corona de Aragón*, ed. Ángel Canellas López, 3 vols. to date (Zaragoza [1610] 1967ff.), lib. II, ch. 69, and lib. III, ch. 1; Ferran Soldevila, "A propòsit del servei del bovatge," *AEM*, I (1964), 573-587; Antoni M. Aragó Cabañas, "La col·lecta del bovatge del 1327," *Estudis d'història medieval*, III (1970), 41-51. Bisson relates its origins to the Peace of God and sound coinage movements, identifying its early form with *monedatge* (see above, n. 79).

[109] "No figuran por nada en las pueblas del [siglo] xiii: a partir del siglo siguiente van apareciendo gradualmente, hasta constituir en el xv y xvi una de las obligaciones más onerosas" (Gual Camarena, "Mudéjares valencianos, aportaciones," p. 181).

[110] Dozy and Engelmann, *Glossaire*, pp. 227-228 (*azofra*, the Castilian form). Neuvonen, *Arabismos del español*, p. 107. Martí, *Vocabulista in arabico*, p. 116. The precise meaning of *sofra* baffled Villarroya (*Real Maestrazgo de Montesa*, I, 57n.); Macho y Ortega, Torres Balbás, and others differ in its application (see below). On "service," see Rodón Binué, *Lenguaje técnico del feudalismo*, p. 235. On personal

Sofra fell both on persons and on their animals, in such forms as a day's contributed labor (*jornals*), haulage, repair work, and plowing. Documents speak more frequently of a *sofra* "on wood and water." Logically this had to be provisioning of the lord's house, and possibly irrigation for his fields, or the equivalent money. Thus the Mudejars at Huesa in Aragon had their obligation explained as a specific number of "boxes" of wood per farmer each month, or for those who had animals an equivalent number of "loads." At Nabal the Mudejars "do *sofra*, and this means to bring to the castle every Saturday wood or whatever other thing, and besides they also do service to the castle on other days of transporting and of equipment when there is need."[111] The traditional term *opera* had been applied to the Mudejars at Tortosa in 1174, when they were dispensed from labor service. The same term applied again in 1258 at Aldea above Valencia's border, this time as formally identified with *sofra*; each Muslim owning a house had to contribute one day's labor a month "to our needs." The Hospitallers undertook to feed the workers

---

services to Castilian rural lords (*operas, labores, sernas, fazendera, vereda, castellaria*), see García de Valdeavellano, *Instituciones españolas*, pp. 251-252. *Servitium* or *servitutes*, generically whatever one owed the lord or landowner, could mean labor or rents; without a qualifier it is ambiguous, as in a 1265 entry: "item recepit de quodam sarraceno de Liria pro servicio 1 solidos" (Arch. Crown, James I, Reg. Canc. 17, fol. 66), or at Pego that year "item de serviciis, lix solidos, iii denarios" (*ibid.*; the "item de Jahep açofra" in these lists may possibly represent a personal name). Christian charters for Catalonia can identify the word with labor as in "servitiis agradables seu forsats, nec teneantur facere opera, traginas, trots, viatichos, nec aliquas servitutes . . . excepta communia que fiant ad opus ecclesie Sancti Ylari" (*Cartas de población de Cataluña*, 1, doc. 557, San Hilario de Sacalm [May 26, 1337]); there are further examples of *servitium caseorum, servitium pensi, servitium censuum et tributorum*, and the like in this collection. Though bizarre spellings of the tax might seem to include *ceyffa*, that was rather the fixed, annual *peita* when given in kind, according to Macho y Ortega ("Mudéjares aragoneses," p. 201): see, e.g., the 1263 crown exemption to the Moors of Borgia near Zaragoza from the *civana* given as *ceyffa* in August of each year, "racione cavalleriarum et de azemile quas per cavalleris" [*sic*] they paid (*Itinerari*, p. 334).

111 The Mudejar taxes of Huesa, just north of Montalbán, in 1294 included: "item çaffra de lenna en esta manera es assaber aquellos qui han bestias sendas cargas cada mes, et los otros qui no han bestias sendas faxes de lenna cada mes" (*Rentas de Aragón*, p. 214). At Nabal in 1294, "fazen [moros] çafre, et es assaber aduzir al castiello todos sabados lenna o qualquiera otra cosa et encara fazen tambien los otros dias servicio al castiello de carriar et pertrechos necesarios quen es menester" (p. 301). *Pertrechi* (Catalan *pertrets*) are the tackle and tools required for a given job. The word *sofra* should not be confused with the identical, but etymologically different, Catalan forms for "sulfur" (*sofra, sofre*) and for "cantle."

gratis that day; men who fell ill ceased to owe work until they had recovered.[112]

The duty of *sofra* was prominent enough in Mudejar Valencia, a link with the Islamic past both semantically and in life. The Uxó pact formally dismissed it both for persons and animals. The charter for Eslida, Veo, and other towns freed Mudejars from *sofres* on wood, beasts, and waters. The Templars' seignorial charter at Chivert on the other hand extended exemption only to persons, wives, children, and animals of the civic and religious leaders of local communities—those with the status of *qā'id*, *faqīh*, or imam. Játiva Muslims paid it; the king exempted a merchant and his family there from *sofra* and other taxes, on condition of his settling at Játiva, which meant nothing if the other Moors already possessed exemption.[113] The Mudejars of Peñíscola had to give "*sofra* of wood . . . every month."[114] At Almizra in 1260 one Muḥammad the Red renewed for his son and heir the lifetime exemption he had held by

[112] Aldea Charter: "teneantur in unoquoque mense operare unum diem in nostris necessariis et nos in ipso die teneamur eis dare victum"; this *opus* is then referred to as "dictam çoffram." The Tortosa Convention of 1174 used both feminine and neuter forms of *opera* for Mudejar personal service: "[non] faciat operam aliquo modo nobis neque successoribus nostris in Dertuse neque deforis neque in castris nec in aliquibus locis per nos neque per baiulos nostros sed sint sani et quieti ab omni opere." On the great estates of Spain during the late period of the Roman empire, personal services on the owner's area were called *opera et iugera*; in medieval Spain *opera* remained one designation for personal labor (García de Valdeavellano, *Instituciones españolas*, pp. 133, 251). The term does not appear among the many hundreds in Rodón Binué's *Lenguaje técnico del feudalismo*, nor among the medieval meanings assigned to *obra* in the exhaustive Alcover *Diccionari català-valencià-balear*, VIII, 134-136.

[113] Uxó Charter: "zofris." Eslida Charter: "azofres." Chivert Charter: "açofram" for a wall, and the more general "açoffres," exempting "alfachinus[,] alcaydus cum suis successoribus et çabacalonis." Perhaps the Templars required a day's work every month from their other Chivert Muslims, as they did at Villastar just west of Valencia's frontier; see Forey, *Templars*, pp. 203-204. The Tudela Charter of 1119 freed its Mudejars from *azofra* on man and beast. For Játiva see Arch. Crown, James I, Reg. Canc. 9, fol. 53 (Sept. 7, 1273): "et de çofra."

[114] Arch. Crown, James I, Reg. Canc. 11, fols. 182v-183 (Oct. 26, 1260): "vobis universis et singulis sarracenis qui nunc estis in Peniscola et successoribus . . . [quod] teneamini pro çofra lignorum alcaido nostro Euse de Peniscola [sed non detis] de çofra lignorum unquam [nisi semel] in unoquoque mense." The manuscript is badly worn, and my reconstruction is represented in the bracketed parts; the date is borrowed from the entry immediately above. Since this document is a concession, yet imposes *sofra*, it probably represents a diminution as reconstructed. A further concession concerned "leudam ab aliquo ligno vel barcha inde transeunte," where *lignum* was used in its meaning as ship (see Chapter VI, n. 30).

Battle at Puig

Imaginative representation of the main pitched battle of the Valencian crusade, Puig in 1237. Marçal de Sas (Martial de Sax), the German artist of the Cologne school who transformed Valencian painting during his dozen years in the kingdom (1392-1410), puts King James at the battle for symbolic effect, with St. George fighting at his left side. This painting is a section of an altarpiece. (Crown Copyright, Victoria & Albert Museum, London.)

Arnold Sa Morera,
Bailiff General of Valencia,
Receiving Taxes (1338)

Painted in blue and red on the yellow leather binding of his account book, *Libre de apoqites.* Note the money bags, coffer at lower right, and heraldic tree representing his name (*morera*, mulberry tree). (Archivo General del Reino de Valencia, sección Real, number 622, codex Àpoques de la baylia.)

Islamic-Mudejar Baths at Valencia City

"Baths of 'Abd al-Malik," probably the same as those of Ibn Mālik (Dabenmelich) and called by the Christians "Baths of the Admiral." Declared a national monument in 1944, and restored in 1963, they are the only extant baths at the capital. This is the main or steam-bath room. (Archivo Mas.)

MUDEJARESQUE CERAMICS
Varied Themes

From the extensive ceramics collection at Valencia city. Mudejar craftsmen continued the Islamic traditions at Paterna, outside Valencia city, soon joined by Christians. These twelfth- or thirteenth-century plates and bowls may be exclusively the work of Muslims, who often handled animal or human figures. The themes here are Arabic-calligraphic, peacock and fish, and woman's half-concealed face. Though the fish and peacock may be heraldic, some see them as representing the Christian attack on, or coexistence with, Valencian Islam. The originals are in the Museo Nacional de Cerámica "González Martí" de Valencia, Paterna cycle, numbers 244, 517, 653.

MUDEJARESQUE CERAMICS
Castle in the Pines

Probably the work of Mudejar crafts-man, and in the Islamic tradition, thirteenth century. A castle of this shape was a common heraldic device, though it may here represent simply a decorative castle. The original is in the Museo Nacional de Cerámica "González Martí" de Valencia, Paterna cycle, number 538.

Nobleman of Paterna

Thirteenth century, probably by Mudejar craftsman. The warrior carries the coat of arms, half-moon with stars, of the Luna family, lords of Paterna from shortly after the crusade. The original is in the Museo Nacional de Cerámica "González Martí" de Valencia, Paterna cycle, number 638.

Valencian Money of King James

Expressly coined as a colonial expedient, "to remake [the kingdom of Valencia] according to the ways of the Christians." The profile facing left indicates the second or subsequent minting. (Drawing, from *Geografía general del reino de Valencia*, Establecimiento Editorial de Alberto Martín [Barcelona, 1918].)

Entering Accounts at the Royal Exchequer

From the *Leges palatinae* of the kingdom of Majorca, early fourteenth century. More specialized and organized by then, both the Majorcan and mainland systems made entries under the direction of a *mestre racional* and four assistants, affording some idea of thirteenth-century procedure from which it was evolving. Note the abacus. (Bibliothèque Royale Albert Ier, Brussels, Manuscript 898, codex Leges palatinae.)

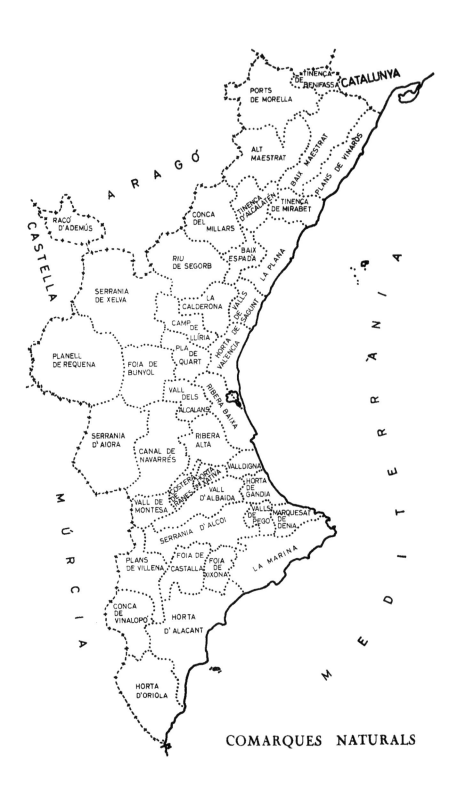

COMARQUES NATURALS

Factors such as geography, history, economy, and language shaped the Valencian kingdom into immemorial natural regions, not necessarily conterminous with administrative boundaries. Geographers and historians today group these regions variously, combining or dividing them according to the priority assigned to the several shaping factors. Vicente Badía Marín (1955) schematizes the component subunits into over a hundred *comarques*, Jaime Marco Baidal (1963) into over eighty, Manuel Sanchis Guarner (1966) into twenty-two (excluding areas not speaking Catalan), and most recently (1973) José Climent Barber into thirty-two. The illustration here, from the *Geografia elemental del regne de València*, reproduced with permission of its author Emili Beüt i Belenguer, arranges the kingdom at its largest historical extension into forty-one "very distinct" regions.

The Spanish toponyms equivalent to his Catalan forms are, by rows left-to-right: Puertos de Morella, Tinenza de Benifasa(r) /Alto Maestrazgo, Bajo Maestrazgo, Llanos de Vinaroz / Cuenca de Mijares, Tinenza (Señorío) de Alcalatén, Tinenza de Mirabet / Río de Segorbe, Bajo Espadán, La Plana [de Castellón] / Rincón de Ademuz, Serranía de Chelva, Campo de Liria, La Calderona, Valles de Sagunto [Murviedro] / Meseta de Requena, Hoya de Buñol, Llano de Cuart, Huerta de Valencia / Valle de Alcaláns, Ribera Baja [del Júcar] / Serranía de Ayora, Canal de Navarrés, Ribera Alta / Valle de Montesa, La Costera de Ranes, Huerta de Játiva, Valldigna / Valle de Albaida, Huerta de Gandía / Serranía de Alcoy, Valles de Pego, Marquesado de Denia / Llanos de Villena, Hoya de Castalla, Hoya de Jijona, La Marina / Cuenca de Vinalopó, Huerta de Alicante / Huerta de Orihuela.

The Kingdom of Valencia

Showing the major natural divisions as grouped administratively in the Tomás López map of 1788. (Reprinted from Robert I. Burns S.J., *Islam under the Crusaders*, Princeton University Press.)

formal charter, so that he was not "to give *sofra*, by reason of the aforesaid property, for himself or for his animals, at any time of his life."[115] In conveying the castles and countrysides of Cocentaina and Alcoy in 1258, King James decreed "that all the Saracens of the aforesaid castles and their regions, future as well as present, are to make *sofres* there of water and wood."[116] The king referred in 1263 to the *sofres* "that we have and ought to have in Biar, from the Saracens resident there."[117] Collection was made as well at aljamas like Alfandech,[118] Chulilla,[119] Confrides,[120] Gallinera with Alcalá,[121] Luchente, Montaberner, Serra, Torres Torres, Vallada, and throughout a region comprising "Denia, Segárria, Vall de Laguart, Pop, Jalón, Calpe, Olocaiba, and Polop."[122] A general document for 1264

[115] *Ibid.*, fols. 192v-193 (Feb. 5, 1260): "laudamus . . . tibi Mahometo el Ruvio de Villena sarraceno franquitatem . . . et quod non donet ipse vel filius suus pro se nec pro bestiis suis çofram aliquo tempore vite sue ratione predicte hereditatis." The concession had previously made clear that it applied also to "filius tuus sive filia," in case a daughter inherited. His epithet, "the Red," was probably al-Aḥmar.

[116] *Ibid.*, Reg. Canc. 10, fol. 68 (June 28, 1258): "volumus etiam et mandamus quod sarraceni omnes iam dictorum castrorum et terminorum eorum presentes atque futuri faciant ibi çofras de aqua et lignis."

[117] *Ibid.*, Reg. Canc. 12, fol. 119 (Oct. 1, 1263): "çofras . . . et omnia alia iura que nos in Biar et a sarracenis ibidem habitantibus habemus et habere debemus."

[118] *Ibid.*, Reg. Canc. 20, fol. 245 (April 27, 1275): "soffram."

[119] *Ibid.*, Reg. Canc. 16, fol. 229v (Jan. 28, 1270): "ab omni scilicet . . . çofra . . . et eorum redempcionibus et ab omni alio servicio, exaccione, seu demanda regali." This exemption for a Mudejar resident argues the general obligation.

[120] *Ibid.*, Reg. Canc. 10, fol. 140 (May 29, 1259): "çofram."

[121] *Ibid.*, Reg. Canc. 15, fol. 88 (March 1, 1267): "aliame sarracenorum de Galinera et de Alcalano . . . ratione reddituum, exituum, . . . zofre nec alicuius alterius exaccionis regalis." The *sofra* occurs here in a context of general revenue farming for a two-year period.

[122] *Ibid.*, Reg. Canc. 16, fol. 254v (June 6, 1271): "cum . . . çofris (Serra, Torres Torres). Reg. Canc. 19, fols. 126v-127 (April 20, 1274): "et cum zofris" (Vallada). Peter III, Reg. Canc. 40, fol. 66v (Feb. 19, 1277): "coffris" (Luchente). Alfonso III, Reg. Canc. 63, fol. 18 (Jan. 13, 1286): "soffris" (Montaberner). The regional reference is in James I, Reg. Canc. 10, fol. 20v (Sept. 24, 1257): "de omnibus redditibus . . . çofris . . . de castris et villis Denie, Segarrie, Alaguar, Pop, Exalo, Calp, Olocayba, et Polop." Segarrie is not nearby Sagra but the hill region and valley named Segárria, which bounded the old marquisate of Denia at the north; the name also appears without accent, and in the Catalan form Segària. The Martínez Ferrando catalogue regularly gives it as Segarra. Laguart is also Lauar and Lahuár as well as archaic Alaguar. See the similar document in Reg. Canc. 9, fol. 39r,v (Sept. 19, 1257): "castra et villas de Alguarr et de Exalone, cum . . . ço[fris] . . . et aliis iuribus omnibus . . . çofras"; the grantee can settle Moors temporarily or permanently there. James I transferred the *sofra* for Sagra to a lord, Raymond of Villanueva (Arch. Nac. Madrid, Ords. milits., Uclés, caj. 301, no. 1 [Sept. 26, 1296]).

concerns its collection at all the aljamas below the Júcar River.[123] It appears too in the formulary contract among the burdens normally imposed upon late medieval Valencian Mudejars.[124]

Sometimes this labor service appears in an obviously physical guise. King James in 1260 reduced the "çofram" owed by Muslims of the Castellón region in northern Valencia to their lord, the prior of St. Vincent's, down to "only one day in each month [by] each household." They had to carry "wood for the operation of his kitchen" but only when the prior was "personally in residence" at the town of Castellón.[125] Here the service was tailored to actual needs, specifically the cookery needs of the landowner. Equally clearly, a series of documents for southern Valencia displays commutation into money. The sums do not appear singly in that set of accounts, but rather as lumped with the obligation to provide one's lord with chickens; occasionally other taxes were also reckoned into the total under this one entry or item.

At Benigánim, for example, "sofra and chickens" brought 32 solidi and 6 pence. At Jaraco and Jeresa together the two taxes came to 37 solidi and 6 pence, and at Benirredrá and a companion town to 40 solidi. At Sumacárcel in 1268 "sofra and besant and chickens and oven" for twenty-four households totaled 268 solidi or a little over $11\frac{1}{2}$ solidi per house; subtracting the besant, the other three taxes averaged out at just under 8 solidi per house, the oven probably accounting for most of this. The next year the same entry rose to 290 solidi but rather because of a higher assessment: 12 solidi and 1 pence "for each house." In a separate listing for sofra and chickens, the Moors of Martin Sanchis brought 10 solidi, those of Isabel 25 solidi, and those of La Xarquia 35 solidi, while "a poor Moor" gave 2 solidi and 6 pence. A similar auxiliary list in 1269 had "the Moors of Don

---

[123] Arch. Crown, James I, Reg. Canc. 14, fol. 55v (May 30, 1264): "in castris, [villis], et locis totius baiulie regni Valentie quam pro nobis tenebatis a rivo Xuchari ultra tam videlicet de . . . çofris, serviciis . . . et computavistis nobiscum de opere turris de Biar et de tota missione quam in ea fecistis." The revenues were probably mixed Christian and Mudejar; the Biar repair work may have been involved with that locale's sofra (see above, n. 117).

[124] *Formularium diversorum contractuum*, fol. xxviiii: "*çofris.*"

[125] *Itinerari*, p. 308 (Nov. 5, 1260), copied from Arch. Nac. Madrid, manuscripts of Poblet monastery: "non teneamini facere çofram priori . . . nisi tantum unusquisque casatus vestrum unam diem in unoquoque mense . . . ; concedimus etiam vobis quod non teneamini dare eidem priori et suis successoribus ligna ad opus coquine sue nisi tantum quando ipsi fuerint in Castilione personaliter constituti."

Blasco" giving 45 solidi for the two taxes, while those of neighboring landholders gave respectively 20, 40, 5, 20, 25, 30, 35, 5, and 5 solidi.[126] Both labor and chickens appear in these accounts as specific sums of money, sometimes in terms allowing the reader to prorate the total by households. Under the circumstances, it seems unlikely that only the poultry half of the average entry was paid in kind and its price added to the money commutation of *sofra*. In some places, however, the chickens were actual fowl; unless the Valldigna monastery estates had evolved a different tax pattern in later years, their custom of taking live chickens may serve as illustration.[127] The connection between *sofra* and chickens is too constant in the records to be extrinsic. Another meaning of *sofra*, in fact, and the dominant meaning at a later period in Aragon proper, was the surrender of a fixed number of chickens or their money equivalent.[128] Perhaps a logical relation may be traced through evolution of *sofra* as pro-

[126] Arch. Crown, James I, Reg. Canc. 35, fols. 3-4 and fols. 7-8 (1268, 1269, 1270), a series of accounts, loosely dated: "B[e]nig[a]na, çofra e gallin[es], xx[x]ii sous, vi diners; [. . .], çofra e gallines, xl sous; Benerida [e] Alcana, çofra e gallines, lii sous, vi diners"; "Exaracho [cum] Exeresa, çofra e gallines, xxxvii sous, vi diners." Fol. 7: "rendas de Somacarcel: çofra e besa[nt] e gallines e forn, xxiiii cases, cclxviii sous." Fol. 7v: "[ren]das del raval de [Car]cel e de Sueca . . . [çofra] e [g]allines, ii sous, vi diners"; "de las alcherias del terme de Somacarcel, item l'alcantera, çofra e gallines, xx sous; item don Pere Çabata, çofra e gallines, xx sous; item Anabairon, çofra e gallines, xx sous; item dona Soriana, çofra e gallines, xlv sous; [item] de do M[ar]ti Sanchis, çofra e gallines, x sous; item de do Pere Sanchis [çofra e gallines, xx sous]; item de do Guillem P[eres] çofra e [. . .]." Fol. 8: "item de [d]ona Isabel, çofra e gallines, xxxv sous; item de La Exarquia, çofra e gallines, xxxv sous; item d'En Bartolomeu, çofra e gallines, v sous; item de i moro pobre, ii sous, vi diners." Fol. 8v: "[re]membrança de lo que prisimos de los moros del terme [de Carcel e de Çuecha] . . . los moros de don Blascho P[eres], çofra e gallines, xlv sous; [item de] do Pere [Çabata], çofra e gallines, xx sous; [item de dona] Soriana, çofra e gallines, xl sous; [item de] do Marti Sanchis, çofra e gallines, v sous; [item de do] Pere [San]chis, ç[ofra] e gallines, xx sous; [item de do] Guillem Peres, ço[fra] e gallines, xxxv sous; [item de] dona Isabel, çofra e gallines, xxx sous; [item de La E]xarquia, ço[fra] e gallines, xxxv sous; [item d'En Bartolomeu], çofr[a] e gallines, v sous; [item . . . , çofra] e gallines, v sous." Since the last list is explicitly only Moorish rents, and the preceding is identical in form and in several specific entries, both must be unmixed Moorish accounts. "Anabairon" might be "a Na Bairon" on the analogy of the one "En" that replaces "don," but it may well be a Mudejar name beginning "an-N," as in an-Nuwayrī.

[127] The tenants of Valldigna protested against the monastery's attempt to collect money instead of chickens (Casey, "Moriscos," p. 33).

[128] Macho y Ortega could describe the fifteenth-century *sofra*: "variaba en significación, pero generalmente se refería al pago de un numero determinado de gallinas por cada familia," or a money equivalent ("Mudéjares aragoneses," p. 203).

167

visioning, or supplying one's lord, somewhat along the line of the *cena* levy discussed below. Since the chicken played a noble role in the tax structure of contemporary Egypt, perhaps its prominence in Mudejar Valencia echoes a more universal feature of medieval Islam's rural economy.[129] Fowl such as chickens, peacocks, and doves did hold a special place in the heart of the Spanish Muslim.[130] During various surrender negotiations of the Valencian crusade, King James and the Muslim agents dined on chicken as well as on mutton and game; during raids the king could count on sweeping up "many fowl" from Islamic villages.[131]

As a service demand, chickens sometimes stand in the accounts unaccompanied by the companion entry of *sofra*; the place or person involved may have held exemption from one of the two charges. Thus a Pego entry in 1268 recorded 45 besants or some 168 solidi for "the chickens"; two entries the following year divided the collection into 7 besants for chickens, and 97 besants for oven and chickens. Cárcer and Sueca entered "the besant and chickens for twenty households" together as one item.[132] In the Aldea Charter the nexus between chickens and labor service becomes explicit: "those who make the said *sofra* are obliged to give us one chicken at Christmas every year." This fell upon households, and elsewhere was a pair of chickens.[133] The price of a chicken, at least for a wealthy and pre-

---

[129] Rabie, *Financial System of Egypt*, p. 103; during the thirteenth century the Ayyubid state distributed chicks to the *fallāḥīn* to raise, later collecting two-thirds of the adult birds in recompense as a tax, taking care also to make the sale or growing of chickens a state monopoly.

[130] Vicens Vives, *Economic History of Spain*, p. 112.

[131] Burns, *Islam under the Crusaders*, ch. 5, part 3, with citations to the *Llibre dels feyts* of King James.

[132] Arch. Crown, James I, Reg. Canc. 35, fol. 3 (1268): "item las gallines, xlv besants"; fol. 4 (1269): "item gallines, vii besants; item forno e gallines, xcvii besants, viii millareses, [e] colidura ix besants, viii millareses"; fol. 7 (1268): "besant e gallines de vii moros barranis, xxx [. . .] sous, v [diners]"; fol. 8 (1269): "besa[n]t e gallines de xx casados del [r]aval, vii sous, viii diners." The *barranis* were residents lacking true domicile, usually resident aliens; another case is on fol. 8 for Sumacárcel with Sueca: "besant e gallines de xii [moros] barranis, lx sous."

[133] Aldea Charter: "illi qui dictam çoffram fecerint, teneantur nobis dare unam gallinam in festo natalis domini singulis annis." At Avencalles near Tortosan Ulldecona, in 1257, the Christian settlement charter required "pro capmasio par gallinarum annuatim in natale domini persolvendum," but this was a kind of acknowledgement for the bit of *farraginal*, or grazing land for the domestic animals, given to each house (*Cartas de población de Cataluña*, I, part 1, doc. 302); *capmàs* meant

sumably more extravagant household, ranged from 8 to 11 pence, the better part of a solidus, though a pullet might cost as little as 3 pence.[184]

A special form of labor involved periodic forays into vineyards; hoeing around vines or gathering faggots were prime examples of this tax. Its name, *venema* or the garbled *verema*, represents a corruption of Latin *vindemia* or harvest. The Uxó charter freed its Muslims from such obligation.[135] At Alcira the crown collected it along with *calonias* and *servicia*.[136] A document issued by King James, in dispensing Játiva's Moors from this very labor in 1262, discloses its existence in that region. "We grant to all you Saracens in the greater Moorish quarter of Játiva, present and future, and to your descendants forever," it ran, "that you or yours are never to be bound to dig around the vines that we had you plant in the district of Játiva for our purposes; nor are you or yours bound to plant any vine for us ever again nor to contribute any work in the said vineyard existing or to be made, nor to go to any other expense."[137] Vineyard labor service continued into the next century. Chelva's authorities expected from each Mudejar house two men to dig around vines, but did provide a salary of eight pence apiece. Cheste in 1371 required digging and similar labor, recompensed with twelve pence daily.[138] The money may have represented the lord's obligation to feed each worker, as seen above in the Aldea charter.

Another form of labor, not commonly considered personal service, was the haulage or delivery of taxes in kind; thus the Chivert

---

head of a farm household. Here the Christians' chicken tax was double that of the Mudejars.

[134] Soldevila, *Pere el Gran*, part 1, iii, appendix 2; the cost at Lérida was 9 pence, at Barcelona and Monzón 8 pence; see also ii, 162, n. 158 (pullet).

[135] Uxó Charter: "la venema dels arbres." Early in the next century the revenues for Aspe record the tithes falling on the tax of *verema* as a hundred solidi yearly.

[136] Arch. Crown, Reg. Canc. 17, fol. 27 (Dec. 30, 1263): "vindemia, calonie, et servicia" in mixed Moorish-Christian returns.

[137] *Ibid.*, Reg. Canc. 12, fol. 40v (May 6, 1262): "concedimus vobis omnibus sarracenis in ravallo maiori Xative comorantibus presentibus et futuris et vestris imperpetuum quod nunquam vos vel vestri teneamini fodere vineas quas fecimus vobis plantare in termino Xative ad opus nostrum, nec teneamini vos vel vestri plantare aliquam vineam pro nobis decetero nec aliquid laboris facere in dictam vineam factam nec faciendam nec aliquam aliam missionem facere."

[138] Gual Camarena, "Mudéjares valencianos, aportaciones," pp. 181-183.

charter twice adverted to *sofra* but took up separately the requirement of carting up to the castle the Hospitallers' share of produce
and vintage. The same obligation of delivering tax in kind sometimes fell on peasants in Islam, though there was opposition to this
burden. Here in Valencia it represented continuity from Islamic
into crusader times.[139]

Another category of labor, far more important and widespread
than the rural obligations but subtly removed from them in context
and status, affected community utilities or resources. This was obligatory, even in the cities, upon every class of citizen. In 1251 the king
admonished Christians of all classes at Valencia city, including
clergy and nobles, not to refuse their obligatory share "in the building
and repair of [city] walls and moat, the building, repair, and cleaning . . . of the public roads and bridges, and the care of the city."
The kingdom's *Furs* incorporated his demand in much the same
words.[140] Such duties weighed also upon the Mudejars. In the crusader states of the Holy Land, where Islamic rural taxes continued
unchanged under the new lords, the only labor service explicitly
revealed by surviving evidence was precisely this kind of work on
public resources.[141] Contemporary Islamic Egypt also required personal labor, work animals, and provisions from the *fallāḥīn* for construction and repair of the larger dams, an obligation that could also
be redeemed by money. Presumably the local authorities responsible for lesser projects arranged for similar participation; in 1283
the sultan, Qalā'ūn, went out to a province to supervise canal digging

[139] Chivert Charter: "aportent ubi fratres voluerint intus castro"; "de vindemia
similiter . . . aportent ad trullum intus castro ubi fratres voluerint"; *trull* is a wine-
press. On haulage in Egypt see Løkkegaard, *Islamic Taxation*, p. 119. For this transport charge among Christians, found in northern Valencia only at Cervera, see
García y García, *Estado económico-social de Castellón*, p. 43. Haulage as a labor
service was commonly referred to as *traginum* in northern Christian documents.
See *Cartas de población de Cataluña*, I, doc. 223 (1207): "traginum, id est servitium
asinorum aliarumque bestiarum"; doc. 322 (1273): "facere traginum nisi bis traginum in annum, unum scilicet per duos dies in anno ad bladum defferendum . . . nec
facere teneantur aliquod opus vel operam . . . nisi tantum de fusta." These seem, in
part at least, the equivalent of the Mudejar *sofra*.

[140] *Fori antiqui Valentiae,* rub. cxxiv, no. 16. *Colección diplomática,* doc. 399
(June 19, 1251): "ad construccionem et reparacionem murorum et vallis, construccionem, reparacionem et mundacionem et ad instrucciones et mundaciones viarum
publicarum et poncium et civitatis custodiam."

[141] Cahen, "Régime rural syrien," p. 297.

himself.[142] In a more local context, of course, such work on utilities shaded into labor service, acquiring the taint and sometimes the name of that more inferior charge. Thus at Chivert, where the overlord Hospitallers undertook to construct a segregating wall between their castle and the Moorish quarter, they agreed not to require from the Mudejars "contribution of money or *sofra* of their persons."[143] Repair of walls provided so common an occasion for *sofra* that Torres Balbás, an authority on medieval Spanish cities, viewed the latter too closely in that context.[144]

Community service of this more elevated kind resembled repair of one's own home; it involved one's immediate environs or related somehow to one's own welfare. King Peter underlined this character in a directive of 1280. "You are not to bring legal pressure on the Saracens of Cabanes to construct the bridges in their districts that the lord king ordered to be constructed for carrying the roadways, unless the said Saracens at some time shall wish to make use of the aforesaid roads."[145] Earlier that year the king had occasion to commend a crown project to those Muslims inhabiting the Valencian kingdom down to the Júcar River: an extramural palace-with-park (*real*) at the capital's northeast. They had to contribute their services. "Know that we have appointed Vives b. Vives, our Jew of Valencia, to administer the project of our residence in Valencia; wherefore we command all those among you, whom the said Vives considers needed for the aforesaid work, to help him and it."[146]

The military work already discussed, such as repair of fortifica-

---

[142] Rabie, *Financial System of Egypt*, pp. 70-71, 115.

[143] Chivert Charter. In the early fourteenth century at Aspe 200 solidi were returned to local authorities every year "en reparacio dels murs del loch," an entry that must have come under the heading of *sofra* (*Rentas de Aragón*, p. 126).

[144] *Resumen histórico del urbanismo en España* (Madrid, 1954), p. 77.

[145] Arch. Crown, Peter III, Reg. Canc. 48, fol. 187 (Nov. 28, 1280): "non compellare sarracenos de Cabanes ad aptandum pontes terminorum suorum quos dominus rex aptari mandavit ad opus carreriarum, nisi dicti sarraceni aliquo tempore se iuvare voluerint de carreriis predictis." *Compello* in the first conjugation ("to accost" or "to abuse") bears a juridical meaning of arraigning or accusing.

[146] *Ibid.*, fol. 67 (June 26, 1280): "noveritis nos posuisse Vives Abenvives iudeum nostrum Valencie pro custode in opere regali nostri Valencie; quare mandamus vobis quatenus omnes illi vestrum quos dictus Vives in predicto opere necessarios habuerit ut . . . iuvetis eundem ac eidem." The order is directed to "universis babtizatis et sarracenis" of Valencia "a rivo Xucar citra," thus demanding Mudejar service from convert Moors.

tions, mounting of local guard, and provision of pack animals for campaigns, related somewhat to this community labor service; so did the upkeep of any public facilities, repair of mosques or churches, maintenance of irrigation ditches, or labor at the saltworks.[147] Perhaps the "bridge *òbols*," or subpennies levied as toll on every loaded animal entering a city, until construction costs for a new bridge were met, assumed in the eyes of residents at places like Valencia city or Alcira the nature of a commuted labor service, especially since the bridge charge could enter a list of farmed taxes as though it were itself a straightforward tax.[148]

As time went on, *sofra* grew heavier. By the sixteenth century the complex of services under that title comprised a burden peculiarly Morisco, persisting even after a Muslim's conversion; it rendered the condition of Valencia's Moors "almost servile."[149] In

[147] At Nabal in 1294, not a Valencian place, the Moors not only paid the usual "calonias de sal," but worked in and coadministered the six saltworks—"tambien christianos infançones o otros como moros tienan, lauran, et aministrean todas las ditas salinas" (*Rentas de Aragón*, pp. 303-304). Mudejar work on Christian churches, apparently rare in Valencia, may have fallen under a similar rubric of public works or may have represented a substitute for labor owed as rent; Alfonso X in 1267 ordered all available Mudejar carpenters, sawyers, and masons to work two days in repairing Cordova cathedral, with meals supplied free, a program widened to involve Mudejars generally for two days a year by King Sancho in 1282 (Miguel A. Orti Belmonte, "El fuero de Córdoba y las clases sociales en la ciudad: mudéjares y judíos en la edad media," *Boletín de la real academia de Córdoba*, xxv [1954], 41-42).

[148] Arch. Crown, James I, Reg. Canc. 10, fols. 25v-26 (Nov. 28, 1257): "obulos pontis, censualia, percasia, aventuras, servicia, cu[m] redditibus seu tributis sarracenorum" at Alcira; the list occurs again later in the document. See also fols. 33v-34 (Feb. 9, 1258): "obulos pontis" to a different tax farmer at Alcira. At Valencia city, from 1243, each loaded animal, whether of resident Christian or Moor or of outsider, had to pay a penny for entering, until the pennies had paid for the new bridge (Arch. Mun. Val., perg. James I, sig. no. 9). Johannes Vincke has a study in hand on the crown's deliberate control of bridge construction, its political significance, and the fees. This construction fee was distinct from *pontatge* (Latin *pontaticum*) a transit fee related to *cespaticus* (see Rodón Binué, *Lenguaje técnico del feudalismo*, pp. 54, 199).

[149] Even in the late thirteenth-century the crown had to restrain authorities at Gallinera for increasing the *sofres*; it rebuked demands for early payment of agricultural thirds from Mudejars there, then added: "mandamus insuper vobis quatenus in açofris vel aliis servitutibus exigendis vel recipiendis ab eis non gravetis eos vel aliquem eorum noviter, nec exigatis aliud ab eis nisi ea tantum que dare actenus consueverunt" (Arch. Crown, Alfonso III, Reg. Canc. 85, fol. 127v [March 28, 1291]). For the later era see Tulio Halperín Donghi, "Recouvrements de civilisation: les morisques du royaume de Valence au xvie siècle," *Annales, économies, so-*

thirteenth-century Valencia, however, the light nature of the service where visible, the frequency of commutation, and the small sums involved, argue to an obligation relatively negligible.

HOSPITALITY AND COURT FINES

Cena or procurations had its origin in the hospitality owed to a royal court constantly on the move. It had its counterpart in hospitality obligations of vassals toward their lords. The term designated the most burdensome aspect of the obligation, the provisioning or victualing of the royal party, sometimes commuted to a money payment. Wherever this commutation became a permanent, fixed tax, an evolution encouraged by the growing sophistication of crown administration, the functional *cena de presència* became the fictional hospitality called *cena de absència* or simply *cena*. In practice, each town on the *cena* tax list paid a set, unchanging sum annually. The crown heir had the right to a parallel *cena del primogènit* from certain places; by an analogous development, the bishop of Valencia collected ecclesiastical *cena* from his parochial rectors.[150]

---

ciétés, civilisations, XI (1956), 159: "presque servile." At Perpunchent in 1334 the commander could requisition Muslims and their mules for repairs or new buildings as often as he wanted, paying 6 pence for each day's work, plus 6 to 12 pence more if an ass or mule were involved; at Cheste in 1371 each Moor had to "fer çofra a nos e als nostres, tota hora que nos e los nostres vos hauren menester," receiving only daily bread and any animal's forage; at Ribesalbes each household had to give two days' work free, after which the lord could demand work usually only within a distance of five leagues and according to a pay schedule running between 1 and 1⅔ solidi (Gual Camarena, "Mudéjares valencianos, aportaciones," pp. 181-183). The 1370 Chelva Charter required a large commutation: "item por zofra cuatro sueldos por casa, los cuales seades tenidos pagar un año en dos pagas," half in January and half in August.

[150] Bofarull explains the categories of *cena* in the introduction to his *Rentas de Aragón*, pp. ix-x, xiii-xiv. See also Branchát, *Derechos y regalías de Valencia*, ch. 10, no. 25; Asso, *Economía política de Aragón*, p. 297; García de Valdeavellano, *Instituciones españolas*, pp. 252, 393, 603; Piles Ros, *Bayle general de Valencia*, pp. 87-88; Rodón Binué, *Lenguaje técnico del feudalismo*, pp. ix, 15, 182, 187, 217-218; Nilda Guglielmi, "Posada y yantar, contribución al estudio del léxico de las instituciones medievales," *Hispania*, XXVI (1966), 5-40, 165-219. *Alberga, comestion, freda, hospedera, hospedaje, mansionatici, ostalitas, paratae, pausitaria, recepti*, and *yantar* are among the synonyms, related terms, and more generalized origins for the victualing tax; the closest equivalent for Castile was *yantar*. On ecclesiastical *cena*, see Burns, *Crusader Valencia*, I, 32. For an example of a Christian charter imposing only the *cena de presència* (100 cafizes of wheat) see *Cartas de población de Cata-*

A series of four annual lists of *cena* "in the absence" of the king survives for the kingdom of Valencia from the early fourteenth century. The thirty-six towns or administrative entities recurring in it comprise a map of the kingdom. Each of the four military orders with the largest holdings in Valencia contributed a lump sum. Muslims apparently joined their Christian neighbors in local payment, but separate listing was provided for the aljamas of Beniopa, Gallinera, Játiva, and Valencia city. Jewish aljamas merged into the larger communities in the same fashion, only Valencia city furnishing a separate entry for Jews. The series remained steady both as to towns named (though one was exempted and seven disappeared from the final lists) and as to sums demanded. Two places paid over 300 solidi each; seven gave 200 or more; twenty paid between 100 and 166 apiece; and five fell into the category of 66 solidi. Specifically Mudejar entries ranged over several categories, Valencia city's aljama yielding a figure below all others—33 solidi—while the Beniopa and Gallinera communities came under the central grouping, and Játiva paid 200 solidi. This larger picture, though fifty years too late for direct evidence, may help orient the fragmentary information on the *cena* from thirteenth-century Muslims.[151]

---

luña, I, doc. 308 (Almacellas, 1260), and of the double tax, hospitality plus provisioning, "de alberga et de cena et de albergando in domibus vestris," see doc. 335 (Palamós, 1279). In the *corts* or parliament of 1251 at Barcelona, King James decreed an end of claiming "cenas, albergas, vel acapita" on the land of knights, barons, or churchmen (*Cortes de Aragón y de Valencia*, I, part 1, p. 144). Edmund Ohlendorf, in his "Zur 'cena in presentia' des Königs von Aragon" (*Gesammelte Aufsätze zur Kulturgeschichte Spaniens*, xxi [1963], 155-161) discusses an aspect of *cena* under Alfonso III, 1286-1287; see also Johannes Vincke, "Die Gastungsrecht der aragonischen Krone im hohen Mittelalter" (*ibid.*, xix-xx [1962], 161-170).

[151] *Rentas de Aragón*, pp. 428-449, lists of 1327-1330; collected in Valencian solidi. The last two lists do not have Beniopa, Cullera, Gallinera, Gandía, Guadalest, Pego, and Uxó; Castalla was exempt. The sums are arbitrary, apparently representing a prorating of normal expenses according to categories of ability to pay. Arch. Reino Val., Real Cancillería, 612, Libre de titols de les rendes e drets reals del regne de Valencia, codex 3, fols. 60-61v, is a fifteenth-century list of *cenae*. It includes "la moreria de Valencia" at 100 solidi, enters Christian Játiva for 1,000 solidi but the Játiva aljama for 600, the "aliama sarracenorum de Guallinera" or Gallinera for 300, and the "aliama sarracenorum de Beniopa prope Guandia" or Gandía for 300. Either Christian or mixed *cena* from Morella came to 1,000 solidi, from Burriana and Murviedro 700 apiece, from Cullera 500, and from Uxó 300. Arch. Crown, James I, Reg. Canc. 8, fol. 59 (April 28, 1262) gives the *cena* being collected in neighboring Aragon, with twenty-five places contributing in the Zaragoza bailiate alone; five paid 100 solidi each, five paid 150, five paid 200, another five 300, four paid 400,

No clear evidence has survived showing a Valencian aljama giving *cena de presència*, though some must have done so; collateral evidence of such an obligation does turn up for Aragon proper. Perhaps one approbation of accounts by King James in 1275 conceals such a reference for Valencia; the king had received *cena* from his Christian and Muslim subjects at various places "on the route after we departed from Lérida up to the time we were in Valencia."[152] Commuted or as tax, the *cena* occurs in Mudejar records for Almizra in 1260,[153] for Biar in 1258 and 1267,[154] for Pego in 1268,[155] for Alcalá and Gallinera in 1267,[156] for "Alcira, Gandía, and other places" in 1273,[157]

and one paid 500, with the only Mudejar group being the "sarraceni de Terrer" at 150 solidi. On the following folio, the bailiwicks for Barbastro, Exea, Huesca, and Jaca do not single out Mudejar communities at all. Felipe Mateu y Llopis studies an earlier equally well-organized effort, in his "Colecta de la cena en el reino de Valencia en 1292-1295" (*BSCC*, xlvi [1970], 215-236); of 41 Valencian places paying in 1292, only five were explicitly and purely Mudejar: Guadalest at 300 solidi, Játiva at 500, Tárbena at 300, Uxó at 150 (and 200 remitted), and Valencia city at 150. The sums, repeated in the 1293 collection, compare with such (mixed Moorish and Christian?) totals as: Ayora 700, Burriana 800, Chivert 600, and Denia 800.

[152] *Itinerari*, p. 528 (Feb. 4, 1275): "in itinere postquam recessimus de Ilerda usque fuimus in Valencia." Francisco Macho y Ortega provides a late document (June 23, 1414) illustrating an abuse of the *cena de presència*. The entourage of the prince forcibly lodged themselves with the Moors of Zaragoza in Aragon proper; they in turn complained to the king both of the indignity and of shameful talk about their wives ("uxores vestri dictorum serracenorum iniuste remanent diffamare"); calling this aljama "thesaurus noster," the king forbade anyone connected with the crown to quarter there "nisi illos de officio alguatzirii nostri et dicti primogeniti nostri" in the personal presence of king or prince ("Documentos relativos a la condición social y jurídica de los mudéjares aragoneses," *Revista de ciencias jurídicas y sociales*, v [1922], 159-160). See also his "Mudéjares aragoneses," pp. 183-184. A Mudejar delegation from "Almonezir" waited on King Alfonso in 1291 to insist that they had to give *cena* only "si contingat nos [Alfonso] ire ad dictum locum" (Arch. Crown, Alfonso III, Reg. Canc. 85, fol. 182 [June 9, 1291]); though cited as Valencian in Rafael Gallofre Guinovart's catalogue, *Documentos del reinado de Alfonso III de Aragón relativos al antiguo reino de Valencia y contenidos en los registros de la corona de Aragón* (Valencia, 1968), no. 2,209, this is the same Almonacid de la Sierra, in Aragon, which confused Martínez Ferrando above in n. 59.

[153] Arch. Crown, James I, Reg. Canc. 11, fols. 192v-193 (Feb. 5, 1260): "cena," an individual exemption.

[154] *Ibid.*, Reg. Canc. 10, fol. 103v (June 16, 1258): "cenas," farming them to the aljama. Reg. Canc. 15, fol. 84 (March 1267): "atque cenas."

[155] *Ibid.*, Reg. Canc. 35, fol. 3v (1268): "item cena de caste[ll de Pego] . . . bisantios."

[156] *Ibid.*, Reg. Canc. 15, fol. 88 (March 1, 1267): "de Galinera et Alcolano."

[157] *Ibid.*, Reg. Canc. 19, fol. 107 (Feb. 23, 1273): "in Algezira, Gandia, et aliis locis."

for Mudejar settlers along the Alcira irrigation system in a 1274 exemption,[158] and at Játiva in 1273 and 1282.[159] *Cena*, whether of presence or absence, was not on the list of regalian demands expected as a matter of course from Valencian Mudejar communities in the fifteenth century.[160] An allied tax deriving from obligations of hospitality was the landlord's privilege of buying from his tenants common food at fixed prices. Gual Camarena believes this appeared in Valencia only in the fourteenth century, eventually becoming burdensome.[161]

Justice, a medieval saying went, was great profit. Money fines in civil and criminal courts could mount to an impressive total. *Calònia* (Latin *calonia* or *calum[p]nia*) meant such fines and more particularly the share collected by an overlord.[162] The king's share might run to a third or a fourth on regalian lands. Though not properly a tax, it was processed as such in royal accounting and appeared commonly in lists of tax obligations. Mudejar charters take due notice of this important income. At Eslida "fines are to be given according to their Law." At Játiva the Muslim functionary who supervised the prison "is to have a tenth part of the *calònies* [in payment] for his work." At Tales these "civil and criminal fines" were to be imposed only "according to the aforesaid Sunna of the Saracens." At Alfandech the charter dealt with "*calònies* of pennies and also judicial fees." Manslaughter, theft, and rapine must have proved particularly lucrative for the courts, since the crown retained these when allow-

---

[158] *Ibid.*, fol. 124 (April 16, 1274): "sarracenos qui populabunt . . . subtus cequiam Algezire . . . [ab] cena ac qualibet alia exaccione sive demanda regali."

[159] *Ibid.*, fol. 53 (Sept. 7, 1273): "ab omni . . . cena"; again in Peter III, Reg. Canc. 60, fol. 26 (Feb. 11, 1282), a thousand solidi: "fuit missa litera aliame sarracenorum Xative quod visis presentibus dent et solvant . . . mille solidos regalium pro cena, alias mandat eidem per ipsos inde compellat."

[160] *Formularium diversorum contractuum*, fol. xxviiii-xxx.

[161] Gual Camarena, "Mudéjares valencianos, aportaciones," pp. 183-185, with lists and prices; these tend to be chickens or eggs, with occasionally wood or a goat, and may relate rather to the *çofra* of fowl already seen.

[162] On the Islamic court system of the Mudejars in Valencia and its complex relationships with the crusader authorities, see Burns, *Islam under the Crusaders*, ch. 11. On *calònia*, derived from an evolution of the secondary meanings of the classical word, see Rodón Binué, *Lenguaje técnico del feudalismo*, p. 47; García de Valdeavellano, *Instituciones españolas*, pp. 247, 441, 602-603; García y García, *Estado económico-social de Castellón*, p. 68. In its origins it included indemnity or recompense for causing another's death. See also *Fori antiqui Valentiae*, rub. IV, nos. 5 and 6.

ing Játiva a two-year exemption from paying the royal share of fines. Paternity suits brought the crown twenty solidi from convicted male delinquents; single women "found pregnant" gave only five solidi apiece. The later Chelva charter regulated civil and criminal fines according to Islamic custom, but retained them in whole or part for the lord. Fines of all kinds continued to be a normal income for holders of Mudejar villages even in the fifteenth century.[163]

Prince Peter received accounts in 1272 of the *calònies* owed by Almonacid's Muslims.[164] Records of collection exist also for Biar in 1258,[165] for Alcira and Onteniente in 1263,[166] for Pego both in 1268

---

[163] Eslida Charter: "et caloniae dentur secundum legem ipsorum." Játiva Charter: "et habeat decimam partem caloniarum pro labore suo"; "non teneamini dare aliquem censum . . . nisi pro morte hominum vel pro furto aut rapina"; "si aliqua sarracena fuerit inventa pregnans, que maritum non habeat, solvat nobis quinque solidos, et quod omnis sarracenus qui negaverit filium vel filiam, quem vel quam habuerit ab aliqua, solvat viginti solidos nobis, si mater probare poterit." Tales Charter: "pro aliqua calonia . . . nisi secundum çunam predictam sarracenorum"; "pro . . . calonia civili et criminali." Alfandech Charter: "calonias denariorum ac iusticias"; *denarii* here may stand generically for money; *iustitias* meant the revenues claimed by a lord in connection with his administering or executing justice (Rodón Binué, *Lenguaje técnico del feudalismo*, pp. 157-158), but the word was also used in our documents as a synonym for *calumnia* or as a more general, allied term to reinforce and extend it. Chelva Charter: "que vuestras cuestiones e calonias sean . . . alcadi, segun zuna o xara de moros"; "calonias civiles e criminales." The fifteenth-century norm is in the *Formularium diversorum contractuum*, fols. xxviiii-xxx: "penis, caloniis, atque multis civilibus et criminalibus." The non-Valencian Masones Privilege had "iustitie civiles et criminales" among its taxes or revenues. Catalan Christian charters had such phrases as "firmancias, iustitias, calu[m]pnias, et alias dominationes et iurisdictiones," and "sine aliqua iustitia et firmancia et calumpnia" (*Cartas de población de Cataluña*, i, contemporary docs. 261, 302). An exemption from *calònies* for Valencia city's Jews in 1239 retained the "calonia homicidii" (*Itinerari*, p. 139).

[164] Arch. Crown, James I, Reg. Canc. 37, fol. 47v (Feb. 29, 1272): "super caloniis quas dicti sarraceni . . . fecerunt."

[165] *Ibid.*, Reg. Canc. 10, fol. 103v (June 16, 1258): "calonias . . . tam a christianis quam a sarracenis," the criminal fees not reserved. In Reg. Canc. 15, fol. 84 (March 1267) the "calonias [et] iustitias" were farmed, "exceptis homicidiis."

[166] *Ibid.*, Reg. Canc. 17, fol. 27 (Dec. 30, 1263): "calonie sarracenorum, xxiii solidos et medium"; a later entry in the list lumps six taxes, including "mostaçafia, oleum, vindemia, calonie, et servicia," at 286 solidi, perhaps representing Christian fines or a mixed category from other courts. Fol. 29v (Dec. 31, 1263) at Onteniente: "calonie sarracenorum" of 20 solidi. Corbera's fines came to 50 solidi, probably mixed Christian and Mudejar (fol. 27, Dec. 30). Cullera's similar entry has "calonie, quarti, et servicia, clxxx solidos minus ii denariis," followed by "calonia, i kafiz ordei et alium frumenti que faciunt xii solidos" (fol. 29, Dec. 31). Finally, an un-

and 1269, Cárcer with Sueca in 1270,[167] "Alfandech and its valley" in 1275,[168] and Uxó and Pego at the end of the century.[169] In a rental of revenues at Alfandech in 1270, the king took care to "except from this sale administration of justice with its profits and revenues."[170] In the aljamas of Algar, Callosa, Castell, Confrides, Guadalest, Jalón, Pop, Sagra, and Vall de Laguart the crown farmed all *calònies* in 1282, except for "criminal fines."[171] An occasional entry speaks ambiguously of a "*calònia* of the saltworks" or "of vines and vegetable farms." This practice may represent misuse of the term, but more probably relates to specialized fines along the line of the *calònies* collected for infringement of water regulations in the irrigation network. Thus the "*calònia* for wine" at Játiva refers apparently to a fine on selling wine directly to the householder, bypassing the public monopoly and control at the tavern.[172] Specific sums collected for *calònia* at any given place rarely appear in the records. One such entry for 1269 lists 37 besants or some 138 solidi, plus a collection charge of 3 besants. Another amounts to 75 besants, and a third to only 7 solidi. After the turn of the century, Novelda yielded 500 solidi a year, Elda 400, and Aspe 250.[173] In granting amnesty for all crimes to the Muslims surrending Uxó, King James conceded that "*perres* not be demanded for those said crimes or penalties."[174] Considering

---

dated list of cereals on fol. 31 under the heading "bladum mercati" ends with an entry for wine and for "calonie, v solidos" (see n. 172 and text, on possible usage as "fee").

[167] *Ibid.*, Reg. Canc. 35, fol. 3v (1268): "item calonias, [lxxv] besants." Fol. 4 (1269): "item calonias, xxxvii besants, ii millareses; colidura, iii besants, vii millareses." Fol. 8 (1270): "item las calonias, vii sous."

[168] *Ibid.*, Reg. Canc. 20, fol. 245 (April 27, 1275): "sarracenis de Alfandech et vallis eiusdem."

[169] Martínez y Martínez, "Pego," pp. 68-69 (1300).

[170] Arch. Crown, James I, Reg. Canc. 35, fol. 56v (March 19, 1270): "excipimus tamen de ista vendicione iusticiatum cum proventibus et exitibus eiusdem."

[171] Document in n. 35: "calonias . . . exceptis iusticiis criminalibus."

[172] Játiva Charter: "[non] dare caloniam pro vino quod habuerit vel emerit in domo sua," a privilege. At Nabal in Aragon proper, the revenue lists give not only "las calonias de christianos et de moros," but also "las calonias de las salinas" and "el tierço de las calonias de vinnas et de huertos" (*Rentas de Aragón*, p. 301).

[173] See the sums in nn. 166 and 167. For Aspe, Elda, and Novelda ("valen cascun any les calonies quels dits moros paguen tro a"), see *Rentas de Aragón*, pp. 122-124 (1315).

[174] Uxó Charter: "remetem a aquells tots crims o penes . . . , e perres non fosen de aquells dits crims o penes demanats." *Perra* can be a small copper coin (*perra*

the legal context, *perres* or *perras* may derive from the Castilian coin of that name, or by a misstroke represent *peites* for punitive taxes. A Mudejar fee for "homicides," perhaps meaning fines related to manslaughter, turns up at Gallinera and at Alcalá.[175]

Though lacking in detail, this picture of Mudejar Valencia continuing its obviously elaborate structure of fines under Christian lordship casts light also upon the judicial system of precrusade Islamic Valencia. The spectrum of varied fines reviewed in the chapter affords views into both Islamic and Mudejar society, especially into those strata involved in irrigation communities, professional stock raising, and farm work. The salt, coinage, and war demands open a particularly broad vista, since they affected everyone. Each tax in the list represented a point of contact with Christian neighbors, and at times a point of shared discontent; as a pattern, with novel modalities, they functioned both as continuity and point of departure for the conquered people.

---

grossa or *perra menuda*, respectively ten and five *centims*), or a form of *pedra*, rock or stone (quarrying fee?). *Perro* was the watchdog levied for military guard, or a common term of abuse against Muslims; during the revolt of 1276, when the settlers added two dogs to the garrison of Guadalest castle, the crown contributed 120 solidi for dog food during the coming year, or a hefty five solidi per month per dog (Soldevila, *Pere el Gran*, part 2, 1, appendix, doc. 13 [Sept. 1, 1276]). Context classifies *perra* here; elsewhere in the registers *peita* can easily be misread as *perra*, when the bar of the *t* carries over the preceding *i*, to resemble double *r*.

[175] Arch. Crown, James I, Reg. Canc. 15, fol. 88 (March 1, 1267): "retinemus tamen, in predictis, nobis . . . homicidia et venditionem salis nostri. . . ."

CHAPTER VI

Treasure, Tithe, Fees, and Miscellany

No MATTER HOW infrequent or trivial, any tax can illumine the daily life of its supporters. Some charges are of so bizarre a nature, or so obscure in the surviving records, as to call for treatment apart. Most Mudejars did not pay tithe; few chanced upon buried treasure; and those who contributed toward the vice taxes remained, one piously trusts, a minority. Yet each of these revenue sources tells something about Valencia's Mudejars. Entering upon marriage, on the other hand, drawing a will, gathering firewood, buying property, or traveling overseas were more common undertakings, shared by a goodly percentage of the population. The sparse fiscal data bearing on such ordinary activities, though unrevealing as a whole, can be more confidently generalized. Both categories of imposition, the bizarre and the ill-documented, round out the picture of Mudejar life.

TREASURE HUNTING

Treasure hunting has fascinated people from Roman times to our own. It had special relevance in an age when the affluent were apt to bury their valuables before fleeing from raiders. During unstable times, too, the aged or ill might hoard their savings in the ground for security, and die before disposing of them. When the crusaders of King James were advancing in Valencia, the *qā'id* Maḥmūd (Mamud) of Benimamet buried 200,000 gold pieces and fled; two centuries later the fortune enriched its Morisco discoverer.[1] A non-

[1] Gaspar Escolano, *Décadas de la historia de la insigne y coronada ciudad y reino de Valencia*, ed. Juan B. Perales, 3 vols. (Valencia, [1610-1611] 1878-1880), II, lib. VII, c.4. See also Martínez Aloy in *Geografía general del reino de Valencia [Provincia de Valencia]*, I, 841; and José Sanchis y Sivera, *Nomenclátor geográfico-eclesiástico de los pueblos de la diócesis de Valencia con los nombres antiguos y modernos . . . , notas históricas . . .* (Valencia, 1922), p. 128. In 1899 a farmer at Jalón found a treasure of Islamic moneys. For Rome and as a survey of European practice see George F. Hill, *Treasure Trove in Law and Practice from the Earliest*

Valencian but neighboring example of such treasure was the 3,000 gold pieces unearthed during construction of the Alhambra ramparts, at the site where a Jewish treasurer to a sultan had lived.[2] Even in the territory of Barcelona the name of a town, Auro Invento, long commemorated a rich find of the tenth century.[3] In Christian and Islamic Spain alike, authorities required a license for the professional treasure hunter and also demanded a generous share of his resulting treasure trove. It may be instructive to pause over this tax, viewing it comparatively in the two societies, and conjecturing the sense of continuity or discontinuity experienced by the Mudejar passing from one rule of law to another. Treasure (*troba*, Latin *thesaurus, troba,* or *inventio*) provided a rare instance of a Christian tax supplanting the Islamic in Mudejar society, possibly because the case affected very few people and those only once or twice.

Spanish Muslims kept an eye open for bonanzas, from the era of the Moorish conquest up to the Reconquest by the Christians. During the period of consolidation, around 718, Spain's ruler al-Ḥurr looked upon the multiplying treasure enthusiasts as a public nuisance and punished them to curtail their numbers,[4] though a Christian chronicler asserts rather that al-Ḥurr tortured fellow Muslims "so they would reveal their hidden treasure."[5] Either interpretation confers an ancient pedigree on Spanish treasure hunting. Six centuries later Ibn Khaldūn, the North African of Sevillian antecedents, went out of his way to rebuke treasure hunting as a mania engaging the enthusiasm of "many weak-minded persons" in all parts of Islam. He explained it as rooted in the assumption that families of a people being conquered naturally buried their wealth to protect it. Professional Berber swindlers "get their sustenance" by disclosing false

---

Times to the Present Day (Oxford, 1936); the brief section on medieval Spain is confused and misleading (pp. 116-122), and of course Islamic practice is omitted.

[2] Goitein, *Mediterranean Society*, I, 265; he also cites a Tunisian Jewish merchant who buried his brother's capital in 1052, gaining security at the temporary cost of profit.

[3] José Balari Jovany, *Orígenes históricos de Cataluña*, 2 vols. (San Cugat, [1899] 1964), II, 708-709; references begin in 961 and end in 1064, without Romance equivalent.

[4] Edward P. Colbert, *The Martyrs of Córdoba (850-859): A Study of the Sources* (Washington, D.C., 1962), p. 41.

[5] *Historia arabum*, ed. Francisco de Lorenzana, attributed to the thirteenth-century primate of Spain, Rodrigo Jiménez de Rada, in his *Opera*, 1 vol. to date (Valencia, [1793] 1968), ch. 10: "eos afflixit ut absconditos thesauros revelarent."

clue-maps to the gullible and by other "astounding techniques." Many victims labored harder for treasure than if they worked for a living, unaware that treasure is found "rarely and by chance, not by systematic search"; greedy governments connived at the absurdity, "and a tax has to be paid by those stupid and deluded persons."[6]

Besides this license fee, Muslims in Spain as everywhere in Islam had to return to the state treasury a share of the valuables found. Islamic jurists wrangled over the appropriate tax to apply. Generally they distinguished treasure from lost-and-found articles and assimilated it to the products of mines, recommending the non-*shari'a* tax of a fifth. Some, however, subjected it rather to the canonical *zakāt* or tithe. The jurists complicated these basic positions with any number of distinctions. Malikites, the dominant school in Almohad Spain at the time of the Valencian crusade, argued that a trove fell under the fifth if it was of pre-Islamic or doubtful origin, no matter what its quantity or the status of its finder, but that it shifted to fall under the *zakāt* if its recovery entailed great expense or toil. A certain kind of infidel under protection had to surrender his entire find to the state. Authorities differed as to who claimed the four-fifths when the treasure lay on privately owned land. Some held for the former owner at the era of conquest or for his heirs, since he had sold only the property's surface; if he were unknown, the state could claim. Others reasoned that the distributors of land at the conquest, in order to effect a just division, must have disregarded possible treasure, and therefore the finder had sole claim.[7] Qudāma devoted a considerable portion of his book on taxes to treasure trove, minerals for mining, pearls, sea finds, and related questions. Abū 'Ubayd Allāh cited over thirty conflicting traditions on treasure trove and mineral finds, and Abu Yūsuf gave the subject serious consideration.[8]

Christian Spain had inherited a more confusing, double tradition. Roman law, sometimes disregarding treasure as an accident of pri-

---

[6] *Muqaddimah*, II, 319-326.

[7] Aghnides, *Mohammedan Theories of Finance*, p. 201 (*zakāt* vs. *shari'a* theories); part 2, ch. 8, section on *rikāz* (underground wealth) and *kanz* (treasure trove); and p. 525. Siddiqi, *Public Finance in Islam*, pp. 10ff., 120-122.

[8] Qudāma, *Kitāb al-kharāj*, ch. 11 on minerals and treasure trove, ch. 12 on pearls and sea-findings, ch. 14 on lost-and-found treasure, and ch. 1 (p. 24) on treasure as pre-Islamic. Abū Yūsuf, *Kitāb al-kharāj*, pp. 54-55; and on Abū 'Ubayd in Ben-Shemesh's introduction there, p. 18.

vate property and sometimes confiscating it as abandoned goods, had solved the problem in the code of Justinian by awarding half to the finder and half to the landowner, the state taking nothing unless it owned the treasure-infested parcel of land.[9] This position, of some influence in early medieval times but increasingly prominent during the Roman law renaissance of the twelfth and thirteenth centuries, clashed with customary laws that appropriated treasure to such common goods as mines, rivers, and fish, making the local lord and later the king either sole or main beneficiary. Historians of law sometimes use this opposition as a touchstone for gauging the influence of Roman law on a given code, a technique not without its perils.

In 1064 the parliament of Barcelona had issued a decree, which entered that region's celebrated *Usatges* in 1068, forcing any "countryman" who found gold or silver, or a mule or articles of any kind, to surrender all to "its lord" and accept whatever "reward" the lord cared to give.[10] This immemorial custom, once planted in writing,

[9] J. Arias Ramos, *Derecho romano*, 2 vols., 11th edn. rev., ed. J. A. Arias Bonet (Madrid, 1969), 1, 250-251. The law used by Justinian had been the solution attributed to Emperor Hadrian. Gary Hanekamp, a Los Angeles businessman looking for treasure on a piece of city property in 1971, apparently encountered this same tradition; the Board of Commissioners allowed him twenty-five percent up to the first $500 and half thereafter, but stipulated use of hand tools only, refill of land, and a $300,000 liability insurance policy against accidents. Electronic devices for finding buried treasure are marketed cheaply for individuals by half a dozen firms in the United States today, and at least one national association of treasure hunters caters to the many hobbyists of buried treasure.

[10] *Cortes de Aragón y de Valencia*, 1, part 1, no. 112, p. 38 *bis* (1064, Raymond Berengar I): "rusticus vero si invenerit aurum vel argentum [et] quod vulgo dicitur bonas . . . statim denunciet domino suo et demonstret et reddat et accipiat ab eo qualem mercedem inde ei senior dare voluerit." *Usatges de Barcelona*, in the *text antic*, no. 97, p. 118: "pagès, si troba or ni argent ni aver en bonetes, o caval o mul o sarraí o ostor, mantinent o diga e o mostre a son senyor, e dón-li-o, e prena ço que son senyor dar-li volrà per guardó." As the editor notes, this makes equivalent "els tresors ocults" and "les coses abandonades"; on the latter classification, res *derelictae* or res *nullius* in the strict sense in Roman law, and their ownership by "occupation," see Arias Ramos, *Derecho romano*, 1, 242-244; see also his comments here on booty taken during a raid, either for the group or for the individual soldier (p. 244). "Treasure" and "finds" (*trobes, trobadures*) are frequently synonyms, or at least species and genus, in the formulas; see, e.g.: "medietatem omnium trobarum super terram vel subtus terram" (Balari Jovany, *Orígenes*, p. 554). The treasurer of England, Richard of Ely (d. 1198), in his *Dialogus de scaccario*, a volume on conducting the exchequer and fiscal affairs of the kingdom, brusquely included "treasure trove, whether found by digging or otherwise" among revenues automatically confiscated

spread broadly as an item in the laws of Catalonia.[11] At Daroca in Aragon proper, on the other hand, the Catalan count approved a code in 1142 that let the finder of treasure "have and hold it in peace."[12] The code of Teruel in Aragon similarly gave treasure to its finder, tax-free and without interference by lord or king; it did require that treasure found on another's property be shared equally with the landowner.[13] At conquered Tortosa, just north of Valencia, this half-and-half policy also prevailed.[14]

The public code of the Valencian kingdom, Roman in its exaltation of royal power but medieval in its greed for rents, demanded a full three-fourths for the crown; if the treasure lay on alien property, the finder had to deduct expenses and damages of the search from his own fourth and then split the remainder with the landowner. If the finder did not notify the crown within ten days of discovery, disposition of both treasure and delinquent was at the king's mercy. This law was an afterthought, inserted into the code by King James I during a subsequent revision; the circumstance suggests that men had been finding treasure in the wake of the crusaders' recent conquest.[15] A decade after James's death, the crown reversed this

in full by the state; the finder must submit it voluntarily, "etiamsi summonitia nulla precesserit" (*The Course of the Exchequer*, ed. and trans. Charles Johnson [London, 1950], p. 98, text, and 98 *bis*). The thirteenth-century English jurists Glanville and Bracton both saw concealment of treasure as theft and akin to treason ("quasi crimen furti"); see Bracton's *De legibus et consuetudine Angliae*, ed. G. E. Woodbine, trans. S. E. Thorne, 2 vols. to date (Cambridge, Mass., 1968), I, 47, 167, 344; and Frederick Pollock and Frederic Maitland, *The History of English Law Before the Time of Edward I*, 2 vols., 2d edn. (Cambridge, 1923), II, 499-500. *The Liber Augustalis, or Constitutions of Melfi Promulgated by the Emperor Frederick II for the Kingdom of Sicily in 1231*, trans. J. M. Powell (Syracuse, N.Y., 1971), displays the same mentality, despite its Roman bias (see tit. 35, and on shipwreck tit. 29).

[11] *Usages y demás derechos de Cataluña* . . . , ed. P. N. Vives y Cebriá, 2d edn. rev., 5 vols. (Madrid, 1861-1867), II, lib. IV, tit. xxxii, no. 2, p. 137.

[12] *Colección de fueros municipales*, p. 559, *fuero* of Daroca (1142): "si quis tesaurum invenerit, habeat et teneat illum in pace."

[13] *Forum Turolii, regnante in Aragonia Adefonso rege, anno dominice nativitatis mclxxvi*, ed. Francisco Aznar y Navarro (Zaragoza, 1905), no. 422, p. 222: "quicumque thesaurum veterem invenerit . . . ipsum habeat inmunem et liberum, et pro ipso domino regi non respondeat sive alio domino. . . ."

[14] *Cartas de población de Cataluña*, I, doc. 293 (1251): "consuetudinem dertusensem."

[15] *Fori antiqui Valentiae*, rub. cxxiv, no. 17: "facimus forum novum quod si quis in suo thesaurum absconditum invenerit, quod inde quartam partem habeat, et nos

principle for the Balearics, decreeing: "let the treasure [belong to] him who found it, as is contained in the Roman law."[16] Albarracín, on Valencia's western flank, similarly incorporated a proviso into its code, by which treasure went entirely to the discoverer or, on another's property, was shared with the landowner equally.[17]

While the realms of Aragon underwent these juristic variations, the lands that became Castile evolved their own, eventually assigning three-fourths of such finds to the crown.[18] A Palencia law of 824 had divided treasure between count and finder, however, while the influential eleventh-century code of Sepúlveda yielded everything to the finder; the far more important Cuenca code of the twelfth century excluded the authorities and divided treasure between finder and landowner equally.[19] The closet-code of Alfonso the Learned gave the finder all treasure on his own land; treasure on another's land went wholly to that other if the finder had deliberately searched the alien land, but was split between finder and owner if it had turned up only by happy chance.[20]

---

tres inde habeamus; et si in alieno invenerit, quod illud quartum dividatur inter inventorem et dominum loci, restitutis tamen communiter expensis et dampnis datis, factis in inveniendo . . . ; et si . . . non notificabit hoc nobis vel tenenti locum nostrum infra x dies ex quo invenerit, quod sit ad mercedem nostram." See also Branchát, *Derechos y regalías de Valencia*, I, 449-452 (treasure), 452-453 (lost or abandoned articles), 444-449 (mines); García de Cáceres, *Impuestos de Valencia*, p. 31; Ferraz Penelas, *Maestre racional y la hacienda foral valenciana*, pp. 25-27; Piles Ros, *Bayle general de Valencia*, pp. 86-87. Christian A. Fischer discussed early-modern treasure hunters in Valencia, in his *A Picture of Valencia, Taken on the Spot; Comprehending a Description of that Province . . .* , trans. anon., 2d edn. (London, 1811), pp. 132-134.

[16] Archivo Histórico de Mallorca, codex Sant Pere, fol. 138 (1285 or 1286), in Jaime Salvá, "Instituciones políticas y sociales otorgadas por Jaime I a los pobladores de Mallorca," in J. Mascaró Pasarius *et alii, Historia de Mallorca*, 4 vols. projected (Palma de Mallorca, 1970), III, 400: "que sia lo tresor del qui el trobarà com és contengut en la llei romana."

[17] *Carta de población de la ciudad de Santa María de Albarracín*, ed. Carlos Riba y García (Zaragoza, 1915), p. 172: "qual quiere que trasoro uieyo trobare en todo el termino dalbarazin ayo lo quito e franco, e por el non responda. . . ."

[18] Rafael Gibert, *Historia general del derecho español*, I vol. to date (Granada, 1968), I, 246.

[19] *Colección de fueros municipales*, p. 17, *fuero* of Brañosera (Palencia): "de ipsa rem quam invenerint inter suos terminos habeant foro illa medietate ad comite[m], altera medietate ad omes de villa Brana Ossaria"; *fuero* of Sepúlveda (p. 284): "subtus terra, nihil det regi, neque seniori." See also Gibert, *Historia del derecho español*, pp. 30, 34, 468 (Cuenca).

[20] Alfonso X of Castile, *Las siete partidas*, ed. Gregorio López (1555), in *Colec-*

Shipwreck, with its flotsam and jetsam, did not properly come under treasure. Those tempted to see such a windfall in that light had to be restrained by law. The maritime code prevailing along Spain's Mediterranean coast required finders to turn these articles over to the authorities, to be held for "a year and a day" as lost-and-found; if unclaimed, the finder took half and the authorities a fourth, while a fourth was applied for the souls of the owners presumed lost at sea.[21] The earliest code of Valencia took care to spell out the owner's continuing right; nothing must be taken or kept in case of shipwreck.[22] Presumably the year-and-a-day rule held, with some reward for the finder of unclaimed goods. "Precious stones, gems, and other items, which are found along the seashore will immediately belong to the finder, as long as the owner of such things does not show up"; this provision of the Valencian code, though legally unrelated to shipwreck or treasure, assumed for the layman an adventitious connection.[23] The code of Alfonso the Learned contained a similar proviso. In the case of shipwreck, the laws of Majorca stated flatly: "no one is to make shipwreck-claim at any time in the regions of the aforesaid island."[24] It became necessary, nevertheless,

---

ción de códigos y leyes de España, códigos antiguos, ed. Esteban Pinel and Alberto Aguilero y Velasco, 2 vols. (Madrid, 1865), II, part. III, tit. xxviii, ley 45: "thesoros fallan los omes . . . por aventura o buscandolos"; the section is long and detailed. López de Ayala summarizes it in *Contribuciones é impuestos en León y Castilla,* pp. 315-316.

[21] *Costumes de la mar,* compiled around 1250, prefixed by Ferran Valls i Taverner to his edition of the *Consolat de mar,* 3 vols. (Barcelona, 1930-1933), I, 87-88, no. 98, really about anything drifting ashore "en plaja o en port o en ribera, que vaja sobre aygua o que la mar la hagués exaugada en terra."

[22] *Fori antiqui Valentiae,* rub. cxxviii, no. 1: "iure vel occasione naufragii a navibus, lignis, rebus, et mercibus, et hominibus unumcumque [*for* undecumque] fuerint extraneis et privatis . . . aliquid a nobis vel nostris vel ab aliquibus nullatenus accipiatur vel extingatur, et si occupata fuerint, restituantur dominis eorum." A variant form, specifying the ships, appears in the *Aureum opus,* doc. 16, fol. 7 (Sept. 24, 1243): "a navibus et buciis, galeis, taridis, galiotis, sagitis, et quibuslibet aliis barchis et lignis." See also Piles Ros, *Bayle general de Valencia,* pp. 34-35; and see p. 46 for *trobaduríes,* etymologically related to *trobas,* a reward fee obligatory from owners whose fugitive Moorish slaves had been "found" for them.

[23] *Fori antiqui Valentiae,* rub. cxxiv, no. 8.: "lapilli, gemme, et cetera que in litore maris inveniuntur, statim inventoris fuerint quamdiu ipsarum rerum dominus non aparuerit"; this follows Justinian's *Digest* closely.

[24] "Carta de franquesa," Majorca (March 1, 1230), ed. Benet Pons Fàbregues, in Mascaró Passarius, *Historia de Mallorca,* III, 462, no. 5: "naufragi negú no ferà negun temps en les parts de la ila damunt dita."

to issue an extensive prohibition for all Catalan coasts in 1286 against making off with ships or cargo as though they were treasure.[25] A variety of documents, more immediately tied to reality than were the codes, show the treasure laws in action. Some gifts of property to a Catalan monastery included the lord's right to "finds from land and from sea."[26] Settlement charters for Catalan towns sometimes conveyed the seignorial right to all or half or two-thirds of treasure.[27] Farming of revenues in Valencia on occasion retained the crown's treasure share.[28] In the Valencian kingdom the Catí charter yielded all claim to the finder; Pulpis retained it all for the lord; Cabanes, Cervera, and Rosell split it equally, dismissing as negligible any claims less than five solidi.[29] One case of shipwreck, at Denia, entered Valencian administrative records.[30]

[25] *Privilegios reales concedidos a la ciudad de Barcelona*, ed. Antonio Aragó Cabañas and Mercedes Costa, directed by Federico Udina Martorell, *Colección de documentos inéditos del archivo [general] de la corona de Aragón*, second series, I [old XLIII] (Barcelona, 1971), doc. 29 (March 29, 1286), indication: "trobadures."

[26] *Cartulario de "Sant Cugat" del Vallés*, ed. José Rius Serra, 3 vols. (Barcelona, 1945-1947), III, doc. 946 (March 17, 1143): a castle "cum trobis de mare et de stagnis, de montibus et vallis et de pratis et de marinis"; and another castle "cum cunctis exiis et trobis et venacionibus de terra et de mare"; here fishing, treasure, shore-finds and the like are equivalent. Doc. 1117 (May 1, 1178): "et cum venacionibus et trobes"; doc. 1326 (July 28, 1234): "invencionibus"; doc. 1348 (Oct. 21, 1238). As with the *fueros*, these gifts and testaments more frequently omit any reference to treasure.

[27] *Cartas de población de Cataluña*, I, doc. 72 (Aug. 9, 1149): "trobas"; doc. 134 (July 26, 1168): "donamus vobis . . . duas partes . . . de forciis, trobis, et de omnibus"; doc. 175 (Jan. 1185): "et des michi tres partes in . . . trobis et in omnibus"; doc. 184 (March 22, 1190): "et trobas"; doc. 291 (March 5, 1250): "de omnibus siquidem inventionibus vel trobis habeat inde medietatem inventor et nobis aliam retinemus"; doc. 293 (May 9, 1251): "et medietatem in trobis secundum consuetudinem dertusensem"; doc. 318 (March 27, 1270): "inventis in trobas."

[28] Arch. Crown, James I, Reg. Canc. 11, fol. 197v (March 27, 1261): the Denia rents and taxes for ten years, retaining only the confiscated property of heretics and "pecuniam seu thesaurum inventum." Fol. 204 (April 20, 1261): the Murviedro rents for five years, "exceptis inde bonis hereticorum et pecunia seu thesaurum [*sic*] inventum que nobis et nostris retinemus." Reg. Canc. 12, fol. 147v (1263): the Játiva rents for five years, except heretics' property "et pecunia seu tresauro invento." Reg. Canc. 15, fol. 97 (May 1, 1268): "et thesauro invento, que nobis et nostris penitus retinemus" at Murviedro.

[29] García y García, *Estado económico-social de Castellón*, p. 63, gathering details from all the charters of northern Valencia. The Cabanes Charter is in *Cartas de población de Cataluña*, doc. 281 (June 19, 1243): "de omnibus siquidem inventionibus vel trobis habeat inde medietatem inventor et nobis aliam retinemus."

[30] Arch. Crown, James I, Reg. Canc. 14, fol. 55v (May 30, 1264): "tam de redditibus . . . quam de eo quod habuistis de ligno quod fregit apud Deniam." A *lignum*

Though the chance finder of a treasure had only to notify authorities or to apply for a condonation if he had failed to do so in time, the true hunter had to take out a license; this could target a specific trove, or else allow for general treasure search or for mineral prospecting over designated areas. For example, a license in 1265 allowed the Tarazona sacristan "free permission to search out treasure under the earth," reserving two-thirds to the crown; unfortunately this unworthy cleric seems to have taken the license in order to mask his extensive counterfeiting activities.[31] An example of condonation was the case of Mathew Corbató, who neglected to notify the crown of his considerable find at Daroca; accusations against him and his

---

or *lleny* can be any seagoing vessel, but technically was the long-distance coastal ship, lighter than the cargo ship *tarida* but smaller than the galley.

[31] *Itinerari*, p. 366 (Feb. 17, 1265): "liberam potestatem querendi thesaurum subtus terram." On the sacristan and his crime see Burns, *Crusader Valencia*, I, 114, II, 424, with the trial record cited from Zaragoza's Diputación del Reino de Aragón, manuscript collection. King James recounts the story at length in his *Llibre dels feyts*, chs. 465-470. See also Zurita, *Anales de la corona de Aragón*, lib. III, c. 72. Antonio M. Aragó Cabañas studies the fourteenth- and fifteenth-century license and condonation in the realms of Aragon, from ten documents that he reproduces in full (1330-1484), "Licencias para buscar tesoros en la corona de Aragón," *Martínez Ferrando miscelánea*, pp. 7-10, documents on pp. 10-21. Doc. 2 (1335) concerned Ismā'īl, a Mudejar of Plasencia, jailed for concealing his newly discovered treasure; for 1,000 solidi of Jaca the crown condoned the crime, but with the possibility of further evidence bringing local prosecution or adjustment "prout christianis in casu simili servarentur." Doc. 3 (1371) licensed the Castilian Jew Jahuda and three fellow Jews to find treasure in Valencia at Bocairente and the Mariola hills, the crown taking half, after expenses. Doc. 5 (1385) allowed two courtiers to seek jewels, gold, and silver in and around Tarragona, dividing any finds into nine parts, four for the finders, two for the king, and one each for queen, heir, and a pair of citizens named. Doc. 6 (1388) licensed the seignorial lady Violant of Urrea to search anywhere in her jurisdictions for "tesauri absconditi ab antiquo, qui potuerunt de facili reperiri et extrahi a locis in quibus fuerunt et sunt reclusi" according to rumor; the crown yielded two-thirds of finds. Doc. 7 (1392) involved a Tarazona man and a courtier from Teruel in a search for "magnus thesaurus absconditus ab antiquo"; it notes that none can search for treasure or share it "absque nostra licencia"; the two were personally to lead their men and to give the crown a fifth after expenses and damages. Doc. 9 (1406) teamed a Mudejar and a Knight Hospitaller in search of "aurum absconditum, hominum ingenio vel natura in mineris," half going to the crown. Doc. 10 (1484) sent a knight washing gold in several rivers: "ius perquirendi et piscandi aurum in rivo." Obviously the crown adjusted its claims to persons and circumstances, as did the Castilian crown (see doc. of 1447, pp. 1-2n.). Piles Ros summarizes some fifteenth-century treasure licenses in his *Bayle general de Valencia*, appendix, docs. 19 (1404), 32 (1406), 299 (1427), 355 (1429), 499 (1432).

Christian and Jewish friends led in 1257 to a flurry of condonations from the crown.[32]

Mudejars were prominent among treasure enthusiasts in the realms of Aragon.[33] Very little documentation has survived from the thirteenth century, however, covering actual cases of treasure hunting; one highly successful episode drew the personal attention of King Peter in 1283. A Mudejar at Játiva was the lucky man. Peter notified the bailiff and justiciar of that town: "we understand that Yaḥyā al-Bajjanī [Jafia Alpatzeni], a Saracen of Játiva, has found treasure." The king ordered his officials, on receipt of this letter "to conduct an investigation into that affair and into everything else touching that affair in any way." They were to speed the results "in all haste to us, locked under protection of your seal." Yaḥyā appears to have struck it rich.[34] Another echo of Mudejar interest in treasure troves turns up in a tax-farming contract of 1281 to nine aljamas; the crown "specially" retained the treasure share along with water tax

---

[32] *Colección diplomática*, doc. 617 (Oct. 29, 1257): appointing a judge "super thesauro qui fuit inventus," to cite to court "omnes illos tam christianos quam iudeos et sarracenos qui in facto isto sciunt vel tenent de isto thesauro seu peccunia aliquid ad dicendum." Doc. 680 (Dec. 18, 1257): "diffinimus tibi Aprili de Perdicibus . . . demandam quam tibi vel rebus tuis possemus facere racione vel occasione illius thesauri quem Matheus Corbaton habitator Daroce dicebat et asserebat se invenisse et inde tibi partem dedisse"; Miret y Sans reads the name incorrectly as Corbací. Doc. 685 (Dec. 19, 1257): to four Jews, brothers, in the same sense, "cum super facto dicti thesauri inquisicionem diligenter fecerimus et non potuerimus invenire aliquam certitudinem nec aliqua signa vera" to prove the charge; doc. 686 (Dec. 19, 1257): to the same four, receipting acceptance of 1,100 solidi of Jaca as compensation or quittance to the crown because of the legal doubt, but undertaking to return this sum if the four could ever clear themselves in the future.

[33] Arguing from their number in the next two centuries. See Aragó Cabañas, "Licencias para buscar tesoros," p. 9: "abundan sobre todo los judíos y sarracenos."

[34] Arch. Crown, Peter III, Reg. Canc. 60, fol. 91 (April 18, 1283): "baiulo et iusticie Xative, cum intelleximus quod Iafia Alpatzeni sarracenus Xative invenit thesaurum, mandamus vobis quatenus visis presentibus, super ipso negotio et omnibus aliis ipsum negotium tangentibus aliquomodo, faciatis inquisicionem et ipsa inquisicione facta indessinenter nobis mittatis et sub vestri sigilli munimine interclusam; datum Cesarauguste, xiiii kalendas Madii, idem [1283]." Martínez Ferrando read the first name as Jafra. The surname recalls the tenth-century Andalusian Abū 'Abd Allāh b. Sa'īd al-Bajjanī (Lévi-Provençal, *España musulmana*, v, 48); both probably derived their name from the nuclear city for the port of Almería, Bajjāna, an interpretation strengthened by considering the evolution of the Arabic into Latin and Romance Pechina and into the modern (Puerta de) Purchena.

and court fines, a conjunction suggesting great expectations from local treasure hunters.[35]

THE TITHE

More significant was the Christian tithe, indirectly augmented by all Mudejars but paid directly by a growing minority.[36] The tithe was peculiarly valuable in Valencia both to secular and diocesan authorities. Bishops, relatively poor here in estates, relied upon it for support; parishes yielded their own claims so as to sustain the central organism. By the crusader's patronage right, King James sequestered a third, sometimes a half or more, to his civil purposes. Enforceable by law, the tithe amounted roughly to ten percent of income—personal, commercial, industrial, and particularly agricultural. It affected such diverse items as fishing, mining, transient flocks, mills, ovens, livestock, and wine; often it drew upon the same commodity more than once, touching wheat at the harvest, the mill, and the oven. Permanent and universal, the tithe proved a godsend to the tax-hungry feudal monarchy of Aragon.

A Christian landlord expected to pay his own tithes to the church for everything he had received from his Mudejars by taxes, rents, or other income. Muslims themselves, on the other hand, by definition had no obligation to support the Christian church; personally exempt, they came under the burden only by abusive local custom or by acquiring property not immemorially Muslim. At Tarazona in Aragon in 1167, for example, barons and townsmen alike had avoided tithes by bringing in Mudejar tenants as *exarici*, while Muslims were siphoning other properties off the tithe rolls both by purchase and by foreclosure on defaulting debtors. Alfonso II therefore ordered tithes taken from all three categories and in general

[35] Arch. Crown, Peter III, Reg. Canc. 51, fol. 27 (March 3, 1281), for Callosa, Castell, Confrides, Guadalest, Jalón, Pop, and other areas: "exceptis iusticiis criminalibus, alphardis, et thesauro invento que nobis specialiter retinemus ad nostram voluntatem faciendam."

[36] See Burns, "A Mediaeval Income Tax: The Tithe in the Thirteenth-Century Kingdom of Valencia," *Speculum*, XLI (1966), pp. 438-452, and *Crusader Valencia*, I, 144-172; each includes full bibliographical background. López de Ayala sums the data for thirteenth-century Castile in *Contribuciones é impuestos en León y Castilla*, pp. 327-332, 347, 352, 370-371. In Valencia the allied firstfruits amounted to a thirty-ninth of produce, reckoned on the pretithe total; the tithe varied according to crops, being a fifteenth on saffron and dried figs, for example, and a tenth on olives.

from any lands "that formerly belonged to Saracens and later came or will come into Christian hands, on which the church took tithes once."[37] Throughout the conquered kingdom of Valencia, the mass of agricultural owners and laborers were Muslims; the coffers of both church and state consequently suffered. To the Christian eye also, "paganism" seemed to gain favored status by immunity from tithe and its allied firstfruits. Greed and right reason, respectably allied with power, promised ill for the future of the Mudejars.

Throughout Valencia, however, Muslim communities who surrendered did keep exemption. As early as 1240 the bishop-elect for the central part of the kingdom solemnized this traditional arrangement for Mudejars "who are subject to you on terms, while they remain in that status, but Saracens brought onto [*populati*] lands freely acquired are to give the full tithe on everything." The bishop of Segorbe, ensconced in a heavily Muslim sector of Valencia, found himself so poverty stricken by lack of tithes that Christians made him a figure of fun. The case of an obscure region within his diocese was typical; witnesses in a jurisdictional dispute after the passage of almost a century deposed that many towns still "do not pay tithes or anything to the church," because they remain "peopled by Saracens." A similar list taken at these hearings characterized its places as containing "no Christians, but Saracens," and underlined its point by adding: "nor do they pay church tithes."[38]

[37] Fernández y González, *Mudejares de Castilla*, appendix, doc. 8: "potestates et alii milites, necnon et burgenses, dabant hereditates suas et honores ad excolendum et laborandum suis exarichis sarracenis, nec dabant decimam vel primiciam de illa parte hereditatum. . . . Similiter sarraceni de hereditatibus quas emebant a christianis vel accipiebant in pignore decimas vel primitias non solvebant. . . . [Hereditates] que fuerunt quondam sarracenorum et postea in manum christianorum devenerunt vel devenerint [dent decimas]." The king does not advert to properties granted to Christians but co-owned by preconquest Moors, the common situation later in Valencia; in Valencia also, however, all classes were introducing fresh Muslim tenants in considerable numbers during the postcrusade decades; see Burns, "Immigrants from Islam: The Crusaders' Use of Muslims as Settlers in Thirteenth-Century Spain," *American Historical Review*, LXXX (1975), 21-42. Torres Fontes found the tithe demanded from Mudejars at Murcia, "though not in all places" there, and cites as well a concession of 1289 to the Cartagena church of tithes and firstfruits from Jews and Moors ("Mudéjares murcianos" [offprint], p. 13). In the crusader Holy Land, Muslims were exempt from tithe; indeed, despite the efforts of European churchmen, non-Latin Christians never paid tithes (Cahen, "Régime rural syrien," p. 301).

[38] Arch. Cat., perg. 1,304 (June 1, 1240): "que sunt vobis cum conditione subiecti, dum tali modo permaneant"; "sarraceni vero populati in terris libere acquisitis . . . dent integram decimam de omnibus." Francisco de Asís Aguilar y Serrat, *Noticias*

A serpent lurked in this tax garden. Muslims had to continue paying tithes due from Valencian lands newly acquired from Christians, lest property slip from tithe rolls by purchase or defaulted mortgage. This understandable arrangement became more onerous when extended to all newly taken up properties, including freshly opened farmland along expanding irrigation systems, grants to loyal Muslims, abandoned estates transferred to Mudejar neighbors after rebellion, areas settled by Moorish immigrants from abroad or from other Valencian towns, and the various bits purchased from Christians or converts normally in the lively Valencian land market. When King James took over a barony in 1270, consequently, he made clear to its Mudejars that newly broken lands came under the tithe. "If you, or any one of you, receive or freshly break virgin land," the rents were to include giving "the tithe and firstfruits on it" as with similar acquisitions. "And if perchance you or any one of you buy any holdings from Christians, you are obliged to come to us and ours and make arrangements with us and ours concerning those holdings that you bought from Christians." Receiving an account for all the rents of Biar from its *amín* in 1275, King James reminded the Muslim "that you have to pay the tithe-officer the tithe of the Valencian bishop." It is improbable that this tithe was the negligible sum owed by the few Christians at that far southern post; more likely it included both Christian holdings and postcrusade Mudejar acquisitions.[39]

---

de Segorbe y de su obispado, 2 vols. (Segorbe 1890), I, 146: "in locis seu castris de Cucheira, de Castro, de Bonazulona, Xinquer, Caudet, Fansara, L'Alcudia, et Lompa, que quidem loca sunt populata sarracenis, non solvunt decimas nec aliquid ecclesie"; p. 141: "item ponit quod in predictis locis de Montan, et de Montanejos, et de Aranyol, Cirat, Pandiel, Tormo, Torrechiva, Tuega, Spadiella, Ballat, Fuentes, Ayodar, Berniches et Argelita, non habitant christiani sed sarraceni nec solvunt ecclesie decimas."

[39] Arch. Crown, James I, Reg. Canc. 16, fol. 213 (Sept. 21, 1270): "universis et singulis sarracenis de Suyllana et de Trulars . . . si vos vel aliquis vestrum recipiatis seu scaliaveritis terram heremam . . . de omnibus fructibus dicte terre quam recipiatis seu scaliaveritis . . . detis inde decimam et primiciam. . . . Et si forte vos vel aliquis vestrum emeritis aliquas possessiones a christianis, teneamini venire ad nos et nostros et componere nobiscum vel cum nostris de ipsis possessionibus quas emeritis a christianis ut est dictum." *Scaliare* is the same as Catalan *escaliar*, to break land, reducing it to cultivation. The renegotiating of rents with the crown followed too, since they lay outside the privileges agreed upon at surrender. Reg. Canc. 20, fol. 327 (March 3, 1275): "tu Mahomat Avincelim, alaminus de Biar, computavisti nunc

This was merely a chapter in the wider story of Christendom. Church authorities for centuries had professed the principle of taking tithes from ex-Christian property, particularly in the case of Jews; the puzzling factor of immemorial ownership, legalisms like the replacement of a purchased building by new and perhaps exempt constructions, and the complicated interplay of the established Jewish community with local authorities in the matter of more general taxation, had led to compromises, the Jews sometimes paying an agreed sum such as six pence per male head on all property acquired to date.[40] In addressing himself to the problem at the beginning of the thirteenth century, Pope Innocent III had coupled the Jews with Spain's Mudejars, rebuking Alfonso VIII of Castile who "not only was unwilling to make them pay tithes but even gave them freer license to buy properties and not pay tithes"; he warned that the king thus "seemed to exalt the synagogue and the mosque."[41] The 1215 ecumenical council of the Lateran gave new vigor to tithe claims, explicitly treating only the more universal question of properties that "had under some title or other passed into Jewish hands."[42] A little over a decade later, follow-up councils at Valladolid for León and Castile, and at Lérida for the realms of Aragon, saw the

---

nobiscum . . . et est sciendum quod tu debes . . . solvere decimario decimam episcopi valentini."

[40] Solomon Grayzel outlines the history and conveniently gathers the main documents, adding a translation, in *The Church and the Jews in the XIIIth Century: A Study of Their Relations During the Years 1198-1254, Based on the Papal Letters and the Conciliar Decrees of the Period*, 2d edn. rev. (New York, 1966), pp. 36-38, 112, 122, 124, 126, 142, 144, 148, 182, 188, 194, 286, 308, 318, 320, 326. See Grayzel's interpretation of the Narbonne provincial council of 1227 and the Beziers council of 1246 on the six pence compromise (pp. 319n., 332), and the 1218 truce between Archbishop Rodrigo Jiménez de Rada and the Jews, exempting land currently held (summed on p. 147). See also Demetrio Mansilla Reoyo, *Iglesia castellano-leonesa y curia romana en los tiempos del rey San Fernando, estudio documental sacado de los registros vaticanos* (Madrid, 1945), pp. 144-145; *La documentación pontificia*, docs. 193 (1199) and 312 (1205); *Colección de cánones y de todos los concilios de la iglesia de España y de América*, ed. Juan Tejada y Ramiro, 7 vols. (Madrid, 1859-1863), III, 335. See also Baron's remarks on the problem in Spain, *Social and Religious History of the Jews*, x, 121, 355; with cross references to the more general discussion in volume IV.

[41] Grayzel, *Church and Jews*, doc. 17, p. 112 (May 5, 1205): "synagogam ac moskitam extollere videaris."

[42] *Sacrorum conciliorum nova et amplissima collectio*, ed. J. D. Mansi, *et alii*, 53 vols. (Leipzig, 1903-1927), XXII, col. 1,055; Grayzel, *Church and Jews*, conciliar section, doc. 4.

papal legate apply this fresh concern to Spain's Mudejars, ordering Muslims as well "to pay to the churches the tithes and firstfruits [*oblationes*] owed for lands and buildings and other possessions that came into their hands from Christians in any fashion."⁴³

By the end of the Valencian crusade the tithe question was in the forefront of Christian consciousness. It would erupt after mid-century, without reference to claims against Mudejars, into a passionate controversy among all classes of Christians in the new realm.⁴⁴ Valencia's Mudejars were caught up in the fringe of this storm. After King James had restored calm by his arbitral decision in April 1268, he took up the allied problem of Valencian tithes owed by Jews and Muslims, ordering every *amīn* "of the Saracens of towns and places in the kingdom of Valencia" to pay "the tithes, revenues, and income" owed to bishop and clergy. Context clarified this obligation as tithes and firstfruits incumbent upon land acquired from Christians. Wherever Muslims might refuse to meet their obligation, the general bailiff for southern Valencia and his counterpart north of the Júcar River were to compel obedience.⁴⁵ For the special case of Cocentaina, perhaps exempted for lands acquired to date, the king decreed: "if Saracens present or future shall purchase properties from Christians, from now on, they are to pay and give tithes and firstfruits in full on their income, just as Christians are bound to do."⁴⁶

⁴³ Grayzel, *Church and Jews*, conciliar section, doc. 20 (Valladolid, 1228); doc. 21 (Lérida, 1229); summation in *Sacrorum conciliorum nova collectio*, XXIII, col. 2,056; see also XII, col. 1,091. See also the *Fueros* of Aragon (*Incipiunt fori editi per dominum Iacobum regem Aragonum in curiis aragonensibus celebratis in ciuitate Osce* [Zaragoza, 1496]), II, lib. VII, "De decimis iudeorum et sarracenorum"; Tourtoulon, *Jaime I*, II, 160; and on the problem at Cordova, Orti Belmonte's "Fuero de Córdoba: mudéjares," pp. 38, 40 (tithe "to the king and the church" from aljamas), 42, with Grayzel's doc. 126 from Innocent IV to the Cordova church (March 28, 1254) on "some Saracens" refusing the tithe from lands got from Christians. The Valladolid cortes of 1295 sought a final solution by ordering Mudejars to divest themselves of properties previously Christian (Fernández y González, *Mudejares de Castilla*, p. 209).

⁴⁴ Burns, *Crusader Valencia*, I, chs. 8, 9.

⁴⁵ Arch. Cat., perg. 5,997 (June 30, 1269): "alamini sarracenorum villarum et locorum regni Valencie respondeant de decimis, redditibus, et exitibus."

⁴⁶ *Ibid.*: "sicut christiani facere tenentur." Though Huici publishes this order, he adjoins an identical decision affecting the "sarraceni de Unceria"; Unceria is not a Valencian place but a miscopy of Concentania, for Cocentaina, in a simple copy of the first document (*Colección diplomática*, docs. 959 and 961).

The pope felt it necessary to warn the Valencian church, lest "by the settling of Saracens the church herself be defrauded somewhat of her tithes and other rights in some places."[47] This probably explains the unusual condition in Peter of Castellnou's charter of 1260 to his Mudejar colony at Tales. "You are also to give the church of Onda the firstfruits, namely out of thirty measures of grain one, and so of all other things from which it is the custom to give firstfruits"; Moors on tithable lands stood, by tithe logic, accountable as well for firstfruits.[48] Muslim settlers coming to Villarreal in 1280 held a two-year tax exemption plus the privileges of Mudejars already settled in the realm; "however, you are to pay the tithe and firstfruits just as the Christians resident in the same place give that tithe and firstfruits."[49]

Certain records concerning "tithes of the Saracens" must be understood in the sense of indirect payment eventually contributed by their landlord from his own receipts. Because of extended disputes over the amount of tithe the crusader patrons might retain, a number of arbitrations spelled out the landlord's obligation. Peter of Montagut, lord of Alfarp and Carlet, agreed in 1241 to pay tithes to the church "not only from the tenth but from all [revenues] that you have from the Saracens of that castle in any just or customary manner." The tenth here tithed was the civil tribute or rent, a tax whose identical Latin name can cause confusion in discussions of the church tenth.[50] William Raymond of Moncada, lord of Nules, though he wrested a full half of the tithe into his own coffers, explicitly conceded his income from "Saracen" tenants as tithable.[51] Artal of Luna, on the other hand, stubbornly refused any payment for nearly

---

[47] Arch. Vat., Reg. Vat. IX, Innocent IV, fol. 133v, ep. 146 (Dec. 23, 1251): "quod per populationem sarracenorum ecclesia ipsa decimis et aliis suis iuribus in locis aliquibus aliquatenus non fraudetur."

[48] Tales Charter: "item detis ecclesie de Onda primiciam"; the measure of grain is *barchilla*.

[49] Arch. Crown, Peter III, Reg. Canc. 48, fol. 20v (May 13, 1280): "tamen solventibus decimam et primiciam prout christiani residentes in eodem loco dant ipsam decimam et primiciam."

[50] Arch. Cat., perg. 2,341 (Feb. 7, 1241): "decima predicta debet deduci non tantum de decima sed de omnibus quae vos haberetis a sarracenis illius castri aliquo iusto vel consueto modo."

[51] Arch. Cat. Tortosa, cajón Obispo, nos. 8, 35, 39, 52; cartulary no. 8, fols. 147, 149. These include a renewal of the agreement in 1306 by his descendant, Raymond Moncada.

twenty years "from either his Christians or his Saracens" of Paterna and Manises until brought to heel in 1257.[52] The magnate Simon Pérez of Arenós, while yielding much of his tithe from Christian tenants, by a convenient quirk of reasoning retained all tithes drawn on income from his more numerous Mudejars.[53]

A bastard of King James, Peter Ferdinand, withheld the tithe at Buñol and Ribarroja; later he conceded an annual compensatory sum of 300 solidi for his Mudejar rents, while yielding the diocesan share of tithes from Christian rents.[54] Berengar of Entenza, baron of Chiva, agreed "to satisfy the tithe that the Saracen residents of the said castle area and its jurisdiction were bound and are bound to pay you, or the lord for them." The wording, understandable in context of this series of documents, suggests a natural confusion by which in the future the burden may have shifted onto some Mudejars.[55] An agreement between the Valencian diocese and the Knights Hospitaller in 1264 included the tithe on rents paid to the order by their Mudejars. Since the Knights as patrons kept half, diocesan profits correspondingly shrank; tithes from Mudejar revenues at Silla town and countryside were waived. A like agreement for the northern part of the new kingdom, between the Tortosa diocese and the knights, speaks of tithes from the Muslims of Oropesa and on Mudejar revenues at Miravet.[56] Individual landlords, like the canon

[52] Arch. Cat., perg. 2,432 (June 14, 1257): "ab eo vel a christianis sive sarracenis."

[53] Ibid., perg. 2,413 (Aug. 29, 1260): renewed in perg. 2,322 by his son Blasco (Feb. 10, 1268).

[54] Ibid., perg. 2,370 (Feb. 7, 1260).

[55] Ibid., perg. 2,412 (1314, but treating of an accord between Bishop Ferrer and Berengar of Entenza in our period): "concedimus vobis [episcopo] . . . quod sarraceni habitantes in dicto castro et eius termino qui nunc sunt vel pro tempore fuerint, in recompensacione, satisfaccione et emenda decime quam tenebantur et tenentur vobis solvere vel dominus pro eisdem . . . quod . . . fideliter decimas solvere teneantur." Again, e.g., in perg. 2,413 (Aug. 29, 1260): "et omnis fructus decimarum sarracenorum existentium in predictis locis."

[56] Samper, Montesa ilustrada, part 4, art. 4, document of August 5, 1243: "sarraceni de Miravetero." Not an error for Murivetero (Murviedro), this is very probably the Templar commandery near Tortosa, or possibly the small Valencian castle just northwest of Oropesa near Cabanes, both lying within the Tortosa diocese; it is not the Templar castle of Miravete in southern Aragon near the western Valencian border. Cartulaire général de l'ordre des hospitaliers de S. Jean de Jérusalem (1100-1310), ed. Joseph Delaville le Roulx, 4 vols. (Paris, 1894-1901), III, doc. 3,091 (April 8, 1264). The Mudejar tithe quarrels echoed in subsequent reigns. See, e.g., Arch. Crown, Peter III, Reg. Canc. 43, fol. 119 (Feb. 5, 1284): "mandamus vobis quatenus

Roderick Díaz for Almonacid Valley and Benaguacil, routinely surrendered the diocesan share of tithes "both from Christians and from Saracens."[57]

Though Christian authorities respected the principle of Muslim nonpayment, they managed in practice eventually to extend the tithe. Investigating this metamorphosis in connection with an early twelfth-century Aragonese conquest, Lacarra observed that within one or two generations after the conquest the Moors there were all paying tithes as though they were Christians; yet exemption for Muslim-held land remained as a principle and became incorporated into the Huesca law code of 1247! Lacarra suggests that some Muslims may have volunteered the tithe to keep the king's good will, that documents soon confused as tithe the rents paid by Muslim vassals of the church, that the civil tithe due to the king was sometimes given to the church, and that much land changed hands between the Muslims themselves (especially as wealthier owners sold their property and left the country) thus breaking the former contract and its exemption.[58] Each of these elements may have been at work; more radical perhaps, as the phrasing of Entenza's tithe document suggests, was the expedient of shifting the lord's burden by prorating that section of his personal tithe affecting Mudejar rents. Such a transformation did not occur in Valencia on any large scale, however, at least within the crusade century.

Some perspective on the general situation can be gained by viewing it from a terminal date. In 1314 bishop and chapter reported how "certain Saracens and almost all [Christians] resident in the places of the aforesaid diocese of Valencia" owed tithes; some, however, "refused these to the bishop and chapter and other clergy of the same diocese." The recalcitrants acted "maliciously and unjustly"; to judge from the impatience of James II, they constituted a long-standing problem that had resisted previous reform efforts by

---

super facto decime sarracenorum de Chiva non compellatis ipsos sarracenos," because the matter is in litigation.

[57] Arch. Cat., perg. 2,431 (Jan. 19, 1263): "tam a sarracenis quam a christianis."

[58] José M. Lacarra, "La restauración eclesiástica en las tierras conquistadas por Alfonso el Batallador (1118-1134)," *Revista portuguesa de história*, IV (1948-1949), 277-280. See also his "Documentos para la reconquista del valle del Ebro" (part 2), doc. 269, and Hinojosa, "Mezquinos y exáricos," p. 529.

the crown. After examining the laws of James I, the king sharply ordered his officials to enforce payment from recusant Muslims "in such wise that we do not see the said bishop and chapter or the aforesaid clerics bringing complaints on this matter in the future."[59]

A much later assessment of ecclesiastical tithes owed by Mudejar communities, drawn in 1330, is ambiguous; it affords only a partial list and by this time probably included resident converts. Since Muslim officials collected tithes at these places, there seems to be no question of Christian immigrant communities. Omitting the small change of the manuscript and reducing its solidi to round numbers, Albalat paid 80; Almácera, 102; Callosa, 554; Castell, 456; Confrides, 366; Finestrat, 159; Guadalest Valley, 680; Polop, 434; Tárbena, 273; Vall de Laguart with Pedil, 157; and Chirles (?Xarli), 166. The *amin* of each place stood responsible, directly or through the bailiff general.[60] Unlike more prosaic taxes, such tithe figures hint at the underlying social tensions within this mixed kingdom.

FEES AND MISCELLANY

Mudejars could sell their lands at will, and purchase properties anywhere in the kingdom. The crown allowed Christian land to pass into Mudejar hands, as the many disputes over the continuing obligation of such lands to pay tithe demonstrates; but it tried to inhibit traffic of real estate in the other direction. Theoretically all land was held by Christian owners, though served by Muslim tenants or sharecroppers; in practice Mudejars were masters of their own

[59] Arch. Cat., perg. 2,397 (July 28, 1314): "a quibusdam sarracenis et quasi ab omnibus habitantibus in locis predicte diocesis valentine; aliqui tamen . . . contradicunt eisdem episcopo et capitulo et aliis clericis eiusdem diocesis dare et solvere"; "maliciose et contra iusticiam"; "taliter quod dictos episcopum et capitulum aut prefatos non videamus hac de causa ulterius querelantes." The document concerns firstfruits, but these fell only on tithable land.

[60] *Ibid.*, perg. 2,447 (May 2, 1330). Is Xarli Chirles? In 1487, responding to the plea that peaceful reconquest could be had by promising mitigated taxation to Granadan aljamas under attack, and that the crown badly needed money, Pope Innocent VIII conceded the Saracen "tenths" in such places to the Spanish crown, without ecclesiastical interference, "prout etiam in diversis Aragonum et Valentiae regnorum locis, quae vulgariter Mendejas nuncupantur." The pope makes comparison twice again with Valencia's Mudejar situation. Context leaves it unclear whether these are the civil tenths taken over from Granada's king, and here denied to possible ecclesiastical claimants under title of tithe, or a special tithe situation (Fernández y González, *Mudejares de Castilla*, appendix, doc. 82).

properties, their rents assuming the nature of taxes. Alienation of such inherited land altered revenue conditions, raised problems about tithes and firstfruits, confused the structure of privilege and exemption, and sometimes played havoc with the smooth functioning of local society. Alienation to knights or ecclesiastics particularly threatened crown revenues. The Játiva charter therefore made it clear that Muslims could sell their properties, "possessed or to be possessed," only "to Saracens and not to Christians."[61] At Pego a grant of land and houses placed this restriction: "you may sell them to Saracens, and otherwise do as you wish with them," just as the other Mudejars of that valley do.[62]

Special privilege could dispense a Moor from restrictions on his sale. Thus the qāḍī of Valencia city, who held a shop in the quarter without fee, was permitted in 1273 to dispose of it by rental or sale either to Muslim or Christian; like Valencian Christians, he could not alienate to knight or cleric.[63] During the confused years just after the crusade, when many Muslims took advantage of the privilege of selling their properties and leaving the country, Christians seem to have purchased such lands freely. At Alcira the king had to interfere in order to correct and regulate the resulting arguments over title; he assigned a board of Muslims and Christians to adjudicate. "Christians who had, have, or will have from us permission to purchase properties from Saracens at Alcira" were to refrain from invading Mudejar holdings illegally and were to surrender any property for which they could not show a bill of sale in Arabic from the original owner.[64]

The seller of real property had to contend with two fees. *Fadiga* or *fatica* designated the option, held by lord or king, of preempting purchase during a set number of days if he could meet a buyer's

[61] Játiva Charter: "habitas et habendas . . . sarracenis et non christianis."

[62] Arch. Crown, James I, Reg. Canc. 37, fol. 48 (June 25, 1272): "et possitis ipsum vendere sarracenis et alias tuas voluntates facere sicut alii sarraceni eiusdem vallis possint facere de hereditatibus suis." Cuart Muslims had a similar restriction (Reg. Canc. 10, fol. 8 [Aug. 11, 1257]).

[63] *Ibid.*, Reg. Canc. 19, fol. 30v (July 8, 1273); on alienation to knight or cleric, see Burns, *Crusader Valencia*, I, 10.

[64] *Colección diplomática*, doc. 304 (Aug. 5, 1246): "statuimus quod sarraceni recuperarent hereditates suas, quas christiani intraverunt violenter, nisi christiani emissent eas a sarracenis dominis earundem cum cartis sarracen[ic]is. . . . Statuimus autem quod christiani qui habuerunt, habent, vel habebunt a nobis licenciam emendi hereditates a sarracenis in Aliasira, non emant hereditates assignatas . . . christianis."

price; in practice it might be a fee for the normal waiving of this option. *Lluïsme* (Latin *laudimium*) was a charge or share of purchase price, incurred at the sale of real property. Both applied also in case of mortgage, exchange, pledge, or gift, but were waived for property being transferred into a dowry or inheritance.[65] They affected any real property, including oven or garden. Contemporary Christian charters might set "an option of twenty days" or ten days, and a sales tax of one-tenth the price or perhaps twelve pence per pound involved in mortgage and two solidi per pound from sale.[66] The Chivert charter waived all fees on sale of "farm or house or other things to an equal Saracen."[67] The Uxó charter stipulated sale "of any of their possessions and goods to Moors alone and that they cannot sell them at any time to any Christian."[68] Eslida's charter contained a similar proviso.[69] Aldea had a more

[65] On waiving, see *Aureum opus*, doc. 39, fol. 12v (June 26, 1251): "faticham," "laudimium." Neither term appears in Rodón Binué, *Lenguaje técnico del feudalismo*, except as misnomers, *fatiga* as a variant of the legal *fatigatio* and *laudimium* as a variant for *laudamentum* as arbitration-decision or consent (pp. 114, 159).

[66] *Cartas de población de Cataluña*, 1, doc. 271 (1237): "laudismium nec firmamentum"; doc. 302 (1257): "tertium, laudismium nec firmamentum"; doc. 318 (1270): "et detis nobis per lodismum decimum"; doc. 334 (1279): "faciat in me . . . prius faticam decem dierum, et si infra spatium istorum dierum retinere voluerimus, habeamus sicut alter"; doc. 335 (1279): "ratione laudismi vel foriscapii," the latter being the opposite of the "accapta" below in note 73, and "laudismium . . . nisi ad rationem duodecim denariorum pro libra, et de emptionibus . . . tantum duos solidos pro libra, et nichil aliud detur"; doc. 361 (1297): "laudimiis et foriscapiis venditionum et emptionum domorum, terrarum, vinearum, ortorum, et possessionum sive honorum."

[67] Chivert Charter: "et possit vendere domos et honores et alias res et de hac venditione [et] guidatico fratres eis nil petant nec possint petere," for a Muslim leaving the country; for all others: "de nulla vendicione quam faciant . . . eis petant neque petere possint"; and for all: "sit licitum . . . vendere honorem suam vel domum vel alias res suo pare sarraceno et de hac vendicione nichil ipsis dare aut facere teneantur." "Equal" may refer to class (See Burns, *Islam under the Crusaders*, ch. 5). The *precaria* or counterpresent might come under agrarian rents, forced grants, or more plausibly fees. It was an obligatory gift signifying claim to usufruct of land not one's own. At Masones in 1263 the crown exempted Mudejars from the *precaria*; it is not explicitly mentioned for Valencian aljamas, at least under that name (Masones Privilege); Rodón Binué, *Lenguaje técnico del feudalismo*, pp. 203-204.

[68] Uxó Charter: "e que pusquen vendre totes lurs possessions e bens als moros tan solament e que nols pusquen vendre a alcun christia nulls temps."

[69] Eslida Charter: "possint vendere hereditates suas et res sarracenis ibidem habitantibus, . . . nec sarraceni propter hoc faciant aliquam missionem"; guaranteeing emigrants' rights, this probably applied also to the ordinary resident.

complex system. Its charter allowed the Mudejar to market newly acquired lands freely; but in disposing of an original holding he had to give the Hospitallers a fifth of the price as fee, and he could not sell such heartland under compulsion of debts owed to a Jew or Christian. By purchasing Christian properties he obliged himself to whatever services already attached. Each Aldean could maintain an extra, small garden, tax-free, which he could also sell without fee.[70] Mudejars at Pego had to pay *lluïsme*.[71] Their accounts for 1269 list "the tenth from land sold: 48 besants, 2 *millareses*."[72] The purchaser paid a corresponding fee. *Intrada* and *entrada* (Latin *intrata*) was an entry fee on the occasion of *acapta* or actual taking of possession. When Prince Peter gave the Mudejars of Pego a region or considerable estate, formerly belonging to Peter Mir, the entry fee for assuming ownership came to 3,000 solidi.[73] Both *lluïsme* and *fadiga*, rare in Mudejar Valencia during the thirteenth century, increased in incidence during the fourteenth.[74]

Renewing a privilege required a special fee. This must have been negligible except in the case of the kingdom's code. In 1261 King James demanded the huge sum of "100,000 solidi from the Christians

[70] Aldea Charter: "et si aliquis vestrum vendiderit honorem alicui, teneatur facere illud quod christianus faciebat pro eo . . . et quod ipsum honorem possitis vendere christiano vel sarraceno sine aliqua parte nostra"; "item volumus quod quisque eorum qui ibi tenebunt hospitium, ut habeant unam tafulam de terra in qua possint facere ortos et parrales et arbores . . . francham et liberam . . . ubicumque eis placuerit infra terminos de Aldeya, et possint vendere alter altero dictam tafulam sine aliqua parte Hospitalis quam ibi non accipiat"; this was one-sixth of a fanecate, for "vegetables, grapes, and trees."

[71] Martínez y Martínez, "Pego," pp. 68-69, document of 1300. A standard formulary set for Valencian Christian charters dismisses claims for *fatiga, laudimium,* or other *questie* owed to the king (*Documentos inéditos de España,* XVIII, 50-51).

[72] Arch. Crown, James I, Reg. Canc. 35, fol. 4 (1269): "item diesmo de terra vendida, xlviii besants, ii millareses." Fol. 3v (1268) has a similar item for Pego. See also Reg. Canc. 17, fol. 28 (Dec. 30, 1263), mixed revenues from Gandía: "laudoysmum cuiusdam molendini, lx solidi."

[73] *Ibid.*, Reg. Canc. 37, fol. 57v (Dec. 22, 1272): "pro intrata." A Christian sale involved "illas xvi maçemutinas iucefias censuales . . . percipiendas annuatim perpetuo pro acapte sive intrata domorum vestrarum quas eidem . . . stabilistis." *Acapta,* whence the fee *acapte,* was "taking possession"; it and *intrata* here refer rather to the permanent rent.

[74] Gual Camarena, "Mudéjares valencianos, aportaciones," p. 188. In the fourteenth and fifteenth centuries too the purchase of property was often restricted to residents, and the residency requirements absurdly inflated (pp. 172, 188).

and Saracens of the said kingdom of Valencia" for "confirming the
Furs of the said kingdom." A form letter sent by King Peter in 1278
demanded from eighty-six Mudejar communities the payment overdue for certain charters drawn by his chancellery, apparently confirmations of their privileges routinely issued after the recent revolt.
The graduated fees, annotated with adjustments for actual payment,
required 2,000 solidi from Montesa, capital of Valencian Mudejarism
since Játiva's decline; 1,000 each from Chelva, Denia, Bétera with
Bufilla, and Gallinera with Alcalá; 500 each from Aguilar, Alfon-
deguilla, Benaguacil, Carbonera, Castell, Dos Aguas, Eslida, Guada-
lest, Serra, Tous and Vall de Laguart; 550 each from Chivel with
Cortes [de Pallars], Paterna with Manises and Rafalell (? Rafals),
and Villamarchante; 300 each from Andilla or Antella (Andila),
Artana, Beselga near Estivella, Carlet, Cheste with Calpe, Laccum
(?), Monserrat, Olocaiba, Olocau, Pedralba, Picasent, Segorbe,
Villalonga, and Villamalur (? Benimalur); 200 each from Agres,
Alfandech, Aljub, Almedíjar, Almonacid, Anna, Azuébar with
Soneja, Beniopa, Bolbaite, Chella, Cheste, Chulilla, Domeño, Garg,
Masalavés, Montroy, Penáguila, Perpunchent, Polop, Relleu, Sanet,
Segárria, and Sueras; 150 each from Algar, Alpuente, Cinqueros,
Fanzara, Liria, Millares, Náquera, Nules, Quesa, Serra de Tous, and
Sot; and 100 each from Alarch, Benilloba or Benillup (? Benisop),
Bicorp, Cocentaina, Espioca, Llombart with Margarida, Navarrés,
Otanel, and Serrella. The list is studded with small and even obscure
places; presumably most of the important aljamas had paid
promptly.[75]

[75] Arch. Crown, James I, Reg. Canc. 11, fol. 233 (April 13, 1261): "pro confirmatione furorum dicti regni"; "dicta centum millia solidorum regalium abeamus
tantum a christianis et sarracenis dicti regni Valencie." *Tantum* suggests the context,
privilege of exemption for all Jewish communities. See the confirmation itself on
fol. 202v (April 11), which entered the *Aureum opus*, doc. 60, fol. 18r,v; and fol.
203 (April 13), an episode in collecting this, with a list of principal places on which
it fell. Arch. Crown, Peter III, Reg. Canc. 22, fols. 107v-108 (Sept. 25, 1278): "fidelibus suis aliame sarracenorum de Eslida . . . visis presentibus, solvatis nobis d solidos
ratione cartarum quas habuistis de scribania nostra." The attached list concerns
Mudejars alone, since it forms a unit with this exemplar (Eslida itself is repeated in
the list, for the same sum) and refers again at the end to the exemplar's collector,
James Panicer; it explicitly mentions only "los moros de Sogorp." The tax called
forum, which the Mudejars of Gallinera and Alcalá paid, and which the crown
reserved when farming all taxes to the aljama, normally appeared in charters as
meaning the prevailing law code, but as a tax it meant the fee or share owed to

In 1271 King James charged Ḥāmid b. Hūd of Uxó 100 solidi for confirming purchase of a property worth only 130 solidi, a disproportion suggesting legal battles and clearance of title. No fee is expressed in some confirmations. ʿIsā had bought a farm and buildings for 800 solidi from the *amīn* of Cuart, had secured a confirmation from King James, and had prudently put these papers on deposit in the Moorish quarter of Valencia, where rioting between Christians and Mudejars caused their destruction; on presentation of circumstantial proof of ownership in 1277, ʿIsā won a second confirmation from King Peter. The Mudejar community of Pego won a general confirmation from Peter as prince in 1272 for all their holdings, "according to the form of the grants and concessions made for you by the aforesaid [King] James and just as they are entered in the Saracen receipts you have, sealed with the seal of the aforesaid James."

The Arabic contracts described indirectly in such confirmations were turned out in abundance by local Mudejar scribes. The scribal function, as important in its own way in Islam as the notariate was in Christian towns, yielded yet another fee to lord or king. The single reference for early Mudejars covers a large segment of the Valencian kingdom; the king offered to satisfy a debt to one of his crossbowmen for 2,190 solidi by means of "services, alaminates, and scribal offices of the towns and places of the kingdom of Valencia below the Júcar." The context of *çofra* and of the *amīn*, in this heavily Islamic region, indicates that the scribal office of Mudejar towns is meant.[76]

---

the lord for confirming the privilege of a market; see Reg. Canc. 15, fol. 88 (March 1, 1267): "vobis alamino et aliame sarracenorum . . . [nisi] forum." "Forum sive mercatum" appears as reserved also in some Christian charters; see also Rodón Binué, *Lenguaje técnico del feudalismo*, pp. 124 (*forum*) and 176 (*mercatus*).

[76] Arch. Crown, James I, Reg. Canc. 16, fol. 268v (April 8, 1271): "confirmamus tibi Hamet Abennut sarraceno de Uxon venditionem quam Bernardus Scriba . . . fecit de quadam hereditate in termino de Uxon cum instrumento sarracenico pro c et xxx solidis, volentes et concedentes quod dictam hereditatem habeatis tu et tui . . . ut in dicto instrumento melius et plenius continetur." Peter III, Reg. Canc. 39, fol. 218 (July 1, 1277): "intellecto per te Eyçam filium de Ahomet Abinamis quod emeras ab Abrafim Embona alamino de Cuart cum carta publica hereditatem . . . precio dccc solidorum et quod dominus rex inclite recordationis pater noster confirmaverat . . . et quod predictas cartas amis[er]as in barrigio morararie [*sic*] Valencie in qua ipsas cartas deposueras in comanda, attendentes siquidem te sufficien-

Under both Islamic and European law, the estates of intestate or heirless subjects tended to drift into the public treasury; the role of authority in both societies was more supervisory than fiscal, though revenue did accrue. For the Mudejar it was far more important that his extremely complex inheritance procedures be respected and that no death duty be taken from the estate.[77] The surrender charters carefully guaranteed ancient Islamic practice in this.[78] Christian subjects of King James resented both *intestia,* or confiscation of a third or half the movables of those dying without a will, and *exorchia* or confiscation of a portion of an estate lacking heirs. Any number of charters gave exemption from these "bad customs"; but they were to persist until the late fifteenth century.[79] Contemporary Islamic

ter probasse . . . confirmamus tibi predicto Eyça. . . ." Martínez Ferrando read *Bilium* or *filium* as "Bluny" (*Catálogo,* II, no. 247); the scribe does seem to have interpreted this as part of the name. On the riot, see Burns, "Social Riots on the Christian-Moslem Frontier: Thirteenth-Century Valencia," *American Historical Review,* LXVI (1961), 378-400. Arch. Crown, James I, Reg. Canc. 37, fol. 56v (Dec. 5, 1272): "secundum formam donacionum et concessionum vobis factarum a predicto Iacobo et prout contine[n]tur in albaranis sarracenis quos inde habetis cum sigillo predicti Iacobi sigillatas." Reg. Canc. 14, fol. 72v (April 30, 1265): "super çofris, alaminatibus, et scribaniis villarum et locorum regni Va[lencie] ultra Xucarum"; the three sources failed to meet the debt, and the king was assigning other revenue. The Christian secretariates did yield revenue (García de Cáceres, *Impuestos de la ciudad de Valencia,* p. 26); perhaps both *amin* and scribe returned something during their first years in office or even regularly, but neither source of revenue appears again in the Mudejar documentation.

[77] On Islamic inheritance laws, see Siddiqi, *Public Finance in Islam,* p. 12; Aghnides, *Mohammedan Theories of Finance,* pp. 201, 422; Qudāma, *Kitāb al-kharāj,* ch. 15; but especially Rabie as cited below in n. 80. See also Burns, *Islam under the Crusaders,* ch. 10, part 1, and the works cited there.

[78] Alfandech Charter. Chivert Charter. Eslida Charter ("divisionibus"). In the same tradition Almería's surrender charter in 1490 included: "hayamos de llevar e llevemos e gocemos de las herencias . . . segund que las llevaban los reyes moros que han sido" (Fernández y González, *Mudejares de Castilla,* appendix, doc. 85).

[79] Rodón Binué, *Lenguaje técnico del feudalismo,* pp. 108-109; García de Valdeavellano, *Instituciones españolas,* pp. 253-254, as *malos usos.* Exorchia derives from the Catalan *xorch, xorcha,* for sterile or childless; its ultimate derivation is moot, but probably relates to the *jorcos* of Gaul. *Cartas de población de Cataluña* has any number of enfranchisements from these taxes: I, doc. 297 (1252), doc. 299 (1255), doc. 300 (1256), docs. 315 and 316 (1267), doc. 329 (1277), doc. 332 (1278), doc. 335 (1279). In doc. 313 (1263) an abbot confesses that the two taxes "sunt plurimum hodiose," have impoverished or driven away many, have inhibited fresh settlement, and have already been annulled for the "maior pars villarum et hominum domini regis" in the Gerona diocese; consequently he sold them forever to the town for

Egypt had not only reinstated the corresponding tax for Muslims, but was even levying severe death duties, up to a third of the legacy, to the considerable enrichment of the public treasury.[80] King James probably collected the legal Islamic tax, since Christian and Islamic practice converged here; but there is nothing to indicate that he took whatever death-duties may have crept into the fiscal practices of disintegrating Almohad Spain, unless these are concealed under the rubric of past Islamic custom. If a Muslim converted to Christianity, however, James obliged himself by the Játiva charter to confiscate his movable property: "and we can give this to Saracens but not to Christians." Eventually this policy had to be rescinded, under pressure from the church, and the whole question of the convert's relation to Mudejar taxation had to be fought out.[81]

The so-called vice taxes included imposts and fees on wine, already considered, and a fee from prostitutes. Here again Christian and Islamic experience converged. The instinct to suppress vice and renounce all profit from it struggled against the commonsense counsel to regulate and punitively tax it; thus the tax on prostitution in contemporary Egypt was abolished by a reforming sultan in 1269, was restored soon afterwards under his successor, and was abolished again in 1315.[82] In much the same fashion, the celebrated Catalan canonist Raymond of Penyafort insisted, against reformist lawyers, that prostitution be tithed, lest exemption from tax amount to en-

---

6,070 solidi of Barcelona, which he needed for debts. Doc. 261 (1233) has an ample description of how *intestia* was applied in practice.

[80] Rabie, *Financial System of Egypt*, pp. 127-132; "this source of revenue often produced high yields, especially during the frequent epidemics." See p. 132 on the resultant growth of the pious foundation (*waqf*) as a device for avoiding confiscatory death-duties.

[81] Játiva Charter: "possit habere suppellectilia et alia bona mobilia sua omnia, sed hereditates sint nostrae et nostrorum et possimus eas dare sarracenis et non christianis." This development will be taken up in my sequel on Islamic-Christian relations; meanwhile see Burns, "Journey from Islam: Incipient Cultural Transition in the Conquered Kingdom of Valencia (1240-1280)," *Speculum*, xxxv (1960), 337-356. For inheritance tax in Valencia generally, see Piles Ros, *Bayle general de Valencia*, p. 46, and the "collector of inheritances belonging to the lord king" in doc. 99 (p. 145). That the crown earlier took the inheritance tax is suggested by the standard formula for Mudejar taxes two centuries later: "herenciis" (*Formularium diversorum contractuum*, fols. xxviiii-xxx; it also includes "laudimiis, faticis").

[82] Rabie, *Financial System of Egypt*, ch. 3, part G, "Taxes on Vice," esp. pp. 120-121.

couragement of vice.[83] Spanish Islam taxed and regulated its prostitutes, a policy that carried over into Valencian Mudejar society.[84]

The crown did not discountenance Valencian reformist movements, and allowed Biar's Muslims in 1258 to expel "all the Saracen whores or prostitutes without any person impeding";[85] but it continued the custom of enrolling prostitutes and taking a tax on their professional activities. One tax of 1281 "on Saracen women prostitutes" of the kingdom was so high as to be punitive: "20 solidi for each."[86] The revenue accounts for Sumacárcel in 1268 include an item of 12 solidi for "one prostitute" and 14 solidi for "the other prostitute." The two items were combined in 1269 lists: "from two prostitutes, 16 solidi." Similar accounts for Pego in 1268 put down 9 besants, or some 33 solidi, for "the prostitutes," and in a mixed item for the next year 25 besants.[87]

Empriu (Latin *ademprivium*) stood for any fee paid for using materials, especially of a community nature: collecting firewood or construction materials, drawing water, benefiting from local pasturage, enjoying egress or right of passage, dwelling in a house, and the like. These privileges sometimes shaded off into other taxes with their proper names, and at times the term *empriu* stood among the generic "demands" and "services" and "forced taxes" so disliked by con-

---

[83] Ramón de Peñafort (Penyafort), *Summa*, ed. H. V. Laget (Verona, 1744), lib. 1, tit. xv, no. 4. Manuel Carboneres was unable to find pre-fourteenth-century data for his history of Valencian prostitution in the Middle Ages, *Picaronas y alcahuetes ó la mancebía de Valencia. Apuntes para la historia de la prostitución desde principios del siglo xiv hasta poco antes de la abolición de los fueros, con profusión de notas y copias de documentos oficiales* (Valencia, 1876); taking up the story from about 1311, however, he supplies valuable background on the situation as it had developed about seven decades after the crusade. See also Burns, *Crusader Valencia*, 1, 128, 145, 235, and 11, 430, 485.

[84] Lévi-Provençal, *España musulmana*, v, 289-290; and see the authors cited in Burns, *Islam under the Crusaders*, ch. 5, n. 21, as well as Piles Ros, *Bayle general de Valencia*, p. 36 on Mudejar prostitution, with documents 9, 10, and 12.

[85] *Itinerari*, pp. 275-276 (June 16, 1258): "omnes putas seu meretrices sarracenas sine impedimento alicuius persone."

[86] Arch. Crown, Peter III, Reg. Canc. 50, fol. 231 (Jan. 17, 1281): "de mulieribus sarracenibus meretricibus viginti solidos pro qualibet"; this was the highest rate assigned for the special tax on Mudejar households in Valencia, and the only class or stratum of society singled out for special treatment in this tax otherwise adjusted according to property values. Possibly brothels are meant, rather than individuals.

[87] *Ibid.*, James I, Reg. Canc. 35, fol. 3v (1268): "item las putas, ix besants"; fol. 4 (1269): "item la tarquena e las putas, xxv besants"; fol. 7v (1268): "una puta de la exarquia, xii sous," and "otra puta, [x]iiii sous"; fol. 8 (1269): "item de ii putas, xvi [sous]."

temporaries. The word itself does not appear, at least in thirteenth-century Mudejar documents, but the reality does.[88] Islamic jurists had long discussed the right of villagers to common pasturage, firewood, and water, as well as wider rights to such elements in the public domain as roads, markets, and streets, and the circumstances that limited such rights.[89] Christian charters frequently waived fees upon amenities or materials, acknowledging in effect that feudal ownership had yielded to public domain.[90]

Valencia's Mudejar charters handled both general concessions and the occasional reservation of a fee, in patterns undoubtedly representing precrusade Almohad taxation. The Chivert charter gave "the right of breaking or cutting wood from pines and all other trees in the waste lands, for covering their houses and for making doorposts, doors, thresholds, and roofs and for all other work that may be necessary for them." Játiva's charter specified that plazas be free, in a context suggesting that open places in the maze of streets were meant, where potters, ceramicists, and hawkers displayed the modest domestic production unsuitable for the general market place of larger commerce.

In line with Islamic tax practice, Játiva's charter expressly conceded mosques, cemeteries, and schools, without fees. Aldea gave away mosque, cemetery, and especially the regalian monopoly of communal bakehouse that formed part of the *waqf* or exempt properties supporting the mosque. Uxó similarly exempted "the rents of the mosques for the upkeep of the said mosques, just as was done

---

[88] *Formularium diversorum contractuum*, fol. xxviiii: "et ademprimis" [*sic*]. Rodón Binué, *Lenguaje técnico del feudalismo*, pp. 9-10. García de Valdeavellano, *Instituciones españolas*, p. 250. Variants include *aempriu, ampriu,* and *emparamentum*; it derives from a crossbreeding of Latin *imperare* and *imparare*. Mixed Muslim-Christian taxes for Vall de Laguart (Alaguar) and Jalón do retain "ademprivia" (Arch. Crown, James I, Reg. Canc. 9, fol. 39 [Sept. 19, 1257]). The *boalar* or communal pasturage for village or town was a fairly universal concession under the *empriu* rubric; see the *devesia* or waste conceded for this along the sea side of the road in the Aldea Charter, "sine aliquo logerio" (*logerium* or *locatio,* Catalan *lloguer,* is rental or payment). Similarly fishing and hunting, touched upon in Chapter III, part 1, could also be put under *empriu*.

[89] Aghnides, *Mohammedan Theories of Finance,* pp. 513-524.

[90] *Cartas de población de Cataluña,* i, passim; doc. 318 (1270) does retain "plenum ademprivium in pascuis, silvis, lignis, et aquis," its major applications; doc. 262 (1234) concerns "adempramentum de boscho et de lignis et de aquis et petris et lignis et rippariis et etiam de omnibus universis . . ."; doc. 319 (1271) retains "ademprivium quod consuevimus habere ibi in aquis videlicet et pasturis."

[here] in olden times." Chivert gave major and minor mosques, their pools of ablution with water needs, and cemeteries, "in such wise that they are not to pay any rent or tax or fees." Eslida's charter included similar provisions, both for domestic and religious requirements; it contained a special proviso that "the dead may be buried in their cemeteries without hindrance or fees."[91]

For those who could afford it, marriage in Islamic Spain had been an expensive business, sometimes amounting to "a magnificent spectacle." Jurists had fulminated against the extravagances of the week-long ceremonies.[92] No data survives concerning possible fees levied by the authorities in precrusade Valencia; the corresponding Christian taxes, a *lluïsme* on properties involved in the dowry, and a gift (*dona, sponsalicium*) or confirmation fee to the lord, were on the wane during the crusade century.[93] The Mudejar charter for Chivert expressly allowed "that every Saracen of the said castle and its jurisdiction can take a wife, or Saracen woman take a husband,

[91] Chivert Charter: "omnes habitatores castri Exiverti habeant posse frangendi vel talliandi fusta de pinis et aliis arboribus omnibus in heremo ad cohoperiendum domos suas et faciendum postes, portas, limina et tegellos et ad omnia opera que sint eis necessaria"; "suam mesquitam maiorem cum omnibus oratoriis . . . et omnia ciminteria cum plateis suis et honoribus heremis et populatis et omnibus domibus et casalibus . . . et dicta mezquita cum oratoriis suis omnibus, ciminteriis, et plateis, et aljupo, et honoribus sit francha et libera, ita quod nullum censum vel tributum sive missiones non faciant." Játiva Charter: "et quod habeatis plateas franchas et liberas, sine aliqua servitute." Aldea Charter: "damus masquide sarracenorum de Aldeya furnum meum de Aldeya, et aliquis alius christianus vel sarracenus non possint ibi aliquem furnum construere nec possint coquere panem aliunde." Uxó Charter: "sien les rendes de les mezquites a ops de les dites mezquites axi com ere antigament." Eslida Charter: "et mortui sepeliantur in eorum ciminteriis sine contrario et missione." There is an ambiguous entry on wood for burning in the communal oven, in Arch. Crown, James I, Reg. Canc. 35, fol. 3 (1268): "item avie de la fusta que vino de Carcel, que metieron l'aliama en el forno, que avian cremado, liii sous e vii diners, que son xvi besants, iii millareses." Fol. 7v (1268) has an entry for Cárcer and Sueca: "item el logero de la fusta, x sous" (for *lloguer* see above, n. 88). On mosques, cemeteries, religious properties, marriage, and religious customs, see Burns, *Islam under the Crusaders*, ch. 9, and *Crusader Valencia*, i, ch. 4, part 3; to the Valencian materials cited there, add the later but instructive document edited by Peregrín Lloréns y Raga, "La morería de Segorbe, rentas de su mezquita a fines del siglo xiv," *BSCC*, xlix (1973), 303-324.

[92] Lévi-Provençal, *España musulmana*, v, 260-261.

[93] *Cartas de población de Cataluña*, i, doc. 271 (1237): "quod de obligatione dotis et donationis propter nuptias et sponsalicii, non teneamini dare laudismium nec firmamentum"; doc. 290 (1248): "ratione dotis et sponsalici[i] sive donationis propter nuptias"; and other documents passim.

whomsoever each wishes, without any gift, sum, or fee." It also provided for the introduction of a wife or husband from an alien jurisdiction "without any gift or fee." At Uxó marriages were left entirely to Islamic custom, no fee being mentioned; at Eslida it was joined to inheritance and purchases as regulated "by their Law."[94] A century later, however, the Chivert authorities were to introduce a tax of five solidi; in 1371 at Cheste this *almería* amounted to eight solidi.[95]

A considerable source of revenue was the safeconduct or flag of protection. This *guiatge*, awarded by the crown to Christian or Muslim, to community or individual, and to merchant, traveler or undifferentiated subject, guaranteed the recipient against harassment or violence, under severe monetary and other penalties. The *guiatge* served many purposes, from passport, authorization, and pardon for crime or debt, to a kind of mercantile insurance. Valencian Mudejars enjoyed their share of these protective documents, some of which involved payment of a fee; but documentation of this facet of their society will be deferred to a sequel volume on Christian-Muslim interaction. Emigration or any voyage to a foreign land, common for Valencian Mudejars, involved a fee. The Játiva charter required a besant from any immigrant who left after having established residence "for two or more years." Muslims ejected after revolt seem to have paid "two silver besants" apiece.[96] An ambiguous item at Pego was several varieties of *mercat* (Latin *mercadum*), probably referring rather to marketing charges on the commodities specified than to a fee for the privilege of a market.[97]

---

[94] Chivert Charter: "unumcumque voluerit, sine aliquo dono, precio, et missione"; "liceat eis facere sine aliquo dono et missione." Uxó Charter. Eslida Charter. *Missio* means output or expenditure, commonly "expenses" but here "fee."

[95] Gual Camarena, "Mudéjares valencianos, aportaciones," p. 185, quoting charters of Chivert for 1359, Cheste for 1371, and Ribesalbes for 1405; the Cheste charter calls this *dret de almería*.

[96] Játiva Charter: "possit id facere secure, dando tamen unum bisancium." Arch. Crown, James I, Reg. Canc. 9, fol. 28 (May 1, 1258): "pro qualibet personarum ipsarum duos bisancios bonos argenti," plus the usual local fee or "[tabule] de Denia"; Reg. Canc. 10, fol. 62v (May 1, 1258), similar phrasing; both concern mass expulsion after revolt. On voyages see also Piles Ros, *Bayle general de Valencia*, pp. 37-39.

[97] Arch. Crown, James I, Reg. Canc. 35, fol. 3v (1268), at Pego: "item el mercado de [los molendinarios], v besants minus i diner"; "[el] mercado del junto, xli besants, iii millareses e medio"; "item el mercado de la farin[a], xv besants." See

A profusion of taxes or impositions has passed in review through-out these chapters. Pieced together from random survival of documentation, they form a fairly complete mosaic but with small bits inevitably missing. Men of that era were ingenious in devising casual fees, while unspoken tradition could conceal any number of small charges expected as a matter of course. It is imprudent to assume that a tax does not exist because charters omitted it; charter interpretation ran according to the precrusade customs in force at a given locality. Mudejars had to contend with intra-aljama expenses as well, though the continuity of religious public foundations saved them from serious outlay, while such sums as payment to a scribe were rather part of living costs than of public taxation and revenue. A number of taxes imposed in neighboring regions or in subsequent generations do not appear in postcrusade Mudejar charters and revenue documents.[98] Allowing for all exceptions, however, the intricate net of small fees, services, and taxes weighing upon the Mudejar comprised a structure not very different from that imposed upon Valencian Christians. Though multiple, these charges were not onerous by contemporary standards; in terms of omnivorous modern taxes they were moderate. They bear witness frequently both to Valencia's general prosperity and to continuity with her Islamic past.

Rodón Binué, *Lenguaje técnico del feudalismo*, p. 124 (*forum*, or *mercatum*) and p. 176 (*mercatum*).

[98] For example, the obligation of weaving, upon married women or single women owning their own houses, imposed by fourteenth-century seignorial charters of Valencia: "sia tenguda filar, sens alcun lloguer, una lliura de lli" (Gual Camarena, "Mudéjares valencianos, aportaciones," p. 187); and the *herrería* for metal-working (p. 192). A number of the taxes or fees in the *Cartas de población de Cataluña* or in García de Valdeavellano, *Instituciones españolas*, or in a list like that of Antoni Pons Pastor, *Historia de Mallorca, instituciones, cultura, y costumbres del reino (s. xii-xv)* (Palma de Mallorca, 1965; pp. 134-135) do not appear in postcrusade Valencia. An occasional detailed document accounting for minor taxes as well as major can turn up a number of odd entries. *Alfarra* and *alferra*, for example, may sometimes be misreadings for *alfetrá*, a variant of *cabeçatge*; Alcover puzzles over *alfarra*, suggesting that it was a variant of *alfarda* (*Diccionari català-valencià-balear*, I, 489) and omits *alfetra*. *Alfarra* may be related to *alfarràs* and *alfarrasament* or fee for price-setting on certain commodities by a public committee of Moors and Christians (Gual Camarena, "Mudéjares valencianos, aportaciones," p. 190); cf. Catalan *alfarrassar* (Castilian *alfarrazar*), meaning to assess or evaluate. It occurs, e.g., in the lists of Arch. Crown, James I, Reg. Canc. 35, fols. 3-4, 7-8 (1268 and 1269), passim; and see above, Chapter V, n. 48. Contributions in the same lists include "el rio, vii besants"; "item castelon . . .", with *soffra* and chickens; "item toroncas, ii denarios"; and separate items for various kinds of farm produce.

CHAPTER VII

Harvesting the Taxes

THE ADMINISTRATIVE structure of King James's realms was as yet rudimentary, his bureaucracy embryonic and thinly staffed. How then could he manage so many taxes? Mudejar custom provided the framework for solution at the local level. Mechanisms within aljamas, moreover, could be preserved and somehow controlled. The kingdom-wide scale of collection posed a special problem. The formative status of Valencia insured as well a certain amount of squabbling. Complicating the study of all facets of Mudejar tax collection is a chronological factor. During the fluid first phases of colonial government, especially in areas dominantly Mudejar, it made sense to intrude as few Christian officials as possible; with the passing decades, however, authorities could progressively rationalize, systematize, and control these early arrangements. The factors of scale, novelty, and rapid change affected both the collecting agencies and the taxpaying Mudejars. A preliminary sketch of the tax-collecting mechanisms, without pause for detail or documentation, will set the stage.

MECHANISMS OF COLLECTION

Where relatively few Christian settlers had as yet penetrated, or where the combined numbers of both communities were required to comprise a viable accounting unit, the collectors took taxes indifferently from Christian and Muslim alike, so that a modern investigator cannot discern the uniquely Mudejar elements. More commonly the separate Arabic and Romance accounts for either community became merged as the upper echelons of the collection hierarchy consolidated their disparate entries into manageable gross sums for auditing by the crown; here again the phenomenon of mixed revenues obscures the Mudejar scene proper. From the relatively independent seignorial jurisdictions, more circumscribed and in the hinterland more Mudejar in character, and even from the lands controlled by the church, few records have survived that clarify this early revenue scene.

The tax records that do remain by reason of having been regis-tered by the crown comprise a chaotic mass of detail. A bewildering flood of transient appointments and assignations of debt gives the impression initially that the king conducted his government hig-gledy piggledy as a vast confusion of small loans. The circumstance that the crown lumped together its state revenues and those from personal or domanial properties, and both public expenditures and private debts, further confuses the picture. Despite all advances in banking and administrative technique, the money affairs of so kaleidoscopically changing and commercially lively a land were not yet susceptible to tidy management. An investigator plunging into the luxuriant undergrowth of disparate records is soon lost; even-tually he can manage to mark out paths and to discern the eccentric ecology of this tax jungle, but much of it is intractable to systematic mapping.[1]

[1] Soldevila, dean of Catalan historians, complains that studying the revenues and revenue system even of the heir, Prince Peter, is "una empresa difícil, per no dir impossible" owing to the sporadic and partial nature of the documentation; the wider "organització financera del estats catalano-aragonesos," he regrets, is "tan poc estudiada" for this early period (*Pere el Gran*, part 1, 1, 79). Ludwig Klüpfel devotes his *Verwaltungsgeschichte des Königreichs Aragon zu Ende des 13. Jahrhunderts* (Berlin, 1915) to an analysis of court functionaries as they later evolved under Alfonso III from 1285 to 1291, outlining as well the finance ministers and the super-vising of collection; see esp. pp. 82ff. on the bailiff, and ch. 5 on finances. See also the more accessible Catalan translation: "El règim de la confederació catalano-aragonesa a finals del segle xiii" (title varies), *Revista jurídica de Catalunya*, xxxv (1921), 36-40 (purchase of bailiates by all classes), 203-205 (overlapping roles of treasurer and chamberlain), 301-313 (bailiffs), 321-326 (Jews; cf. 39-40), and xxxvi (1930), 97-135 (finances in general, esp. 119-120 on auctioning bailiates). The treas-urer or receiver general administered the bailiates and assignations, but the cham-berlain also sent out collectors and operated independently in his guise of controller of the king's expenditures, while the *scriptor rationalis* reviewed and receipted loan assignments. Klüpfel wryly concluded that "en treiem la impressió que el sistema de finances de la Confederació no havia arribat encara a un alt grau de perfecció" (xxxv, p. 219). He has nothing about Mudejar taxes. Karl Schwarz carries this story through the grand reorganization by which Peter the Ceremonious later transformed the crown bureaucracy, in *Aragonische Hofordnungen in 13. und 14. Jahrhundert: Studien zur Geschichte der Hofämter und Zentralbehörden des Königreichs Aragon* (Berlin, 1914), esp. pp. 41ff. After the reigns of Kings James and Peter, when tax documents had mixed into a kaleidoscope of every kind of royal business, the crown began to register different categories into separate codices, thus facilitating the mod-ern scholar's task. López de Ayala, in the standard treatment for the kingdom of Castile, *Contribuciones é impuestos en León y Castilla*, offers almost nothing on Mudejar taxes or their collection, while his few comments on tax collection in gen-eral derive largely from the *Siete partidas* (see pp. 282, 301-302, 334, 343, 348, 356, 373, 381-382, 390-391).

The collectory mechanisms revealed fall naturally into two categories: the receiving-auditing and the sparsely documented gathering of money or produce; the bailiff, castellan, tax farmer, and king's agent inhabited the upper region, while the staff of working collectors busied themselves in the lower. The crown could choose to take a tax directly, by agents who might or might not operate through aljama officials like the *amin* and his helpers; or it could designate a tax farmer, or a coordinate set or expandable consortium of tax farmers, who in turn might subfarm areas or individual taxes; or it could accept a reasonable compromise sum from, or impose an arbitrary or agreed sum upon, a taxpayer group, allowing the aljama to collect this directly or by subfarming for its own profit. The supervisory agent or tax farmer might receive one tax throughout the kingdom, or a tax at one locality, or several taxes in an arbitrary mix covering a large district. The financier-supervisory function included the office of bailiff for a given locality and could be exercised by wealthy tax farmers or creditors.

In theory the moneylender was not part of the financial machinery and participated only from the outside as an investor. Theoretically also tax farming was avoided in favor of appointed collectors who received a share salary. In fact, however, the crown did sometimes accept a lump sum and then appoint the creditor as office-holding tax collector, instead of merely assigning his debt with its incorporated interest or profit to be paid by a more legitimate officeholder. More commonly the crown engaged in speculative contract-farming, accepting the promise of an agreed sum to be recovered by the officeholder along with an additional profit from the taxpayers of up to ten percent. The profit, especially for a small community contract-farming its own taxes, could also be stated in terms of partial tax exemption. The crown could auction rents, accepting the bidder satisfied with the lowest margin of profit; in this case it frequently succumbed to the temptation to auction or sell the office itself, letting the officeholder squeeze out of the taxpayers, with all the juridical machinery of his office, as much of his possible ten percent as he could, abandoning the merciful discretion proper to his function.

Where a creditor or pensioner merely received his share as designated by crown authority, he was rather a beneficiary than a farmer of taxes; in practice it is not always easy to distinguish the holder of such a *violari* or corody from a collector. To the Mudejar both the tax farmer's concession and the beneficiary's assignation must have looked much like the Islamic *iqṭāʿ* or money fief in its non-agricultural form.[2] All varieties of loan, assignment, contract, or pension required an outpouring of paper work. Designation of a tax farmer sometimes included specific instructions to call in the warrants of indebtedness as soon as he retired an attributed debt.

Of the several formats available, it is hard to decide which the crown used most frequently; after all, authorities were more likely to register important instruments of debt and to be concerned rather with general than with local and detailed accounts. If a document went unregistered, the transaction dropped into oblivion after the crown recovered and destroyed its note acknowledging the debt. Here as elsewhere, the historian is at the mercy of surviving documentation, but he can retain a healthy skepticism concerning generalizations of pattern, including his own. From the taxpayer's point of view, one administrative device was much like any other, since he paid his full tax according to a fairly constant schedule, except in anomalous situations like war crises or modifications of obligation due to hardship. Though the individual was the direct target of a tax, in cases of preagreed lump sums the community bore ultimate responsibility *in solidum*.

Though Mudejars like Christians paid most of their taxes in money, they satisfied the obligation of agricultural shares, especially of grain, in kind. Thus Eslida's charter specified that "wheat, barley, millet, flax, and vegetables" be left on the harvesting ground (*in era*), and not stored until the tax men had taken their share. The practice accorded with Islamic custom, as well as with the civil and ecclesiastical system of collecting tithes in kind from Christian-owned fields in Valencia. It involved calculations as to prededucted expenses, an order of priority for multiple taxes, a network of transport and storage facilities, a statement of money equivalent for the auditors, and eventually a merchandising operation. In much the same manner, collectors might take pasturage or livestock taxes in animals rather than money.[3] To be properly understood, this review

[2] See contemporary examples of the money fief in Islam in Rabie, *Financial System of Egypt*, pp. 43-44. See also Cahen, "*Iḳṭāʿ*," *EI*[2], iii, 1,088-1,091, and below, n. 21.

[3] Eslida Charter: "decima tritici, ordei, panicii, milii, lini, et leguminis, et decima persolvatur in era." For gathering of tithes in kind on the field by Valencian district

of the essential mechanisms must be restated concretely in terms of the bailiff's office and then related to the collecting mechanisms within the Mudejar aljamas.

THE BAILIFF

At the purely administrative level, the basic unit for supervising collection was the local bailiff, traditional custodian of temporalities and revenues acting for king or lord.[4] Protector of the crown's property and interests, and supervisor of crown income, the bailiff had acquired the judicial powers necessary for his office and, as the most prominent local representative of the crown, had taken on governing functions as well. His governing powers varied according to time and place, constricting in the presence of strong town and castellan government. Allied functions of the most varied sort accrued, until the bailiff's role ramified into maritime affairs, fortification, commercial licensing, and supervision of Jews and Moors.

---

collectors and bailiffs, see Burns, *Crusader Valencia*, I, 147, 153. See too the various receipts in kind mixed into the money receipts in the accounting for Prince Peter's holdings in 1274 (Soldevila, *Pere el Gran*, part I, III, appendix, doc. 41 [Feb. 24, 1274]).

[4] Jesús Lalinde Abadía studies the bailiff in his origins and evolution, in *La jurisdicción real inferior en Cataluña ("corts, veguers, batlles")* (Barcelona, 1966), esp. pp. 56-69, 83-89, 125-153, 213-215, 237-256. Piles Ros, though concerned with the office after the mid-fourteenth century, reviews the thirteenth-century background and the several positions of historians in his *Bayle general de Valencia*, ch. I, noting the slight attention given by historians to this office. On the duties and jurisdiction of the capital city's bailiff, more an embryo bailiff general until the 1280's, see the *Fori antiqui Valentiae*, rub. III, no. 8. Piles Ros rebuts the positions of Tourtoulon's *Jaime I* on the bailiff; but of older authors Branchát is still useful, *Derechos y regalías de Valencia*, I, esp. ch. I, and Matheu y Sanz, *De regimine regni Valentiae*, ch. 2, part 4. See too Font y Rius, "Régimen municipal," pp. 248-254; García de Valdeavellano, *Instituciones españolas*, pp. 515-517, 524-525, 592; Rodón Binué, *Lenguaje técnico del feudalismo*, pp. 33-38; Antonio M. Aragó Cabañas, "La institución 'baiulus regis' en Cataluña, en la época de Alfonso el Casto," *Congrés VII*, III, 139-142. See also Burns, *Islam under the Crusaders*, ch. 3, part I, and ch. 15, part 3. At the court of the king the procurator in charge of finances evolved into the celebrated *mestre racional* around 1285, probably on the model of contemporary Sicily, then coming under Catalan control; under him in the fourteenth century a remarkably rationalized fiscal system developed, in which the regional bailiff generals played their role. See, e.g., the description by Eiximenis, ed. Jill R. Webster, "Francesc Eiximenis on Royal Officials: A View of Fourteenth-Century Aragon," *Mediaeval Studies*, XXXI (1969), 246-248, from his *Lo chrestià*, ch. 747.

He was essentially a local figure. The bailiff general left him largely to his own devices in his specific locality or for his special tax; the subbailiff below him was not an assistant but a lesser bailiff of smaller scope. This pattern of bailiffs below bailiffs, with the aggregate of bailiffs varying so widely in the range and importance of their powers, makes it difficult to treat the bailiate[5] in an abstract, univocal sense. Seignorial bailiffs more easily split the basic functions, becoming either administrative alter egos of the lord or mere tax collectors; some lords thus had two quite different bailiffs, one of them a renter-bailiff or tax farmer.

The crown bailiff was not a castellan, though he might hold a castle as well as its bailiwick, nor was the castellan a bailiff by reason of acquiring a district's rent; both cases confuse the eye and must sometimes have merged into a single reality. Nor was the bailiff a tax farmer or loaner of money, at least not by virtue of his office. Here theory does part with practice, however, and many bailiffs purchased their bailiwicks with a previous or a parallel loan. A bailiff could not be a Jew, Muslim, or heretic, again in theory; in practice, from the mid-twelfth century on, the Arago-Catalan kings frequently appointed Jews. The bailiff's traditional salary was a tenth of the revenue he supervised, the *retrodecima* or *redelme*. The lowest collector took a tenth of his small amount, and the bailiff general took a tenth from the conglomerate sum or from as much as pertained to his own activity, all collectors and bailiffs down the line reckoning such tenths in their assessment as an expense added to the basic tax return expected by the crown.[6]

---

[5] "Bailiate" in English stresses the total office, "bailiwick" the region or the defined revenues assigned; Latin *baiulia* covers both.

[6] In Valencia, King James assigned such a *redelme* in 1261 to William Bertrand, for example, when granting him the collection of the crown's third of the church tithe in Peñíscola and its district: "recipias pro nobis totam partem nostram decimarum . . . in Peniscola et suis alqueriis et terminis suis, panis videlicet et vini et carnium et quorumlibet aliorum, cum tuis propriis missionibus et expensis; et habeas et percipias inde ad opus tuum, pro tuo officio et labore redecimam integre . . . omnibus diebus vite tue" (Arch. Crown, James I, Reg. Canc. 11, fol. 204v [May 4, 1261]). In 1258, giving "baiuliam eiusdem ville de Alcoy et terminorum eius, ita quod tu colligas et recipias ac colligi et recipi facias" all revenues "que pertineant ad officium baiulie," King James included "retrodecimam de omnibus que ibi colliges et colligi facies, pro tuo officio et labore" (Reg. Canc. 9, fol. 30 [May 5, 1258]). The lifetime tenure as bailiff of Murviedro, however, awarded to Robau or Rotbald of Voltarasc in 1251, paid a fifteenth: "pro vestro officio et labore quindecimam partem omnium predictorum redituum nostrorum" (*Itinerari*, p. 211 [Feb. 11, 1251]). The general

Although a bailiwick might consist of a valley with its towns and castles, a cumulus of several cities, a mountain region, or one kingdom-wide tax, the usual unit was a town with its natural countryside or jurisdiction; a subbailiff might then take a component village or cluster of outlying castles.

"Bailiff" was a very flexible term, therefore, ranging from the courtier aristocrat at the king's side, who acted as treasurer or overseer, to the grubby speculator illegally turning administration into tax farming with the blessing of the crown. Aside from his core duties as fiscal administrator and specialized judge, the bailiff's activities as executive of the ruler depended on the scope afforded by his locality or circumstances and upon the extent of the mandate accorded him. The bailiff general who evolved at Valencia city, and his lieutenant bailiffs respectively above and below the Júcar River, enjoyed broad powers on such matters as repair of defenses, concern for Moors and Jews as wards of the crown, issuance of commercial licenses and passports, and the smooth functioning of utilities like baths and bakehouses. Conversely, a local bailiff out in the countryside and cooperating with a ruling castellan might find himself attending to little more than supervising tax collections during a brief year in office.

The bailiff's field of action easily overlapped those of other authorities, especially of the king's lieutenants, the ubiquitous justiciars, the municipal jurates and officers, and the castellans in their

---

practice outside Valencia is revealed at Lérida, for example, where the longtime bailiff was told in 1225 to continue collecting all revenues "sicut levari et teneri *consuevit* hucusque a vobis vel a quolibet alio baiulo Ylerde, ita videlicet . . . sicut in prima carta commande baiulie predicte . . . , salvo vobis vestro retrodecimo quod de predictis omnibus baiulus Ylerde *semper* accipere consuevit" (*Colección diplomática,* doc. 45 [Nov. 12, 1225], italics mine). That this affected even the bailiffs general, and was the rule in the realms of Aragon under the kings preceding James I, is evident from doc. 16 (June 19, 1220); giving the Templar William total supervision of revenues and bailiffs throughout Catalonia, with a matching Templar for Aragon, each having "plenariam potestatem" to collect, audit, appoint, and remove, King James added: "preterea eidem dedimus plenam licenciam et potestatem, ut in omnibus exitibus et redditibus nostris, sicut est a nostris predecessoribus constitutum, decimam recipiat." Where a salary or sum is specified instead, examination often shows these also to be roughly a tenth. See also Lalinde Abadía, *Jurisdicción real inferior,* pp. 254, 258; Rodón Binué, *Lenguaje técnico del feudalismo,* p. 37 and n.; and on the tenth for underlings, below, Chapter VIII, part 4. On Islamic custom in paying tax collectors, see Aghnides, *Mohammedan Theories of Finance,* pp. 395-396, 443-445, and, below, part 3.

castellanies. At its most developed stage, the office was typically medieval, an asymmetrical congeries of functions around a fiscal-cum-executive core, with sufficient authority attached to get the job done but with an extent of mandate sufficiently vague to ensure continuous bickering with coauthorities. The bailiff might be a castellan or baron, professional courtier or favored civil servant, merchant, Jew, or cleric, all ranged in parallel rather than hierarchically, constituting a welter of regional and local functionaries of unequal competence and disparate background.

A recent interpretation of the bailiff stresses his role as a civil authority, who rarely and only incidentally made loans himself, a professional valued by the crown for his ability but especially for his loyalty; he administered on a nonprofiteering plane essentially removed from that of the tax farmer who acquired the rents, bailiff and farmer making "a complete bifurcation." The bailiff's reward, in this view, came in the form of land grants from a grateful monarch, or from his incidental loans at high interest to his indigent taxpayers; he did not profit from the taxes directly like the farmer.[7] This scheme comprises a supporting argument for a wider and more persuasive thesis on the role of the Jews, considered below, and rests upon the mistaken premise that bailiffs did not receive a generous return from the taxes, and that speculative, contract purchase of the office was a rarity. The latter distinction was true in theory. The moneylender stood outside the administrative, bailiff system; his notes were assigned for payment by some local bailiff as an encumbrance or disbursement charged to that bailiwick. The lender, whose interest or profit was included in his note, waited at home until one of the king's bailiffs either discharged the obligation, recalling and voiding the note, or else renegotiated it. In fact, however, the public office itself frequently—even normally—became an object of speculation.

Just as the king sold all or part of a locality's revenues by way of

<hr />

[7] Jerome Lee Shneidman, *The Rise of the Aragonese-Catalan Empire, 1200-1350,* 2 vols. (New York, 1970), ii, ch. 14, esp. pp. 472, 474-475. Against too enthusiastic a stress on the bailiff as civil governor, see the decree of James I, which serves as text for treatment of the office by Matheu y Sanz, excluding the bailiff from all jurisdiction except those "que seran sobre los censals nostres, o les altres rendes nostres" (*De regimine regni Valentiae,* ch. 2, part 4, text); but see also nos. 10-11 on jurisdiction over Jews and Mudejars and on the progressive amplification of his powers.

assignment to tax speculators, so he often sold or granted as a rent charge the bailiate itself, in effect the office with its ten percent profit. The speculator bailiff submitted as high a bid as he dared, during the annual auctioning of bailiwicks. He reckoned closely all pre-deductable expenses, salaries, and encumbrances; contracted to pay his estimated total according to a precise schedule; and secured his venture with his own and his backers' properties and chattels. Such a contract farmer risked ruin at the start of his career, but he could operate with a minimum of ready money, swiftly building a tidy fortune. The bailiff's customary tenth, less than the maximum theoretical interest allowed on private loans, came close to the market interest actually prevailing and profitably involved large sums with fast return.

The contractor-bailiff enlarged his total bid as grossly as was consistent with the real taxes available by nonextortionate means, thus affording the highest income to the crown and profit from his tenth; but he had to reckon the tax potential closely, allow for delinquents as well as for a poor year coming up, and figure nicely the smaller tenths deducted by any subordinates before they passed along their own collection. A total too low could lose out in the bidding. A total too high meant at least diminution or loss of the profit-tenth. If the renter-bailiff overextended himself and failed to meet the obligations of his contract, the crown regarded all his possessions plus those of his formal backers as a kind of collateral or rather surety to be confiscated. Desperate borrowing and even debtors' prison followed. Spreading the risk either by consortium or via sub-farming lessened the profit; if the colleagues or subfarmers failed, the principal was himself in deep trouble. With care, energy, and some luck, however, a man of modest means could rise by contract farming of taxes, but especially of the bailiate itself, to the status of merchant-prince.

A variation of selling, by auction or by grant of favor, was the payment of debts by assigning not only the revenues, as was normal, but even the bailiate itself until the debt was discharged. A bailiff might also manage taxes administratively for his profitable tenth but simultaneously take over as tax farmer for specified revenues; thus the general bailiff for Valencia north of the Júcar in 1262 transmitted crown taxes, disbursed public funds to the king's treasurers, and also dabbled in loans to the crown and their recovery in tax farming.[8] Not only did the king auction bailiwicks on a grand scale, but major bailiffs conducted such auctions to select lesser bailiffs; thus the Barcelona bailiff each May personally conducted open bidding for all comers during ten continuous days for the revenues of one town, the winner becoming bailiff.[9] The equivalent *amīn* of a Valencian Mudejar community probably auctioned separate rents or areas, as was the later Mudejar custom in Aragon "by public bidding."[10]

The sale of bailiwicks attracted a considerable number of speculators unequal to their attached judicial and governing duties. The resulting outcry for reform forced King Peter to promise at his 1283 parliament: "in the sales of revenues that we shall conduct henceforth, we shall not sell the magistracy, the bailiate, or even the

[8] Eximèn (Simon) Pérez of Arenós in 1262 or 1263 held the revenues of Burriana, the castle of Alfandech, the Albufera saltworks, the mills of Campanar, and the taxes of Valencia city's Jews—all "pignori obligata cum quodam instrumento nostro" for 66,702 solidi of Valencia; he contracted to farm for the following year or so a similar cluster of revenues for 63,401 solidi of Jaca (Arch. Crown, James I, Reg. Canc. 12, fol. 17r,v [March 3]). At the same time, in his capacity as bailiff for other revenues he did not farm to himself, he paid out "de omnibus redditibus et exitibus tabule nostre Valencie" in five assignments to creditors 21,500 solidi, of which 16,500 went to Eximèn of Foces (Reg. Canc. 14, fol. 13v [March 1, 1262-1263]); in assignments on the revenues of Uxó 3,700 solidi to Bernard Escrivá, "solutis missionibus castri d'Uxone" (fol. 13v, another document of the same date); in assignments on Murviedro 7,500 solidi to the same Bernard, "pro quibus . . . fuerunt venditi omnes redditus et exitus dicti castri et ville" (fol. 13, same date); and from the Valencia city bailiwick 15,500 solidi divided between the same Bernard and Arnold of Font (fol. 13, same date).

[9] *Colección diplomática*, doc. 656 (Nov. 28, 1257): "mensis madii annis singulis in encanto," either at the town or in the Barcelona bailiff's presence elsewhere, "per decem dies continuos . . . [et] sit baiulus eiusdem ville et non alius, et ipse colligat et recipiat ipsos redditus, exitus, et proventus per totum illud tempus per quod sibi venditi fuerint."

[10] This was the custom for at least some taxes in a better documented era (Jan. 18, 1402), when the queen sent a rebuke "al alami e vells de la aliama de los moros de la val d'Almonetzir," because "no sguardant lo profit nostre e de la dita aliama, havets vendut calladament e fraudulosa *sens subastacio alguna* la renda o dret appellat almaxita, lo qual se acostuma vendre cascun any al mas donant al encant publich" (italics mine); actually the custom had been observed and the rebuke was subsequently revoked (Macho y Ortega, "Documentos de los mudéjares," p. 154); the place seems to be Almonacid de la Sierra in Aragon. In another rebuke, collectors are revealed to have taxed nonresident merchants also: "sed etiam extranei sarraceni venientes ad villam eamdem . . . ementes et vendentes seu quomodolibet contractantes" (p. 146 [Feb. 17, 1399]).

vicariate, since in that way justice can be destroyed and [our] subjects oppressed."[11] The selling continued unabated, however, and a decade later became so great a scandal that the crown had to order all *contract bailiffs dismissed and any purchase price restored to* them, an expedient that did not halt the illegal sales.[12]

Arago-Catalan monarchs would in fact pawn away a great deal of the crown's patrimony everywhere with increasing recklessness, for a century more, selling not only bailiwicks and rents but mills, ovens, castles, and fiefs. Throughout the fourteenth century this process often took the form of a gracious, free gift, disguising the operation itself but especially allowing freer disposal by the principal beneficiary; this recipient in turn pledged himself to surrender the property on demand, or after a specified few years, for the return of the original sum, so that in effect he enjoyed a yearly interest until such time as the crown could restore his capital. The device had points of resemblance to the open *violari* and pension, discussed below as an encumbrance upon revenues, but it was more grossly and deceptively a raid upon the crown's basic resources. The kingdom of Valencia differed from the other segments of the Arago-Catalan realm, in this game of loans disguised as grants, in that it

---

[11] *Cortes de Aragón y de Valencia*, I, part 1, p. 148 (Barcelona, 1283): "item quod in vendicionibus reddituum quas de cetero faciemus, non vendamus curiam, baiuliam, vel etiam vicariam, cum ex hoc si fieret posset iusticia deperire et subditi opprimerentur." The reference to justice, as well as the intention to continue selling the revenues themselves, makes it clear that the word *baiuliam* here means the office with its jurisdiction and not just the rents. See also I, 94, no. 15, Lérida *cortes* of 1214, where "nullus christianus, nec iudeus, nec aliqua alia persona [sarracenus?] pignori accipiant aut per aliquem titulum adquirant aliqua de hiis que tenent in feudum, sine dominorum assensu et voluntate." Thus in cases where the crown had installed a castellan or lord but retained regalian taxes, it had to consult the lord before intruding its chosen bailiff; in many cases the lord or castellan himself had the revenue-collecting prerogative and would merely transfer the due amount to the royal bailiff. On the practice of selling, auctioning, pledging, and enfeoffing the bailiate itself, despite frequent protest and promises to desist, see Lalinde Abadía, *Jurisdicción real inferior*, pp. 191-194; see also p. 86.

[12] *Cortes de Aragón y de Valencia*, I, part 1, p. 156 (Barcelona, 1292). The "customary" sale of Valencian rents, as opposed to sale of the bailiate office, is described for example in *Colección diplomática*, doc. 618 (Oct. 29, 1257); each year the king's bailiff of Játiva "sells or assigns" them to "buyers," who in turn obligate themselves to the castellan for sums assigned by the king to him. Accounts by bailiffs were commonly approved by a document describing the audit and waiving the crown's rights to recover at law or to confiscate the bailiff's property in case discrepancies turned up in future.

lost rents alone nearly as often as it did jurisdictions or fiefs, a process visible as much in its south as in its central portion.[13]

The plethora of crown bailiffs over Valencia, each with his *curia* or staff, had a markedly scattered character, unlike the superficially more rational system in France of crown agents supervising large areas. This disparate arrangement was further complicated, not only by the coexistence of seignorial and some ecclesiastical revenue autonomies under their own bailiffs, but by the circumstance that James's new kingdom required some time to evolve a true bailiff general with more than a semblance of hierarchical order and with his own regional subdivisions operating above and below the Júcar River. Some historians see the full appearance of the bailiff general as coming late in the reign of King Peter; others, from Branchát down to Piles Ros, argue that he functioned from the very fall of Valencia city with sweeping but relatively undefined powers.[14]

General bailiffs appear in action both above and below the Júcar River at least from 1262, possibly representing division of a more general jurisdiction long held by the Valencian bailiff as treated in the kingdom's law code. King James appointed Giles Eximèn of Teruel in 1262 "into the bailiate of the city of Valencia and of all castles, towns, and places of the aforesaid kingdom from the Júcar River up, in such wise that he be thenceforth bailiff for us and establish [other] bailiffs there in his place, whomsoever he shall wish, and these [bailiffs] are to receive our rents and income of the aforesaid places." Everyone was to receive "him and all those he chooses as bailiffs" and to pay them all the king's revenues "that you are accustomed and bound to pay to our bailiffs." The appointee was to swear on the Gospels to collect revenues honestly and to pay off the king's creditors as ordered. A matching document went to Arnold of Monzón for the region "from the Júcar River down."[15]

[13] M. T. Ferrer i Mallol, "El patrimoni reial i la recuperació dels senyorius jurisdiccionals en els estats catalano-aragonesos a la fi del segle xiv," *AEM*, vii (1970-1971), 352, 368, 400-408.

[14] Piles Ros, *Bayle general de Valencia*, pp. 13, 21. David Romano Ventura, "Los funcionarios judíos de Pedro el Grande de Aragón," *BRABLB*, xxviii (1969-1970), p. 20. Branchát, *Derechos y regalías de Valencia*, i, 83-84.

[15] Arch. Crown, James I, Reg. Canc. 12, fol. 50 (May 4, 1262): "universitati hominum civitatis Valencie et omnium castrorum, villarum, et locorum totius regni Valencie a rivo Xuqari citra . . . sciatis quod nos constituimus Egidium Ximeni de Turolio in baiulum civitatis Valencie et omnium castrorum . . . que sunt a dicto rivo Xuqari citra, ita quod ipse sit inde baiulus pro nobis et ponat et constituat ibi

During these early years, before the development of a hierarchical method of financial administration, accounting followed an eccentric, fragmented pattern, various regions reporting to the king severally. Thus, the bailiff for Gandía and Palma in 1276 had to send his accounts to the king, which in fact went "in our stead" to Bishop James of Huesca.[16] Other Valencian references to this auditing speak of the account books kept by each bailiff and, in the case of loans, of receipts given Mudejars in Arabic. In 1283 Judah b. Manasseh had to present himself or a proxy before the king or his treasurer Conrad Lancia, bringing along the books, instruments of debt, "and all other writings that pertain to your accounts."[17] Mudejar fiscal authorities throughout Valencia also kept such "account books," but in Arabic, and probably in terms of Islamic moneys; later, a well-salaried supervisor "translated" them out of "the Moorish tabulations" for the Christian records. Such translation would have involved, besides language, the Arabic numerals still avoided in European public finance as unfamiliar to many conservative officials.[18]

---

baiulos, quoscumque voluerit loco sui, et recipiant omnes redditus et exitus nostros predictorum locorum . . . ; ipse enim iurabit super sancta dei evangelia statim . . . quod respondeat et respondi faciat bene et fideliter. . . ." Fol. 50v (same date): "sub eadem forma, quarto nonas Madii anno predicto fecit dominus rex Arnaldo de Munço instrumentum a rivo Xucaris ultra, videlicet in forma instrumenti Egidii Eximeni."

[16] *Ibid.*, Reg. Canc. 22, fol. 63v (July 14, 1276): "loco nostri." The bailiffs of Valencia kingdom at times submitted their accounts to review by Joseph Ravaya (see p. 284). The *Colección diplomática* includes a number of non-Valencian audits with procedural details, some in the king's presence; see docs. 45 (Nov. 12, 1225), 217 (July 28, 1240), 222 (Feb. 17, 1241), and 767 (Feb. 26, 1258). For making accounts of local taxes to a town's *cort*, see docs. 261 (Sept. 22, 1243), 366 (Jan. 19, 1250), and 413 (Feb. 12, 1252), all on Valencia.

[17] Romano, "Hermanos Abenmenassé," document of June 23, 1283: "cum quaternis vestris, albaranis, et omnibus aliis scripturis que pertinent ad vestrum compotum." For a receipt, see p. 256 (April 29, 1280): "in Algezira sigillamus quandam literam sarracenicam . . . recognitionis sarracenorum Xative, videlicet quod solverant domino regi octingentas quadraginta duplas." King Alfonso later speaks of the account books kept by local Christian authorities throughout the kingdom, presumably also for mixed populations, but apparently only for current accounts and debts: "fuit mandatum universis scriptoribus curiarum et iustitiarum regni Valencie quod ostendatis dicto Raimundo Fivellerii libros dictarum curiarum quandocumque a dicto Raimundo fuerint recquisiti, ob hoc ut certificare se possit de debitis et quitiis que debeantur domino regi qualibet ratione de temporibus preteritis in regno Valencie" (Arch. Crown, Reg. Canc. 82, fol. 83 [Nov. 20, 1290]).

[18] See, e.g., Johannes Vincke, "Königtum und Sklaverei im aragonischen Staatenbund während des 14. Jahrhunderts," *Gesammelte Aufsätze zur Kulturgeschichte*

Alongside or below the supervisory level of bailiffs, Islamic officials and procedures fitted easily into such a disparate system, either continuing immemorially or adapting to the new overlord and allowing for some intrusive novelties. Many regular taxes had their special collectors—such as customs, transit, market, and notarial charges; others came to a similar local collector on their way to a higher receiver—fees for bath, oven, mill, fonduk, irrigation, and the like. Many taxes and rents fell in lump installments twice or thrice a year,[19] in operations requiring organization through designated local agents under the eyes of aljama officials and representatives of lord or farmer. Behind all this lay the methods for assessing,[20] local lists of taxpayers, arrangements for a compromise sum, and the lowest classes of subfarmer. In Valencia the prominent supervisor of taxes in each Mudejar aljama was its *amīn*, a functionary who will receive closer attention in the next chapter.

Spaniens, xxv (1970), doc. 41 (Oct. 6, 1340), an order to release an illegally seized Mudejar of Valldigna with his "libri compotum." Mudejar accounts from Valencia kingdom below the Júcar were translated in 1315 by a Christian functionary at the high salary of 400 solidi (see the document quoted in Chapter VIII, n. 196). Both examples are late, but it is highly improbable, especially given the anti-Mudejar spirit growing in early fourteenth-century officialdom, that they represent an innovation.

[19] Any number of examples have been included in chapters above. In the rents for Aragon proper for 1294 one finds the Mudejar tribute of Tarazona given in three installments at the beginning of May, September, and January; at Borgia it came twice, on St. Michael's and Christmas; Magallón collected it once, on St. Michael's; and Aranda took it in four unequal sets (*Rentas de Aragón*, pp. 219, 224, 233, 240). Collation of the Valencian examples in the present book might establish a more logical pattern. Perhaps, like collection in at least some Islamic regions, taxes connected with the harvest were collected by the solar year, and many independent fees by the lunar calendar (Rabie, *Financial System of Egypt*, p. 105).

[20] The complicated method of assessing and collecting from Christians the local and regalian taxes at Valencia city is described in a privilege of 1252, with each parish electing men for the double task under supervision of the city council, excluding the bailiff or any royal official at this stage, and with the assessors under both oath and peril of confiscation of property. The collector could serve only once, enjoyed tax exemption, and had to maintain secret even from the king the share owed by each (*Colección diplomática*, doc. 413 [Feb. 12, 1252]). See also Arch. Crown, James I, Reg. Canc. 9, fol. 25 (March 7, 1257), where the king allows Valencians "quatenus eligatis duos probos homines, qui nom[inentur] secretarii, qui duo petant, accipiant et audiant computum omnium iurium que pertinent communitati civitatis, et quod teneant caxiam privilegiis . . . qui tamen duo dent et teneantur reddere compotum coram dictis electis de parrochiis, quotienscumque ab eis fuerint requisiti." Reg. Canc. 10, fol. 61 (April 28, 1258), a revenue document, addresses not only bailiffs but "collectoribus [et] portariis."

In governmental-jurisdictional terms, the manner of collecting could differ on crown land (to which the outline above applies eminently), seignorial or ecclesiastical small holdings, and the few sweeping estates distinguished by size and independence, including those areas reserved, for example, to support the heir apparent of the crown. At the local level, below any overarching but loose control, local dispositions could differ in accordance with antecedent tradition, a shifting emigration pattern, or the degree of self-government retained within a relatively undisturbed ambience.

ISLAMIC TAX COLLECTION

From the Islamic side, nothing survives of Valencian practice, except what finds reflection in Christian postcrusade sources. Clues come from other regions of Islam, and from other times, including caliphal Spain, as well as from the heavily theoretical tax treatises. These often represent a different tradition, economy, or governmental organization. The clearest picture of thirteenth-century tax collection comes from Egypt, unfortunately for our purposes the most atypical of Islamic administrations. In its areas of *iqtā'*, a kind of military money fief, each village had a staff of several clerks directly responsible to the fief holder, though tax farming was also used. The sultan collected his own revenues both by farming and by direct action of his central financial office under the vizier; civil servants staffed over a dozen subordinate offices, each under its hierarchy from controller to lowly clerk or *amīn*, and each specializing in some segment of the revenue.[21]

General studies on Islamic tax practices are disappointing and lack detail on actual procedure. Like the juristic theorists, they tend to give a textbook overview of public treasury and common revenues, taken by collectors according to their specific authorization and

---

[21] Rabie, *Financial System of Egypt*, ch. 4 on tax collection and financial administration; ch. 2, part C, on the *iqtā'* as a method of collecting taxes. Until 1315 the sultan's taxes such as the *zakāt* were collected on *iqtā'* lands under supervision of agents from the central treasury, with the fief-holder's taxes a system apart, but the status of the holder (from prince to simple soldier) and other circumstances varied the actual situation considerably. As Bernard Lewis notes in the preface, Egypt was "sharply defined by both geography and history, with a degree of administrative cohesion and continuity unparalleled elsewhere in the Islamic world." On the elaborate paper work connected with the Nile land tax, see pp. 73-74.

traditions.[22] In the mixed society of the Near Eastern crusader states, where taxes and their collection changed name rather than substance, Cahen found that the absentee Frank acted much like his Islamic predecessor, holding the village of noncommunal farms responsible as a unit for its taxes, and acting either through a dragoman-scribe or more usually through an overseer or *ra'is*. The scribe provided one obvious point of local reference, given the importance of written accounts in Islamic society. The *ra'is* was that common product of crisis periods, the local notable who served as liaison to the changing administrative superstructure; his district or *raisagium* soon became hereditary in his family.[23]

In records reflecting a broad spectrum of Islamic countries and times, up into the thirteenth century, Goitein finds that "the farming of revenues of all descriptions pervaded from top to bottom the system of administration and economy," whether by contract or regular farming or by prearranged kickback; the ruler, higher tax farmer, notable holding a tax, or the local tax office could issue patents of appointment by lease or sublease. Competition was intense; during times of low public morality bidding was rampant, and severe losses to tax farmers were "not infrequent." Despite its "pernicious" aspects, however, and unlike the oppressive tax farming of the ancient Roman and Persian empires, the Islamic system via a more controlled and mercantile stratum "fitted well into the general framework of the economy and society."[24]

[22] Løkkegaard, *Islamic Taxation*, ch. 4 on tax farming, drawn especially from early Iraq; and see pp. 109, 147-148, 175. Aghnides, *Mohammedan Theories of Finance*, ch. 3, parts 1 and 2 on collection of the *zakāt*, with the distinctions and speculative arabesques of the several schools of thought; see also pp. 396-397, 443, 498. Poliak, "Feodalité islamique," pp. 253-256, with the *iqtā'* beneficiary not seeing much difference between his grant as a farming privilege or as a property, though the theoretical distinction was clear.

[23] Cahen, "Régime rural syrien," pp. 302, 304-307, 309. The Latin dragoman in his *drugmannagia* was found only on seignorial lands; the *ra'is* (Latinized sometimes as *regulus*) was more universal and in Islamic areas of the crusader states always a Muslim. In his "La féodalité et les institutions politiques de l'orient latin," *Atti del convegno di scienze morali, storiche, e filologiche, tema: oriente ed occidente nel medio evo* (Rome, 1957), Cahen remarks on similarities there between Islamic and feudal taxes (pp. 185-186), and on how the Latin lord apparently came to regard his Muslim *ra'is* as a low subvassal, a receptacle of local power with oath of homage to him (p. 187).

[24] Goitein, *Mediterranean Society*, II, 358-363, 377-378.

In Spain during the long caliphal era, three systems of revenue collection coexisted in parallel: the direct conveyance of rents or income from the caliph's personal holdings into his private or household account, the administration of rents from pious and philanthropic foundations by the chief *qāḍī* for religio-social needs, and the workings of the main or public treasury. The finance ministry was one of four major departments of state, each under its own vizier and responsible to the prime minister or *ḥājib*, the equivalent of the powerful vizier in states of eastern Islam. The revenue hierarchy ranged downward from chief secretary, through director of collection and disbursement, to provincial overseers and local collectors. The town tax agent, as well as the customs man in each main city and the receiver of specific revenues such as market tolls, passed his receipts through district headquarters to his respective provincial capital; each capital, after deducting expenditures, passed the residue to Cordova. The pattern was complicated both by the usual evolutions within the organization itself and by tax farming, special arrangements, and local differences. The neat pattern accommodated itself to the vagaries of the many unwieldy bureaucracies it comprised.[25]

The circumstances of Almohad Spain, and particularly of the fragmented post-Almohad principalities, differed greatly from those of the caliphal era. The economic organization of the Valencian territory, moreover, varied widely from that of a contemporary region like Seville with its *latifundia* estates. Badly documented and scarcely studied, the precrusade period remains largely a matter of hints and conjecture. Ibn 'Abdūn, dealing with twelfth-century Seville, tells how landowners paid the salaries of appointed tax

---

[25] Lévi-Provençal, *España musulmana*, v, 22, 24-25. García de Valdeavellano, *Instituciones españolas*, pp. 672-673. Imamuddin, *Socio-Economic and Cultural History of Muslim Spain*, pp. 45-47, 53-55. Any number of details in general Islamic or in Spanish-Islamic practice resemble details of Christian collection procedures, either by reason of common origin in Roman and Byzantine antecedents, or in response to similar practical necessities by men of the same era, or by cultural osmosis and borrowings. Even the separateness of *waqf* collection had its counterpart in ecclesiastical tithes and widespread exempt properties, as with religious orders. Both Islamic and Christian collectors of agricultural shares visited the field for their portion immediately after harvesting and before any of the produce left the field; both authorities reduced or wrote off some taxes in response to hardship or to win goodwill; and the yearly land tax in either area might be taken in three installments.

assessors; in a jeremiad against this abuse, he urged that the government pay, and the *qāḍī* control the activities of, the irreligious assessor class. From fixed assessments and prepared tax lists the actual
collectors did their job, helped by local authorities, especially by the
village head or district leader (*'āmil*); all these men, Ibn 'Abdūn
complains, tended to evil. Distinguished from them was the collector
of market, sales, and similar taxes within a fixed area—"the worst of
the creatures Allah has put on earth." Ibn 'Abdūn includes a note on
renting a shop, mill, bathing establishment, or boat from public
authorities.[26] For neighboring North Africa, a system of collecting
taxes through a functionary called the *amīn* existed alongside a
parallel tax-farming method.[27]

Valencian Mudejar practice, much of it carried over from precrusade times, furnishes contrasts and analogies at the local level, and
comparisons in the matter of tax farming. Certain revenues remained fully in Mudejar hands—those received as his own by a
Muslim feudatory or landlord, those required for aljama administration, and those allied with worship and philanthropic institutions.
The postcrusade tax scene presents another facet for study, in the
need for recurrent adjustment in assessments and fixed lists. A tax
set by custom or decree might require further assessment so as to
reapportion the burden. This involved reckoning the population,
judging values, enlarging lump sums to accord with recent expansion, designating the individuals for sharing, and making allowance
for hardship. Christian and Mudejar precedent counseled the use of
local officials or locally elected assessors. Such had been the system
functioning at Tortosa, when in 1174 the crown provided for substitution of money in place of certain physical labors. Two Muslims,
counseled by aljama notables, were to adjust tax increment according
to future population increase, or to diminish it in the event—"perish
the thought!"—of population loss.[28] As the first settlers entered
Valencia, quarrels immediately arose in the Alcira region, with rents
a prominent cause; King James intervened, ordering the conflict
resolved by two Christians and two Muslims "suitable and legal,"

[26] Ibn 'Abdūn, *Séville musulmane, le traité*, pp. xi-xii, 10-12, 66-70, 142n., 149n.

[27] Idris, *Berbérie orientale*, ii, 616-619 on collecting; Hopkins, *Medieval Muslim
Government in Barbary*, ch. 4 on collection, esp. pp. 56-57 on the two systems.

[28] Tortosa Convention: "si vero quod absit minuerit, minuant mazemudine." The
ṣāḥib al-madīna an-Nājī (Nage), the *qāḍī* Muhammad, and unspecified local notables
were to serve as adjusters.

under oath, inquiring into antecedent custom and arbitrating.[29] A revised assessment for one levy, affecting all the aljamas of Valencia, was carried through in 1281 by "arrangement" with "all the Saracens" of the kingdom. Later in this decade the crown undertook a grand review of all taxes paid, from the late 1260's through 1289, during the reigns of James, Peter, and Alfonso, by the Mudejars and few Christians at Segárria. A like inquisition covered "the sixteen years past, every year" at Callosa, Jalón, Vall de Laguart, and other dominantly Mudejar places. Since no continuous records had been preserved locally, officials were to "summon witnesses by notary public" and "interrogate the witnesses according to the form in the document sent to you."[30]

Variations within the pattern abounded, including appointment of a special administrator to gather some specific tax, assignment of collecting to the local community itself, designation of a group of entrepreneurs, or recognition of some local politico as the responsible agent. Seignorial estates hardly required an elaborate system; their case will be separately considered. At each level of the crown system it was possible to intrude either a subfarmer or a salaried official. Seen from the king's vantage, the procedure proved relatively simple and effective; an observer attempting to describe its multiple vagaries for any given year, however, and hard put to encompass its patchwork improvisations, might prefer to limit his narration to a selection of typical cases.

---

[29] "Sección de documentos," p. 404, doc. 56 (July 18, 1245): "qui redditus arbitrentur a duobus christianis et duobus sarracenis ydoneys et legalibus prestito ab eis tamen iuramento."

[30] For the 1281 levy see the document in n. 38. Arch. Crown, Alfonso III, Reg. Canc. 80, fol. 85r,v (Nov. 4, 1289): "Bernardo de Libiano baiulo montanearum sarracenorum regni Valencie, mandamus vobis quatenus incontinenti, recepta presenti litera, recipiatis vel recipi faciatis per notarium publicum testes tam sarracenos quam christianos . . . [quantum] valuit redditus vallis de Alaguar vel consuevit valere a sexdecim annis citra, quolibet anno, nobis vel antecessoribus nostris cum omnibus serviciis, servitutibus et tributis que nos vel antecessores nostri quolibet unquam modo accipiebamus"; "item quantum valuit a dicto tempore in xvi annos citra quolibet anno vallis de Xalo; item quantum valuit a dicto tempore xvi annorum citra quolibet anno locus de Verdia cum suo termino, scilicet Callosa. . . ." Fol. 93 (Nov. 6, 1289): "Bernardo de Libiano baiulo montanearum sarracenorum regni Valencie . . . recipere faciatis per notarium puplicum testes . . . quantum valuit locus de Segarria cum terminis et pertinentiis suis a viginti annis ultra, et interrogetis testes secundum formam littere ad vos misse; item. . . ." On Bernard and the *montanea* see Chapter VIII, n. 34.

MUDEJAR TAX FARMERS

Muslim theorists, in common with their Christian counterparts, deplored tax farming even while resigned to it as the most practicable system of collecting. "I am against tax farmers," wrote one of Islam's greatest jurists, Abū Yūsuf of Bagdad, in his treatise on taxes; "they rob the taxpayers by imposing on them what they do not owe, and punish them in repulsive ways to secure their profits." A practical man, Abū Yūsuf then outlined a system of tax farming under the control of some saintly tax administrator, assisted by a staff from the local military garrison. This supervisor, distinct from subsidiary profiteering concessionaires, was to get a salary from the caliph.[31]

The crown, in deploying various forms of tax farming in Valencia, from debt recovery to prior contract, adjusted the manner of Mudejar participation to fit the form chosen. When a Christian or Jewish tax farmer distributed his subfarming contracts, and the subfarmers in turn made arrangements with collectors even lower down the scale, the *amīn* found his place either as salaried supervisory collector or as subfarmer at the most localized level; the responsible upper members of the pyramid had no reason to report on his very subordinate role or to preserve his accounts after incorporating these into their own. When the crown bypassed intermediate agents, farming all, some, or one tax directly to an aljama, the ultimate effect within the Mudejar community was much the same: the *amīn* managed the collection, reporting this time either to the king or to his designated local representative such as the castellan. Even in the case of a direct collector sent by the crown to gather a single tax from Christian and Muslim alike, the collectory mechanism of the *amīn* undoubtedly came into play.

The practice of direct farming, under various arrangements, can be seen in a number of surviving contracts. The Muslims of Alcira "bought" their taxes from King James in the closing year of the crusade, for a "rental" price, thus effecting a saving while sparing the king the bother of introducing his own collectors at this critical

---

[31] Ya'qūb b. Ibrāhīm, Abū Yūsuf al-Anṣārī (d. 798), *Kitāb al-kharāj*, trans. Ben-Shemesh in his *Taxation in Islam*, II, 74, under "Tax Farming and Appointments." Goitein has some information on tax farmers in *Mediterranean Society*, I, 269-270 and passim. On tax collecting by king and church from Valencia's Christians as seen in the ubiquitous tithe, see Burns, *Crusader Valencia*, I, chs. 8-9, esp. pp. 142-144.

time.[32] The Pego Valley Muslims purchased all their revenues without exception in 1262. By the transferal "we sell to you the aljama of the Saracens of Pego," and to any individual subfarmer or group of subfarmers, "the revenues, income, profits, and other receipts that for any reason we have or ought to have in Pego, from the first of January for one year," for 5,500 solidi. The contract designated Peter of Berbegal, archpriest of Daroca and castellan of Pego, to gather this sum "in our stead," no schedule of payment being specified. The archpriest had received the military custody of Pego castle in the summer of 1260 with the promise of 700 solidi a year in salaries for the garrison. Probably an absentee financier who retained his own bailiff at Pego, he had made large loans to the crown, the most recent amounting to 2,000 solidi; he was receiving the revenues of another castle as well, and 1,000 solidi yearly from Solomon of Daroca at the crown salt monopoly of Arcos. The Pego aljama had to pay the archpriest, over and above the flat rate of 5,500 solidi, "all expenditures and expenses of garrisoning the said castle for the said one year." A final clause warned the Muslims against prededucting certain specified expenses or exemptions.[33]

An odd case turns up for 1267. King James "had allotted to the Saracens" of Guadalest Valley all the local taxes and rents "for 7,000 solidi by a document, just as is contained in it" in fuller detail. Some unspecified irregularity or scandal caused the king to void this agreement: "we utterly revoke the aforesaid grant of the said revenues, made to the said Saracens, because it was done fraudulently against

[32] "Sección de documentos," doc. 56 (1245), cited above in n. 29: "de tributo seu logerio quod sarraceni debent nobis dare et facere pro emptione reddituum Algezire."

[33] Arch. Crown, James I, Reg. Canc. 14, fol. 17 (Feb. 5, 1262): vendimus vobis aliame sarracenorum de Pego, et cui vel quibus volueritis, a kalendis Ianuarii . . . ad unum annum additus [sic], exitus, proventus, et alia iura que habeamus et habere debemus qualibet racione in Pego . . . sed vos ultra dictum precium solvatis dicto Petro de Berbegal omnes missiones et expensas custodie dicti castri per dictum unum annum." Reg. Canc. 11, fol. 176 (July 12, 1260) has the archpriest's charter "quod teneatis in custodia et retencione castri de Pego quattuor homines et unam bestiam," receiving the salaries "in redditibus et exitibus nostris de Pego." Reg. Canc. 14, fol. 14 (March 6, 1262) is the assignation of Pego revenues "sicut in carta quam inde vobis fecimus continetur," of Çancharies castle and of Arcos "et salinas ipsius loci." The non-Valencian Masones Muslims in 1263 purchased all their regalian taxes in perpetuity except fines, moneyage, and herbage, at a flat 1,500 solidi of Jaca, to be paid in tri-annual installments (perg. 1,738 [April 12, 1263]).

us [*in fraudem nostram*]." James transferred the terms of the original agreement, but with a price 500 solidi higher, to "the citizen of Valencia, Bernard Taberner." Bernard rendered his accounts the following year "in the valley of Albaida in the settlement that the lord king is making there," but retained his post as "castellan of Guadalest" until 1272.[34] The Mudejar community of Gallinera and Alcalá agreed in 1267 to pay the crown 2,500 besants or over 9,300 solidi a year, half in August and half in December, for two years, in return for "the revenues, income, hospitality charges, bakeries, [and] mills of Gallinera and Alcalá, and all other receipts that we ought every year to collect and have from you."[35]

"The valley of Alaguar and its district," or modern Vall de Laguart in southern Valencia, had brought the crown 5,000 solidi from Christian farmers in 1264; in 1279 the valley's Mudejars farmed their own revenues, paying the crown only 3,400 solidi.[36] The drop in value may represent ravages of war; after the revolt of the late 1270's had come under control, King Peter ordered Vall de Laguart's castle dismantled. In 1281 the aljamas of the surrounding regions joined together to purchase the bulk of the crown revenues for Callosa, Castell, Confrides, Guadalest, Jalón, Polop, Sagra, and Vall de Laguart, contracting to pay half the price in September and half

[34] *Ibid.*, Reg. Canc. 15, fol. 71 (Nov. 18, 1267): "vendimus et concedimus et tributamus vobis Bernardo Tavernarii civi Valencie et vestris redditus, exitus, proventus, et iura omnia . . . in Godalest . . . et attributaveramus aliame sarracenorum eiusdem loci pro septem millibus solidorum, cum carta prout in ea continetur; ita scilicet quod volumus et concedimus vobis quod habeatis et percipiatis ipsos per totum illud tempus ad quod eos attributaveramus dictis sarracenis, secundum quod sarracenis ipsis eos concesseramus et in carta quam inde a nobis habent plenius continetur . . . ; nos autem predictam concessionem de dictis redditibus factam dictis sarracenis, quia facta fuit in fraudem nostram, penitus revocamus; mandantes christianis et sarracenis universis de Godalest quod vobis de redditibus . . . respondere tenentur et de omnibus in dicta carta contentis et concessis [a] nobis dictis sarracenis respondeant vobis." See also *Itinerari*, p. 449 (May 26, 1271), where King James approved the accounts of Taberner, "alcaidus de Godalest," at the new town of Montaberner, "in valle de Albayda in populacione quam dominus rex ibi fecit."

[35] Arch. Crown, James I, Reg. Canc. 15, fol. 88 (March 1, 1267): "redditus, exitus, . . . de Galinera et Alcolano et omnia alia iura que a vobis debemus quolibet anno percipere et habere."

[36] *Ibid.*, Reg. Canc. 13, fol. 174v (May 21, 1264): "de valle de Al[a]guar et terminis eiusdem," later in the document simply as "dicte vallis de Alaguar." Peter III, Reg. Canc. 42, fol. 215v (Feb. 8, 1279). This should not be confused with Algar de Palancia near Sagunto (Murviedro).

in January, with separate listing of revenues for these localities.[37] At this time too the crown arranged a compromise or "indemnity" with all the Mudejar communities of the kingdom of Valencia; each household, whether headed by Muslim man or woman, was to pay a graduated tax of six to twenty solidi. Judah b. Manasseh arrived with an authorizing letter to undertake this kingdom-wide task, doubtless through each local *amīn*.[38]

In 1279 Mogente's aljama and *amīn* received instructions concerning the same house tax,[39] with the local castellan Martin William of Biot acting as overseer.[40] Játiva's Muslims farmed their own *alfarda* in 1283.[41] Where an Islamic lord survived for a time with semiautonomous status, much like a Christian vassal or castellan, the crown sometimes alienated the revenues to him. In 1257 the *qā'id* of Montesa secured control of the herbage on transient sheep in his crossroads region.[42] A quarter-century later, after Montesa was reduced to a dependent aljama like the others, it too farmed its range of revenues from time to time: "the lord king sold to the aljama of the Saracens of Montesa all revenues, income and profits of the town and holdings of Montesa."[43] Perhaps the two episodes differ radically, one involving the Mudejar lord acting as financier, the other involving the community itself in an economizing move.

[37] *Ibid.*, Peter III, Reg. Canc. 51, fol. 27 (March 3, 1281): "de Çagra, de Alaguar . . . omnes redditus"; the order to dismantle went out in September 1283.

[38] *Ibid.*, Reg. Canc. 50, fol. 231 (Jan. 17, 1281): "universis sarracenis in regno Valentie commorantibus . . . noveritis quod nos commisimus . . . Abenmenasse . . . quod colligit pro nobis omnes illos denarios quos racione compositionibus [*sic*] quam nobiscum fescistis dare nobis teneamini quolibet anno." On Judah and his brother Samuel, see Chapter VIII, part 5.

[39] Arch. Crown, Peter III, Reg. Canc. 42, fol. 163 (Nov. 3, 1279), confirming a privilege from James I and allowing those not owning houses to pay "segond lur poder."

[40] *Ibid.*, fol. 175v (Nov. 19, 1279): "al alcayt de Muxen," here unnamed, "que cascu dels moros casats de Muxen donassen vi solidos." He succeeded Peter of Ahones in 1276, with an income of 1,500 solidi a year; see fol. 177 (Nov. 23, 1279), and Reg. Canc. 38, fols. 17 (Oct. 14, 1276) and 84 (Oct. 28, 1276).

[41] *Ibid.*, Reg. Canc. 60, fol. 91 (April 18, 1283): "illi sarraceni Xative qui collegerunt alfardas"; the crown is investigating excessive collection, beyond the sum owed.

[42] Doc. in Chapter V, n. 96.

[43] Arch. Crown, Peter III, Reg. Canc. 51, fol. 24 (Jan. 11, 1281): "dominus rex vendidit aliame sarracenorum Muntesie omnes redditus, exitus, et proventus ville et possessionum de Muntesa."

An early example of a Mudejar lord receiving crown taxes is the contract given the Moorish castellan of the Tárbena region in 1264. The *qā'id* Muḥammad 'Amr b. Isḥāq (Emnebenezach) had succeeded in 1259 to this small principality, so troublesome to the crown in the several Mudejar revolts of the thirteenth century; from late 1264 his nephew Bakrūn (Bocharon) took over the rule of a segment of the region. In November 1264 King James reached an agreement giving "to you, the *qā'id* Muḥammad, and to yours, the entire castle of Tárbena completely, with its villages, districts, and appurtenances, and with all the revenues and income of the same castle." Muḥammad was to collect these, then split them with the crown: "we are to have half, and you and yours to have the other half, without any gainsaying." From the "common" total or gross, the *qā'id* was to prededuct "a suitable expenditure for the task of custody of the same castle."[44] This was not a matter of the king's surrendering half his crown income in order to conciliate a powerful Muslim baron and ensure his zeal in collecting taxes; it represented, rather, an intrusion of the king into what had been an alodial or financially independent situation up to 1258. The great Mudejar barons had held their castles free of rents, or else surrendered a tributary share. The ex-ruler Abū Zayd, for example, obliged himself in 1229 and in 1236 to pay the king a fourth of revenues from all castles conquered by the Muslim allies of the crusaders, while the famed rebel lord of southern Valencia, al-Azraq, had at first kept his six main castles free and quit of all taxes.[45] Thus the Tárbena contract signals a decline in status from alodial tributary to taxed vassal.

A similar case was "the castle and town of Polop with its districts," together with three towns of the Jalón region. Here again the Mudejar lord and his Muslims were "frank and free," but had to pay the

[44] *Ibid.*, James I, Reg. Canc. 13, fol. 236 (Nov. 5, 1264): "damus et concedimus vobis alcaydo Mahomet et vestris totum castrum integriter de Tarbana cum alqueriis, terminis, et pertinentiis suis, et cum omnibus iuribus eiusdem, ita tamen quod de omnibus redditibus et exitibus ipsius castri, deducta competenti missione ad opus custodie dicti castri de communi, habeamus nos medietatem et vos et vestri aliam medietatem libere et sine aliqua contradiccione." The full story of this fief and of the role Muḥammad played is told in Burns, *Islam under the Crusaders*, ch. 13, part 3.

[45] *Colección diplomática*, doc. 151 (April 20, 1229, renewed May 28, 1236): "dabimus vobis semper quartam partem libere, sine vestra expensa et missione, omnium exituum, reddituum, et proventuum . . . salva semper vestra quarta parte." For al-Azraq, see the documentation in Burns, *Islam under the Crusaders*, ch. 14, part 1.

small sum of 300 solidi twice a year.[46] All such cases, though not really involving even that kind of farming by which a reasonably corresponding lump sum was guaranteed by the aljama, do bear a resemblance to it and do give some appearance of buying off. Finally a number of individual Mudejars paid some taxes directly, or at least they entered the final accounting as important specific items. At Alfandech Valley, for example, "besides the 9,000 solidi" collected generally, the crown "received in money from the village of a certain Saracen from Murcia 201 solidi and 6 pence." The entries following consist of seven Mudejars, each with his tax contribution, the sums ranging from 100 solidi, through 76 and 20, to 10.[47] Similarly at Ribarroja an item appended to the general reckoning reads: "received from a certain Saracen of Liria, for a service tax, 50 solidi." At Alcira in 1280 King Peter put his seal to a receipt prepared for the Mudejars of Játiva, witnessing that they had paid the crown 5,076 solidi.[48]

A prominent Mudejar collector, acting as a superbailiff over an extensive grouping of bailiates near Denia called "the mountain district," discussed below, was "our Saracen, Ibrāhīm b. Ṣumādiḥ [Abençumada]." Under the titles *amīn, muḥtasib*, and probably *mushrif*, he supervised collections here regularly during the early 1280's. In 1284, for example, he delivered "2,400 solidi from the bailiate of Pop" to the king's treasurer at Tarazona. Later that year he transferred 3,000 solidi, just gathered "from the Saracens of the mountains of the kingdom of Valencia" to defray "the expenses and requirements" of a commission returning prisoners of war to the sultan of Granada. By November he was himself a prisoner, seemingly on charges of financial misconduct, with law officers of Valencia city and of the crown vying for his person. Restored to favor, Ibrāhīm formally reentered the office of collector for the mountains

[46] Arch. Crown, James I, Reg. Canc. 12, fol. 118v (Sept. 30, 1263), a detailed conveyance of Polop and Altea "francham et liberam . . . cum introitibus et exitibus." Reg. Canc. 16, fol. 156 (April 22, 1269): "ita scilicet quod tu pro predictis tenearis facere et facias nobis et nostris annuatim de cetero, et loco nostri alcaydo castri de Berdia, ad retentionem ipsius castri, sexcentos solidos regalium Valencie annuales, per tres terminos"; the thirds fell due respectively on St. John's Day, in October, and in January.

[47] *Ibid.*, Reg. Canc. 17, fol. 66 (1265): "item ultra dicta ix millia solidorum recepit in denariis de alqueria cuiusdam sarraceni de Murcia, cci solidos, vi denarios."

[48] *Ibid.*, fol. 66v (1265): "item recepit de quodam sarraceno de Liria pro servicio, l solidos." The Alcira document is above in Chapter II, n. 26.

in March of 1286, only to fall under a cloud again within six months. By this time the Mudejar tax system throughout the Valencian kingdom was suffering a crisis of disorganization, necessitating a reform tour by the king's own treasurer. During this turmoil, Ibrāhīm drops from view, soon replaced by the first of a series of Christian superintendents over the "mountain" bailiates.[49]

ENCUMBRANCES, CREDITORS, AND THE *Violari*

Bailiwick administrative control, as well as any tax farming contract, was usually encumbered by small salaries, pensions, and subordinate debts having nothing to do with the tax operation itself. The crown attached debts to bailiwicks as a convenient way of consolidating multiple small obligations. Islamic tax administration employed a similar "assignation" (*ḥawāla*).[50] In Arago-Catalonia the technique constituted an important element in the total operation of collection and disbursement. Since the creditor did not have to arrange any part of the farming but merely waited for his money, he was not a tax farmer but an investor; in terms of objective activity, however, he had an essential role in keeping the system flexible. Borrowing comprised only a part of the king's financial arrangements, and was usually rather a credit operation, with tax receipts themselves the main direct source of money. In his own way the

[49] Arch. Crown, Peter III, Reg. Canc. 52, fol. 89 (Oct. 26, 1284): "quatenus recipiatis in computum Abrafim Abinçumada duos [*sic*] millia et quadringentos solidorum regalium de baiulia de Pop, quos tradidit in Tirasona fideli nostro thesaurario Bernardo Scribe loco nostri." Fol. 66v (Oct. 28, 1284): "magistro racionali domus nostre sarracenos captivos . . . [et] quod per Abrahim Abençumada sarracenum alaminum nostrum faciatis dari . . . tria millia solidorum regalium . . . a sarracenis montanearum dicti regni Valencie pro expensis et necessariis suis . . . in viatico quod pro nobis facit ad regem Granate." Reg. Canc. 43, fol. 74 (Nov. 22, 1284): "vos cepistis et captum tenetis Abraphim Abensumada sarracenum nostrum." Fol. 81 (Dec. 9, 1284): "et quod faciat inquisitionem contra Abrafim Abençumada super hiis de quibus inculpabatur." Reg. Canc. 56, fol. 93v (May 4, 1285), published in Romano, "Hermanos Abenmenassé," appendix, doc. 17. Arch. Crown, Alfonso III, Reg. Canc. 65, fol. 114 (March 26, 1286): "Abrahim Abencumade collectori reddituum nostrorum morariarum sive locorum sarracenorum in montaneis regni Valencie." Reg. 67, fol. 40 (June 23, 1286): "Abrafimo mostalafio et universis sarracenis dictarum montanearum." On the "mountain district," the Mudejar tax crisis of 1286, and the *mushrif* title, see Chapter VIII, nn. 33, 34, and text. See also Burns, *Islam under the Crusaders*, p. 261n.

[50] Halil İnalcık, "Hawāla," *EI²*, 11, 283-285.

lender was the obverse side of the bailiate network, supplying short-term loans or loans in the form of credit for the crown's day-to-day operations.

The king signed a steady stream of promissory notes or bonds, for everything from purchase of a mule to payment of a salary, much like a modern businessman signing a check. His treasurer then assigned and reassigned these against imminent revenues or against the sums pledged by their buyers, expressing the loan or debt at a higher figure to cover interest or profit. When interest compounded on a delayed debt, the creditor might discount it, accepting a reduced sum in order to get a cash settlement. This system, in which barons and bishops of the highest rank enthusiastically played the role of disguised moneylender along with the lower orders, prevailed alike in England and in the realms of Aragon.[51]

A device for bestowing patronage, but sometimes for arranging a concealed loan, was a kind of rent charge called a *violari*, from Latin *vivolarium*, for "lifetime use." It attached to a given tax as an annuity to be paid by the collector and entered his books after the fashion of an expense to defray. Beneficiaries could obtain these, for a time or more usually for life, either by outright purchase or by a gift of capital to the king in return for a conveyance phrased as a free grant. Like the corodies they resembled, which the crown imposed on ecclesiastical establishments, *violaris* had become a common phenomenon by this century.

Technically a purchase of income or taxes, and therefore exclud-

---

[51] On governmental credit operations see also *Cambridge Economic History of Europe*, III, ch. 7; Usher, *Early History of Deposit Banking in Mediterranean Europe*, I, part 1, passim. On credit operations by forced and voluntary loans, see also Bowsky, *Finance of the Commune of Siena*, chs. 7, 8. M. M. Fryde rejects the charge that assignations were ruinous or at the root of other evils in financial administration. Admitting that they were "unfortunate" by their chaotic nature, he concludes that contemporary circumstances made them "inevitable" if authorities wanted to operate beyond current or ordinary income; they had positive good effects "as a kind of check circulation, decreasing the costs and risks, and increasing the possibilities of quicker use of the revenues, often to be collected in distant territories" ("Public Credit of German Principalities and Towns in the Middle Ages," pp. 233-235); he cautions against confusing assignment either with farming or with pledges. For the system at work in twelfth and thirteenth-century England, see Richardson, *English Jewry under Angevin Kings*, ch. 2, "The King's Borrowings." Jews were a minority in this moneylending; and since they may not have received interest on these loans in England, they were reluctant to hazard their capital so unprofitably (p. 65).

ing interest and usury, the *violari* paid over fourteen percent interest on the capital surrendered, or double the interest of a perpetual annuity or *censal mort*. It was redeemable only at the seller's will; the government preferred to retire it soon, often by selling others at a more favorable rate, thus converting the long-term investment of the creditor into a short-term loan. It was tax-exempt, and negotiable in the primitive sense that it could be resold from hand to hand. Beginning as a gratuity or annuity of provision, probably from the late twelfth century in Catalonia, for a period of two or more life-times, it had matured into a commercialized purchase of capital funds. The single life-period now common, reckoned on an adjustable scale, ordinarily ran from seven to fourteen years. The *violari* found a ready market from all classes, especially from the modest or timid investor. It was to spread throughout the realms of Aragon as the preferred device for municipal credit from about 1340.[52]

Crown records for Valencia disclose a number of Mudejar rent charges or *violaris*. In 1258, for example, King James granted to Muḥammad, a resident of Gandía, "thirty solidi of Valencia as annuity . . . from the community levy" of the Beniopa Muslims.[53] The king made a like grant in 1260 to another Muḥammad, drawing from the industrial tax on the famed paper industry of Játiva. "For us and ours we give and grant to you, Muḥammad of Morella, *qāḍī* of the Saracens of the Moorish quarter of Játiva, a hundred solidi of Valencia each year while you hold the *qāḍī* function for the said Saracens; in such wise that you are to have and receive the money every year, from our revenues and income from the mill tax on paper that the said Saracens pay."[54] The letter affords

[52] Rodón Binué, *Lenguaje técnico del feudalismo*, pp. 257-258. Usher, *Early History of Deposit Banking in Mediterranean Europe*, I, 530-531, under *censal*, and text, pp. 143-159. On analogous monastic corodies, see the extensive treatment in Burns, *Crusader Valencia*, I, ch. 15. A list of tax accounts of 1315 supplies a comprehensive view of such *violaris* and claims throughout the kingdom of Valencia. Above the Júcar River 47,000 solidi went to *violaris*, to assigned salaries of higher officials, and to burdens such as rebates for use in public works; they included three claims on the city granary and one "sobre les dites rendes de la moreria per violari"; below the Júcar the total was 57,000 (*Rentas de Aragón*, pp. 95-105, 116-119).

[53] Arch. Crown, James I, Reg. Canc. 9, fol. 29v (May 4, 1258): "triginta solidos regalium Valencie censuales . . . super peyta." On this Muḥammad see Chapter IV, n. 67.

[54] Arch. Crown, James I, Reg. Canc. 11, fol. 191v (Jan. 20, 1260): "per nos et nostros damus et concedimus tibi Mahometo Almorelli alcadi [*sic*] sarracenorum ra-

as well a rare glimpse of the Mudejar-manned paper industry, still flourishing in the 1260's.

A similar case to that of Muḥammad was the life annuity awarded in 1267 to Sa'īd b. Yaḥyā from the butchery utilities. "For us and ours we give and concede to you Sa'īd b. Yaḥyā, leader of the Saracens of the city of Valencia, throughout your life a hundred solidi of Valencia, to be had and received yearly from our revenues and receipts from the meat stalls of the Saracens of Valencia, because of your aforesaid office of *qāḍī*." This was to be paid him "in such wise that you will have, and are to have and get, the said hundred solidi from our revenues and receipts in the meat stalls, every year henceforth all your life, as long as you exercise the said office and conduct yourself well and faithfully in it," specifically as salary "for your labor and office as is contained above." In closing his directive, King James "firmly" ordered "our bailiff at Valencia that you be given and paid from our aforesaid revenues and receipts of the aforesaid meat stalls annually a hundred solidi."[55]

In 1277 King Peter confirmed one of his father's *violaris*: "Peter by the grace of God etc. to his faithful bailiff of Beniopa, health and favor; we order that you pay those thirty solidi of Valencia that Muḥammad b. Yumn [Abeniumen], Saracen of Beniopa, is accustomed to receive, [and that] he claims, showing a charter of the said James of happy memory, king of the Aragonese, our father, from the revenues of Beniopa annually, as you will see contained in the

---

valli Xative c solidos regalium quolibet anno dum alcadiam dictorum sarracenorum tenueris, ita quod habeas ipsos et recipias quolibet anno in redditibus et exitibus nostris de almaxeram [*sic*] papyri quem dicti sarraceni faciunt." Note the form *alcadus* here rather than *alcaydus*, indicating a *qāḍī* rather than a *qā'id* or castellan, though *alcaidia* occurs once later in the document.

[55] *Ibid.*, Reg. Canc. 15, fol. 85 (March 14, 1267). "Per nos et nostros damus et concedimus tibi Çahato Abinhaia alcaydo sarracenorum civitatis Valentie in tota vita tua centum solidos regalium habendos et percipiendos annuatim in redditibus et iuribus nostris carnicerie sarracenorum Valentie ratione predicti officii tui alcaydi. Ita quod tu singulis annis de cetero in vita tua, dum dictum officium exerceris et in ipso bene et fideliter te habebis, habeas et percipias dictos c solidos de redditibus et iuribus nostris carnicerie . . . pro labore et offico tuo ut superius continetur. Mandantes firmiter baiulo nostro Valentie . . . quod de redditibus et iuribus nostris predictis carnicerie predicte donetur et solvatur tibi ut dictum est annuatim c solidos." The name Abenhaia might suggest something like Ibn Ḥayyān, but three variants elsewhere for the same man afford a wider base of interpretation.

said charter."[56] One Ibrāhīm received assignments during the 1280's to recover substantial loans to the crown, once for nearly 3,000 solidi and once for 20,000.[57] Mudejar creditors of the crown turn up both within tax farming contracts and more loosely in documents like precontract lists of debtors. In an accounting of 1262 with the bailiff for the Valencian kingdom below the Júcar River, concerning returns from the office of weights and measures for both Christians and Mudejars, King James approved an outlay of 21,100 solidi for debts. Of this, 16,500 may represent the farming price prepaid by Simon of Foces, lieutenant or procurator general of Valencia kingdom; at any rate his

[56] *Ibid.*, Peter III, Reg. Canc. 40, fol. 26 (Oct. 7, 1277). "Petrus dei gratia etc. fideli suo baiulo Beniope salutem et gratiam. Mandamus vobis quatenus illos triginta solidos regalium, quos Mahomet Abeniumen sarracenus de Beniopa recipere consuevit ut asserit cum carta dicti Iacobi inclite recordacionis regis Aragonum patris nostri de redditibus Beniope, ipsos sibi solvatis annuatim ut in dicta carta videbitis contineri."

[57] *Ibid.*, Alfonso III, Reg. Canc. 67, fol. 7v (May 10, 1286), for 20,000 solidi; and see the details on his family in the gift from Peter III, renewed by Alfonso in Reg. 63, fol. 40 (Feb. 2, 1286): "tradimus vobis Axie sarracene, uxori quondam Haiçe sarraceni, et Abrafim Bellido genero tuo et filiis vestris reallum nostrum Valencie tenendum dum nobis placuerit, secundum quod illustrissimus dominus Petrus . . . pater noster vobis commendaverat reallum predictum." Reg. Canc. 82, fol. 89v (Dec. 13, 1290): "collectoribus alfardarum sarracenorum Valencie, Xative, et Uxonis quod observent Abraymo Bellido assignationem sibi factam per Arnaldum de Bastida de quibusdam pecunie quantitatibus ut in albarano dicti Abraymi de Bellido continetur." Fol. 170 (Dec. 18, 1290): "assignet Abraymo Bellido . . . duo millia xx solidorum . . . item cccc solidos, qui debebantur eidem Abraymo ratione illorum apparatiorum que se tenet cum alfondico regni Valencie." In 1338 Peter IV was to give his court entertainer, the Játiva Mudejar "Çahat Mascum, mimum seu juglar de Exabeba," a hundred solidi yearly from the revenues of Játiva, to cover his expenses for as long as he accompanied the court; he made the same provision "pro Ali Eziqua sarraceno de Jativa, mimo seu juglar de rabeu" (*Documents per l'historia de la cultura catalana mig-eval*, ed. Antoni Rubió y Lluch, 2 vols. [Barcelona 1908-1921], I, doc. 100); Catalan *xabeba* is a shepherd's pipe; *rabeuet* is a three-stringed rebec. The Mudejars exploited the *violari* concept individually in order to amass ready capital, often fleeing if bankruptcy threatened; by the early fifteenth century such misadventures were causing serious loss of Valencian Mudejar taxpayers, so that the crown thenceforth required a license from the bailiff general for this kind of operation. See the *Aureum opus*, Alfonso IV, doc. 31, fol. 184v: "loca sarracenorum nostrorum regni Valencie deteriorant nimis in eorum populis propter ea inter alia quia ob facilitatem quam inveniunt diversorum emptorum et volencium emere censualia et violaria super dictos sarracenos et eorum bona; dicti sarraceni vendunt super se et bonis suis censualia et violaria emptoribus predictis, et demum nolentibus aut nequeuntibus solvere . . . coguntur derelinquere loca nostra predicta et de facto se transferunt alibi," to be safe from prosecution.

testator received that much for the deceased Simon's estate. Of the remaining 4,600 shared out to three distinguished public figures and one Mudejar, the largest sum or 1,400 solidi went to the latter, "the Saracen of Jérica, Waḍḍaḥ [Ouetar]. The Mudejar held the highest debt from the crown, save one; considering the documentary company he kept, he must have been a major figure among Valencia's Muslims.[58]

Sometimes the notice of debt lacks circumstance. Thus in 1268 King James drew up an elaborate instrument of debt in favor of Arnold of Romaní, who had both loaned money to the king and paid a large number of debts for him, to the extent of 19,435 solidi plus 750 besants, all to be taken by tax farming Játiva; James noted that the financier had "now loaned to us in Valencia 4,000 solidi to supplement the payment that we have now made to the $q\bar{a}'id$ Muḥammad."[59] On the face of it, this might represent a standard loan from one of many Muslim leaders named Muḥammad; but very probably it relates to the project seen in a similar lengthy consolidation of debts into a tax-farming instrument drawn on the revenues of Murviedro only a few weeks later for a consortium of financiers led by three Christians. This list includes "12,000 solidi that you have now loaned us to make the payment that we ought to make to the $q\bar{a}'id$ Muḥammad for [purchasing from him] the castle and town of Tárbena." Apparently embroiled in an abortive revolt, Muḥammad was about to depart the kingdom under safeguard, and King James wished to purchase his castle as a gift for the current royal mistress, Berengaria Alfonso.[60]

[58] Arch. Crown, James I, Reg. Canc. 14, fol. 13v (March 1, 1262): "de omnibus redditibus et exitibus tabule Valencie anni preteriti, ita quod solvistis de mandato nostro . . . Ouetar sarraceno de Xerica m et cccc solidos." Carroz, lord of Rebollet, got 1,000 solidi, as did the castellan of Almenara; William of Plana, a financier regularly farming large revenues, collected 1,200 solidi. See also fol. 9 (Feb. 20, 1262), where the *tabula* of this document is specified as the "tabula nostra pensi Valencie." Eximèn (Llop) of Foces was fifth in the line of Valencia's procurators, from 1257. If the pronunciation of the Mudejar's name stressed the labial, reconstruction might yield 'Ubāda, 'Ubayda.

[59] *Ibid.*, Reg. Canc. 15, fol. 99 (March 4, 1268): "item ex alia parte debemus vobis dicto Arnaldo de Romanino et vestris quattuor millia solidorum regalium quos modo in Valencia mutuastis ad complementum solucionis quam modo fecimus alcaydo Mahometo." The date, "quarto [nonas] Marcii," is filled out from extrinsic evidence.

[60] *Ibid.*, fol. 97 (May 1, 1268): "videlicet de duodecim millibus solidorum que

Simple debts could be handled after the general pattern of loan-debts and *violaris*, the crown assigning them either as disbursements or as remissions of the full sum owed. Remissions might also represent reduction of tax due to hardship or bad harvest, or a gesture of favor or conciliation toward an aljama, or indeed an adjustment or reassessment of any kind; consequently it is often difficult to discern cases where remission was used to retire small debts. One such item occurs at Buñol in 1257 concerning 400 besants owed: "the Saracens kept this at the command of the lord king to pay for the goats that he ordered to be given to them."[61] Fifteen hundred solidi worth of goats seems an uncommonly large supply of that commodity to donate to a single town, enough indeed to provide four knight's fiefs if invested in that direction. Since Buñol was a castle, however, it seems possible that the gift had something to do with its surrender after the crusade or after the recent revolt, unless it represented some investment or resettlement project such as King James was mounting among Valencia's Mudejars elsewhere.

This same list has 800 besants left in the hands of Alfandech's Moors, "because of the sale" of their own revenues to them as a tax farm. Of the twenty-seven monetary totals received from thirty Mudejar centers, no less than nineteen sums were remitted in whole or in part, of which three (representing four places) went to specifically named individuals. Alcira had its 100 dismissed, Burriana its 100, Carbonera its 600, Cheroles and Seta 150 of their 200, Chulilla 50 of its 150, Jijona 100 of its 300, Mogente 100 of its 400, Onda its 100, Relleu its 200, Sumacárcel and Cárcer 50 of their 100, Tous and Tárbena 300 of their 400, and Valencia city's quarter 50 of its 200. These figures must be multiplied three to four times to give the same sums in Valencian solidi. Calpe returned its 100 to the castellan, while Confrides' 100, Guadalest's 500, and Segorbe's 100, some 3,000 solidi in all, went to individuals who were presumably creditors. The king's agent (*porter*) Peter William was general collector over all these Mudejar returns.[62]

---

nunc nobis mutuastis ad faciendam solucionem quam alcaydo Mahometi facere debebamus pro castro et villa de Tarbena."

[61] *Ibid.*, Reg. Canc. 8, fol. 36 (Nov. 24, 1257): "cccc bisantios, quos retinuerunt sarraceni de mandato domini regis ratione caprarum quas eis da[ri mandavit]."

[62] *Ibid.* The document uses *remisit* ten times, *dimisit* four, perhaps indicating repayment as against antecedent dismissal, but perhaps merely a careless usage for

Sometimes a remission or debt would appear in the more orthodox guise of a disbursement, arranged separately from the revenue list. A 1264 survey of Gandía's revenues under nearly fifty headings had such a series of disbursements appended under twelve headings, the largest item being 3,000 solidi to William of Castellnou. "The Moors of Beniopa" got 400 solidi, actually a remission repeated from the income list where they paid 6,000 solidi. "Ṭalḥa [Talpha], Saracen of Beniopa" received 50 solidi. "Al-Azraq [Aladrach] the wood-worker," who had appeared among the taxpayers as giving 3 solidi and 4 pence for his shop, got 30 solidi; this seems to be a payment for work, since it is followed by entries of 30 solidi "to repair the bakehouses" and 104 solidi "to repair the houses."[63] Such debts, expenditures for local public repairs, and small bills owed must not be confused with the expenses and salaries of the collection itself.

Though detailed evidence is hard to come by, Mudejar participation in financial and loan activities in general is attested by their inclusion in the Christian law code of Valencia from its earliest form, and on the same level of interest per loan as were Christians and Jews. When Mudejar, Jew, or Christian transgressed these legal limits they committed usury in civil law—as in demanding interest beyond a five-year period, taking more after interest had come to equal the principal, or increasing by any means the maximum of twenty percent interest per year.[64] Presence of a debtors' category at

___

the identical reality. On *dimittere* as the common verb in wills for leaving legacies, enfeoffing, and the like, see Rodón Binué, *Lenguaje técnico del feudalismo*, pp. 81-83. The castellan of Calpe, Peter Martin of Pedrissol (de Pedrixola) had received the castellany at a salary of 150 solidi a year on February 26, and was assigned here 750 solidi, probably a loan reimbursed. On Peter Martin see Chapter VIII, n. 140.

[63] Arch. Crown, James I, Reg. Canc. 17, fols. 37-38 (July 2, 1265, concerning 1264): "item lexa lo seyor infant . . . als moros de Beniopa, cccc sous"; "item an Talpha sarray de Beniopa, l sous; item an Aladrach fuster, xxx sous; item a adobar los forns, xxx sous; item a adobar les cases . . . ciiii sous."

[64] *Fori antiqui Valentiae*, rub. LXVII, no. 1: "christiani, iudei, sarraceni non acci-piant pro usuris nisi tantum iiii^or denarios in mense de xx solidis"; this applied, whatever prior agreement or collateral might be involved. Thus in Valencia 4 pence per month could be taken by anyone for every loan of 240 pence, amounting to 48 pence or twenty percent per year. Elsewhere in James's realms civil law codes allowed Christians to take twelve percent on private loans, and Jews and Muslims up to twenty percent; if the loan ran longer than a year, the interest rate could rise to nearly seventeen percent. In practice, though the local market price controlled the value of money taken at loan, so that it fluctuated, the twenty percent maximum may have applied to the net profit on the full run of a financier's lending; lenders

the Mudejar-conducted prison in Chivert's charter also indicates loan activity, at least at the local and small-loan level. The practice of publicly regulated debt slavery, especially when used to acquire capital for a business venture, is another indicator.[65] A debt extension in 1258, though as general in tone as the law's statute, reinforces the legal presumption of coequal role in moneylending. In it King James enjoined the creditors of three Játiva residents, Bernard of

commonly, and in some places legally from the 1260's on, concealed the interest within the loan and then took compound interest on overdue loans rather than refinance them (Richard W. Emery, *The Jews of Perpignan in the Thirteenth Century, an Economic Study Based on Notarial Records* [New York, 1959], pp. 82, 86-88, 100). Emery's research shows an average ten percent profit on fixed rental charges on property, and therefore suggests that twenty percent on risk loans did not reflect the higher actual rate. Perpignan lay within the realms of Aragon, but constituted an unusual situation at the time, lacking sufficient capital in an expanding economy (pp. 95-98, 106-107, 126), and its almost exclusively moneylending Jewish stratum (pp. 25, 79) was equally anomalous. The crown issued, to its own profit, waivers of prosecution when a financier exceeded the regulated rates and was caught. Canon law and civil codes diverged in their application of usury theory to circumstanced life; the consequent dialogue of spirited action and counteraction, though widely noted, has not been examined with any degree of legal sophistication. See also Tourtoulon, *Jaime I*, II, 127-128, and the Balearics law similar to the Valencian in *Colección diplomática*, doc. 402 (Aug. 20, 1251). Usury was also against the tenets of Islam.

[65] By a law of James I, no one could enslave a Mudejar on account of a debt; voluntarily to enter such slavery in order to liquidate a debt required a license from the king's bailiff. Vicenta Cortés offers early background and fifteenth-century details in *La esclavitud en Valencia durante el reinado de los Reyes Católicos (1479-1516)* (Valencia, 1964), pp. 40-43; see also *Aureum opus*, doc. 88, fol. 27, as cited there. Mudejars commonly entered debt slavery in the Balearics in the thirteenth century, either to pay debts or as part of a debt-scheme to acquire capital for business ventures; psychologically and materially these temporary slaves differed from real slaves. They could stave off default and permanent slavery by fresh borrowing, and the creditor could "sell" or otherwise deploy them as a financial asset. See Lourie, "Free Moslems in the Balearics," pp. 634-635; as she remarks, Charles Verlinden was unable to find examples of it in mainland documentation in the thirteenth century (see his *L'esclavage dans l'Europe médiévale*, 1 vol. to date, on Spain and France [Bruges, 1955], p. 275), though a document of 1438 referred to it as of ancient custom among Valencia's Muslims (*Aureum opus*, John II, doc. 2, fol. 204: "consuetudinem sarracenorum valde antiquatam et observatam in regno Valentie," applying also to their minor children). Even at Barcelona the Mudejars required "debt instruments" for overseas trade, written in Arabic, on such a scale as to justify licensing these as a monopoly: "Iahudanum filium Astrugi Bonisenioris iudeum Barchinone . . . [ad] conficiendum instrumenta debitoria arabice facienda per sarracenos" (*Documents de la cultura catalana mig-eval*, 1, doc. 12 [Dec. 13, 1294]).

Pamies, Bernard of Soler and Raymond Colteller, from seizing their persons or real property, or the several kinds of movable properties listed, "to pay any debts that they may owe anywhere, either by themselves or for others, to Christians, Jews, or Saracens."[66]

King James himself reveals that Muslim financiers held a large number of crown rents at the time of his accession. "All the revenues" of Aragon and Catalonia were mortgaged in whole or in part "to the Jews and to the Saracens."[67] This text poses some difficulties, though a minimal reading would still give Mudejar financiers a role in crown finance. Shneidman has recently challenged the text, on the grounds that so overwhelming a role for the Jews so early in the reign is improbable; he suggests that the king's memory failed him here.[68] His point as to the Jews, and implicitly as to Mudejars, is well taken, if perhaps overstated in its details; but the solution may lie rather in a universal misunderstanding of the text than in the king's memory. James compiled this early part of his memoirs in his prime, at Játiva in 1244, showed himself remarkably careful in such details, drew upon the witness of his former counselors as well as upon his memory, was not trying to make some side point here or writing under the influence of an extrinsic emotion, and was describing the single greatest government crisis of his early years, a mortgaging amply documented by other evidence.[69] He may have exaggerated, of course, to heighten the reader's sympathy; some scribe or later rewriter might just possibly have interpolated the "tro" phrase in question.

On the other hand, one can argue that the current understanding of the phrase is correct. There are no registers, and few parchments about Jews, until after mid-century, so that the absence of evidence about Jewish financiers loses force as an argument for suspecting the text's correctness. Moreover, Jews had more potential as finan-

---

[66] Arch. Crown, James I, Reg. Canc. 10, fol. 62 (April 28, 1258): "non compellatis nec compelli permittatis Bernardum . . . habitantes de Xativa nec bona eorum ad solvenda aliqua debita que ipsi debeant in aliqua parte christianis, iudeis, vel sarracenis tam pro se quam pro aliquo alio, ipsis tamen assecurantibus quod dicto termino solvant."

[67] *Llibre dels feyts*, ch. 11: "e toda la renda . . . era empenyorada tro als iueus e als sarraïns, e encara les honors, que eren set-centes cavalleries en aquell temps, e nostre pare lo rei don Pere havia-les totes donades, e venudes de cent trenta enfora."

[68] *Rise of the Aragonese-Catalan Empire*, II, 439-440, 456.

[69] See above, Chapter II, part I.

ciers at this time than the skeptical interpretation allows them, especially since men of modest means combined into *consortia* to farm taxes, while others used land (which Jews owned plentifully in Catalonia) to secure their contract type of tax farm. After all this has been said, nevertheless, it still seems highly improbable that the kingdom's Jews and Moors could have held all the revenues, impoverishing the government in the way James describes; the majority of loans, even at the height of Jewish wealth, came from Christians.[70]

The text in fact can support a milder reading. The original manuscript, displaying a bare minimum of punctuation, seems to call for two pauses;[71] if one supplies a comma before "tro" (no edition does) and a comma after "sarraïns" (Soldevila does, while Casacuberta prefers a semicolon), and if one then avoids translating "tro als" as merely "als," a satisfactory understanding emerges. From Latin *intro*, and equivalent to Catalan *fins* or Castilian *hasta*, "tro" means "to," "until," or by extension "(even) including"; here it can make the phrase mean "the revenues all were mortgaged, even to Jews and Saracens," or perhaps "were pledged [to lenders], including the Jews and Saracens." The sentence thus makes sense for the first time, both structurally and in its use of "tro"; the sense of the whole is that all revenues, and the rashly distributed fiefs as well, had been mortgaged to various lenders, "all the way to Jews and Saracens," giving even the aliens a share in this national disgrace.

Mudejars also collected some taxes from local Christians during the postcrusade years, as has been seen; but this happened rarely and only in mixed situations where common sense recommended it. Though Mudejars engaged in international and domestic commerce, could join with Christian partners in business ventures, and loaned money to the crown against public revenues, they undoubtedly had to operate more discreetly than the Jews in financial and official affairs of state. History had not prepared for them a situation like that in the homeland of King James's queen, Violant or Yolanda of Hun-

---

[70] See below, Chapter VIII, part 6.

[71] Bibl. Univ. Barc., MSS, no. 1, is by far the best manuscript of the king's memoirs. It can now be examined in photographic reproduction, *Libre dels feyts del rey en Jacme, edición facsímil del manuscrito de Poblet* (1343) *conservado en la biblioteca universitaria de Barcelona*, ed. Martín de Riquer (Barcelona, 1972); see fol. 6.

gary, where Muslims held Christian office and even intermarried with Christians.[72] The early *Furs* of Valencia took care to exclude Muslims not only from "town government or any public office" but specifically from "the bailiate."[73]

[72] Gregory IX protested the Hungarian practice; Grayzel conveniently gathers several of these condemnations (*Church and Jews*, doc. 53 [Aug. 23, 1225], doc. 61 [March 3, 1231], and doc. 73 [Aug. 12, 1233]). In the relatively autonomous enclaves described in Burns, *Islam under the Crusaders* (chs. 13-14), a Christian vassal or farmer could find himself accepting his holding from a Muslim. Violant or Yolant is the Castilian Yolanda or Violante, and sometimes English Yolanda.

[73] *Fori antiqui Valentiae*, rub. cxxix, no. 3: "publici usurarii, nec iudei, [nec] sarraceni baiuliam vel curiam vel aliquod officium publicum non teneant." The original law referred to Valencia city, but probably applied elsewhere as the code was extended; it did not, in any case, prohibit Muslims from playing the loanfinancier through others serving as actual bailiffs. See also *Colección diplomática*, doc. 236 (Nov. 11, 1241), or *Aureum opus*, doc. 13, fols. 4v-5v, where James outlined at length the procedures to follow when the borrower is a Christian or the loan is between Christians, adding "in debitis iudeorum et sarracenorum non ponimus aliquam formam in presenti, preterito, et futuro, sed componant inter se, sicut voluerint, et fiant soluciones eis secundum quod in instrumento iudeorum continetur." Cf. doc. 223 (Feb. 25, 1241), also in *Aureum opus*, doc. 11, fols. 3-4, though the Mudejars are not considered there.

CHAPTER VIII

Collectories: Muslim, Christian, Jew

DESPITE THE general evidence of Mudejars acting as financiers and tax farmers, there is a dearth of specific detail and examples. Did the Muslim work at so low a collecting level, or at so peripheral a fringe, as not to enter the overall tax records? Were his accounts all assumed and transformed as part of some intermediary Christian's accounts? Or is he lying concealed in surviving documents under a different formality and name?

THE PIVOTAL FINANCIER: THE *Amīn*

Approaching the problem aprioristically, one explanation might be that the *amīn* receiving an aljama's revenues was in fact an entrepreneurial tax farmer, like his counterpart the Christian or Jewish bailiff. Just as the appointed official under the title bailiff had purchased or contracted for some revenue share, so a profit-hungry notable of an aljama may well have applied for the corresponding contract and dignity at the local level. Conversely the *amīn* already collecting when the crusaders appeared may quite naturally have assimilated his role to that of the bailiff and have adjusted his activities accordingly. Both developments may have occurred in parallel. If the *amīn* confined his role to the local, aljama level, his manuscripts of contract would normally have disappeared eventually along with the welter of similar subcontracts by Christian and Jewish bailiffs; larger or comprehensive operations, and those arranged more directly with the crown, had a far better chance to survive in the official registers. The ambiguity of expressing a tax farm as a debt, and the expedient of attaching lesser debts to the obligations assumed by the larger tax farmer, may also serve to conceal Muslim financiers. Given the disapproval of canon law, the crown would not have been disposed to advertise Mudejar participation in collecting at any level except the intra-aljama.

Confirmation of this view of the *amīn* as a kind of bailiff-entrepreneur comes by merest chance in a document of 1259 from an obscure Valencian locality. One of the earliest surviving transactions recording local tax recovery processes, it owes its preservation not to an archives but to inclusion in a textbook or handbook used by medieval notaries for legal formulas; thus it forms a vivid example of a mass of lost documents neither registered nor copied. At the same time it reveals the collecting system at work at its lowest level, in two insignificant fortified villages. The subject of this exemplar contract, aljamas named Montes and Carrícola, had previously given their taxes to the Catalan knight Raymond of Timor, who held both places as a crusader's reward until his recent death. Carrícola stood between Alcoy and Játiva; with Montes it appears several times in the royal registers. The tower of Montes, for example, had a castellan answerable to Artal of Foces in 1258.[1] A decade later, Carrícola went to James's mistress Berengaria Alfonso, in a grant that shows it as the center of other townships; these with Tárbena paid Berengaria 30,000 morabatins.[2]

The formulary's document concerned the sale "to you Muḥammad [b.] Wāra [b.] Ghānim [Mafomat Huarat Ganim] and Yūsuf [b.] Wāra [b.] Sa'd [Huarat Zoot or Zaat] and Shāfi' al-Mawṣilī [b.] Ḥafṣ [Jafid Amosela Ha(fs)], artificers of Montes, and to the whole aljama—those who choose to associate themselves in the purchase— of Carrícola and Montes, which belong to Raymond of Timor, [of] all the revenues" at both places "for the three years coming succes- sively."[3] The three artisans were to pay the new Christian owner of

---

[1] Arch. Crown, James I, Reg. Canc. 10, fol. 100v (July 4, 1258): "diffinimus im- perpetuum vobis, dilecto nostro Artallo de Focibus, et per vos universis alcaydis et hominibus qui pro vobis teneant castra de Penacadel . . . et de Montes, omnem petitionem, questionem, et demandam quam vobis facere possimus ratione quod vos dictus Artallus non solvistis Romeo Martini illos mille morabetinos quos ratione dictorum [octo] castrorum de mandato nostro ei solvere debebatis . . . , ita quod . . . vos et dicti alcaydi . . . [sitis] penitus absoluti."

[2] *Ibid.*, Reg. Canc. 16, fol. 187 (Aug. 18, 1269): "xxx millia morabatinorum." For this and allied documentation see Burns, *Islam under the Crusaders*, ch. 13, part 3.

[3] "Repàs d'un manual notarial del temps del rey en Jaume I," ed. Joan Segura, *Congrés I*, p. 310, doc. 1 (1259): "vendimus vobis Mafomat Huarat Ganim et Jucef Huarat Zoot [?] et Jafid Amosela Ha[fs?] fabris de Muntis et omni alzama (qui in ista emptione velint esse) de Carricola et de Muntis . . . omnes redditus . . . usque ad iii annos continue venturos." The editorial interrogatory is Segura's. The recon- struction of names here is highly conjectural in their latter segments; there are no connectives (ibn, abū), and the transcription may well have been faulty. Huarat may relate to Hawwāra, after the prominent Berber tribe in Spain; Huarat was a com- mon forename, appearing under that form alone fifteen times in personal and town names in the *Repartimiento de Murcia*.

these revenues or his bailiff 900 solidi a year, in two equal parts in early March and late September. The cost of maintaining and garrisoning the local "tower" or fort fell on the collectors. An accompanying order selected one of the three as *amīn* and directed the aljama to accord him the rights of that office. Though the *amīn* appears as the pivotal figure even at this local level, his office attaches casually to the likeliest candidate for farming the taxes. The hint of a company of shareholders buying into the project at so small a place, in numbers limited only by membership in the local aljama, is itself a valuable discovery.

Such a document goes far to clarify the status of the mysterious figure the Valencians called an *amīn*. The name in itself reveals nothing; a generic term for "trustworthy," it attached carelessly to a bewildering variety of minor offices throughout Islam. In the Valencian Mudejar experience, however, the *alamí* was a specific officer of the aljama, exercising a function called *alaminatge*; he later came to be the main administrator over each aljama, presiding at the local council, conducting a court of justice, and directing the daily routine of the community. Scholarly descriptions of aljama governance throughout the realms of Aragon routinely designate him, with his aides (*adelantats*), as the wielder or coordinator of local political power and as the main political institution common to all aljamas. There may well have been many another *amīn* of the several traditional or possible sorts within the economic and bureaucratic structure of the aljama; given the undifferentiated nature of Islamic society, moreover, other offices and functions may easily have accrued to that of the central *amīn*. But Christian documents focus upon a precise function and a definite personage. The mystery arises from the fact that this *amīn* did not enjoy the central role during the postcrusade generation. The governance of the aljama at that time resided either in a *qāḍī* or in a *qā'id*—a system I have described elsewhere along with the minor, political-juridical participation of the *amīn*.[4] Since circumstance or policy elevated him fairly rapidly thereafter, the key to his evolution probably lies back within those postcrusade years.

[4] Burns, *Islam under the Crusaders*, ch. 16, part 1, with full documentation, bibliographical notes, and review of scholarly opinion; on the judicial function, see ch. 10, part 2. See also Claude Cahen, "Amīn," *El²*, 1, 147; Dozy and Engelmann, *Glossaire*, p. 56. The Valencian *amīn* of this period sometimes received as well the independent office and income of the *scribania*.

250

Given only the common denominator of meaning underlying the use of *amīn* in contemporary Islam, as well as the unsettled late-Almohad situation and then the radical reorientation of tax collection under the Christians, the modern investigator might reasonably anticipate the rise of some local figure like the *amīn* to prominence and eventually to control. The clue in each premise is the logic of fiscal responsibility in a mixed society during crisis. Consequently an analysis of that facet of the *amīn* belongs here, just as detailed examination of his political and juridical facets belonged to my previous book on Valencian Islam in transition.

The responsibility or trust implied by the name, in itself, translated most frequently into financial responsibility, or administration of something connected with trade or the market place, or custody with a strong hint of money matters. *Amīn* was used for estate steward, head of a craft group, legal representative for minors, a customs officer, treasurer, clerk in one of the state tax offices, director of a segment of irrigation network, or regulator of weights and measures. Even more than *ra'īs* in the Near Eastern crusader states, it would have made an apt title for the local notable (farmer, artisan, or wealthy merchant) who emerged in times of crisis and conquest as tax functionary mediating between community and current alien overlords. Unlike the Near Eastern *ra'īs*, his further evolution as point of liaison, spokesman both to and from the overlords, and inevitable receptacle of real powers, was impeded in Valencia by the unique, antecedent development of the *qāḍī* in secular functions and civil governance, as well as by the stratum of Muslim strongmen or castellans who survived for a time in the wake of the crusade.[5]

The Christians did not have to preside over the creation of a revenue officer; such a go-between had emerged in Almohad Spain, especially at the regional or the city level, in the person of the local notable serving as aide to the foreign Berber appointee over a given place; consistent with the necessarily tax-oriented nature of his office, he went under the more blatantly fiscal title of *mushrif* or treasurer.[6] At Valencia, a hundred and fifty years before King James, the victorious Cid maintained at least two figures in his entourage bear-

[5] Cahen, "Régime rurale syrien," pp. 306-307, on *ra'īs*; the Valencian *qāḍī* and *qā'id* are treated extensively in Burns, *Islam under the Crusaders*, ch. 10, parts 2, 3; ch. 15, part 3; and ch. 16, part 1.

[6] Évariste Lévi-Provençal, *Conférences sur l'Espagne musulmane* (Cairo, 1951), p. 81.

ing the significant title *mushrif*: Ibn 'Abdūs (Ben Abduz) and Mūsā; the Cid made the latter his vizier over the conquered kingdom.[7]

King James encountered this finance minister briefly only at the level of princely government, especially in Valencia city at the moment of its surrender and at Játiva; but he did find the ubiquitous local representatives or counterparts of this dignitary throughout Valencia under the name *amīn*. The charters of Alfandech, Játiva, and Uxó ranked him just after the *qāḍī*. Chivert's charter described his duties as "administering and collecting the taxes of the lord," the Templars. Aldea, just over the northern border, probably had the same functionary; the Hospitaller castellan of Amposta, receiving the Mudejar *alfarda* in 1250, got the concomitant privilege of appointing his own collector or collectors during the following twenty years.[8] The Játiva charter directed the local *amīn* to "collect and receive our taxes" from the aljama there.[9]

Was the *amīn* merely a revenue officer, or do his judicial functions and his obvious eminence in aljama affairs, at the time the crusaders arrived to draw the charters, point to some collateral dignity? The presence of the traditional market inspector and guardian of public ethics, the *muḥtasib*, combined with the strange paucity of reference to him, especially in the charters, raises the suspicion that the revenue duties may have lodged in that personage at many localities. *Alamín* in Castilian and *alamí* in Catalan has as its primary definition the custodian of weights and measures, which had been a main concern of the *muḥtasib* in Islamic Spain; and at times the two titles seem to converge.[10] Whatever the merits of this line of thought, the connec-

---

[7] Menéndez Pidal, *España del Cid*, ii, 554.

[8] Chivert Charter: "habeant aluminum ad incautandum et recipiendum iura dominorum fratrum." Aldea Charter, mentioning the *amīn* in his judicial context. *Itinerari*, pp. 206-207 (July 15, 1250): "ille vel illi, quem vel quos, vos vel vestri successores elegeritis ad colligendam." On the Valencian and Jativan *mushrif* see nn. 24, 25.

[9] Játiva Charter: "colligat et recipiat iura nostra raballi predicti."

[10] On the *muḥtasib* see Burns, *Islam under the Crusaders*, ch. 10, part 2. Conversely, the office had declined in importance in Spain by this time; and Cahen notes that colonial documents in the Near East hardly mention the *muḥtasib*, probably relating him merely to internal conduct by the aljama ("Féodalité et les institutions," p. 187). Ibn 'Abdūn treats of the *amīn* who regulated measures as *muḥtasib*; and a fifteenth century Valencian document concerns election of "hun alami, que es appellat mustaçaf" (*Islam under the Crusaders*, ch. 10, nn. 44, 65, and reference to Gual Camarena's thesis); but use of generic *amīn* in such cases is suggestive rather

tion of the Valencian *amīn* with tax collecting crops up recurrently during the postcrusade decades. Even after he had become firmly established in later centuries as the aljama's main ruler, his duties of governance continued to be balanced by his equally important position as administrator of the lord's revenues and keeper of the tax records.[11] In postcrusade Valencia he was clearly the appointee of lord or crown and rather clearly the equivalent of the Christian bailiff or guardian of taxes, temporalities, and rights of the lord.

King James, arranging to have the revenues of Alcira, Alfandech, and Pego surrendered to a Christian in 1263 up to the sum of 20,000 solidi, conveyed to him also the corresponding right "to install bailiffs, whether *amīn* or castellan" at the castles of Alfandech and Pego, to handle or subfarm the constitutive taxes.[12] Three years later he devised a similar transference of all taxes for Ribarroja, Alfandech, and Pego, again authorizing installation of every "bailiff, castellan, or *amīn*" necessary for their collection.[13] King Peter directed a tax instruction to every "*amīn* and collector of the Saracen communities of Játiva and of all our other places of the kingdom of Valencia beyond the Júcar";[14] he subjoined separate orders for their colleagues above the Júcar.[15] In 1279 he instructed the *amīn* of

than probative. The judicial prerogatives are susceptible of other explanations, including acquisition of *maẓālim* audiences by the *amīn* (ch. 16, n. 45).

[11] Macho y Ortega, "Mudéjares aragoneses," p. 156. An Eslida outline of the office of *amīn* in 1425 expressly forbade his reception of rents or taxes, a negative indication of the same role.

[12] Arch. Crown, James I, Reg. Canc. 17, fol. 43v (April 30, 1263): "concedentes vobis quod . . . possitis instituere baiulos, sive alaminos sive alcaydos." In this and the following text a different intrusion of punctuation would alter the meaning slightly, setting three equal choices, rather than dividing bailiffs into a castellan and an *amīn* class. The Latin plurals in this and the next two notes are translated in the text by singular forms in an implied plural sense, to avoid Arabic plurals.

[13] *Ibid.*, fol. 67r,v (April 28, 1266): "possitis ponere et instituere baiulos, alcaydos sive alaminos."

[14] *Ibid.*, Peter III, Reg. Canc. 57, fol. 225v (Oct. 25, 1285): "suis alaminis et collectoribus aliamarum sarracenorum de Xativa et omnium aliorum locorum nostrorum regni Valencie ultra Xucharam." A covering instruction to the lieutenant of the king's procurator is on fol. 126, ordering him to enforce the order "alaminis, collectoribus, et aliamis sarracenorum." Similar letters with covering instructions are indicated there, for five non-Valencian Mudejar communities—at Huesca, Lérida, Tarazona, Tortosa, and Zaragoza.

[15] *Ibid.*, fol. 225 (same date): "similiter fiat alaminis et collectoribus aliamarum sarracenorum morarie Valencie et omnium locorum regni Valencie citra Xucharum." Covering instructions are indicated on fol. 226. Note the respective centrality of Valencia city's and Jativa's Mudejar communities above and below the river.

Mogente concerning the household tax.[16] James farmed the revenues of Gallinera and Alcalá in 1267 to their *"amīn* and aljama of Saracens" for two years at 2,500 solidi a year; again the *amīn* comes to the fore in tax business.[17] When farming all the revenues of Cocentaina to Guic William for three years at 1,500 solidi a year in 1260, James required that he collect them after the same fashion as the present tax farmer "and the *amīn* of Cocentaina."[18]

In 1257 at Cuart, when the king sold a large estate to the Mudejar community, "to give, divide, and sell among yourselves," he addressed the grant "to you, Aḥmad an-Najjār [Ahamet Anayar] the *amīn*, and to the whole aljama of the Saracens."[19] At one point James, farming some rents below the Júcar for a return of 2,192 solidi, included the "alaminates" of all the towns and places there; since these revenues did not meet the sum required, the king had to assign fresh tax sources in 1265; the relatively small amount of money spread over much of the kingdom suggests that the office of *amīn* itself returned some trifling annual fee at each place, or possibly that some share of salary was rebated to the crown by new and recent appointees.[20] A tax dispute of 1282 similarly involved the *amīn* responsible for collection.[21] During the crusade itself, when James promised the turncoat Muḥammad at Elche both "the town and all the revenues," he made the Muslim in effect the local *amīn*.[22]

[16] *Ibid.*, Reg. Canc. 42, fol. 163 (Nov. 3, 1279): "alamino et aliame sarracenorum de Moixen."

[17] *Ibid.*, James I, Reg. Canc. 15, fol. 88 (March 1, 1267): "attributamus vobis alamino et aliame sarracenorum."

[18] *Ibid.*, Reg. Canc. 11, fol. 173 (May 21, 1260): "concedimus vobis Guicco Guillelmi quod . . . teneatis pro nobis castrum et villam de Cocentania, et quod percipiatis et habeatis omnes redditus . . . prout melius et plenius Romeus Martini et alaminus Cocentanie modo ipsos percipiunt pro nobis." Guich or Guic, a family name in Catalonia, probably derives from Gui, Guiu, as a form of Guy, or less probably from the German name Giki.

[19] *Ibid.*, Reg. Canc. 10, fol. 8 (Aug. 11, 1257): "concedimus tibi Ahamet Anayar alamino et toti aliame sarracenorum . . . dare, dividere, vendere inter vos." The name is "Azmet Anajar sarraceno, alaminatum," in Reg. Canc. 12, fol. 63v (June 9, 1262).

[20] *Ibid.*, Reg. Canc. 13, fol. 177r,v (May 23, 1265): "super çofris, redditibus, et alaminatibus et scribaniis."

[21] *Ibid.*, Peter III, Reg. Canc. 46, fol. 78v (April 11, 1282): "alamino et sarracenorum Benioppe."

[22] *Llibre dels feyts*, ch. 417: "que tenria per nos la vila e tots les rendes" permanently. The Valencian documents throughout the reign of Alfonso III continue to address the *amīn* of each locality in tax matters. Even the hue and cry addressed

The *Mushrif*

What was the relation of *amīn* to *mushrif* or treasurer—the go-between seen above—and where does the latter fit into Mudejar Valencia? Ibn 'Abdūn, in his treatise on twelfth-century Seville, names the *mushrif* as controller of the fisc there, entitled to a copy of the tax lists;[23] he does not mention the *amīn* as a tax officer. In fact, however, an *amīn* was local representative of the central or provincial *mushrif*. Within the late-Almohad Valencian principality, the *mushrif* or treasurer resided at Valencia city, with an *amīn* apparently presiding over tax receipts, public disbursement, and forwarding of surplus at each district center. The title *mushrif* disappears from Valencian records during these postcrusade decades. When James's conquest of Valencia city drove the current *wālī* and his household into exile, the *mushrif* abandoned his "buildings" at the capital; he entered Christian property listings as 'Abd Allāh al-Baṭṭāl (Abdala Ambadel).[24] Since Játiva survived as a semi-independent feudal enclave for a few years, its *mushrif* Ibn al-'Arab (Abenhalara) kept his property until a postrevolutionary confiscation in 1248.[25] Each of these luminaries may well have been much more than a finance minister; the *mushrif* across the waters at Tunis during the

---

to "universis baiulis, iusticiis, alaminis, et aliis officialibus," when Giles Gonzálvez "manu armata invasit . . . et rapuit dompnam Feliciam," was a revenue affair; driven from the land "propter sonum sive appelido qui fuit inde emissus," he was now to lose any possessions these officials could confiscate (Arch. Crown, Alfonso III, Reg. Canc. 85, fol. 142 [April 20, 1291]).

[23] *Séville musulmane, le traité*, p. 69. See also Imamuddin, *Socio-Economic and Cultural History of Muslim Spain*, p. 193. On the *mushrif* as liaison between Spanish Muslims and Berber rulers, see Lévi-Provençal as cited above, n. 6.

[24] *Repartimiento de Valencia*, p. 221: "qui erat almaxarif Valentie." Ambadel might stand for any number of names, from al-Baṭṭāl or Ibn (Aben) 'Aṭā'llah to compression-distortion of a form like al-Muffaḍḍal. On the local precrusade *amīn* in general see García de Valdeavellano, *Instituciones españolas*, p. 672; more persuasive for our time and place, of course, is the actual presence of the revenue *amīn* in Valencian charters and documentation.

[25] The *repartimiento* manuscript (Arch. Crown, Reg. Canc. 6, fol. 89v [May 4, 1248]) reads: "domos in Xativa que fuerunt de almoxarif et generi sui cum turre in eis sita, que sunt [in?] algefria et affrontat ex una parte in domibus que fuerunt alterius generi dicti almoxarif . . . et ex alia in muro algefrie." *Algeferia* is a form of *Aljaferia*, both Catalan for the Zaragozan castle built by and named for Abū Ja'far; was it applied here to the castle or a palace? The entry for n. 24 is an interlinear item in Reg. Canc. 5, fol. 50.

reigns of James and Peter was not only "master of customs" with his own staff and building, but a diplomat who negotiated treaties of commerce and peace, acting as plenipotentiary for the Hafsid caliph.[26] King James does not apply the term to anyone functioning in his Valencian Mudejar system, though his autobiography gives prominence to the powerful *mushrif* (*moxerif* or *moixerif*) of neighboring Minorca, Abū 'Uthmān Sa'īd b. Ḥakam al-Qurashī, a literary figure from Seville and brother of the island's ruler; he became tributary governor of Minorca for James, proudly retaining the appellation *moixerif*, his son succeeding to both governance and strange title until he betrayed Peter III.[27] A pseudo-*moixerif* for Játiva's Muslims entered history via a misprint in James's memoirs.[28]

Absence of the title among Valencia's Mudejars has a certain significance, reinforcing the impression that while the tax-collecting infrastructure survived the crusade, its central bureaucracy was supplanted by that of the Christians. The title itself was not alien to the Christian fisc. Rare in its Castilian form before the thirteenth

[26] *Traités de paix et de commerce et documents divers concernant les relations des chrétiens avec les arabes de l'Afrique septentrionale au moyen âge*, ed. Louis [Comte de] Mas Latrie, 2 vols. (New York, ca. 1963), II, 280-284 (Feb. 14, 1271), drawn in Catalan at Valencia but preserved in a copy made at Tunis in 1278 by William of Bonastre "mandato Bolphaçen, moxeriffi Tunicii, et instantia senum officialium curie Tunicii, hoc instrumentum, in domo dicti moxeriffi fideliter scribendo scripsit, translatavit ab originali et clausit." The same man, "Yayam Benabdelmec dictum Bolasem, chaytum [*alcaidum*] dugane Tunexis" negotiated a treaty with Genoa (II, 122-125 [Nov. 6, 1272]). King James's treaty with Tunis in 1278 was signed "in domo dicti moxeriffi Tunicii," whose name is slightly garbled as "Ya-Ya Ebni Abidel Malech" (II, 187-188).

[27] *Llibre dels feyts*, chs. 119-121; Muntaner, *Crònica*, ch. 50; al-Ḥimyarī, *Kitāb ar-rawḍ al-mi'ṭār*, pp. 371-372. As late as 1510, when Argel in Bugia surrendered, the principal men making the treaty were "el Xeque y el Almoxarife, y el Alcadi y el Mufti, el Alfaqui principal, y otros alfaquis" (Fernández y González, *Mudejares de Castilla*, appendix, doc. 94). José Conde errs in making Abū 'Uthmān the first ruler of Majorca, transferred then to Minorca; he does give the four main subleaders of Minorca and Ibiza; see his *Historia de la dominación de los árabes en España, sacada de varios manuscritos y memorias arábigas* (Madrid, 1874), p. 263. The surrender treaty of Minorca in 1231 was done in the name of "alfaqui Aboabdille Mafomet, filius domini alfaqui Abolança Aly Abineixem," who adds to his recurrent main title *alfaqui* three more—"alcayd et alcadi et almoxariff" (*Traités de paix*, II, 182-185 [June 17, 1231], erroneously applied to Majorca); this was apparently the *qāḍī* Abū 'Abd Allāh Muḥammad b. Aḥmad b. Hishām, who revolted against James's puppet Abū 'Uthmān.

[28] The "almofarix" in the 1557 edition of the *Llibre*, conjectured by Gayangos to be a *moixerif*, is really "Almofois," for al-Mufawwiz or al-Mufawwaz, of Játiva.

century, it suddenly abounded within that period. Castilians called the Jew who conducted their kingdom's finance-secretariate and the farming of regalian income the *almojarife*, and his charge in Latin an *almuisserifatum*;[29] his title would shift to the equivalent *tesorero* from 1317. In Andalusia and Murcia especially, the Castilian collectors of customs also assumed the title,[30] but *almojarifazgo* soon widened as a more general term applying to some other taxes. The director of any Catalan fonduk or commercial concession at a North African port went under the title *moixerif*.[31]

Valencia's Mudejars paid a trifling tax called the *moixerifat*, discussed in Chapter IV as possibly related to customs or to commercial taxes; possibly also it was like the *alaminatum* tax just seen, relating somehow to the privilege of controlling one's own tax-collecting mechanisms. The Mudejar community of Aledo, just south of Valencia city, in 1271 paid a similarly named tax to their overlords, the Knights of Santiago; there it seemed to stand for the taxes as such. The *moixerifat* taken at Alfandech, a thousand solidi each year between 1268 and 1273, amounts to a small fraction of that valley's taxes even during a bad year. At any rate, the *mushrif* seems

---

[29] Julio González discusses the office for Castile and especially for the Seville region in his edition of the *Repartimiento de Sevilla*, I, 366-368. See also his *El reino de Castilla en la época de Alfonso VIII*, 3 vols. (Madrid, 1960), I, 249-250, on the "almosserifatum meum, redditus scilicet regales," and on the Jews holding that post, who directed also regional *almojarifes*. Neuvonen treats of the word's entry into Spanish in *Arabismos del español*, pp. 157-158. See also Dubler, *Wirtschaftsleben*, p. 147; Dozy and Engelmann, *Glossaire*, p. 179; García de Valdeavellano, *Instituciones españolas*, pp. 592ff., 596, 604-605.

[30] López de Ayala, *Contribuciones é impuestos en León y Castilla*, pp. 282, 294; Seville and other towns had a customs center or *almojarifazgo mayor*, while internal transit duties constituted an *almojarifazgo menor*. One Iñigo functioned as *"almojarife* of Murcia" after the conquest of 1266 (Fernández y González, *Mudéjares de Castilla*, appendix, doc. 46). In Murcia, Berengar of Moncada "era almoxeriff" for a time, and Jordan of Puig had half of Beninabia "que los almoxeriffes le dieron" (*Repartimiento de Murcia*, p. 214). See also the *Repartimiento de Sevilla*: "don Abrahan fijo del almoxarife," Meir b. Shoshan (II, 65), Don Zulema the king's *almojarife* (II, 342), and Don Zag (I, 280). For the *almojarifazgo* paid at Cordova see Orti Belmonte, "Fuero de Córdoba: mudéjares," p. 40. Macanaz noted in 1713 that the word *mojarifazgo* had ceased to be used except on the Andalusian frontier (*Regalías de Aragón*, pp. 68-69).

[31] Dufourcq, *L'Espagne catalane et le Maghrib*, pp. 321-324. For movement of the term south from Spain into North Africa see Hopkins, *Medieval Muslim Government in Barbary*, pp. 51-52. Catalan spellings vary, from *moxerif* of the *Llibre dels feyts* (ch. 119) to modern *(al)moixerif*.

to have given way to the corresponding bureaucracy of James I. The term may have survived within the aljama as a private title for the *amīn*, however, since the word list for this time and place attributed to the Dominican friar Martí not only includes it but equates it with *baiulus*.[32]

If the *amīn* was the pivot between the Mudejar collectory mechanisms within the aljama and the local Christian bailiff or higher authorities, did some general functionary serve as expediter for Mudejar taxes alone, either regionally or over the kingdom? Leaving aside the situation where a separate collector might acquire one or more Mudejar taxes over a broad region, it is possible that the crown's Arabic secretary, or someone recommended by him, intervened in the anomalous Valencian Mudejar tax scene, facilitating and reviewing the transfer of funds and accounts from *amīn* through bailiff to king. The documents, especially for the more developed decade of King Peter's reign, do speak occasionally of a "collector of Saracen taxes of the kingdom of Valencia," or "collector of Saracen pennies of the kingdom of Valencia," or "collector of our revenues of the Moorish quarters or Saracen places in the mountains of the kingdom of Valencia."

This Mudejar "mountain" collectory emerges clearly into light during the reign of Peter's successor, Alfonso III. It covered the rocky region to the southeast of Játiva, roughly the outthrust of coast comprising the areas of Denia-Pego and Guadalest-La Marina, possibly extending westward into the inhospitable hinterland areas like Albaida and Alcoy. Alfonso describes it in 1286 as "places in the kingdom of Valencia called the mountains [*montanea*], in which places is the place named Denia, and the place called Vall de Laguart, and the place named Ebo Valley, and the place named Alcalá, and Gallinera, and Pop, and Jalón Valley, and the place named Castell,

---

[32] Fernández y González, *Mudejares de Castilla*, appendix, doc. 49 (1271): "moneda que nos rescibieremos de las rentas del almojarifazgo, mientre fuere Alaedo de moros." A military order or secular lord could have *almojarifes*; thus the *Repartimiento de Murcia* gave "a don Çuleman Catorçe, almoxerif de don Gil García, un palomar con i realejo," bordered by a mosque and a canal (p. 200). At Elche, after the turn of the century, the local *almoxerifat* was described as a customs tax (see the document in Chapter IV, n. 50). For Alfandech see Arch. Crown, James I, Reg. Canc. 37, fol. 64v (May 10, 1273): "compotum de almoxerifato v annorum [4,798 solidorum] . . . retentis et levatis vobis iure collectorum et salario vestro." Martí is in *Vocabulista in arabico*, p. 265.

and Tárbena Valley, with all the appurtenances of those places, and other places also which we have in the said realm which are called the mountains." In that year the Mudejar, Ibrāhīm b. Ṣumādiḥ, emerged from his legal troubles to resume his post as "collector of our revenues of the Moorish communities or places of the Saracens" here.[33] By the late 1280's each *amīn* and bailiff in these mountains was reporting to the first of the Christian superintendents who replaced Ibrāhīm; was the Christian's title of *moixerif* a reflection of his predecessor's Arabic title? It remains distinctive in crown documents for this region, despite the fact that a *moixerifat* fee was collected elsewhere in the kingdom. Do title and region comprise a paradigm for similar collectories now hidden from us; or were they idiosyncratic, an atypical grouping?

Whether a nexus can be established between Ibrāhīm as *mushrif* and the *moixerif* title of succeeding years, the change in personnel and title came about through a general tax crisis in 1286. King Alfonso detached his "faithful treasurer," Peter of Llibiá, "a respected citizen of Valencia, substantial and experienced" who had previously served King Peter in high affairs of state and had been justiciar at Valencia city, as inspector and reformer. The treasurer traveled "in my name over all my Moorish communities of the kingdom of Valencia," with a mandate to regulate their disordered finances. On the heels of this reorganization, Alfonso appointed a relative of his agent, Bernard of Llibiá, to be the first Christian "*moixerif* of the Saracens of the mountains" below the Júcar River. Typical business finds him processing crown debts assigned by the treasurer "on the mountains of our Saracens of Jalón, Castell, Tárbena, Callosa, Vall de Laguart, [and Vall de] Guadalest," together

---

[33] Arch. Crown, Alfonso III, Reg. Canc. 67, fols. 52v-53 (July 23, 1286): "in redditibus, exitibus, et proventibus locorum nostrorum que habemus in regno Valencie et que vocantur montanea, in quibus locis est locus qui dicitur de Denia, et locus vocatus vallis de Alaguar, et locus qui dicitur vallis de Ebo, et locus qui dicitur de Alchalano, et de Gallinera, et de Pop, et de valle de Exalo, et locus qui dicitur Castel, et vallis Tarbene, cum omnibus pertinentiis ipsorum locorum, et alia etiam loca que habemus in dicto regno que nuncupantur montanea." The Low Latin *montanea* had its exact equivalent in Catalan *muntanya*, for a mountain or mountainous region. For Ibrāhīm b. Ṣumādiḥ see Chapter VII, n. 49. See also Romano, "Hermanos Abenmenassé," pp. 269, 270: "collectori iurium sarracenorum regni Valencie"; "collectori denariorum sarracenorum regni Valencie"; "collectori reddituum nostrorum morariarum sive locorum sarracenorum in montaneis regni Valencie."

with the *alfarda* due at Gallinera, Játiva, and Uxó. Significantly, this superbailiff could also be called "bailiff of the mountains of the kingdom of Valencia." He went on to become bailiff and procurator for resettlement at Tortosa.

In 1290 Bernard Sabater succeeded him in charge of "the *moixerifat* of the mountains of the kingdom of Valencia below the Júcar, for three years"; he supervised all Mudejar revenues there "and also the [sale] prices of their bailiates," submitting his account directly to the king or to whatever agent he might appoint. "For your salary and work you are to receive what other *moixerifs* have been accustomed to receive." As "*moixerif* of the Moorish communities," presumably the only collector with such a title, Bernard was soon busy overseeing an assessment on the aljamas of Gallinera with Ebo, Guadalest, Jalón, Játiva, Tárbena, and Vall de Laguart.[34]

[34] Arch. Crown, Alfonso III, Reg. Canc. 66, fol. 51v (April 26, 1286): "fideli tesaurario nostro Petro de Libiano quod viderat nomine nostro super omnibus morariis nostris regni Valencie, et quantum poterit dirigat eas et redigat ad bonum statum prout ei melius visum fuerit." Reg. Canc. 78, fol. 24 (Jan. 13, 1289): "in montaneis sarracenorum nostrorum de Xalone, de Castel, et de Tarbena, de Cayllosa, de Alaguarre, et Vall de Godalest . . . et super alfardis . . ."; "item Bernardus de Libiano almoxerifo montanearum nostrarum quod respondeat dicto Bernardo de omnibus iuribus sarracenorum predictorum." Fol. 26 (Dec. 23, 1289): "Bernardo de Libiano almoxarifo sarracenorum montanearum [*sic*] quod observet . . . assignationem." Fol. 38 (Jan. 27, 1289): "Alfonsus etc. Bernardo de Libiano almoxeriffo montanearum nostrarum ultra Xucarum, cum nos deberemus. . . ." Reg. Canc. 80, fol. 137 (Dec. 17, 1289): "Bernardo de Libiano baiulo montanearum regni Valencie," with other examples in Chapter VII, n. 30. Reg. Canc. 81, fol. 185v (Sept. 5, 1290): "confitemur et recognoscimus vobis fideli nostro Bernardo Sabaterii nostrum baiulum quod cum nos commendaverimus vobis almoxerifatum montanearum regni Valencie ultra Xucarum habendum et tenendum pro nobis per tres annos. . . ." Reg. Canc. 82, fol. 69v (same date): "fuit mandatum al [*sic*] alamino et moxerif et sarracenis dicti loci"; "Bernardo Sabaterii et moxerifo." Reg. Canc. 83, fol. 81v (same date): "commendamus vobis fideli Bernardo Sabaterii civi Barchinone almoxerifatum montanearum nostrarum regni Valencie ultra Xucarum . . . et officium almoxerifatus predicti exerceatis per dictum tempus et obligatis et recipiatis vos nostros redditus et quelibet alia iura a sarracenis nostris montanearum predictarum et etiam precia baiularum eorum [*sic*] . . . concedentes vobis quod recipiatis pro salario et labore vestro id quod per alios almoxerifos est recipi consuetum." *Ibid.*, a note: "fuit scriptum sarracenis ipsarum montanearum quod habeant ipsum Bernardum pro almoxerifo infra tempus predictum, et eidem respondeant de omnibus de quibus tenentur domino regi respondere." Reg. Canc. 82, fol. 71 (Sept. 7, 1290): "almoxerifo montanearum regni Valencie . . . super redditibus . . . alcharee de Petro [Patró] que est in valle de Gallinera . . . mandantes almoxerifo seu alamino et aliis sarracenis de alcharee." Reg. Canc. 85, fol. 131v (April 1, 1291): "alamino et aliame sarracenorum . . . [quod] respondeatis incontinenti Bernardo Çabaterii al-

Area Example: Biar

The role of *amīn*, aljama, castellan-bailiff, regional bailiff, and crown can best be studied in a local example. A run of revenue documents for Biar between 1258 and 1275 comprises a mini-cartulary that can serve as such a sample. Biar was hardly a typical Mudejar area, however, and its contract-farming, or more exactly collection according to a deliberately low and agreed sum, may not have been fully characteristic of other aljamas. Biar castle stood on a podium of land at the southwest corner of the Valencian kingdom; under its *qā'id* Mūsā al-Murābiṭ (Almoravit) it had surrendered on good terms to the crusaders after a long siege in 1245.[35] Biar was not only an anchor for the southern defenses but an inland port for merchandise crossing the frontier; these circumstances rather than its negligible population lent it major importance.

In June 1258 King James sold "to you the whole aljama of Biar," perhaps for the third or fourth time, all the rents of the district, except criminal fines and tavern income, over the next two years. This covered not only Mudejar but Christian taxes. Though canon law forbade Muslims to farm Christian revenues, in practice the prohibition broke down; besides, lawyers could overlook the case of dominantly Islamic towns in a recently conquered kingdom as an

---

moxeriffo morariarum," a form letter. Sometimes these individual bailiates were farmed or sold indirectly to the several aljamas (Reg. Canc. 78, fols. 25v-26 [Jan. 14, 1289]): "aliame sarracenorum ravalli de Tarbena, sciatis quod eo quod ullus baiulus seu emptor redituum non faciat nobis impedimentum super redditibus quos nobis dare tenemini, mandavimus retineri vobis ad opus vestri reddditus supradictos quoscumque ad presentem annum, precio videlicet mille septingentorum solidorum . . . [et eos] colligatis ac colligi faciatis," presenting accounts to the *moixerif* Bernard of Llibiá. Identical form letters went to six other aljamas here. A series of allied documents for the previous spring names the actual agents acting for the respective aljamas purchasing (Reg. Canc. 74, fol. 104v [March 27, 1288]): "venditionem factam per Guillelmum Colrati, Abdulmega alamino, et Aberola Abensibi et Iuçeffo Abenhyals sarracenis de Gallinera et de Alcala et suis ementibus pro se et tota aliama sarracenorum dictorum locorum," indicating an aljama and collectory of multiple units. At Callosa and Vall de Laguart the sale was made to: "Mahometo Abnaxer alamino de Callosa et Dalaguer et Açmeto Abencaçim et Abrahim Ablexar." The quotation about Peter of Llibiá is in Muntaner, *Crònica*, ch. 172: "un honrat ciutadà de València . . . molt prohom e savi"; cf. ch. 279.

[35] *Llibre dels feyts*, chs. 355-359. Carlos Sarthou Carreres, *Castillos de España (su pasado y su presente)*, 4th edn. rev. (Madrid, 1963), pp. 454, 457.

exception, by recourse to the principle of epieikeia.[36] Subsequent
contracts omitted this proviso concerning Christians, possibly because
of increased local immigration or better rationalization of procedures
for collecting Christian taxes in the south. The deposit price was
about 4,400 solidi each year, expressed as "1,200 besants minus 25
besants, according to the manner in which besants are paid in
Valencia"; the latter condition referred perhaps to procedures for
collecting the poll tax, to be applied here. Starting that summer, the
aljama was to pay half the year's sum in January and half the next
August, "and if the aforesaid sale exceeds in profit the aforesaid
price, or will exceed it, we give you and yours that full amount that
exceeds or will exceed, to do with freely as you will." They could
also subfarm "to any person or persons you wish." The conveyance
does not mention the *amīn* or any individual Mudejar, assigning
reception or accounting "to me and mine and to him or those whom
we shall order."[37]

The contract ran until August 1261, but in August 1260 Arnold of
Monzón, castellan and tax farmer at Biar and two other castles,
rendered his own accounts to the crown; these covered "the expenses
you [Arnold] incurred in the aforesaid castle and all the expenditures you made for me and at my order from the said revenues and
income, from that day when you took over the castle for me up until
this day," yet left the bailiff with a debt and claim on the crown for
3,280 solidi. Thus the aljama had collected the taxes of Christian and
Moor, forwarded out of them the sum of 1,175 besants, rendered
their accounts, and then relied on Arnold to review and pass these
accounts on, either directly or as incorporated into the larger accounts of Játiva or some bailiff higher in the echelon.[38] Arnold

---

[36] *Corpus iuris canonici*, ed. Emil Friedberg and E. L. Richter, 2d edn., 2 vols.
(Leipzig, 1879-1881), Decretales, lib. v, tit. vi, c. 18. Epikeia or epieikeia relates to
equity.

[37] Arch. Crown, James I, Reg. Canc. 10, fol. 103v (June 16, 1258): "vendimus
vobis toti aliame sarracenorum de Biar et vestris, et cui vel quibus vos volueritis, a
kalendis mensis Augusti proximo venturi ad tres annos primos venturos . . . proventus et omnia alia iura nostra que nos habemus et percipimus et percipere et
habere debemus in villa de Biar tam a christianis quam a sarracenis aliquo modo,
exceptis homicidiis et taberna, precio videlicet mille et ducentorum [bisanciorum]
minus xxv bisancii . . . secundum morem quo solvuntur bisancii in Valencia . . . ; et
si predicta venditio plus valet vel valebit precio antedicto, totum illud quod plus
valet vel valebit damus vobis et vestris ad vestras voluntates libere faciendas."

[38] *Ibid.*, Reg. Canc. 11, fol. 178v (Aug. 25, 1260): "vos Arnaldus de Monsso

continued to hold Biar castle, adding to it in 1262 and 1263 the lucrative office of regional bailiff over the southern half of the kingdom, below the Júcar;[39] the king approved his accounts for the various bailiffs under him in that region, and in 1264 again assigned Biar to recompense him for his partially unrecovered deposit.[40]

At this point the Mudejar community again comes to the fore, renewing in 1263 the terms of the 1258 rental, this time at a price revealing a much expanded revenue base. They were to pay 6,000 solidi each year for the next two years "to me and in my place to the bailiff of the said locality." Just as the earlier rental spoke of the aljama as subject, without reference to *amīn* or local authorities, this conveyance was aimed only at Muḥammed b. al-Balawī (? Abnabu-lay); unless Muḥammad was an important financier, improbably appearing only once in all the realm's tax affairs, he was the local *amīn* acting for his community.[41] Arnold of Monzón served as castellan for Biar and Alcoy, as well as bailiff for the Játiva area, from 1264 to 1267, presenting his accounts in 1267, perhaps for the last time. He had to cope with the debt or loan of 20,000 morabatins for the king's mistress, laid upon the revenues of Biar and Castalla castles over an indefinite period, probably as a *violari* encumbering the tax farmer's gross intake.[42] By 1270 Peter of Segura had replaced

---

alcaydus de Biar reddidistis nobis rectum et legale compotum de omnibus recep-tionibus quas fecistis de redditibus et exitibus castri de Biar et castri de Almizra et [castri] de Beniamar et terminorum suorum, [et] de omnibus missionibus quas fecistis in predictis castris qualibet ratione et de omnibus datis quas pro nobis et mandato nostro fecistis de dictis redditibus."

[39] *Ibid.*, Reg. Canc. 12, fol. 50v (May 4, 1262): "fecit dominus rex Arnaldo de Munço instrumentum a rivo Xucaris ultra. . . ."

[40] *Ibid.*, Reg. Canc. 14, fol. 55v (May 30, 1264): "rectum et legale compotum de omnibus recepcionibus . . . in castris, [villis], et locis tocius baiulie regni Valencie quam pro nobis tenebatis a rivo Xuchari ultra . . . ; pro quibus omnibus denariis [10,760 solidi] obligamus et impignoramus vobis et vestris omnes redditus et exitus . . . in castro et villa de Biar . . . [et] de Castalla. . . ."

[41] *Ibid.*, Reg. Canc. 12, fol. 119 (Oct. 1, 1263): "vendimus tibi Mahometo Abna-bulhay de Biar . . . omnia alia iura que nos in Biar et a sarracenis ibidem habitanti-bus habemus . . . quos solvas nobis et loco nostri baiulo dicti loci." The name form, quite clear in the manuscript, could sustain less probable interpretations, such as al-Balkhī, but none seems really satisfactory. The combination "ibn abu" was not unacceptable as a medieval form, though uncommon, and opens the way to larger conjecture, e.g., Ibn Abu 'l-Hajj.

[42] *Ibid.*, Reg. Canc. 15, fol. 54 (April 9, 1267), accounts, including expenses "de Billena et guerre sarracenorum." Fol. 24v (July 29, 1266), published in Joseph Soler

Arnold as bailiff. The Muslims continued to pay their taxes by agreed assessment or contract-farm. King James in 1267 conferred "on you the Saracen aljama of Biar and all Saracens of the same aljama, present and future, from the month of January recently past, up through the four years immediately ahead in unbroken series," all taxes and revenues, in return for 5,000 solidi each year, paid "half in each month of August and the other half in each month of December."[43]

Not long before King James's death, he concluded a final accounting with Biar's Mudejar population through its *amīn*. In early March of 1275 he acknowledged "that you, Muḥammad b. Sālim [Avincelim], the *amīn* of Biar, have rendered account now to me concerning all my revenues, income, and other taxes of Biar of this year up to this present day, and concerning all expenditures, payments, costs, and expenses handled there for me within the said time." The king receipted these accounts, and confessed himself "well satisfied with you." Somehow the net revenue did not cover the initial assessment and farming price given the crown: "and thus, balancing receipts against disbursements, costs, and expenses, I conclude that I ought to refund to you, the aforesaid *amīn* Muḥammad, 393 solidi and 7 pence of Valencia." This sum the *amīn* was to deduct from crown taxes of the following year. James concluded with a reminder that the *amīn* was bound to see that Michael Garcés got his share of Biar's revenues and to take care of the church tithe on the crown's income from Biar.[44]

---

y Palet, "Un aspecte de la vida privada de Jaume I," *Congrés I*, pp. 557-558, with allied documents.

[43] Arch. Crown, James I, Reg. Canc. 15, fol. 84 (1267): "indulgemus vobis aliame sarracenorum de Biar et universis sarracenis eiusdem aliame presentibus et futuris . . . usque ad iiii⁰ʳ annos primo venturos et continue completos . . . et omnes alios redditus, exitus, ac iura nostra de quibus nobis tenemini respondere [non dentur sed] pro omnibus predictis detis in unoquoque dictorum quattuor annorum pro tributo predictorum nobis et loco nostro alcaydo de Biar quinque millia solidorum regalium Valencie, medietatem in unoquoque mense Augusti et aliam medietatem in unoquoque mense Decembris."

[44] *Ibid.*, Reg. Canc. 20, fol. 327 (March 3, 1275): "nos Iacobus etc. recognoscimus et confitemur quod tu Mahomat Avincelim alaminus de Biar computavisti nunc nobiscum de omnibus redditibus, exitibus, ac aliis iuribus nostris de Biar istius anni usque in hunc presentem diem et de omnibus datis, solucionibus, missionibus, et expensis ibidem factis pro nobis infra dictum tempus, de quo computo concedimus nos esse a te bene paccatos; et sic coequatis recepcionibus cum datis, missionibus, et

Peter of Segura was castellan-bailiff at the time; later that same month he submitted his own accounts for Biar, covering the past two years. Two months afterward, the bishop of Huesca in Aragon received in farm the future revenues of Biar and Alcira to cover his sale of wheat to Prince Peter; the conveyance allowed the bishop to name his own temporary castellan at Biar and bailiff at Alcira. Biar's world now turned upside down. The great Mudejar revolt shook the kingdom of Valencia, sweeping Biar into the rebel ranks. As James died on his battle-torn frontier, and Peter fought stubbornly to win southern Valencia "a second time," Biar's revenues lay once more at the service of Islam. It held out almost to the end, collapsing finally in September 1277. Now the crown sought to drain off Mudejar population from this strategic point toward attractive new settlements farther north, to bring in Christian settlers for proper defense, and to strengthen Biar's works and garrison.[45]

UNDERLINGS AND PROTECTION

At the lower end of the tax-collecting structure, assisting the district *amīn*, a staff of assistants and clerks lies in a documentary penumbra.[46] Only a few documents specify the collection costs, much

---

expensis, remanet quod debemus tornare tibi Mahomat, alamino predicto, cccxciii solidos et viii denarios regalium, quos assignamus tibi habendos et percipiendos in redditibus et exitibus nostris de Biar anni proximi venturi." On *paccatus* see Rodón Binué, *Lenguaje técnico del feudalismo*, p. 184.

[45] Details of the war are in Burns, *Islam under the Crusaders*, ch. 2, part 3, and ch. 14, parts 1 and 2 passim and esp. part 3. The contemporary Muntaner says of Peter: "segurament hom pot be dir, que dit senyor infant En Pere conqués altra vegada partida del regne de València" (*Crònica*, ch. 10). On James's movement of Biar Mudejars northward, see Fernández y González, *Mudejares de Castilla*, appendix, doc. 51 (1279). For the surrender of rebel Biar, see Soldevila, *Pere el Gran*, part 2, 1, appendix, doc. 95 (Sept. 8, 1277).

[46] Roca Traver adverts to the *clavario*, who became the local treasurer in Valencian Christian communities, and implies a place for him in Mudejar society ("Vida mudéjar," p. 130; and on the Christian officer see García de Cáceres, *Impuestos de la ciudad de Valencia*, pp. 61-62, including his *arca* or deposit box at the cathedral sacristy). The Chivert Charter comes closest, with "saionem et ianitorem sive portarium"; but this would semantically rather be a *ḥājib*, and realistically is probably the gate custodian described by Ibn 'Abdūn (*Séville musulmane, le traité*, pp. 71-73). Aldea's charter closes with a protective clause against Jews or Christians selling a Muslim's property to recover a debt, then adds: "volumus et concedimus quod semper instituatis et habeatis sayonem sarracenum," perhaps indicating a

less expenses,[47] actually involved at the lowest level—in effect the recompense given to the collector of the individual tax. Thus the *alfarda* for Beniopa and its countryside in 1268 cost 100 besants to bring in. Since the total tax came to 1,100 besants, with the entry of 100 besants subscribed, one might reasonably see the latter as in fact a note of expenditure, a refund to meet costs. In fact it seems to have been a tax in itself, a surcharge of roughly ten percent, reckoned beyond the officially stated tax total.[48] As with higher officials, the lower collectors were taking the usual tenth as salary, adding also their expenses.[49]

The pattern can be seen again at Pego in 1269, where the "salary of the collector" for taking 930 besants from as many sectors of land

---

fiscal role for the latter. A non-Valencian account does describe the "saionem, qui colligit prescriptos directos et somoneisse los mauros in açofra, et tenet las claues de las portas de la villa [de Cortes] et abre la porta et serra de nocte" ("Documentos para la reconquista del valle del Ebro," part 3, *EEMCA*, v [1952], doc. 399 [1234]). Macho y Ortega found that the very large aljamas in Aragon proper in subsequent centuries had a *clavario* as treasurer, who administered all taxes, income, and disbursements, drew up the accounts for the year, and was well paid ("Mudéjares aragoneses," p. 160). López de Ayala merely asserts, without details or proof, that the Moorish aljamas in the kingdom of Castile managed all the intra-aljama collection, "con verdadera independencia administrativa" (*Contribuciones é impuestos en León y Castilla*, p. 479). An interesting survival of collection techniques unrelated to public taxes at Valencia city is the statement of shares owed for Ramaḍān by a brotherhood there in 1515, done in Arabic by the mosque's custodian (Fernández y González, *Mudejares de Castilla*, appendix, doc. 97).

[47] Arch. Crown, James I, Reg. Canc. 17, fol. 29v (Dec. 31, 1263): "item pro expensis ordei et frumenti de aportacione, xlvi solidos minus ii denariis"; "pro baiulia, ccc solidos"; "item pro expensis ordei et frumenti de mensuratione, viii solidos"; "item logerium domus ordei et frumenti, viii solidos" (a storage rental); fol. 30: "de quibus levamus pro missionibus vinee domini regis et vini," 55 solidi and 5 pence. Expenses of the oven ran to 22½ solidi, and on fol. 28v to 25¾ solidi; "pro aptanda carniceria" cost almost 25 solidi, and on fol. 27v "pro missionibus balneorum, carnicerie et furnorum" came to 81 solidi.

[48] *Ibid.*, Reg. Canc. 35, fol. 3 (1268): "item lalfarda de Beniopa e del termino, m besants c; [item] colidura, c besants." Fol. 4 (1268), Pego: "item ossera del collidor, cxiii besants, de los quals dic al colidor xxxviii besants, assi finca als seior infant lxxv besants." *Collidor* or collector and *collidura* or collecting derive from Latin *colligere* through Romance *collir*. At least in later years *collida* was a surcharge or fee to meet the collector's salary and costs; see Mateu y Llopis, *Materiales para un glosario de diplomática*, p. 26. The later *collidors* of crown rents continued to be "frequently Moors and Jews"; see Mateu y Llopis, "Para el estudio del monedaje," p. 318, though his illustration seems rather our *amín*: "Juce Dulmelich, moro de Borja [Aragon], cullidor e receptor de nostras rendas e dreytos que havemos en la dita villa e sus terminos."

[49] See Chapter VII, n. 6.

266

came to exactly 93 besants. Pego's "tithe and *lleuda* together" was 80 besants, its "collecting" 8. The "market" brought 180 besants and its "collecting" 18. Subsequent entries in the same list balance a tax of 25 besants against a "collection" of 2 besants and 5 *millareses*, followed by a balance of 1 *millarès* to the collector for every besant taken—6 *millareses* for 6 besants, 7 for 7, and 18 for 18. For collecting 53 besants in head tax the collector got 5 besants and 3 *millareses*. For 97 besants and 8 *millareses* from oven and chickens, the collecting fee came to 9 besants and 8 *millareses*. The pattern continues down the list: 13 besants and 5 *millareses* against 13 *millareses* and 2 pence, 17 besants and 6 *millareses* against 17 *millareses* and 2 pence, 37 besants and 2 *millareses* against 3 besants and 7 *millareses*, 28 besants and 2 *millareses* against 2 besants and 8 *millareses*, and 107 besants and 3 *millareses* against 10 besants and 7 *millareses*. The collector's take then dipped as several taxes-in-kind were reckoned in money, the difference perhaps allowing for the greater trouble, expense, and fluctuating prices of such commodities. Here 187½ besants balanced against 12½ for collecting, and 375 besants against 25. The pattern returned with the *alfarda*, at 600 against 60.[50]

The crown protected its Muslims from greedy or overzealous collectors, if only as a commonsense dictate of tax husbandry. Officials or tax farmers occasionally attempted to increase their levies unilaterally. The extra taxes imposed on Muslim tenants in the next century, especially by seignorial landlords, had their ominous foreshadowing even in the thirteenth. By 1279 these attempts had so agitated Játiva's Moors that they appealed to the king. Peter responded in July with a rebuke to the local bailiff and justiciar: "I hear that some are molesting the Saracens of the Játiva aljama by new taxes and in other ways." He ordered officials to consult and follow the charters (*instrumenta*) conceded by James I and by himself.[51]

---

[50] Arch. Crown, James I, Reg. Canc. 35, fol. 4 (1269): "soldada de colidor"; "diesmo e leuda del iunto . . . item collidura"; "el mercado . . . item cuillidura," and so through the list.

[51] *Ibid.*, Peter III, Reg. Canc. 41, fol. 101v (July 3, 1279): "intelleximus quod aliqui aggravant sarracenos aliame de Xativa in novis peticionibus et aliis, quatenus mandamus. . . ." See also Chapter VII, nn. 34, 41. The crown later assured Mudejar immigrants to Játiva that taxes remained as they had been in the days of King James: "et quod ipsi etiam dent et solvant tributa que consueverunt solvere tempore dicti domini regis Iacobi et postmodum usque nunc"; see Arch. Crown, Alfonso III,

When war with France upset the crown budget, leading to public outcry over tax innovations, King Peter cut back the new taxes.[52] Around the same time he addressed himself to the problem of profiteers among the tax farmers of Mudejar revenues. He issued instructions in 1285 designed to inhibit fraud on the part of collectors, taking care to have a copy sent to every *amīn* throughout the kingdom of Valencia.[53] Underlining his concern, he made a separate document directing the lieutenant of the crown's procurator below the Júcar River to present these instructions. Among other provisos, accounts had to be submitted in the first week of the coming December.[54] A number of such instructions, designed to protect Muslims from greedy collectors, went out from the royal chancellery.[55] On Christmas Day of 1282 Peter had cautioned the Jew Samuel to observe instructions for collecting Mudejar taxes.[56] The

---

Reg. Canc. 75, fol. 5 (May 3, 1287). In Reg. Canc. 83, fol. 66 (July 30, 1290) Alfonso warned his officials: "cum sarraceni vallis de Uxo asserunt habere privilegia ab illustrissimo domino Iacobo avo nostro et domino Petro patre nostro, eorum videlicet que debent dare seu peitare nobis . . . mandamus vobis quatenus . . . observetis." In Reg. Canc. 85, fol. 127v (March 28, 1291) he rebuked Bernard William of Villafranca: "intelleximus per sarracenos eiusdem loci [de Gallinera] quod vos gravatis eos pro eo quia compellitis ipsos et bona sua ad solvendum tercias reddituum et aliorum iurium que dare debent ante terminum"; Bernard was to desist from this demand for premature payment, respecting the "terminis quibus eas solvere teneantur et consueverunt." In Reg. Canc. 80, fol. 137 (Dec. 17, 1289) Alfonso suspended a collection temporarily on one tax to ease collection of military obligations: "quod supersedeat exigere monetaticum a sarracenis morerie regni Valencie usque ad festum Pasche et quod compellat omnes christianos et sarracenos a villa Gandie ultra ad solvendum partem suam in excubiis et talais"; on military *excubia* see below, n. 59; Catalan *talaia* is a guard. In Reg. Canc. 63, fol. 14 (Jan. 7, 1286), he intervened to protect the "sarracenos de Villamarchante qui obligati sunt in debitis aliquibus iudeis" against paying "pro lucro seu usura ipsorum debitum aliquid ultra constitutionem per predecessores nostros editatam . . . et si quidam receperint ab ipsis sarracenis . . . restitui faciat."

[52] Martínez Aloy, *Diputación de Valencia*, pp. 34-35.

[53] Arch. Crown, Peter III, Reg. Canc. 57, fol. 225v (Oct. 25, 1285): "con nos havian entes que alcuns de vos altres han fetes . . . enganns dels maiors als menors e dels menors als mijans por no acominalar dels peytes"; *acominalar* means to assess or share equally, and an *engan de mitges* means fraudulently to understate by half.

[54] *Ibid.*: "manam vos que la primera setmana del mes de Desembre proxime vinent siats denant nos en quelque loco nos siam, e quens aportets . . . tot ço que cullit haiats de les aljames, ço assaber cascuns de nostres logars, e tot ço que haiats taylar regitat sobre les dites aljames."

[55] See also n. 90, and Chapter VII, n. 34.

[56] Arch. Crown, Peter III, Reg. Canc. 59, fol. 188 (Dec. 25, 1282): "contra ipsam ordinationem [regis Iacobi] non gravatis seu permittatis in aliquo adgravari."

next year the king warned his brother, Judah b. Manasseh, collector at the Chella aljama, not to demand a return in excess of the amount owed.[57]

King James had intervened similarly on a grand scale in 1259. He ordered "that you suspend for the Saracens of the kingdom of Valencia the taxes that you required of them, until the feast of St. John in June soon to come, namely those taxes that you have not as yet collected; and you are to receive and take from them taxes as you see these contained below." The king included an interim schedule of modest taxes: 300 besants each from two aljamas, 200 each from four others, 100 each from seven, and nothing from a final seven; whatever had already been collected was to be reckoned as paid on this new schedule. The submission of accounts by local bailiffs was "prorogued" until such times as the king, or his special representative, was personally "in the kingdom of Valencia." Meanwhile "you are to investigate the truth of the matter from Saracens" and other residents of the castles and jurisdictions involved, as to how much was owed at each place, and to prepare a written report.[58] In 1273, when the royal chancellery lost the document obliging Crevillente's Moors to pay a tax, King James waived that tax forever.[59]

[57] *Ibid.*, Reg. Canc. 60, fol. 94 (April 18, 1283): "Iafudano Avenmenaçe . . . quod vos compellitis sarracenos det [*sic*] Xella qui sunt Iacobi de Oblitis ad solvendum vobis maiorem quantitatem pecunie quam deberent pro quolibet casato contra ordinationem domini regis." On the Manasseh brothers see below, part 5.

[58] Arch. Crown, James I, Reg. Canc. 10, fol. 108 (April 14, 1259). "Volumus enim quod elongetis sarracenos regni Valencie de peytis quas ab eis petistis usque ad festum Sancti Iohannis Iunii proxime venturum, de illis videlicet peytis quas adhuc non collegistis, et recipiatis ac habeatis ab eis peytas prout inferius videbitis contineri; compotum enim alcaydorum volumus quod prorogetur quousque nos vel Eximinus de Focibus simus in regno Valencie. Interim enim petatis veritatem a sarracenis et hominibus habitantibus in terminis castrorum que dicti alcaydi tenent pro nobis, quid et quantum eisdem alcaydis dederunt, et illud scribatis taliter quod possitis illud nobis hostendere."

[59] See the incident and document below, in Chapter IX, n. 49. Arch. Reino Val., Real Canc., codex 659, Llibre negre, fols. 79v-80v (April 24, 1342), is a crown document revealing that the farmer of Valencia city's Moorish quarter had some responsibility for protecting it, "ex antiqua consuetudine observata in moraria civitatis Valencie." This aimed at security connected with tax collecting probably, and would seem to have dated from our earlier period; "consueverunt baiudulus seu arrendator iurium baiulie dicte morerie facere et instituere certas limitatas excubias tam in dicta moreria, quam prope et extra, antiquitus designa[tas] ad conservacionem interne [?] et detentionem ipsius morarie, et prout est et fuit et diutius observatum licitumque sit ipsi baiulo pro exercicio sui officii arma deffere prohibita"; the document also calls the tax farmer "baiulum seu emptorem." On *excubia* see

ROLE OF THE JEWS

Jews had long enjoyed a distinguished, if modest, role in governmental circles of the realms of Aragon. Treasurers, bailiffs, or royal
physicians, they served also as executive agents, counselors, and diplomats. During the chaotic opening years of King James's reign, as
Pope Innocent III notified the world, a much needed peace was
negotiated "between the Saracens and the realm of Aragon by the
Jew Isaac," commissioned by the cardinal-legate helping to reorgan-
ize the kingdom.[60] James valued his prosperous Jewish communities

---

Rodón Binué, *Lenguaje técnico del feudalismo*, p. 126 with note; see also *Cartas de
población de Cataluña*, 1, docs. 1 (801) and 2 (844): "explorationes et excubias quod
usitato vocabulo wactas dicunt." A form of the defense tax *guaita* (from *wahten*),
the Latin *excubia* or *escubia* is unrelated to Catalan *escubia* and uncommon at our
period. On the bailiff of Valencia city's Moorish quarter, a lieutenant of the city's
bailiff, under James I, see Piles Ros, *Bayle general de Valencia*, p. 35.

[60] *La documentación pontificia*, doc. 537 (Jan. 23, 1216): "et treuge similiter inter
sarracenos et regnum Aragonum per Azacum iudeum de mandato ipsius cardinalis
statute serventur"; see also Soldevila, *Primers temps de Jaume I*, p. 95 and appendix,
doc. 1. On Jewish bailiffs in Aragon and Valencia see David Romano Ventura,
"Los funcionarios judíos de Pedro el Grande de Aragón," *BRABLB*, xxviii (1969-
1970), 5-41; his summary under the same title in *Congrés VII*, ii, 561; and his
"Hermanos Abenmenassé," pp. 243-292. His *Estudio histórico de la familia Ravaya,
bailes de los reyes de Aragón en el siglo xiii* (1951) and his *Contribución a la
historia de los judíos de la corona de Aragón durante el reinado de Pedro el Grande*
(1960) are completed but as yet unpublished. See also Jerome Lee Shneidman,
"Jews as Royal Bailiffs in Thirteenth-Century Aragon," *Historia judaica*, xix (1957),
55-66; his *Rise of the Aragonese-Catalan Empire*, ii, chs. 13-14; and the bibliography
for his latter chapters, ii, 557-563. Helene Wieruszowski's "Peter der Grosse von
Katalonien-Aragon und die Juden," *Estudis universitaris catalans*, xxii (1936), 239-
262, has been reprinted in German in her *Politics and Culture in Medieval Spain
and Italy* (Rome, 1971), ch. 7. For background, see the older work of José Amador
de los Ríos, *Historia social, política, y religiosa de los judíos de España y Portugal*,
2 vols. (Buenos Aires, [1875-1876] 1943), i, book 1, ch. 9 on James I, and book 2,
ch. 1 for Peter III; Neuman, *Jews in Spain*, ii, ch. 20, and the recent Baer, *Jews in
Christian Spain*, i, ch. 4, especially as cited below, as well as the more general
European context in Baron, *Social and Religious History of the Jews*, analytical
index to first eight volumes, *sub* "Taxation," and x, ch. 44. A panoramic if superficial view of the Jewish contribution can be gained from the pertinent entries in
Martínez Ferrando's *Catálogo*, but especially from Jean Regné, "Catalogue des actes
de Jaime Ier, Pedro III, et Alfonso III, rois d'Aragon, concernant les juifs," *Revue
des études juives*, lx (1910), 161-201, progressing through subsequent issues and
gathered into offprint book form (Paris, 1911-1914), then continuing through
James II (1291-1327), lxxv (1922), 140-178 and following issues. Emery's *Jews of
Perpignan in the Thirteenth Century*, though describing an area belonging to the

and even mounted an immigration movement to expand them. He multiplied the number of Jewish officials in his service, possibly as a maneuver to increase crown autonomy;[61] his son gave them such prominence as to provoke a baronial reaction toward restoring constitutional balance. During the final twenty years of James's rule and the ten of Peter's, over fifty such officials move about in the crown records.

The uncritical observer tends to suppose that such power must have derived from their role as moneylenders and financiers, as clannish aliens excluded from more normal occupations and useful as fiscal milch-cows. The stereotype does not fit the Jews of James's realms. Owners of estates, farms, and livestock, and engaged in the occupations common to their Christian neighbors, with even the urban artisans a semiagrarian class, they did not dominate either the merchant or the moneylending fields. They did comprise their own community, with substantial legal and political autonomy, after the pattern employed by Christian and Islamic governments around the Mediterranean; but the privileged Jewish quarters were not then ghettos, and antisemitism was still a cloud on the horizon.

The sunny scene darkened with the century's advance; but despite a share of tribulation and trauma the years under James and Peter are rightly called a Golden Age for the Jews of Spain. Their courtier and administrative role expanded with these passing years, especially deriving from a base as local or as more general bailiff. As the Arabic section of the royal chancery they took on ever greater importance when the Reconquest annexed princely realms to the crown and spread Arago-Catalan influence over North Africa. The importance of Jewish financier-counselors of the king peaked during the first two-thirds of Peter's reign, and then began to wane.

Valencia, especially its Mudejar situation, had much to do with the expanded participation of Jews in royal and local government. It not only provided broad new fields of action in management, commerce, and service to the crown, but presented a specialized area of problems and opportunities in the form of a prosperous, dissident majority locked into its Arabic culture and language. With the

---

crown of Aragon, has "next to nothing" about Jewish participation in royal finance (p. 40) and treats besides of an exceptional situation (see above, Chapter VII, n. 64).

[61] Shneidman, *Rise of the Aragonese-Catalan Empire*, II, ch. 15, esp. p. 485.

passing decades Valencia became increasingly important to Jewish financiers, as opportunities in Catalonia diminished and as progressive expropriation of Muslim rebels together with the increasing prosperity of peacetime Valencia opened fresh prospects. Jews with administrative skills, capital, a grasp of Arabic, or all three advantages, found Valencia a land of challenge and promise. Some of those who won lands and status here may have belonged to families held over from Islamic Valencia; some undoubtedly brought to the Mudejar enterprise a unique knowledge of Spanish and North African Islamic ways, rooted not merely in commercial experience but in far-flung connections of family and friendship in Islamic states. Name forms like Alconstantini (al-Quṣṭanṭīnī) or Abinafia (Ibn Yaḥyā) reflect this dimension.

Jews were not alone in possessing exotic qualifications, since there was a greater degree of intermingling between the Islamic and Christian worlds than is commonly realized; at the local level, moreover, a *qāḍī* or *amīn* with a command of Romance comprised an effective bridge between Muslim taxpayer and Christian collector. But the Jewish community probably held the larger share of available educated men endowed with the language and expertise so valuable, though not absolutely necessary, for supervising the collection of Mudejar taxes. Their Arabic was often a true second language, moreover, rather than the pragmatic or minimal commercial tool. Spanish monarchs trusted them as men whose horizons of political ambition were necessarily limited and who existed as wards of the crown, aliens under a permanent but separate constitution, unlikely to ally with the baronage or local church in power struggles. Valencia consequently offered a fertile field of action for Jewish civil servants; they persisted here in the role of local bailiffs even after their participation elsewhere in that office had decreased, later in the century.

Valencia differed from the other realms of Aragon in not developing an effective bailiff general over all the local bailiffs until late in Peter's reign. The Valencia city bailiff did exercise an embryonic general function from the start, and a similar general bureaucrat did appear very early for the region below the Júcar, as we have seen.[62] Certain Jews were particularly active in this more

[62] See Chapter VII, part 2.

general way, such as Moses Alconstantini for a time at Valencia city. Joseph Ravaya supplied a kind of overseer function as King Peter's treasurer, and during the annual sale of rents or local bailiwicks by the regional bailiff general he handled those pertaining to the Valencian kingdom. Aaron b. Yahya as bailiff general for Aragon proper briefly had responsibility over the Ademuz, Alpuente, and Liria bailiates. This relatively underdeveloped structure increased the importance of the local bailiff in this frontier kingdom. During the period of greatest Jewish participation, under King Peter, the historian Romano distinguishes four patterns of operation in Valencia: different Jews alternating as bailiff, as at Alcira, Játiva, and Sagunto; Jewish bailiffs appearing as isolated instances in a series of Christian bailiffs, as at Carbonera, Denia, and Segorbe; the single long tenure of Solomon Vidal for six years at Villarreal; and the biennium, like that of Moses Alconstantini at Valencia city, or triennium, like that of Samuel b. Vives in the Alfandech Valley.[63]

In friendly dispute with Romano, Shneidman contends that Jews controlled the economic wealth of the crown estates and the financial administration of the government, from 1265 to 1283, a centrality deliberately engineered by King James in order to wrest power from his feudal lords. In this scheme the Jewish bailiff was civil servant, only occasionally or incidentally plunging as moneylender into rent speculation; his wealth derived, not from antecedent capital but from profits and gifts consequent upon his role as bailiff. Both Romano and Shneidman agree that the eventual reaction against Jewish bailiffs under Peter derived from baronial determination to redress the balance of power or governmental control in their own favor, rather than from antisemitism.[64] Whatever the resolution of these larger issues, the considerable importance of the Jews in collecting Christian, mixed Christian-Mudejar, and Mudejar taxes is evident.

A series of financial and loan operations so localized and under transient custody, conducted by many individuals and surviving for us in so casual, disjointed a type of record, can best be examined by reconstructing the Mudejar role of the more prominent, representative Jews. These were often members of powerful dynasties within the Jewish communities of Arago-Catalonia. Such families formed

---

[63] "Funcionarios judíos de Pedro el Grande" [*BRABLB*], pp. 14-15, 22-23.
[64] Shneidman, *Rise of the Aragonese-Catalan Empire*, II, 432-440, 485, and Romano, "Funcionarios judíos" [*BRABLB*], pp. 8n., 9.

an oligarchy, split by factions and rivalries, which had come to dominate the big city communities by the early thirteenth century. Their aristocratic members, like the equivalent Muslim notables or Christian knights, engaged heavily in commerce and financial investments. They entered *partnerships of every description*, with Christians, Muslims, or other Jews, frequently to exploit some passing opportunity. Especially as an informally leagued family partnership, however, each great house comprised a pool of capital, credit, influence, and permanence, strengthened by a multitude of transient partnerships between individual members, like some powerful firm.

The great houses represented in Valencia had their roots generally in northern communities, but some individuals or families seem to have belonged to Islamic Valencia. Ashtor and Beinart believe that 162 Jewish households stayed on in Valencia city alone after its surrender, a community of respectable size, and that a hundred new households soon joined them as settlers; by 1300, when confrontation between the great houses and the other classes of the Jewish community at Valencia city over tax assessment brought royal intervention, there were some 250 taxpaying households. But if the courtier and great family class looms large in the supervisory records of the crown, ordinary artisans could also profit from Valencian taxes by way of investment, entering a consortium, or advancing a loan against village revenues.[65]

Members of the celebrated Cavallería clan, whose Romance name derived from past connection with the Templars, appear on the Valencian scene. The patriarch of the family, Judah b. Lavi, bailiff of Zaragoza and "treasurer of the realm" of Aragon proper, owned properties at Valencia city both in and out of the Jewish quarter, and as early as 1260 agreed to settle one of his four sons, "whichever one you wish, in the kingdom of Valencia." In 1273 he won as a favor free grazing rights for a thousand sheep belonging to his Valencian Mudejar *exarici*. As bailiff of Valencia some time before 1275, he assigned a large property in the Moorish quarter near the king's "baths of the aforesaid Moorish quarter" and hard by an

---

[65] On the aristocratic families and the conflict within Arago-Catalan Jewry, see Baer, *Jews in Christian Spain*, I, 211ff.; on numbers see I, 194, and Shneidman, *Rise of the Aragonese-Catalan Empire*, II, 419-420. See also Haim Beinart, "Valencia," *Encyclopaedia judaica*, 16 vols. (Jerusalem, 1971-1972), XVI, 54-58. On family partnerships of the great Jewish families, see Goitein, *Mediterranean Society*, I, 180-183.

Islamic cemetery.[66] No specific records connect him with the Mudejars, though their taxes and persons fell under his jurisdiction in the
region of the capital city. His son Solomon b. Lavi received in 1273
"the bailiate of Murviedro and Segorbe, Onda and Uxó and Almonacid as long as it pleases us," and maintained his "headquarters" by
royal order "in the castle of Murviedro"; later in the document these
appear as separate "bailiates." King James directed "each and every
man of the said places, namely Christians and Saracens, to answer to
you in our place for all our revenues, income, and taxes."[67] Presumably these Mudejars conveyed the taxes of their several aljamas here
through the respective *amīn* of each. In March 1275 Solomon presented his accounts for fourteen months as bailiff of Murviedro and
for two months as bailiff of Almonacid.[68]

As eminent as the Cavallería family were the Alconstantini, their
rivals for predominance over the Zaragoza Jewish community, the
leading community of Aragon proper. The family name suggests
that they came from Constantine in North Africa. They roused
angry reaction against their pretensions to judicial authority over all

[66] Arch. Crown, James I, Reg. Canc. 11, fol. 186v (Dec. 19, 1260): "donationem
vobis facimus in hunc modum quod unum de filiis vestris, quemcumque volueritis,
in regno Valencie populatis." His first appearance in Valencian records comes in
Reg. Canc. 10, fol. 18 (Sept. 6, 1257): "fideli suo Iahudano de Cavalleria, baiulo
Cesarauguste . . . sciatis quod nos assignavimus Iohanni Dominici civi valentino
super peyta de Alfayerino quingentos solidos iaccenses." Reg. Canc. 20, fol. 311
(Jan. 17, 1275): "patuum terre ad opus domorum quod Iahudanus de Cavalleria
baiulus noster Valencie tibi assignavit supra [*sic*] moreriam Valencie, et habet in
longum xx bracias et in latitudinem vi bracias, et affrontat . . . cum balneis morerie
predicte." *Supra* may indicate that it stood just outside the quarter, as the cemetery
also suggests but does not demand. For an outline of the family tree, the great trial
of 1266 for blasphemy, and the fifteenth-century family schism as many converted
to Christianity, see Francisca Vendrell Gallostra, "Aportación documental para el
estudio de la familia La Caballería," *Sefarad*, III (1943) 115-154, and Haim Beinart, "Cavalleria (Caballería), de la," *Encyclopaedia judaica*, V, 261-265. See also
Bofarull, "Jaime I y los judíos," pp. 833-836, 921-922; Baer, *Jews in Christian Spain*,
I, 85, 406-407.

[67] *Colección diplomática*, doc. 1,408 (Aug. 31, 1273): "baiuliam Muriveteris et
Segorbi, Onde et Uxoni et de Almonecid, dum nobis placuerit, ita scilicet quod tu
sis baiulus . . . baiularum suarum . . . et habeas staticum tuum in castro Muriveteris . . . ; mandantes firmiter universis et singulis hominibus dictorum locorum,
christianis scilicet et sarracenis, quod tibi loco nostri, vel cui volueris loco tui,
respondeant de redditibus et exitibus ac iuribus nostris omnibus." Both Bofarull
("Jaime I y los judíos") and Huici (*Colección diplomática*) have published a number of documents touching on Judah's career.

[68] *Itinerari*, p. 516 (March 29, 1275).

Aragonese Jewry; in one of his rare intrusions into Jewish domestic politics, King James canceled this writ-supported claim. The first of the Alconstantini to be connected with Valencia was the rabbi Bahiel, Arabic secretary to the crown, who helped negotiate the surrenders of Majorca, Játiva, and Murcia; his brother Solomon assisted at Minorca's submission. Bahiel's sons Moses and Solomon embarked on eminent careers in the bailiates of Valencia. Moses acted as chief judicial authority for the Jews of the Valencian kingdom from 1258.

Like his father Bahiel, who struggled against the Cavallería clan at Zaragoza and led the fight for the study of Maimonides in an intra-aljama dispute, Moses had his share of battles. Suing the Zaragoza community, he had half his property confiscated for forging a document of evidence. Rising thereafter to the posts of treasurer, Arabic secretary, and in 1277 through 1281 bailiff of Valencia city, he survived a number of embroilments with Valencian officials but was ultimately ousted and punished on charges of unscrupulousness brought by Valencian Jews and Christians. He was also implicated in the beating of a rabbi who had given a legal opinion to King Peter about the feuds between the leading Jewish families. He did win pardon, and restoration of his confiscated properties, but his star had declined and he died six years later. His long tenure of the Valencia city bailiate had involved some wider administrative powers, and of course he had supervised local Mudejar as well as Christian taxes. His brother Solomon held bailiates at Murviedro and Montesa in 1278 and 1279, and collected the kingdom's herbage in 1283; all these offices affected the Mudejar population. He held high office within the Zaragoza Jewish community too, and was proposed by the queen of Aragon for crown rabbi and chief justice. Mudejar affairs in Valencia, as well as Christian, benefited from the caliber and energies of such strong figures and from their family strength.[69]

[69] Baer, *Jews in Christian Spain*, I, 105-106, 138-139, 143, 146, 163, 172, 223-224, 242, 409, 411. *Llibre dels feyts*, chs. 74, 118, 325. Bofarull, "Jaime I y los judíos," pp. 835-838, with documents published. Haim Beinart, "Alconstantini," *Encyclopaedia judaica*, II, 550-551; the family moved to Turkey after the Spanish expulsion, later settling at Ancona in Italy as the Constantini. In Arch. Crown, James I, Reg. Canc. 13, fol. 167 (March 29, 1264) the crown confirmed to "Mosse filio Bahiel alfaquimi nostri quondam et vestris imperpetuum illam partem hereditatis vobis pertinen[t]em ex partitione facta inter Salamonam alfaquimum nostrum et vos ac fratres vestros,

A remarkable figure among the Jewish bailiffs in Valencia was Vives b. Joseph b. Vives, or Vives Abenvives. He first appears in 1261 as an affluent "Jew of the city of Valencia," purchasing from a knight "buildings, farms, vineyards, and an estate."[70] His public career, as a finance official for Peter both as prince and later as king, first becomes visible in a loan of 1,000 solidi to the prince in 1267, continues strongly through the next fifteen years, and fades to an occasional echo during the final years of the century.[71] Vives became deeply involved in Mudejar taxes, especially in the Alfandech Valley and Pego. In 1267 Prince Peter "sells to you Vives, son of Joseph b. Vives, our Jew, and to anyone you wish," for 4,600 solidi, all the revenues due in Ribarroja "and from the Saracens of Liria."[72] On the same day Vives received "our revenues and income from the Saracens of Alfandech" to repay his previous loan of 4,000 solidi; he was to collect these himself.[73]

In August of the following year the prince itemized nearly a dozen loans and expenditures by Vives in his service to a total of 22,714 solidi, "which we assign to you and yours to have and receive in all our revenues and income of Alfandech de Marignén," with priority over all previous assignations of debt made there in favor of

---

videlicet quasdam domos et vineas in Muroveteri et terminis suis, et alchaream in Albacer . . . et vineas in termino Muriveteris . . . et in Conillera, et domos in Valentia . . . et hereditatem . . . in Algezira . . . et ortum quem habetis in Alcanicia et molendinum in termino Algezire . . . et domos in Algezira."

[70] Arch. Crown, James I, Reg. Canc. 11, fol. 199v-200 (April 9, 1261): to Vives and a colleague, "iudeis civitatis Valencie," "omnes domos, ortos, vineas, et heredi-tatem . . . que omnia sunt in territorio civitatis Valencie," of "Martinus Sancii de Loriz miles et Maria Diaz uxor eius." On Vives see Baer, *Jews in Christian Spain*, I, 407, 411. Jerome Lee Shneidman, "Abenvives," *Encyclopaedia judaica*, 11, 70 and his *Rise of the Aragonese-Catalan Empire*, 11, 473-474, 484.

[71] Arch. Crown, James I, Reg. Canc. 17, fol. 22v (Sept. 1, 1267): "[kalendas] Septembris mcclx septimo fecit infans Arnaldo de Romanino baiulo Valencie albara-num septem [mille et lx s]olidorum regalium Valencie, in quibus . . . sunt compu-tati in eisdem mille solidi quos dominus infans deb[e]bat Vives iudeo cum albarano."

[72] *Ibid.*, Reg. Canc. 35, fol. 11 (March 12, 1267): "vendimus vobis Vives filio Iucefi Abenvives iudeo nostro et cui volueritis omnes redditus . . . in Rib[a] Roya et terminis suis et a sarracenis de Liria." Peter ordered Vives to pay 3,000 to a creditor, the Lady Bella, "et residuos secundum [quod in] libro compoti [con]tinetur."

[73] *Ibid.*, fol. 13 (March 12, 1267): "in redditibus et exitibus nostris sarra[cen]orum de Alfandech quos pro nobis debetis [h]act[enus] percipere et colligere." The loan "quos nobis mutua[stis bono] amore, et de mandato nostro tradidistis Iacobo de [L]inars scriptori nostro," has later cancellation marks to indicate fulfillment.

"some knights of ours"; Vives was to prededuct a salary of 950 solidi yearly for the governing castellan, Arnold of Fores.[74] These large sums were essentially taxes from Alfandech's Mudejars. In an accounting in the following spring, as "our bailiff for Alfandech, for Ribarroja, and for Liria," Vives presented accounts for the past year and submitted a list of outstanding expenditures totaling 8,314 solidi (including 15 solidi to bring falcons from Alfandech): he renewed his control of Alfandech's revenues for another year, again excepting the salary of castellan Arnold.[75] Continuing as bailiff of Alfandech, he assumed as well the bailiwick of Sollana and Trullás in 1270-1271 and 1275, and perhaps for the intervening years. In 1270 he rented "all the revenues, profits, income, and proceeds . . . of Alcira and of the Saracens of its Moorish quarter and countryside," a gross receipt of 13,000 solidi per annum to be deposited with the prince in three equal payments.[76]

The interplay between governing castellan of a Mudejar region and fiscal bailiff, where the two did not coincide in the same man, can be seen at Alfandech in May 1272. Prince Peter notified Vives, "bailiff of Alfandech de Marignén," that Arnold of Fores had a successor as castellan there, Peter of Sant Climent; "and we desire that he hold the said castle for us, and receive or cause to be received all revenues, income, proceeds, and whatever other taxes we collect or ought to collect in the valley and jurisdiction of the said castle for any reason from Saracens or anyone else." As bailiff, Vives would "henceforth answer to him or his delegate faithfully and entirely

[74] *Ibid.*, fol. 14 (Aug. 9, 1268): "confitemur nos debere vobis, Vives filio Iucefi Aben Vives, baiulo nostro de Alfandech ix millia dc[ccclxiv] solidorum . . . et sic sunt in summa xxii millia dccxiiii solidorum regalium, quos assignamus vobis habendos et percipiendos in universis redditibus et exitibus nostris de Alfandech de Marayen, non obstantibus assignationibus ibi factis aliquibus militibus nostris, . . . exceptis dccccl solidis quos Arnaldus de Foresio, alcaydus castri de Alfandech debet percipere quolibet anno pro salario suo et custodia dicti castri, quos solvere teneamini eidem de redditibus et ex[iti]bus antedictis." An annotation reads: "solutum est et recuperatum."

[75] *Ibid.*, fol. 14v (April 20, 1269): "confitemur vobis . . . baiulo nostro de Alfandec, de Riba Roya, et de Liria, quod dedistis c[c]cxxix solidos et vi denarios qu[os] nobis debebatis tornare de compoto reddituum [pre]dictorum locorum anni preteriti. . . . Et sic sunt in summa octo millia cccxiiii solidorum"; "item xv solidos quos dedistis illis qui extraxerunt falcones [de] Alfandec." See fol. 15 (April 20, 1277): "vobis Vives baiulo nostro de Alfandec, de Ripa Roya et de Liria."

[76] *Ibid.*, Reg. Canc. 37, fol. 14v (March 19, 1270): "omnes redditus, fructus, et exitus, proventus . . . Algazire et sarracenorum morarie et termini."

about all our aforesaid revenues, income, proceeds, and claims, and not to anyone else." The arrangement especially affected approval of loan assignments, now to be confirmed and processed by the castellan "according to the tenor of the bill" each creditor held from the prince. Vives was to "sell or pay" only with "the consent and mandate of the said Peter."[77] Vives continued to hold the post of Alfandech, presenting accounts to the prince in July 1272 and a general accounting for the past five years in May 1273. He also made a separate "accounting for the *moixerifat* for five years at Alfandech," a total of 4,698 solidi after Vives had deducted "the pay of the collectors and your salary," presumably the usual ten percent.[78]

Meanwhile Vives had acquired another valuable bailiwick, again very largely Mudejar. In October 1272 the prince drafted an authorization by which "we sell to you Vives, son of Joseph b. Vives, our bailiff," the 12,500 solidi "that the Saracens of Pego Valley are obliged to give and pay us as tribute or for the purchase they made of the revenues, income, and proceeds of this coming year." This was a classic tax-farming arrangement, with the added circumstance that the Mudejars had "bought" their own revenues; the Mudejar purchase in this instance amounted to preagreement on a lump assessment for future collection, probably with the ten percent surcharge or commission at the lower levels of collection going to aljama delegates. In return for owning this future 12,500 solidi, Vives had to "pay immediately" to the prince's general bailiff, Joseph Ravaya, 11,000 solidi. Thus the profit for Vives came to 1,500 solidi

[77] *Ibid.*, Reg. Canc. 35, fol. 18 (May 16, 1272): to Vives, "baiulo de Alfandec de Marayen, salutem et graciam; noveritis quod nos tradimus castrum nostrum de Alfandec fideli scriptori nostro Petro de Sancto Clemente, et volumus quod ipse dictum castrum [habeat] pro nobis, et recipiat seu recipi faciat omnes redditus, exitus, proventus et quelibet alia iura que in valle et terminis dicti castri percipimus seu percipere debemus a sarracenis vel quibuslibet aliis aliqua racione, quare mandamus vobis firmiter quatenus ab odierna die lune in antea respondeatis eidem de cetero vel cui voluerit fideliter et integre de omnibus predictis redditibus . . . et mandamus inde quod ipse solvat assignaciones factas per nos in eis hucusque secundum tenorem albaranorum que a nobis habent . . . [et] non vendatis aliquid vel solvatis nisi de consensu et mandato dicti Petri de Sancto Clemento."

[78] *Ibid.*, Reg. Canc. 37, fol. 64v (Feb. 29, 1272): "quod reddidistis nobis computum de almoxerifatu v annorum de Alfandec . . . , et tradidistis nobis de dictis quinque annis quattuor millia sexcentos nonaginta et octo solidorum, et novem denarios regalium, retentis et levatis vobis iure collectorum [et] salario vestro." The small total shows either that a single tax or tax group is involved, or less probably that disbursements to creditors ate up all revenues except this small sum.

instead of the normal tenth of 1,250. Peter insured his bailiff's investment, "firmly ordering the same Saracens to answer to you in our stead for this [sum, and] giving you authority to use [legal] force upon those Saracens and their possessions for the paying of the said tax."[79]

For Vives 1272 was a good year. He also acquired Christian and Mudejar taxes at Alcira, and all taxes of Mudejars "resident [at Beniopa] and in its district"; Beniopa, under the castellan Sancho Roiz of Corella, brought 15,000 solidi yearly, again a profit for Vives of 1,500 after expenses.[80] He continues to appear in the records as bailiff of Alfandech, Pego, and Sollana in 1275 and 1276, and as a fiscal agent of the crown in other responsible capacities deep into the 1280's.

Two reports of January and February 1274 offer a view of Vives' operations as they fit into the larger picture of the prince's loan system at a given moment. After an episode of rebellion against his father, Prince Peter reorganized his finances with King James's help. The king audited and approved Peter's debts to Vives, to the total of 64,700 solidi of Valencia; he recalled the several bills from Vives and drafted a consolidated new form, assigning the actual revenues of Pego and Alfandech until the debt was satisfied. Vives in turn submitted to James his accounts on Alfandech for the past year: he had taken in 23,000 solidi, disbursed some two-thirds in expenses and assignments to creditors upon the prince's order, and was now transferring the residue to creditors at Alcira to pay part of the prince's 13,623 solidi debt there. Judah b. Lavi (de la Cavallería) held yet another 9,680 solidi of Jaca in debts, but Vives had paid 12,878 Valencian solidi on this in the prince's behalf and had secured a receipt, leaving Judah a surplus to apply on other loans. The Valencian citizen Peter Mir had loaned 10,000 solidi, still outstanding; and the prince's secretary Pericon had loaned 400.

<hr/>

[79] *Ibid.*, fols. 51v-52 (Oct. 12, 1272): "vendimus vobis Vives filio Iucefi Abenvives baiulo nostro illos . . . solidos regalium quos sarraceni vallis de Pego nobis tenentur dare et solvere pro tributo sive empcione quam fecerunt nobis reddituum . . . ; quam vendicionem vobis facimus per totum annum predictum pro undecim millibus solidorum regalium Valencie, quos incontinenti solvistis Iucefo Ravaya fideli baiulo nostro; . . . [quos] percipiatis a predictis sarracenis; mandantes firmiter eisdem quod vobis respondeant de ipsis loco nostri, dantes vobis licentiam compellendi ipsos sarracenos et bona eorum ad solvendum tributum predictum."

[80] *Ibid.*, fol. 6ov (June 23, 1272): "qui morantur ibidem et in terminis."

Besides all this, Vives held further bills of his own for 51,000 solidi, 1,300 solidi, 1,000 solidi, 400 solidi, and 200 solidi respectively. Nor was this the full extent of Prince Peter's indebtedness. A detailed list of some three dozen items reveals a total well above 200,000 solidi, with a cutoff date preventing the more recent debts on loans from being included in this current reckoning. Jews held some of this, but the bulk was owed to Christians, including 6,470 to a draper and 5,722 to the bishop of Barcelona; several were assigned on Mudejar taxes at Alfandech, with the notation that they had previously had priority over Vives' claims.[81]

Vives apparently promoted the interests of his relatives Samuel and Abraham, who appear a half-dozen times in the crown registers; but his success seems to have remained personal, without the dynastic dimension of some of the other bailiffs. Vives had many responsibilities in the kingdom of Valencia, especially as supervisor over fortifications of the Valencian palace, and he must have made enemies. During his incumbency at Alfandech in 1274, four Jews and a Mudejar lodged charges against him of exploiting the Mudejars. "You loaned or caused to be loaned to these Saracens, at great usury beyond our permitted level, pennies and other money"; for good measure his accusers charged him of "the vice of sodomy."[82] He soon won acquittal. Vives was never so important a man in governmental circles as Moses Alconstantini or Joseph Ravaya, but his career is particularly worth reviewing in the present context since it focused on the Valencian kingdom, was about equally divided between the reigns of James and Peter, and was identified with the heavily Mudejar Alfandech and Pego.[83]

[81] Soldevila, *Pere el Gran*, part 1, III, appendix, doc. 38 (Jan. 7, 1274), and the list comprising doc. 41 (Feb. 24, 1274), the latter with notations like: "e assignatz a el sobre Alfandech, e a·n albara, e es primer que en Vives," or "e es abans del deute d·en Vives." See the accompanying documents on Vives at this juncture.

[82] *Itinerari*, p. 506 (Aug. 9, 1274): "tu mutuabas vel faciebas mutuari eisdem sarracenis ad usuras magnas ultra cotum nostrum denarios et aliam peccuniam et quod de vicio sodomitico culpabilis eras."

[83] The famous Mudejar lord under James I, al-Azraq, had given Pego in southern Valencia to the crown, but his strength still dominated the region and around 1258 he recaptured the town briefly (see Burns, *Islam under the Crusaders*, ch. 14, part 1). Christian settlement long remained weak here. Alfandech, with a very strong Mudejar population, became a center of the 1277 revolt; at the turn of the century King James II chose it as a "worthy" site for a Cistercian monastery, whence the name Valldigna according to folk etymology, a circumstance which argues a somewhat remote wildness.

The brothers Manasseh represent another family, probably native to Islamic Valencia, which centered its financial activities on Valencia, especially the south. Samuel and Judah b. Manasseh, sons of Abraham b. Nahmias b. Manasseh, rose high in the service of King Peter. Samuel held a lifetime appointment both as royal physician and as chancellor for Islamic affairs.[84] He collected Mudejar rents, though his activities in this direction are known more from later charges of peculation than from details as to specific taxes taken. Constantly involved in Mudejar affairs, he raised the armies of Valencian Muslims sent in 1283 to defend the realms of Aragon against the great French invasion. During Samuel's absence with King Peter in the Arago-Catalan invasion of Sicily, his brother Judah held the substitute appointment as Arabic chancellor. More involved with Mudejar taxes than Samuel, he was bailiff at Játiva and elsewhere around 1281. His letter of authorization in January 1282, "to receive and collect for us" the household tax of Muslims throughout the kingdom, is a prime source for our understanding of that tax. King Peter addressed the letter "to all his Saracen subjects resident in the kingdom of Valencia," excepting those on crown lands without an intervening landlord; he requested them to pay Judah "all that money that you are bound to give us each year by reason of the agreements you made," regulating this household tax on a sliding scale, under penalty of confiscation and legal action against delinquents to be initiated by Judah.[85]

A year later the crown again designated Judah "for collecting that amount of money that, according to the decree of the lord king, the Saracens of the same kingdom of Valencia must pay every year to the lord king" for every household; castellans, bailiffs, and other officials

---

[84] Samuel held "alfaquimatum nostrum et scribaniam nostram de arabico," acting as "alfaquimus et fisicus noster et de domo nostra, et scriptor noster maior de arabico" (Romano, "Hermanos Abenmenassé," appendix, doc. 1 [Feb. 13, 1279]).

[85] *Ibid.*, pp. 243-292, and appendix, doc. 4 (Jan. 17, 1282): "fidelibus suis sarracenis in regno Valencie comorantibus salutem et gratiam; noveritis quod nos committimus Iahudano Abinemasse . . . quod recipiat et colligat pro nobis omnes illos denarios quos racione composicionibus quam nobiscum fecistis dare nobis tenemini quolibet anno . . . ; alias mandamus eidem quod inde vos et bona vestra pignoret et compellat." Another document refers to him as "collectori iurium sarracenorum regni Valencie." See also Haim Beinart, "Abenmenasse." *Encyclopaedia judaica*, 11, 70; Baer, *Jews in Christian Spain*, 1, 165; Shneidman, *Rise of the Aragonese-Catalan Empire*, 1, 32, 38.

were to give him "advice and help" whenever asked.[86] When King Peter issued an injunction in 1284 protecting some "buildings" belonging to Judah at Játiva against seizure by private persons, apparently creditors, the crown order also guaranteed that "those Saracens of the Játiva jurisdiction possessing or working any estates or farms" belonging to Judah would pay their share-rent to him as landlord and not to the creditors.[87] Samuel's Valencian lands and villages, with "all Christians and Saracens" as tenants there, became forever tax exempt by special privilege granted that year in gratitude for services "long" rendered.[88]

An episode in the collecting at Játiva in 1283 is particularly instructive. Judah formed a consortium of Mudejars, Jews, and Christians of Játiva, to buy that area's taxes on a farm contract requiring future payment. As bailiff he then auctioned or distributed the burden among subfarmers; when they were slow to contribute their share, Judah found himself in debtor's prison. Though overextended, his own position as a creditor indicated that he could meet his obligations if released and given a moratorium. A few months later, he narrowly avoided having his properties, stock, and slaves confiscated as a kind of forfeited collateral; Samuel persuaded the king to revoke a decision to foreclose, in favor of constraining the colleagues and subfarmers to pay their share.[89] In 1286 disaster struck. Either because Judah had died, or because Samuel acted as head of the family for all in time of crisis, Samuel bore the brunt of financial collapse at Játiva. Out of office since the coming of the new king, Alfonso, he also suffered attack from other quarters: charges "both by Christians and by Saracens" that Samuel had been guilty of "many unseemly and exorbitant extortions from the Saracens of

[86] Romano, "Hermanos Abenmenassé," appendix, doc. 8 (Jan. 29, 1283): "super colligenda illa quantitate pecunie quam, iuxta ordinacionem domini regis, sarraceni regni Valencie eiusdem domino regi quolibet anno dare tenentur pro quolibet casato sarracenorum."

[87] Ibid., doc. 12 (July 4, 1284): "illos sarracenos de ravalli Xative tenentes vel colentes aliquos honores vel hereditates dicti alfaquimi, ad solvendum eidem vel procuratori suo."

[88] Ibid., doc. 14 (Dec. 30, 1284): "propter multa grata et servicia ydonea que vos ... nobis diu fecistis ... concedimus ... per hereditatem propriam, francham, et liberam ... [cum] omnibus christianis et sarracenis qui ibi sunt vel erunt." See also doc. 13 (Dec. 28, 1284).

[89] Ibid., pp. 273-274, with documents.

Montesa and many others," and that he had "pocketed many sums that he had collected."[90] By this time Samuel and a Christian colleague were in debtor's jail, with the crown preparing to confiscate and liquidate Samuel's extensive Valencian possessions in order to meet Judah's default of the Játiva contract.

Moses (Musa) of Portella represented a courtier family of Aragon proper. Tax farmer and bailiff at Tarazona during the last years of King James, he rose to be bailiff general for Aragon proper under King Peter, and died at the hand of an assassin while serving as fiscal agent for King Alfonso in 1286. He controlled Mudejar and Christian taxation over much of northern Valencia, under both James and Peter, as "bailiff of Murviedro, Segorbe, Onda, Villarreal, Morella, and Peñíscola," especially around 1275. Among other public services, Moses negotiated the surrender of Valencian Mudejar rebels around Montesa for King Peter. His relatives Solomon and especially Ishmael collected non-Valencian taxes and enjoyed high status into the early fourteenth century.[91]

The Ravaya or Ravalla family of Gerona had achieved prominence in Catalonia proper just as Jewish political influence there began its decline; Astruc with his sons Joseph and Moses became national figures both as financial and as innovating administrative officers. Joseph functioned as a kind of royal chancellor, and controlled the bailiff general of each region. His brother Moses was bailiff general over Catalonia; his father Astruc served as bailiff of Gerona from 1276 to 1281. Joseph's supervision of the Valencian kingdom was especially firm, once King Peter's centralizing system went into operation, since the local bailiffs there rendered accounts

---

[90] *Ibid.*, appendix, doc. 18 (May 27, 1286): "ex relatione plurium tam christianorum quam sarracenorum . . . Samuel alfaquimum in pluribus que gerebat et tractabat seu administrabat . . . plures fecisse extorsiones indebitas et inmoderatas tam a sarracenis Montesie et pluribus aliis, etiam plures retinuisse quantitates quas exegerat." The crown was appointing a team of two men to conduct a "diligent" investigation and audit; the two were to return their conclusions in a confidential report, "locked under" their respective seals.

[91] Bofarull, "Jaime I y los judíos," doc. 166 (Feb. 5, 1275). Baer, *Jews in Christian Spain*, I, 165. Romano, "Funcionarios judíos de Pedro el Grande" [*BRABLB*], pp. 14-15, 18-19. Haim Beinart, "Portella, de," *Encyclopaedia judaica*, XIII, 910. Shneidman, *Rise of the Aragonese-Catalan Empire*, II, 467, 471, 483-484. He had the backing of King James's clandestine wife, the "holy queen" Teresa Giles of Vidaure. See also *Itinerari*, p. 492 (Jan. 17, 1274). Portella was a common place and family name, deriving from the diminutive for gate, opening, or pass.

directly more often than through their own bailiff general. Para-doxically, both Moses of Portella and Joseph Ravaya exercised more control over the tax administration of Valencia's Mudejars than did men like Ben Vives, but the more immediate control of the district bailiff was naturally better documented as to local details.[92] The administration of Joseph Ravaya marks the high-water mark of Jewish influence in the fiscal affairs of Valencia and of the realms as a whole.

Other luminaries had a hand in the finances of the new kingdom. Astruc Jacob Shishon (Xixon), "Jew of Tortosa" just north of the Valencian kingdom, served a number of years over Valencia's bailiwicks of Morella and Peñíscola. King James gave Astruc, "our faithful bailiff of Tortosa," the castle of Peñíscola in 1263 with all its Christian and Mudejar taxes, including the salt monopoly, to allow recovery of a 9,000 solidi loan.[93] As bailiff of Peñíscola therefore Astruc made an elaborate accounting to the king at Barcelona the following November, much of it in produce reckoned at "that [money] price that prevailed at Valencia" on the day of delivery. The king returned to Astruc the excess, amounting to 21,307 solidi of Jaca, 10,000 quarters of wine, and much grain, to be recovered through the bailiwicks of Morella and Peñíscola.[94] As "bailiff of Morella and Peñíscola" in 1267 he loaned 2,320 solidi of Jaca to construct a trebuchet or counterweighted catapult for the king's army.[95]

[92] Baer, *Jews in Christian Spain*, I, 164, 409. Romano, "Funcionarios judíos de Pedro el Grande" [*BRABLB*], esp. pp. 14-15, 20, 23. Haim Beinart, "Ravaya (Ravalia, Ravaylla)," *Encyclopaedia judaica*, XIII, 1,581. Shneidman, *Rise of the Aragonese-Catalan Empire*, II, 442-443, 458. In January 1278 and August 1281, for example, the crown ordered all Valencian bailiffs to submit their annual accounts to Joseph Ravaya; in October 1282 Joseph rented the bailiwicks over Valencia, as well as Aragon and Catalonia, for a year.

[93] Arch. Crown, James I, Reg. Canc. 10, fol. 25 (June 15, 1263): "pro quibus obligamus et impignoramus vobis castrum et villam de Paniscola, cum omnibus redditibus . . . , simul cum alio debito quod vobis debemus." Reg. Canc. 12, fol. 119v (Sept. 26, 1263): "donatis et solvatis fideli baiulo nostro Dertuse, Astrugo Iacob Xixon, per quinque annos . . . quingentos solidos annuatim . . . ad opus operis castri nostri de Peniscola." Xixons is a family name in several places of Catalonia.

[94] *Ibid.*, Reg. Canc. 14, fol. 67 (Nov. 7, 1264): "de qua baiuliam Dertuse et Penis-cole pro nobis emparastis . . . [et] debemus vobis tornare xx unum millia cccvii solidorum iachsensium."

[95] *Ibid.*, fol. 90 (June 10, 1267): "baiulo Morelle et Peniscole . . . racione bricole

As "our bailiff of Burriana" as well, Astruc worked through his "lieutenant," Musquet (Mus'ad?) Mordecai;[96] he remained bailiff of Burriana for over five years, and continued or reappeared in the post as late as 1280. Similarly he retook the Peñíscola and Morella bailiates in a series over the years, and held for a time such bailiates as Segorbe and Onda. A lengthy document of 1269, misdated 1260, shows Astruc turning in accounts for his five years at Peñíscola from 1264 to 1269, for his four years at Morella from 1265 to 1269, and for taxes collected recently at specified places "north of the Júcar River," as well as for public expenditures.[97]

Any number of other Jews had supervisory or loan-assignment connections with Valencia and its Mudejars. Two dozen documents trace the activities of Aaron b. Yahya (Abinafia or Ibn Yaḥyā) of Calatayud, bailiff general for southeast Aragon proper, whose jurisdiction spilled over the Valencian border to include the bailiwicks of Ademuz, Alpuente, Castielfabib, and Liria. By renting Segorbe's revenues in 1276, Aaron took that bailiate too. His brother Abraham replaced him as an important crown official during Alfonso's reign. A confirmation by Prince Peter in 1272 "approves all the notices of loan that our faithful bailiff Aaron b. Yahya will make to the Saracens of Almonacid," concerning taxes "that the said Saracens have made up until the present day in any way"; the prince confirmed such instruments of credit beforehand "according to the form of

---

quam pro nobis . . . fecistis apud Dertusam, et ratione alcofolli, et ratione aliorum aparamentorum predicte bricole." This is the Catalan *brigola*; *alcofoll* means lead ore.

[96] *Ibid.*, Reg. Canc. 15, fol. 107v (Feb. 17, 1267): "tibi Muscheto Mordofay iudeo tenenti locum Astrug Iacob Sixo baiuli nostri Borriane."

[97] *Ibid.*, Reg. Canc. 14, fol. 166 (Dec. 1, 126[9]): "et de denariis finaliter quas recepistis . . . citra Xucarum, videlicet de Borriana, de Onda, de Almenara, de Segorb, de Morella, de Peniscola, de Castelhabib, de Ademuz, de Alpuent, et de Archos . . . et de cenis similiter . . . a iudeis vel sarracenis Dertuse." See also his role in the prince's indebtedness as specified in Soldevila, *Pere el Gran*, part 1, 111, appendix, doc. 41 (Feb. 24, 1274): "remembrança que reebe N'Astruch Xixo seguns que el atorga, del deute," and similar entries. See also Baer, *Jews in Christian Spain*, 1, 407; Bofarull, "Jaime I y los judíos," pp. 837, 872. The Romance name Astrug or Astruc(h), derived from late Latin for "star," was common to Jew and Christian; for women it favored the form Astruca. Cosmopolitan Jews often had three names, one each in Hebrew, Arabic, and Romance. Astruc owned lands in Catalonia, plus an estate, baths, and mills in Valencia; on one holding he built a synagogue. As a mark of royal favor he held exemption from the jurisdiction of any Jewish aljama or laws, except for the capital offense of informing on Jews.

loan-notices that the said Aaron will make to the aforesaid Saracens."
Here the Mudejars of the Almonacid Valley seem to have been in
the position of subrenting or directly farming their own revenues.[98]

Joseph b. Shaprut (Avinçaprut or Ibn Shaprūṭ), in a public career
stretching through the 1270's and 1280's, became especially identified
with Murviedro; he was bailiff there, probably continuously, from
1276 through 1280, and bailiff briefly at Segorbe. His brother Solomon was associated with him in his later activities. The mixed revenues of his bailiwicks included Mudejar contributions, and one
crown authorization concerned specifically the money owed by
Segorbe Muslims.[99]

The tragic figure of David Mascarán or Almascarani appears
among Valencia's Mudejar tax personnel. In May 1271 King James
collected six outstanding notices of loan from him, including one
already assigned "on the Saracens of Uxó." The king assigned the
consolidated total of 4,420 solidi "to be collected from the full increase that you and your father made for us, in the revenues and
income and our rights of the castles of Guadalest, Confrides, Penáguila, and Castell, beyond what we ordinarily receive and have
there."[100] Prince Peter meanwhile ran up a debt of 6,000 solidi to
David, assigned on February 1274 on the revenues of Cárcer and
Sumacárcel.[101] King James ordered his bailiffs at Játiva and Beniopa, "on reading this, immediately to release to David Mascarán,

[98] Arch. Crown, James I, Reg. Canc. 37, fol. 47v (February 29, 1272): "laudamus
et approbamus omnes albaranos diffinicionum quos fidelis baíulus noster Aaron
Abinafia faciet sarracenis de Almonezir super caloniis quas dicti sarraceni usque in
presentem diem quoquo modo fecerunt . . . ; nos ratam habemus secundum formam
albaranorum que dictus Aaron faciet sarracenis predictis." See also Romano, "Funcionarios judíos de Pedro el Grande" [*BRABLB*], pp. 19-20, 21n., 22n., Baer, *Jews
in Christian Spain*, I, 163, 165, 166, 410, 412.

[99] Romano, "Funcionarios judíos de Pedro el Grande" [*BRABLB*], pp. 22-23.
Itinerari, pp. 458 (Jan. 29, 1272), 483 (June 16, 1273). Shneidman, *Rise of the
Aragonese-Catalan Empire*, II, 453, 481-482. Joseph died in 1302.

[100] Arch. Crown, James I, Reg. Canc. 14, fol. 120 (May 29, 1271): "cum alio
albarano nostro super sarracenis de Uxone . . . , quos quidem et certe assignamus
tibi habendos et percipiendos in toto augmento quod tu et pater tuus fecistis nobis
in redditibus et exitibus ac iuribus nostris castrorum de Godalesto et de Confrides
et de Penaguila et de Castello, ultra illud quod nos inde recipere consuevimus et
habere, quod quidem augmentum habeas et recipias." See also Baer, *Jews in
Christian Spain*, I, 176, 242, 440. There were Christians named Mascaró, and in the
Valencian *Repartimiento* a Muḥammad "Almascaro."

[101] Soldevila, *Pere el Gran*, part I, III, appendix, doc. 41 (Feb. 24, 1274): "item
deu l'infant a en David Almascaran, jueu, sobre Carcel vi millia sous de reals."

or anyone he chooses in his stead, the bailiate of Cárcer and of Sumacárcel and of the hamlet of Beniamira."[102] Areas such as Castell, Guadalest, Penáguila, and to a lesser extent Cárcer were heavily Mudejar at this date. Mascarán, a highhanded and powerful courtier, became embroiled in factional fighting within Aragonese Jewry; twenty years after his first appearance in the fiscal records he was assassinated.

Moses (Musa or Mūsā) Ales held revenues and then the bailiate of Alcira several times between 1276 and 1282. Maimon of Pontons briefly held Onteniente's bailiwick in 1276, and that of Valencia city in 1288. Solomon Vidal was bailiff of Villarreal at least from late 1276 to early 1281. Moses Almateri (al-Maṭarī) was bailiff of Játiva around 1279, and later collected Alcira's revenues; Peter ordered him "to demand from the Saracens of Játiva and its district, both [those belonging to] knights as well as to other [classes], the besants and all other taxes that they are obliged to give or pay us."[103] Vidal Aborrabe (Abu 'r-Rabī') had Onda's bailiate from 1276 apparently through 1279 or 1280; at one point he had charge of recovering the goods of Mudejars stolen at Onda during a civil disturbance.[104] In 1267 one Meir was bailiff of Gandía, and sold a number

[102] *Colección diplomática,* doc. 1,430 (Feb. 26, 1274): "visis presentibus, incontinenti desemparetis David Mascharani vel cui voluerit loco sui baiuliam de Carcel et de Somacarcel et de rahal de Beniamirra, quam tenebat . . . racione sui debiti obligatam; et ipse teneatur computare inde. . . ." King James had given an estate in conquered Valencia "Abrahe Mascarani iudeo et Davidi filio suo, subtus cequiam novam Algezire," which they eventually forfeited by not taking possession (Arch. Crown, James I, Reg. Canc. 19, fol. 85 [Dec. 13, 1273]).

[103] Arch. Crown, Peter III, Reg. Canc. 42, fol. 226v (Feb. 20, 1279): "Petrus Mosse Almateri baiulo Xative quod exigat a sarracenis Xative et termini eiusdem, tam militum quam aliorum, bisancia et omnia alia iura que nobis dare sive solvere teneantur" (this is the entire document except for date). Moses of Portella, "baiulus et merinus" at Zaragoza (Reg. Canc. 39, fol. 234v [July 28, 1277]), became more active in Valencian tax collection during 1286 under Alfonso; one document refers back to the towns King Peter had granted to him as an estate: "sarracenis qui consueverunt morari apud Benibuqer et Alcudiam mandamus quatenus mandatum per dictum dominum regem patrem nostrum . . . quod veniretis apud Aldandech [sic] et computaretis cum Samuele Abenvives . . . de redditibus . . . de tempore quo dictus Samuel ipsas alcherias tenuit pro Muça de Portella" (Reg. Canc. 85, fol. 132 [April 4, 1291]).

[104] Soldevila, *Pere el Gran,* part 2, 1, appendix, doc. 34 (Oct. 25, 1276): "que fuerunt ablate sarracenis Onde . . . tradatis incontinenti Vitali Aborrabe, baiulo dicti loci." Martínez Ferrando read the name in two manuscripts as Abenrabe, which would yield Ibn ar-Rabī' rather than Abu 'r-Rabī' (*Catálogo,* II, nos. 881, 911).

of commercial taxes "from Christians and Jews as well as from Saracens" to the town's justiciar for 3,300 solidi, "just as is contained in the document drawn for you by the said Meir." King James made one exception: "in such wise that the Saracens of Beniopa are not bound to contribute to the market fee, market license, transit tax, [and] measuring fee except according to the [Islamic] legal customs of Montesa which we granted them to have."[105]

Bonet of Zaragoza, a Jew resident at Murviedro, collected grazing fees or herbage in the Valencian kingdom in 1279; his supervisory post would have included the Mudejar aljamas.[106] Salima (Çaleme) of Daroca, a Jew of Monzón, became creditor to the crown in 1257 for the large sum of 5,000 gold Alfonsine morabatins, when King James assumed that debt on the death of the magnate, William of Entenza; in recompense Salima received the castle and revenues of Arcos de Jalón, just beyond Valencia's western frontier, with its salt monopoly in Valencia, thus involving himself in a number of Mudejar fees.[107] To recover another debt in 1263 he had his son-in-law Samuel continue as director of the celebrated salt monopoly for "the coming four years." King James required 7,000 solidi for the crown every year, with the remaining 5,000 going to Salima; the schedule for the current year differed, with Samuel getting only 2,300 after

---

[105] Arch. Crown, James I, Reg. Canc. 17, fol. 114v (March 12, 1267): "confirmamus tibi, Petro de Blita iusticie Gandie, vendicionem quam Mayr, quondam baiulus noster ipsius loci tibi fecit per istum unum annum in quo modo sumus, de merchato, lezda, pedatico, et mensuratico ville de Gandia et omnium terminorum eius que nos ibidem debemus percipere et habere tam a christianis [et] iudeis quam sarracenis, pro iii millibus ccc solidorum regalium Valencie . . . prout in carta dicti Mayr tibi facta continetur; . . . ita tamen quod sarraceni de Beniopa non teneantur dare pro mercato, lezda, vel pedatico [vel] mensuratico nisi secundum forum Muntese quem nos eis concessimus habendum." Montesa was then a Mudejar fief under the Banū 'Īsā (see Burns, Islam under the Crusaders, ch. 14, part 3); the document consequently is important for Mudejar legal history. In Reg. Canc. 16, fol. 198v (July 1, 1270) Meir was involved in a lawsuit with the Knights of Santiago, "dicens se esse paratum facere iusticie complementum magistro ordinis" and giving two barons as his guarantors.

[106] Arch. Crown, Peter III, Reg. Canc. 42, fol. 227 (Feb. 22 and 23, 1279), two documents. Abraham Abençumada, apparently a similarly obscure Jewish collector, was in fact a Muslim; see n. 33 and especially Chapter VII, n. 49.

[107] Arch. Crown James I, Reg. Canc. 10, fol. 1 (July 25, 1257): "obligamus vobis et vestris castrum et villam de Archubus, cum omnibus suis redditibus, exitibus, et proventibus, peytis, cenis, redemptionibus exercituum, et caloniis que in dicto castro et villa . . . debemus percipere quoquomodo, et specialiter salinas . . . "; after expenses, he was to retain all tax moneys until the debt was satisfied.

assignations and expenses.[108] Salima received a special document for himself, describing his recent loan as 8,850 gold Alfonsine morabatins, "minus 51 solidi of Jaca," and made an accounting for the previous years.[109]

Even the most important financial managers and district bailiffs are sparsely documented; more peripheral figures like Salima flicker briefly in the records, most details of their business forever lost. Particularly transient were the letters of debt assignment, called in and routinely destroyed by the bailiff after the debt had been satisfied, with the crown occasionally registering or adverting to them. The crown registers usually deal in generalities, recording a bulk of mixed Christian and Mudejar taxes received, a district accounted for, an operation authorized or successfully concluded, or an action constituting only one element of a larger transition. At this supervisory level, the connection with Mudejars often remains implicit. Sufficient hints or open statements survive, however, to suggest the outline of Jewish participation in Mudejar tax collection.

Six years after the crusade had ended, Jews were either so important in the kingdom already or else regarded as so potentially dominant, that King James conceded to the settlers a privilege against them: "we grant and pact in good faith that never again can any Jew be a bailiff, subbailiff, or vicar or subvicar, justiciar, or judge in all the kingdom of Valencia, nor hold or have any public office or any jurisdiction."[110] The Lateran ecumenical council of 1215 had laid down a universal law against Jews holding "public office" in Christian affairs, explicitly renewing an ancient Spanish law from the third council of Toledo, and had also "extended" this to include

---

[108] *Ibid.*, Reg. Canc. 14, fol. 18 *bis* (May 8, 1263): "salinas nostras de Archos, et quod teneatis caldiras in quibus decoquitur sal ipsarum salinarum, et domos, et terium, sicut iam consuevistis tenere . . . in solucionem debitorum que nos debemus Çaleme socero vestro . . . sic quod illi qui emerint sal de dictis salinis teneantur dare xv denarios iaccenses pro qualibet fanecha, sive cruda fuerit sive decocta."

[109] *Ibid.*, fol. 41 (Sept. 14, 1263): "minus quinquaginta et unum solidos iaccenses . . . pro omnibus debitis que unquam vobis debuimus usque in hunc diem cum cartis; facto inde legaliter compoto inter nos et vos . . . obligamus et impignoramus vobis et vestris . . . iura nostra salinarum de Arcos."

[110] *Aureum opus*, doc. 41 (Nov. 28, 1251), and *Colección diplomática*, doc. 408 (corrected date, Sept. 28, 1251): "promittimus, concedimus, et convenimus bona fide quod nunquam de cetero aliquis iudeus sit baiulus, subbaiulus, vel vicarius, vel subvicarius, iusticia, curia, vel iudex in toto regno Valencie, nec teneat vel habeat aliquod officium publicum vel aliquam iurisdiccionem." See the corresponding law in the *Furs*, above in Chapter VII, n. 73.

Muslims; but King James goes farther, not so much by strong and specific language as by conveying this obtrusive privilege against Jews instead of relegating the point only to passing mention in the inclusive law code of Valencia.[111] The ensuing thirty years saw a growth of Jewish officeholders and administrative influence in the realms of Aragon, especially under King Peter, unparalleled in previous European history. From the end of 1283 a reaction set in. The baronage particularly attacked the Jewish role as strengthening the crown against their own interests. Popular pressure again legislated the exclusion of Jews from public office and particularly from that of bailiff; the crown continued to use them as before, avoiding use of titles, but Jewish influence in Valencian governmental finances gradually diminished.

Valencian Mudejars did not always take kindly to Jewish tax collectors. The Játiva Muslims, though excluding Christians and Jews alike from running bakeries or ovens in their community, incorporated a special proviso into their charter against Jews as tax officials: "no Jew can ever be your bailiff or collector of our [royal] revenues."[112] On the other hand Judah b. Manasseh did serve as their bailiff in 1282 and was involved with their regalian revenues. Either the crown satisfied its obligation by excluding Jews at the lower levels of Mudejar collecting, or occasionally disregarded Muslim objections just as it overrode Christian protest.

CHRISTIAN FINANCIERS AND COLLECTORS

As in the rest of Western Europe, Christians comprised the bulk of financiers, moneylenders, and revenue officers. Their predominant

[111] Grayzel publishes the decrees with a translation in his *Church and Jews*, conciliar section, doc. 11 (Nov. 11, 1215), and see doc. 3, Montpellier Council (Dec. 1195); "officium publicum," "hoc idem extendimus ad paganos."

[112] Játiva Charter; for *pideus* read *iudeus*. The Latin emphasizes the negative: "statuentes quod aliquis pideus non possit esse unquam baiulus vester, nec collector reddituum nostrorum ravalli praedicti." For continuing influence of Jews into the next century in both diplomatic and commercial life, see Dufourcq, *L'Espagne catalane et le Maghrib*, pp. 139-144, 211-213, 230-235, 597-601. As late as 1308 at Elche the Jewish notary who kept the Moorish tax records was replaced by a Christian (Baer, *Jews in Christian Spain*, ii, 4). At the capitulation of the kingdom of Granada in 1491 the Muslims excluded the use of Jews in tax collecting: "item, es asentado e concordado que ningund judío non sea recabdador nin receptor, nin tenga mando nin juridición sobrellos" (Fernández y González, *Mudejares de Castilla*, appendix, doc. 86 [Nov. 25, 1491]).

role, correspondingly bulkier, is more difficult both to research and to reduce to presentable order. The prevalence of mixed-tax appointments at the better documented supervisory levels again enters as a factor to frustrate systematic inquiry into Mudejar rents alone. The introduction of representative individuals and of those separate accountings still available will have to serve.

Adam of Paterna makes a suitable point of entry into this busy world of finance, suspended as he was between the strata of baron or courtier financiers and the strata of the less affluent aspirants in this career. Under the spell of the myth that high financiers in the Middle Ages were seldom Christians, the distinguished historian of Catalonia Ferran Soldevila concluded that Adam "must have been a wealthy Jew" engaged in "extensive speculation" with the revenues of king, prince, and barons. Torres Fontes also records him as a Jew. So obscure is this important moneyman that his very name puzzles historians.[113] A review of his appearances in disparate financial dealings reveals him as a Christian named Adam, not Catalan Ad, Ada, or At. His alternate surname, "of Castellar" is too common a toponymic to locate his origins; with other indications it may suggest a connection with the crusader Raymond of Castellá or Castellar from the neighborhood of Huesca in Aragon. Adam's Valencian residence, Paterna, a short distance upstream from the capital, explains his designation as "a citizen of Valencia [city]."

In the earliest notice of his existence, he is seen purchasing from the crown for 4,000 solidi, in August of 1248, "the castle of Segart [de Albalat] near Beselga, in free alod"; he already owned, or soon acquired the castle and town of Beselga itself, today long abandoned and in ruins. Both castles lie about a dozen miles west of Murviedro. King James so esteemed the "many and valued services you have previously done and daily [still] do," that in April 1258 he bestowed as an alod "the village of Benifallim, which is in the jurisdiction of the castle of Penáguila, with its strongholds, houses, outbuildings,

---

[113] Soldevila, *Pere el Gran*, part 1, 1, 121: "devia ésser un jueu opulent que va especular llargament." Juan Torres Fontes, *La reconquista de Murcia en 1266 por Jaime I de Aragón* (Murcia, 1967), p. 103. Martínez Ferrando prefers the name Ade, with a cross-reference from alternate Adam; Miret y Sans, in his single passing reference, chooses Ada over Adam (*Itinerari*, p. 274), and Soldevila Adam. No discussion of Adam exists beyond such brief animadversions. The form Ade is in fact the genitive and dative of Adam, normally indeclinable but here following patristic precedent in assuming first-declension endings.

farms," and all appurtenances and revenues.[114] When Adam's ward, John Sánchez, "wickedly killed" one of the king's Muslims, Adam secured for the murderer that same month "remission and absolution" from criminal or civil charges.[115]

King James exempted Adam for life from all taxes; more exactly he ordered his collectors to write in such taxes as though paid, in effect returning them.[116] As a further grace, James conferred a "tower" or fortified place "on the frontiers of the Valencian kingdom," whether Adam himself or the king's forces were to reconquer it from the Mudejar rebels.[117] The following decade proved lucrative for Adam the financier, but by 1270 he was dead. A tombstone from the Hospitaller church at Valencia city mourns the simultaneous passing of Adam of Paterna and Peter Adam of Paterna, whose knightly coat of arms featured a castle along with a bell or perhaps a pear. Adam left behind him tangled money affairs and a last

[114] Arch. Crown, James I, Reg. Canc. 6, fol. 96 (July 29, 1248): "castrum de Segart iuxta Biselcam," a *repartimiento* entry sometimes misread as Buselgam. Reg. Canc. 10, fol. 61v (April 28, 1258): "attendentes multa et grata servitia que vos fidelis noster Adam de Paterna nobis olim fecistis et [cotidi]e facitis . . . assignamus per hereditatem propriam, francham, et liberam vobis et vestris imperpetuum alqueriam de Benihalim, que est in termino castri de Beniaguila, cum sua fortalicia, casis, casalibus. . . ."

[115] *Ibid.*, Reg. Canc. 10, fol. 62v (April 29, 1258): "diffinimus tibi Ioanni Sancii, alumpno Ade [*sic*] de Paterna, et tuis imperpetuum omnem actionem . . . ratione Avingamerro sarraceni nostri, quem olim nequiter occidisti."

[116] *Ibid.*, Reg. Canc. 10, fol. 61 (April 28, 1258), a separate document from those in notes 114, 117, and 119: "confirmamus vobis Ade de Paterna cartam franquitatis quam v[obis] fecimus in vita vestra de . . . exactionibus regalibus, prout in instrumento . . . continetur; volentes et concedentes quod pars que vobis competat in predictis vel eorum aliquid semper cedat in compotum et solutionem nostram . . . et [baiuli] iamdictam partem vobis competentem in predictis recipiant in compotum et solutionem nostram."

[117] *Ibid.* (same date): "concedimus vobis Ade de Paterna et Raimundo de Mirambello quod si sarraceni vobis reddant turr[em] de Massa[. . .]s que est in finibus regni Valencie, vel ipsam ab eis vel aliis quibuslibet personis quocumque modo pot[ueritis] recuperare . . . habeatis et teneatis ad vestras voluntates . . . [etiamsi] forte eam recuperare possimus." The description does not fit Masanasa, which in any case the Calatrava knights already held (Burns, *Crusader Valencia*, 1, 180-181), not Masalavés; could it be the puzzling Massanera in western Valencia (*Itinerari*, p. 452 [Aug. 3, 1271])? Masamagrell is the closest to Adam's own castles, if the realm's *fines* are taken in a somewhat rhetorical sense of guerrilla battle zone; but the final s has no place here, and the lacuna is perhaps too short. Massalconill, Massalfassar, Massamardá, and Masarojos, all near Valencia city, are not very promising candidates either, nor are Massalet near Carlet, La Massara near Bocairente, Font de Massil near Gandía, and Els Massils near Tárbena.

testament providing for the care of his deceased son Peregrine's children, under the tutelage of his other son, Bartholomew of Castellar. Since Bartholomew's status as direct heir to Adam's wealth involved a conflict of interest with the claims of his wards, a long court battle eventually unseated him from his guardianship. The legal record reveals that Adam had adopted the four small children of his dead son Peregrine as wards: the boy Arnold and the girls Elvirette, Raymondette, and Jacmette. Later his own testament had passed them, still "underage," into the care of his surviving son Bartholomew.[118]

Adam of Paterna turns up in the crown registers in the last days of 1258, already in full career. King James consolidated his current debt to Adam at this period, 13,580 solidi, with a fresh borrowing of 4,420 solidi "that you are now loaning me at Valencia"; destroying the old bond, James assigned the new total of 18,000 solidi to be taken from "all revenues and income of the Moorish quarter of Valencia city with all its appurtenances, and [from] the revenues and income of all those shops of the *qaiṣārīya* that were [in the hands] of William of Porciá." The assignment waived all claims by other creditors, and forbade "any Jew, Saracen, or convert" to open a shop elsewhere, until this debt was satisfied. "And for your greater security," the king had two of his household clerics on his behalf swear an oath on his soul that the king would observe all the provisions of the assignment.[119]

[118] Arch. Crown, Reg. Canc. 16, fol. 225v (Nov. 27, 1270): "attendentes quod cum Adam de Paterna, dictus aliter Adam de Castellario, esset tutor testamentarius Arnaldi, Elvirete, Raimundete, et Jacmete filiarum impuberum Peregrini de Castellario quondam filii eiusdem Ade, et processu temporis dictus Adam ab hoc seculo transmigrasset, et post obitum ipsius Ade esset tutor legitimus dictorum impuberum seu pupillorum Bartholomeus de Castellario filius eiusdem Ade. . . ." In an old miscellany of data about Paterna, a town held from 1237 by the powerful Luna family of Aragon, José Martínez Aloy mentioned the tombstone in passing, "por si alguien puede aprovechar la referencia"; kept in the Museo de San Carlos of Valencia city, it displayed the date 1260 (for 1270?) and as arms a castle and bell (*Geografía general del reino de Valencia* [*Provincia*], I, 198). If the bell shape represents a pear, these heraldic devices recall respectively the Aragonese crusader Raymond of Castellá and his wife, a Pérez, thus strengthening the suspicion of a family connection arising from the name Castella(r).

[119] Arch. Crown, James I, Reg. Canc. 10, fol. 61 (April 28, 1258): "quos vobis debebamus cum instrumento nostro quod nunc recuperamus a vobis, et quattuor millia quadringintos viginti solidos quos vos nunc in Valencia mutuastis; et sic debemus vobis inter hoc totum decem et octo millia solidorum regalium, pro quibus

The confusion between dates in incarnational and nativity calendars for the first months of any year make it difficult to inter-relate certain of Adam's accounts. Some of the following may over-lap or follow a slightly different sequence. In the spring of 1262 or 1263 King James had just repaid Adam 1,800 solidi at Zaragoza on a debt of 12,000 solidi, and was assigning Murviedro's mixed Christian-Muslim revenues for recovery of the remainder, "until you and yours are fully satisfied." Meanwhile Prince Peter borrowed 20,000 solidi from Adam in January of 1262 or 1263, "without any concealed or manifest interest," assigning for a year with the king's permission Alfandech castle and region at 11,500 solidi, Pego castle and region at 6,000, and Alcira for the remainder; from Alfandech and Pego, however, he deducted the castellan's salary and the tithe. Adam himself was to install each bailiff, Muslim *amīn*, and castellan at these places.[120] In 1264 the king approved the assignment of Vall de Laguart made by one of his greatest Valencian feudatories, Carroz of Rebollet, for a debt of 5,000 solidi, which that lord owed Adam.[121] Murviedro's mixed revenues followed, to help Adam recover 3,000 solidi lent for outfitting a warship of the king at Valencia.[122]

omnibus obligamus et tradimus vobis redditus omnes et exitus morarie Valencie cum omnibus pertinentiis suis, et redditus ac exitus omnium illorum operatoriorum alcaçerie que fuerunt Guillelmi de Porciano. . . . Et ad maiorem etiam vestri securi-tatem, facimus iurare in animam nostram Martinum Lupi de Bolas et Matheum Baboti clericos nostros quod nos predicta omnia et singula attendamus. . . ." The oath of the two clerics is appended. On *alcaçeria* in this and a subsequent document as meaning *qaiṣārīya*, not merchandise, see Chapter III, n. 96, with the phrase also: "nullus iudeus, sarracenus, vel babtizatus."

[120] Arch. Crown, James I, Reg. Canc. 14, fol. 142 (March 1, 1262 or 1263): "con-fitemur debere vobis Ade de Paterna et vestris x millia cc solidorum regalium, qui vobis remanent ad solvendum de xii millibus solidorum, quos vobis debebamus cum alba[rano] quem modo recuperavimus in Cesaraugusta a Bernardo Scribe . . . ; assignamus vobis . . . in redditibus et exitibus Muriveteris." Reg. Canc. 17, fol. 43r,v (Jan. 24, 1262 or 1263): "nobis bono amore mutuastis sine aliqua usura ficta vel manifesta"; *usura* also bore the meaning "interest," as probably here. The document is lengthy and detailed. Reg. Canc. 14, fol. 47v (Jan. 26, 1262 or 1263) is the king's confirmation: "ad unum annum de redditibus et exitibus Aliazire, Alfandech de Marinenyn [*sic*], et de Pego."

[121] *Ibid.*, Reg. Canc. 13, fol. 174v (May 21, 1264): confirming to Adam "obliga-cionem quam Carrocius dominus Rebolleti vobis fecit de valle de Al[a]guar et terminis eiusdem pro quinque millibus solidorum regalium Valencie, prout in carta ab ipso vobis facta continetur."

[122] *Ibid.*, Reg. Canc. 14, fol. 55 (May 26, 1264): "tria millia solidorum regalium Valencie, quos nobis accomod[avi]stis ad emendum xarciam et alia necessaria ad

In 1265 the prince still owed Adam nearly 8,000 solidi of the 20,000 previously borrowed; he had also borrowed 7,105 more, 3,000 in cash and the rest in meat, wine, and cattle; and he was receiving at the moment of audit another 5,300 solidi, all to a grand total of over 20,000. This rose in a few months to some 38,000 solidi, of which over 12,000 were assigned on the Moors and Christians of Alfandech and Pego valleys, Alcira, and Ribarroja.[123] The ebb and flow of loans and revenues left the total debt outstanding to Adam by spring of 1266 at 31,413 solidi and 9 pence, of which 4,000 was being borrowed in the present instrument. Again the prince assigned the predominantly Mudejar incomes of Alfandech, Pego, and Ribarroja, and again he surrendered to Adam the power to assign any bailiff, castellan, or amín at these places.[124]

Adam returned a report on the Alfandech revenues, largely Moorish, estimating a net receipt of 11,000 solidi after expenses, of which he assigned 733 solidi as the bishop's two-thirds of the tithe on the prince's income, and 1,200 solidi for garrisoning and maintaining the castle. Adam included a series of additional payments specifically from Alfandech's Muslims, a dozen items in all, to a total of 618 solidi. Ṭalḥa (Talha) gave 10 solidi, for example, Yaḥyā al-Balawī (Jafia Albelahuy) 10, 'Alī al-Ḥaddād (Ali Alfadet) 76, "a certain Saracen, 3 solidi," and two freedmen 30.[125] Adam's receipts for 1264

---

opus galee nostra, quam nunc fieri facimus in Valencia." Catalan eixàrcia means rigging and tackle.

[123] Ibid., Reg. Canc. 17, fol. 33v (April, 1265): "compotavit Adam [sic] de Paterna cum Matheo Baboti de omnibus debitis que dominus infans debet ei"; the list includes "xx vachas, mdccccv solidos" and "ccc quarteros de vino a ii solidis, dc solidos," and a horse at 300 solidi. Fol. 65 contains bonds and audits on the prince's borrowings from Adam, dated July 12, November 4, and September 21 and 23, 1265; the assignment to the four places is detailed, e.g., "item mdclv solidos regalium Valencie quos vobis cum alio albarano debemus, facto ii idus Iulii anno predicto . . . pro quibus [omnibus debitis] tenetis a nobis castra et villas d'Alfandech de Marayen, de Pego, de Algezira, et de Riba Roya obligata." Fol. 65v (Nov. 5, 1265) has the price of a horse from Adam assigned to these same revenues, "solutis assignationibus ibi factis."

[124] Ibid., fol. 67r,v (April 28, 1266): "confitemur debere vobis Ade de Paterna et vestris triginta unum millia ccccxiii solidorum [et] ix denarios regalium Valencie, videlicet . . . ; [et] possitis ponere et instituere baiulos, alcaydos, sive alaminos."

[125] Ibid., fol. 66 (April 27, 1266, covering 1265): "de quibus levamus pro duabus partibus decime dccxxxiii solidos iiii denarios, item pro custodia castri mille cc solidos." The additional list includes 301 solidi "de alqueria cuiusdam sarraceni de Murcia" in the Alfandech valley; "item de Ali Alchexeix, xx solidos, item de quo-

from the overwhelmingly Mudejar Pego Valley came to 6,000 solidi; but he had "waived 300 solidi so that the Saracens would return," presumably as part of a resettlement scheme in that year of war panic. He had also paid out 2,040 solidi for the castle's ten knights and its other expenses. His personal recovery of money for repaying the loan amounted eventually to 3,680 solidi.[126] Five bonds of Prince Peter are listed for Adam in April 1266 and two from "the queen," for a total loan of over 38,000 solidi outstanding.[127]

Early in 1267 Adam made an accounting for revenues collected against the earlier sum of 33,413 solidi. He had taken 3,000 solidi from Pego Valley after expenses, but found only 730 solidi actually in hand after paying off the garrison and improving the castle; he included as a castle expense "8 pence for keys to open doors." Alcira brought 1,630 solidi, Ribarroja 2,000, except for 133 solidi of two-thirds' tithe and 150 for its one-man garrison, and Alfandech 11,500 solidi, except for 750 for the castle and 766 for the partial tithe.[128] At this time the prince issued Adam a bond of indebtedness for 22,705 solidi for all loans outstanding, "with or without bonds," promising to pay 14,000 by Christmas and the remainder by the following Christmas. "As security for the loan," he gave Adam the castle and valley of Alfandech "with all revenues" to hold until paid in full.[129]

---

dam sarraceno de Pinet, c denarios, item Jucef Axarrab, xxvi solidos minus unum denarium, item Ali Alfadet, lxxvi solidos viii denarios, item de Jafia Albelahuy x solidos . . . , item de Jahep Açofra x solidos, item de quodam sarraceno iii solidos."

[126] *Ibid.* (same date, but covering 1264): "vi millia solidorum, de quibus dimisit ut redirent sarraceni ccc solidos." The details for Alcira in 1265 follow in a separate "compotum . . . de eo quod recepit Adam," and then Ribarroja's for a period of 8½ months in 1265.

[127] *Ibid.* (April 27, 1266): "item in alio albarano, xii millia cccclxxv solidorum . . . item cum albarano domine regine, ii millia solidorum," and so on. Two more documents of borrowing from Adam are on fols. 36v and 67v (April 28, 1266). The "queen" here is the prince's wife, Constance (Hohenstaufen) of Sicily, who had that title in her household accounts from 1266 onwards, after Manfred's death at the battle of Benevento.

[128] *Ibid.*, fol. 79 (Feb. 3, 1267, covering 1266): "et deductis cc solidis de decima, et [deducta] custodia castri v hominum per unum annum, qui faciunt dccl solidos, et pro duobus aliis hominibus exceptis istis v pro tribus mensibus, lxxv solidos . . . et pro clavibus ad aprandum [*sic*, aperiendum?] portas, octo denarios." From internal evidence the date is not 1266 (covering 1265), already given above.

[129] *Ibid.*, fol. 79v (Feb. 3, 1267): "cum albaranis et sine albaranis, que a vobis recuperavimus"; "obligamus vobis et vestris et in posse vestro mittimus titulo pigno-

Particularly interesting is the debt of 35,120 solidi bonded in 1267, of which 25,000 represented a fresh loan handed over by Adam's agent; the prince secured it with his wife's crown, crafted by Muslims. To insure its return, Prince Peter described in detail this "crown which is of thirteen gold sections, of Saracen workmanship, and there are in it seventeen precious stones called rubies," fifty-three pearls, and other jewels. Unless repaid in time, Adam could "sell or mortgage" this crown, which meanwhile would remain in his possession.[130] The next year the king recognized his own debt of 6,593 solidi and borrowed a fresh sum of 13,407, just sufficient to round out his indebtedness at 20,000 solidi.

King James had at hand a suitable assignation for the formidable sum. He had just confiscated the Mudejar fief of Tárbena castle and valley from Muḥammad 'Amr b. Isḥāq and conferred it on his mistress Berengaria Alfonso and their potential issue. James now gave the revenues of this Mudejar stronghold to Adam for as long as necessary to recover the loans. Once again Adam "can put in the said places a castellan or castellans, bailiff or bailiffs, whom you wish in your place, who may hold the aforesaid castle, valley, towns, and places for you and yours, and who may collect whole and entire their revenues, income, and taxes in your stead." The king added an instruction "to each and every Saracen of the same castle, valley, towns, and places" to accept Adam's bailiffs and pay all taxes to them.[131]

---

ris castrum et vallem de Alfandech de Marayen cum omnibus redditibus . . . [et] teneatis titulo firmi pignoris." He was to maintain "in dicto castros [*sic*] pro custodia iiii[or] homines, ut consuetum est." The ambiguous date cannot be 1266, when related to the other documents on Adam.

[130] *Ibid.*, Reg. Canc. 28, fol. 30 (same date): "nos infans Petrus . . . et nos domina Constan[cia uxor eius] . . . recognoscimus vobis Ade [de] Paterna, licet absenti, quod debemus vobis . . ."; "quandam coronam que est de tresdecim peciis auri, de opere sarracenico, et sunt in ea decem et septem lapides preciosi qui dicuntur rubis [*sic*] et septem lapides preciosi qui dicuntur manicdes[?] et quinquaginta tres paerles, et in capite dicte corone sunt asiblays de serico livido cum perlis et turquesiis in auro . . . [et] possitis dictam coronam vendere vel impignorare." If the price received for the forfeited crown did not meet the obligation, the debtors had to supply the difference.

[131] *Ibid.*, Reg. Canc. 14, fol. 95 (April 5, 1268): "et sic debemus vobis inter omnia xx milia solidorum regalium, pro quibus obligamus et impignoramus vobis et vestris castrum et villam de Tarbana et vallem de Tarbana et omnes alias villas et loca. . . . Concedimus insuper vobis quod possitis in dictis locis ponere alcaidum et alcaidos, baiulum et baiulos, quem et quos volueritis loco vestri, qui predictum

Adam of Paterna died within the next two years, throwing the affair of the borrowed crown and the tutelage of his grandsons into the hands of his executors and thence into the courts. His heirs finally received satisfaction for the debt on the crown in 1281. Adam's documented career, one of many such careers, extends over only a decade. It bridges for us the functions of loan-financier and bailiff, since the lender at this exalted level did not stand outside the bailiate system, humbly awaiting his assigned small-debt, but aggressively took over the king's privilege of naming, installing, and controlling bailiffs and castellans alike. Adam never took on the presumably lower function of bailiff himself, nor did he move in the sphere and records of either courtiers or barons. Though he had responsibility for the taxes of some of the more important Mudejar regions in Valencia, it seems unlikely that he ever worked personally with the local *amīn* who collected and reported to Adam's subbailiffs and bailiffs.

An examination of the first five hundred documents registered for the new kingdom of Valencia, accomplished not by a review of the often inexact catalogue but directly from reconstruction of the manuscripts themselves, affords innumerable examples of Christian loans and collections. They are not arranged within the neater frame provided by an individual financier such as Adam, but appear in the original process of jumble and constant shift over a period of six to seven years from early 1257 to late 1263. Since the upper and supervisory levels, comprising the bulk of tax reports registered, dealt with consolidated general categories of both Christian and Mudejar taxes, the only way to avoid a book-length study of general tax collection will be to select the specifically Mudejar material wherever it crops up and to handle data on mixed or unspecified taxes sparingly and by illustrative selection. The many individual grants and agreements must also be bypassed.

The earliest document on Valencia in the crown registers is a list of *peites* taken in 1255 from twenty-six towns or regions. The sums,

---

castrum, vallem, villas, et loca teneant pro vobis et vestris, et redditus, exitus, et iura ipsorum percipiant integre atque plene loco vestri . . . , mandantes universis et singulis sarracenis eorumdem castri, vallis, villarum, et locorum quod . . . teneant de cetero pro alcaido et in baiulum et baiulos. . . ." *Alcaidus* has varied meanings; here both "castellan" and *qāʾid* are applicable. On the fief, its downfall and transfer, and Muḥammad himself, see Burns, *Islam under the Crusaders*, ch. xiii, part 3.

ranging from 500 at Almizra to 30,000 at Valencia city, total 90,500 solidi. Dominic Cavall, who owned a meat stall in the Valencia city Mudejar quarter, collected at the first thirteen places, from the capital south; John Borgia, crown *porter* or agent who soon received a bakery in the same Mudejar quarter, collected at the remaining thirteen more northerly places.[132] A few subcollectors appear along with their towns, and two assignees.

In August of 1257 the crown assigned repayment of a loan of 2,700 solidi from "the citizen of Valencia," Bernard of Cogulles, to be delivered to him by Bernard Escrivá, bailiff of Valencia city, "from the first moneys you receive from the bailiwick of Valencia."[133] A small debt to the king's *repositarius*, 300 solidi of Jaca for a horse, fell "on the bailiwick of Játiva," held by a high courtier.[134] In September the crown turned over both the castle of Polop and all its revenues, "for maintaining the said castle," until the Mudejar revolt there had ended;[135] these revenues were Mudejar, so the Muslims were financing their own subjection. In giving the Valencian castles of Jalón, Pop, and Vall de Laguart with all their revenues to the

---

[132] Arch. Crown, James I, Reg. Canc. 8, fol. 21v (Nov. 26, 1255); entries include: "Corbera, md solidorum, Dominicus Enegriz; Cullera, ii millia solidorum; Gandia, iii millia solidorum, in opere murorum"; "Eslida, m solidorum, tenet Gaucerandus in pignore." Borgia's oven is in Reg. Canc. 10, fol. 59v (April 8, 1258): "unum furnum ad coquendum in moraria Valencie." On Dominic de Caballo, and the meat shop he had "prope portam morerie sarracenorum de Roteros de Valencia," see *Itinerari*, p. 199 (Sept. 13, 1249); the gate may be in the Mudejar quarter facing in the Roteros direction, or be in Roteros' Mudejar quarter. The document presented by the Martínez Ferrando *Catálogo* (1, no. 1) as the earliest registered for Valencia is rather a confirmation entered nearly forty years later; like the catalogue, I exclude from my reckoning the grants noted for the *Repartimiento*.

[133] Arch. Crown, James I, Reg. Canc. 10, fol. 1v (Aug. 9, 1257): "de primis denariis quos recipietis de baiulia Valencie donetis et solvatis Bernardo de Coguellis civi Valencie." The name "de Coguellis" is a puzzle and its owner obscure; he may belong to the Catalan Cogull family; a William de Cogoyla received a grant after the Valencian crusade. An assignment of 1,300 solidi loaned by the Valencian citizens Peter Sanz and Ferrer Matoses, to be recovered by the city bailiff for them "de decima vindemie et panicii," is on fol. 1 (Aug. 11), as is another for 500 solidi owed Peter Mercer and William of Na Gilcen "de censualibus nostris operatoriorum draperie Valentie."

[134] *Ibid.*, fol. 16v (Aug. 21, 1257): "Pascasio Lupi de Stella, repositario nostro . . . pro uno roncino . . . super baiulia Xative quam tenetis." An incorrect title makes him "Peter." The Catalan *reboster* was akin to the English royal butler, a dignitary.

[135] *Ibid.*, Reg. Canc. 9, fol. 37v (Sept. 17, 1257): "universis hominibus de Polop . . . quod vos teneatis et custodiatis castrum de Polop . . . [et] accipiatis redditus et exitus dicti castri . . . pro custodia dicti castri."

baron Carroz for life, at this time, the crown required the taxes only from Pop; the seeming beneficence was really purchase of a rent charge on Mudejar taxes in return for a gift by Carroz of 40,000 solidi. Since this was a solidly Mudejar region, Carroz was allowed to settle only Mudejars there.[136]

The crown had recently bought back a rent charge of 500 solidi per annum, on the castle of Planes, from the Valencian citizen who was son and heir of the original beneficiary; the price, 5,000 solidi, was only half-paid by September 1257, so the "Christians and Saracens" of Olocaiba castle and region had all their taxes assigned to liquidate the debt.[137] The arrangement excluded intermediate bailiff or auditor between the recipient and the king's court; it illustrates a common phenomenon, in which the castellan, though he might appoint a collector-bailiff responsible to himself, was in effect the king's authority and bailiff.[138]

A different situation existed at Játiva that year, where the king's bailiff "sold and assigned" all the rents to "buyers," who in turn swore to the castellan that they would respect the sums due him as income from various mixed taxes and from "the Moorish quarter of the same place."[139] In November, assigning specific amounts on

[136] *Ibid.*, fol. 39r,v (Sept. 19, 1257): "pro hiis autem donationibus, confitemur nos habuisse et recepisse a vobis xl millia solidorum regalium . . . [et possitis] stabilire sarracenis et sarracenabus tantum domos et hereditates." Carroz also submitted his accounts directly to the king, for all revenues of the castles and regions of Denia, Segárria, Algar, Pop, Jalón, Olocaiba, and Polop, "et de omnibus aliis locis que unquam pro nobis tenuistis usque in hodiernum diem," the result being that "ita remanemus equaliter quod nichil alter alteri debet restituere nec tenetur" (Reg. Canc. 10, fol. 20v [Sept. 24, 1257]).

[137] *Ibid.*, Reg. Canc. 10, fol. 19v (Sept. 21, 1257): "pro emenda d solidorum regalium quos olim dederamus annuales imperpetuum Bartholomeo [de Roma] patri vestro"; "tam christianis quam sarracenis." The beneficiary's heir, Bernard of Rome, was bound "computare nobiscum et non cum aliqua alia persona."

[138] Another example was Alpuente castle given at this time to Palahí (Palaí, Latin Palazino) de Foces with the obligation of garrisoning it with ten men at 150 solidi each, "inter comestionem et soldatam" (*ibid.*, fol. 20 [Sept. 21, 1257]). He brought his accounts to the king at Lérida for audit, receiving the usual confirmation and waiver of possible prosecution as well as a promise by the king to make up a deficit of 2,000 solidi of Jaca (*ibid.*, same date: "facto recto et diligenti computo de omnibus").

[139] *Ibid.*, Reg. Canc. 9, fol. 43v (Oct. 30, 1257): "super denariis baiulie Xative et super denariis salis, tinturarie, et morarie eiusdem, ita quod postquam redditus . . . annis singulis per baiulum nostrum venditi fuerunt et collocati, emptores eorum intrent vobis per manus et obligent se pro pretiis. . . ." The bailiff would collect the surplus, too, or supply for any deficit.

thirty Mudejar aljamas throughout the kingdom, the king named the crown agent (*porter*) Peter William as collector; no subcollectors appear, and only four assignees, with Alfandech exempt as having arranged its own taxes at farm for a price.[140] Four days later, when contract-farming almost all the revenues of the Alcira region for one year to a consortium of three Christians, "at that price for which they were sold last year and for a thousand solidi besides that," the king included "the revenues or tributes of the Saracens."[141]

In making another assignment of debt for 2,090 solidi of Jaca, he promised to take the sum "from the first taxes [*peites*] we impose in the kingdom of Valencia on Christians or Saracens," and so ordered "the collector or collectors of these taxes."[142] Another castellan received nearly all the taxes from the regions of Sumacárcel, Cárcer, Tous, and Tárbena "both from Christians and from Saracens," for four years, at a price of 1,000 solidi a year and with the obligation of garrisoning and defending these castles at his own expense.[143] From

---

[140] *Ibid.*, Reg. Canc. 8, fol. 36 (Nov. 24, 1257): "has peytas sarracenis civitatis et regni [Valencie], quas colligit Petrus Guillelmi portarius suus." One of the assignees, for Calpe, was castellan there: "habuit Petrus Martini Pedrixolo, alcaydus"; see the grant of his fief in Reg. Canc. 9, fol. 41. King James in his *Llibre dels feyts* (ch. 30) introduces this otherwise obscure figure as "Don Martí de Peroxolo qui era nostre merino." Variants of the name Pedrissol include Pedrixols, Pereixols, Peroixolo, and the Latin Petrisolus. For Segorbe's hundred besants the list notes: "habuit Michael Violeta." Director of the royal secretariate, Violeta figures prominently as notary and secretary in a run of crown documents from 1260 to 1275, though Miret y Sans believes he was displaced as main counselor and director of secretarial affairs by James of Sarroca in 1270 (*Itinerari*, p. 303). In 1266 he and the lieutenant of Montpellier were the diplomats negotiating the marriage of Prince James to Beatrice of Savoy. In 1262 he got for life the revenues and control of the salt monopoly and notariate of Zaragoza. The final assignee was Bernard of Mataró; several members of this knightly family turn up in the military and business affairs of the new kingdom. He may be the same Barcelonan whose name occurs in crown business in 1257 and 1274 (*Itinerari*, pp. 264, 509).

[141] Arch. Crown, James I, Reg. Canc. 10, fol. 25v-26 (Nov. 28, 1257): "cum redditibus seu tributis sarracenorum . . . ; vendimus pro illo precio pro quo anno transacto ea fuerunt vendita et pro mille solidis regalium [Valencie] ultra illud." The same contract, with the same wording on Mudejar revenues was sold on the ambiguous date of February 9, 1257 or 1258, to García Peter of Castalla for a year at 7,000 solidi or rather for a net of just over 6,000, to pay a debt (fols. 33v-34).

[142] *Ibid.*, fol. 35 (Feb. 10, 1257): "super primis peytis quas iactabimus in regno Valencie christianis vel sarracenis, mandantes collectori seu collectoribus peitarum ipsarum. . . ."

[143] *Ibid.*, fol. 40 (Feb. 22, 1257): "et a christianis et a sarracenis." Another rental of these areas is on fol. 64r,v (April 30, 1258) with the same reference to Mudejars

the Mudejar taxes of Liria, James assigned repayment of a debt of 5,500 solidi owed to Raymond of Mirambell.[144] Even in areas where Mudejar taxes predominated, however, the king rarely paused to include them by that name in his writs; thus John Escrivá of Alcoy was simply appointed "bailiff of the same town of Alcoy and its jurisdictions, in such wise that you collect and receive, and cause to be collected and received" all taxes "pertaining to the office of bailiff," remaining in that Mudejar region for life.[145] Similarly Galceran of Moncada received heavily Mudejar Eslida in July 1258, by a short note appended to his list of loans to the crown; for a total debt of 5,833 solidi and 3 pence, Galceran was "to hold the castle of Eslida and receive its revenues, from the past Easter for two years."[146] At this time also, without specifying the overwhelming Mudejar ambience, Artal of Foces "held the castles of Peñacadiel, Palma, Carbonera, Rugat, Borró, Vilella, Beldesa, and Montes," with his own castellans installed.[147]

---

and reserving the "peitam quam iactabimus sarracenis et christianis dictorum castrorum."

[144] *Ibid.*, fol. 40 (March 7, 1257): "in tributo quod nobis faciebant sarraceni Lirie."

[145] *Ibid.*, Reg. Canc. 9, fol. 30 (May 5, 1258): "Iohanni scriptori de Alcoy, baiuliam eiusdem ville de Alcoy et terminorum eius, ita quod tu colligas et accipias, ac colligi et recipi facias . . . que pertineant ad officium baiulie." *Scriptor* may be his scribal occupation rather than his name, but the Escrivá family held important posts throughout Valencia, especially Arnold (procurator general) and Bernard (bailiff of Valencia). *I have found no other mention of this John. Five years later, however,* a crown document about Alcoy and neighboring castles refers to a debt being recovered from "alaminatibus et scribaniis villarum et locorum regni Valencie ultra Xucarum" and the revenues "alaminatuum et scribaniarum" there, one of which John may have held (Reg. Canc. 13, fols. 177r,v [May 23, 1264]).

[146] *Ibid.*, Reg. Canc. 11, fol. 266v (July 1, 1258): "et debet tenere Gaucerandus [de Montecatheno] castrum de Eslida et eius fructus recipere de pasch[al]e transacto ad duos annos cum suis expensis." See also Reg. Canc. 10, fol. 131 (Feb. 23, 1260) where "Galserandus" has handed in his accounts:. "et si predicti redditus suffecerint ad solutionem debiti," the receiver is to transfer the castle to William of Anglesola. The Christian name (also Galcerà, Garceran) is a form of the German Gauzhramn.

[147] *Ibid.*, Reg. Canc. 10, fol. 100v (July 4, 1258), concerning a complaint that "non solvistis Romeo Martini illos mille morabetinos quos ratione dictorum castrorum de mandato nostro ei solvere debebatis"; the remission of penalty here applies also to "universis alcaydis et hominibus qui pro vobis teneant castra de Penacadel . . . de Beldixa" and the others. In a complex transfer on fol. 90 (Dec. 31, 1258), the former *walī* of Valencia had given the castle of Ibi to cover a loan of 4,000 solidi from Berengar of Plana; but when King James subsequently awarded that

Other documents do advert to the Muslim residents, however, as when the king gave the castle and region of Pego to the knight Arnold of Romaní in May 1258, to recover "10,000 solidi of Valencia that you are loaning us in Valencia," drawing the sum from all the crown revenues "both from Christians and from Saracens." This type of commission, where a creditor took over the castle and district, employing his own bailiff-collectors and wielding political authority, was technically illegal; the waiver of prosecution probably given in all such cases is appended to Arnold's writ, because "according to the code of Spain vassals ought not to hold castles from their natural lords by reason of a debt."[148] Another debt of 10,000 solidi was assigned to Peter Zapata by the king at Játiva, two days later, on the revenues "of Christians and Saracens of Gandía."[149] In the same month, King James "sold" by contract to Gonzalvo Ferdinand, for a future "price of 1,200 besants" over two years, all the rents "both from Christians and Saracens" at the castles of Seta and Cheroles. Though the king expressed this contract as a simple mortgage of rents, perhaps to avoid the complication of illegally conferring castellanship as in Arnold's case, in fact he did make Gonzalvo castel-

---

castle to García Peter of Castalla, he (James) moved this assignment of debt, assuming it as his own, to the castle and region of Peñíscola, "ita quod Guillelmus de Plana frater vester teneat dictum castrum et villam, et percipiat omnes redditus, exitus, et proventus" until repaid.

[148] *Ibid.*, fol. 66 (May 14, 1258): "x millia solidorum regalium Valencie, quos nobis in Valencia mutuastis, pro quibus impignoramus, tradimus et obligamus vobis in presenti castrum et villam de Pego cum omnibus terminis [et redditibus] . . . et a christianis et sarracenis"; "absolventes vos . . . [quia] secundum forum yspanie naturales non debent suis dominis naturalibus castra pro debito retinere." On the meaning of "natural" see Luis García de Valdeavellano, "Las instituciones feudales en España," corrective study attached to the Spanish translation of F. L. Ganshof, *El feudalismo* (Barcelona, 1963), pp. 247, 253. Castles fell under the *"fuero* de España" in a number of respects.

[149] Arch. Crown, James I, Reg. Canc. 10, fol. 66v (May 16, 1258): "dominus rex debet Petro Çabata x millia solidorum regalium, pro quibus tradidit et impignoravit sibi omnes redditus et exitus de Candia christianorum et sarracenorum." Zapata, resident at Alcira and a wealthy landholder, apparently belonged to the influential knightly clan of that name. Four years later he had recovered the debt and had submitted his accounts by the king's order to Carroz, "lord of Rebollet," for all revenues of the Gandía district "tam a christianis quam a sarracenis," for the 10,000 solidi "quos nobis accomodaveratis"; he was returning the king's bond (*albaranum*) to him at Zaragoza (Reg. Canc. 14, fol. 11 [Feb. 22, 1262-1263]).

lan, as a query about these revenues the following year makes evident.[150]

Other negotiations also included the Mudejars when describing mixed taxes, as when assigning for credit in June 1258 the castles of Alcoy, Cocentaina, and Villanueva de Castellón.[151] The following month, settling accounts with the Knights Templar, who had recovered a loan of a thousand silver marks from "the castles of Liria, Eslida, Veo, Ahín, Tales, Burriana, Onda, [and] Peñíscola," as well as with some non-Valencian income and with "our profit from the money of Valencia," King James records that he took collection "from Christians, Jews, and Saracens."[152] To Arnold of Montroig, that same month, the king "promised that if ever [your] debt is not satisfied by the aforesaid rent, we will impose a tax on the Saracens of the kingdom of Valencia, and that we will pay those 600 solidi to you from these taxes."[153] Sometimes a collector held his commission only for a Mudejar tax or a Mudejar town, as has been seen; and some taxes were proper only to Muslims and others only to Christians, as with the besant or the tithe. But in general it seems clear that the formula "Christians and Saracens" did not distinguish a more universal mode of collection; inserted or omitted at random, it

[150] *Ibid.*, Reg. Canc. 10, fol. 103v (May 22, 1258): "vendimus vobis Gonzalbo Ferrandi . . . [redditus] in castris de Seta et de Cherolis et eorum terminis, et a christianis [et] sarracenis . . . precio mille cc bisanciorum." See also fol. 108v (April 4, 1259), where Gonzalvo is addressed as "alcaydo de Ceta et de Cheroles."

[151] *Ibid.*, fol. 68 (June 28, 1258), a bill of 2,250 solidi for 500 sheep and 540 solidi for 120 sheep; the creditor Romeo Martin was to hold Villanueva de Castellón castle with its revenues until satisfied. A document of the same date (*ibid.*) gave Alcoy and Cocentaina "donec inde sitis plenarie persoluti." Both documents ordered "quod sarraceni omnes iamdictorum castrorum et terminorum eorum" add castle services.

[152] *Ibid.*, fols. 82v-83 (July 1, 1258): "a christianis, iudeis, et sarracenis."

[153] *Ibid.*, fol. 69v (July 8, 1258): "promittimus etiam vobis quod si unquam de dicto debito in predicto censu vobis [non] fuerit satisfactum, peitas sarracenis regni iactaverimus, [et] quod de dictis peitis ipsos dc solidos persolvamus." Context made it clear that this was not to be an extraordinary levy but one of the usual taxes. See also Reg. Canc. 11, fol. 239v (April 13, 1261), a debt of 4,513 Valencian solidi remaining to the baron William of Rocafull, sometime king's lieutenant of Montpellier, from a complex of taxes owed to his brother, comprising 22,700 solidi of Valencia, 2,480 of Jaca, and 5,000 of Barcelona; the crown assigned the debt to the castle of Planes and its taxes "tam a christianis quam a sarracenis." In Reg. Canc. 12, fol. 13 (Feb. 22, 1262) King James gave Prince Peter the revenues of Pego "tam [de] christianis quam sarracenis," and the appointing to bailiff and castellan posts.

applied to almost all taxes at this level of more general audit and report.[154]

The tax items thus far selected, covering only a year and a half, expose the pattern of borrowing, assignment, and collection. From here on, a more summary review will suffice. In a list of Valencian towns for March 1259, along with the sums collected from each for some unspecified tax, the crown *porter* or executive agent Raymond Helies collected over 65,000 solidi from twelve places above the Júcar, and Bernard of Puigdàlber over 26,000 from twenty-one places in the south. Possibly the discrepancy indicates that this was a tax on Christians, more numerous in the north.[155] In April King James halted a troubled collection of Mudejar taxes, by his agent Bonanat of Guia, until he could arrive to examine the books and the problem himself. Bonanat was allowed to proceed with his operation, however, at over a dozen places with their total of 20,000 besants due.[156] On the same day the king rectified a badly managed sale of revenues in the strongly Mudejar district of Pego. Bonanat of Guia had in-

[154] Thus "Guillelmus de Narbona, repositarius," whom the king sent "ad regnum Valentie pro colligendo erbagium omnium ganatorum per totum regnum predictum, tam de villis et locis ordinum religiosorum, clericorum, militum quam domini regis," surely received Mudejar herbage as well as Christian, perhaps through the local *amin* and subbailiffs (*ibid.*, Reg. Canc. 8, fol. 76v [Nov. 25, 1262]). William soon headed a consortium of five investors to contract-farm the salt monopoly "de rivo de Uldecona usque ad gradum Oropesie" for four years at 1,500 solidi yearly in the various bailiwicks, fiefs, and districts where this "gabellam nostram salis Paniscole" ran (Reg. Canc. 12, fol. 153 [March 10, 1263]). In 1264 he became bailiff for the Valencian kingdom below the Júcar River. Even with tithes, those few Muslims who had purchased Christian lands had to contend with the local *decimarii* of bishop and king; at a district level these too could have their designated collectors, like the William Bertrand, "habitator Peniscole," collector for life of all the king's share in Peñíscola and its territory. William received a tenth of the share ("retrodecimam integre") and had paid 200 solidi of Jaca "pro hac donatione et concessione" (Reg. Canc. 11, fol. 204v [May 4, 1261]). In collecting the rents for Alcira's shops, the shops of Jews ("Muca iudeus, unum operatorium, unum morabatinum") and of Muslims ("Mahomet alcadi, i operatorium, i bisancium") were included in the overwhelmingly Christian list; there were eight Mudejar owners as against sixty-four others (Reg. Canc. 17, fol. 26r,v [Dec. 30, 1263]).

[155] *Ibid.*, Reg. Canc. 8, fol. 44v (March 14, 1259): "istas colligit Raimundus Helies," followed by such entries as "Valencie, xx millia solidorum, accrevit xxx millia solidorum"; Játiva has only 7,000 solidi. Helies or Elies, English Elias, was a family in places as divergent as Barcelona and Alcoy. Puigdàlber is near Villafranca del Panedés in Catalonia.

[156] *Ibid.*, Reg. Canc. 10, fol. 108 (April 4, 1259): "alongetis sarracenos regni Valencie de peytis quam ab eis petitis"; the family name probably derives either from Gothic *wida* or Frankish *witan*.

formed him that the purchaser there, the knight Arnold of Romaní, had contracted to pay 8,000 solidi a year for three years; "since the said sale was effected beyond half of the just price, and we were deceived," however, the king proceded to recover the castle and return the money "that you loaned us on the said castle."[157]

In May the king sold to Vidal of Sarriá, for two years at 600 besants a year, the revenues of Confrides "from Christians and Saracens."[158] In July King James installed James of Alarí in "the bailiwick of Almenar and its territories," to collect "all revenues"; Mudejar revenues were included, though unnamed.[159] The knight Peter Martin of Luna bought for life the castle of Almonacid, with its revenues from "men and women Christians and Saracens"; the contract forbade his introducing new taxation on either people.[160] Artal of Foces, as a creditor, received a commission to go collect the revenues of Beldesa, Carbonera, Rugat, and Vilella until the debt was satisfied, in effect becoming a renter-bailiff for "all Christians and Saracens."[161] In May 1260 the king sold the castle and revenues of Cocentaina to Guic William for three years at 1,500 solidi a year, noting that "Romeo Martin and the *amīn* of Cocentaina now collect these [revenues] for me."[162]

[157] *Ibid.*, fol. 108v (April 4, 1259): "unde cum dicta vendicio sit facta ultra dimidiam iusti precii, et nos simus inde decepti"; "quam nobis accomodastis super dicto castro." The last verb may be a form of *accomodavistis* instead. Arnold was very active in Valencian finance and became bailiff of Valencia city.

[158] *Ibid.*, fol. 140 (May 29, 1259): "a christianis et sarracenis ibi habitantibus et habitaturis" at a "precium." See the similar sale to him of Confrides' revenues "a christianis et sarracenis" in Reg. Canc. 11, fol. 174 (Aug. 18, [1261?]); this involved a "debitum quod vobis debemus."

[159] *Ibid.*, Reg. Canc. 10, fol. 137v (July 21, 1259): "baiuliam de Almenar . . . et colligas et recipias pro nobis omnes redditus. . . ." Alarí is from the form Alarih of the German Alaric, and is a family name both in Catalonia and Valencia.

[160] *Ibid.*, fol. 147r,v (Feb. 13, 1259): "ab hominibus et feminis christianis et sarracenis"; "non iactetis peytas hominibus dicti castri et ville vel feminis, christianis vel sarracenis." The purchase price is illegible. A similar prohibition against a castellan introducing new taxes on Mudejars is found at Chulilla, in the form of a guarantee by the king: "non donetis nec dare teneamini nobis nec alcaydo" any tax not obligatory on all the Mudejars of the Valencian kingdom (Reg. Canc. 11, fol. 186 [Dec. 17, 1260]).

[161] *Ibid.*, Reg. Canc. 10, fol. 130v (Feb. 23, 1259): "fidelibus suis universis christianis et sarracenis de Carbonera, de Beldesa, de Rugat, et de Villela, terminis de Penacadel . . . visis presentibus respondeatis . . . [pro] omnibus redditibus, exitibus, et iuribus nostris . . . quoniam volumus quod predicta recipiat in solucionem debiti quod sibi debemus." The following letter, for Palma, is to Christians alone (*ibid.*).

[162] *Ibid.*, Reg. Canc. 11, fol. 173 (May 21, 1260), quoted above in n. 18.

A major sale in 1261 affected all the taxes of Denia and its region, with special reference to collecting "the *lleuda* from all resident Saracens" on local sales and to settling of new Mudejar taxpayers. The king sold these taxes for ten years, at 10,000 solidi per year, to a consortium comprising his secret wife, Teresa Giles of Vidaure, together with the bailiff of Valencia, Bernard Escrivá, and the royal secretary Peter of Capellades, as well as Peter John of Gerona, Peter of Pocullull, and "a resident of Castellón de Burriana" named Bernard of Almazora. They could "establish in Denia and all its districts a bailiff or bailiffs, whom you choose, whenever and however often it pleases you, on your own authority" to collect from these Christians and Mudejars.[163]

In what may have been a forced loan, King James borrowed for his abortive crusade to the Holy Land 48,000 solidi from the city of Valencia, surrendering a number of castles as surety; in April 1261 he recovered the castles and assigned the debt to the fee he was collecting from all classes for confirmation of the kingdom's laws. At first sight this would seem to have nothing to do with Mudejars, but an exemption granted to the Jews reveals in passing that "the Saracens of the entire kingdom of Valencia" had to join in paying. "The king's intention was and is" to collect a total of 100,000 solidi not only from Christians but "from the Saracens of the said kingdom," a much more numerous group. This confirmation of 1261 possibly covered as well all Mudejar laws and privileges. Since the assignation of nearly half this sum, the debt, fell on Valencia city and huerta, together with the districts of Castellón de Burriana, Corbera, Cullera, Gandía, Liria, Onda, and Villafamés, and on Mudejars, ecclesiastics, knights, and townsmen alike, perhaps these areas together represented forty-eight percent of the new kingdom's mixed Mudejar-Christian wealth.[164]

[163] *Ibid.*, fols. 197v-198 (March 27, 1261): "vendimus vobis dilecte nostre Taresie Egidii de Vidaure . . . concedentes vobis quod possitis in Denia et in omnibus terminis suis constituere baiulum seu baiulos, illum vel illos, quem vel quos volueritis, quandocumque et quotienscumque vobis placuerit, vestra auctoritate propria, qui predicta omnia et singula teneant . . . ; recipiatis lezdam ab omnibus sarracenis habitantibus in locis et terminis." A few lesser taxes were reserved.

[164] *Ibid.*, fol. 203 (April 13, 1261): "confitemur nos recuperasse a vobis probis hominibus civitatis Valencie omnia castra, que a nobis tenebatis obligata in regno Valencie, pro xl octo millibus solidorum regalium Valencie, quos nobis mutuastis ad opus viatici . . . [et assignamus] in universis et singulis denariis quos nunc habere debemus pro confirmatione furorum Valencie ab universis et singulis hominibus . . .

A list of presumably mixed *quèsties* from all over the Valencian kingdom in 1262 noted that Bernard of Puigdàlber had collected 41,000 solidi from fifteen towns above the Júcar and had dismissed an additional 11,000 solidi, while below that river Peter Bonastruc took 16,500 solidi from seventeen towns, plus Játiva's contribution, and dismissed 3,500 more.[165] In giving Alcira, Alfandech, Burriana, Cárcer, Corbera, Gandía, Liria, Onteniente, and Pego castles and districts, with all their revenues, to Prince Peter in 1262, King James ordered "all Christians, Jews, and Saracens" in eight of the nine towns and "all Saracens of Liria" to pay their taxes to the new lord and his agents.[166]

At this time too, King James received an accounting for the Valencia city Moorish quarter and other taxes from Arnold of Font, "citizen of Valencia." Finding a deficit in Arnold's favor, the king reassigned the Moorish quarter, along with "the new Jewry," dye works, and other taxes, to recover 15,000 solidi within two years.[167] This Arnold of Font recurs in tax records. He acted for King James in several important cases, loaned money to build a warship, approved the accounts of the collector at Burriana, and submitted accounts for places like Buñol, Murviedro, and Onda. Another entrepreneur, the knight William, contracted for the revenues of

mandantes collectoribus dictorum denariorum quod . . . vobis de predictis denariis solvant." Fol. 233 (same date): "quos a christianis et sarracenis tocius regni Valencie predicti habere volumus pro confirmacione furorum dicti regni"; "intencionis nostre fuit et est quod dicta centum millia solidorum regalium abeamus a christianis et sarracenis dicti regni Valencie." The exemption of the Jews may have been due to a private "composition" or agreement, like that at Zaragoza in 1269 where the Jewish community gave "20,000 solidi of Jaca" toward the king's crusade to the Holy Land in return for tax exemption over the next three years (*Colección diplomática*, doc. 1,318 [May 2, 1269]). See above, Chapter VI, n. 75.

[165] Arch. Crown, James I, Reg. Canc. 8, fols. 61v-62 (Oct. 20, 1262): "iactavit dominus rex questias regni Valentie, et collegit a rivo Xucari citra Bernardus de Puydalber et ultra Xucarum Petrus Bonastruc." 20,000 solidi above the Júcar were assigned to the Jewish creditor Benvenist de Porta; three other assignments in all were made, to a total of 3,300 Jaca solidi plus 11,767 Valencian.

[166] *Ibid.*, Reg. Canc. 14, fol. 10v (Feb. 22, 1262): "universis bonis hominibus, tam christianis tam iudeis quam sarracenis . . . et universis sarracenis de Liria . . . [quod] impendeatis inde filio nostro vel cui mandaverit loco sui."

[167] *Ibid.*, fol. 12v (Feb. 28, 1262): "Arnaldo de Fonte civi Valentie quod reddidistis nobis compotum . . . de redditibus . . . nostris Muriveteris et de tintureria, moreria, iudaria nova, almudino . . . civitatis Valencie . . . ; et vendimus vobis . . . , ad duos annos primos venturos et completos, omnes redditus, exitus, et quelibet alia iura nostra morarie . . . civitatis Valencie."

both Christians and Mudejars of the Játiva district, plus the salt monopoly for all southern Valencia from "Christians, Jews, and Saracens, and equally [from] the subjects of knights, religious orders, clerics, or ourselves," for 150,000 solidi or 30,000 per year in two installments annually; he assumed the office of bailiff there as well.[168]

One could extend this survey of revenue documentation in either of two directions: by adding many more reports of presumably mixed taxes, or by tediously plodding forward with random descriptions drawn from the next two thousand Valencian manuscripts in James's registers. Neither course would expand much further our knowledge of Mudejar taxation and its collection. It may be better to close this section with several examples, of a specifically Mudejar orientation, taken from the continuing records.

In December 1263 Bartholomew, bailiff of Alcira, submitted accounts that included Mudejar "revenues" of 199 solidi, plus 329 solidi for the besant tax, and 23½ solidi in fines; for Corbera the bailiff Mathew Babot reported 5,400 solidi as Mudejar "revenues"; for Onteniente the bailiff Dominic of Castellar listed 76 solidi as "of the Saracens." Most taxes in the lists were mixed, however, so these items reflect only fragments.[169] In May 1264 Peter Blasch received a commission to take his castellan's salary at Bergia annually from Mudejar taxes at Guadalest and Gallinera; the respective Muslim *amin* at each place was to pay. The same taxes were drawn upon to pay a debt of 5,408 solidi of Jaca to the king's archer Bernard William.[170] In November the king assured the Muslims within Játiva

---

[168] *Ibid.*, Reg. Canc. 12, fol. 147v (Nov. 29, 1263 ?): "tam christianos quam iudeos et tam sarracenos, et tam homines militum, ordinum, clericorum [et] nostrorum quam quorumlibet aliorum"; "servantibus etiam sarracenis eorum açunam prout tempore sarracenorum eisdem servabantur"; "prout recipere in computo consuevimus ab aliis qui baiuliam predictam pro nobis tenuerint." No date is given; the Martínez Ferrando *Catálogo* (1, nos. 447, 499) erroneously lists the document under "1262-1263" and later again as a separate item under the conjectural date given above. The knight's name, illegible, I reconstruct as William of Bielsa, who was bailiff for Valencia below the Júcar.

[169] Arch. Crown, James I, Reg. Canc. 17, fols. 27-32 (Dec. 30, 1263): "computavit Bartholomeus baiulus Algezire cum Martino Lupi de Bolaz notario domini infantis et cum Matheo Baboti, mandato dicti infantis de omnibus redditibus Algezire."

[170] *Ibid.*, Reg. Canc. 13, fol. 176 (May 23, 1264): "super çofra, alaminatu, et scribania de Godalech et de Gallinera, mandantes alamino de Gallinera et alamino de Godalech et aliamis locorum predictorum quod . . . solvant pro nobis vobis." Fol. 177r,v (same date): "super [çofris, redditibus] et alaminatibus et scribaniis."

city that "all Saracens living in the huerta and territories of Játiva are bound to pay taxes together with you in everything and to put in their share."[171] The Moorish quarter of Alcira had its 626 solidi, plus its contribution to mixed taxes, collected in 1265 by the bailiff Berengar Cesposes (de Pausis).[172]

An April 1266 contract of sale suggests how sweeping was the traffic in all rents. Prince Peter, with the king's permission, sold "the whole bailiwick of Valencia," all revenues, and the bailiate itself to two "citizens of Valencia" who often farmed rents together in a consortium. Of the total sale price, 100,000 solidi for the two years, the contractors had paid a deposit of 20,000 solidi; besides this price they had to shoulder all *violaris* and burdens outstanding, beginning with a debt of 40,000 solidi for the king. Arnold of Romaní already held the bailiate under the same conditions; they were to succeed him, and to adopt the same contract. For surety they received the castle of Alfandech. The two were to put their own men in office for collecting the rents "and they are to obey and report to you, and not to us or ours." Two weeks later King James in a long and tendentiously detailed document effectively revoked the prince's appointment by making Arnold of Romaní bailiff for life, with permanent right to appoint a substitute bailiff in his stead.[173] The

[171] *Ibid.*, fol. 236 (Nov. 6, 1264): "quod omnes sarraceni habitantes in orta et terminis Xative teneantur simul vobiscum peytare in omnibus et ponere partem suam."

[172] *Ibid.*, Reg. Canc. 17, fols. 38v-39 (July 2, 1265): "moreria, dcxxvi solidos, v denarios." Berengar's salary was 700 solidi, roughly a tenth of the total 6,215 after expenses.

[173] *Ibid.*, fol. 108 (April 29, 1266): "vobis Ferrario Matosis et Petro Sancii civibus Valencie et cui vel quibus volueritis totam baiuliam Valencie, cum omnibus redditibus . . . ad ipsam baiuliam pertinentibus . . . ; et vos et vestri possitis quoslibet homines volueritis in predicta baiulia mittere et ponere . . . et inde vobis attendant et respondeant et non interim nobis neque nostris." Ferrer appears in crown records as early as 1249, receiving a lifetime rent charge in Valencia from the crown drapers' shops, and was still active under both Peter and his successor Alfonso. He was a jurate of Valencia city and in 1270 justiciar. Of his several litigations, he lost the case in which he and relatives had attacked a Valencian banker, had bloodied his head with knife cuts, and had made off with the money they claimed; the Matoses clan had to pay court charges, medical fees, a severe fine, and restitution. See *Colección diplomática*, doc. 1,422 (Dec. 18, 1273); and see *Itinerari*, pp. 198 (1249), 384 (1266), and 490 (1273). For Arnold's appointment, see Arch. Crown, James I, Reg. Canc. 15, fol. 15r,v (May 12, 1266): "diebus omnibus vite vestre baiuliam civitatis Valencie, ita videlicet quod [vos vel] quem volueritis loco vestri sitis baiulus." In fol. 25v (Aug. 7, 1266) James alienated the town of Collada in

conflict does not lessen the interest of each document for both Christian and Mudejar collections. In November 1267 the crown sold to Bernard Taberner the revenues of Guadalest, which it had "rented to the aljama of the Saracens of the same place." The price was the same in both past and current cases, 7,000 solidi, and like his Mudejar predecessors Bernard was to collect from Christian and Muslim alike. The previous Mudejar purchase of the valley's taxes had been terminated "because it was fraudulently drawn."[174]

When the king found himself saddled with a debt of 26,210 silver besants for the Murcian war, he reduced the exchange rate and converted the sum to 78,630 solidi at 3 solidi per besant, and "assigned them to you to have and receive from the taxes on Saracens in the kingdom of Valencia," as well as from three castles and his share of the papal crusade tithe.[175] In 1269 King James gave Roderick Martin of Azagra and the crown functionary Peter Diego (Didaci) for five years "all our taxes of the Mudejar quarter of Cocentaina" at 2,000 solidi every year. The king promised not to impose any outside tax "on the said Saracens," and ordered them to pay everything to Roderick. He imposed a condition on the two owners: "in this wise, namely, that you improve the said Mudejar quarter" or forfeit 3,000 solidi "in penalty."[176] In 1269 too the prince's secretary James of

---

Albaida Valley, with all the rents "que in dicta alqueria et sarracenis ibi comorantibus habemus."

[174] Arch. Crown, James I, Reg. Canc. 15, fol. 71 (Nov. 18, 1267): "vendimus et concedimus et tributamus vobis Bernardo Tavernarii civi Valencie et vestris redditus . . . [que] attributaveramus aliame sarracenorum eiusdem loci; . . . quia facta fuit in fraudem nostram penitus revocamus." Fraud in this case could have consisted of underestimating the amount owed in taxes by the people. See the document more fully in Chap. VII, n. 34.

[175] Ibid., Reg. Canc. 14, fol. 83v (Jan. 16, 1266 or 1267): "assignamus vobis habendos et percipiendos in peytis sarracenorum regni Valencie."

[176] Ibid., Reg. Canc. 15, fol. 136 (Feb. 10, 1269): "ac iura nostra omnia morerie de Cocentania . . . ; est tamen sciendum quod hoc attributamentum vobis facimus . . . in hunc scilicet modum quod vos dictam moreriam melioretis"; "in pena." The improvement was to consist in doubling the number of Mudejar taxpayers there. Roderick Martín of Azagra had properties in Valencia and Navarre, over which he fought lawsuits against his relatives Batholomew Martín and Romeo Martín; in 1270 he held the taxes of Alcalá and Gallinera for the next four years and in 1282 the castellanship of Montesa, Ayora, and Teresa for one year. A dozen documents in the registers for James and Peter follow the family's important role in Valencia from 1268 to 1283, after which their activity there apparently declined. See also *Itinerari*, pp. 482 (1273), 458 (1272).

Linars was collector of the *alfarda* from the Mudejars of Alcira, Beniopa, Sumacárcel, and Pego, while Arnold of Romaní took that of Alfandech.[177]

To gather the moneyage, an occasional and unusual tax, from "both Christians and Saracens belonging to the order of Calatrava," King James in 1271 simply commissioned the Alcañiz commander of those military knights, stipulating the order's properties as surety. For the wider coverage, however, the king appointed the castellan of Uxó, Berengar of Albiol, specifically for the Mudejars alone in the northern part of Valencia kingdom, and Peter Simon (Eximén) of Espluga, sometime bailiff of Burriana, for the southern or sub-Júcar Mudejars. Each man had jurisdiction for this tax not only over crown Mudejars but "of all the Moors of the church, and of knights, and of orders, and of other persons" such as "the men of the towns" but excluding Mudejars belonging to those "castles of high barons, or of knights, or of townsmen" that had a countryside or territory juridically annexed. Thus each collector took the moneyage in crown districts as well as from Muslims either unattached or else belonging to districts not alodial in their effect. Presumably the castle districts of noncrown or of alodial towns and nobles received their own collection, as in the anomalous case of Calatrava above.[178]

A subbailiff or collector-bailiff turns up at Valencia city late in 1275, formally appointed by the crown and instructed to present his accounts for auditing by the real or main bailiff there; this specialization may reflect the growing complexity of the office of bailiff for the

[177] Arch. Crown, James I, Reg. Canc. 35, fol. 32 (Nov. 18, 1269): "dominus infans saccavit sarracenis suis regni Valencie alfardas inferius nominatas, quas colligit Iacobus de Linariis, excepta alfarda de Alfandech de Marayen [*sic*] quam debet recipere Arnaldus de Romanino." Arnold had wide holdings in the kingdom and served for a time as bailiff of Valencia. James was bailiff of Pego Valley and then of a large region centering on Gandía, Palma, and Beniopa from about 1272 into the 1280's; he held the Mudejar fifths at Beniopa in 1276.

[178] *Ibid.*, Reg. Canc. 16, fol. 248 (July 18, 1271): "universis hominibus tam christianis quam sarracenis qui sunt ordinis Calatrave . . . presens monetaticum." Reg. Canc. 18, fols. 94v-95 (Dec. 1, 1272): "et colligit ipsum a rivo Xucari citra Berengarius de Albiol alcaydus Uxoni," a dozen aljamas being designated by name; "item de tots los moros de la eglesia e de cavalers e de d'ordens e altres persones . . . si no son de castels ab termens de richs homens o de cavalers o de ciutadans." The sub-Júcar region had twenty-nine aljamas designated by name, or nearly two and a half times as many as for the northern half of the kingdom. Moreover, though multiple-town aljamas or entries here are rare for the north, they are common in the south: two as against nineteen.

region above the Júcar. The king conceded "to you, Perico Sabadí, the office of collecting our rents in Valencia [city], and the revenues and all our receipts of the Moorish and Jewish quarters there throughout your life, as long as you conduct yourself well and faithfully in this office."[179] The incumbent seems not to have enjoyed length of days. A similar contract, narrower in scope and duration, replaced the first in 1276: "we give etc. to you, Berengar of Far, that you be the collector of our revenues and receipts in our Moorish quarter of Valencia as long as it will please us and as long as you conduct yourself in the said office well and faithfully."[180] Berengar received the salary customarily given to collectors.

These two letters may represent the better organization of the later period, in a realm already consolidated; comparison with other citations indicates that the several forms of collection nevertheless persisted. Perhaps there is only question here of two coordinate levels of the collection machinery. More complex organization, specialization, and rationalization may also explain the separate "sale of revenues, income, and claims of the castles, places, and towns of the Saracens of the kingdom of Valencia," as against "the sale of revenues" of equivalent Christian groupings in late 1274. The auctioneer was Arnold Escrivá, duly delegated by writ; "if Arnold Escrivá himself cannot be present for conducting the aforesaid sales," then the provisionally delegated Berengar Dalmau and Artal Esquerre were to join in taking his place.[181]

The patterns continued under King Peter; a few examples will suffice. The baron Peter Martin of Luna, lord of Almonacid and

[179] *Ibid.*, Reg. Canc. 20, fol. 287 (Sept. 15, 1275): "concedimus vobis Pericono Zabadia officium colligendi censualia nostra Valencie, et redditus ac iura nostra omnia morerie et iuderie eiusdem tota in tota vita tua, dum bene et fideliter in ipso officio te habebis." Pericó is a diminutive of Pere (like Peterkin); Sabadí or Çabadi shared a grant of open land outside the Valencia city walls with a minor crown functionary, a class to which he too probably belonged.

[180] *Ibid.*, fol. 337 (April 9, 1276): "damus etc. tibi Berengario de Faro quod tu sis collector reddituum et iurium nostrorum morerie nostre Valencie dum nobis placuerit et bene et fideliter in dicto officio te habebis." Is he from Faura near Murviedro? If not, the family probably represents the Fa or Far name found in Catalonia and Majorca, unless a variant of Fer is involved.

[181] *Ibid.*, Reg. Canc. 19, fol. 186v (Nov. 18, 1274): "item alia [carta] de vendicione reddituum, exituum, et iurium castrorum, locorum, et villarum sarracenorum regni Valencie; item similia tria instrumenta fuerunt missa . . . ob hoc quia si ipse Arnaldus Scriba non posset esse ad vendiciones predictas faciendas quod ipse Berengarius possit vendere simul cum predicto Artallo."

counselor to the crown for a quarter-century, controlled Almonacid's crown revenues for over fifteen years, though this castle and valley remained under litigation the whole time. He also oversaw regalian tax collection for a time at Alfandech Valley. Only in 1276 did he receive specific authorization to do so in his own fief; at this time he seems to have been losing control of the property, and perhaps the king's confirmation of his tax farming was meant to stabilize or compensate. Simon López of Embún, another crown dignitary, acquired two-thirds of the 1278 *alfarda* paid by the Moors of Gallinera Valley. John Pérez of Vitoria, former justiciar of Calatayud and property holder in Valencia, collected the 1279 regalian dues at Eslida, and was involved in Mudejar tax business also at Valencia city and Peñíscola.

Early in 1275 the knight Matthew of Montreal, holder of baths, mills, and an oven at Valencia city along with other properties, joined with his brother Guarner to loan the crown 30,000 solidi; in return he took the castellanship of Alcalá and Gallinera castles with their territories. Though the documentation does not always make it clear, the taxes for both places were almost wholly Mudejar. Matthew proved unlucky. The Mudejar revolt and Petrine reconstruction tied up tax resources, so that he was still retrieving his investment from both castles almost a decade later, his efforts paralleled by a series of instructions from the king's court. The wealthy crown official Berengar of Conques took 3,000 solidi from Mudejar revenues in 1284. William Elias received the revenues from the Moorish aljama of Almonacid Valley in 1285. After the turn of the century the crown conveyed to one of its functionaries all the hospitality tax (*cena*), in an instruction sent to thirty-six localities or tax units, including five Mudejar aljamas.[182]

COLLECTORIES

How were the numerous Mudejar towns arranged into effective units of collection? The district or supervisory accounts merely in-

[182] *Ibid.*, Peter III, Reg. Canc. 52, fol. 81 (Dec. 12, 1284), on Berengar, who took his name from Conques rather than Cuenca and once held the Valencia bailiate (see Burns, *Crusader Valencia*, I, 293, 299, and II, 514). Reg. Canc. 54, fol. 194 (Sept. 3, 1285), on Elias. A run of half a dozen documents follows Matthew of Montreal and his Mudejar rents at the two castles after James's death, in Peter's registers. For the fourteenth-century case see Chapter V, n. 151.

cluded all Mudejar sums as lumped together; where the district was densely Mudejar, with few Christians, an occasional account might specify certain centers. Tax lists of purely Mudejar collections provide some notion as to how the treasury grouped such communities; lists are infrequent, vary in their arrangements, and may well have been idiosyncratic.

The districts or regions serving normally as collectories probably centered for convenience around dominant Mudejar aljamas, somewhat like the corresponding Jewish *collectae*. Unlike the Jews, of course, Mudejars comprised the mass of the kingdom's population, and therefore required less of the extrinsic interrelating proper to the smaller, more scattered Jewish centers. The Muslims already possessed some kind of collection mechanism, which the conquerors undoubtedly preserved as far as feasible in accordance with their fixed policy of maintaining the existing aljama institutions. Aprioristic conjecture would favor collectories corresponding to the *termini* or countryside jurisdictions surrounding each village, which were englobed in turn by the wider countryside of a large town, the whole delimited by some natural feature in an immemorial pattern.

Since the structure for Jews is both clear and accessible, it can serve as a point of analogy or comparison. Within each kingdom of the crown of Aragon, the Jews divided into *collectae* or groupings of communities bearing the name of the most important Jewry of an area, the sum assigned each *collecta* being then subdivided among its component localities. Apart from this revenue device the Jewish aljamas remained mutually autonomous; at the end of King James's reign and during King Peter's, representatives occasionally gathered as a kind of Jewish parliament to counsel on new levies. Within the several Valencian *collectae* Jewish officials normally cared for actual collecting, despite assignment of the total to a farmer or creditor. If the excitement at Zaragoza in 1264 can serve as an index, the rich normally preferred to have assessment judged by appointed local men, while the poor demanded a computation based on the individual's declaration under oath before elected assessors. Valencian Jews often complained that the rich shifted tax burdens to the poor; in 1300 the individual declaration was therefore imposed.[183]

[183] David Romano Ventura, "El reparto del subsidio de 1282 entre las aljamas catalanas," *Sefarad*, XII (1953), esp. p. 76. Neuman, *Jews in Spain*, I, 61-63. Baer, *Jews in Christian Spain*, I, 215-217, 222-223.

Drawing from hundreds of *responsa* or rabbinical opinions of the celebrated Ben Adret of Barcelona, Epstein has described the system at our period. After the king fixed the sum for each collectory, sometimes consulting Jewish representatives, the aljamas comprising the collectory sent two or three delegates apiece to a meeting arranged by the collectory's principal town or by the king, to settle quotas and procedure, drafting a constitution and sealing it with their oaths. Actual assessment and collection at the local, final stage varied; usually each aljama in a collectory set up a tax commission of two treasurers and three property-assessors (honorific posts, coveted even though this *collegium* had to make personal surety for the community's debt). The commissioners then drew up tax rolls for all over fifteen years, lumping properties of wife and children under the father. They either received and examined the personal declaration of profits and holdings, or actually investigated and estimated these. In either case, local custom modified details, Lérida exempting one's residence and productive capital, for example, and Zaragoza reckoning excess profits, while spirited dispute prevailed on such topics as how to treat loans still out or properties owned elsewhere.

During a conference of delegates called at the local synagogue, regulations were drawn up and then transcribed into the communal register to serve as precedent in law. Minor local officials might then collect the share assigned each taxpayer, this function falling to the synagogue beadle in very small communities; alternatively, every person deposited his tax in a community chest, kept under multiple lock at the synagogue, in the presence of guards at a stated time. The tax commissioners or the agent in charge of a given tax remitted the chest to the king's bailiff or appointee, sometimes conveying it to a special place at a designated time, for ultimate transfer to the king's treasury. The whole rigmarole applied only to direct taxes, and could be bypassed in case of haste by reapplying past assessment.[184]

Not only the Jews but the Valencian church had a special map for taxes; to collect the tithe, a third of which went to the king, the combined crown and diocesan collectors worked through "tithe-

---

[184] Isidore Epstein, *The "Responsa" of Rabbi Solomon Ben Adreth of Barcelona (1235-1310) as a Source of the History of Spain. Studies in the Communal Life of the Jews in Spain as Reflected in the "Responsa."* . . . (New York, [1925] 1968), ch. 3.

ships" or "rectorates," perhaps conterminous with the parishes.[185] A hint of some collectory system for the Mudejars too may lie in the instruction of 1272 to the Muslims of Ayelo: "you are bound to pay taxes to us according to the code or Sunna of the Saracens of Montesa," perhaps a reference to a regional custom and grouping.[186] When the Beniarjó Muslims paid a major tax directly to the king, they became embroiled in a dispute with the district tax collectors, described as "the *amīn* and community of the Saracens of Beniopa," a town to which Beniarjó was obviously subordinate.[187] Similarly, in 1264 King James allowed as a permanent privilege to "all Saracens living in the huerta and countryside of Cocentaina" that they could participate with Cocentaina's Moorish quarter when paying taxes, "and contribute their portion." Perhaps the rustic Muslim did not always share the privileges of the countryside's main town, so that collection mechanisms may have differed. The same privilege in the same wording, however, did go to "all Saracens resident" in the Játiva district.[188] Whatever the theoretical pattern, multiple assignments against a locality's taxes disturbed it badly; alien collectors might intrude for a given sum or tax, or the crown might remove jurisdiction over it to a more important bailiff designated to handle that assignment. In 1286 the king directed "the *amīn* and Saracens of [Raço de l']Alburgir that they ought to answer to Peter of Puigroig, bailiff of Alcira, for all revenues and claims of the Lady Andrea."[189]

[185] Burns, *Crusader Valencia*, I, 147.

[186] Arch. Crown, James I, Reg. Canc. 37, fol. 52v (Oct. 18, 1272): "teneamini nobis contribuere ad forum sive çunam sarracenorum Muntesie."

[187] *Ibid.*, Peter III, Reg. Canc. 46, fol. 78v (April 11, 1282): "alamino et aliame sarracenorum Benioppe: intelleximus per Iacobum Castellani quod vos compellitis sarracenos suos de Benijarion ad contribuendum simile vobiscum in ista quantitate . . . ; mandamus vobis quatenus non compellatis eos."

[188] *Ibid.*, James I, Reg. Canc. 13, fol. 236 (Nov. 6, 1264): "preterea damus et concedimus vobis et vestris imperpetuum quod omnes sarraceni habitantes in orta et terminis Concentanie teneantur simul vobiscum peytare in omnibus et ponere partem suam." The Játiva document is on the same fol. (same date).

[189] *Ibid.*, Alfonso III, Reg. Canc. 67, fol. 78 (Sept. 21, 1286): "fuit scriptum alamino et sarracenis del Alburgi quod de omnibus redditibus et iuribus, de quibus debent respondere dompne Andree [de Arnedo] respondeant Petro de Podio Rubeo baiulo Algezire." When a population dispersed, owing to war or catastrophe, the king held it to the payment of current taxes, especially where a purchase of a complex of taxes by the local Mudejars had left the king anticipating a lump sum. Thus, Alfonso ordered all his "dominis seu alcaydis castrorum regni Valencie" to

The word *collecta* in Mudejar tax documents sometimes meant only "collection";[190] but at least once it defined a tax district and was moreover synonymous with *terminus*.[191] Thus the Mudejar unit or *collecta* may normally have been identical with a larger town's jurisdictional countryside, with each component aljama and its collecting *amīn* acting as subordinate or responsible to the more important *amīn*, exceptions being allowed for any aljama or *amīn* of a town to contract-farm more directly to the king's bailiff. "The aljama of Saracens of Pego," for example, seems to coincide with the tax area of "Pego and the whole valley and its jurisdictions."[192] Assignations of mixed taxes to a debt or to a supervising bailiff, of course, were stated often in terms of such *termini*, though this says nothing about their constitutive elements, Christian or Mudejar, where the subbailiffs and the underling collectors labored.[193] The "Saracens of the mountains" with their special *moixerif* have already been discussed; apparently a late and localized supervisory development, it left the component bailiate groupings undisturbed.

The connection of an *amīn* with his surrounding countryside, or

---

return such fugitives to Montesa or else have them send their taxes: "ut tornent habitare in ipso loco de Muntesia vel quod solvant ipse aliame de Muntesia illud quod per eosdem tacxati fuerint in illa pecunie quantitate quam ipsa aliama nobis quolibet anno dare et solvere tenetur prout de predictis illustrissimus dominus Petrus inclite recordationis pater noster. . . . [mandavit]" (Reg. Canc. 63, fol. 40v [Feb. 2, 1286]). Similarly the fugitives from Villarreal had to pay what they owed under the recently deceased King Peter: "compellatis omnes sarracenos qui fuerunt de moraria Ville Regalis . . . ad solvendum vobis loco nostro denarios quos debebant illustrissimo domino regi patri nostro."

[190] *Ibid.*, James I, Reg. Canc. 10, fol. 23 (Oct. 29, 1257): "in primis collectis quas facietis pro nobis." Reg. Canc. 15, fols. 40v-41 (Jan. 9, 1266): "et de omnibus collectis et assignationibus . . . tam super christianis . . . quam etiam sarracenis." Reg. Canc. 14, fol. 80v (April 18, 1266): "percipiendos in omnibus collectis quas faciet . . . tam a christianis [et] iudeis quam sarracenis."

[191] *Ibid.*, Reg. Canc. 9, fol. 33v (Sept. 4, 1257): "sive vinum sit de termino et collecta de Biar sive aliunde apportetur," in connection with sale of wine in the Biar fonduk. This meaning does not seem to have passed into Catalan *collecta*; for a later, special sense, however, see Mateu i Llopis, *Materiales para un glosario de diplomática*, p. 26.

[192] Arch. Crown, James I, Reg. Canc. 14, fol. 7 (Feb. 5, 1262): "aliame sarracenorum de Pego . . . [redditus] in Pego et tota valle ac terminis eius."

[193] For example, "baiuliam Muriveteris et tocius termini eiusdem . . . sicut baiulus accipere consuevit," for life, to Robau of Voltarasch (*Colección diplomática*, doc. 390 [Feb. 11, 1251]). Robau, whose name derives from Hrotbald, was a nephew of the German count, Carrós or Carroz, lord of Rebollet.

terminus with its villages, turns up also in nontax contexts; when the military order of Montesa was settling Muslims throughout several districts of Perpunchent in 1316, it entrusted actual division or assignation of the residences and farms to "our *amīn*." Thus the ubiquitous *alaminatum* (Catalan *alaminatge*) would seem to have designated not only the office but usually also a territory. Like the term *baiulia*, which often held both these same meanings simultaneously, it was flexible enough also to apply to the smallest unit of superintendence, as at Carrícola; the *collecta* under an *amīn* therefore would have coexisted with a patchwork of *ad hoc* and even of component Mudejar entities, each boasting its own functionary of that name.[194]

The major division effected by the Júcar River, important in Christian collections, was utilized for certain Mudejar taxes as marking at least supervisory districts. Special collectors stood outside the framework; for example, Mudejars who paid tithes and first-fruits on land purchased from Christians had to deal with the diocesan bailiffs. King James insisted on this in 1269: each *amīn* "of the Saracens of towns and places of the kingdom of Valencia is to answer" to the bishop, chapter, and clergy "or to their bailiffs." The king's bailiff at Valencia city would enforce this upon Muslims north of the Júcar, where applicable and necessary, while his bailiff at Játiva would similarly serve sub-Júcar Valencia.[195]

Later documentation does not safely illustrate thirteenth-century methods, even in so traditional a society. For what light it may cast, some fourteenth-century evidence may nevertheless be cited. The highest echelons at that time saw a rapid evolution in accounting

[194] Arch. Nac. Madrid, Ords. milits., Montesa, 542 C, Libro registro de poblaciones i privilegios, fol. xix (1316), on Perpunchent: "prout per alaminum nostrum sunt vobis assignate." For Carrícola, see above, p. 250. The *qāḍī* in Valencia soon came to have, anomalously, an appeals territory (Burns, *Islam under the Crusaders*, ch. 10, part 3), providing perhaps some analogy here. Besides the references above to individual "alaminates," see the general reference to all those below the Júcar as a universalized system, above in n. 145.

[195] *Colección diplomática*, doc. 959 (June 30, 1269), about lands "bought or acquired" from Christians "postquam nos habuimus ipsa loca." The particular case explained, King James ordered generally "quod alamini sarracenorum, villarum, et locorum regni Valencie respondeant de decimis, redditibus, et exitibus episcopo et capitulo ac clericis ecclesie valentine vel baiulis eorundem; alias quod distringantur citra Xucarum per baiulum Valencie, ultra Xucarum per baiulum Xative, secundum instrumenta et mandata nostra, prout in ipsis instrumentis plenius continetur."

methods, specialization of personnel, and general rationalization of method. This does not seem to have affected local operations substantially. A case from the early part of the century involved the collection of twenty-four crown taxes in the Valencian kingdom below the Júcar. Of the eleven taxes designated there as Mudejar, five provided for prededuction of lower echelon salaries, under formulas like "subtracting salaries and expenses," or "subtracting the salary of the collector," or in the case of water (*laygua*) "subtracting the salaries of the procurators and the collectors."

For this region, Arnold Torrelles received 3,000 solidi under title of procuration (plus 6,000 as castellan at Orihuela), while his assessor got 1,460, the bailiff general 2,000, bailiffs for separate subregions 300 or 200 each, a port scribe 304, the Christian who "received the Moorish [Arabic] accounts and translated them into Christian" 400, and "the Moorish *alcaldes* for the salary of the *alcaldía*" 180 solidi apiece. Perhaps the six taxes for which neither salary nor expense appear came to the crown coffers via tax farmers or special collectors. *Cena* was handled apart from these eleven Mudejar taxes; a letter went out to each of thirty-six Valencian collectories, prorating the total owed, designating the Christian supervisor and threatening seizure of person and property in case of nonpayment. Though most *cena* collectories were mixed, five were exclusively Mudejar.[196]

Another fourteenth-century case involved moneyage, whose collection rights the king assigned to his son. The prince in turn appointed the Valencian merchant Arnold of Vallejola for that kingdom. Arnold began collecting at Michaelmas through subcollectors—for example, at Morella, Játiva, and Alcira. If procedure was the same at mid-century as in 1385, Arnold's subcollectors went from village to village in their area, notifying those subject to the

---

[196] *Rentas de Aragón*, pp. 109ff.: "assi comensen les rendes . . . della el riu de Xuquer"; "abatut lo salari del cullidor"; "abatuts salaris del procuradors et cullidors"; "abatuts salaris et messions." The rents, which include mixed taxes like pasturage for flocks and commercial duties, are followed by a list of six *castellans* who draw nearly 15,000 solidi from the revenues, nine specific salaries as distinguished from the general annotations for underlings given above, ten *violaris* to a total of 7,486 solidi, and six assignations of debt for 42,270 solidi plus three assignations for castle improvements. Salaries include: "pren Narnau Torrelles por salari de la dita procuracio, cascun any, iii millia solidos . . . lo assessor del dit procurador por salari de la assessoria, mcccclx solidos . . . lo batle general . . . la batlia de Oriola . . . Nalffonso G. por salari de reebre los comptes murischs et trasladar aquells en christianesch, cccc solidos," and so on.

tax, and convoking meetings during which local officials collaborated and swore oaths. Whatever this procedure reveals about the systematic nature of Arago-Catalan tax collecting, it may have applied only to Christian and to mixed communities, with modifications for purely Mudejar aljamas or *collectae* according to the evidences just examined.[197]

In arranging available information on tax harvesting, the highest or supervisory echelons stand out clearest, as does each aljama's participation under its *amīn*. How the hierarchy of bailiff general through subbailiffs meshed with special crown agents or with tax farmers and concessionaires is obscure. Finally, one can see pensioners burdening an income, creditors drawing from it, patronage figures like a local Muslim lord endowed with control of an area, and particularized procurators like the operator of a fonduk or the administrator for crown shares of the kingdom's baths.[198]

Collectories, even disparate sets of them for the several taxes, can be reconciled with quite different procedures for other taxes—the booth at the city gate, the dignitary and his staff roaming a region in the interests of a single regalian fee, or the village buying its own revenues at a set sum. All these elements make sense. Fitting them further into a single pattern that can exclude other dispositions for the same material is not possible. Marshaling the data and reasonably interrelating it may represent the only accessible control in studying so essentially chaotic a system. The remaining intransigent materials serve to remind us of the patchwork nature of much medieval administration.

[197] Russell, "Monedatge," pp. 487-488. Vallejola may be a misreading for the Valleriola family prominent in Valencia then.
[198] See Chapter III, part 3.

CHAPTER IX

Delinquents, Anomalies, and Exemptions

IF THE REVENUE collector's lot is not a happy one, much less so is the path of the tax delinquent. What happened when Mudejars found themselves in straitened circumstances or refused to pay the rent? Several lines of retreat lay open: public reduction of the community's debt, personal or group exemption, temporary postponement of the obligation, borrowing from the local usurer, or flight.

DEBTORS

Private or public, debt was a serious fault. The tax collector was empowered to confiscate the delinquent's assets until he paid and even to auction them off. As a final dire fate for Christian or Muslim the gates of prison yawned, though the confined wretch then sank deeper into his predicament due to charges for room and board. Mudejar debtors could declare a kind of bankruptcy before the bailiff, receiving legal remission of all debts either permanently or in the form of a moratorium, under the title *guiatge de deudes*. Confiscation of goods as pledge, which could also be forestalled by depositing a sort of bail, was handled by the local *amīn*.[1]

Chivert's charter took a firm line with debtors. "The prison in the quarter" of the Mudejars included debtors among "bad men" expected to lodge there. The charter's general amnesty moreover deliberately excluded any "dispute or contest over debts or estates."[2]

---

[1] Piles Ros, "Moros de realengo en Valencia," pp. 264-265, and his *Bayle general de Valencia*, pp. 42-43, 53, 77, applicable also to Christians and Jews. His examples are from later generations, but this form of *guiatge* belonged to the pardons for crime, a type existing also for Moors of our earlier period. Permanent pardon for debt was rare in the case of taxes owed to the crown. Some prisons of Arago-Catalonia were free, but most charged several pennies a day; see, e.g., *Cortes de Aragón y de Valencia*, I, part I, p. 265, and cf. p. 224.

[2] Chivert Charter: "habeant dicti mauri carcerem in suo arravallo, in quo malefactores, debitores, et ali[i] mali homines distringantur"; "clamor vel querela de debitis et honoribus."

In collecting taxes, agents received wide discretion for seizure of chattels. Uxó's Muslims, during confirmation of their charter after the troubles of the late forties, cannily slipped in an absolution from debts owed to Jews. Perhaps these included rental debts to the local farmer of taxes. More probably these were private obligations; their inclusion in a basic charter or constitution indicates the sternness of contemporary authorities toward all debtors.[3]

A debtor's episode in 1284 involved Muslims who fled, deliberately leaving their debts behind them. Unhappily for the delinquents, their overlord was Samuel b. Manasseh, distinguished chancellor for Arabic documents and affairs, counselor and physician to the king, and brother of the influential Judah b. Manasseh. With such a figure as Samuel involved, pursuit got under way. "Wherever our Arabic secretary Samuel will indicate to you the Saracens who were cultivating lands as tenants [exarici] for the said Samuel," the royal writ ordered, "arrest and hold them until they have paid to the said secretary the money that they owe him."[4] Since no more is heard, presumably the culprits were apprehended.

A strange case occurred in 1280. For some reason collectors had neglected to take the besant from Albalat's Muslims; seeking to force tardy payment, local officials fastened onto their possessions. At this point the Christian lord intervened, complaining to the king. The royal decision, couched in official jargon, soon arrived. "We understand from Gonsalvo López of Pomar that you, or those who held the bailiate of Murviedro in previous years, are requiring the besant of past years from the Saracens of the place of Albalat that belongs to the said Gonsalvo; wherefore, since you did not require the said besant at the time when you ought, we wish you to refrain from requiring the same besant, from the present until we shall have ordered otherwise." The collector was ordered to restore the pledges he had taken.[5]

---

[3] Uxó Charter: "ne sien demanats de alcuns deutes que fossen deguts á alcuns juheus per alcuna manera."

[4] Arch. Crown, Peter III, Reg. Canc. 43, fol. 17v (Aug. 10, 1284): "quod ubicumque Samuel alfaquimus noster vobis hostenderit sarracenos quos [for qui] tenebant . . . hereditates ad exariquias a dicto Samuele, ipsos capiatis incontinente et ipsos captos teneatis donec solverint dicto alfaquimo denarios. . . ."

[5] Ibid., Reg. Canc. 48, fol. 159 (Sept. 24, 1280). "Intelleximus per Gonçalbum Luppe de Pomar quod vos, seu illi qui annis preteritis tenuerunt baiuliam Muriveteris, petitis a sarracenis loci de Albalat qui est dicti Gonçalbi bisancium annorum

SEIGNORIAL LANDS

The situation on seignorial lands is sparsely documented. It does merit a special word, however, to bring the Mudejar tax structure into sharper focus. On crown lands not permanently subinfeuded, the principle prevailed that the Muslim "is not bound to serve any person except us and ours."[6] Elsewhere on crown lands many a grant progressively moved through the hands of a series of owners; the registers are filled with such transactions. Mudejar tenants serving this latter category, though possessing their liberties, may well have had to make successive adjustment to the Christian landlords in the matter of smaller rents or fees.

This financial topic does not require a full review of the peculiar nature of Valencian feudalism, but it must posit clearly that this was feudalism with a difference. Landlord, lord, and alodial farmer assimilated to each other. "The term lord stood equally for landlord, farmer-owner, and [feudal] lord," as Tourtoulon observes, contrasting it with the French situation especially in the simplification of the rent and tax patterns.[7] The *Furs* insidiously spread an influence for more uniformity in this direction. In revenue terms, one should not look for a neat picture of alodial baronies practically independent of the crown, followed by a linked series of levels of vassalage estates relatively dependent either on a lord or on the king-as-lord, a set of crown estates managed by employee-bailiffs or castellans, and among the mass of tenantry sustaining all these estates a sprinkling of alodial small farmers or knights. Valencian lords did not form such a hierarchy, nor was the status of their land or the nature of their rents sharply distinct from those of burghers or nonnobles, aside

---

preteritorum. Unde, cum dictum bisancium non petistis tempore quo debuistis, volumus quod a peticione eiusdem bisancii abstineatis ad presens donec nos aliud mandaverimus." See also the problem of Onda's Muslims in arrears (Reg. Canc. 59, fol. 79v [Sept. 2, 1282]). Gonzalvo López was in the entourage of James I in 1264, 1270, and 1273; he received a small grant in 1263 and 13,500 solidi as dowry for his wife Milia in 1269 (*Itinerari*, pp. 332, 348, 427, 440, 487).

[6] Arch. Crown, James I, Reg. Canc. 15, fol. 81v (Feb. 26, 1267): "non teneatur alicui persone servire nisi nobis et nostris."

[7] Tourtoulon, *Jaime I*, II, 198-201. See especially Burns, *Islam under the Crusaders*, ch. 12, part 1, where the nature of Valencian feudalism is more closely examined, and Burns, "The Muslim in the Christian Feudal Order: The Kingdom of Valencia, 1240-1280," *Studies in Medieval Culture*, v (1975), 105-126.

from tax exemptions enjoyed. A few barons did display great estates, with courts, armed retainers, and subholdings; the mass of knights, including 380 created especially for Valencia by King James, had lesser fiefs or rather small holdings. Where vassalage existed, its structure remained shallow and weak, rather like a landlord-tenant relationship.

The more usual situation was of large and small landlords, over farms relatively independent of each other and differing little from the neighboring farm of nonnoble connections. A farmer could subdivide, or a lord cut up his property for vassals, but neither could make ties toward a higher lord except to the king, and the resultant tenants or vassals could leave simply by returning the property-portion to landlord or lord. This weakened the feudal orientation both at top and bottom, reinforcing the assimilative pressures. Further diluting the feudal status was the circumstance that nonnoble landlords kept rights to justice inherent in the estates they held, as much as feudal lords did, having the court of first instance, with appeal to the justiciar.

Barons and knights did refuse to pay most crown or local taxes, a position James tried vainly to undermine. When they or ecclesiastics bought crown lands, the king tried to insist they pay taxes; but by 1271 he had abandoned this attempt. While consolidation was going forward, the tax practice remained fluid, involving strong claims, frequent exemptions, reluctant concessions, and a varied practical result. From seignorial lands at such a time King James could hope for only a limited number of taxes—some fines, levies, and commercial fees. Even the besants of the Muslims on these lands eventually went, after a sharp quarrel with King Peter, to the lords. What the lord received as rents from his Mudejar town or his farmer tenant, whether on land held by grant or on lands bought away from and therefore lost to the crown, was probably not much different from that paid to the king by Muslims on crown lands. An anomalous situation, not uncommon during the earliest years of postcrusade Valencia, was the granting of lordship and rents to a Christian by a Muslim lord or feudatory. A rare notice of the practice comes in King James's confirmation of the suburb given to Dominic Marqués by Abū Bakr b. 'Īsā, lord of Játiva, "by a Saracen document" that more fully explained the holding, with its "revenues

[and] income."[8] Doubtless the Mudejar farmers continued to pay their usual taxes.

The crown owned the largest bloc of land in Valencia, retaining all territories that it had not expressly given away. The king might alienate lands to a vassal or to a nonnoble tenant, receiving feudal services from him as would any lord, plus regalian taxes from the nonnoble. In the case of direct sale or grant the land easily became equivalent to an alod, economically a free property beyond rent or recovery—despite King James's early attempts to claim at least ten solidi per jovate of land. Purchased land, like awarded land, still paid regalian taxes if its buyer were nonnoble. There is a strangely democratic air about all these holdings, whether feudal or alodial, high or low: each owner, lord or mere landlord, stood in relation to his holding and to his renters, if any, in much the same way. Each could cut up his lands ad infinitum and dispose of them as he wished. Only the personal status of the owner made a real difference, in the freedom of knight and cleric from taxes to crown and to local administrative bodies; when these privileged men bought lands from nonnobles they insisted on extending this right. In the same way, nonnobles as well as nobles exercised justice on their equivalently alodial properties; full justice, or *merum et mixtum imperium*, was rare.

The landlord as well as the lord could make his contract with

[8] Arch. Crown, James I, Reg. Canc. 11, fol. 199 (April 9, 1261): "confirmamus per hereditatem propriam, francham, et liberam vobis Domenico March[esii] habitatori Xative et vestris imperpetuum totum rahallum qui d[icitur] Aqualatella, qui est in termino de Carbonera, cum omnibus pertinenciis suis, quem vos tenetis et habetis [ex don]acione alcaydi Xative quondam nomine Abovecor, confirmantes vobis illam [d]onacionem quam de dicto raphallo vobis fecit dictus alcaydus, prout in instrumento sarracenico quod inde vobis fecit plenius continetur . . . cum introitibus, exitibus. . . ." Though the Martínez Ferrando *Catálogo* gives the Christian as March, the mutilated name is undoubtedly Marqués, a Játiva resident who appears elsewhere in the crown records, for example, as buying a horse for 1,500 solidi of Valencia in the king's name (Reg. Canc. 17, fol. 36 [July 13, 1265]: "vobis Domenico Marchesii md solidos") and as king's judge at Játiva settling a boundary litigation between several towns (*Itinerari*, p. 420 [1269]). The royal secretary Peter Marqués seems to be a relative. The Muslim lord, transcribed as Abenetos by Martínez Ferrando, was Abū Bakr Muḥammad b. Yaḥyā b. ʿĪsā, elsewhere called Abubequer, the vizier and relative who succeeded Yaḥyā; see Burns, "Le royaume chrétien de Valence et ses vassaux musulmans (1240-1280)," *Annales, économies, sociétés, civilisations*, XXVIII (1973), p. 218-219.

laborers or with renters of his property. The basic economic situation on Valencian lands was not complex; tenants of lords or of landlords, or the many small holding free-owner farmers with no lord but the king, paid charges according to the private law or agreement prevailing at a given place; landowners who were not knights gave regalian and local taxes, as did every householder with respect to certain taxes. Applied to the Mudejar population, this meant that almost all Muslims of large towns or on crown lands paid the regalian taxes and tenant fees to the crown; those on crown lands held by non-nobles paid the regalian taxes to the crown, and the feudal fees or services to their landlords and townships; those on noble lands paid all taxes and fees to their lords, except for a scattering of fines and commercial taxes or levies. Slightly complicating this picture was the city law of Valencia, applied at first to a sweep of territory from Murviedro to Cullera and inland to Chiva, except for scattered holdings of knights. This law also applied beyond the enclave, to other municipalities and their regions, though in some it could meet resistance. The important towns were mostly royal. A number of towns however were seignorial—for example, the Hospitallers held half of Cullera, the Alagón family briefly Morella, and a series of owners Segorbe; but the grip of the crown's overlord authority and the influence of the city law of Valencia both remained strong.

The Mudejar community might fall under the city law of a royal or seignorial town, or comprise a royal aljama directly under the king, or serve as tenants on estates and farms owned by nonnobles; all such communities and individuals had obligations and status roughly equivalent. They proved less profitable to the crown as communities or tenants under a lord or ecclesiastical body; their privileges, status, and taxes were not substantially different, but they answered in most things not to the king but to their lord. To the lord went their fees for mills, ovens, baths, butcheries, cloth-dyeing, local commerce, weights and measures, and the like, except for express retentions by the granting king. Unless such a Muslim became involved in a criminal or important case, or one with unusual dimensions, or engaged in commerce, he might pass his life without paying anything to the crown or else only minor taxes like salt fee, moneyage, and sheep-movement charges. From the king's point of view, all Muslims came under both his protection and his mechanism of legal appeals from local bodies; the large mass came under his system of regalian taxes.

The usual status of seignorial Muslims—not counting craftsmen, petty functionaries, hired labor, and the like—was the exaricate. Presumably the *exaricus* on seignorial land, especially under an Aragonese rather than a Catalan lord, experienced a stricter regime than did his crown colleague. Whatever the differences between the two, however, they must not be exaggerated. Custom was a strong controlling force in the society presided over by King James, and long-established custom dictated the Mudejar structure in its essentials. Enlightened self-interest too in this century would have ruled out extremes of exploitation by lords. Valencian fiefs could not escape being influenced and limited by the spirit of crown charters of privilege. Many were too small, moreover, to encourage a structure of feudal impositions.

The Tales charter was a seignorial contract issued in 1260 by the crown vassal Peter of Castellnou, bishop of Gerona; despite that status, it compares favorably with the run of royal charters, including one to Christians in the same neighborhood. Castellnou gave his Muslims perpetual ownership at the moderate rate of a tenth of crops; every tafulla of land paid an annual twenty pennies in two installments; livestock, but not draft animals, yielded a penny a head. There was the king's besant (which later legislation returned to the lord), justice fines to the lord according to the precrusade law, and a fee for using his wheat mill. Each household gave also a tribute of three solidi every Christmas, but no other tribute or service.[9]

Another seignorial constitution, granted by the provincial master of the Templars, Raymond Patot, with his chapter, was the Chivert charter. Its minute detail puts it among the most valuable surviving. Local minor commerce went free, as did marriage, sale of property,

[9] Arcadio García Sanz gives background to this charter in his "Tales y sus cartas pueblas" (*BSCC*, xxviii [1952], 439-442). Compare the king's charter of April 28, 1248, v (1924), 283-285, by which two men were to settle three hundred immigrants at Tales and Onda; see also *Itinerari*, p. 191 and crown disposal of Tales rents as late as 1258, p. 276. On the Tales Mudejar charter see also the interpretation of García y García, *Estado económico-social de Castellón*, p. 74. On Peter of Castellnou, bishop of Gerona, see Burns, *Crusader Valencia*, ii, 380, and on measurements and their practical nuances i, xii. An ideal fanecate, a sixth of a cafizate, was 831 square meters, so that in theory a tafulla, from Arabic for a piece of land, approximated 138 square meters.

preparation and marketing of meat, pasturage on wastelands, and collecting of branches for building houses. A tribute of one-sixth fell on crops and wine, plus their transport; this was remitted for the first two years. A fourth of any hunting bag and a penny per head on livestock completed the agrarian picture. These Muslims enjoyed free hospitality at Tortosa when traveling, free water supply for their mosques, exemption from host and cavalcade, and all the usual economic and tax arrangements. Precrusade custom doubtless carried over some minor fees unmentioned, but the charter was liberal. Special circumstances of strategic location, of surrender to an ecclesiastical lord, and of subvassalage to the crown may have helped insure good terms.[10]

The Aldea charter similarly showed itself generous, except that rent rose to a fourth of crops.[11] The circumstance of ecclesiastical origin, since it came from the Knights Hospitaller, and its motive of luring new settlers, complicate its interpretation. For other seignorial holdings, argument can only proceed from analogy. As the crown treated its Muslims on a rough parity with its Christians, so these early lords probably handled both peoples according to relatively equivalent tax norms. In short, the lords' charters were more demanding with both Muslims and Christians than were the king's, though not to the point of exploitation or ill-usage.

Beyond whatever regalian dues and rents a lord received in the grant of an estate, he could expect any number of fees because of custom at his place of origin. Muslim and lord arranged these fees between them, subsequent to the grant, as happened for example in the rural areas of Valencia city and again in James Matera's settlement at Vall de Laguart "according to the agreement worked out" with his Muslims.[12] Probably the barons applied the public law of their place of origin, especially in its economic aspects, to their Moorish holdings. They insisted on this strongly for their Christian settlers, and there is no reason to exempt Mudejars from inclusion in these sentiments. A law of 1283 ratified existing practice and effectively blocked royal interference at this level, either for mitigating required services or for imposing uniformity. Inserted into the

[10] Chivert Charter. See Burns, *Islam under the Crusaders*, ch. 6, part 1.
[11] Aldea Charter.
[12] Arch. Crown, Peter III, Reg. Canc. 42, fol. 187 (Dec. 8, 1279): "sibi respondeant de redditibus et aliis iuribus prout cum eo composuerint."

Valencian *Furs* when the barons forced revision of novel crown taxes on their Muslims, it decreed for the whole realm "that Saracen farmers are obliged to give the lord of the property whatever shall be agreed upon between them."[13]

On the point of freedom from regalian dues for seignorial Muslims, a grant by King James in 1268 offers some clarification. "You and yours are to have the aforesaid twenty households of Saracens frank and free," he wrote the baron William of Rocafull, "in just the same way as the other nobles and knights holding castles [and] settlements in the realm of Valencia hold their Saracens frank and free."[14] In the universal statements of taxation, therefore, does an implied exception lurk for noncrown lands held by such barons? Were these taxes a bone of contention between barons and crown, either on their original grants or on those later secured from the royal domain? Certainly noncrown lands went free of at least some royal dues; if they were waived entirely rather than transferred to the lord, this compensated the Muslims perhaps for other seignorial exactions. A waiver like this is too much to believe, since the lords were used to having one or other of these taxes from their Christians. When the Mudejars finally left Chulilla, displaced by Christian settlers in 1340, the bishop of Valencia hurried to retain for himself among other taxes the town curia, notariate, castellany, bailiate, all mills and ovens, host, cavalcade, castle guard, moneyage, herbage, and civil and criminal justice![15]

A distinction might be drawn between barons and orders who held by right of conquest or by almost independent status, and on the other hand those knights to whom the king divided his domain as though to sublandlords. Such a distinction helps only a little since the indirect knight-landlord class seems to have acquired eventually many tax privileges of the exempt baronial caste. A letter of 1273

[13] *Furs*, lib. viii, rub. viii, c. 28: "et quod sarraceni laboratores teneantur domino hereditatis quicquid comentum fuerit inter eos." See also there the proviso: "quilibet homo civitatis et regni possit mittere sarracenos laboratores ad laborandum in hereditatibus suis ad certum tempus, vel imperpetuum, et quod ipsi sarraceni vel qui iam habitant in eisdem non teneantur dare domino regi, nec alicui alio, illos . . . solidos."

[14] Arch. Crown, James I, Reg. Canc. 15, fol. 115v (Aug. 27, 1268): "predictos viginti casatos sarracenorum habeatis vos et vestros [*for* vestri] franchos et liberos perpetuo sicut alii nobiles et milites habentes castra et alquerias in regno Valentie habent franchos et liberos suos sarracenos."

[15] Arch. Cat., perg. 2,450 (Feb. 8, 1340).

may help to clarify the question. Prince Peter had been holding Alcira, Alfandech de Marignén, Bairén, Beniopa, Burriana, Cárcer, Corbera, Cullera, Gandía, Onteniente, Palma de Gandía, Pego, and Sumacárcel. When the king as overlord recovered them all late in 1273 or early in 1274,[16] the knights holding fiefs in the neighborhood of these places, themselves unaffected by the change, saw an opportunity for abolishing certain regalian taxes falling on their own Mudejar tenants. Their report to King James conceded that Prince Peter like other barons had collected "*quèsties*, hospitality duty, and other regalian taxes" from their estates "just as he did from our [the king's] Saracens of the said places that he [Peter] held." Two species of Muslim tenants on regalian lands are uncovered here—those directly under the crown and those under its enfeoffed knights; both species were paying regalian taxes to the prince. The knights now petitioned to waive these taxes, leaving "nothing else except what the Saracens pay who belong to knights possessing estates and Saracens in Valencia, Játiva, and other places of the kingdom of Valencia."[17]

[16] Soldevila, *Pere el Gran*, part 1, III, appendix, doc. 37 (between Dec. 11, 1273 and Jan. 4, 1274). Palma castle was acquired in exchange for Ribarroja.

[17] *Ibid.*, doc. 40a (Feb. 23, 1274). "Relatum fuisset ex parte militum qui habent hereditates et sarracenos in Algezira, Gandia et aliis locis que infans Petrus habebat et tenebat pro nobis in regno Valencie, quod dictus infans petebat et recipiebat a sarracenis suis . . . questias, cenas, et alias exacciones regales prout faciebat a sarracenis nostris dictorum locorum que ipse tenebat. Et nobis ex parte dictorum militum humiliter supplicatum fuisset quod dictos sarracenos absolveremus . . . Inclinati supplicacioni iamdicte . . . absolvimus, quitiamus . . ."; "nisi prout faciunt sarraceni illorum militum qui habent hereditates et sarracenos in Valencia, Xativa, et in aliis locis regni Valencie." A clear statement of exemption for nonregalian knights and their Mudejars was issued by King James as early as 1259, during a process of land-survey and confirmation; by way of amnesty or privilege it covered also lands thus far acquired otherwise than by crown grant. James conceded "vobis universis militibus et infancionibus populatoribus regni Valencie et vestris imperpetuum omnes emptiones et permutaciones quas fecistis cum cartis et sine cartis ab aliquibus christianis in regno Valencie . . . [et] habeatis vos et vestri francas et liberas perpetuo et immunes; concedimus etiam quod aliqui christiani vel sarraceni excolentes seu laborantes hereditates quas habetis in regno Valencie tam ex donacione nostra quam qualibet alia racione non teneantur dare nec solvere nobis vel nostris vel alicui alio nomine nostro nisi tantum quilibet sarracenus unum bisancium quolibet anno, et solventibus dictum bisancium nichil aliud nobis dare teneantur christiani et sarraceni racione peite aut cuiuslibet alterius exaccionis regalis, set sint inde franchi perpetuo et ymunes nisi aliquid tenuerint de realencho pro quo nobis servire teneantur sicut alii homines regni Valencie." See Josep Baicells i Reig, "València a

Knights on crown property or at least over a great expanse of crown property, in brief, came to pay few if any regalian taxes. Since the knights won their point, presumably only the alternate class, the relatively direct Mudejar tenants, eventually paid full regalian dues into crown coffers. Of the three kinds of land then—baronial or religious, regalian but permanently enfeoffed, and crown controlled—only the latter was to continue yielding much in regalian taxes to the king, though this category was very extensive. As the protest of 1283 shows, the king nevertheless attempted to intrude taxes of a nature the barons denounced as illegal. Sometimes Mudejar communities were "frank and free" where the phrase covered little more than a stable arrangement for farming revenues by the community or its lord. This was the case at Polop in 1269 where the Muslim lord got the local revenues in return for 600 solidi per annum, yet the "Saracens dwelling in the said places are frank and free."[18] Simon of Foces, then procurator or lieutenant over the kingdom of Valencia, was allowed an estate in 1258, settled with Muslims; here the tenants paid the besant alone, "and beside this they are to give or pay nothing else to us or ours, nor are they bound to pay or give."[19] A similar situation prevailed at Tales in 1260, and in 1258 at the Onda villages belonging to Bernard of Juneta.[20]

The distinction between crown and seignorial is legitimate up to a point. Like the cherished distinction between urban and rural, however, it can lose its usefulness as a tool and turn into a trap. It frames the data neatly, allowing for orderly understanding of juridical and other organizational forms. In a matter like taxes, and even more in daily life—social, political, religious, and economic—

---

l'arxiu de la catedral de Barcelona," *Primer congreso de historia del país valenciano*, 1 vol. to date (Valencia, 1973), doc. 4 (Nov. 26, 1259).

[18] Arch. Crown, James I, Reg. Canc. 16, fol. 156 (April 22, 1269): "et concedimus tibi quod sarraceni habitantes in dictis locis sint franchi et liberi."

[19] *Ibid.*, Reg. Canc. 10, fol. 82 (June 28, 1258): "et preter hoc nichil aliud nobis vel nostris donent donent [*sic*] vel faciant, nec teneantur facere vel donare." On Ximèn or Eximèn of Foces, see Josefina Mateu Ibars, *Los virreyes de Valencia: Fuentes para su estudio* (Valencia, 1963), pp. 53-54; he is prominent in the king's circle from 1237.

[20] Arch. Crown, James I, Reg. Canc. 10, fol. 79 (June 30 incorrectly for May 31, 1258). The name of this obscure beneficiary is: "vobis B[er]n[ardo] de Juneta habitatori Onde," not to be confused with the crown functionary Peter of Juneda, though perhaps by confusion of a copyist the same as the Bertrand de Juneda in the *Repartimiento de Valencia*. Tales Charter.

it directs attention away from the central realities. A more pertinent distinction can be derived from the differences affecting Muslims in areas of heavy Christian settlement, of light settlement, and of Muslim dominance. The psychology and rate of acculturation at each point could display marked divergence. Muslims of the huerta as against those of the "mountains," those of the north as differing from those in the south part of the kingdom, or the contrasting classes comprising the Valencian social structure, also provide more meaningful contrasts. In these categories the surviving data is less easily discerned, however, and more difficult to fit into a pattern.

For the moment one can only cultivate awareness of such basic differences, refusing to have one's horizons closed by older formulas. In the matter of taxes, the crown-seignorial dichotomy has a limited use for the thirteenth century. In the next two centuries the situation of seignorial Moors worsened dramatically, so that the formula acquired more meaning.[21] The Renaissance Mudejar began to lose his liberty of movement, suffered a variety of novel taxes as well as labor services, and saw previous taxes increase in amount. The thirteenth-century Muslim, on the other hand, seems to have paid much the same taxes through his *amīn*, no matter what the juridical status of his landlord or who the beneficiary.

EXEMPTIONS

A remarkable number of Muslims in one way or another became frank and free from various taxes, though on seignorial land such

[21] Gual Camarena, "Mudéjares valencianos en la época del Magnánimo," p. 471. See also the seignorial Chelva Charter (1371) and Palma del Río Charter (1370). In some places the lord confiscated all goods of Muslims dying intestate. When the crown had alienated many Valencian bailiates by way of pledge-leases disguised as loans, the Mudejar communities helped the crown buy off the creditor-lords oppressing them; in 1405 the Muslim delegates signed for Almonacid Valley (Mahomat Galop or Muḥammad Ghālib), the Eslida sierra (Abolaix Fayçubi or Abu 'l-'Aysh al-Fasawī?), Uxó Valley (Abdelaziz Ali or 'Abd al-'Azīz 'Alī), Benaguacil (Abdalla Abenamir or 'Abd Allāh b. 'Āmir), and Castro Valley (Maymo Galip or Maymūn Ghālib), all of which districts had been especially hard hit. The *morerías* of Valencia city and Játiva, respectively 60 and 300 hearths or over 1500 souls, contributed heavily to the repurchase. Below the Júcar, areas like Alcoy were also involved as pawns. See Ferrer i Mallol, "Patrimoni reial i la recuperació dels senyorius," pp. 402-404. As with Arago-Catalonia, Castile too saw oppressive tax burdens increase for its Mudejars in these centuries (López de Ayala, *Contribuciones é impuestos en León y Castilla*, pp. 553-554).

334

exemptions probably profited master more often than subject. Here again the Mudejar experience paralleled to some extent the previous Islamic practice; just as sultans punished tax evasion, so they waived taxes in whole or part to remedy calamities, to adjust during bad times for the farmer, or even to gain popularity.[22] Contemporary Arago-Catalan documents, for Christian and Mudejar alike, implied personal, social, and economic liberty by such phrases as "liberos et ingenuos," "liberi et franchi," "franchi et liberi penitus ac immunes." This freedom more commonly attached to settlers on crown lands and in cities than to the farmers on seignorial lands.[23] Mudejar charters normally included a certain number of express exemptions granted in the course of negotiations or taken over from previous Islamic custom.

Muslims on the Burriana lands of the Knights of Calatrava were "frank and free" of crown dues, and paid neither moneyage nor besant.[24] Hospitaller lands won similar exemption, if a 1221 privilege had practical effect; it freed all Hospitaller subjects whether Christian, Jew, or Muslim from bovage, herbage, host, cavalcade, moneyage, tariff, portage, rents, *peita, quèstia, força, tolta,* or "any other fee

[22] Lévi-Provençal, *España musulmana,* v, 22. Aghnides, *Mohammedan Theories of Finance,* pp. 302-303, 328.

[23] Font y Rius, "Régimen municipal," part 1, pp. 517-518 and notes. Liauzu, misunderstanding the *exaricus* status, posits a privileged, exempt class in the Ebro Valley ("Musulmans dans l'Aragon chrétien," p. 190). On communal and individual exemptions for Jews at our period, see Epstein, *"Responsa" of Rabbi Solomon Ben Adreth,* ch. 4, "Tax Exemptions." A typical "frank and free" grant, with limited rental exemption of a private nature, was the gift made to three Muslims by King James during the siege of Alcalá: "per nos damus et concedimus per hereditatem propriam, francham, et liberam vobis Abzeit Aventablia, Cahat Avinoahe[s], et Juceph Avinçalamon sarracenis et vestris imperpetuum domos et vi iovatas terre in regadivo, in alqueria de A[l]cudia, termino de Navarres, videlicet unicuique vestrorum domos et ii iovatas . . . franchas et liberas"; they could not be alienated "nisi tantum filiis vel parentibus vestris sarracenis" (Arch. Crown, James I, Reg. Canc. 10, fol. 79v [June 1, 1258]). Exemptions in the Eslida Charter included freedom from services, especially to the castle, from tax on fruit grown or on vines or on selling property, plus a full year's general tax exemption. Uxó Charter gave the year's general freedom and dismissed the egg levy ("dret del ous"). Játiva Charter included two years' freedom from taxes, exempted vegetables (presumably noncommercial), and dismissed certain transit and commercial fees. The Aldea Charter allowed each Muslim his house and one tafulla of land free.

[24] El *"Repartiment" de Burriana y Villarreal,* pp. 71-72, doc. from Arch. Nac. Madrid in translation (March 26, 1258).

regalian or local."[25] A concession so inclusive may have been designed for putting new lands into cultivation. On Templar lands crown officials could not take transit tax "from any men of the Temple—Jews, Christians, or Saracens—as long as they are not merchants."[26] Diocesan authorities held exemptions, as did important lords.[27] The magnate Blasco Simon of Arenós paid neither tariff nor transit tax for "your subjects whom you have in the kingdom of Valencia, both Christians and Saracens, on anything they carry," except on professional merchandise.[28] Arnold of Romaní held the same concession "for your lifetime."[29] Religious orders sometimes collected and retained regalian taxes as a form of exemption.[30]

The crown in 1262 permanently dispensed "some Saracens on certain lands" held by Jews in the kingdom of Valencia from the besant.[31] These were neither slaves, who did not pay the tax, nor the

[25] *Colección diplomática*, doc. 1,013 (Dec. 23, 1221): "nullamque aliam exaccionem regalem vel vicinalem."

[26] *Ibid.*, doc. 292 (Jan. 12, 1246): "de aliquibus hominibus Templi, iudeis, christianis, seu sarracenis . . . dummodo non sunt mercatores." See also the discussion by Forey, *Templars in the Corona de Aragón*, pp. 113-115.

[27] Arch. Crown, James I, perg. 1,466 (Jan. 18, 1257): "pedagium, portaticum, neque lezdam" for all Christian and Saracen subjects throughout the Valencian kingdom. Renewed in Peter III, Reg. Canc. 39, fol. 230 (July 21, 1277): "noveritis nos vidisse quoddam instrumentum domini Iacobi . . . tam christiani quam sarraceni residentes in aliquibus locis eorum [episcopi et capituli] non teneanter solvere . . . denarios seu aliquod pedagium, portaticum, sive lezdam, pro aliquibus mercibus seu rebus quas emerent, venderent, seu portarent, nisi essent mercatores."

[28] *Ibid.*, James I, Reg. Canc. 15, fol. 87v (March 29, 1262): "damus et concedimus vobis Blasco Eximini de Arenoso et vestris, imperpetuum, quod homines vestri quos habetis in regno Valencie, tam christiani quam sarraceni, non donent pedagium neque lezdam de aliquibus rebus quas portaverint nisi uterentur de mercatura prout hoc est in Valencia usitatum [*sic*]."

[29] Document above in Chapter IV, n. 42 (1275). On at least one occasion Mudejars were expressly excluded from a local exemption, in this case on merchandise moving in and out of Játiva: "in hac tamen gratia non intendimus sarracenos nec iudeos Xative nec de eorum mercibus sive rebus si per christianos deferentur" (Arch. Crown, Alfonso III, Reg. Canc. 64, fol. 120 [Sept. 20, 1286]). More usual are the inclusive exemptions such as that given for a series of taxes at Villarreal on fol. 126 or at Murviedro on fol. 132v.

[30] See, for example, Chapter V, n. 16 with text.

[31] Arch. Crown, James I, Reg. Canc. 12, fol. 44v (May 10, 1262): "aliqui sarraceni . . . in aliquibus hereditatibus vestris totius regni Valencie." A number of Jews held Valencian estates tenanted by Muslims; Samuel b. Manasseh secured an order from Peter to enforce rental payment from "illos sarracenos de ravalli Xative tenentes vel colentes aliquos honores vel hereditates dicti alfaquimi" (Romano, "Hermanos Abenmenassé," appendix, doc. 12 [July 4, 1284]).

generality of Muslims on Jewish estates. Since the privilege went both to Jews and to the Moorish aljamas or communities, its restrictive *aliqui* must refer to a class or classes of Muslims—domestic or craft workers perhaps, or wealthier or specialized groups—presumably designated with clarity in a counterdocument held by Valencian Jews. It would be idle to conjecture further, because the effect of the exemption may only have been to transfer this income from the crown to the landlords rather than to the apparent beneficiaries. Exemptions sprang from a variety of causes. Valencian Mudejars who helped defend Gerona against French invaders won dispensation from the military levy imposed upon their colleagues who stayed at home.[32] Other exemptions have already been cited in the context of specific taxes—to promote trade, to tide a weakened aljama past a difficult period, or for some *ad hoc* reason.

Individuals could gain general and permanent exemption, especially for performance of a signal service. The Muslim officer in the rebel army at Biar who helped the captured Templar master to escape was honored in this way. His citation of 1277 read: "we enfranchise and make you frank, free, [and] immune, 'Abd Allāh Blaq [Abdella Blech], Saracen, with your wife and household, from all community levy, service, and any other royal tax, all the days of your life, with all your goods, in such wise that from now on you are not bound to contribute anything to our community tax, or to perform services, or to pay your part in any taxes, but you are to be frank of them with all your goods." The king granted this favor "because of your efforts in liberating the master of the Temple whom the Saracens had captured."[33] The battle took place in late June of 1276 and the escape "some days later," followed by the grant of exemption in October of the next year at Valencia.[34]

---

[32] See Burns, *Islam under the Crusaders*, ch. 12, n. 55.

[33] Arch. Crown, Peter III, Reg. Canc. 22, fol. 76 (Oct. 21, 1277). "Infranquimus et franchum, liberum, immunem facimus te Abdella Blech sarracenum, cum uxore et domicilio tuo, ab omni peyta, servicio, et qualibet exaccione regali, in diebus omnibus vite tue, cum omnibus bonis tuis . . . , ita quod ex nunc non tenearis aliquod in peitis nostris contribuere, nec servicia facere, nec in aliquibus exaccionibus solvere partem tuam, set sis inde cum omnibus bonis tuis franchus. . . . Hanc siquidem graciam tibi concedimus eo quia dedisti operam ad liberandum magistrum Templi quem captivaverant sarraceni."

[34] On the battle of Luchente and this episode see *Llibre dels feyts*, ch. 559. The name Blech, clear in the manuscript, may derive from an Arabic variant like Balkh

Another Muslim, either the king's creditor or else someone in his favor, turns up in an exemption in 1259. Because he was a tradesman, his status is doubly interesting. "We make you 'Alī of Gallinera frank, quit, and immune all the days of your life; however, you are to give and pay us 600 solidi of Jaca when you shall get this money from your trade as a barber." 'Alī may have plied his profession in the Gallinera Valley, just north of Pego, or he may have removed from the place that conferred his surname. In either case, his hair-dressing skills had made him prosperous. The transaction may represent a purchase of exemption, but this was not normal; more probably it involved a concession to attract crafts into an area being settled or reconstructed, or a favor mixed with a small immediate profit for the crown.[35] Two other craftsmen appear in an exemption that same year. "We enfranchise and make you frank and free, Muḥammad the painter and 'Abd Allāh the woodworker, Saracen brothers." From now on the two were to pay no Mudejar tax or regalian fee.[36]

Reasons for exemption were not always specified. King James in 1273 exempted "you Sa'd b. Yaḥyā, Saracen leader [alcaydus] of the Valencian Moorish quarter, and yours forever, from those two morabatins of rent that you are obliged to pay us annually for our shop . . . in the Moorish quarter of Valencia."[37] Gifts to individual Moors sometimes carried an attached exemption. The king confirmed such

---

or be related to the Catalan family name Blach; Bellech, for Romance Vélez (Málaga), or Abu 'l-'Aysh if the final letters are soft, also suggest possibilities.

[35] Arch. Crown, James I, Reg. Canc. 11, fol. 157v (Dec. 21, 1259): "nos dei gratia etc. facimus te Ali de Galinera . . . franchum, quitum, ac immunem . . . diebus omnibus vite tue . . . , te tamen dante et solvente nobis sexcentos solidos iaccensium prout ipsos lucratus fueris de officio tuo barbitonsorie."

[36] Ibid., fol. 154 (Oct. 10, 1259): "per nos et nostros enffranquimus et franchos et liberos facimus vos Mahometum pictorem et Abdela fusterium [?] fratres sarracenos." 'Abd Allāh was probably more than a "carpenter"; artistic woodworking was to be a Spanish Mudejar specialty.

[37] Ibid., Reg. Canc. 19, fol. 30v (July 8, 1273): "absolvimus tibi Çahat Abenache sarraceno, alcaydo morerie Valencie, et tuis imperpetuum illos duos morabatinos censuales quos annuatim nobis facere teneris pro nostro operatorio scito [sic] in moreria Valencie." Çahat can also represent Sa'īd, as with the Granadan ambassador to James II in 1294, given as "Çahat" b. Muḥammad. The surname Abenacha (in the nominative) is not some form like Ḥakīm but a variant for Abinahia and Abiniafia; the Valencia city alcaydus Çahat appears under the latter names in documents respectively of 1258 and 1267, though Martínez Ferrando mistook "Abenache" as a different man (Catálogo, I, no. 1, 491).

a privileged grant in 1260 to a certain Muḥammad. In 1259 a jovate
of land went to the *qā'id* of Montesa "as a perpetual holding, frank
and free."[38] And in 1270 Muḥammad b. Muḥammad b. Zabr (Aben-
zabr) got a grant of properties free from regalian taxes "for the
buildings and acreage we are now granting you," through his lifetime.[39] In 1258, when King James gave to this man's relatives, at-
Tīfāshī and his son Sa'd, the castles of Orcheta, Finestrat, and Torres
"frank and free," he also gave at-Tīfāshī a broader personal exemption "all the days of your life from all *peita, quèstia*, demand, hospitality tax, army and cavalcade and their redemptions, and from
every other regalian tax."[40]

A whole class of workers, possessed of valued industrial talents,
might also win exemption. Thus King James gave "to you, the
community of Saracens of Játiva, that each and every master of dyes
who shall come to Játiva," and establish residence there, "is to be
frank and free from payments of our besants."[41] Such a privilege
could broaden for an individual, as when King James dispensed
" 'Alī the Saracen," dye master at Játiva, from all regalian taxes.
Some months earlier the king had proclaimed "that we enfranchise
and make frank and free you 'Alī al-Lūrī [Ali Allauri], silk worker,
coming now into Játiva."[42] In 1270 "we enfranchise and make frank

[38] Arch. Crown, Reg. Canc. 11, fol. 192v (Feb. 5, 1260): "franquitatem . . . de
hereditate." Fol. 152 (Sept. 29, 1259): "per hereditatem perpetuam, francham, et
liberam" in detail.

[39] *Ibid.*, Reg. Canc. 16, fol. 208 (July 26, 1270): "tibi Mahomat Abenmahomat
Abenzabre sarraceno, nepoti Tovicini [*sic*], et tuis imperpetuum domos . . . et xxx
kaficiatas terre . . . , [et] quod diebus omnibus vite tue sis franchus ab omni peyta,
questia, cena, et exercitu et cavalcata et redempcione eorum et etiam ab omni alia
qualibet exaccione regali . . . pro domibus et kaficiatis terre quas nunc tibi damus."

[40] *Ibid.*, Reg. Canc. 10, fol. 77r,v (June 16, 1258): "tibi Teviçino et filio tuo
Çahat . . . ; concedimus etiam tibi Teviçino iam dicto quod sis franchus et liber
diebus omnibus vite tue ab omni peyta et questia, pedido, cena, exercitu et cavalcata
ac eorum redempcionibus, et ab omni alio servicio et exaccione regali, ita quod de
premissis vel eorum aliquibus non tenearis dare aut solvere aliquid, set sis inde
cum omnibus bonis . . . franchus, liber, et quitius quamdiu tibi vita fuerit comes."
On this Mudejar fief, see Burns, *Islam under the Crusaders*, ch. 13, part 3.

[41] Arch. Crown, James I, Reg. Canc. 21, fol. 141 (June 7, 1273): "indulgemus
vobis, aliame sarracenorum Xative, . . . quod omnes et singuli . . . magistratus
purpurarum qui venient apud Xativam et ibi residenciam fecerint . . . sint franchi
et liberi a prestatione bisanciorum nostrorum."

[42] *Ibid.*, Reg. Canc. 19, fol. 53 (Sept. 7, 1273): "noveritis universi quod nos . . .
enfranquimus et franchos et liberos facimus te Ali Allauri sederium . . . venientes
modo Xativam." (See above, Chapter IV, n. 71, on the range of this exemption and
on the alternate name form al-Ḥurr).

and free, and absolutely immune, 'Īsā al-Waṣī [Ayça Alauxi] of Chulilla," for life, "from every regalian tax, exaction, and demand."[43]

Settlement projects, designed to lure the Muslim immigrant, offered initial periods of tax-free residency or else reduced taxes to a minimum. This was advantageous to the Muslim moving onto crown lands; but when a lord, rather than his Muslims, received the dispensation, it probably helped the lord fatten his own tax demands. King James did a favor for a baron, for example, in exempting "men and women Saracens you settle," so that "each household of Saracens" gave a silver besant yearly "and besides this, nothing else to us or ours."[44] Another lord was beneficiary in the exemption "from giving the besant and from all other tax," granted for "all Saracens whom you've settled or will settle" in a town near Alcoy.[45] One exemption was definitely for an outsider's benefit: a royal promise in 1268, phrased as a concession to Cocentaina's Muslims, not to impose fresh taxes during the five-year period of tax farming held by two courtiers.[46] A similar background may explain the grant or clarification sent by King James in 1273: "we grant to you James Castellá, citizen of Valencia, and to yours, that the Saracens resident in our village called Beniarjó, located in the district of Gandía, are not bound to give, nor do they give or do for us ... anything except that which they were accustomed to give or do before we had granted Gandía to Prince Peter."[47]

[43] *Ibid.*, Reg. Canc. 16, fol. 229v (Jan. 28, 1270): "franchum et liberum facimus penitus et immunem te Ayça Alauxi sarracenum de Xulela toto tempore vite tue ab omni scilicet questia . . . et ab omni alio servicio, exaccione seu demanda regali." The name is close enough to Allauri to suspect a scribal slip; even if caught correctly by the scribe, it lends itself to other reconstructions, like al-Awzāʿī.

[44] *Ibid.*, Reg. Canc. 10, fol. 82 (June 28, 1258): "populatis sarracenos et sarracenas, quotcumque et quoscumque velitis, et cuiuscumque ipsi sint; ita tamen quod . . . [donet quisque] unum bisancium argenti, et preter hoc nihil aliud nobis vel nostris donent."

[45] *Ibid.*, fol. 83r,v (July 1, 1258): "enfranquimus etiam *imperpetuum* omnes sarracenos qui populati sunt . . . de prestatione bisancii et ab omni alio servicio."

[46] *Ibid.*, Reg. Canc. 15, fol. 136 (Feb. 10, 1268): "promittentes quod nos a dictis sarracenis aliqua ratione peite . . . aut alterius exactionis regalis, non petemus per totum predictum tempus."

[47] *Ibid.*, Reg. Canc. 19, fol. 109v (Feb. 26, 1273): "nos Iacobus . . . concedimus vobis, Iacobo Castellani civi Valencie, et vestris quod sarraceni habitantes in alqueria nostra vocata Benizaryo, sita in termino Candie, non teneantur dare, nec donent, nec faciant nobis vel alcaydo seu baiulo alicui nostro, aliquid nisi illud quod facere et dare consueverunt antequam karissimo filio nostro infanti Petro dedissemus Candiam." "Castellanus" may be "of Castile," or represent "castellan" or a prosaic family

An extensive exemption might appear in the registers without explanation, as with King James's order of 1259 to his agent "not to accept or demand from the Saracens of Navarrés those 200 besants that we had imposed on them as *peita*."[48] In one case the crown authorities, challenged as to their claim, had to write off a tax for Crevillente aljama, a Mudejar principality, "because we can't find" the Arabic document proving the obligation; "and if the document should [later] be found, let it be considered null and void" in light of the present decision.[49] Another instrument casting light on the methodology of collecting is the decree that Mudejar workers at Campanar, "who do not have farms or any holdings there," cannot be forced to pay more than a yearly besant or "to give anything for any tax to any officials of ours."[50] A similar case in 1257 at Huesca in Aragon proper involved the Mudejars of Sigena monastery who lived in town, refused to pay taxes, and were consequently excluded from the mosques. King James heard the civil lawsuit on appeal and decreed that the outsiders must pay any tax benefiting the whole community, defined as including themselves, but were exempt from all other local and all regalian taxes, presumably giving their share via Sigena; they were to have full access to mosques and cemeteries.[51]

---

name; its owner, who appears several times in the registers, held Beniopa and Beniarjó and seems to belong to the same Castellá or Castellar clan of Huesca as Adam of Paterna (see p. 292).

[48] *Ibid.*, Reg. Canc. 10, fol. 108v (April 8, 1259): "fideli portario suo Bonanato de Guia salutem et gratiam: mandamus vobis firmiter quatenus non accipiatis, nec exigatis, a sarracenis de Navarres illos cc bisantios quos eis iactaveramus pro peyta."

[49] *Ibid.*, Reg. Canc. 19, fol. 98v (Feb. 5, 1273): "absolvimus et clamamus quitios vos Hamet Avenhuda, sarracenum de Crivellen, et aliama eiusdem loci, et omnia bona vestra a solucione illorum bisanciorum argenti in quibus vos nobis tenebamini cum carta sarracenica, quam non possumus invenire; . . . et si dicta carta inveniretur, pro cassa et irrita habeatur." Pierre Guichard has researched this Mudejar principality, which surrendered to King James in 1265, and the name forms of its several rulers; this is the *ra'īs* Aḥmad b. Hudayr. See his "Un seigneur musulman dans l'Espagne chrétienne: le 'ra'īs' de Crevillente (1243-1318)," *Mélanges de la casa de Velázquez* IX (1973), pp. 291-295, the family tree on p. 332, and the early fourteenth-century tax administration on p. 311 (castellan, bailiff, collector, assignation of 3,000 solidi yearly for three knights' fiefs, and a tithe quarrel).

[50] Arch. Crown, Reg. Canc. 16, fol. 217 (Oct. 2, 1270): "qui non habetis heredi-tates seu possessiones aliquas ibidem . . . ut facere consuevistis, nec teneamini dare aliquid pro servitio alicui officiali nostro." *Servitium* here may mean labor or other services, or more probably any fee or tax.

[51] *Colección diplomática*, doc. 566 (Aug. 30, 1257).

An exemption could be bought; probably a number of apparently gratuitous dispensations conceal such a transaction. Thus King James in 1273 dispensed "you the Saracens of Uxó" from a regalian tax in perpetuity, "acknowledging that we received from you for this concession and enfranchisement 400 solidi."[52] A privilege to Onda's Moors in 1259 removed all taxes in return for a flat two besants per family each year; and if any poor Muslim could not pay, "all of you will give and pay those two besants for him."[53] Lists of Mudejar taxes frequently "remit" or "dismiss" all or part of the sum stated. Since no reason is given usually, these reductions may represent merely reassignments to the aljama, as for debts or castle repair; but since the latter seem to have their separate manner of expression, such notations probably represent rather an adjusting of taxes to ability to pay.[54]

Funds needed for public works or to recoup from disaster were charged off against current taxes, allowing an aljama to repair or improve its material surroundings. When Onteniente suffered severely from an earthquake in 1258, the king remedied "the extensive destruction" by a two-year exemption "from every regalian tax and

[52] Arch. Crown, James I, Reg. Canc. 21, fol. 148v (May 20, 1273): "concedimus vobis sarracenis de Uxo, quod non teneamini unquam [dare almoxerifatum] . . . , set sitis franchi et liberi . . . , recognoscentes nos habuisse a vobis pro huiusmodi concessione et franquitate quadringentos solidos regalium de quibus bene paccati sumus."

[53] Ibid., Reg. Canc. 11, fol. 168v (Sept. 1, 1259): "et si aliquis casatus vestrum non poterit solvere dictos duos bisancios, vos omnes ipsos duos bisancios pro eo donetis et solvatis; et vobis dantibus nobis et nostris annuatim ut dictum est predictos duos bisancios, non teneamini dare nobis vel nostris aliquam questiam sive peytam nec aliquam regalem exactionem, set sitis inde . . . liberi et penitus perpetuo absoluti."

[54] Ibid., Reg. Canc. 8, fol. 21v (Nov. 26, 1255), is a list of Mudejar taxes with two assignations of repair ("in opere murorum" and "pro opere castri") and a notation that "remisit iiii millia" of the 10,000 solidi due from Játiva. On fol. 36 (Nov. 24, 1257), another Mudejar tax list, there are eight "remisit" entries for all or part of the tax, out of twenty-eight, four "dimisit" reductions of part, and two "remisit" items with explanation as assignment. A similar relaxation of sums due is encountered within lists of mixed taxes; thus the Gandía lists for Christians has: "item los moros de Beniopa, vi mils sous, dels quals a fet lexa l'ifant cccc sous" (Reg. Canc. 17, fol. 37 [July 2, 1265]). Sometimes the crown drafted a special notification to collectors, explaining an exemption: "sciatis quod remisimus ipsis sarracenis propter eorum paupertatem ccccl solidos, quare mandamus vobis quatenus . . . non compellatis eos ad amplius persolvendum" (Alfonso III, Reg. Canc. 85, fol. 142 [April 19, 1291]).

demand."[55] To judge from later episodes in Valencia, the beneficiaries of an exemption presented their documentation to the Christian authorities to demand compliance or redress; cases are on record of humble Mudejars at places like Catí and Eslida thus forcing tax officials to restore small sums like ten solidi or a few goats, and in one instance at Segorbe of causing the crown collector to be jailed until he made restitution.[56]

The exemptions reflect concern for Muslim subjects, another manifestation of parity between Christian and Muslim Valencians. The whole policy bears the stamp of frontier conditions, both remotely in the Mudejar tradition inherited from past frontiers, and more immediately in the determination to keep Mudejar skills at the paper and dye industries as well as in the spreading farms. There was a level at which Muslims were valued subjects as much as any Christian, and even sought after. Though this aspect of relations between the two peoples might be discerned in the older, now settled frontiers, it is in Valencia that it becomes prominent. Too vast a land had been captured, at a time when opportunity beckoned in too many other quarters for the men of Catalonia; the crusaders consequently esteemed the native population at this economic level. The value of the ordinary Muslim of Valencia may even have risen with the coming of the Christian power, because war-wracked, uncertain communities had now entered a period of relative stability and security.

[55] *Ibid.*, James I, Reg. Canc. 10, fol. 52v (March 26, 1258): "considerantes dampnum maximum quod vos . . . recepistis et sustinuistis propter terre motum." These had to be mixed taxes, at this location so early. The Martínez Ferrando *Catálogo* notes an exemption but erroneously explains it as covering damage from war.

[56] Piles Ros, "Moros de realengo en Valencia," p. 241; before collecting a tax the agent had also to present a formal order signed by king or bailiff general (p. 234).

CHAPTER X

The Human Factor

MONEY TALKS; but its conversational range is limited. Tax records cannot recreate the full life of Valencia's Mudejar community. They tell little about its spiritual or intellectual dynamics. The cautionary tale of its interrelations with Christians, issuing both in violent riots and in curiously osmotic adaptations, lies in a penumbra just beyond the field of vision afforded by revenue rolls. What insights they do contribute are considerable, however; had circumstances destroyed all other documentation, tax materials alone would suffice to discover whole facets of that society. They reveal it moreover from a novel vantage, uncovering a view not otherwise accessible. Even in specific details, they eavesdrop where other records disdain to go. If their voice is not rich, discoursing on complex insights that hold and move the soul, it does ring out as authoritative, voluble, candid, and highly informative.

Such a voice might have arisen from the older centers of Mudejarism, but thinly. The geographical extent of this new kingdom, the demographic weight of its Islamic majority, and the sophistication of its complex communities, with the consequent volume and variety of records, lends unique range and value. Heard from any later period in Valencia, the sound would emerge from a mutilated organism whose identity was half worn away, desperately clinging to life. The thirteenth-century society, however, wounded but vigorous, still stood whole, warmed by the setting sun of a half-millennial culture. If its tax voice were somehow silenced, whole areas of the Mudejar experience would fall into obscurity, leaving us thereby the poorer.

At their most obvious, the taxes demonstrate the essential fairness and flexibility of the century's Mudejarism. They had not yet become onerously exploitative, but compared well with the taxes weighing upon neighboring Christian settlements. This holds true even in detail, apparent in parallel charters or lists. On the other hand, Mudejar tax summations are too partial, and Christian taxes as yet too neglected, to invite comparison in terms of relative totals. The benign conclusion does not exculpate the crusaders, whose colonial system incorporated grosser, psychologically more wearing forms of oppression; but it clarifies the picture. Probably the conquerors maintained a more rationalized and tolerable system than the squabbling late-Almohad lordlings managed.

The taxes themselves identified in large degree with precrusade impositions, ironically supplying continuity with the Muslim's past, so that they served less as acculturative bludgeon than as much-needed boundary preservative. Crusade vagaries or local circumstance ensured against an iron, univocal system, while the disparate, more controlled precedents from older frontiers guaranteed a humane adaptation of logic to life. The accumulation of taxes would have appalled the nineteenth-century historian, who could only have pitied Christian and Muslim alike. More instructed in community sharing of resources, and bowed under a tax yoke heavier than medieval farmers knew, men of the present century judge with a different eye.

A revenue approach to Mudejar history challenges other assumptions—the sharp opposition of regalian and seignorial, the arbitrary lump-sum adjustments of a later era as reflecting normal practice, and the relegation of subject Muslims to agricultural hinterlands. Mudejar Valencia only later devolved into a peasant-farmer class, losing its nation of shopkeepers and merchants; the rural-urban dichotomy only gradually strengthened, replacing a more subtle symbiosis of the two. Tax materials uncover other surprises. The linked castles of some outlying valley, for example, could produce as much revenue as a city *morería* and consequently seem as valuable to its masters. The tithe situation emerges as more straightforward than later developments, or even contemporary parallels elsewhere, might suggest. The shift to European control appears clearly in a given institution like the fonduk, even its placement reflecting the changes as the century wore on; at the same time, the stratum of Christian financiers linked itself into such utilities from an early date, giving influential Catalans a stake in Mudejar prosperity. The meshing of both societies, in activities from financing down to collecting, illustrates how taxes became a bond, not only at the top, but at multiple interim points. This in turn reflects a wider if superficial assimilation of the two peoples—to be neither exaggerated nor dismissed—at the realistic level of economic life.

The rich returns specified by tax records had implications beyond the boundaries of the Valencian kingdom. The realms of Aragon gained more than territory and glory. Not only was Valencia wealthier already than the Catalan heartland, with the crown the largest landholder, but the tax base was wider in these early years, narrowing with the growth of privilege and alodial developments as time went on. The relation of this income to public activities has yet to be coordinated. It is clear nevertheless that Valencian revenues were decisive in Arago-Catalonia's rise as a world (or Mediterranean world) power later in the century. We are not fully informed on the whole subject of thirteenth-century Christian taxation; many small fees remain obscure, along with the collectory mechanisms, area totals, and exemption pattern. Since the small bibliography available has hardly broached the subject, knowledge of Mudejar taxation can play a feedback role in clarifying Christian taxation in the realms of Aragon, with its unsystematic formalities in assessory and collection phases, its technicalities like the *violari*, and its exciting complexity as a game of high finance or public investment with many players.

Examination of the revenue processes elicits admiration for their professionalism. This does not appear so clearly in the uncoordinated tax mechanisms, which reflect the codified confusion of life rather than the rationalized system of a planner. It does stand out in the impersonal fairness, assiduity and attention to detail, careful linking of tax to essential activities, manipulation of exemptions and protection, flexibility in readjusting assessments, respect for Muslims' susceptibilities by awarding privileges to the notable class, long-range attitude toward some tax problems, restraint in order to promote morale or favor Muslim immigration, and all the elements of measured procedure in a consciously legalistic framework. To examine the system alongside the contemporary, highly sophisticated papal organization of taxes, whose agents were visible in James's realms especially in connection with crusade levies, would be instructive but not to our present purpose. Perhaps one could trace social crises and revolts, using taxes as seismograph, though such reflexive studies must wait their turn. The history of Aragon's Jews forms one area that has profited already from Valencia's Mudejar tax records, and that can draw further information.

A kind of tax ecology emerges from this data—an interpenetrating, interdependent mélange of taxes and the social functions they affected. A social psychologist, anthropologist or sociologist, sympathetic to developmentalist structuralism, might see here a method or key to understanding the whole society from a narrow but novel perspective.[1] These records also trace a profile of the realm's economy, accessible in no other way, including the familial environment of the lowly farmer. The range of Valencian products in field or shop, the proud irrigation system with something of related medieval hygiene, moral attitudes as in treatment of debtors or delinquents, the degree of freedom implied by merchandising laws and rules for land sale, the tolerance involved in dietary or *waqf* regulations, the glimpses of an impressive stock industry, along with hunting and fishing, the traces of artisan activity caught in a chance document or two, from ceramics to hairdressing, the extent and location of wine or sheep enterprises, the minor role of labor services and the central role of money, the Mudejar nobiliary survivals and the military activity allotted to ordinary Muslims—all this and more has become lodged in tax manuscripts like prehistoric bones in a tar pit, awaiting reassembly at our later day. The early date, moreover, with its minimal Christian impact, ensures that not merely Mudejarism but even much of obscure Almohad Valencia lies exposed to our gaze. Through this material we can begin to map its important communities in their original character, its sheepwalks and fisheries, its diet and trade, and more of its commonplace life than weightier documents cared to preserve.

All this was to change. Taxes eventually altered in their physiognomy and relative weight. The balance of Mudejars on crown as against seignorial lands shifted. Mudejar social structure and modes of local government suffered startling mutations. And impositions grew increasingly heavier, consequent upon the hard times and hardening social arteries of the Early Renaissance. If marching to the faint beat of a different drum inevitably alarms one's unattuned neighbors, the reverberating din of an entire ambience addicted to alien rhythms can convey to colonial overseers a sense of mortal peril.

[1] This forms one theme of my "Spanish Islam in Transition: Acculturative Survival and Its Price in the Christian Kingdom of Valencia, 1240-1280," an address at the Fourth Biennial Giorgio Levi della Vida Conference, of the Near Eastern Center of the University of California, Los Angeles, published with the other addresses as *Islam and Cultural Change in the Middle Ages*, ed. Speros Vyronis, Jr. (Wiesbaden, 1975).

Dark days lay ahead. Their ominous elements stand clearly visible even during the thirteenth century, but suspended by countervailing hopes and needs. The human factors predominated yet, effecting in this prehumanist time a more humane balance. Far from ideal, that balance compares favorably with eras presumably more civilized.

BIBLIOGRAPHY

My *Crusader Kingdom of Valencia* and its sequel *Islam under the Crusaders* supply direct and background bibliography on thirteenth-century Valencia. Consult their more ambitious listings for topics like the Valencian crusade, Islamic institutions, Hispano-Islamic and North African history, Christian and Muslim chroniclers, problems of acculturation and interrelation, settlement and colonial patterns, or bibliographies and finding aids. The supplementary list below merely allows the reader to identify the principal titles cited in the footnotes of the present book. A handful of other works has been added, to round out an introductory, but only an introductory, bibliography on its main themes. All the essential studies on early Mudejar economy and taxation are included.

PRIMARY SOURCES

Manuscript

Of the thirty-five archival collections discussed in the bibliography of my *Crusader Valencia*, many of which are relevant here, only the following ten have been cited directly.

> Archivio Segreto Vaticano, Rome.
> Archivo de la Catedral, Tortosa.
> Archivo de la Catedral, Valencia.
> Archivo de la Corona de Aragón, Barcelona.
> Archivo General del Reino, Valencia.
> Archivo Histórico Nacional, Madrid.
> Archivo Municipal, Alcira.
> Archivo Municipal, Valencia.
> Biblioteca Nacional, Madrid.
> *Biblioteca, Universidad de Valencia.*

Published

Aldea Charter. Carta puebla de Aldea, February 12, 1258. In "Colección de cartas pueblas," no. 60. *Boletín de la sociedad castellonense de cultura*, XVI (1935), 289-291. Also in *Cartas de población y franquicia* (*q.v.*), I, doc. 303.

Alfandech Charter. Carta puebla de Alfandech, April 15, 1277. See primary sources, manuscript: Archivo de la Corona de Aragón [James II, Reg. Canc. 196, fol. 164].

Alfonso X the Learned (Wise), King of Castile. *Las siete partidas*. Editor, Gregorio López (1555). In *Colección de códigos y leyes de España, códigos antiguos*, editors Esteban Piñel and Alberto Aguilero y Velasco. 4 vols. Vol. II. Madrid: R. Labajos, 1865-1866.

Aureum opus regalium priuilegiorum ciuitatis et regni Valentie cum historia cristianissimi regis Jacobi ipsius primi conquistatoris. Editor, Luis de Alanya. Valencia: Diego de Gumiel, 1515.

Ben (Ibn) Adret. See secondary sources, Epstein.

Ben-Shemesh. See *Taxation*.

Carta de franquesa de Majorca. Editor, Benet Pons Fàbregues. In Mascaró Pasarius, *Historia de Mallorca* (*q.v.*, secondary sources), III, 459-473.

Carta de población de la ciudad de Santa María de Albarracín. Editor, Carlos Riba y García. Colección de documentos para el estudio de la historia de Aragón, 10. Zaragoza: Pedro Carra, 1915.

Cartas de población y franquicia de Cataluña. Editor, José M. Font y Rius. 1 vol. to date. Instituto Jerónimo Zurita, Sección de Barcelona, 17. Madrid: Consejo superior de investigaciones científicas, 1969.

Cartulaire général de l'ordre des hospitaliers de S. Jean de Jérusalem (1100-1310). Editor, Joseph Delaville le Roulx. 4 vols. Paris: E. Leroux, 1894-1901.

Cartulario de "Sant Cugat" del Vallés. Editor, José Rius Serra. 3 vols. Textos y estudios de la corona de Aragón, 3, 4, 5. Barcelona: Consejo superior de investigaciones científicas, 1945-1947.

Censo de Catalunya ordenado en tiempo del rey Don Pedro el Ceremonioso. Editor, Próspero de Bofarull y Mascaró. *Colección de documentos inéditos del archivo general de la corona de Aragón* (*q.v.*), vol. XII.

Chelva Charter. Carta puebla de Chelva, August 17, 1370. In *Colección de documentos inéditos de España* (*q.v.*), XVIII, 69-74. Also in Fernández y González, *Mudejares de Castilla* (*q.v.*), appendix, doc. 71.

Chivert Charter. Carta puebla de Chivert, April 28, 1234. In "Colección de cartas pueblas," no. 76. *Boletín de la sociedad castellonense de cultura*, XXIV (1948), 226-230. Also in *Homenaje á Codera* (*q.v.*), pp. 28-33.

Código de las costumbres de Tortosa. Editor, Bienvenido Oliver. In his *Historia del derecho en Cataluña* (*q.v.*, secondary sources), vol. IV.

Colección de cánones y de todos los concilios de la iglesia de España y de América. Editor, Juan Tejada y Ramiro. 7 vols. Madrid: Imprenta de Pedro Montero, 1859-1863.

Colección de documentos inéditos del archivo general de la corona de Aragón. Editors, Próspero de Bofarull y Mascaró *et alii*. 41 vols. Barcelona: Imprenta del archivo, 1847-1910. Second series; editor, Federico Udina Martorell. 1 vol. to date, Barcelona: El Archivo, 1971.

Colección de documentos inéditos para la historia de España. Editors, Martín Fernández Navarrete, Miguel Salvá, Pedro Sáinz de Baranda *et alii*. 112 vols. Madrid: Viuda de Calera *et alibi*, 1842-1896.

Colección de documentos para la historia del reino de Murcia. Editor, Juan Torres Fontes. 2 vols. to date. Murcia: Academia Alfonso X el Sabio, 1963ff.

Colección de fueros municipales y cartas pueblas de los reinos de Castilla, León, corona de Aragón y Navarra coordinada y anotada. Editor, Tomás Muñoz y Romero. (Vol. I, *unicum*.) Madrid: J. M. Alonso, [1847] 1970.

Colección de los documentos justificativos de los derechos y regalías que corresponden al real patrimonio en el reyno de Valencia y de la jurisdicción del intendente como subrogado en lugar del antiguo bayle general. 2 vols. In Branchát, *Tratado de los derechos y regalías de Valencia* (*q.v.*, secondary sources). Vols. II, III.

Colección diplomática. Short citation used only for Huici, immediately below.

Colección diplomática de Jaime I, el Conquistador. Editor, Ambrosio Huici Miranda. 3 vols. Valencia: Hijo de Francisco Vives Mora, 1916-1920; Renovación tipográfica, 1922.

Colección diplomática de los documentos a que se refiere la disertación del feudalismo particular e irredimible de los pueblos del feudalismo del reino de Valencia, de donde salieron expulsos los moriscos en el año 1609. Editors, Miguel Salvá and Pedro Sáinz de Baranda. In *Colección de documentos inéditos de España* (*q.v.*), vol. XVIII.

Consolat de mar. Editor, Ferran Valls i Taverner. 3 vols. Els nostres clàssics, series A, 27, 37, 41. Barcelona: Editorial Barcino, 1930-1933.

Corpus iuris canonici. Editors, Emil Friedberg and E. L. Richter. 2d edn. 2 vols. Leipzig: B. Tauchnitz, 1879-1881.

Cortes de los antiguos reinos de Aragón y de Valencia y principado de Cataluña. 26 vols. in 27. Madrid: Real academia de la historia, 1896-1922.

Costumes de la mar. In *Consolat de mar* (*q.v.*), I, 29-92.

Costums de Tortosa. See *Código*.

Ad-Dāwūdī, *Kitāb al-amwāl* [partial]. Editors and translators, H. H. Abdul Wahab and F. Dachraoui. In "Le régime foncier en Sicile au moyen âge (ix et x siècles)." *Études d'orientalisme* (*q.v.*, secondary sources), II, 401-404.

Desclot, Bernat. *Crònica*. Editor, Miguel Coll y Alentorn. 5 vols. Els nostres clàssics, series A, 62, 63, 64, 66, 69-70. Barcelona: Editorial Barcino, 1949-1951. Also in *Les quatre grans cròniques* (*q.v.*), pp. 403-664.

Dialogus de scaccario. See Richard Fitz Nigel.

La documentación pontificia hasta Inocencio III (925-1216). Editor, Demetrio Mansilla Reoyo. Monumenta Hispaniae vaticana, I. Rome: Instituto español de estudios eclesiásticos, 1955.

Documentos de Alfonso X el Sabio. In *Colección de documentos de Murcia (q.v.),* vol. I.

Documentos inéditos de Aragón. See *Colección de documentos inéditos del archivo general de la corona de Aragón.*

"Documentos para el estudio de la reconquista y repoblación del valle del Ebro." Editor, José M. Lacarra. *Estudios de edad media de la corona de Aragón,* II (1946), 469-574; III (1947-1948), 499-727; V (1952), 511-668.

"Documentos relativos a la condición social y jurídica de los mudéjares aragoneses." Editor, Francisco Macho y Ortega. *Revista de ciencias jurídicas y sociales,* V (1922), 143-160, 444-464.

Eslida Charter. Carta puebla de Eslida, May 29, 1242. In "Colección de cartas pueblas," no. 63. *Boletín de la sociedad castellonense de cultura,* XVIII (1943), 159-160. Also in *Colección de documentos inéditos de España (q.v.),* XVIII, 55-58; *Colección diplomática (q.v.),* doc. 241; 17. See also Second Eslida Charter.

Fernández y González, *Mudejares de Castilla (q.v.),* appendix, doc.

Fori antiqui Valentiae. Editor, Manuel Dualde Serrano. Escuela de estudios medievales, textos, 22. Valencia: Consejo superior de investigaciones científicas, 1967.

Fori regni Valentiae. Editors, Francesc J. Pastor and P. J. de Capdevila. 2 vols. Monzón: Impressi imperiali, 1547-1548.

Formularium diversorum contractuum et instrumentorum secundum pratiquam et consuetudinem civitatis et regni Valentie. Valencia: n. p., 1499(?).

Forum Turolii, regnante in Aragonia Adefonso rege, anno dominice nativitatis mclxxvi. Editor, Francisco Aznar y Navarro. Colección de documentos para el estudio de la historia de Aragón, 2. Zaragoza: Mariano Escar, 1905.

Fuero de Córdoba. Editor, M. A. Orti Belmonte. In Orti Belmonte, "El fuero de Córdoba" *(q.v.,* secondary sources), pp. 67-84.

[Fueros de Aragón]. *Incipiunt fori editi per dominum Iacobum regem Aragonum in curiis aragonensibus celebratis in ciuitate Osce.* Zaragoza: Paulus Hurus, 1496.

Furs de València. Editors, Germán Colón and Arcadio García. 2 vols. to date. Els nostres clàssics, series A, 101. Barcelona: Editorial Barcino, 1970ff. Complete Catalan version is *Fori regni Valentiae (q.v.).*

BIBLIOGRAPHY

Al-Ḥimyarī (Muḥammad b. Muḥammad b. 'Abd al-Mun'im, al-Ḥimyarī). *Kitāb ar-rawḍ al-mi'ṭār.* Translator, M. P. Maestro González. Textos medievales, 10. Valencia: Gráficas Bautista, 1963.

———. *La péninsule ibérique au moyen-âge d'après le Kitāb ar-rawḍ al-mi'ṭār fī ḥabar al-aḳṭār d'Ibn 'Abd al-Mun'im al-Ḥimyarī. Texte arabe des notices relatives à l'Espagne, au Portugal et au sud-ouest de la France, publié avec une introduction, un répertoire analytique, une traduction annotée, un glossaire et une carte.* Editor and translator, Évariste Lévi-Provençal. Publications de la fondation de Goeje, 12. Leiden: E. J. Brill, 1938.

Hoenerbach. See *Spanisch-islamische Urkunden.*

Huici. See *Colección diplomática*; see also secondary sources, Huici.

Ibn 'Abdūn (Muḥammad b. Aḥmad b. 'Abdūn, at-Tujībī). *Séville musulmane au début du xiie siècle, le traité d'Ibn 'Abdūn traduite avec une introduction et des notes.* Translator, Évariste Lévi-Provençal. Paris: Editions G. P. Maisonneuve, 1947.

Ibn Baṭṭūṭa (Muḥammad b. 'Abd Allāh b. Muḥammad b. Ibrāhīm b. Baṭṭūṭa, aṭ-Ṭanjī). *Travels.* Translator, H.A.R. Gibb. 3 vols. Hakluyt Society Publications, second series, 110, 117, 141. Cambridge: Cambridge University Press, 1958-1971.

Ibn Khaldūn ('Abd ar-Raḥmān b. Muḥammad Walī ad-Dīn·b. Khaldūn). *The Muqaddimah: An Introduction to History.* Translator, Franz Rosenthal. Bollingen Series, 43. 3 vols. 2d edn. Princeton: Princeton University Press, 1967.

Ibn Sa'īd ('Alī b. Mūsā b. Sa'īd, al-Andalusī al-Maghribī). *Moorish Poetry: A Translation of the Pennants, an Anthology Compiled in 1243 by the Andalusian Ibn Sa'īd.* Translator, A. J. Arberry. Cambridge: Cambridge University Press, 1953.

Itinerari. See secondary sources, Miret y Sans.

James I, King (Spanish Jaime; Catalan Jacme or Jaume). *Crònica [Llibre dels feyts],* Editor, Josep M. de Casacuberta. 9 vols. in 2. Col·lecció popular barcino, 12, 15, 21, 185, 186, 196, 197, 199, 200. Barcelona: Editorial Barcino, 1926-1962. Also in *Les quatre grans cròniques (q.v.),* pp. 7-402.

———. *Libre dels feyts del rey en Jacme, edición facsímil del manuscrito de Poblet (1343) conservado en la biblioteca universitaria de Barcelona.* Editor, Martín de Riquer. Barcelona: University of Barcelona, 1972.

———. *The Chronicle of James I, King of Aragon, Surnamed the Conqueror (Written by Himself).* Translator, John Forster; introduction, notes, appendix, and glossary by Pascual de Gayangos. 2 vols. London: Chapman and Hall, 1883.

353

Játiva Charter. Carta puebla de Játiva, January 23, 1251 or 1252. In *Colección de documentos inéditos de España* (*q.v.*), xviii, 62. Also in *Colección diplomática* (*q.v.*), doc. 412; Fernández y González, *Mudejares de Castilla* (*q.v.*), appendix, doc. 24.

Jiménez de Rada, Rodrigo (attribution moot). *Historia arabum*. Editor, Francisco de Lorenzana. In his *Opera*, editor, M. D. Cabanes Pecourt, 1 vol. to date. Textos medievales, 22. Valencia: Editorial Anubar, [1793] 1968. Also editor, José Lozano Sánchez. Serie: Filosofía y Letras, no. 21. Seville: University of Seville, 1974.

Libros de tesorería de la casa real de Aragón. Editor, Eduardo González Hurtebise. (Vol. I, *unicum*.) Barcelona: Luis Benaiges, 1911.

Llibre de privilegis de Ulldecona. See secondary sources, Bayerri.

Llibre dels feyts. See James I.

Martí, Ramón. See *Vocabulista*.

Masones Privilege. Tax exemption to Mudejars of Masones in Aragon, 1263. In Fernández y González, *Mudejares de Castilla* (*q.v.*), appendix, doc. 45.

Muntaner, Ramón. *Crònica*. Editor, Enrique Bagué. 9 vols. in 2. Collecció popular barcino, 19, 141-148. Barcelona: Editorial Barcino, 1927-1952. Also in *Les quatre grans cròniques* (*q.v.*), pp. 665-1000.

Palma del Río Charter. Carta puebla de Palma del Río, 1371. In Fernández y González, *Mudejares de Castilla* (*q.v.*), appendix, doc. 72.

Penyafort [Peñafort], Ramón de. *Summa*. Editor, Honoratus Vincentius Laget. Verona: Ex typographia seminarii, 1744.

"Primera contribución conocida impuesta a los moros del reino de Valencia." Editor, Roque Chabás y Lloréns. *El archivo*, I (1886), 255-256.

Privilegios reales concedidos a la ciudad de Barcelona. Editors, Federico Udina Martorell, Antonio M. Aragó Cabañas, and Mercedes Costa. In *Colección de documentos inéditos [del archivo general] de la corona de Aragón* (*q.v.*), [xliii] second series, I, 1971.

Les quatre grans cròniques: Jaume I, Bernat Desclot, Ramon Muntaner, Pere III. Editor, Ferran Soldevila. Biblioteca perenne, 26, Barcelona: Editorial selecta, 1971.

Qudāma b. Jaʿfar b. Qudāma, al-Kātib al-Baghdādī. *Kitāb al-kharāj*, part 7. In *Taxation in Islam* (*q.v.*), ii, 17-68.

Rationes decimarum Hispaniae (1279-1280). Editor, José Rius Serra. Textos y estudios de la corona de Aragón, 7, 8. Barcelona: Consejo superior de investigaciones científicas, 1946-1947.

Rentas de la antigua corona de Aragón. Editor, Manuel de Bofarull y de Sartorio. *Colección de documentos inéditos del archivo general de la corona de Aragón* (*q.v.*), vol. xxxix.

El "Repartiment" de Burriana y Villarreal. Editor, Ramón de María. Valencia: J. Nácher, 1935.

Repartiment de Valencia. Facsimile edition. Editor, Julián Ribera y Tarragó. Valencia: Centro de cultura valenciana, 1939.

Repartimiento de Mallorca. Editor, Próspero de Bofarull y Mascaró. In *Colección de documentos inéditos del archivo general de la corona de Aragón (q.v.),* XIII, 1-141.

Repartimiento de Murcia. Editor, Juan Torres Fontes. Escuela de estudios medievales, textos, 31. Madrid: Consejo superior de investigaciones científicas, 1960.

Repartimiento de Sevilla. Editor, Julio González. 2 vols. Escuela de estudios medievales, textos, 15, 16. Madrid: Consejo superior de investigaciones científicas, 1951.

Repartimiento de Valencia. Editor, Próspero de Bofarull y Mascaró. In *Colección de documentos inéditos del archivo general de la corona de Aragón (q.v.),* XI, 143-656.

"Repàs d'un manual notarial del temps del rey en Jaume I." Editor, Joan Segura. *Congrés I (q.v.,* secondary sources), pp. 300-326.

Richard [of Ely] Fitz Nigel. *De necessariis observantiis scaccarii dialogus, qui vulgo dicitur Dialogus de scaccario.* [*The Course of the Exchequer*]. Editor and translator, Charles Johnson. Medieval Classics. London: Thomas Nelson and Sons, 1950.

Sacrorum conciliorum nova et amplissima collectio. Editors, J. D. Mansi *et alii.* 53 vols. (plus those irregularly numbered). Leipzig: H. Walter, 1903-1927.

"Sección de documentos." Editor, Roque Chabás. Series irregularly published in *El archivo.*

Second Eslida Charter. Carta puebla de Eslida, June 27, 1276. See primary sources, manuscript: Archivo de la Corona de Aragón [James I, Reg. Canc. 83, fol. 3v].

Siete partidas. See Alfonso.

Spanisch-islamische Urkunden aus der Zeit der Naṣriden und Moriscos. Editor, Wilhelm Hoenerbach. University of California Publications, Near Eastern Studies, 3 [Bonner orientalistische Studien, neue serie, bd. 15, Orientalischen seminars der Universität Bonn]. Berkeley: University of California Press, 1965.

Tales Charter. Carta puebla de Tales, May 27, 1260. In "Colección de cartas pueblas," no. 84. *Boletín de la sociedad castellonense de cultura,* XXVIII (1952), 437-438.

Taxation in Islam. Editor and translator, Aharon Ben-Shemesh. 3 vols. to date. 2nd edn. rev. Leiden: E. J. Brill, 1965ff.

Tortosa Charter. Carta puebla de Tortosa, December 1148. In *Colección de documentos inéditos del archivo general de la corona de Aragón* (*q.v.*), IV, 130-134. Also in Fernández y González, *Mudejares de Castilla* (*q.v.*), appendix, doc. 5.

Tortosa Convention, June 18, 1174. In *Colección de documentos inéditos del archivo general de la corona de Aragón* (*q.v.*), VIII, 50-52. Also in Fernández y González, *Mudejares de Castilla* (*q.v.*), appendix, doc. 9.

Tudela Charter. Carta puebla de Tudela, 1119. In *Colección de fueros municipales y cartas pueblas* (*q.v.*), p. 415. Also in Fernández y González, *Mudejares de Castilla* (*q.v.*), appendix, doc. 2.

Usatges de Barcelona i commemoracions de Pere Albert. Editor, Josep Rovira i Ermengol. Els nostres clàssics, series A, 43, 44. Barcelona: Editorial Barcino, 1933.

Uxó Charter. Carta puebla de Uxó, August 1250. In *Colección de documentos inéditos de España* (*q.v.*), XVIII, 42-50. Also in *Colección diplomática* (*q.v.*), doc. 383; Fernández y González, *Mudejares de Castilla* (*q.v.*), appendix, doc. 23.

Valencia Capitulation. Surrender treaty for Valencia city, September 28, 1238. In *Colección de documentos inéditos de España* (*q.v.*), XVIII, 84-86. Also in Fernández y González, *Mudejares de Castilla* (*q.v.*), appendix, doc. 15; Tourtoulon, *Don Jaime el Conquistador* (*q.v.*), I, appendix, doc. 15.

Vocabulista in arabico, pubblicato per la prima volta sopra un codice della biblioteca riccardiana di Firenze. Dubious attribution to Ramón Martí. Editor, Celestino Schiaparelli. Florence: Successori Le Monnier, 1871.

Yaḥyā b. Ādam b. Sulaymān, Abū Zakariyā, al-Qurashī al-Kūfī. *Kitāb al-kharāj.* In *Taxation in Islam* (*q.v.*), vol. 1.

Ya'qūb b. Ibrāhīm, Abū Yūsuf, al-Anṣārī. *Kitāb al-kharāj.* Abridged in *Taxation in Islam* (*q.v.*), II, 69-78.

SECONDARY SOURCES

Aghnides, Nicolas P. *Mohammedan Theories of Finance, with an Introduction to Mohammedan Law and a Bibliography.* Studies in History, Economics, and Public Law, 70. New York: Columbia University Press, 1916.

Aguilar y Serrat, Francisco de Asís. *Noticias de Segorbe y de su obispado.* 2 vols. Segorbe: F. Romaní y Suay, 1890.

Alcover. See *Diccionari.*

Aliaga Girbés, José. "Moralidad de las exacciones tributarias del reino de Valencia en el siglo xvi según Miguel Bartolomé Salón O.S.A. (1539?-1621)." *Anthologica annua*, xvi (1968), 103-173.

———. *Los tributos e impuestos valencianos en el siglo xvi: Su justicia y moralidad según Fr. Miguel Bartolomé Salón, O.S.A. (1539?-1621)*. Rome: Instituto español de historia eclesiástica, 1972.

Á[lvarez] de Cienfuegos, Isabel. "Régimen tributario del reino mudéjar de Granada (la hacienda de los nasríes granadinos)." *Miscelánea de estudios árabes y hebraicos*, viii (1959), 99-124.

Amador de los Ríos, José. *Historia social, política y religiosa de los judíos de España y Portugal*. 2 vols. Buenos Aires: Editorial Bajel, [1875-1876] 1943.

Aragó Cabañas, Antoni M. "La col·lecta del bovatge del 1327." *Estudis d'història medieval*, iii (1970), 41-51.

———. "La institución 'baiulus regis' en Cataluña, en la época de Alfonso el Casto." *Congrés VII (q.v.)*, iii, 139-142.

———. "Licencias para buscar tesoros en la corona de Aragón." *Martínez Ferrando miscelánea (q.v.)*, pp. 7-21.

Arié, Rachel. *L'Espagne musulmane au temps des nasrides (1232-1492)*. Paris: Editions de Boccard, 1973.

Arroyo Ilera, Rafael. "El mercado de Valencia en el siglo xiii, notas para su estudio." *Congrés VII (q.v.)*, ii, 399-405.

———. "La sal en Aragón y Valencia durante el reinado de Jaime I." *Saitabi*, xi (1961), 253-261.

Ashtor, Eliyahu. *Histoire des prix et des salaires dans l'orient médiéval*. Monnaie, prix, conjuncture, 8. Paris: S.E.V.P.E.N., 1969.

Asso, Ignacio de. *Historia de la economía política de Aragón*. Zaragoza: Francisco Magallón, [1798] 1947.

Baer, Yitzhak [Fritz]. *A History of the Jews in Christian Spain*. Translator, Louis Schoffman *et alii*. 2 vols. Philadelphia: Jewish Publication Society of America, 1966.

Balari Jovany, José. *Orígenes históricos de Cataluña*. 2 vols. Biblioteca filológica-histórica, 10. San Cugat del Vallés: Instituto internacional de cultura románica, [1899] 1964.

Barabier, É. *Enquêtes sur les droits et revenus de Charles Ier d'Anjou en Provence, 1252 et 1278, avec une étude sur le domaine comtal et les seigneuries de Provence au xiiie siècle*. Documents inédits sur l'histoire de France, 4. Paris: Bibliothèque nationale, 1969.

Baron, Salo W. *A Social and Religious History of the Jews*. 2d edn. rev. 15 vols. to date. New York: Columbia University Press, 1952ff.

Bayerri y Bertoméu, Enrique. *Historia de Tortosa y su comarca.* 8 vols. to date. Tortosa: Algueró y Baíges, 1933ff.

———. *Llibre de privilegis de la vila de Ulldecona, cartulario de la militar y soberana orden de San Juan de Jerusalén (ahora de Malta) en su comendadoría de Ulldecona desde mediados del siglo xii hasta finales del xvi.* Tortosa: Imprenta Blanch, 1951.

Ben-Shemesh. See primary sources, *Taxation in Islam.*

Benton, John F. "The Revenue of Louis VII." *Speculum,* XLII (1967), 84-91.

Bisson, Thomas N. "Negotiations for Taxes under Alfonse of Poitiers [1220-1271]." *XIIᵉ Congrès international des sciences historiques,* pp. 77-101. Paris: Béatrice-Nauwelaerts, 1966.

———. "Sur les origines du *monedatge*: quelques textes inédits." *Annales du midi,* LXXXV (1973), 91-104.

Bofarull y Sans, Francisco de A. de. "Jaime I y los judíos." *Congrés I* (*q.v.*), pp. 818-943.

———. *Los judíos en el territorio de Barcelona (siglos x al xiii), reinado de Jaime I, 1213-1276.* Barcelona: F. J. Altés, 1910.

Boronat y Barrachina, Pascual. *Los moriscos españoles y su expulsión, estudio histórico-crítico.* 2 vols. Valencia: Francisco Vives Mora, 1901.

Bosch Vilá, Jacinto. "Referencias a moneda en los documentos árabes y hebreos de Aragón y Navarra." *Estudios de edad media de la corona de Aragón,* VI (1956), 228-246.

Botet y Sisó, Joaquín. *Les monedes catalanes.* 3 vols. Barcelona: Institut d'estudis catalans, 1908-1911.

———. "Nota sobre la encunyació de monedes aràbigues pêl rey Don Jaume." *Congrés I* (*q.v.*), pp. 944-963.

Bowsky, William N. *The Finance of the Commune of Siena, 1287-1355.* Oxford: Oxford University Press, 1970.

Branchát, Vicente. *Tratado de los derechos y regalías que corresponden al real patrimonio en el reyno de Valencia y de la jurisdicción del intendente como subrogado en lugar del antiguo bayle general.* 3 vols. Valencia: José y Tomás de Orga, 1784-1786.

Brown, Elizabeth A. R. "Taxation and Morality in the Thirteenth and Fourteenth Centuries: Conscience and Political Power and the Kings of France." *French Historical Studies,* VIII (1973), 1-28.

Brunschvig, Robert. *La Berbérie orientale sous les ḥafṣides.* 2 vols. Publications de l'institut d'études orientales (d'Alger), 8, 11. Paris: Adrien-Maisonneuve, 1940-1947.

Burns, Robert Ignatius. "Baths and Caravanserais in Crusader Valencia." *Speculum,* XLVI (1971), 443-458.

———. "Christian-Islamic Confrontation in the West: The Thirteenth-Century Dream of Conversion." *American Historical Review*, LXXVI, (1971), 1386-1434.

———. *The Crusader Kingdom of Valencia: Reconstruction on a Thirteenth-Century Frontier*. 2 vols. Cambridge: Harvard University Press, 1967.

———. "Immigrants from Islam: The Crusaders' Use of Muslims as Settlers in Thirteenth-Century Spain." *American Historical Review*, LXXX (1975), 21-42.

———. "Irrigation Taxes in Early Mudejar Valencia: The Problem of the *Alfarda*." *Speculum*, XLIV (1969), 560-567.

———. "Islam [as an Established Religion] in the Kingdom of Valencia." *Studies in Mediaevalia and Americana. Essays in Honor of William Lyle Davis, S. J*. Editors, G. G. Steckler and L. D. Davis. Spokane: Gonzaga University Press, 1973.

———. *Islam under the Crusaders: Colonial Survival in the Thirteenth-Century Kingdom of Valencia*. Princeton: Princeton University Press, 1973.

———. "Journey From Islam: Incipient Cultural Transition in the Conquered Kingdom of Valencia (1240-1280)." *Speculum*, XXXV (1960), 337-356.

———. "Los hospitales del reino de Valencia en el siglo xiii." *Anuario de estudios medievales*, II (1965), 135-154.

———. "A Mediaeval Income Tax: The Tithe in the Thirteenth-Century Kingdom of Valencia." *Speculum*, XLI (1966), 438-452.

———. "Mudejar Life and Work: Colonial Tax Structure in the Thirteenth-Century Kingdom of Valencia." *Primer congreso de historia del país valenciano*, II, in press. I vol. to date. Valencia: University of Valencia, 1973.

———. "The Muslim in the Christian Feudal Order: The Kingdom of Valencia, 1240-1280." *Studies in Medieval Culture*, V (1975), 105-126.

———. "Renegades, Adventurers, and Sharp Businessmen: The Thirteenth-Century Spaniard in the Cause of Islam." *Catholic Historical Review*, LVIII (1972), 341-366.

———. "Le royaume chrétien de Valence et ses vassaux musulmans (1240-1280)." *Annales, économies, sociétés, civilisations*, XXVIII (1973), 199-225.

———. "Social Riots on the Christian-Moslem Frontier: Thirteenth-Century Valencia." *American Historical Review*, LXVI (1961), 378-400.

———. "Spanish Islam in Transition: Acculturative Survival and Its Price in the Christian Kingdom of Valencia, 1240-1280." *Islam and Cultural*

Change in the Middle Ages. Editor, Speros Vryonis, Jr., pp. 87-105. Wiesbaden: Otto Harrassowitz, 1975.

Burriel de Orueta, Eugenio L. *La huerta de Valencia, zona sur, estudio de geografía agraria.* Instituto de geografía, 6. Valencia: Institución Alfonso el Magnánimo, and Diputación provincial, 1971.

Cagigas, Isidro de las. *Los mozárabes.* 2 vols. Minorías étnico-religiosas de la edad media española, 1, 2. Madrid: Consejo superior de investigaciones científicas, 1947-1948.

——. *Los mudejares.* 2 vols. Minorías étnico-religiosas de la edad media española, 3, 4. Madrid: Consejo superior de investigaciones científicas, 1948-1949.

Cahen, Claude. "Djizya." *Encyclopaedia of Islam,* 2d edn. (*q.v.*), II, 559-562.

——. "La féodalité et les institutions politiques de l'orient latin." *Atti del convegno di scienze morali, storiche, e filologiche, 27 Maggio-1 Giugno 1956, tema: oriente ed occidente nel medio evo,* pp. 167-197. Rome: Accademia nazionale dei Lincei, 1957.

——. "Iḳṭāʿ," *Encyclopaedia of Islam,* 2d edn. (*q.v.*) III, 1,088-1,091.

——. "Notes sur l'histoire des croisades et de l'orient latin: orient latin et commerce du Levant." *Bulletin de la faculté des lettres de Strasbourg,* XXIX (1951), 328-346.

——. "Notes sur l'histoire des croisades et de l'orient latin: le régime rural syrien au temps de la domination franque." *Bulletin de la faculté des lettres de Strasbourg,* XXIX (1951), 286-310.

Casas Torres, José M. *La vivienda y los núcleos de población rurales de la huerta de Valencia.* Madrid: Consejo superior de investigaciones científicas, 1944.

Castañeda y Alcover, Vicente. *Relaciones geográficas, topográficas e históricas del reino de Valencia hechas en el siglo xviii a ruego de Don Tomás López.* 2 vols. Madrid: Revista de archivos, bibliotecas, y museos, 1919-1922.

Cavanilles, Antonio J. *Observaciones sobre la historia natural, geografía, agricultura, población y frutos del reyno de Valencia.* 2 vols. Madrid: Imprenta real, 1795-1797. (Reprint, much reduced in maps and size, 2 vols. Zaragoza: Consejo superior de investigaciones científicas, 1958.)

Chabás y Lloréns, Roque. "Çeit Abu Çeit." *El archivo,* IV (1890), 215-221, V (1891), 143-166, 288-304, 362-376.

——. "Glosario de algunas voces oscuras usadas en el derecho foral valenciano." *Anales del centro de cultura valenciana,* XII (1944), 3-27, 76-79, 128-150. Repaged offprint, Valencia: Imprenta Diana, 1946.

———. "El libro del repartimiento de la ciudad y reino de Valencia." *El archivo*, III (1888-1889), 73-98, 217-225; VI (1892), 240-250; VII (1893), 365-372.

———. See also primary sources, "Primera contribución" and "Sección de documentos."

Chalmeta, Pedro. *El "señor del zoco" en España: edades media y moderna, contribución al estudio de la historia del mercado*. Madrid: Instituto hispano-árabe de cultura, 1973.

Chejne, Anwar G. *Muslim Spain: Its History and Culture*. Minneapolis: University of Minnesota Press, 1974.

Cienfuegos. See Álvarez de Cienfuegos.

Cipolla, Carlo M. *Money, Prices, and Civilization in the Mediterranean World, Fifth to Seventeenth Century*. New York: Gordian Press, 1967.

Congrés [I] d'història de la corona d'Aragó, dedicat al rey En Jaume I y a la seua época. 2 vols. paginated as one. Barcelona: Ayuntamiento de Barcelona, 1909-1913.

III Congrés d'història de la corona d'Aragó, dedicat al període compres entre la mort de Jaume I i la proclamació del rey Don Ferran d'Antequera. 2 vols. Valencia: Diputación provincial, 1923.

IV Congrés d'història de la corona d'Aragó. 2 vols. I, Palma de Mallorca: Diputación provincial, 1959; II, Barcelona: Archivo de la corona de Aragón, 1970.

VII Congrés d'història de la corona d'Aragó. 3 vols. Barcelona: Ayuntamiento de Barcelona, 1963-1964.

Cortés, Vicenta. *La esclavitud en Valencia durante el reinado de los Reyes Católicos (1479-1516)*. Archivo municipal de Valencia, Estudios monográficos, series 3, new section, 1. Valencia: Ayuntamiento de Valencia, 1964.

Cortés Muñoz, Fermín. "Aportación al estudio de las instituciones mercantiles de la Valencia foral, la condición jurídica de los mercaderes." *Boletín de la sociedad castellonense de cultura*, XXIV (1948), 218-225.

Coy Cotonat, Agustín. "El derecho llamado 'furnatico' en el siglo xiii." *Congrés I* (*q.v.*), pp. 190-193.

Cuvillier, Jean Pierre. "La propriété de l'eau et l'utilisation des ouvrages hydrauliques dans la Catalogne médiévale (xiiie et xive siècles): essai d'histoire économique et sociale." *Miscellània històrica catalana*, III (1970) [*Homenatge al Pare Jaume Finestres*; and Scriptorium populeti, no. 3], 243-257.

Diccionari català-valencià-balear, inventari lexicogràfic i etimològic de la llengua catalana en totes les seves formes literàries i dialectals, re-

collides de documents i textos. Editors, Antoni M. Alcover, Francesc de B. Moll, Manuel Sanchis Guarner, and Anna Moll Marquès. 10 vols. Palma de Mallorca: M. Alcover, 1930-1962.

Dozy, Reinhart P. A. and Willem H. Engelmann. *Glossaire des mots espagnols et portugais dérivés de l'arabe.* 2d edn. rev. Leiden: E. J. Brill, [1869] 1965.

Dubler, César E. *Über das Wirtschaftsleben auf der iberischen Halbinsel vom xi. zum xiii. Jahrhundert, Beitrag zu den islamisch-christlichen Beziehungen.* Romanica helvetica, series linguistica, 22. Erlenbach-Zurich: Eugen Rentsch Verlag, 1943.

Dufourcq, Charles Emmanuel. "Les consulats catalans de Tunis et de Bougie au temps de Jacques le Conquérant." *Anuario de estudios medievales,* III (1966), 469-479.

——. *L'Espagne catalane et le Maghrib aux xiiie et xive siècles, de la bataille de Las Navas de Tolosa (1212) à l'avènement du sultan mérinide Abou-l-Hasan (1313).* Bibliothèque de l'école des hautes études hispaniques, Université de Bordeaux, 37. Paris: Presses universitaires de France, 1966.

Duri, Abdel Aziz ('Abd al-'Azīz ad-Dūrī). "Notes on Taxation in Early Islam." *Journal of the Economic and Social History of the Orient,* XVII (1974), 136-144.

Emery, Richard W. *The Jews of Perpignan in the Thirteenth Century, an Economic Study Based on Notarial Records.* New York: Columbia University Press, 1959.

Encyclopaedia of Islam. A Dictionary of the Geography, Ethnography, and Biography of the Muhmmadan Peoples. Editors, H. M. Houtsma *et alii.* 4 vols. plus supplement. Leiden: E. J. Brill, 1913-1936. 2d edn. rev. [*EI²*]. Editors, H.A.R. Gibb, J. H. Kramers, É. Lévi-Provençal *et alii.* 4 vols. to date. Leiden: E. J. Brill, 1960ff.

Epstein, Isidore. *The "Responsa" of Rabbi Solomon Ben Adreth of Barcelona (1235-1310) as a Source of the History of Spain. Studies in the Communal Life of the Jews in Spain as Reflected in the "Responsa." And the Responsa of Rabbi Simon B. Zemah Duran as a Source of the History of the Jews in North Africa.* 2 books in one. New York: KTAV Publishing House, [1925-1930] 1968.

Escolano, Gaspar. *Décadas de la historia de la insigne y coronada ciudad y reino de Valencia.* Editor, Juan B. Perales. 3 vols. Valencia: Terraza, Aliena y Compañía, [1610-1611] 1878-1880.

Études d'orientalisme dediées à la mémoire de Lévi-Provençal. 2 vols. Paris: G. P. Maisonneuve et Larose, 1962.

Fernández y González, Francisco. *Estado social y político de los mude-jares de Castilla, considerados en sí mismos y respecto de la civilización española.* Madrid: Real academia de la historia, 1866.

Ferraz Penelas, Félix M. *El maestre racional y la hacienda foral valenciana.* Valencia: Tipografía moderna, 1913.

Ferrer i Mallol, M. T. "El patrimoni reial i la recuperació dels senyorius jurisdiccionals en els estats catalano-aragonesos a la fi del segle xiv." *Anuario de estudios medievales,* VII (1970-1971), 351-492.

Finances et comptabilité urbaines du xiiie au xvie siècle; colloque international. Collection histoire, 7. Brussels: Pro civitate, 1964.

Fischer, Christian Augustus. *A Picture of Valencia, Taken on the Spot; Comprehending a Description of that Province, its Inhabitants, Manners and Customs, Productions, Commerce, Manufactures, etc., with an Appendix, Containing a Geographical and Statistical Survey of Valencia and of the Balearic and Pithyusian Islands; Together with Remarks on the Moors in Spain.* 2d edn., trans. anon. London: Henry Colburn, 1811.

Font y Rius, José M. *Instituciones medievales españolas: la organización política, económica y social de los reinos cristianos de la reconquista.* Madrid: Consejo superior de investigaciones científicas, 1949.

———. "Orígenes del régimen municipal de Cataluña." *Anuario de historia del derecho español,* XVI (1945), 389-529, XVII (1946), 229-585.

———. See primary sources, *Cartas de población.*

Fontavella González, Vicente. *La huerta de Gandía.* Zaragoza: Consejo superior de investigaciones científicas, 1952.

Foster, Alice. *The Geographic Structure of the Vega of Valencia.* Chicago: University of Chicago Libraries, 1936.

Fryde, Matthew M. "Studies in the History of Public Credit of German Principalities and Towns in the Middle Ages." *Studies in Medieval and Renaissance History,* I (1964), 221-292.

Gallardo Fernández, Francisco. *Origen, progresos y estado de las rentas de la corona de España, su gobierno y administración.* 7 vols. Madrid: Imprenta real, 1805-1808.

Gallofre Guinovart, Rafael. *Documentos del reinado de Alfonso III de Aragón relativos al antiguo reino de Valencia y contenidos en los registros de la corona de Aragón.* Valencia: Diputación provincial, 1968.

García Cárcel, Ricardo, and Eduardo Ciscar Pallarés. *Moriscos y agermanats.* La unitat, 14. Valencia: L'Estel, 1974.

García de Cáceres, Francisco. *Impuestos de la ciudad de Valencia durante la época foral.* Valencia: Librería de Ángel Aguilar, 1909.

G[arcía] de Valdeavellano y Arcimís, Luis. *Curso de historia de las insti tuciones españolas de los orígenes al final de la edad media.* 2d edn. rev. Madrid: Revista de occidente, 1968.

García y García, Honorio. *Estado económico-social de los vasallos en la gobernación foral de Castellón.* Vich: Imprenta Ausetana, 1943.

――――. *Notas para la historia de Vall de Uxó.* Vall de Uxó: Ayuntamiento de Uxó, 1962.

García Sanz, A. "Mudéjares y moriscos en Castellón." *Boletín de la socie-dad castellonense de cultura,* xxviii (1952), 94-114.

――――. "Tales y sus cartas pueblas." *Boletín de la sociedad castellonense de cultura,* xxviii (1952), 439-442.

Garrison, Frances. "Les hôtes et l'hébergement des étrangers au moyen âge, quelques solutions de droit comparé." *Études d'histoire du droit privé offertes à Pierre Petot.* Paris: Librairie générale de droit et de jurisprudence, 1959.

Gayangos, Pascual de. See primary sources, James I (Forster translation).

Geografía general del reino de Valencia. Editor, Francisco Carreras y Candi. 5 vols. Barcelona: Alberto Martín, 1920-1927.

Gibert y Sánchez de la Vega, Rafael. "Los contratos agrarios en el derecho medieval." *Boletín de la universidad de Granada,* xxii (1950), 305-330.

――――. *Historia general del derecho español.* 1 vol. to date. Granada: F. Roman, 1968.

Giménez Soler, Andrés. *La edad media en la corona de Aragón.* 2d edn. rev. Colección Labor, ciencias históricas, 223, 224. Barcelona: Editorial Labor, 1944.

Glick, Thomas F. *Irrigation and Society in Medieval Valencia.* Cam-bridge: Harvard University Press, 1970.

――――. "Levels and Levelers: Surveying Irrigation Canals in Medieval Valencia." *Technology and Culture,* ix (1968), 165-180.

Glossarium mediae latinitatis Cataloniae, voces latinas y romances docu-mentados en fuentes catalanas del año 800 al 1100. Editors, Mariano Bassols de Climent *et alii.* 1 vol. to date. Barcelona: Universidad de Barcelona, 1960.

Goffart, Walter. "From Roman Taxation to Medieval Seigneurie, Three Notes." *Speculum,* xlvii (1972), 165-187, 373-394.

Goitein, Solomon D. *A Mediterranean Society: The Jewish Communities of the Arab World as Portrayed in the Documents of the Cairo Ge-niza.* 2 vols. to date. Berkeley: University of California Press, 1967ff.

Gómez Serrano, N. P. "Contribució al estudio de la molinería valenciana mijeval." *Congrés III (q.v.),* ii, 695-766.

Grayzel, Solomon. *The Church and the Jews in the XIIIth Century: A Study of Their Relations During the Years 1198-1254, Based on the*

Papal Letters and the Conciliar Decrees of the Period. 2d edn. rev. New York: Hermon Press, 1966.

Gual Camarena, Miguel. "El hospedaje hispano-medieval, aportaciones para su estudio." *Anuario de historia del derecho español,* xxxii (1962), 527-541.

––––. "Mudéjares valencianos, aportaciones para su estudio." *Saitabi,* vii (1949), 165-199.

––––. "Los mudéjares valencianos en la época del Magnánimo." *Congrés IV (q.v.),* pp. 467-494.

––––. "Para un mapa de la sal hispánica en la edad media." *Homenaje a Vives,* i, 483-497. 2 vols. Editor, J. Maluquer de Motes. Barcelona: Universidad de Barcelona, 1965.

––––. "Precedentes de la reconquista valenciana." *Estudios medievales* [Valencia], i (1952), 167-246. Repaged offprint, Valencia: Consejo superior de investigaciones científicas, 1953.

––––. "Reconquista de la zona castellonense." *Boletín de la sociedad castellonense de cultura,* xxv (1949), 417-441.

––––. *Vocabulario del comercio medieval, colección de aranceles aduaneros de la corona de Aragón (siglos xiii y xiv).* Tarragona: Diputación provincial, 1968.

Guglielmi, Nilda. "Posada y yantar, contribución al estudio del léxico de las instituciones medievales." *Hispania,* xxvi (1966), 5-40, 165-219.

Guichard, Pierre. "Un seigneur musulman dans l'Espagne chrétienne: Le 'ra'îs' de Crevillente (1243-1318)." *Mélanges de la casa de Velázquez,* ix (1973), 283-334.

Halperín Donghi, Tulio. "Un conflicto nacional: moriscos y cristianos viejos en Valencia." *Cuadernos de historia de España,* xxiv-xxv (1955), 5-115; xxv-xxvi (1957), 82-250.

––––. "Recouvrements de civilisation: les morisques du royaume de Valence au xvie siècle." *Annales, économies, sociétés, civilisations,* xi (1956), 154-182.

Hamilton, Earl J. *Money, Prices, and Wages in Valencia, Aragon and Navarre, 1351-1500.* Harvard Economic Studies, 51. Cambridge: Harvard University Press, 1936.

Hill, George F. *Treasure Trove in Law and Practice from the Earliest Time to the Present Day.* Oxford: Clarendon Press, 1936.

Hinojosa, Eduardo de. "Mezquinos y exáricos, datos para la historia de la servidumbre en Navarra y Aragón." *Homenaje á Codera (q.v.),* pp. 523-531.

––––. *El régimen señorial y la cuestión agraria en Cataluña durante la edad media.* Madrid: Victoriano Suárez, 1905.

Homenaje á D. Francisco Codera en su jubilación del profesorado. Estudios de erudición oriental. Editors, Eduardo Saavedra *et alii.* Zaragoza: Mariano Escar, 1904.

Homenaje a Millás-Vallicrosa. 2 vols. Barcelona: Consejo superior de investigaciones científicas, 1954-1956.

Hopkins, J.F.P. *Medieval Muslim Government in Barbary until the Sixth Century of the Hijra.* London: Luzac and Co. Ltd., 1958.

Houston, J. M. "Land Use and Society in the Plain of Valencia." In *Geographical Essays in Memory of Alan G. Ogilvie,* editors R. Miller and J. W. Watson, pp. 166-194. London: Thomas Nelson and Sons Ltd., 1959.

Huici Miranda, Ambrosio. *Historia musulmana de Valencia y su región, novedades y rectificaciones.* 3 vols. Valencia: Ayuntamiento de Valencia, 1970.

———. *Historia política del imperio almohade.* Tetuán: Instituto General Franco de estudios e investigación hispano-árabe, 1956-1957.

———. See also primary sources, *Colección diplomática.*

Idris, Hady Roger. *La Berbérie orientale sous les zīrīdes, xe-xiie siècles.* 2 vols. Publications de l'institut d'études orientales (d'Alger), 22. Paris: Adrien-Maisonneuve, 1962.

Imamuddin [Imām ad-Dīn], S. M. *Some Aspects of the Socio-Economic and Cultural History of Muslim Spain, 711-1492 A.D.* Medieval Iberian Peninsula Texts and Studies, 2. Leiden: E. J. Brill, 1965.

Islamic Taxation: Two Studies. See Løkkegaard.

Kaeuper, Richard W. *Bankers to the Crown: The Riccardi of Lucca and Edward I.* Princeton: Princeton University Press, 1973.

Klüpfel, Ludwig. *Verwaltungsgeschichte des Königreichs Aragon zu Ende des 13. Jahrhunderts.* Abhandlungen zur mittleren und neueren Geschichte, 35. Berlin: W. Kohlhammer, 1915.

Küchler, Winfried. "Besteuerung der Juden und Mauren in den Ländern der Krone Aragons während des 15. Jahrhunderts." *Gesammelte Aufsätze zur Kulturgeschichte Spaniens,* XXIV (1968), 227-256.

Lacarra, José M. See primary sources, "Documentos . . . del Ebro."

Ladero Quesada, Miguel Ángel. "Dos temas de la Granada nazarí." In *Estudios sobre la sociedad castellana en la baja edad media,* editor Salvador de Moxó, pp. 321-345; Cuadernos de historia, 3 (supplement to *Hispania*). Madrid: Consejo superior de investigaciones científicas, 1969.

———. *La hacienda real castellana entre 1480 y 1492.* Departamento de historia medieval, estudios y documentos, 26. Valladolid: Universidad de Valladolid, 1967.

Lalinde Abadía, Jesús. *La jurisdicción real inferior en Cataluña* (*"corts, veguers, batlles"*). Museo de historia de la ciudad, Seminario de arqueología e historia de la ciudad, 14 [Estudios, 1]. Barcelona, Ayuntamiento de Barcelona, 1966.

Lapidus, Ira M. *Muslim Cities in the Later Middle Ages.* Harvard Middle Eastern Studies, 11. Cambridge: Harvard University Press, 1967.

——, editor. See *Middle Eastern Cities.*

Le Tourneau, Roger. "Funduḳ." *Encyclopaedia of Islam*, 2d edn. (*q.v.*), II, 945.

Lévi-Provençal, Évariste. *Histoire de l'Espagne musulmane.* 3 vols. 2d edn. rev. Paris: G. P. Maisonneuve, 1950-1953. Revised and translated by Emilio García Gómez, *España musulmana hasta la caída del califato de Córdoba (711-1031 de J.C.).* 2 vols. In Ramón Menéndez Pidal *et alii, Historia de España,* 12 vols. to date, vols. IV, V. Madrid: Espasa-Calpe, 1957ff.

——. *Péninsule ibérique.* See primary sources, al-Ḥimyarī.

——. *Séville musulmane.* See primary sources, Ibn 'Abdūn.

Lewis, Bernard, and Roger Le Tourneau. "Bayt al-Māl," *Encyclopaedia of Islam,* 2d edn. (*q.v.*), I, 1,141-1,149.

Liauzu, Jean-Guy. "Un aspect de la reconquête de la vallée de l'Ebre aux xie et xiie siècles, l'agriculture irriguée et l'héritage de l'Islam." *Hespéris-Tamuda,* V (1964), 5-13.

——. "La condition des musulmans dans l'Aragon chrétien aux xie et xiie siècles." *Hespéris-Tamuda,* IX (1968), 185-200.

Llorens y Raga, Peregrín L. "La morería de Segorbe, rentas de su mezquita a fines del siglo xvi." *Boletin de la sociedad castellonense de cultura,* XLIX (1973), 303-324.

Løkkegaard (Loekkegaard), Frede. *Islamic Taxation in the Classic Period with Special Reference to Circumstances in Iraq.* Copenhagen: Branner and Korch, 1950. Also in *Islamic Taxation: Two Studies* (New York: Arno Press, 1973).

Lombard, Maurice. "La chasse et les produits de la chasse dans le monde musulman (viiie-xie siècle)." *Annales, économies, sociétés, civilisations,* XXIV (1969), 572-592.

López de Ayala Álvarez de Toledo y del Hierro, Jerónimo (conde de Cedillo). *Contribuciones é impuestos en León y Castilla durante la edad media.* Madrid: Real academia de ciencias morales y políticas, 1896.

López Martínez, Celestino. *Mudéjares y moriscos sevillanos: páginas históricas.* Seville: Rodríguez, Giménez y Compañía, 1935.

Lourie, Elena. "Free Moslems in the Balearics under Christian Rule in the Thirteenth Century." *Speculum,* XLV (1970), 624-649.

Lyon, Bryce, and A. E. Verhulst, *Medieval Finance: A Comparison of Financial Institutions in Northwestern Europe.* University of Ghent, Belgium, Faculty of Letters Publications, 143. Providence: Brown University Press, 1967.

Macanaz, Melchor [Rafael] de. *Regalías de los señores reyes de Aragón, discurso jurídico, histórico, político* [1713]. Editor, Joaquín Maldonado Macanaz. Biblioteca jurídica de autores espanoles, 1. Madrid: Imprenta de la revista de legislación, 1879.

Macho y Ortega, Francisco. "Condición social de los mudéjares aragoneses (siglo xv)." *Memorias de la facultad de filosofía y letras de la universidad de Zaragoza,* 1 (1922-1923), 137-319.

———. See primary sources, "Documentos de los mudéjares."

Martínez Ferrando archivero: miscelánea de estudios dedicados a su memoria. Editor, anon. Barcelona: Asociación nacional de bibliotecarios, archiveros y arqueólogos, 1968.

Martínez Ferrando, Jesús E. *Catálogo de la documentación relativa al antiguo reino de Valencia contenida en los registros de la cancillería real.* 2 vols. Madrid: Cuerpo facultativo de archiveros, bibliotecarios, y arqueólogos, 1934.

Martínez y Martínez, Francisco. "Pego, su población y primeros señores." *Congrés I (q.v.),* pp. 63-69.

Mascaró Pasarius, J. *et alii. Historia de Mallorca.* 1, iii, iv, of 4 projected. Palma de Mallorca: Gráficas Miramar, 1970.

Mateu Ibars, Josefina. *Los virreyes de Valencia: Fuentes para su estudio.* Archivo municipal de Valencia, 3d series, 2. Valencia: Ayuntamiento de Valencia, 1963.

Mateu y Llopis, Felipe. *Bibliografía de Felipe Mateu y Llopis, reunida en su lxx aniversario, mcmlxxi.* Barcelona: University of Barcelona, 1972.

———. *La ceca de Valencia y las acuñaciones valencianas de los siglos xiii al xviii: Ensayo sobre una casa real de moneda de uno de los estados de la corona de Aragón.* Valencia: Imprenta de la viuda de Miguel Sanchis, 1929.

———. "La circulación monetaria en las diócesis de Tortosa y Segorbe-Albarracín en el reino de Valencia, según la decima de 1279-1280." *Boletín de la sociedad castellonense de cultura,* xxii (1946), 494-501.

———. "Colecta de la cena en el reino de Valencia en 1292-1295." *Boletín de la sociedad castellonense de cultura,* xlvi (1970), 215-236.

———. *Glosario hispánico de numismática.* Barcelona: Consejo superior de investigaciones científicas, 1964.

———. *Materiales para un glosario de diplomática hispánica, corona de Aragón, reino de Valencia.* Obras de investigación histórica, 34. Castellón de la Plana: Sociedad castellonense de cultura, 1957.

———. "Nómina de los musulmanes de las montañas de Coll de Rates del reino de Valencia en 1409." *Al-Andalus*, vi (1942), 299-335.

———. "Para el estudio del monedaje en Aragón, Tortosa y Lérida en el siglo xiv." *Martínez Ferrando miscelánea* (*q.v.*), pp. 315-322.

———. "La regalía monetaria en la corona de Aragón y en especial en el reino de Valencia hasta Fernando el Católico." *Cuadernos de historia Jerónimo Zurita*, iv-v (1956), 55-79.

———. "Les relacions monetàries entre Catalunya i València des de 1276 a 1376." *Boletín de la sociedad castellonense de cultura*, xii (1931), 27-39.

———. "La repoblación musulmana del reino de Valencia en el siglo xiii y las monedas de tipo almohade." *Boletín de la sociedad castellonense de cultura*, xxviii (1952), 29-43.

———. "Sobre el curso legal de la moneda en Aragón, Cataluña, Valencia, y Mallorca, siglos xiii y xiv." *Congrés VII* (*q.v.*), ii, 517-528.

———. "Sobre la política monetaria de Jaime I y las acuñaciones valencianas de 1247 y 1271." *Anales del centro de cultura valenciana*, xv (1947), 233-261.

———. "'Solidi' y 'denarii' en los reinos cristianos occidentales del siglo xiii, en torno de dos documentos del concejo de Molina Seca, de 1277 y 1282." *Acta numismática*, i (1971), 115-127.

———. "'Super monetatico' o 'morabetino' (breve noticia documental sobre el impuesto de monedaje en Aragón, Cataluña, Valencia, Mallorca, y Murcia, 1205-1327)." *Mélanges offerts à René Crozet*, editors Pierre Gallais and Yves-Jean Riou, 2 vols., ii, 1115-1120. Poitiers: Société d'études médiévales, 1966.

———. "Valores monetarios valencianos." *Boletín de la sociedad castellonense de cultura*, vii (1926), 287-294.

Mat[t]heu y Sanz, Lorenzo. *Tractatus de regimine [urbis et] regni Valentiae, sive selectarum interpretationum ad principaliores foros eiusdem.* Lyons: Anisson and Jean Posuel, [1654] 1704.

Mazahéri, Aly Akbar. *La vie quotidienne des musulmans au moyen âge, xe au xiiie siècle.* Paris: Librairie Hachette, 1951.

Menéndez Pidal, Ramón. *La España del Cid.* 2 vols. 4th edn. rev. Obras completas, 6, 7. Madrid: Espasa-Calpe, 1947.

Middle Eastern Cities: A Symposium on Ancient, Islamic, and Contemporary Middle Eastern Urbanism. Editor, Ira Lapidus. Berkeley: University of California Press, 1969.

Milián Boix, Manuel. "Tasas y sobreprecios en el siglo xiv por tierras de Morella." *Boletín de la sociedad castellonense de cultura*, xxv (1949), 787-798.

Miret y Sans, Joaquín. *Itinerari de Jaume I "el Conqueridor."* Barcelona: Institut d'estudis catalans, 1918.

Mitchell, Sydney K. *Taxation in Medieval England.* Editor, Sidney Painter. Yale Historical Publications, Studies, 15. New Haven: Yale University Press, 1951.

Momblanch y Gonzálbez, Francisco de P. *Historia de la Albufera de Valencia.* Valencia: Ayuntamiento de Valencia, 1960.

Monroe, James T. *Islam and the Arabs in Spanish Scholarship (Sixteenth Century to the Present).* Medieval Iberian Texts and Studies, 3. Leiden: E. J. Brill, 1970.

Moxó, Salvador de. *La alcabala, sobre sus orígenes, concepto y naturaleza.* Madrid: Consejo superior de investigaciones científicas, 1963.

Neuman, Abraham A. *The Jews in Spain: Their Social, Political and Cultural Life During the Middle Ages.* 2 vols. Philadelphia: Jewish Publication Society of America, 1942.

Neuvonen, Eero K. *Los arabismos del español en el siglo xiii.* Helsinki: University of Helsinki, 1941.

O'Callaghan, Joseph F. "The Cortes and Royal Taxation during the Reign of Alfonso X of Castile." *Traditio*, xxvii (1971), 379-398.

———. *A History of Medieval Spain.* Ithaca, New York: Cornell University Press, 1975.

Ohlendorf, Edmund. "Zur 'cena in presentia' des Königs von Aragon." *Gesammelte Aufsätze zur Kulturgeschichte Spaniens*, xvi (1963), 155-161.

Oliver, Bienvenido. *Historia del derecho en Cataluña, Mallorca y Valencia. Código de las costumbres de Tortosa.* 4 vols. Madrid: Miguel Ginesta, 1876-1881.

Orti Belmonte, Miguel A. "El fuero de Córdoba y las clases sociales en la ciudad: mudéjares y judíos en la edad media." *Boletín de la real academia de Córdoba*, xxv (1954), 5-94.

Palomeque Torres, Antonio. "Contribución al estudio del ejército en los estados de la reconquista." *Anuario de historia del derecho español*, xv (1944), 205-351.

Pastor de Togneri, Reyna. "La sal en Castilla y León, un problema de la alimentación y del trabajo y una política fiscal (siglos x-xiii)." *Cuadernos de historia de España*, xxxvii-xxxviii (1963), 42-87.

Piles Ibars, Andrés. *Valencia árabe.* (Vol. i, *unicum*). Valencia: Manuel Alafre, 1901.

Piles Ros, Leopoldo. *Estudio documental sobre el bayle general de Valencia, su autoridad y jurisdicción.* Valencia: Consejo superior de investigaciones científicas, and Diputación de Valencia, 1970.

370

———. "La situación de los moros de realengo en la Valencia del siglo xv." *Estudios de historia social de España*, i (1949), 225-274.

Poliak, A. N. "Classification of Lands in the Islamic Law and Its Technical Terms." *American Journal of Semitic Languages and Literatures*, LVII (1940), 50-62.

Poliakov, Léon. *Les banchieri juifs et le saint-siège du xiiie au xviie siècle.* École pratique des hautes études, vi^e section, affaires et gens d'affaires, 30. Paris: S.E.V.P.E.N., 1965.

Pons Pastor, Antoni. *Historia de Mallorca, instituciones, cultura, y costumbres del reino (s. xii-xv).* Colección Ángel, 2. Palma de Mallorca: Imprenta Mossén Alcover, 1965.

Powers, James F. "The Origins and Development of Municipal Military Service in the Leonese and Castilian Reconquest, 800-1250." *Traditio*, XXVI (1970), 91-111.

Prestwich, Michael. *War, Politics and Finance under Edward I.* London: Faber and Faber, 1972.

Rabie (Rabīʿ), Hassanein. *The Financial System of Egypt, A.H. 564-741 / A.D. 1169-1341.* [University of] London Oriental Series, 25. London: Oxford University Press, 1972.

Ribera y Tarragó, Julián. *Historia árabe valenciana.* Fourteen studies republished as part 3 of his *Disertaciones y opúsculos*, 2 vols. Madrid: Estanislao Maestre, 1928.

Richardson, H. G. *The English Jewry under Angevin Kings.* London: Methuen and Co., 1960.

Roca Traver, Francisco A. "Un siglo de vida mudéjar en la Valencia medieval (1238-1338)." *Estudios de edad media de la corona de Aragón*, v (1952), 115-208.

Rodón Binué, Eulalia. *El lenguaje técnico del feudalismo en el siglo xi en Cataluña (contribución al estudio del latín medieval).* Filología clásica, 16. Barcelona: Consejo superior de investigaciones científicas, 1957.

Rodrigo y Pertegás, José. "La morería de Valencia, ensayo de descripción topográficohistórica de la misma." *Boletín de la real academia de la historia*, LXXXVI (1925), 229-251.

Romano Ventura, David. "Los funcionarios judíos de Pedro el Grande de Aragón." *Boletín de la real academia de buenas letras de Barcelona*, XXVIII (1969-1970), 5-41.

———. "Los funcionarios judíos de Pedro el Grande de Aragón." *Congrés VII (q.v.)*, II, 561.

———. "Los hermanos Abenmenassé al servicio de Pedro el Grande de Aragón." *Homenaje a Millás-Vallicrosa*, II, 243-292. 2 vols. Barcelona: Consejo superior de investigaciones científicas, 1954-1956.

Romano Ventura, David. "El reparto del subsidio de 1282 entre las aljamas catalanas." *Sefarad*, XIII (1953), 73-86.

Ruiz-Moreno, Anibal. "Los baños públicos en los fueros municipales españoles." *Cuadernos de historia de España*, III (1945), 152-157.

Russell, J. C. "The Medieval Monedatge of Aragon and Valencia." *Proceedings of the American Philosophical Society*, CVI (1962), 483-504.

Salvá, Jaime. "Instituciones políticas y sociales otorgadas por Jaime I a los pobladores de Mallorca." Mascaró Pasarius *et alii, Historia de Mallorca* (*q.v.*), III, 361-473.

Samper, Hipólito (de). *Montesa ilustrada. Origen, fundación, principios, institutos, casos, progresos, jurisdicción, derechos, privilegios, preeminencias, dignidades, oficios, beneficios, héroes y varones ilustres de la real, ínclita y nobilissima religión militar de N. S. Santa María de Montesa y San George de Alfama.* 2 vols. Valencia: Jerónimo Vilagrasa, 1669.

Sánchez-Albornoz y Menduiña, Claudio. *La España musulmana según los autores islamitas y cristianos medievales.* 2d edn. rev. 2 vols. Barcelona: El ateneo, 1960.

———. "Notas para el estudio del 'petitum.'" *Homenaje a Don Ramón Carande*, pp. 383-418. Madrid: Sociedad de estudios y publicaciones, 1963.

Sánchez de Ocaña, Ramón. *Contribuciones é impuestos en León y Castilla durante la edad media.* Madrid: Real academia de ciencias morales y políticas, 1896.

Sanchis Guarner, Manuel. "Època musulmana." In Tarradell *et alii, Història del país valencià* (*q.v.*), I, part 2.

Sanchis y Sivera, José. "Los baños públicos (vida íntima de los valencianos en la época foral)." *Anales del centro de cultura valenciana*, VIII (1935), 1-13.

———. *Nomenclátor geográfico-eclesiástico de los pueblos de la diócesis de Valencia con los nombres antiguos y modernos de los que existen o han existido, notas históricas y estadísticas.* . . . Valencia: Casa de beneficencia, 1922.

Sauvaget, Jean. "Les caravansérails syriens du Ḥadjāj du Constantinople." *Ars islamica*, IV (1937), 98-121.

———. "Les caravansérails syriens du moyen âge." *Ars islamica*, VI (1939), 48-56; VII (1940), 1-20.

Schact, Joseph. "Zakāt." *Encyclopaedia of Islam*, 1st edn. (*q.v.*) IV, part 2, 1202-1205.

Schiaparelli. See primary sources, *Vocabulista*.

Schwarz, Karl. *Aragonische Hofordnungen im 13. und 14. Jahrhundert: Studien zur Geschichte der Hofämter und Zentralbehörden des Königreichs Aragon.* Berlin: W. Rothschild, 1914.

Shaw, Stanford J. *The Financial and Administrative Organization and Development of Ottoman Egypt, 1517-1798.* Princeton Oriental Studies, 19. Princeton: Princeton University Press, 1962.

Shneidman, Jerome Lee. "Jews as Royal Bailiffs in Thirteenth-Century Aragon." *Historia judaica,* XIX (1957), 55-66.

———. *The Rise of the Aragonese-Catalan Empire, 1200-1350.* 2 vols. New York: New York University Press, 1970.

Siddiqi, S. A. *Public Finance in Islam.* Lahore, Pakistan: Shaikh Muhammad Ashraf, 1952.

Soldevila, Ferran. "A propòsit del servei del bovatge." *Anuario de estudios medievales,* I (1964), 573-587.

———. *Història de Catalunya.* 2d edn. rev. 3 vols. Barcelona: Alpha, 1962.

———. *Pere el Gran.* 2 parts in 4 vols. Memòries de la secció històrico-arqueològica, 11, 13, 16, 22. Barcelona: Institut d'estudis catalans, 1950-1962.

———. *Els primers temps de Jaume I.* Memòries de la secció històrico-arqueològica, 27. Barcelona: Institut d'estudis catalans, 1968.

———. *Vida de Jaume I el Conqueridor.* Biblioteca biogràfica catalana, 14. Barcelona: Editorial Aedos, 1958.

———. *Vida de Pere el Gran i d'Alfons el Liberal.* Biblioteca biogràfica catalana, 35. Barcelona: Editorial Aedos, 1963.

———. See primary sources, *Les quatre grans cròniques.*

Steiger, Arnald. *Contribución a la fonética del hispano-árabe y de los arabismos en el iber-románico y el siciliano.* Madrid: Revista de filología española [supplement 17], 1932.

Strayer, Joseph R. and Charles H. Taylor. *Studies in Early French Taxation.* Harvard Historical Monographs, 12. Cambridge: Harvard University Press, 1939.

Streck, M. "Ḳaiṣārīya." *Encyclopaedia of Islam,* 1st edn. (*q.v.*), II, part 2, 659-670.

Tarradell Mateu, Miguel *et alii. Història del país valencià.* I vol. to date. Estudis e documents, 5. Barcelona: Edicions 62, 1965.

Toledo Girau, José. *Las aguas de riego en la historia de Valldigna.* Obras de investigación histórica, 35. Castellón de la Plana: Sociedad castellonense de cultura, 1958.

———. *El castell i la vall d'Alfandech de Marinyèn des de sa reconquesta per Jaume I, fins la fundació del monestir de Valldigna per Jaume II.* Obras de investigación histórica, 11. Castellón de la Plana: Sociedad castellonense de cultura, 1936.

Tormo y Monzó, Elías. "Los baños árabes del Almirante, en Valencia." *Boletín de la real academia de la historia,* CXIII (1943), 241-248.

Torres Balbás, Leopoldo. "Alcaicerías." *Al-Andalus,* XIV (1949), 431-455.

———. "Algunos aspectos de la casa hispanomusulmana: almacerías, algorfas y salezidos." *Al-Andalus,* XV (1950), 179-191.

———. *Algunos aspectos del mudejarismo urbano medieval.* Madrid: Academia de la historia, 1954.

———. "Las alhondigas hispanomusulmanas." *Al-Andalus,* XI (1946), 447-480.

———. "El baño de Torres Torres (Valencia) y otras levantinas." *Al-Andalus,* XVIII (1952), 176-186.

———. "Los baños públicos en los fueros municipales españoles." *Al-Andalus,* XI (1946), 443-445.

———. *Ciudades hispanomusulmanas.* Editor, Henri Terrasse. 2 vols. Madrid: Instituto hispano-árabe de cultura, 1971.

———. "Los edificios hispanomusulmanes." *Revista del instituto egipcio de estudios islámicos en Madrid,* I (1953), 92-121.

———. "Plazas, zocos y tiendas de las ciudades hispanomusulmanas." *Al-Andalus,* XII (1947), 437-476.

——— et alii. *Resumen histórico del urbanismo en España.* Madrid: Instituto de estudios de administración local, 1954.

Torres Fontes, Juan. "Los mudéjares murcianos en el siglo xiii." *Murgetana,* XVII (1961), 57-90.

———. *La reconquista de Murcia en 1266 por Jaime I de Aragón.* Murcia: Diputación de Murcia, 1967.

———. See also primary sources, *Colección de documentos de Murcia* and *Repartimiento de Murcia.*

Torres Morera, Juan R. *Repoblación del reino de Valencia, después de la expulsión de los moriscos.* Valencia: Ayuntamiento de Valencia, 1969.

Tourtoulon, Charles (baron de). *Don Jaime I el Conquistador, rey de Aragón, conde de Barcelona, señor de Montpeller, según las crónicas y documentos inéditos.* Rev. in translation. Translator, Teodoro Llorente y Olivares. 2 vols. Valencia: José Domenech, 1874.

Traver Tomas, Vicente. *Antigüedades de Castellón de la Plana, estudios histórico-monográficos de la villa y su vecindario[,] riqueza y monumentos.* Castellón de la Plana: Ayuntamiento de Castellón de la Plana, 1958.

Ubieto Arteta, Antonio. *Ciclos económicos en la edad media española.* Valencia: Anubar, 1969.

Ulloa, Modesto. *La hacienda real de Castilla en el reinado de Felipe II.* Rome: Centro del libro español, 1963.

Usher, Abbott Payson. *The Early History of Deposit Banking in Mediterranean Europe.* 1 vol. to date. Harvard Economic Studies, 75. Cambridge: Harvard University Press, 1943.

Valdeavellano. See G[arcía] de Valdeavellano.

Verlinden, Charles. *L'esclavage dans l'Europe médiévale.* 1 vol. to date, *Péninsule ibérique, France.* Rijksuniversiteit te Gent, faculteit van de letteren, 119. Bruges: Universiteit te Gent [Ghent], 1955.

Viard, Paul. *Histoire de la dîme ecclésiastique dans le royaume de France au xiie et xiiie siècles (1150-1313).* Paris: A. Picard, 1912.

Vicens Vives, Jaime. *An Economic History of Spain.* Translator, F. M. López-Morillas. Princeton: Princeton University Press, 1969.

Vicent Cortina, Vicente. *Bibliografía geográfica del reino de Valencia.* Departamento de geografía aplicada del instituto Elcano, serie regional 1, no. 7. Zaragoza: Consejo superior de investigaciones científicas, 1964.

Villarroya, Joseph. *Real maestrazgo de Montesa, tratado de todos los derechos, bienes y pertenencias del patrimonio y maestrazgo de la real y militar orden de Montesa y S. Jorge de Alfama.* 2 vols. Valencia: Benito Monfort, 1787.

Vincke, Johannes. "Königtum und Sklaverei im aragonischen Staatenbund während des 14. Jahrhunderts." *Gesammelte Aufsätze zur Kulturgeschichte Spaniens,* xxv (1970), 19-112.

———. "Die Gastungsrecht der aragonischen Krone im hohen Mittelalter." *Gesammelte Aufsätze zur Kulturgeschichte Spaniens,* xix-xx (1962), 161-170.

Wahab, H. and F. Dachraoui, "Régime foncier en Sicile." See primary sources, ad-Dāwūdī.

Zayas, Farishta G. de. *The Law and Philosophy of Zakat: The Islamic Social Welfare System.* Damascus: al-Jadidah Press, 1960.

INDEX

Aaron (b. Yaḥyā), 273, 286-87
'Abd al-'Azīz, 92
'Abd Allāh (woodworker), 338
'Abd Allāh ad-Dāyah, 56
'Abd Allāh al-Baṭṭāl, 255
'Abd Allāh Blach, 337
Abraham b. Vives, 281
Abraham (b. Yaḥyā), 286
Abū Bakr, 61
Abū Bakr b. 'Īsā, 326
Abū Ja'far b. Sa'īd, 57n, 149
Abū 'Ubayd Allāh, 182
Abū 'Uthmān Sa'īd b. Ḥakam
  al-Qurashī, 256
Abū Yūsuf, xivn, 9, 182, 230
Abū Zayd, 5-6, 97, 109, 234
acapta (taking possession of land), 201
Ādam (Edam), 113
Adam of Paterna, 292-99
Ad-Dāwūdī, xvn
adelantat (local official), 13
Ademuz, 102, 143, 273, 286
Adret, Solomon b. Abraham b., rabbi,
  317
Africa, North, 5, 31; agricultural
  rents, 111; fonduks, 65n; shops
  and markets, 35; trade with, 71
Aghnides, Nicolas P., xivn, 86n,
  111n, 155n, 182n, 207n, 217n, 226n,
  335n
agrarian rents, 105, 107-20, 199
agricultural produce as tax or rent,
  34, 110-18, 214
Aguilar y Serrat, Francisco de Asís,
  191-92n
Ahín, 141, 305
Aḥmad an-Najjār, 254
Alacuas, 131
Alagón family, 328
alamí (local official), 13, 250; see also
  amīn
alaminatum (tax-collecting territory),
  320
Albaida, 102, 143, 152, 232
Albalat, 32n, 82, 198, 324
Albarracín, 185
Albigensian crusade, 4

Albufera lagoon, 46, 146
Alcalá, 149; fines, 179; tax collection,
  232, 254, 258, 315; taxes and revenue,
  23, 33, 88, 106, 136, 141, 175
Alcañiz, 313
Alcira, 7, 14, 15, 74n, 80, 87, 332;
  agrarian rents, 108, 118; bakeries,
  51; convent, 54; fees for land use
  and sale, 199; fines, 177; fonduks,
  65n; irrigation system, 122, 123,
  124, 141; labor service, 169, 172;
  meat and fish markets, 44; military
  obligations, 141, 143; saltworks, 146;
  shops, 35-36, 39n; tariffs, 89, 90,
  93, 94; tax collection, 230, 235, 242,
  253, 265, 273, 278, 280, 288, 295, 296,
  297, 302, 309, 310, 311, 313, 321;
  taxes and finance, 21, 23-36, 31n,
  50n, 82, 84, 99, 101, 102, 103, 132,
  133, 136, 137, 175, 176
Alconstantini, Bahiel, 276
Alconstantini, Moses, 273, 276, 281
Alconstantini, Solomon (brother of
  Bahiel), 276
Alconstantini, Solomon (brother of
  Moses), 276
Alconstantini family, 275-76
Alcover, Antonio, 76n, 104, 125n,
  127n, 156n, 159n, 164n, 210n
Alcoy, 102, 143, 146, 165; tax collection,
  263, 303, 305
Alcudia, 115
Aldaya, 116, 131
Aldea, 34, 252; agrarian rents, 116,
  120; bakeries, 51; charter, 34n, 39n,
  45, 51n, 92, 120, 168, 201, 265n, 330;
  fees for land use and sale, 200-01;
  labor service, 163, 168; livestock
  taxes, 158, 161; mosque property
  exempt from fees, 207
Aledo, 257
Aleppo, 58n
Ales, Moses, 288
Alfamén, 142
Alfandech (and Valley), 31, 119,
  165, 311, 332; charter, 148, 176, 252;
  fines, 176, 178; mills, 56; tax collec-

LIBRARY OF CONGRESS CATALOGING IN PUBLICATION DATA
Burns, Robert Ignatius.
    Medieval colonialism.

    Bibliography: p.
    Includes index.
    1. Valencia—Economic conditions. 2. Taxation—Va-
lencia—History. 3. Mudejares. 4. Jaime I, King of
Aragon, 1208-1276. 5. Crusades. I. Title.
HC387.V3B87   336.2'00946'76   74-25614
ISBN 0-691-05227-1